Christopher Words\

# The Holy Bible. The Minor Prophets. In the Authorized Version, with Notes and Introductions

## Vol. VI

Christopher Wordsworth

# The Holy Bible. The Minor Prophets. In the Authorized Version, with Notes and Introductions

## Vol. VI

Reprint of the original, first published in 1875.

1st Edition 2024 | ISBN: 978-3-38538-836-9

Verlag (Publisher): Outlook Verlag GmbH, Zeilweg 44, 60439 Frankfurt, Deutschland
Vertretungsberechtigt (Authorized to represent): E. Roepke, Zeilweg 44, 60439 Frankfurt, Deutschland
Druck (Print): Books on Demand GmbH, In de Tarpen 42, 22848 Norderstedt, Deutschland

11 Then shall *his* mind change, and he shall pass over, and offend,
   *ª Imputing* this his power unto his god.
12   ʰ *Art* thou not from everlasting, O Lord my God, mine Holy One ?
We shall not die
  O Lord, ¹ thou hast ordained them for judgment ;
  And, O † mighty God, thou hast † established them for correction.
13 ᵏ *Thou art* of purer eyes than to behold evil, and canst not look on ‖ iniquity :
  ¹ Wherefore lookest thou upon them that deal treacherously,
  *And* holdest thy tongue
  When the wicked devoureth *the man that is* more righteous than he ?
14 And makest men as the fishes of the sea,
  As the ‖ creeping things, *that have* no ruler over them ?
15 They ᵐ take up all of them with the angle,
  They catch them in their net, and gather them in their ‖ drag :
  Therefore they rejoice and are glad ;
16 Therefore ⁿ they sacrifice unto their net, and burn incense unto their drag ;
  Because by them their portion *is* fat, and their meat ‖ † plenteous.
17 Shall they therefore empty their net,
  And not spare continually to slay the nations ?
II. ¹ I will ª stand upon my watch,
  And set me upon the † tower,
  ᵇ And will watch to see what he will say ‖ unto me,
  And what I shall answer ‖ † when I am reproved.
  And the Lord answered me, and said,
  ᶜ Write the vision, and make *it* plain upon tables,

---

11. *Then shall* his *mind change*] Rather, *the wind passes by; that is,* the storm of his violence, compared to a wind, sweeps by, *and passes over* (the land), *and offends; this, its power, is its god.* It defies God, and deifies itself. See above, *v.* 6, and Micah ii. 1, and the description of the Antichristian power in Daniel xi. 36—38.

### THE PROPHET'S QUESTION.

12—17. Art *thou not from everlasting, O* Lord *my God—the nations*] These verses may best be considered together. O Jehovah, my God, the Holy One, the God of Israel, let me derive comfort from the reflection that Thou art from everlasting ; and that whatever the Chaldeans do, is done by the permission of Thee, the Mighty God, or Rock, for our sins, and for our correction ; and therefore *we shall not die.* We shall be chastened, but not killed. But why, O Lord, dost thou use such a power as that of Babylon, which idolizes itself, and imputes all its victories to its own arm, and defies Thee ? Since Thou art of purer eyes than to behold evil with complacency, Why dost Thou look on the Chaldeans, and keep silence while they devour Thy People—which, sinful as many of them are, is more righteous than the Chaldeans ; for many holy men are among them, and they have Thy Temple, and worship Thee ? Why dost Thou make men to be no better than fish and reptiles, where the more powerful and the more venomous hurt and destroy the rest ?

The Chaldeans are allowed by Thee to catch Thy People like fish, with hook and with net. And when they have done it they exult and do outrage to Thee, and, in their brutish idolatry, worship the instruments by which Thou hast permitted them to gain their booty—their net and their drag !

These prophecies concerning the literal Babylon reach onward to our own days, and to the mystical Babylon,—which is Rome. The King of the literal Babylon is compared here to a fisherman, catching men and nations in his net. And it may be observed, that the Head of the mystical Babylon claims to be the successor of an Apostolic fisherman, and is a spiritual "fisher of men ;" and that his decrees, in which he imitates the Chaldean King, and claims universal Supremacy, spiritual and temporal, are issued with this formula—" Datum Romæ apud Sanctum *Petrum* sub annulo *Piscatoris.*" And

he worships his own drag, and makes others worship it ; they must all bow down before his assumed Infallibility, and adore that universal Supremacy in which he encloses the Nations, as in a net. See below, on Rev. xiii., pp. 233, 234 ; and *Dr. Robinson* here, p. 150.

CH. II. 1. *I will stand upon my watch*] The Prophet, likened to a *watchman* (as the Prophets often are ; see Ezek. iii. 17 ; xxxiii. 2. 6. 7. Micah vii. 4. Cant. iii. 3 ; v. 7), stands on his tower, and listens for the reply which God makes to the question which he has just put.

The Prophet raises himself from earthly things, and ascends to the height of spiritual meditation (as Moses did, on the height of Horeb or of Pisgah, and St. Peter on the housetop, and the Saviour Himself, when He went up to the mountain alone to pray) ; and there, with attentive ear, after devout supplication, he hearkens to the Voice of God speaking within him. Cp. *S. Cyril* and *Theodoret* here.

— *what he will say unto me*] Rather, *what He* (God) *will say in me.* He prays that he may hear God's voice speaking within himself.

— *And what I shall answer—reproved*] Rather, *and what* (when I have heard God's voice in me) *I shall answer to my own complaint.* See Sept. here, Targum, and Arabic.

### THE LORD'S ANSWER—WRITE THE VISION.

2. *Write the vision, and make it plain upon tables*] In large letters, to be seen by all, even by those who run, and do not attentively look at it ; even as the Decalogue was written on Tables by God Himself ; and as the Law was written by Joshua on the stones at Sichem (see Josh. viii. 31) ; and as the names of Isaiah's two sons were written by the Prophet.

The Vision (of the future destruction of Babylon) was to be *written* now, in order that, when it came to pass, the people might be witnesses of its fulfilment, and believe in the Prophet's inspiration. *If* it had not been *written* and *published then,* but received for some years in the Prophet's own bosom, and not divulged till it was accomplished, some might say that the Vision had never been seen, and that the prophecy was no prophecy, but had been uttered after the event.

St. Paul appears to allude to these words of Habakkuk in

97

Before
CHRIST
*cir.*
*626.*

d Dan. 10. 14. &
11. 27, 35.

e Heb. 10. 37.

f John 3. 36.
Rom. 1. 17.
Gal. 3. 11.
Heb. 10. 38.

‖ Or, *How much*

That he may run that readeth it.

3 For ᵈ the vision *is* yet for an appointed time,
But at the end it shall speak, and not lie :
Though it tarry, wait for it ;
Because it will ᵉ surely come, it will not tarry.
Behold, his soul *which* is lifted up is not upright in him :
But the ᶠ just shall live by his faith.

‖ Yea also, because he transgresseth by wine,
*He is* a proud man, neither keepeth at home,

---

his Epistle to the Galatians, where he is referring to the large letters in which that Epistle was written by his own hand; which teaches the lesson inculcated by the Prophet here—*the just shall live by his faith.* See below, the note on Gal. vi. 11.

Habakkuk receives a command from God, "*Write the Vision.*" The Vision to be written by the Prophet, related to the literal Babylon, its pride, its idolatry, its fall. St. John, in the isle of Patmos, received a similar command from Christ. "What thou seest, write in a book." See Rev. i. 11.

Habakkuk's Vision concerning the literal Babylon has been fulfilled; so, in due time, St. John's Vision in the Apocalypse, concerning the mystical Babylon (the City and Church of Rome) will be.

3. *the vision* is *yet for an appointed time*] Rather, *the vision* is *for the appointed end, and strives* (or *yearns, pants, and longs ;* see *Fuerst,* 590; *Gesen.* 358; *Hitzig, Keil*) *for the end,* Hebr. *kets,* or *moed kets, the time of the end :* i. e. the time of the Messiah. See Dan. viii. 17. 19 ; xi. 35 ; xii. 4. 13, where the word *kets* is used; and compare the note of *Keil* here.

The sense is, that this prophecy of Habakkuk, concerning the destruction of Babylon, will not only have a literal fulfilment in the overthrow of the Babylon on the Euphrates, but that it reaches onward to the times of the Christian Dispensation, even to the latter days, and will have its perfect accomplishment in the destruction of the mystical Babylon. The Vision of Habakkuk is the preamble to the Apocalypse.

In order that the prophecy of Habakkuk may be duly understood, it must be read throughout with an eye, not only to the literal Jerusalem and the literal Babylon, but with a view also to the spiritual Sion, namely, the Christian Church, and the Antichristian, mysterious, and idolatrous City and Church of Rome, of which (as is shown below, in the notes on the Apocalypse, Rev. xvii.) the literal Babylon was a type.

— *Because it will surely come*] The Author of the Epistle to the Hebrews, grounding his quotation on the *Septuagint* here, paraphrases these words thus—"*He that shall come will come*" (i. e. the Messiah) ; and by this paraphrase he confirms the interpretation given in the preceding note, that this prophecy will have its full accomplishment in the last days. The Prophet is foretelling the Divine Judgment on the spiritual Antichristian Power, which will be finally destroyed by the Second Advent of Christ. See below, on 2 Thess. ii. 8.

— *it will not tarry*] It *will not fail :* literally, it will not lag behind when the proper time comes for its fulfilment. Cp. Judges v. 28. 2 Sam. xx. 5, where the same word occurs.

4. *Behold, his soul* which is *lifted up*] *Behold* (it is) *lifted up,* (and) *not right* (is) *his soul in him ; but the just by his faith shall live.* These words are quoted in the Epistle to the Hebrews (x. 38); and the last clause is cited also in Rom. i. 17. Gal. iii.11, "*The just shall live by faith.*" In the Epistle to the Hebrews (x. 38) the words are represented thus—"*Now the just shall live by faith ;* but if any man draw back, *my soul shall have no pleasure*" (or rather, *my soul is not pleased*) "*in him.*" This form of quotation of the second member of the sentence, "*if he draw back, my soul is not pleased in him,*" is derived from the *Septuagint* Version ; which, as has been already observed more than once (see on Amos ix. 12), was not designed to be a literal Translation, but a Paraphrase. The Author of the Epistle to the Hebrews, for reasons stated below (*Introd.* to Hebrews, pp. 373, 374), used the Septuagint Version in his quotations from the Old Testament ; and in this passage of Habakkuk, that Version gives *the sense and spirit* of Habakkuk, but does *not* attempt to represent *literally the exact words.* The words "*if he draw back,*" are a paraphrastic rendering of the original, "*Behold, his soul is lifted up.*" The word translated "*lifted up*—*uppelah*—(the perfect *pual* of *âphal,* connected with *ôphél,* a hill, an activity ; whence the hill *Ophel* at Jerusalem, on the east of Zion) signifies, in *hiphil,* to *act presumptuously* (see Num. xiv. 44, in which it is so
98

rendered, and which is the only place where it occurs ; and cp. *Gesen.,* 645), is used by the Prophet, meaning to raise himself up from a lower level to a lofty elevation ; and might fitly be represented, as it is in the Septuagint, by a word which the Apostle to the Hebrews adopts as signifying the drawing back of the soul from the proper level of humility and faith in God, and the entrenching itself in an independent spirit of self-reliant presumption, in the lofty fortress of human pride, such as was the characteristic of Babylon and its King. See here i. 11. 16.

That this is the true sense of the word, is shown by *Pocock* (Not. Mis., vol. i. p. 144), who says that the meaning is, the wicked man withdraws himself into the lofty citadel of his own human self-confidence ; but the righteous man has no need of such a citadel ; his castle is faith in God, and he will live and be preserved thereby. See also *Bishop Pearson's* remarks on this passage (Præf. Par. in LXX., vol. i. p. 263, ed. Churton), where he says that the word *áphal* means to withdraw oneself into a lofty tower or dark fortress for safety. Cp. 2 Kings v. 24. With regard to the other portion of the sentence, "*his soul is not upright in him,*" this may mean, as the *Septuagint* paraphrases, "*his soul is not pleasing in him*"—that is, is *not pleasing* to God ; as *Gesenius says* (p. 375, under the verb *yáshar,* here used), "to be *straight* or right in my eyes, signifies it *is pleasing to me, I approve :*" and so *Dr. Pocock,* p. 145, and *Bp. Pearson,* p. 264, explain the phrase here ; and this is paraphrastically represented by "*my soul is not pleased in him.*"

— *But the just shall live by his faith*] Literally, *but the just, by his faith shall he live.* The word rendered *faith,* is *eminah,* from *ômas,* to be firmly rooted and established, supported, and stayed up—as a building on its foundations, or a tree in its roots (see *Gesen.* 58) ; and so may be compared with the Greek and Latin πίστις and *fides* (faith), from πείθομαι and its derivative Latin *fido,* to *rely upon.* Hence the heart of Abraham, the "father of the faithful," is called *neemân* (Neh. ix. 8), in reference to the fact that he *believed* (Hebr. *heemân*) in the Lord, and this was counted to him for righteousness (Gen. xv. 6).

The great truth, therefore, that we derive from this whole passage, is, that there is a characteristic and essential difference between the good and evil man. The evil man, in a proud, presumptuous Chaldean spirit, withdraws and elevates himself in the great and lofty Babylon that he has built for his own glory (Dan. iv. 30). and vaunts his own strength, and imagines himself impregnable there ; but he will be hurled down to destruction in the zenith of his glory, and be made to herd with the beasts of the field (Dan. iv. 32). But the righteous man will not rely on any thing in himself, but will build himself by faith on the solid rock (i. 12) and sure foundation of God's Word, and be rooted, like a firm-set tree, on the soil of His gracious promises ; and, as long as he does this, *he* will *never fall ;* but he *will live*—be preserved eternally, by faith in God's mighty power and love.

5. *Yea also, because he transgresseth by wine*] The Prophet thus applies to the Babylonians what has been said. The better translation is, "*Yea also, because the wine*" (which he drinks, and gives to others to drink) "*is treacherous*" (*Vulg.*)—i. e. betrays and inflames him and them, and excites them to commit sins of insolence, licence, and impiety. Cp. Prov. xxiii. 31, 32.

The Babylonians were notorious for their intemperance : "Babylonii maximè in vinum et quæ ebrietatem sequuntur effusi sunt" (*Curtius,* v. 1).

This prophecy was accomplished in its fullest sense in Belshazzar's feast, when the King and his courtiers were flushed with the wine that they drank profanely from the vessels of the Temple of Jerusalem, and praised their gods of gold and silver, and were destroyed in that night of impious revelry (Dan. v. 1—5 ; 28—30).

— *neither keepeth at home*] Rather, *and he abideth not ;* i. e. is soon swept away by destruction ; whereas the faithful man endureth for ever. Contrast Belshazzar and Daniel here—

VI. ¹ And I turned, and lifted up mine eyes, and looked, and, behold, there <sup>Before CHRIST 518.</sup>
came four chariots out from between two mountains; and the mountains *were*
mountains of brass. ² In the first chariot *were* ᵃ red horses; and in the second <sup>a ch. 1. 8. Rev. 6. 4.</sup>
chariot ᵇ black horses; ³ and in the third chariot ᶜ white horses; and in the <sup>b Rev. 6. 5</sup>
fourth chariot grisled and || bay horses. <sup>|| Or, strong.</sup>

⁴ Then I answered ᵈ and said unto the angel that talked with me, What *are* <sup>d ch. 5. 10.</sup>
these, my lord ?

⁵ And the angel answered and said unto me, ᵉ These *are* the four || spirits of <sup>e Ps. 104. 4. Heb. 1. 7. 14.</sup>
the heavens, which go forth from ᶠ standing before the Lord of all the earth. <sup>|| Or, winds. f 1 Kings 22. 19.</sup>
⁶ The black horses which *are* therein go forth into ᵍ the north country; and <sup>Dan. 7. 10. g ch. 2. 6.</sup>
the white go forth after them; and the grisled go forth toward the south <sup>Luke 1. 19.</sup>
country. ⁷ And the bay went forth, and sought to go that they might ʰ walk <sup>h Gen. 13. 17. ch. 1. 10.</sup>
to and fro through the earth: and he said, Get you hence, walk to and fro
through the earth. So they walked to and fro through the earth.

⁸ Then cried he upon me, and spake unto me, saying, Behold these that go
toward the north country have quieted my ⁱ spirit in the north country. <sup>i Judg. 8. 3. Eccles. 10. 4.</sup>

⁹ And the word of the Lord came unto me, saying, ᵏ Take of *them*
of the captivity, *even* of Heldai, of Tobijah, and of Jedaiah, which are
come from Babylon, and come thou the same day, and go into the house
of Josiah the son of Zephaniah; ¹¹ then take silver and gold, and make
ᵏ crowns, and set *them* upon the head of Joshua the son of Josedech, the high <sup>k Exod. 28. 36. 2 29. 6.</sup>
priest; ¹² and speak unto him, saying, Thus speaketh the Lord of hosts, <sup>Rev. 8. 9. ch. 3. 1.</sup>
saying,

    Behold ˡ the man whose name *is* The ᵐ BRANCH; <sup>l See Luke 1. 78. John 1. 14. m Or, Branch up from under him. n ch. 4. 9.</sup>
    And he shall || grow up out of his place, <sup>Matt. 16. 18.</sup>
    ⁿ And he shall build the temple of the Lord : <sup>Eph. 2. 20, 21, 22. Heb. 3. 8.</sup>
¹³ Even he shall build the temple of the Lord ;

---

Wickedness, or Lawlessness (see *Sept.* here, which has
ἀνομία, and ep. 2 Thess. ii. 8, ὁ ἄνομος), is carried to Babylon and
is settled there, because at Babylon is its proper place (*S. Jerome*).

This Vision, like the other Visions of Zechariah, extends to
Christian times. In the Christian Church Universal, corruptions
have arisen which may find a solemn warning here. The Church
of Rome boasts herself to be Sion : but she is the mystical
Babylon of the Apocalypse (as is shown below, Revelation
xvii., xviii., pp. 210—260). Her Sovereign Pontiff is "the
Lawless one " of St. Paul. See below, on 2 Thess ii. 3—12, pp.
29—32. This prophecy may be applied, and ought to be applied,
as a warning to those who are tempted to communicate with her
in her errors and corruptions. Her doom will be, to be removed
from her place, and to be swept away by the whirlwind of God's
wrath, because she rebels against His Will and Word.

THE FOUR CHARIOTS.

CH. VI. 1—8. *Behold, there come four chariots out from between two mountains—of brass—these—have quieted my spirit
in the north country*] These eight verses will best be considered
together. The four chariots from between two mountains of brass
represent God's instruments of retributive justice going forth
from the fortress of His Power. Brass is a symbol of might
(Job xl. 18. Ps. cvii. 16. Dan. xlv. 2. 32. 39). Chariots are
emblems of rapid march and victorious career.

The four chariots symbolize the four great Empires, already
described by Daniel (ii. 31—43 ; vii. 3—7. See S. *Cyril* here);
and the colours of the horses represent their various attributes
(cp. above, i. 8—10) and their going forth from between two
mountains of brass—not real mountains, but symbolical—shows
that they have one common starting-place, which can be no other
than the Will of God, Who is the Governor of the world. Cp. v. 5.

The words *grisled and bay* would be better rendered *grisled
and strong*. See the *Margin* and *Dr. Pusey* on Daniel, p. 358,
who rightly remarks that "the imagery here, like that above in
i. 18, 19, presupposes the existence of Daniel's prophecies, and is
an argument for their authenticity, and is to be explained from
those prophecies." Of the black horses, the symbol of the Second Empire (the Medo-Persian), it is said, that they have made

mine anger to rest in the north country (i. e. on Babylon),
because of God's judgments executed on Babylon by Cyrus,
who is represented here as God's minister. The third is here
said to *go forth after them*, for the Greeks occupied the region
before held by the Persians. The fourth, the Roman, which is
characterized by grisled and strong horses, corresponds in these
features of mixture and strength with the fourth, or Roman,
Empire, as described by Daniel (ii. 41).

THE CROWNS—FROM THE PEOPLE OF THE CAPTIVITY—
PLACED ON THE HEAD OF JOSHUA THE HIGH PRIEST.

10—14. *Take of them of the captivity—high priest—for a
memorial in the temple of the Lord*] God commands that the
silver and gold, brought as an offering from some of the captives
of Babylon to the Temple at Jerusalem, should be made into
crowns (or rather into *diadems*), encircling one crown (cp. Rev.
xix. 12, and *Kliefoth*, 1¾) and placed, not on the head of Zerubbabel, the *civil Ruler*, but on the head of Joshua the High
Priest. Christ's glory eclipses that of both. Zerubbabel was a
civil Ruler, but not a King ; Joshua was a Priest, not a Ruler;
Christ is the universal King and everlasting Priest.

This was a typical and prophetical act. The *crowns* are
for the *Priest*. This prefigures the future glory of Christ the
Messiah (*Targum*), the *Branch* (v. 12). He grows *up out of His
place*, literally, *from under Him* (cp. Exod. x. 23); the Branch
shall grow up *from under Himself*, that is, by reason of His own
innate power. He, as Man, shall grow up from His eternal
Godhead, and shall put forth divine vigour, and grow up and
flourish and overshadow the earth, like a great tree : as He
Himself says, comparing Himself to a corn of wheat which
dies and brings forth much fruit (John xii. 24), the grain dies,
and the Harvest of the Gentiles springs up from it. By reason
of the union of His Manhood with His Godhead (cp. *A Lapide*
here), He springs up and puts forth His divine power and diffuses His divine Grace in the Universal Church, and therefore
it is added, *He shall build the temple of the Lord*, that is, the
Church in all place and time.

13. *he shall—rule upon his throne—and—be a priest upon*

THE

# HOLY BIBLE,

In the Authorized Version;

## WITH NOTES AND INTRODUCTIONS

BY

## CHR. WORDSWORTH, D.D.

BISHOP OF LINCOLN.

### VOL. VI.

PART II.—THE MINOR PROPHETS.

*NEW EDITION.*

RIVINGTONS,

London, Oxford, and Cambridge.

1875.

# THE MINOR PROPHETS,

In the Authorized Version;

## WITH NOTES AND INTRODUCTIONS

BY

## CHR. WORDSWORTH, D.D.

BISHOP OF LINCOLN.

*NEW EDITION.*

RIVINGTONS,

London, Oxford, and Cambridge.

1875.

# CONTENTS.

# INTRODUCTION TO THE MINOR PROPHETS.

THE twelve Minor Prophets form one book[1]. This is the light in which they were viewed by the ancient Hebrew and Christian Churches; and in order that their works may be profitably studied, they ought not to be regarded as separate writings, but as constituting one harmonious whole.

It is true that each of these prophetical writings has a distinct character of its own; each does its own appointed work. But that appropriate work of each fits in with accurate precision, and is adjusted with beautiful symmetry, to that which is done by the rest and by all[2].

"The goodly fellowship of the prophets" may be compared to a row of statues standing in their niches in the west front of some noble cathedral: each has its proper place; but each has also a relation to the others and to the whole; and together they form a group, graceful in unity as well as in its constituent parts.

The writings of the twelve Minor Hebrew Prophets, as well as those of the four Major Prophets, are arranged in chronological order[3] in the Hebrew Bibles, and in our authorized English Version. Hosea, who stands at the head of the Minor Prophets, was contemporary with Isaiah, who holds the first place among the Major Prophets. The names of both have a similar meaning[4]. Both prophesied in the days of Uzziah, Jotham, Ahaz, and Hezekiah, Kings of Judah[5], that is, at the beginning of the ninth century, and during the greater part of the eighth century before Christ.

The writings of the Minor Prophets extend in a continuous chain with successive links in a parallel line with those of the Major Prophets till the days of the Captivity at Babylon. The series of the Major Prophets ends with Daniel at Babylon. But the line of the Minor Prophets reaches beyond the Captivity to the restoration of the Jews by Cyrus, and to the rebuilding of the Temple of Jerusalem under Zerubbabel and Joshua, and also to the reparation of the walls of the City under Nehemiah and Ezra, in the fifth century before Christ.

The prophets Haggai and Zechariah strengthened the hands of Zerubbabel and Joshua, and stirred up the people to rebuild the Temple. The prophet Malachi saw it rebuilt; and he was a fellow-labourer with Ezra, "the Priest and Scribe," in a still greater work, that of completing the Canon of the Old Testament. Malachi is called by the Jews "the Seal of the Prophets[6]."

---

[1] See Acts vii. 42; xv. 15. *Josephus*, C. Apion. i. 8. *Kimchi* (Præf. ad Hoseam). S. *Greg. Nazianz.* (Carm. xxxiii.) says, "The twelve (prophets) are joined in one book;" and so *Theodoret*, Procem. in Duodecim Prophetas, p. 1308, ed. Schulze. Hal., 1769. Cp. *Hottinger*, Thesaur. Philol. 477. *Keil*, Einleitung, § 81.

[2] Compare *Delitzsch* (Einleitung in die Prophet. Weissagungbucher, prefixed to his Commentary on Isaiah, p. xx); and *Dr. Pusey's* Lectures on Daniel, p. 308, who thus writes:—

"It has been pointed out how the citations of each earlier Prophet by those who came after, presuppose that those former books were of recognized authority. Amos, when he opens and almost closes his prophecy with the words of Joel, or applies a message already recognized as Divine. So also Obadiah, when he uses words of the prophecies of Balaam. Amos, Joel, and a Psalm. Micah alludes emphatically to those parting words of his great predecessor in the Book of Kings, to expressions of the Psalms and Proverbs, to Joshua, to David's elegy over Saul and Jonathan, as well as to the Pentateuch; Habakkuk, Zephaniah, Ezekiel, employ words or thoughts of his. Jonah, by adopting the form *And*, joins on his prophetic history to the sacred histories before him, and blends his mission to the heathen with the history of the people of God.

"Nahum, in the opening of his prophecy against Nineveh, manifestly refers to Jonah's appeal to God in regard to it. For Nahum had to exhibit the stricter side of God's dealings as to that same city. God had said in Jonah how He forgave on repentance; Nahum opens his book by saying in that selfsame form of words, that He was indeed long-suffering, but would not

finally spare the guilty. Nahum and Zephaniah use language of Isaiah. Zephaniah uses that of Habakkuk, as also of Joel, Amos, Micah; Habakkuk's hymn shows one well acquainted with the Psalms. Whom does not Jeremiah employ?

"The appeal in his day to the great prophecy of the destruction of Jerusalem in Micah, in its own words, shows that the book must have been in public use.

"Even before the Captivity, God, by Ezekiel, speaks of the prophets before him as one whole; *Ezek.* xxxviii. 17. '*Thus saith the Lord God, Art thou* (Gog) *he of whom I have spoken in old time by My servants the prophets of Israel which prophesied in those days many years, that I would bring thee against them?*'

"When, then, Daniel, studying Jeremiah's prophecy of the seventy years of the Captivity, says, '*I understood by the books*' (Dan. ix. 2, i. e. the biblia, scriptures), '*the number of the years which the Word of God was to Jeremiah the prophet, to fulfil as to the desolations of Jerusalem seventy years,*' this exactly expresses what we see from the writings of the prophets before the Captivity to have been the fact, that the books of the prophets were collected together.

"The *Captivity* set God's seal on the true prophets of God over against the false prophets, and gained a reverence for them among those also of the people who had derided and persecuted or slain them before. *The former prophets* (Zech. i. 4, 6), is a standing expression for the prophets before the Captivity."

[3] See the Chronological Table at the close of this Preface.

[4] See below, *Preface, Note* to Hosea.

[5] See Isaiah i. 1, and Hosea i. 1.

[6] *Hottinger*, Thes. Phil. 185.

In reading the Hebrew Prophets, it is requisite to have a careful regard to those principles of interpretation which were laid down by our Blessed Lord and by the Apostles, and which were applied by ancient Christian Expositors, such as S. Cyril of Alexandria in the Eastern Church, and S. Jerome and S. Augustine (especially in his work on the City of God) in the Western.

This has been too often forgotten. The system of Interpretation which is more popular in recent times, is that described by St. Paul when he says, "The letter" (that is the letter of Scripture taken alone, without the spirit) "killeth; but the spirit giveth life[1]." This kind of exposition has had the effect of separating Hebrew Prophecy from Christianity, and of isolating it, as if it were a thing to be contemplated at a distance, with which we ourselves have little to do.

The Infidelity now prevalent is due in a great measure to the abandonment of the ancient principles of Interpretation, in the exposition of the Old Testament.

In our own times the Old Testament has been regarded for the most part as a subject for critical disquisitions on matters of History, Geography, and Physics—things most useful and absolutely necessary in themselves, but by no means sufficient for the Interpretation of the Old Testament.

The design of the Old Testament is to prepare the way for Christ; and every reverent expositor of it will make it his principal study to enable the readers of it to see Christ in every part of it.

Unless he does this, he is untrue to his mission; and he is leaving open a wide door for the entrance of Unbelief.

How mean and trivial must many of the incidents in the history of the Patriarchs appear, unless, with St. Paul, S. Justin Martyr, S. Irenæus, S. Jerome, S. Chrysostom, and S. Augustine, and all Christian Antiquity, we read that history by the light of the Gospel, and regard the acts of the Patriarchs as foreshadowings of the history of Christ! As S. Augustine says in his book against Faustus the Manichæan[2], "Not only the words of the Patriarchs were prophetical, but their lives were a prophecy. All the Hebrew Monarchy was like a grand Prophecy of a Mighty One, namely, of Christ. Therefore not only in those things which the Patriarchs said, but also in what they did, and in all things which happened by God's providence to the Hebrew Nation, we ought to search for prophecies concerning Christ and His Church. As the Apostle St. Paul says, 'figuræ nostræ fuerunt,' they were types of us[3].

If we dwell on the letter of the Old Testament, and do not endeavour to penetrate beneath the surface into its inner spiritual meaning—if we look at it merely as a book affording scope for critical, geographical, and historical discussions, we may become what the Manichæans of old were—ingenious disputers about the Old Testament; but we shall not be firm believers in it, nor make others to be so; but perhaps cavillers against it.

Again, how cumbrous, slavish, and even repulsive, will many of the ritual requirements prescribed in the Books of Leviticus and Numbers appear, if considered simply in themselves, without continual reference to Christ, and to the Great Sacrifice of Calvary!

How superfluous, unaccountable, and incredible are the miracles recorded in the Exodus of the Israelites from Egypt—the three days' darkness, the slaying of the first-born of Egypt, the passage through the Red Sea, the Pillar of the Cloud and Fire; and the Giving of the Law, amid thunders, on Mount Sinai, and the Manna coming down from heaven for forty years, and the smitten Rock gushing with water in the wilderness, and the flowing back of the river Jordan at the presence of the Ark, and the falling down of the walls of Jericho at the sound of the trumpets, and the staying of the sunlight at Bethhoron at the command of Joshua—if these things are regarded merely as incidents in the records of the Hebrew Nation, not exceeding the population of London in numbers, and going to take possession of a petty strip of territory, not much larger than Devonshire and Cornwall! Must not every critical reader, and even a thoughtful child, reject such histories as fabulous, if he is not continually invited by the commentator and preacher on the Old Testament, to read the books of Exodus, Numbers, and Joshua, not merely as historical annals of the Hebrew Nation, but as having a spiritual, prophetical, and typical character, and as recording events which were foreshadowings of the Son of God Himself, and of His Death and Resurrection and Victory over Death and Satan, and of the mysteries of the Gospel, which concern the welfare of all men and all Nations in every age and clime, even to the Day of Doom, and in the countless ages of Eternity?

An Expositor of the Old Testament, who does not continually remind his readers of these truths, is surrendering them into the hands of Scepticism.

There may be, and doubtless have been, many fanciful allegorical speculations of wild en-

<hr>

[1] 2 Cor. iii. 6.
[2] Lib. xxii. c. 24.
[3] 1 Cor. x. 6.

[4] See above, for example, the notes on Exodus vii.—xx, and the *Introduction* to Joshua, pp. ix—xxii, for further illustrations of this statement.

thusiasts in the interpretation of the Old Testament, and these are much to be regretted. But the abuse of what is good does not take away its use; and what is here advocated, is that sound, sober, spiritual interpretation of the Old Testament which is commended to our acceptance and imitation by Christ and His Apostles in the New, and by all primitive Antiquity. The right clue for commenting on the Old Testament was put into the hands of the Church by her Divine Master on the Day of His Resurrection, when He had overcome Sin, Satan, and Death by His Divine Power. In His walk to Emmaus with the two disciples on that day He "began with *Moses and all the Prophets*, and expounded unto them *in all the Scriptures* the things *concerning Himself*[1]." And He said to His assembled Apostles, "These are the words which I spake unto you while I was yet with you, that all things must be fulfilled which were written in the law of Moses, and in the Prophets, and in the Psalms concerning Me. Then opened He their understanding that they might understand the Scriptures[2]."

It is evident from these words of Christ Himself, that the primary duty of the Christian Commentator on the Old Testament is to lead his readers to behold Christ "in all the Scriptures;" and that there cannot be any right understanding of the Scriptures, unless their eyes are opened to see Him there. It is much to be feared, therefore, that with all our boasting of greater advances in Biblical Criticism, we have fallen very low from the standard of Apostolic and primitive times, in many of our expositions of the Old Testament. We are wise in the "letter that killeth," but not "in the spirit that giveth life[3]."

We have a warning against this servile system of exposition in the history of Hebrew Criticism. Many of the Jewish Rabbis in our Lord's age had an accurate knowledge of the original language of the Old Testament; they held it in their hands, and heard it read in their synagogues. Many of them dwelt in the country where most of the events took place which it records. But they did not understand it. The great "Hebrew of the Hebrews," the holy Apostle St. Paul[4], expressly affirms that the most learned among the Jews did not *know* (that is, did not comprehend) "the voices of the Prophets" which were read in the synagogues every Sabbath day; and that "they fulfilled those Scriptures by condemning Him" of Whom the Prophets wrote. He affirms that "a veil was on their hearts in the reading of the Old Testament[5]," and he does not hesitate to say, that the manner in which the Spirit giveth life to the reader, is by enabling the inner eye to see Christ in the Old Testament: or, in the Apostle's words, "the veil is done away in Christ, in the Old Testament: When the heart turneth to the Lord, then the veil is taken away from it."

Many in the present day study the Old Testament in a spirit not unlike that of the Hebrew Rabbis. They treat it as a common book; and rely on their own philological skill alone for its interpretation. No wonder that a veil is on their hearts in reading and expounding it.

Holy Scripture cannot be otherwise than a sealed book to the most learned and laborious critics, if they do not approach it with meekness and reverence, but handle it with familiarity, and cavil at it in a self-confident, disdainful, and presumptuous temper, as if they themselves were wiser than St. Paul and St. Peter, and all the prophets, and even than He Who inspired them. That such persons as these should not be permitted to understand Scripture, is no marvel. Rather it would be a marvel if they were permitted to do so. Scripture would not be true, if they could interpret it aright. For Scripture tells us that men cannot understand Scripture except by the help of the Spirit Who wrote it. And the Spirit will not deign to enlighten those who grieve Him by self-confident presumption. God is "the Father of lights[6]." And we cannot see "the wondrous things of His law," unless He vouchsafes to open our eyes and enlighten them. It is only in His light that we can see light. But He will not enlighten the proud. "He resisteth the proud, and giveth grace to the humble[7]." "Surely He scorneth the scorners[8]." "Mysteries are revealed unto the meek[9]." "Them that are meek shall He guide in judgment; and such as are gentle, them shall He learn His way." "The secret of the Lord is with them that fear Him[10]." "He that keepeth the law getteth the understanding thereof[11]." "If any man willeth to do God's will, he shall know of the doctrine[12]." We must become like little children if we would enter the kingdom of God. He hideth mysteries from the wise and prudent, and "revealeth them unto babes[13]." Balaam's ass saw the angel, and rebuked the disobedient prophet who rode upon her, who did not see the angel. Spiritual pride is punished by spiritual blindness. The will must be rectified, and the heart must be purified, if the mind is to be clarified, and if the spirit is to be glorified. "In the Scriptures," says George Herbert[14], "heaven lies flat, subject to every mounter's bended knee." Doubtless the

[1] Luke xxiv. 27.  [2] Luke xxiv.  [3] 2 Cor. iii. 6.  [5] Ecclus. iii. 19.  [10] Ps. xxv. 13.  [11] Ecclus. xxi. 11.
[4] Acts xiii. 27; xv. 21.  [5] 2 Cor. iii. 14.  [6] James i. 17.  [12] John vii. 17.  [13] Matt. xi. 25.  [14] The Temple, Part I
[7] James iv. 6.  1 Pet. v. 5.  [9] Prov. iii. 34.

reader of Scripture, and much more the preacher of God's Word, and the interpreter of Holy Scripture, must use all helps of sound reason and critical learning, and diligent labour, and careful study, for the understanding of that Word. He must use them with as much industry as if every thing depended on his use of them. But he must use them with reverence, humility, and faith, and with constant and fervent prayer for the illumination and guidance of the Holy Spirit. He must use them with continual and loving communion with Christ, Who is ever walking with devout souls to a spiritual Emmaus, and is opening to them the Scriptures, and is making Himself known to them in the "breaking of bread¹." He must use them with devout attention to every whisper of the Holy Spirit, interpreting one portion of Scripture by another, and to His voice in the Church Universal, especially in her Creeds, which we have received from the unanimous consent of undivided Christendom, and which our Reformers commend to our reverent use in the exposition of Scripture². "Faith," says St. Augustine, "opens the door to the understanding; but Unbelief shuts it." "When I was a young man," says that great expositor³, "I approached the study of the Bible with shrewdness of disputation, and not with meekness of inquiry. And thus by my own perverse temper, I closed the door of the Bible against myself, because I sought with pride for what can only be found by humility." The Written Word is like the Incarnate Word, "it is set for the fall and rising again of many in Israel, and for a sign which shall be spoken against⁴." What Christ says of Himself, the Incarnate Word, is true of the Written Word, "Whosoever shall fall on this stone shall be broken, and on whomsoever it shall fall it will grind him to powder⁵." It is like Him, "a stumbling stone and a rock of offence," to some; but to others it is like Him, "Who is the corner stone, elect, precious; and he that believeth in Him shall not be ashamed⁶."

The writer of this Introduction has ventured to dwell longer on this all-important subject in this place, because the present portion of a work in which he has now been permitted to labour for nearly twenty years, affords the last opportunity⁷ which he can expect to have of stating the principles on which it has been his earnest endeavour to compose this Commentary on the Prophetical Books, and on the other parts of the Old Testament.

We may now revert to the point from which we have digressed.

The holy Apostles teach us that "whatever things were written aforetime" (that is, were written in the Old Testament) "were written for our learning, that we, through patience and comfort of the Scriptures might have hope⁸." Whatever the Hebrew Prophets spoke, was not spoken by any private utterance of their own, but by the inspiration of the Holy Ghost, by Whose power they were borne along as on a strong stream⁹. The Apostles teach us that "all the Prophets give witness" to Christ¹⁰, and that the Spirit which was in the Prophets was "the Spirit of Christ¹¹." They assure us that the Prophets "inquired and searched diligently concerning the salvation" purchased for us by Christ, and of the grace vouchsafed to us through Him; and that "it was revealed unto them, that not unto themselves, but unto us, they did minister the things which are now reported unto us, by them that have preached the Gospel unto us, with the Holy Ghost sent down from heaven; which things the angels desire to look into¹²."

It is this characteristic of Hebrew Prophecy which imparts a special interest to it. The Holy Ghost, the Comforter, Who was afterwards sent by Christ to teach the Apostles all things, and to guide them into all truth¹³, speaks to us in the Hebrew Prophets. The Hebrew Prophets were not the original authors of their own prophecies. The Holy Ghost was the Author¹⁴. He speaks in them, by them, and *through* them¹⁵. The prophetic writings are *not sources* from which, but they are *channels* through which, the living waters of the Holy Spirit flow.

The truth therefore is, that we, who live under the Gospel, and have the benefit of the exposition which our Blessed Lord and the Apostles and Evangelists have given us, in the New Testament, of

¹ Luke xxiv. 35.
² See the Reformatio Legum, by Archbishop Cranmer and others, where it is said that the Articles of the Christian Faith set down in the Creeds, ought always ever to be before the eyes of the expositors of Scripture, who ought never to interpret Scripture so as to be at variance with them (Ref. Leg., De Summâ Trinitate, c. 13).
³ S. Aug., Serm. 51.
⁴ Luke ii. 31.
⁵ Matt. xxi. 44. Luke xx. 18.
⁶ 1 Pet. ii. 4—6. Rom. ix. 33; x. 11.
⁷ The Commentary on Daniel, though later in publication, takes an earlier place in this Commentary on the Bible.
⁸ Rom. xv. 4.

¹⁰ Cp. Acts x. 43. As St. Ignatius expresses it, "The prophets lived a Christward life" (ad Magnes. c. 8).
¹¹ 1 Pet. i. 11.
¹² 1 Pet. i. 12.
¹³ John xvi. 13.
¹⁴ See below, on Hos. xi. 1, for some evidence of the unhappy results, in modern days, of the opposite theory.
¹⁵ διὰ = through. This is the preposition used in the passages of the New Testament which describe the agency of the Holy Spirit in the prophetic writings. See below, on Matt. i. 22; ii. 5, 15, 17, 23; iii. 3; iv. 14; viii. 17; xiii. 35; xxiv. 15; xxvii. 9; in all which the preposition διὰ is used; and in the Nicene Creed, "Who spake by" (lit. through) "the prophets."
⁹ See below, on 2 Pet. i. 21.

the meaning of the prophetic writings, and who stand on the vantage-ground of more than two thousand years after them, and see how they have been fulfilled, have a much clearer view of their scope and purport, than the Prophets themselves had, by whose instrumentality they were written[1]. They "searched and inquired diligently" what that meaning was. We know what it is. The Holy Spirit, which was in the Prophets, has revealed it to us in the Gospels and Epistles of the New Testament. He has taught us there what He Himself meant when He spake by the Prophets in the Old, and what the Prophets by whom He spake earnestly longed to know; and therefore our Lord says, "Blessed are your eyes, for they see; for verily I say unto you, that many Prophets have desired to see those things which ye see, and have not seen them[2]."

It would therefore be a low and erroneous notion, to imagine that the Hebrew Prophets have done their work, and that their prophecies belong only to the past. Rather, we may say that they are co-extensive with Christianity, and that they possess a living and growing energy, and are ever adapting themselves to events that are arising from time to time in the Christian Church; and that they will continue to possess this vitality, and to exert this elastic and expansive agency, even to the end.

The Son of Sirach, speaking of them, says, "Let the memorial of the Twelve Prophets be blessed; and let their bones flourish again out of their place[3]." This prayer is verified. By reason of the presence and might of the Holy Spirit moving in them and speaking by them, they have a perpetual freshness, a perennial spring; their prophecies have a luxuriant exuberance, and are ever putting forth new leaves, and buds, and blossoms; and they wait for the full ripeness of their summer season, in the last ages of the Church and the World, when they will bear an abundance of spiritual fruitage to be gathered by the hand of Faith[4].

Hence we need not scruple to say that among all the writings of the Old Testament, none possess a more practical value for all classes of society in the present age, than those of the Hebrew Prophets.

The most illustrious evidence of the divine truth and inspiration of the Hebrew Prophets is reserved to be displayed in the latter days, in the great conflict, which seems even now to be near at hand, between Truth and Error, between Faith and Unbelief, between the Church and the World, between Christ and Antichrist; and in the final victory, which will crown the patience and courage of the faithful, at the consummation of all things, and at the general Resurrection of the dead, and at the Universal Judgment, when Christ will appear in glory. The prophetical writings may be rightly regarded as a Manual, not only for the Christian Preacher, but also for the Christian Citizen, Patriot, and Statesman, who are called to do battle for the Truth in days of doubt and distress, and who may be perplexed and staggered by the temporary success of evil in Civil Polity, and may even be tempted to despair of the cause of piety and of God in the moral government of the world.

If there is any thing which the Hebrew Prophets declare with a more distinct and articulate utterance than another, it is this—that in the latter days of the world, Unbelief and Iniquity will abound, and will triumph for a time; but that eventually all things will be put under the feet of the Divine Governor of the World, the Great Arbiter of the Destinies of Nations; and that all wilful and presumptuous sin will then be punished and crushed; and that Faith, having struggled steadfastly unto the end, will receive a glorious reward.

Thus the Hebrew Prophets supply spiritual comfort to the Christian Confessor in public and private life. They inspire the heart of the soldier of Christ with holy courage, and give him hopes full of immortality.

In the following pages the design has been to supply at the beginning of the work of each several Prophet, a clue to the main purport of his prophecy. The reader is requested to refer to what is there said. But it may be of use to state in a brief synoptical summary what seems to be their leading principle respectively; and thus to exhibit, as it were, in one view the component parts of the whole.

---

[1] See below, on Hos. xi. 1.
[2] Matt. xiii. 16, 17. Luke x. 23, 24.
[3] Ecclus. xlix. 10.
[4] This truth, which is so well expressed by Lord Bacon, (Advancement of Learning, p. 101), ought ever to be present to the mind of the expounder and reader of Hebrew Prophecy. Lord Bacon says, "Divine Prophecies, being of the nature of their Author, 'with Whom a thousand years are as one day,' have springing and germinant accomplishment through many ages." And the same writer well observes (Ibid. p. 267), "that the Scriptures, being written to the thoughts of men and

to the succession of all ages, with a foresight of all heresies, contradictions, and different estates of the Church, are not to be interpreted only according to the latitude of the proper sense of the place, and respectively towards that present occasion whereupon the words were uttered, but have in themselves infinite springs and streams of doctrine to water the Church in every part; and therefore, as the literal sense is, as it were, the main stream, or river, so the moral sense chiefly, and sometimes the allegorical or typical, is that of which the Church has the most use."

The prophet Hosea, who stands at the head of the Minor Prophets, justifies God's dealings with the Hebrew Nation from the beginning to the end.

Hosea, the first of the Prophets, takes up the language of the last preceding Book of Holy Scripture, that of the Canticles, or Song of Solomon[1] In order to show that Hosea's language is not to be understood literally, but spiritually, and that the Marriage between God and Israel is mystical, Israel is represented by Hosea not only as a beloved *Wife* (as the Church is in the Canticles), but also as a dear *Son*, a type of Christ the beloved Son Himself[2].

He treats the relation of God to His People under the endearing figure of that of a Bridegroom to a Bride. The Church of Israel was espoused to God in the Wilderness of Sinai; but, as the Prophet declares, she was unfaithful to Him : she followed strange gods ; and she is therefore charged by Him with spiritual harlotry and adultery. This, he tells us, was the cause of all her misery. No failure of God's love to her—far from it—was the origin of her woe. He was very merciful and long-suffering to her ; but her own sins of unthankfulness and faithlessness to Him, even in those places which had been distinguished by His wonderful acts of love to her, such as the wilderness of Arabia, even Horeb itself, in the first instance, and, when she had been brought by God into the promised Land of Canaan, such places as Beersheba, Bethel, and Gilgal[3], places illustrious in her past history as the scenes of God's miracles of mercy to her fathers, were polluted by her sins, which were the bitter source of all her sorrows.

On account of her long-continued and inveterate sins, the Prophet warns her that she must expect to suffer severe punishment. She will be carried away captive from her own land—the land of promise—and be scattered in a distant region. But even in this captivity and dispersion there will be divine love[4]. By the merciful discipline of chastisement she will be weaned from her idolatry ; she will be made sensible of her misery, and be humbled and brought to repentance[5] ; and she will at last be betrothed again to God, and be restored to Him in Christ.

There will always be a faithful remnant in Israel. Christ Himself will be born of the seed of Abraham. Some of this faithful remnant, especially the Apostles and primitive Preachers of Christ (who were all Jews), will convert the Heathen to the Gospel, which is the fulfilment of the Mosaic Law ; and Gentile Teachers will be employed by God to bring the Jews back to Him in Christ. This will be like a resurrection from the dead[6], a new birth from the grave, into life with God in Christ[7].

Such is a brief summary of Hosea's prophecy. It is a prophetic history of Israel for nearly four thousand years. It teaches us how to read that history ; it gives cheering hopes of the future ; and shows that all God's dealings with Israel have been dictated by righteousness and love. And therefore the Prophet concludes with this question and answer :—

Who is wise ? and he shall understand these things ;
Prudent ? and he shall know them.
For the ways of the Lord are right,
And the just shall walk in them[8].

JOEL, the prophet of Judgment, takes up the message of Hosea, the prophet of Salvation[9].

By a grand and sublime generalization, Joel teaches his readers to regard the Lord God of Israel as ever speaking to Mankind in His judicial character and office, and leads them to recognize and admire Him as Ruler of the natural world, and as Arbiter of the destinies of Nations, according to certain fixed laws of moral government, by which He orders all things, and will continue to order them even to the end of time.

All judicial visitations upon men and nations, whether they be in the natural world, as plagues of locusts, and other physical epidemics, or by means of mighty Empires, which are instruments in God's hands for punishing sins and for working out His own plans—are parts of one great " Day of the Lord." They are only like oscillations of the pendulum, and like faint notes of the clock, which will sound a final alarum with deep and solemn tones in the summons of the World to the Judgment-seat of Christ[10].

Joel proclaims God's offers of mercy and salvation to the penitent and faithful[11] ; and he foretells the first Advent of the Great " Teacher of righteousness[12]," and the outpouring of the Holy Ghost, the fruit of Christ's coming, on all nations, and the overthrow of all enemies of Christ and His Church in the great final conflict, where they will be gathered together, in what is called by a grand

[1] See below, on Hos. i. 2.
[2] Hos. iv. 15; ix. 15; xii. 11. Hosea's words are taken up by Amos (iv. 4; v. 6).
[4] Hos. ii. 14—23; iii. 1.
[6] Hos. vi. 1 - 3; xiii. 14, 14.
[2] S. on Hos. xi. 1.
[3] Hos. xi. 10, 11.
[5] Hos. xi. 10, 11.
[1] See below, on H. s. i. 10, 11; ii. 5.
[3] Hos. xiv. 9. See the note there, p. 28.
[2] On the meaning of their names see on Hos. i. 1; Joel i. 1.
[6] See on Joel, *Prelim. Note*, p. 21.
[5] See Joel ii. 20.
[12] Joel ii. 23.

metaphor "the Valley of Jehoshaphat," (that is, of the Judgment of the Lord) for His great Harvest and Vintage, when they will be crushed by Him with the same ease as sheaves of corn are crushed under the sharp-toothed engine on the threshing floor, or as ripe clusters of grapes are crushed beneath the feet of him who treadeth the wine-press[1].

Then will be the delivery and victory of the faithful; then will be new outpourings of grace, symbolized by the gushing forth of living waters[2] from the House of the Lord, to water the parched and barren places of the earth, as in the vision of Ezekiel[3]; and Judah will dwell safely for ever, for the Lord dwelleth in Zion, the Church militant on earth, to be glorified for ever in heaven[4].

The next prophet, AMOS, takes up the words of Joel[5], and continues the chain of prophecy. Joel had displayed a sublime view of God's judicial majesty in one magnificent panorama. Amos disintegrates that great whole, and represents the divine attribute of Justice, in its visitations on individual Nations. These Nations not only have a literal significance, but are representatives of various forms of hostility to God and His Church in every age, and especially in the latter days. Such were the heathen nations of Syria, Palestine, Tyre, Edom, Ammon, Moab. All of these are typical nations, and find their counterpart in the history of Christendom.

Amos also declares that God will visit with special judicial chastisement all forms of corrupt religion, and all sins of evil living in His Church[6]. Indeed he dwells upon them with special emphasis and with comprehensive fulness, in seven consecutive chapters[7]. Israel, the ancient Church of God, had received signal blessings from Him; but (as Hosea had already shown) it had requited those favours with unthankfulness. Therefore, after long forbearance, God will scatter Israel. But in that dispersion (as Hosea had already declared[8]) there would be mercy. The chastisement will bring Israel to repentance; and Israel will be gathered in Christ and His Church. Then the tabernacle of David, that was fallen, will be reared from its ruins[9]. A faithful remnant of Israel—the Apostles and first Preachers of the Gospel—will go forth and bring the heathen to Christ[10]; and the heathen, in their turn, when they have been converted to Christianity, will assist in restoring the Jews to God in Christ[11]. The Gentiles, having been evangelized by faithful Jews, will evangelize the Jewish Nation; and finally, Jews and Gentiles will dwell together as brethren and fellow-citizens in the spiritual Sion of the Universal Church of Christ.

The prophets Joel and Amos prepared the way for OBADIAH, JONAH, NAHUM, and HABAKKUK. Joel had proclaimed God's judicial majesty in a sublime and comprehensive prophecy, displaying its acts in one grand panorama, embracing all nature and history, civil and ecclesiastical, even to the Day of doom, and the full and final victory of Christ.

Amos had particularized God's judicial workings in the moral government of the world, and in the divine visitations on its several kingdoms, Heathen and Hebrew, and in the ordering all things, even the penal discipline of Israel's dispersion, for the future triumph of the Gospel, and for the reception of all the faithful of all nations into the Christian Church.

The four Prophets, OBADIAH, JONAH, NAHUM, and HABAKKUK, exhibit God's judicial dealings in a still more special and particular manner, in what may be termed a characteristic series of four prophetic *monographics*.

Obadiah directs his prophecy against Edom; Jonah and Nahum address their predictions to Nineveh, the great capital of Assyria. Habakkuk concentrates his utterances on Babylon, the great city which succeeded Nineveh in the Empire of the East.

But it must be remembered that Edom, Nineveh, and Babylon are not merely literal and historical countries and cities, hostile to Israel and Judah; but they have also a prophetic, representative, and symbolical character. They foreshadow three distinct forms of enmity to the Church and people of God. They exhibit three peculiar phases of the Anti-Christianism of the latter days. Edom, the neighbour and kinsman of Israel and Judah, and yet eagerly seizing every opportunity of displaying an unfriendly and unbrotherly spirit toward the Hebrew People of God; exulting with savage and perfidious delight in their distresses, and especially in the fall of Jerusalem and in the captivity of its king and inhabitants by the armies of Babylon, represents the uncharitable temper of those who have some ties of spiritual neighbourhood and alliance with the Church of Christ, and yet, instead of sympathizing with her in her sorrows, and aiding her in her warfare against unbelief and vice, find

[1] Joel iii. 1. 13.　　[2] See on Joel iii. 18, p. 35.　　[8] See above, p. xii., and Hos. xiii. 9.
[3] Ezek. xlvii. 1. Cp. 286.　　[9] Amos ix. 11. Cp. the speech of St. James at the Council of
[4] Joel iii. 20, 21.　　[5] Amos i. 2. Cp. Joel iii. 16.　　Jerusalem, Acts xv. 16, 17.
[6] Amos ii. 4; iii. 1—13; iv. 1—13; v. 1—27.　　[10] Amos ix. 12.
[7] Amos iii.—ix.　　[11] Amos ix. 14.

pleasure in her sufferings, and exert their influence to thwart, hamper, vex, and weaken her. These are the modern Edomites, who are ready to make common cause even with Babylon itself against the Christian Sion; and they may read a solemn warning to themselves in the prophecy of Obadiah. On the other hand, the faithful Church of God, and every true member of it, may find comfort there, in the assurance of future glory and eternal felicity in Christ[1].

The prophet JONAH was sent to preach repentance to Nineveh, the capital of Assyria, the proud and powerful Empire which showed its enmity against Israel and Judah at different times, in the days of successive Assyrian kings, Pul, Tiglath-pileser, Shalmaneser, Sargon, and Sennacherib. God's exceeding kindness, even to His bitterest enemies, was thus displayed. He earnestly desired that Nineveh should repent and be saved; and this divine attribute of mercy towards all nations, even heathen Assyrias, is more clearly exhibited, because it stands in striking contrast to that narrow and exclusive spirit of Judaism which showed itself in Jonah himself, grudging and even censuring the extension of God's compassion to Nineveh[2], and eager to confine His love within the narrow precincts of Palestine.

Jonah himself is a prophecy. The calming of the sea, after his act of self-devotion, was a figure of the peace produced in the troubled sea of the World, after a far greater and more willing Sacrifice. Jonah's three days' burial in the whale's belly, and his resurrection from the sea, and his preaching to Nineveh after that resurrection, and the repentance of Nineveh, and its salvation from the impending doom, was a foreshadowing of the death, burial, and resurrection of a far "greater than Jonah[3]," and of His preaching of repentance after His resurrection from the grave, by the ministry of His Apostles and their successors, with whom He is "present alway, even unto the end of the world[4]."

The Book of Jonah is like a beautiful rainbow of hope, set by God's hand in the dark cloud of human sin and suffering. It shows that whatever judgments are executed by Him on His bitterest enemies, are not consequences of any desire on His part to punish, but are due to their sins, evoking and arming the divine justice against themselves.

The Prophet NAHUM is the complement of Jonah. Nineveh repented at the preaching of Jonah, but it relapsed into sin, and its moral condition became worse than before, by apostasy. God warned it of its doom by Nahum. And Nahum has also a message to men and nations in these latter days. If, having received the message of the Gospel from the divine Jonah, which is Christ, they fall away by unbelief, as it was prophesied by Christ and His Apostles[5] that many would do, then they may see their destiny in the prophecy of Nahum, foretelling the misery and shame, confusion, overthrow, and desolation of the great city of Nineveh, which is the prophetic type of the sin and doom of the Infidel form of Anti-Christianism.

The prophet HABAKKUK completes the series of prophets whose writings consist solely of special prophecies directed against particular countries and cities, opposed to God and His ancient People.

Obadiah had prophesied against Edom; and Jonah and Nahum had prophesied to Nineveh; Habakkuk prophesies against Babylon. He shows that Babylon's victories were not due to itself, but that it was used by God for executing His judicial purposes on the Nations of the world, especially on His own people Judah, for their sins against Him; and that though Babylon was employed as an instrument by God[6], and its power was wielded as a weapon in God's hand, yet that God would visit Babylon also for its presumption and self-confidence[7]; and that though Babylon would prosper and triumph for a time, and though the patience of God's faithful servants would thus be sorely tried, and though the vision of judgment would tarry long, yet it would come at length[8], and the Divine Omnipotence would eventually be shown, by the overthrow of Babylon, the proud mistress of the Eastern World, and then there would be heard a shout of awe-struck and yet joyful adoration from the lips of the faithful: "The Lord is in His holy Temple, let all the Earth keep silence before Him[9]."

These things "were written for our learning." Habakkuk first casts his eye backward to the victories of the Exodus; and in the language of the sublimest poetry[10] he derives faith and hope for the future, from God's past miracles of mercy to His chosen people; and he closes his prophecy with a noble profession of trust in God. However dark may be the prospects of the Church of God, the true believer will never despair[11]; no, whatever her outward condition and circumstance may be, "although the fig-tree shall not blossom, neither shall fruit be in the vines, the labour of the olive

[1] See below, Obadiah 19—21.
[2] See below, *Prelim. Note* to Jonah, p. 62, and Jonah iv. 1 —5.
[3] See on Jonah i. 17.     [4] Matt. xxviii. 19, 20.
[5] Luke xviii. 8. Matt. xxiv. 12, 37. 40.   [1] Tim. iv. 1.
2 Tim. iii. 1.
[6] Hab. i. 6 —11.
[7] Hab. i. 12.
[8] See Hab. i. 12—17; ii. 2—20.
[9] Hab. ii. 20.
[10] See Hab. iii. 1 —15.     [11] See Hab. iii. 17.

shall fail, and the fields shall yield no meat ; the flock shall be cut off from the fold, and there shall be no herd in the stalls, yet," he will say, "I will rejoice in the Lord, I will joy in the God of my salvation[1]."

Habakkuk's prophecy casts its shadow forward to our own days. As the Edom of Obadiah has its antitype in our own times in the treacherous friends and false allies of the Christian Church ; as the Nineveh of Jonah and of Nahum represents the proud self-confident spirit of bold and open Infidelity, so the Babylon of Habakkuk has its counterpart in another form of hostility to God which has long exercised the faith and patience of Christendom.

The Babylon of Habakkuk and of other Hebrew Prophets, especially Isaiah and Jeremiah, is not merely an historical city opposed to the literal Jerusalem, but it has also a typical character. Babylon symbolizes a great Spiritual Power, which is now dominant in the world, and which is called "Babylon" in the New Testament[2]. It resembled that Power in its creature-worship, idolatry, and superstition, combined with a vainglorious profession of spiritual wisdom and sagacity, and of supernatural gifts and abilities to penetrate into the inner mysteries of the unseen world ; and by its claim to perpetuity and universal supremacy ; and by its oppression of God's faithful people ; and by its pride and arrogance and defiance of God, as displayed especially in two critical events, which stand forth in bold relief in the history of Babylon in the pages of Holy writ—namely, first, in the making of the golden image and the setting up of that idol in the plains of Dura, and in the royal decree that it should be worshipped by all nations, on pain of condemnation to death ; and secondly, in that great religious festival (for Belshazzar's feast had this character)[3] when the rulers and nobles of Babylon praised their gods of silver and gold, and outraged the majesty of God by drinking wine in the sacred vessels taken from His Temple in Jerusalem ; and were elated with self-confident joy and exultation, and indulged in festal revelry at a time when the enemy was at their gates, and their own doom was at hand.

The mystical Babylon, which is even now setting up an idol[4] in the person of the Roman Pontiff, to be adored as divine by all, and which has connected that act with a religious festival of her own institution[5], in open defiance of the teaching of Holy Scripture and the primitive Church, and in contravention of the unique sinlessness of Christ, may read her own destiny in the prophecy of Habakkuk ; and all true citizens of the Christian Zion may derive patience and comfort from it, in the present trials of their faith.

The Book of the Prophet Micah is inserted between that of Jonah and Nahum, and is set in beautiful relief and bright contrast against the darkness and gloom which characterize the predictions of Obadiah, Nahum, and Habakkuk, denouncing God's judicial visitations on those who rebel against Him.

Micah is the prophet of divine love. He is the messenger of consolation to all nations. He is the herald of universal salvation to all, through Christ.

Jonah had given vent to feelings of resentment and impatience because God spared Nineveh, the great capital of Assyria, the enemy of God's people, to which Jonah, in the exclusive spirit of Judaism, would have restrained God's favour. God had taught Jonah a lesson of sympathy and largeness of heart ; and Jonah's history and prophecy had imparted that lesson to others. Micah learnt that lesson, and applies it with affectionate fulness in his prophecy. He declares that though God will visit with judicial retribution all forms of hostility which are symbolized by Edom, Assyria, and Babylon, yet He has mercy in store in Christ for all, even for His bitterest enemies, if they will turn to Him with repentance.

Micah proclaims aloud with a thrice repeated appeal, "Hear ye," the solemn truth, that though God is gracious to Zion, if Zion is faithful to God, yet He does not confine His love to her. No, He will chasten Zion, as He punished Nineveh, if she presumes on His grace, and abuses it to an occasion for sin[6]. He will make her desolate, "for the iniquities of her princes, priests, and people ;" "Zion shall be a ploughed field, and Jerusalem shall become heaps, and the mountain of the house," (the Temple itself) "as the high places of the forest[7]." But God will temper judgment with mercy. His promises to David the King of Zion will never fail. The Redeemer will come to Zion, the promised Messiah, God blessed for evermore, He, Whose "goings forth are from everlasting," "He will come forth" as Man "from Bethlehem of Judah[8]." He will come forth as a mighty Conqueror

---

[1] Hab. iii. 18.

[2] The reasons for this identification are given at large below, in the notes on the Book of Revelation, xiii.—xvii. pp. 224—252. All successive investigation, and more recent events, have only served to confirm the writer in the conclusion there stated.

[3] See above, on Isa. xxi. 6.

[4] Cp. note on Zech. xi. 17; and above, on Daniel iii. 1—7.

where reasons are given for the opinion that the idol was an image of the ruler of Babylon himself.

[5] That of the Immaculate Conception, on which day the Roman Council met, Dec. 8, 1869.

[6] Micah i. 2—13; ii. 1—12; iii. 1—12.

[7] Micah iii. 12.

[8] Micah v. 2.

and will overthrow His enemies, symbolized by Assyria[1] the foe of Israel and Judah, and will raise up shepherds to feed His flock, and rulers to guide them and to defend them from their adversaries. In other words, Christ, Very God and Very Man, begotten of His Father from eternity, and born as Man of the Virgin Mary, of the seed of David, of the house of Judah, at Bethlehem, will overthrow the spiritual enemies of all true Israelites. He will vanquish Sin, Satan, and Death. He is "the breaker up" Who will tear asunder the bars of the grave, and raise Himself, and lead forth the glorious army of His saints from the darkness of the tomb. "Their king shall pass before them, and the Lord on the head of them[2]." The result of that glorious victory will be, that "out of Zion will go forth the law, and the Word of God from Jerusalem." The Gospel of Christ will be preached by His Apostles, sent forth by Him from Jerusalem to teach all nations, baptizing them in the name of the Father, and of the Son, and of the Holy Ghost[3]. Jerusalem will be the Mother Church of Christendom. "The mountain of the Lord's house" (that house which will have been laid desolate like a ploughed field for its sins[4]) "shall be established in the top of the mountains, and it shall be exalted above the hills, and all people shall flow unto it, and many nations shall come and say, Come and let us go up to the mountain of the Lord and to the house of the God of Jacob, and He will teach us of His ways and we will walk in His paths."

The Temple of Jerusalem will be destroyed; but out of its ruins will arise a nobler fabric, the Christian Church. The Law will be fulfilled in the Gospel. The Temple will be spiritualized, and Jerusalem will expand and develope herself with living energy and comprehensive universality, and will enfold all nations in the Catholic Church of Christ; and the Jews, once rebels against God[5], will at length be brought by the agency of Gentile Christians into the fold of the One Shepherd.

Therefore well might the Prophet exclaim, with this glorious vision of the future before his eyes, "Who is a God like unto Thee, that pardoneth iniquity? He retaineth not His anger for ever; because He delighteth in mercy. He will turn again, He will have compassion, He will subdue our iniquities, and Thou wilt cast all their sins into the depths of the sea[6]."

The prophet ZEPHANIAH is the ninth of the Minor Prophets, and is the last of that order who prophesied before the Captivity at Babylon.

Zephaniah does for the Two Tribes the same prophetic work which had been done for the Ten Tribes of Israel by Hosea, who stands at the head of the Minor Prophets. He utters a warning voice of coming judgments to Jerusalem, as Hosea had done to Israel: he foretells that Jerusalem will fall, and that Judah will be carried away captive for her sins, as Israel had already been[7].

He declares also that the God of Israel and Judah is supreme Governor of the World, and that the triumphs of Assyria and Babylon over Israel and Judah were not due to their own power, but that the God of Israel and Judah used those mighty nations as His own instruments for vindicating His own majesty, and for manifesting His own glory, and for executing His judgments on His unthankful people.

But Zephaniah also assures Judah, as Hosea had assured Israel, that God's love to His people had never failed, and that it never would fail.

Both these prophets minister spiritual consolation to all God's people in every age, and cheer them with the promise, that all who remain faithful to God will be sheltered in all tempests[8], civil and ecclesiastical, and will be saved in time and eternity.

They also proclaimed God's love to the Gentile Nations of the world.

They foretold that the mighty Empires of the earth will fall, and that their proud Dynasties will be humbled. They declared that God would thus wean the Nations from trusting in their false deities, and prepare them for the reception of a purer faith in the Gospel of Christ; that He would give them "a clean lip," and He would cleanse them from idolatry; and that with those lips, with which they had once worshipped false gods, they would "call upon the Name of the Lord, and serve Him with one consent[9]."

They predicted that the Gentiles, having been converted to Christ by the faithful remnant of Israel (namely by the Apostles and first preachers of the Gospel, going forth from Jerusalem), would in their turn supply Christian Missionaries for the conversion of Israel and Judah, scattered abroad and humbled by captivity and dispersion, and liberated even by that captivity from their besetting sin of idolatry, and healed by that wholesome discipline; and so, in God's due time, Jerusalem, the

---

[1] Micah v. 5.
[2] Micah ii. 13.
[3] Matt. xxviii. 19.
[4] Micah iii. 12.
[5] Micah vii. 12—19.
[6] Micah vii. 18—20.
[7] Zeph. i. 1—18; iii. 1—4.

* The name Zephaniah signifies, Whom the Lord hides; Hosea signifies, Saviour. See on Zeph. i. 1. Hos. i. 1.
* Zeph. iii. 9.

mother of Christendom, would be a praise in all the earth. The Lord her God would be in the midst of her[1]; He would dwell with her for ever in the Christian Church, which had her origin in Sion. The world itself would be a spiritual Jerusalem. Jew and Gentile will dwell together as fellow-citizens and fellow-members of Christ ; and God's words by Zephaniah will then be fulfilled, "I will make you a name and a praise among all the people of the earth[2]."

More than a century passed between the age of Zephaniah and the next following prophet, HAGGAI.

In that interval Jerusalem had been taken, and its king, princes, and people had been carried captive to Babylon[3].

But Babylon also in her turn had felt the power of God. Cyrus, His servant, had done His work, and had punished Babylon for her sins ; and having executed His judgments on Babylon, Cyrus performed God's purpose of love towards His chosen people, by issuing a royal decree for their liberation from Babylon, and for their return to Jerusalem, and for rebuilding the Temple at Jerusalem, and for the restoration of the sacred vessels which had been taken from the Temple by Nebuchadnezzar, and had been placed in his idol's temple, and had been sacrilegiously profaned by Belshazzar at that festal anniversary when Babylon was taken.

These events had been foretold by foregoing Hebrew Prophets, by Isaiah, Micah, Habakkuk, Jeremiah, Zephaniah, and Daniel. Thus the faith of God's People in the inspiration of their own prophets had been confirmed; and their reverence and love for Him Who had spoken by the prophets, and had humbled their powerful enemies, Assyria and Babylon, and had raised up Cyrus, the great conqueror of Babylon, to be His instrument for their good, had been quickened and invigorated; and a pledge and earnest had been given them that the other predictions which God had uttered, or might hereafter utter by His servants the prophets, would in due time be fulfilled also.

This is what imparts a special interest and value to the writings of the three prophets who now follow, HAGGAI, ZECHARIAH, and MALACHI.

The prophetic vista had now been cleared. Israel had been dispersed; Nineveh had fallen; Judah had been scattered ; Babylon had fallen ; Judah had been restored. No great events like these now remained, to arrest the eye and to intercept the view of the faithful in looking at the prospect lying before them, between their own age and the Coming of Christ.

Haggai, Zechariah, and Malachi are in a special manner the prophets of Christ's first Advent, and of its consequences, even till His Second Coming to judge the world.

The mission of Haggai was to stimulate the flagging energies of the exiles who had returned from Babylon. The ancient men among them, who remembered the magnificence of the first Temple, wept when they saw the foundations of the second Temple[4]. But the Prophet cheered them[5], not, indeed, with any promise of material splendour (for the latter house was "as nothing in comparison[6]" with the former), but with the joyful assurance that the glory of the second Temple, which they themselves were building, would be far greater than that of the former, because the Lord of the Temple Himself, "the Desire of all Nations[7]" would come to that Temple, and by coming to it would fill that house with glory; and that in that place He would give peace[8]. This prophecy was fulfilled when Christ, "God manifest in the flesh," came to that latter house. He was presented there ; He taught and healed there; He filled it with the Divine Glory by His Coming, and gave peace and salvation, and promise of eternal bliss by His Presence. Therefore, when this prophecy was accomplished, the devout Simeon was enabled to say in the Spirit, as he took up the infant Saviour in his arms, "Lord, now lettest Thou Thy servant depart in peace, for mine eyes have seen Thy salvation[9]."

The prophet ZECHARIAH was a contemporary of Haggai; and his prophecies are a sequel to those of Haggai, and are continued in a series of prophetic visions from his own days to those of Christ's first Advent, when He came to save, and even to those of His Second Advent, when He will come again to judge.

Zechariah's prophecies are obscure to the Jews ; and no wonder ; because they read them with a veil on their hearts. But "that veil is taken away in Christ[10]." The darkness of these predictions is dispelled by the light of the Gospel.

Here is a striking proof of the inspiration of the prophet Zechariah, and of the truth of the Gospel. Each is fitted to the other. His prophecies are fulfilled in the Gospel, and are made clear by it.

---

[1] Zeph. iii. 17.   [2] Zeph. iii. 20.
[3] Compare below, *Introductory Note* to Haggai, p. 113.
[4] Ezra iii. 12.   [5] Hag. ii. 2—4.
[6] Hag. ii. 3.   [7] See on Hag. ii. 6—9.

[8] The Hebrew word for *peace (shâlôm)* has a far wider sense than our English word (*peace*), by which it is rendered. It means salvation from enemies, and peace after it, and happiness.
[9] Luke ii. 29.   [10] 2 Cor. iii. 1. 15, 16.

The first vision of Zechariah reveals the Divine Presence and Power protecting the Hebrew Nation, at that time in a poor estate, like a lowly grove of myrtles in a valley[1]. But God was with them there, as He was at Horeb, in the burning bush, which represented the Hebrew Nation in Egypt, then like a lowly bush, a bush burning with fire, but not consumed[2].

The Divine Presence is symbolized by a red horse—an emblem of power and battle; and behind him are red horses, His ministers, showing that the Powers of the world are servants of the God of Israel, Who will use them for the defence of His own people[3].

The next vision represents four horns[4], the symbols of aggressive power. These four horns (as the prophecies of Daniel had prepared the readers of Zechariah to understand[5]) are emblems of the four great earthly Monarchies, opposed to the people of God. And as the number *four* is a scriptural symbol of universality in space, these four horns, in a secondary sense, represent all earthly powers antagonistic to the Church of God.

The future overthrow of all such worldly Powers is pre-announced in the next vision of the four *Carpenters*, or *Smiths*, who are shown to the Prophet by the Lord[6].

These four Carpenters, or Smiths, are the spiritual adversaries of the four horns which represent the worldly and irreligious power. As their name intimates, they have not only a destructive commission, but also a constructive office; they not only overthrow what is evil, but they also build up what is good. They "fray and cast out the horns" which had scattered God's people[7].

Their fourfold character displays them as opposed to the four great worldly Monarchies; and also, in a spiritual and secondary sense, as the instruments in God's hands, in all the four corners of the earth. And thus they symbolize the power of the fourfold Gospel preached to all Nations, even to the four winds of heaven, by the Apostles and their successors in every age; and overthrowing the powers of the world, and building up the Church of God[8].

Fitly, therefore, is this vision followed by another which reveals an angel from heaven with a measuring-line in his hand for the building up of Jerusalem[9]. This vision also has both a literal and a spiritual significance. It displays the building up of the literal Jerusalem, notwithstanding the opposition of her enemies; and it foreshadows the building up of the spiritual Jerusalem, the Church of Christ, by divine power in spite of all human antagonism[10], and the perpetual dwelling of the Lord in the midst of her, and the flowing in of all Nations to find a home there.

The next vision reveals another form of conflict between the powers of good and evil. Satan himself is displayed as opposing Joshua the High Priest[11], the spiritual representative of God's ancient people, the Jews, on their return from the Babylonish Captivity to Jerusalem.

In former prophecies it had been revealed, that the Temple at Jerusalem and the walls of the City would be rebuilt, in spite of all worldly hostility. And now it is declared, that, notwithstanding the antagonism of Satan himself, the Priesthood would be preserved, as a brand plucked from the fire by God's hand; and that it would be purified from taint of sin, represented by the filthy garments in which Joshua was clothed; and be invested with dignity and glory[12].

This vision was partly fulfilled in the restoration of the Ritual of the literal Temple at Jerusalem; but its adequate fulfilment is in Christ.

Christ is the Divine Joshua, or Saviour; He is the One Great and Everlasting High Priest; He is ever ministering in the true Holy of Holies. He has exchanged the garments of humility and the robe of "the likeness of sinful flesh[13]," in which for our sakes He vouchsafed to be clothed on earth, for the glorious apparel and splendid mitre of an everlasting Priesthood in the heavenly Jerusalem. Therefore Joshua and his companions are described in the vision as "men to be wondered at[14]." That is, they are types of another and mysterious Priesthood, the Priesthood of Christ, to be contemplated with awe and amazement.

This interpretation throws light on what follows.

The vision of Joshua, the type of Christ's Priesthood, prepares us for the view which is next presented to us, of Christ Himself in His threefold office, as Prophet, Priest, and King; and of Christ's Church, which derives all her light from Him in His two Natures, Very God and Very Man, suffering for the sins of the world, and glorified by suffering.

The beautiful harmonies of Zechariah's prophecies are awakened by the breath of the Holy Spirit in the Gospel, as by a heavenly breeze stirring and attuning the golden strings of a divine harp. The one is adjusted to the other. The one proves the divine origin of the other.

The manifold functions of Christ are displayed in the many names by which He is designated

[1] Zech. i. 8.    [2] Exod. iii. 2.    [3] See Zech. i. 8.    [9] Zech. ii. 1.    [10] Zech. ii. 5-13.    [11] Zech. iii. 1-3.
[4] Zech. i. 18.    [5] See on Zech. i. 18.    [12] Zech. iii. 4, 5.
[6] Zech. i. 20.    [7] Zech. i. 21.    [8] See below. p. 124.    [13] Rom. viii. 3.    [14] See on Zech. iii. 8.

by Zechariah. He is Joshua, because He is our High Priest : He is Zerubbabel, because He is our Prince, of the regal race of Judah. He is also called "the Branch;" "Behold, I will bring forth My Servant the Branch[1]," says the Lord. Christ is the Branch from the root of Jesse and stem of David.

In His Human Nature He is the Lord's "Servant," coming in the flesh in order to do His will. He is also the Stone[2], "the elect Corner Stone," which joins together the two walls of the Jew and Gentile in one ; and the "Stone cut out without hands[3]," which becomes a mountain and fills the earth ; and He is the Stone "engraven with seven eyes," because He is illumined with the sevenfold gifts of the Spirit. And the blessings of redemption and peace which flow from these attributes and offices are described by the Lord Himself : "I will remove the iniquity of the land" (or of the earth) "in one day" (the day of the Messiah). "In that day shall ye call every man his neighbour under the vine and under the fig-tree[4]."

This Vision of Christ is succeeded by a Vision of His Universal Church, symbolized by the seven-branched Candlestick, of pure gold, whose pipes are fed with oil flowing into them from two Olive-trees, standing on the right and left side of it[5]. These two Olive-trees, representing the continuity of that supply by their vitality and verdure, are called "the two anointed ones," or literally, "the two sons of oil," which stand by the Lord of the whole earth[6].

The Candlestick represents the Church of Christ[7]. This explains the circumstance that, together with the candlestick, there is conjoined a mention of the Temple, and of its foundation and completion by the Spirit of God[8]. The reason is, that the Temple and the Candlestick are figures of the Church. The Temple typifies its solidity and symmetry, due to the Spirit of God ; the seven-branched Candlestick of pure gold prefigures the Universal Church of God in the purity of its doctrine, and as diffusing throughout the whole world the light which it receives from the oil of the Spirit. The two Olive-trees, or "Sons of oil," which stand before the God of the whole earth, represent the kingly and priestly offices of Christ. These offices He discharges as Very Man, anointed by the Holy Ghost at His Conception and at His Baptism. Therefore He has the Name Messiah, Christ, or Anointed One[9]. "He is anointed with the oil of gladness above His fellows[10]," and all the unction of Christians flows on them from Christ their Head. "Ye have an unction from the Holy One," says the Apostle[11]. He, the Everlasting King and Priest, "hath made us to become kings and priests to God[12]" by virtue of His Incarnation, Kingdom, and Priesthood, and of our mystical incorporation in Him ; and He "stands before the Lord of the whole earth." He is ever standing at God's right hand, as our King, ruling the world and defending His People ; and as our Priest, making intercession for us ; and "of His fulness have all we received, and grace for grace[13]."

The next vision represents Christ's judicial office. He is merciful and loving to all who believe and obey Him ; but for those who do not believe and obey, there is a sweeping malediction, represented by the flying roll which goeth forth over the face of the whole earth. None can escape it[14]. This is directed against moral delinquencies ; and there is also a special punishment for false doctrine.

The true Church is represented by a woman ; she is the Bride of Christ. The false Church is also represented by a woman, the harlot. Zechariah is explained by St. John in the Apocalypse. This woman, the corrupt Church, is punished by being placed in an ephah[15] ; and she is carried for her sins from Jerusalem to the Land of Shinar, that is, to Babylon[16]. Here, also, Zechariah is again illustrated by St. John in the Apocalypse. The woman carried away from Sion to Babylon, is the corrupt Church of the Apocalypse, who is there called "the woman, the harlot," and "Babylon[17]." Her doom, pronounced by Zechariah, is more fully described by St. John.

The following vision displays the Universal Sovereignty of the Lord God, ruling in all kingdoms of the world, and using them as His instruments for the accomplishment of His purposes, and for the execution of His judgments.

This truth is declared by the four chariots[18], which represent primarily the four great earthly Empires of ancient history ; and secondarily, since the number *four* is the Scriptural symbol of all space[19], these four chariots[20] typify all earthly dynasties. The chariots go forth from the brasen

[1] Zech. iii. 8.
[2] Zech. iii. 9.
[3] Dan. ii. 34.
[4] Zech. iii. 10.
[5] Zech. iv. 2—11.
[6] Zech. iv. 14.
[7] See on Zech. iv. 2.
[8] See verses 6—11 of this chapter.
[9] Cp. Acts iv. 27 ; x. 38. God anointed Jesus of Nazareth with the Holy Ghost.
[10] Heb. i. 9. Ps. xlv. 7.
[11] 1 John ii. 20.
[12] Rev. i. 6 ; v. 10.
[13] John i. 16.
[14] See Zech. v. 1—4.

[15] See on Zech. v. 8. And she is called "wickedness" in the *Sept.*, ἀνομία, a remarkable word, especially when taken in connexion with the ἄνομος of St. Paul, describing the "lawless one" who sits in the Temple of God, i.e. in the Church of Christ, claiming for himself the divine attributes of infallibility and universal supremacy. See below, on 2 Thess. ii. 3.
[16] The *Sept.* here has "the land of *Babylon*."
[17] See Rev. xvii. 1. 3. 5—7. 15, 16.
[18] Zech. vi. 1.
[19] See on Matt. x. 2 ; xxiv. 31. Rev. vii. 1, and Rev. p. 215.
[20] Zech. vi. 5.

mountains of God's might and power; they are compared to winds issuing forth from the Lord of the whole earth[1]. They go forth from His presence like winds let loose from a cave, to sweep over the earth with irresistible power, and to do the work of Him Whose emissaries and servants they are.

This universal kingdom is next represented as given to Christ. He is " the Man Whose Name is the Branch[2]." He is both Priest and King[3]. He was typified by Joshua the Priest, and by Zerubbabel the temporal Ruler and builder of the Temple at Jerusalem. The crowns brought by the people of the Captivity are given to Joshua the Priest[4], in order to signify that the time would come when the Royalty would be united with the Priesthood. This has been fulfilled in Christ. He is the Builder of the True Temple ; He is the Eternal Priest and Universal King of the Spiritual Jerusalem, the Christian Church. What Zechariah foretold is accomplished in Him, " He shall build the Temple of the Lord, and He shall bear the glory, and shall sit and rule upon His throne ; and He shall be a Priest upon His throne[5]."

These visions, which unfold great truths of the Christian Faith, are followed by precepts concerning godly practice. The utter hollowness of all religious professions, and of all ceremonial observances, without the exercise of the moral virtues of truth, justice, mercy, and charity, is declared in strong language[6];" and thus a prophetic protest is delivered against that hypocritical Pharisaism which corroded the vitals of the religion of the Hebrew Nation in later days, especially in our Lord's age, and which also has been one of the most pestilent cankers of the Christian Church.

Almighty God proffers an abundance of blessings to His people ; but the fulfilment of these gracious promises, it is distinctly declared, is contingent on their own acts[7]. If they cleave to Him by faith and obedience, then, it is affirmed, they will be a blessing to themselves and others. The Heathen Nations of the world will be brought into communion with God by their means. " Ten men will take hold out of all nations of the skirt of him that is a Jew, saying, We will go with you, for we have heard that God is with you[8]." This has been fulfilled by Christ and by the faithful remnant of Israel, especially the Apostles, all of whom were Jews, and by other first preachers of Christianity, who were enabled by their commission from Christ, and by the power of the Holy Ghost given to the Church at Pentecost, to be instruments in God's hands for bringing the Heathen Nations to Him ; and the eagerness with which the Heathen embraced the Gospel preached by them is described in the vivid language of the prophet, "Ten men will take hold out of all nations of the skirt of him that is a Jew."

Such is God's purpose of love to the Heathen, if they believe and obey Him. But, as it is in His dealings with the Jews, so it is in His overtures to the Gentiles. There is mercy, on the one hand, to the penitent, but there is retribution to the ungodly. God is ready to be the Saviour of all who believe, both Jew and Gentile ; and He is also the righteous Judge of all.

This truth is declared in what follows. God there reveals His judgments against Heathen Nations relying on their own power, wealth, and wisdom, such as Persia, Syria, Tyre, and Philistia[9]. But even in these chastisements there was compassion. The humiliation of these Nations by the arms of Alexander the Great (who, like Nebuchadnezzar and Cyrus before Alexander, and like the Roman Power after him, was an instrument in God's hands preparing the way for Christianity) broke down their faith in the power of their local and national deities, who, as they found by experience, were not able to help and defend them in their danger; and thus, by a salutary discipline of affliction, predisposed them to receive the Gospel of Christ[10]. Hence, therefore, the Prophet passes from a view of Alexander's conquests to describe the victories of a greater Conqueror, Jesus Christ : just as Zechariah's predecessor, the Evangelical Prophet Isaiah, having described the successes of Cyrus, the conqueror of Babylon and the liberator of the captive Jews, proceeds to hail the victorious career of Christ, subduing all His enemies and redeeming a captive world[11].

How striking is the contrast ! Christ, the Son of God, is seen riding in His triumphal entry into His capital city, Jerusalem, not in a magnificent chariot drawn by snow-white horses, not mounted on a martial charger champing a golden bit, like the Emathian conqueror, Alexander the son of Philip, on his tamed war-horse Bucephalus, but "lowly and meek, riding on an ass, even on the foal of an ass[12]."

This vision is to be the signal of rapturous ecstasy to Jerusalem. " Rejoice greatly, O daughter

---

[1] Zech. vi. 5.   [5] Zech. vi. 12.   [9] Zech. ix. 1—6.
[2] Cp. Zech. iv. 14.   [4] Zech. vi. 11.   [10] See on Zech. ix. 7.
[3] Zech. vi. 1. 13.   [6] Zech. vii. 3 – 14.   [11] See above, Prelim. Note to Isaiah.
[7] Zech. viii. 1.   [8] Zech. viii. 23.   [12] Zech. ix. 9.

of Zion; shout, O daughter of Jerusalem: behold, thy King cometh unto thee: He is just and having salvation; lowly and riding upon an ass, even upon the foal of an ass[1]."

The might of Christ, the King of the Spiritual Zion, is declared to be her sufficient safeguard and support. She is secure under the rule of Him, Who does not need the help of chariots and horses, but rides on in meekness to victory.

The day (it is foretold) is coming, when the Church will be deprived of all earthly helps, supports, and defences. "The chariot will be cut off from Ephraim and the horse from Jerusalem, and the battle-bow shall be cut off[2];" but still, though the World is no longer for her, but against her, Christ's kingdom will be extended to the heathen, who will look on Him as their Saviour. It will be universal in extent and everlasting in duration[3].

This glorious deliverance from the bondage of Sin and Death is to be purchased by blood, "the blood of the covenant," the blood of Christ. This is the price to be paid for the redemption of Zion and of the World from the prison-house in which they lie like captives in a pit. They are freed from it by that redemption; and instead of being prisoners of death, they become "prisoners of hope[4];" and they exchange the dark dungeon of their captivity for the strong fortress of salvation. The battle-bow of earthly power is cut off; but Christ is a victorious Conqueror: He triumphs by His own death; and He is a warlike Archer, riding with a bent bow in His hand, and discharging His arrows against His enemies. Zechariah adopts the imagery of the Psalmist, which is reproduced by St. John in the Apocalypse, where Christ is displayed as riding with a bow in His hand, on His glorious career, "conquering and to conquer[5]."

The arrows of Christ were the Apostles and first preachers of the Gospel. He took these arrows from His quiver and discharged them from His bow, like missiles to subdue His enemies, and to overcome the heathen World, and to make it subject to His peaceful sway. Christ is ever riding as an Archer in Christian Missions; and, in the ordination of Christian Ministers to their apostolical and Evangelical office, He is ever sending forth His arrows, winged with feathers from the plumage of the Divine Dove.

Zechariah's words are ever being fulfilled, "The Lord shall be seen over them" (like a mighty Archer bending His bow and scattering His enemies, who fall backward before Him[6]); "and His arrows shall go forth like lightning; and the Lord God shall blow the trumpet" (the trumpet of the Gospel), "and shall go with whirlwinds of the south" (with irresistible power); "and the Lord God shall defend them; and they shall be like jewels in His crown." And the consequence of this victory will not be carnage and desolation; but salvation and joy, and a feast of spiritual delight in the Word and Sacraments of Christ. "How great is His goodness, and how great is His beauty! corn shall make the young men cheerful, and new wine the maids[7]."

The Prophet returns to contrast this blessed consummation with the evil results of disobedience and idolatry. Evil shepherds—bad rulers, civil and ecclesiastical, will be punished for their sins; and God will take away from them their office and give it to others, namely to faithful Teachers raised up by Christ from the people of God. "Out of him" (that is, from Judah) "Christ will come forth;" He Who is the "corner stone" which supports the fabric of the Church, and in which the two walls of the Jewish and Gentile world meet in one; and "the nail" (or peg) to which the cords of the tent of the Church are braced, and by which it is kept firm in the ground, so as not to be torn up or shaken by storms; and "the battle-bow," by which she overcomes her enemies[8]. By means of the preaching of those whom Christ sends forth, the Heathen will be evangelized; and not only so, but the Jews themselves, scattered abroad in all countries hostile to Israel—which are represented by Egypt in the south and Assyria in the north—will be brought into the True Zion, the Church of Christ[9].

Having thus foretold the future gathering together of Israel, the Prophet goes back, in order to specify the cause of their dispersion, and to account for it.

It might have been supposed, that in Zechariah's days, when the Temple and Walls of Jerusalem had just been rebuilt, and the great Empire of Persia, in the reigns of Cyrus and Artaxerxes, had favoured their restoration, there would be no more scattering of Israel. But the prophet Zechariah, being inspired by the Holy Ghost, reveals the marvellous and almost incredible fact, that Jerusalem would again be destroyed; and that her inhabitants would again be scattered abroad, on account of a sin far greater than any committed by their forefathers, namely the rejection and murder of their True Shepherd, the Messiah, Who is co-equal with Jehovah

---

[1] See on Zech. ix. 9.  [2] See on Zech. ix. 10.  [6] As seen in some of the sculptured monuments of Nineveh.
[3] Zech. ix. 10.  [4] Zech. ix. 12.  See Zech. ix. 13, 14.  [7] Zech. ix. 17.
[5] See below, on Zech. ix. 13, and Rev. vi. 2.  [8] See on Zech. x. 4.  [9] Zech. x. 7—12.

Himself[1]. He foresees the destruction of Jerusalem; he foretells the desolation of all the noble mansions of that city, which had just been rebuilt. "Howl, fir-tree[2]; for the cedar is fallen." He explains the reason of this catastrophe. Her shepherds have been faithless; they have not been true to their commission to feed His flock, but have slaughtered it for the gratification of their own carnal appetites. It has become "a flock of slaughter;" and they glory in their shame[3]. Therefore their commission is revoked. God sends to Jerusalem a faithful Shepherd, "the Good Shepherd," which is Christ. But they will reject Him with scorn; they will appraise His faithful service at the pitiful price of thirty pieces of silver[4]. This is cast to the potter. The Lord rejects them because th reject H i m; and He, the True Shepherd, breaks asunder His pastoral staves, "Beauty and Bands[5]," the symbols of the blessed effects of His pastoral work, which would have invested His people with spiritual grace and glory, and would have bound them to one another and to God[6]. Zechariah reveals the mystery, which has now been cleared up in the eyes of the world, that the Jews would destroy themselves, and be outcasts from God, and be scattered abroad, because they rejected and crucified Christ.

After describing the pastoral work of Christ in the Church, the Prophet proceeds, by a bold contrast, to describe that of an opposite power and person in Christendom, who claims to be a *shepherd*, and yet makes himself to be an "*idol*" in the Church[7]. " Woe to the *idol shepherd*," exclaims Zechariah. The woe which awaits him is described, " Woe to the *idol shepherd* that leaveth the flock ! the sword shall be upon his arm " (in which he trusts, and by which he claims to guide the world), " and upon his right eye" (for he thinks that he alone can see) : " his arm shall be clean dried up, and his right eye shall be utterly darkened[8]."

This prophecy of Zechariah concerning "the *idol shepherd*," seems to be even now in course of fulfilment in Christendom[9]. And here we may recognize another example of the mode in which the words of the prophets adjust themselves to events as they arise, and possess a continuous and increasing power and value for the Christian. And it may be anticipated, that additional evidences of the truth of divine Revelation will be supplied in the latter days, as years pass on, by the fulfilment of utterances in them which are now veiled in obscurity; and that, if we may so speak, the hand of Time will raise new trophies to Holy Scripture, and place fresh crowns on the heads of its writers, in proportion as we approach nearer to Eternity; and that thus, in an age of doubt, the reverent reader of Holy Scripture will have new confirmations of his faith in its Inspiration, and in the Gospel of Jesus Christ the Son of God, which is the end of all Hebrew Prophecy.

Zechariah has next a vision of the last days. He sees a gathering of hostile powers against God and against His Church, which, having been founded at Jerusalem by Christ, will expand itself to enfold the world. The Church, the true Jerusalem, will be assaulted by enemies on all sides, before the End comes. But she will be " a cup of trembling[10]" to all who attack her; she will be " a burdensome stone " to her adversaries. In other words, their own acts in persecuting and oppressing her will recoil upon themselves to their own utter confusion and ruin. God will make her foes to reel like drunken men, and will crush them and grind them to powder beneath the heavy weight of His wrath, and they will be consumed by the fire of His indignation, which will burst forth from her to consume them. The Prophet delivers the gracious assurance that Almighty God will defend His Church, and will strengthen all her faithful members, and will finally crown them with victory and glory. " The feeble among them shall be as David[11]," for they will be strong through the grace of the Divine David, Jesus Christ.

Still further, Zechariah reveals, that not only Heathen Nations, but the Jewish People also, will be converted to Christ. God will pour upon them " the Spirit of grace and supplications;" and God says, that "they will look on Me Whom they pierced[12]"—a clear testimony (as explained in the Gospel[13]) to the Godhead as well as the Manhood of Christ. They will mourn for Him, the true " King of the Jews," as they mourned for the good King of Jerusalem, Josiah[14]. Each family and person will be touched with penitential sorrow, and will confess Him, Whom they crucified, to be Christ and God[15]. Then He will be their Saviour. The fountain opened at Calvary in the wounded side of Christ, to the house of David and to the inhabitants of Jerusalem, will flow freely to them, and they will be cleansed by it. There will be no more idolatry among the Jews, as there was before the Babylonish Captivity. Nor will there be false teaching then, as there was in the days of the Scribes and Pharisees[16].

[1] See on Zech. xi. 1. 13 ; xiii. 7.        [2] Zech. xi. 1. 2.                    [10] Zech. xii. 2.            [11] Zech. xii. 8.
[3] Zech. xi. 4, 5.                        [4] Zech. xi. 13.                     [12] Zech. xii. 10.          [13] John xix. 37. Cp. Rev. i. 7.
Zech. xi. 7, 10. 14.        [6] xi. 7 – 15.        [7] See on xi 15 – 17    [14] See on 2 Kings xxiii. 29, 30.  2 Chron. xxxv. 24.
[8] See on xi. 17, a further exposition of this prophecy.           [15] Zech. xii. 11 – 14.        [16] Zech. xiii. 2 – 4.
[9] See below, on Zech. xi. 17.

It is the ordinary practice of Divine Prophecy, in Holy Scripture, *to recapitulate*[1]. That is, after it has descended to a distant point in the future, it comes back again to its former starting-place, and delivers another prediction which reaches down to still more distant objects than those which it had before attained. So it is here. The Prophet once more returns to describe more particularly the Death of Christ. He speaks of the wounds in His hands—wounds which He received in the house of His friends, even at Jerusalem itself[2]. The Death of Christ, which is foretold by Zechariah (as Christ Himself has assured us[3]), and is described by the Prophet as the death of Him Who is the Shepherd of His People, and also the "fellow," or equal, of Jehovah[4], is represented as due to the sins of His People, but as permitted and effected by God[5]. But God will have a remnant among them; He will bring His "hand upon the little ones," the meek and gentle of Israel. He will defend them and purify them by trial[6].

Thus the Prophet is brought again to the times of the End. He describes the last fierce struggle of infidel Antichristianism against the Lord and His Church. The Church will suffer great distress, as Jerusalem did in the days of its siege by the Romans. But at last the Lord will arise and scatter her enemies[7]. Then shall the End come. Christ will descend from heaven in glory, as He went up from Olivet in His Ascension into heaven. Whether He will literally appear on the Mount of Ascension, the Mount of Olives[8], time will show. His enemies will all be confounded; but His faithful servants will be marvellously preserved[9]. In the latter days, the living waters of the Spirit will be universally diffused over all the earth. There will be no more strifes and parties in religion; there will be "One Lord, and His Name One[10]." The Church will be exalted, extended, and glorified like a lofty plain above the hills of the earth[11], and will be safely inhabited[12]; all her adversaries will be consumed, and she will celebrate an universal and everlasting Feast of Tabernacles[13].

The typical foreshadowings of that great and crowning Festival of the Hebrew year, which spake of God dwelling with His people in the Tabernacle in the Wilderness, and which prefigured the glory that would follow when God Himself would vouchsafe to pitch His Tabernacle in human flesh, and be our Everlasting Emmanuel, will then be realized and consummated.

The Church will celebrate a spiritual Feast of Tabernacles for evermore; for God Himself will ever tabernacle amidst her[14]. Every thing will then be consecrated. The "bells of the horses[15]," the emblems of warfare, will be hallowed; common things will be sanctified[16]. The Church will shine in pure light, and in a bright atmosphere of holiness, and be transfigured and glorified for ever in the heavenly Jerusalem.

The glorious visions of Zechariah are succeeded by the moral homilies of MALACHI; and by this juxtaposition they supply a striking comment on the indispensable necessity of religious practice, and personal holiness, if there is to be a fruition of heavenly glory[17].

In the age of Malachi, Jerusalem rejoiced in her newly-built Temple and its restored Ritual; and she looked with self-complacency and hope for the Coming of the Messiah. But the Holy Spirit, speaking by Malachi, tempers her joy with sober reproofs and solemn warnings. He utters a prophetic protest against that hard, proud, covetous spirit of formalism, which afterwards displayed itself in the blindness of the Priests and in the vainglorious hypocrisy of the Pharisees in our Lord's age. He declares to the Jews—who gloried in their national privileges, but were not alive to the responsibilities, and did not discharge the duties, which those privileges involved—that unless they repented of their sins, their pride, their oppression, their perjury, their adultery, God would loathe all the ritual observances and sacrifices of the Temple at Jerusalem; and that their privileges would be taken from them, on account of their unthankfulness, insensibility, and presumption, and wilful disobedience and moral profligacy, and would be transferred to the Gentiles. The Advent of the Messiah would be a day of sorrow and shame to them, and not of joy and glory.

Thus Malachi, "the Seal of the Prophets," prepared the way for the stern preaching of the second Elias, John the Baptist[18], coming forth in the wilderness in his raiment of camel's hair, with a leathern girdle about his loins, to denounce God's judgments against Priests, Pharisees, and Sadducees, and the People of Jerusalem; and to prepare the way for the Judge[19], Whose Coming is heralded by Malachi: "The Lord Whom ye seek shall suddenly come to His Temple, even the

---

See below, *Introduction* to the Book of Revelation, pp. 151, 152; and *Prelim. Note* to Rev. xx.
[2] This seems to be the true exposition of xiii. 6.
[3] See our Lord's words, Matt. xxvi. 31, verifying this assertion.
[4] Zech. xiii. 7.
[5] Cp. the note on Acts ii. 23. Isa. liii. 10.
[6] Zech. xiii. 9.
[7] Zech. xiv. 1—5.
[8] Zech. xiv. 4. Acts II
[9] Zech. xiv. 4, 5.
[10] Zech. xiv. 9.

[11] Zech. xiv. 10. Cp. on Isa. ii. 2, 3. Ezek. xl. 2.
[12] Zech. xiv. 11.
[13] See on Zech. xiv. 16—19.
[14] The Apocalypse, as usual, takes up Zechariah's words and explains them. See on Rev. vii. 15, and xxi. 3.
[15] Zech. xiv. 20.
[16] Zech. xiv. 20, 21.
[17] See further below, as to this point, in the *Prelim. Note* to Malachi.
[18] Mal. iii. 1; iv. 5.
[19] In the words of St. John the Baptist, Matt. iii. 12, and note.

Messenger of the Covenant Whom ye delight in," and for Whose Coming ye look with desire, but do not prepare yourselves for it by holiness of life. "Behold, He shall come, saith the Lord of Hosts. But who may abide the day of His Coming, and who shall stand when He appeareth?"

Like John the Baptist, whom he announces, Malachi even while he is describing Christ's First Advent, sees the bright glory and awful majesty of His Second Coming; and he darts backward a rapid glance to Mount Sinai, and to the promulgation of the Law of Moses[2], and commands the Hebrew Nation to remember and observe the statutes and judgments which the Lord then delivered to Israel; and he then looks forward to the great and dreadful Day of the Lord[3]. Thus in his vast prophetic panorama he blends the earthly Sinai with the heavenly Sion. And while he assures the faithful and obedient of every age and nation that "the Sun of Righteousness will arise to them with healing in His wings," he ends his prophecy with a solemn call of sinners to repentance, lest God should reveal Himself to them in wrath and indignation, "and smite the earth with a curse[4]."

We have thus been brought by God's help to the close of the prophetical books of the Old Testament. Here we may pause awhile, and take a retrospective view of the ground traversed from the beginning of the Sacred Volume, and consider what reflections are suggested by it with regard to what still lies before us in our passage from time to Eternity.

Holy Scripture, from its first page to the last, reveals a succession of conflicts between good and evil; and of triumphs of good over evil, after severe struggles.

The Creation of the earth itself, in its present form, was a work of restoration by God, after a time of desolation and ruin due to the agency of evil[5]. The Fall of Man was a work of ruin wrought by the Evil One; but it was succeeded by God's promise of Christ, the Seed of the Woman, Who would bruise the serpent's head[6], and would raise men to a loftier condition than that in which they had existed in Adam. The rise in Christ is higher than the fall in Adam was deep.

The Deluge was like another fall, consequent on man's sin; but God graciously enabled him to emerge from it to a higher altitude, with nobler promises.

The building of Babel was like another fall, due to human pride and rebellion against God. Men sought for strength by combination in Babel, which was designed by them to be a centre of unity[7]; but they were punished by dispersion and confusion. God overruled evil for good; their dispersion prepared the way for the colonization and civilization of the World, and for the eventual diffusion of the Gospel of Christ, flowing in the language of all nations; and for the building up the universal Church of Christ, the true Sion, the city of peace—the antithesis of Babel, the city of confusion[8].

The declension of Mankind into idolatry was like another fall, produced by the evil agency of Satan, the author of idolatry[9]. But God called Abraham, the father of the faithful, out of the darkness of heathenism and idolatry[10], and promised that of him Christ should come, in Whom all nations should be blessed; and He made his family to be a depository and witness of truth, and to be the seminary of Christianity.

The selling of Joseph, one of that family, into Egypt by his brethren, and his imprisonment on false accusations, and his subsequent elevation to bear rule in the palace and realm of Egypt, and to become the preserver of life in the seven years' famine, is like a miniature specimen of the declensions and elevations which have their consummation in the Divine Antitype of Joseph, Jesus Christ[11].

The going down of that family into Egypt, the land of idolatry and the house of bondage, was like another fall; but God made it to be the occasion for a great and glorious conflict with the gods of the heathen, whom He visited with plagues[12], and for manifesting the glory of the Lord God of Israel, by the overthrow of their power, and by covering with the waves of the Red Sea the hosts of Egypt, when pursuing after His own people, whom He saved by two miraculous deliverances (both of which were typical and prophetic of mankind's deliverances by Christ, and of our Exodus in Him[13]), first at the Passover, when the firstborn of Egypt were destroyed, and next by the way which He made for them on dry land through the waters of the Red Sea, in which their enemies were overwhelmed.

The rebellion of Israel in the wilderness was like another fall; but it was followed by another

[1] Mal. iii. 1, 2.   [2] Mal. iv. 5.   [3] Mal. iv. 4.
[4] Mal. iv. 6.
[5] See the notes above, on Gen. i. 1, 2.
[6] See Gen. iii. 15.
[7] See the notes above, on Gen. xi. 1—6.
[8] See below, on Acts ii. 5, 6.      [9] See on Matt. iv. 9, 10.
[10] See Gen. xii. 1; and on Josh. xxiv. 2.

[10] See the notes on Genesis xxxvii. 28, and xli. 40, 57, where the points of resemblance are specified.
[12] See on Exodus xii. 12. The first of the ten plagues was executed on the river, which they revered as a deity. See the notes on Exodus vii. 17; viii. 1.
[13] See on Exodus xii, Prelim. Note, and Exodus xiv, Prelim. Note, and the notes on these two chapters throughout.

rise to a higher elevation, in the passage of the river Jordan, and in the conquests of Joshua, the type of Jesus [1], and in his settlement of Israel in Canaan, the figure of heaven.

The days of the Judges were evil; they were days of degeneracy and apostasy, but were followed by those of Samuel the Prophet, and David the King, the anointed of the Lord, "the man after God's own heart," "the sweet Psalmist of Israel," the conqueror of his enemies, the first Hebrew King of Jerusalem, the progenitor and type [2] of Christ; and by the glorious times of Solomon "the Peaceable," the builder of the Temple of Jerusalem, and in these respects the type of Christ the Prince of Peace, the Builder of the true Temple in the everlasting Sion, the universal Church [3].

The dispersion of the Ten Tribes of Israel, and the destruction of Jerusalem, and the captivity of Judah at Babylon (which had been foretold by Isaiah, Micah and Habakkuk, Zephaniah and Jeremiah) for their sins of idolatry, were like another fall. But this was overruled for the gracious purposes of manifesting the majesty and glory of the Lord God of Israel throughout the East, by the deliverance of the three children, who refused to fall down and worship the golden image set up by the King of Babylon [4]; and by the preservation of His faithful prophet Daniel in the lions' den, into which he was cast because he refused to omit his prayers to God, notwithstanding the decree of Darius the king [5]; and by the fulfilment of the prophecies of Isaiah, Jeremiah, and Habakkuk, in the capture of Babylon by Cyrus the Persian, "the shepherd" and "the anointed" of God [6]; and in the deliverance of God's People by him, and in his decree for their return to their own land, and for the restoration of the sacred vessels of the Lord's house, and for the rebuilding of the Temple at Jerusalem—all which events were figurative of still greater mercies in Christ [7], the mighty Deliverer of all faithful Israelites from their captivity, and the Restorer of our nature, which was like a city in ruins.

The destruction of the Temple, and the dispersion of the Hebrew People in distant lands, had the effect of weaning their minds from what was local, material, and transitory in religious worship [8], and of raising their hearts to commune with what is unseen, heavenly, and eternal; and it prepared them by a holy discipline for a purer faith. It rescued them from idolatry, and spiritualized them [9]. It also put an end to the unhappy rivalry and schism between Israel and Judah, and trained them for union in Christ.

The Temple built at Jerusalem after the return from Babylon, was far less glorious in external splendour and grandeur than the Temple of Solomon [10]. But the promise was, that "the glory of the latter house would be greater than that of the former [11]." And why? Because Christ, the Lord of the Temple, would come to it, and fill it with glory. Thus, even the inferiority of the latter house in material respects taught the great truth, that the essence of divine worship, and the glory of the Church, do not consist in external things, however magnificent, but in the presence and in-dwelling of Christ. Here was another progressive step toward that vital and spiritual religion which is taught by Christ in the Gospel [12].

The accomplishment of numerous prophecies which had foretold the sufferings of the Hebrew Nation for sin, and their deliverance and restoration after the fall of Babylon, strengthened their faith in the inspiration of Hebrew Prophecy, and in the power and love of the God of Israel, and stimulated them to look forward to the accomplishment of the other prophecies which were contained in their Scriptures, and especially those prophecies which foretold the Coming of the Messiah to that Temple which was built after the Captivity. The fulfilment of the former prophecies was an earnest and pledge that the latter prophecies would be fulfilled also.

The age of their return from Babylon was succeeded by a debasement and corruption of morals consequent on their vainglorious self-confidence in their own spiritual privileges, and on their disdainful contempt of heathen nations. These were the besetting sins of Judaism after the return from Babylon, even till the days of our Blessed Lord, when they reached their climax, and were punished with spiritual blindness as their inevitable retribution. But when every thing seemed most dark, then "the Sun of Righteousness [13]" arose upon the world. The Son of God Himself appeared in human flesh. The great majority of the Hebrew Nation were unable to recognize the beauty of the promised Messiah in the "Man of Sorrows [14]." "He came unto His own, and His own received Him

---

[1] See above, *Introd.* to Joshua ix.—xix., and notes on Joshua i. 1; v. 1, and throughout the book.
[2] See the notes above, on 2 Sam. vii., and *Prelim. Note* to 1 Chron. xxviii.
[3] See on Psalms lxxi. and lxxii.
[4] Dan. iii.
[5] See above, on Isaiah xliv. 28; xlv. 1.

[6] Dan. vi. 10.

[7] See the notes on 2 Chron. xxxvi. 22, and *Prelim. Note* to Isaiah xl.
[8] See *Introd.* to Ezra, pp. 298, 299.
[9] See *Introd.* to Ezra, p. 299.
[10] Haggai ii. 3. Ezra iii. 12. Zech. iv. 10.
[11] Haggai ii. 7—9. Cp. Malachi iii. 1.
[12] John iv. 23.
[13] Malachi. iv. 2.
[14] Isaiah liii. 3.

not [1]." They rejected and crucified the Holy One of Israel [2]. Thus they fulfilled the prophecies of the Psalms, of Isaiah, and Zechariah; as St. Paul declares, they did not understand the words of the prophets which were read in their own synagogues, and " they fulfilled them by condemning Him [3]."

Thus greater strength accrued to Divine prophecy, even from the unbelief of those who killed the King of Glory. The true remnant of Israel—namely, the Apostles and primitive believers among the Jews—were confirmed in their own faith by the infidelity of the Nation. That infidelity had long before been foretold : " Lord, " exclaimed Isaiah [4] in the name of the Hebrew Prophets, " who hath believed our report ? "

The apostasy of the Jews was punished by the utter destruction of the Temple and City of Jerusalem by the arms of Rome, and by the dispersion of the people into all lands even to this hour. But even this terrible visitation was fraught with mercy. No longer are the eyes of the faithful directed toward any local centre, such as the Temple at Jerusalem. No longer do they sit beneath the shadow of the Levitical Law. The material City and Temple have been levelled to the dust; but Jerusalem still lives and grows, and has been catholicized in the Church of Christ. The Church Universal has risen on the ruins of the Temple on Mount Moriah. The Church is the true Moriah, or, Vision of the Lord, where the abiding presence of the Lord is ever seen by the eye of the faithful [5]. The dim, visionary twilight of the Ceremonial Law has passed away for ever, and has melted away and been absorbed into the glorious sunshine of the Gospel.

The Jews, as a nation, have been rejected for a time, because they rejected Christ ; but even by this rejection the evidence of Christianity has been strengthened; for all these things were foretold by their own Prophets who prophesied of Christ. And there ever has been a faithful remnant in Israel, as those Prophets predicted, amid God's Ancient People. They have been the seminary of Christendom. All the Apostles and first preachers of Christianity were Jews, and were sent forth from Jerusalem by Christ, Who was the personification and consummation of faithful Israel [6]. They went forth, sent by Him, and empowered by the Holy Ghost, given to them at Jerusalem [7], to execute His commission, and to preach to all nations the Gospel, which is the fulfilment of the Law, and to make all men to be citizens of the true and everlasting Zion, which is His Church [8].

The dispersion of the Jews in all lands is a standing and ever-speaking witness, in all places, to the truth of Holy Scripture, which foretold it ; and it is also a testimony to the truth of Christ, because the Prophets, and Christ Himself and His Apostles, predicted that such would be the punishment of the Jews for that rejection, and declared that their only escape from that punishment, which has now lain heavy upon them for eighteen hundred years, is by repentance and faith in Christ. The heinousness of the sin of Unbelief, rejecting Christ, may be seen in the history of the Jews since the fall of Jerusalem even to this day.

But the Prophets also foretold that another triumph still awaits Christianity through this dispersion of the Jews. They foretold that the faithful remnant of the Jews, namely the Apostles and earliest disciples, would first convert the Heathen to Christianity; and that afterwards Preachers and Missionaries of the Gospel would be raised up in heathen nations, and would evangelize the Jews, and bring them also to the fold of Christ [9]. God's love to His Ancient People will be manifested, and they will unite with the Gentiles in adoring Him in the Christian Church [10].

Thus we see, that ever since the Creation, to the Coming of Christ, there has been a succession of conflicts with Evil and of conquests of the Truth, a series of moral falls and moral resurrections, a succession of decompositions and of redintegrations ; and that the tendency has ever been one of progress from what is material, local, and temporal, to what is spiritual, universal, and eternal.

The climax of this gradual ascent is reserved for the latter days. The crisis will be seen on the eve of Christ's Coming to judgment.

All Hebrew Prophecy in the Old Testament, and all Christian Prophecy in the New, concur with the evidence derived from the analogies of history, in testifying to a great coming struggle of Error with Truth, and of a great and final victory of Truth over Error.

The conflict and triumph described in the last chapter of Isaiah [11]; the great battle of Antichristian powers, symbolized by Gog and Magog in Ezekiel [12], and their utter rout and discomfiture;

[1] John i. 11.
[2] See on Acts xiii. 27.
[3] On the meaning of the term *Moriah*, see on Genesis xxi. 2. 14, and the notes on 2 Sam. xxiv. 24. 2 Chron. iii. 1.
[4] See on Hosea xi. 1
[7] Luke xxiv. 47–49. Acts i. 4. 8.
[2] Acts iii. 14. iv. 10.
[4] Isaiah liii. 1.

[8] See on Psalm lxxxvii. Heb. xii. 22.
[9] See on Hosea i. 10, 11 ; ii. 14–23. Amos ix. 9–15.
Rom. xi. 25, 26.
[5] See Rom. xv. 8–12.
[11] Isaiah lxvi. 15–24.
[12] Ezek. xxxviii. and xxxix.

the gathering of the Nations, and the crushing of their pride in the valley of Jehoshaphat, in the magnificent description of Joel[1]; the combination of hostile forces against the spiritual Jerusalem, the Church of God; and the grinding to powder of rebel Nations by the Stone cut out without hands, and their scattering like the dust of the summer threshing-floor, predicted by Daniel[2] in his vision of the Son of Man coming to judgment, and the future Resurrection; and the confederacy of worldly and godless forces against the Church of God, and their final overthrow, foretold by Zechariah[3]; all these and other similar prophecies, together with those which are ever recurring in the Psalms — from the first and second Psalms even to the end of the Book — which speak of the raging[4] of Nations against Christ, and the final subjection of all things beneath His feet; are like parts of one great prophetic drama, which is consummated in the Apocalypse of St. John, in the description of the marshalling of Antichristian forces for a great struggle in the latter days[5], and for the final shout of victory—"Hallelujah, for the LORD God Omnipotent reigneth;" "the kingdoms of this world are become the Kingdom of our LORD and of His CHRIST[6]."

Therefore the social and political phenomena of the present times will not disturb the mind of the Christian. In our own age (as has been truly said) we "live amid falling institutions; the foundations of fabrics have long been giving way, and a visible tottering has begun; and the sounds of great downfalls, and great disruptions come from different quarters; and great crashes are heard, as if some vast masses had just broken off from the rock, and gone down to the chasm below."

But the believer in Christ, with the Bible in his hand, remains unshaken. He knows that "heaven and earth will pass away, but Christ's Word will not pass away[7]." "Jesus Christ is the same yesterday, to-day and for ever[8]." States and Empires will fall; but Christ remains for ever[9]. The Holy Ghost will abide for ever with His Church[10]. The Holy Scriptures will remain; the holy Sacraments will remain; the Creeds of the Universal Church will remain; the Church herself[11] will remain for ever, to preach the Word of God, and to minister the Sacraments, and to fight against error and sin, and to lead men to a blessed immortality.

The faithful Christian will, indeed, mourn over the infatuation of States, abdicating their noblest functions, and forfeiting their most glorious prerogatives by apostasy from Christ[12], as if the everlasting Gospel were a thing which could now be flung aside, as superannuated and obsolete; and as if they could prosper without God's blessing; and as if they could have any blessing from Him unless they maintain His truth and promote His glory. He will deplore the presumption which vaunts that it can educate a nation (as if Education were not a discipline for eternity) without the doctrines and sanctions of religion, and the grace of the Holy Ghost; and by the mere beggarly elements of Secularism, which will have its sure retribution in national anarchy and confusion. He will weep, as Jeremiah wept amid the ruins of Sion, over the fall of national Churches. He will mourn over the breaking up and crumbling away of ancient Monarchies, and over the sweeping away of fallen and ruined Thrones by the fierce hurricane of popular revolutions. But in all these perturbations he will retain a spiritual calm. They will even strengthen, stablish, and settle him in the truth. And why? Because all these things have been foretold by Prophecy, Hebrew and Christian; and because they betoken the approaching consummation of a long series of events, which will culminate in the overthrow of all Error, Unbelief, and Ungodliness, and in the full and final triumph of the Christian Faith, at the Coming of the Lord to judgment. They are signs of the nearness of that Coming, and of its blessed results, which Hebrew and Christian Prophecy have foretold—the Resurrection of the dead, the re-appearing of the bodies of the faithful who have fallen asleep in Him; and the fruition of eternal peace, and the joys of His Church triumphant, glorified for ever in heaven.

Thus the retrospect of the past, from the present time even to the Creation, is full of comfort to the Christian. He knows that "not one good thing has failed" of God's promises, from the first prophecy in Scripture to Adam after the Fall[13], to the present time. It was prophesied that Christ should be born of a woman, that He should come of the seed[14] of Abraham, Isaac, Jacob, and Judah[15], and of David[16], that He should be born of a Virgin[17], and at Bethlehem[18], that He should be a Man of

[1] Joel iii. 19—21.
[2] Daniel ii. 35, 44; vii. 9—14, 26, 27; xii. 1—3.
[3] Zech. xiv. 1—21.
[4] Ps. ii. 4—12; xlv. 5, 6; cx. 1—7.
[5] See Rev. xvi. 10; xx. 9, 10.
[6] Rev. xix. 6; xi. 15.
[7] Matt. xxiv. 35.
[8] Heb. xiii. 8.

[9] Matt. xxviii. 19, 20. 1 Cor. xi. 26.
[10] John xiv. 6.
[11] Matt. xvi. 18.
[12] Rev. xiv. 6.
[13] Gen. iii. 15.
[14] Gen. xii. 3; xviii. 18; xxi. 12; xxii. 18; xxvi. 4; xxviii. 14. Exod. ii. 24.
[15] Gen. xlix. 10.
[16] See 2 Sam. vii. 12. Isa. vii. 14. Micah v. 2.

Sorrows[1], be meek and lowly, and ride on the foal of an ass[2], that His price should be thirty pieces of silver[3], that He should be pierced in His hands and His feet[4], that His raiment should be parted, and lots be cast for His vesture[5], that He should die as a transgressor[6] and be buried by the rich; and yet that He should be no other than the MIGHTY GOD[7], the Prince of Peace, the LORD OUR RIGHTEOUSNESS; that He should come as the Lord to that Temple[8] which was built by Zerubbabel; that He should rise from the dead[9], ascend in glory to the heavens[10], and send down the gift of the Holy Ghost; and that His Word should go forth from Zion[11] into all parts of the world, and that He should enfold the Gentile Nations in His Church.

All these prophecies have been fulfilled. What then shall we say? Since these predictions, so numerous, so circumstantial, so various, have been accomplished, can it be imagined that the other prophecies of the Hebrew and Christian Scriptures shall not be accomplished also? Shall ninety-nine prophecies in the Sacred Volume be fulfilled, and shall the hundredth fail? Assuredly not. The past fulfilment of the many is a pledge of the future fulfilment of the few; especially since these few prophecies which remain to be fulfilled, are not only delivered to us by Hebrew Prophets, but by Christ Himself also, Who is the subject and end of all Prophecy, and the Lord of all the prophets. And what is the great prophecy that remains to be fulfilled, and which Christ Himself has reiterated by Himself and by His Apostles, especially by St. Paul in the Epistles to the Thessalonians[12] and the Corinthians[13] and by St. John in the Apocalypse[14]? The final overthrow of all that is opposed to Christ and the complete victory of the True Faith. This is what lies before us. It will be fulfilled at Christ's Second Advent. "Therefore will we not fear[15], though the Earth be moved, and the hills be carried into the midst of the sea." In all the trials and troubles of private and public life, amid all the winds and waves of popular commotions and tumults, in the distress of nations with perplexity[16], in the fainting of men's hearts through fear, and for looking after those things which are coming on the earth, in the dissolution of Empires, in the disintegration of national Churches, and in the distraction and strife of parties in religion and polity, in the wild frenzy of fanaticism, in the over-flowings of a self-idolizing superstition in the Church itself, in the rebuke and blasphemy of unbelief, the true Christian will cling to this anchor of the soul, sure and steadfast, and will see in the storm itself a sign of eternal calm. When all things seem to be most dark, then, as the Apostles, toiling in the ship on the Sea of Galilee, saw Christ in the fourth watch of the night, walking on the sea amid the storm, and coming to them into the ship, and then the wind ceased, and the ship was at the land whither they went; so at length the faithful will see Him coming to those who are labouring in the Apostolic vessel of His Church, tossed by waves, and buffeted by winds; they will behold His refulgent Form, made more bright by the contrast of the gloom around it, and treading beneath His feet all the foaming billows of human pride and presumption, and speaking to His disciples with a voice of power and love, "Be of good cheer, it is I[18]." And then the ship will be "at the haven where they would be[19],"—the heavenly haven of everlasting peace.

C. LINCOLN.

RISEHOLME, LINCOLN.
Ascension-tide, 1870.

[1] Isaiah liii. 3.  [2] Zech. ix.  [3] Zech. xi. 12.  [12] Isaiah ii. 2—4.  Micah iv. 1, 2.
[4] Psalm xxii. 16.  [5] Psalm xxii. 18.  [13] 1 Thess. iv. 13—18.  2 Thess. ii. 1—8.
[6] Isaiah liii. 12.  [7] Isaiah ix. 6.  [14] 1 Cor. xv. 24—28; 51—58.
[8] Jeremiah xxiii. 6.  [15] Rev. xix. 11 - 21; xx. 8—15.  [16] Psalm xlvi. 2.
[9] Haggai ii. 6—9.  Malachi iii. 1.  [17] Luke xxi. 25, 26.
[10] Psalm ii. 2—6; xvi. 11.  Cp. Acts ii. 29—36.  [18] See Matt. xiv. 23—27.  Mark vi. 47—50.  John vi. 16—21.
[11] Psalm lxviii. 18.  Micah ii. 13.  [19] Psalm cvii. 30.

# CHRONOLOGICAL ORDER OF THE PROPHETS.

Some of the Prophets, e.g. HOSEA and ISAIAH, prophesied during a much longer time than others; and therefore some of their prophecies may be later in date than some of the prophecies of Prophets who began to prophesy after them. Their dates for the most part cannot be precisely determined. It is probable that the books of most of the Prophets contain the substance and pith of prophecies delivered by them at intervals on several occasions. In the following Table, some modifications have been adopted of that order which is exhibited in the Table prefixed to ISAIAH.

| | | |
|---|---|---|
| HOSEA | In the days of Jeroboam II., King of Israel, and Uzziah, Jotham, Ahaz, and Hezekiah, Kings of Judah . . . . . . . | |
| ISAIAH | In the days of Uzziah, Jotham, Ahaz, and Hezekiah, Kings of Judah | These Prophets prophesied in the time between B.C. 810—710. |
| JOEL | Probably in the days of Uzziah, King of Judah . . . . | |
| AMOS | In the days of Jeroboam II., King of Israel, and Uzziah, King of Judah | |
| OBADIAH | Probably in the days of Uzziah . . . . . . . | |
| JONAH | Probably in the days of Uzziah . . . . . . . | |
| MICAH | In the days of Jotham, Ahaz, and Hezekiah, Kings of Judah. Cp. Jer. xxvi. 18 . . . . . . . . . . | |
| NAHUM | Probably in the reign of Hezekiah, King of Judah . . . | 710—625. |
| HABAKKUK | Probably in the reign of Manasseh or Josiah, Kings of Judah . | |
| ZEPHANIAH | In the days of Josiah, King of Judah . . . . . | |
| JEREMIAH | From the thirteenth year of Josiah, and in the reigns of Jehoahaz (Shallum), Jehoiakim, Jehoiachin (Jeconiah, or Coniah), and Zedekiah, Kings of Judah, and after the destruction of Jerusalem . . | 629—580. |
| EZEKIEL | From the fifth year of Jehoiachin's captivity, and in the reign of Zedekiah, and after the destruction of Jerusalem . . . | 595—573. |
| DANIEL | In the days of Nebuchadnezzar, Belshazzar, Darius, and Cyrus . . | 603—534. |
| HAGGAI | In the second year of Darius Hystaspes . . . . . . | 519. |
| ZECHARIAH | Associated with Haggai . . . . . . . . . | 519—487. |
| MALACHI | "The Seal of the Prophets " . . . . . . . . . | 430—400. |

For a synoptical view of the historical events of the above period, the reader is requested to refer to the Chronological Table prefixed to the Books of Kings, pp. xx—xxii, and the *Introduction* to Ezra, p. 295.

The principal Commentaries on the Minor Prophets are those of *S. Jerome*, *S. Cyril of Alexandria* (published in an emended edition by P. E. Pusey, Oxf., 1868), *Theodoret*, *S. Augustine* (De Civitate Dei, lib. xviii.), *Haymo*, *Remigius*, *Theophylact*, *Rupertus Tuitiensis*, *Hugo de S. Caro*, *Albertus Magnus*, *Nicolaus de Lyra*, *Ribera*, *Cornelius a Lapide*.

Among the Rabbis, *R. Salomon ben Isaac*, *Abenezra*, *Kimchi*.

Among the Reformers, *Œcolampadius*, *Luther*, *Calvin*, *Mercer*, *Osiander*.

After the Reformation, *Drusius*, *Sanctius*, *Piscator*, *Tarnovius*, *Calovius*, *Grotius*, *Schmid*, *Marckius*, *Lyserus*, *W. Lowth*, *M. Henry*.

In the eighteenth and nineteenth centuries, *J. H. Michaelis*, *Starck*, *Petersen*, *Dathe*, *Newcome*, *Rosenmüller*, *Umbreit*, *Eichhorn*, *Ackermann*, *Maurer*, *Henderson*, *Hesselberg*, *Hitzig*, *Ewald*, *Schegg*, *Reinke*, *Hengstenberg* (in his Christology), *Dr. Robinson*, *Drake*, *Bassett*, and especially *Dr. Pusey* (a very learned and inestimable Commentary), and *Dr. C. F. Keil* (one of the best works of that erudite Expositor), and *Kleinert*. The expositions of *Dr. Pocock* on Hosea, Joel, Micah, and Malachi are of great value, as are those on Micah and Obadiah by *C. P. Caspari;* and that of *Kliefoth* on Zechariah is written in an excellent spirit of Christian Criticism.

# HOSEA.

I. ¹ THE word of the LORD that came unto Hosea, the son of Beeri, in the days of Uzziah, Jotham, Ahaz, and Hezekiah, kings of Judah, and in the days of Jeroboam the son of Joash, king of Israel. ² The beginning of the word of the LORD by Hosea. And the LORD said to Hosea, ³ Go, take unto thee a wife of whoredoms and children of whoredoms : for ᵇ the land hath committed great whoredom, *departing* from the LORD.

Before
CHRIST
about
785.

a xxi ch. 3. 1.
b Deut. 31. 16.
Ps. 73. 27.
Jer. 2. 13.
Ezek. 23. 3, &c.

CH. I.] On the history and prophecies of HOSEA, see above, INTRODUCTION to the Minor Prophets generally.

The first three chapters of this Book are a prologue to the whole (like the first five chapters of Isaiah: see on Isa. ch. i.), and reach from the age of the Prophet to the last days. It is an uniform principle of divine prophecy,—"semper ad eventum festinat." It passes at once with a rapid flight to the consummation of all things. So at the very beginning of the Apocalypse the writer announces the Second Advent of Christ : "Behold, He cometh with clouds" (Rev. i. 7).

1. *Hosea, the son of Beeri*] HOSEA, who stands at the head of the Minor Prophets in the Canon of Scripture, is to them what Isaiah, whose name signifies *Salvation of Jehovah*, is to the Major Prophets. Both Hosea and Isaiah prophesied *in the days of Uzziah, Jotham, Ahaz, and Hezekiah, kings of Judah*. See above, Isa. i. 1. The word HOSEA signifies *salvation*; and *Beeri* means *my well* (S. Jerome). The words of the Minor Prophets flow down from the well of God's saving power and love, in a continuous stream, parallel to those of the Major Prophets. They rise from a higher point than the words of the Major Prophets, and descend to a lower one, till they bring us down in Haggai, Zechariah, and Malachi, to the days of the Second Temple, in which the Saviour Himself taught, from Whom, as from an exhaustless well-spring, flowed forth the living waters of the Gospel, and the gift of the Holy Spirit of God ; and they reveal to us the glories of the heavenly city, and the crystal sea, and the waters of life flowing from the throne of God.

— *in the days of Uzziah—Jeroboam the son of Joash, king of Israel*] Jeroboam the second, King of Israel, in whose reign the kingdom of the Ten Tribes rose to the highest pitch of prosperity ; by which God graciously proved them whether they would be thankful and obedient to Him, Who gave them their wealth and power (see 2 Kings xiv. 23—27). He reigned contemporaneously with Uzziah, king of Judah, for twenty-six years, and died in the twenty-seventh year of Uzziah, who outlived Jeroboam by twenty-five years.

Since, therefore, Hosea began to prophesy before the twenty-seventh year of Uzziah, and continued to prophesy in the times of Hezekiah, the son and successor of Ahaz, who succeeded Jotham, the son and successor of Uzziah, he must have prophesied for a period of more than sixty years (i.e. from about B.C. 790 to B.C. 725). In the Chronological Table, prefixed to Isaiah, above, p. xxii, the reader is requested to correct 780 into 790. Hosea does not mention any other kings of Israel under whom he prophesied besides Jeroboam II., because the successors of Jeroboam (Zechariah, Shallum, Menahem, Pekahiah, Pekah, the son of Remaliah, Hosea the son of Elah) had no permanent position as kings on the throne of Israel, and several of them were murderers and usurpers, and by their sins brought the kingdom to ruin and desolation, till at last their capital, Samaria, was taken, and the Ten Tribes were carried captive to Assyria.

## ISRAEL'S SPIRITUAL FORNICATION.

2. *Go, take unto thee a wife of whoredoms*] God speaks from the lofty eminence of His foreknowledge. *Go, take to*

VOL. VI. PART II.—1

*thee a wife*, who, I foresee, will be *a wife of whoredoms*; that is, one who will be faithless to thee, and who will thus cease to be worthy to be called thy wife. See ii. 2.

That this is the true interpretation of this much-controverted passage seems to be evident,—

(1) From the fact that the Prophet's wife is designed to symbolize the Israelitish Nation and its relation to God. Now God did not espouse that Nation to Himself *when* it was unfaithful ; but it *became* unfaithful *after* it had been espoused to Him. Cp. Ezek. xxiii. 3.

It is observable that the *Targum* here, and the ancient Versions (*Sept.*, *Vulg.*, *Syriac*) render the words in the *future* tense (as indeed they are in the original), the land *will commit* great whoredom from the Lord; and this confirms that exposition.

(2) From the circumstance that this wife of Hosea is afterwards spoken of as *a woman beloved of her friend* (i.e. by her *husband*, yet *an adulteress* (iii. 1), and, as such, is a figure of Israel, faithless, and yet not wholly cast off by God.

(3) From the great embarrassments which beset the other conflicting interpretations, viz.—

(1) The interpretation which regards the woman whom God's Prophet is commanded to take to himself in marriage, as no other than a common harlot.

(2) The interpretation, which, recoiling from such a supposition, resorts to the theory that the whole transaction had no outward visible reality, but was done only in the Prophet's inner consciousness, and that the names of his wife (Gomer) and of his three children, are mere ideal fictions and visionary phantoms.

Each of these two interpretations has great names to plead in its favour. The former is supported by S. Irenæus, S. Basil, S. Cyril of Alexandria, Theodoret, S. Augustine, by Aquinas, Lyranus, A Lapide, Colerius, Glassius, Pocock, Ewald, Kurtz, and by Dr. Pusey.

The latter interpretation is maintained by S. Jerome, Maimonides, Junius, Drusius, Witsius, Hengstenberg, Keil. For the history of these interpretations, see Marck, Diatribe de Muliere Fornicationum, Lug. Bat. 1696 ; Pfeiffer, Dubia, p. 433 ; Dr. Pocock here ; Dr. Waterland, Scripture Vindicated, p. 264, who, as well as Wm. Lowth and Dr. Wells, gives the preference to the opinion which, on the whole, seems the most reasonable, and says, "I understand here a wife which, *after* marriage, however chaste before, should prove false to her marriage vow ; and so the case of Hosea and Gomer might be the apter parallel to the case of God and His people Israel."

— *the land hath committed great whoredom, departing from the LORD*] In the Hebrew Canon of Scripture the Prophet Hosea follows next, in order of time, after the BOOK OF CANTICLES, or Song of Solomon, which is a prophetic and mystical representation of the *love and marriage of CHRIST and His Church*. See above, *Introd.* to the *Song of Solomon*, pp. 121—124.

The relation of *Marriage*, as a symbol of God's union with His people, serves to connect the prophecies of Hosea with the Song of Solomon ; and the unfaithfulness of Israel to God is

B

Before
CHRIST
about
785.

³ So he went and took Gomer the daughter of Diblaim; which conceived, and bare him a son.

⁴ And the LORD said unto him, Call his name Jezreel; for yet a little *while*, and I will †avenge the blood of Jezreel upon the house of Jehu, ᵈand will cause to cease the kingdom of the house of Israel. ⁵ ᶜAnd it shall come to pass at that day, that I will break the bow of Israel in the valley of Jezreel.

⁶ And she conceived again, and bare a daughter. And *God* said unto him, Call her name ‖ Lo-ruhamah: ᶠfor †I will no more have mercy upon the house of Israel; ‖but I will utterly take them away. ⁷ ᵍBut I will have mercy upon the house of Judah, and will save them by the LORD their God, and ʰwill not save them by bow, nor by sword, nor by battle, by horses, nor by horsemen.

⁸ Now when she had weaned Lo-ruhamah, she conceived, and bare a son.

⁹ Then said *God*, Call his name ‖ Lo-ammi: for ye *are* not my people, and I will not be your *God*.

¹⁰ Yet ⁱthe number of the children of Israel shall be as the sand of the sea,

---

displayed in striking contrast to the love of the Bride in that Divine Book. Cp. *Hengst.*, Proleg. to Canticles, pp. 304, 305; on Cant. ii. 4; and *Thrupp*, on the Song of Solomon, p. 15. See also below, on ii. 2, for another instance of this connexion.

Thus also we recognize another example of the beautiful and harmonious unity of purpose with which the Books of Holy Scripture are joined on successively (like links in a golden chain) to one another.

These are evidences of the *continuity of Scripture*, and are silent proofs of its *Inspiration*. All the Books of Scripture (written at intervals extending over 1500 years) may rightly be regarded as making *one book*; they are all parts of one plan, and are from the mind and hand of Him, with Whom "a thousand years are as one day."

3. *he went and took Gomer the daughter of Diblaim*] The word *Gomer* signifies *completion* (*Pococke*), and also *exhaustion* and *failure* (*Gesen.* 175; *Fuerst*); and it may signify the condition of destitution and helplessness to which the Israelitish Nation had been reduced, especially by the bondage in Egypt, when it was received into covenant with God, and was espoused to Him at Mount Sinai. The name *Gomer* may also have been adopted as connected with heathenism itself (Gen. x. 2. Ezek. xxxviii. 6), as Ezekiel says (xvi. 3): "Thy father was an Amorite, and thy mother a Hittite;" and this is symbolized also by "the daughter of *Diblaim*," or of *two pressed cakes* of figs (*Gesen.* 185), a figure of mere sensual pleasure (S. *Jerome*, *Kimchi*; and it may signify heathen extraction, as connected with *Diblath*, or *Diblathaim*, in the wilderness (Num. xxxiii. 47. Jer. xlviii. 22). See the note above, on Ezek. vi. 11, where *Diblath* is a symbol of what is heathen; and this illustrates the use of the word here.

Such was originally the condition of the Hebrew Nation. It was in a heathen and destitute state, and was mercifully taken up by God, in the wilderness, when it thought of little more than the gratification of its sensual appetites. Even after the Exodus it hankered after "the onions, and leeks, and garlick, and the fleshpots of Egypt" (Exod. xvi. 3. Num. xi. 5).

4. *Call his name Jezreel*] Call his name in memory of Jezreel, situated in the fruitful plain on the north of Kishon (Josh. xvii. 16), but polluted with blood, especially that of Naboth the Jezreelite, for the shedding of which, and other sins, the house of Ahab was threatened with extermination (1 Kings xxi. 14—23); and also because Jezreel was the scene of cruel and sanguinary acts committed by Jehu (2 Kings ix. and x.).

The name *Jezreel* was also prophetic, both of judgment and mercy; of *judgment*, because it means, *God will scatter*, and thus presignified the *dispersion* of Israel; and of *mercy*, because it also means, *God will sow*, and preannounced that the *dispersion* of Israel would be a *dissemination*, and a sowing of themselves in mercy (see ii. 23), and be also a *sowing of the seed* of God's truth in all lands (see above, *Introd.*, to Ezra, p. xv; and below, *Introd.* to the Acts of the Apostles, p. ix), and would prepare the way for the diffusion of the Church of Christ in every land.

It was like the scattering of the tribe of Levi throughout the length and breadth of the Holy Land—a scattering which was threatened in judgment for sin, but was overruled by God's mercy into love. See above, on Gen. xlix. 7. Such (as Hosea shows in these prophecies) is the true character of the dispersion of Israel.

5. *I will break*] By some *signal victory* gained over Israel by Assyria. Cp. below, x. 14.

— *Israel—Jezreel.*] Observe the contrast. By God's grace the Hebrew Nation became *Israel*, *a prince of God*; but by its own sin Israel was changed into *Jezreel*, and was *scattered* by Him.

6. *Lo-ruhamah*] *Not pitied*, *not favoured*. It is rendered *not-beloved* by St. Paul (Rom. ix. 25), and *not having obtained mercy*, by St. Peter (1 Pet. ii. 10). Israel forfeited God's love and pity by unfaithfulness to Him.

— *but I will utterly take them away*] Literally, *for in taking away, I will take away from them*, i.e. all that belongs to them (*Hengst. Pusey*).

7. *Judah*] Judah is contrasted with Israel, which revolted under Jeroboam the first, from the house of David, and set up a rival worship in opposition to that in the Temple at Jerusalem. Judah, therefore, will obtain mercy, but Israel will be deprived of spiritual blessings.

— *will not save them by bow*] Hosea, whose name signifies *salvation*, declares here the only source from which salvation comes (cp. Isa. ix. 6), and thus prepares the way for the prophecy which follows concerning Jesus Christ, the Saviour of the world. Cp. Matt. i. 21. Acts iv. 12.

8. *when she had weaned Lo-ruhamah, she conceived*] The long-suffering of God to Israel is thus symbolized. There was a long interval, like that between childbirth and weaning (see on Gen. xxi. 8. 1 Sam. i. 21), between its forfeiture of mercy and its utter rejection; but at length the birth of *Lo-ruhamah* is succeeded by that of *Lo-ammi*. One sin and punishment was followed by another in a deliberate succession and miserable sequence of births. Cp. James i. 15: "When lust hath conceived, it bringeth forth sin; and sin, when it is finished, bringeth forth death."

10. *the number of the children of Israel shall be as the sand of the sea*] By the reception of all nations into the Church, through faith in Christ, the true *Jezreel*, the Seed of God, and the Seed of Abraham, through Whom the promise was fulfilled, that Abraham's seed should be as the sand on the sea-shore (Gen. xxii. 17; xxxii. 12), and in Whom all families of the earth are blessed (Gen. xii. 3; xxviii. 14), and are joined together in one body and one Head, which is Christ.

That this interpretation of this passage is the true one is evident from the testimony of St. Paul (Rom. ix. 25, 26), and of St. Peter (1 Pet. ii. 10).

Here is an answer to all objections that might be raised against God's dealings with the Jewish Nation. God chose them to be His people; they rebelled against Him; but His purpose in choosing them was not, therefore, frustrate. He scattered them; but their punishment had a salutary effect in weaning many of them from Idolatry, and in bringing them back

2

which cannot be measured nor numbered; ᵏand it shall come to pass, *that*
‖ in the place where it was said unto them, Ye *are* not my people, *there* it
shall be said unto them, Ye *are* ᵐ the sons of the living God.   ¹¹ ˡ Then shall
the children of Judah and the children of Israel be gathered together, and
appoint themselves one head, and they shall come up out of the land: for
great *shall be* the day of Jezreel.

II.  ¹ Say ye unto your brethren, ‖ Ammi ;
And to your sisters, ‖ Ru-hamah.
²  Plead with your mother, plead :
For ᵃ she *is* not my wife, neither *am* I her husband :
Let her therefore put away her ᵇ whoredoms out of her sight,
And her adulteries from between her breasts ;

*(marginal references:)*
Before CHRIST about 785.
k Rom. 9. 25, 26.
1 Pet. 2. 10.
‖ Or, *instead of that.*
l ch. 2. 23.
m John 1. 12.
1 John 3. 1.
n Isa. 11. 12, 13.
Jer. 3. 18.
Ezek. 34. 23, &c 37. 16—24.
‖ That is, *My people.*
‖ That is, *Having obtained mercy.*
a Isa. 50. 1.
b Ezek. 16. 25.

---

to Him.  See ii. 7.  He raised up the Gentiles to be His people
by means of the Gospel of Christ, and His Apostles, who were
*Jews ;* and the Law went forth from *Sion,* and the Word of
God from *Jerusalem,* and thus Jerusalem itself was universalized
and became co-extensive with the world.  And now the duty
and privilege of the Gentiles (who have received the Gospel
from the Jews, and whose spiritual Mother is Jerusalem) is to
bring back Israel in their turn to the Church of God (ii. 1).

This is beautifully expressed in the Book of Canticles or
Song of Solomon (see above, on Cant. viii. 1—9), the connexion
of which book with the prophecies of Hosea has been already
noticed on v. 2.

11.  *Then shall—the children of Israel be gathered together*]
Christ Himself, "the One Head" of whom the Prophet here
speaks, adopts these words, when He says to Jerusalem, "How
often would *I have gathered thy children together*" (Matt.
xxiii. 37).  Cp. John xi. 51, 52, "He should *gather together in
one* the children of God that are scattered abroad ;" and again,
these words are applicable to Christ : "Where the body is, there
will the eagles be *gathered together.*"  See the notes on Matt.
xxiv. 28, Luke xvii. 37, and Eph. i. 10.

*S. Augustine* (De Civ. Dei, vii. 28) thus writes concerning
this passage :—"The Prophet Hosea speaks of deep mysteries,
and is therefore more difficult to follow ; but as to the passage,
where he says, 'It shall come to pass that in the place where
it was said unto them, Ye are not my people, there it shall be
said, Ye are the sons of the living God, we know that the
Apostles themselves understood this prophecy as foretelling the
*calling of the Gentiles,* and that the Prophet says, 'The children of Judah and the children of Israel shall be gathered
together, and shall appoint themselves one head, and come up
out of the land ;' therefore let us think of the Corner-Stone,
Jesus Christ, in Whom the two walls are joined together, and
lean upon Him, Who is the common support of them both"
(*Augustine*).

— *one head*]  Christ.  See above, on Ezek. xxxiv. 23 ; xxxvii.
22 ; and below, iii. 5.

— *shall come up out of the land*]  All nations shall be
*gathered together from out of the land ;* that is, as all the
tribes of Israel were commanded to come up to worship together at Jerusalem at stated annual festivals, so all the tribes
of the spiritual Israel will come up in heart and spirit from all
parts of the whole Earth, to the *Mountain of the Lord,* the
Zion of the Church of God ; that is, they will be joined together
in one faith and worship in the Christian Church.  See above,
Isa. ii. 2, 3 ; and below, Micah iv. 1, 2, which are the best comments on this passage ; and see Ps. lxxxvii.  Isa. lv. 6 ; lxvi.
23.  Jer. iii. 18 ; l. 4 ; and Zech. xiv. 16, 17.  This prophecy
(says *M. Henry*) denotes, not a local remove (for they are said
to be in the same place, v. 10), but a spiritual ascent to Christ.

GREAT SHALL BE THE DAY OF JEZREEL.

— *great shall be the day of Jezreel*]  *Great* shall be the
*day of Jezreel,* the *seed of God.*  The first blood that was
shed at Jezreel was that of Naboth, whose blood cried for his
Vineyard, and which blood brought with it Divine retribution
on those that shed it.  See on v. 4.  Naboth, as is observed by
*S. Jerome* here, was a signal type of CHRIST, shedding His
blood for His Vineyard the Church (the resemblances are specified above in the note on 1 Kings xx. 43).

Naboth's blood brought retribution on those who shed it ;
so did the blood of Christ on those who said, "His blood be

upon us and on our children" (Matt. xxvii. 25).  But Christ's
blood speaks better things than that of Naboth ; His blood is
the *seed of the* Church ; He is the true *Jezreel,* the *seed of God*
(see on v. 4), and *great is the day of Jezreel* in Him.  Great
was the day of Jezreel, when, after His Passion, Burial, Resurrection, Ascension, and sending of the Holy Ghost from heaven,
the Lord added to the Church daily such as should be saved
(Acts ii. 47), then God did great things for it.  "Magnus est
dies *seminis Dei,* qui interpretatur CHRISTUS ; ex quo perspi-
cuum est ideo in typo Naboth Jezraelitis sanguinem processisse,
ut veritas compleretur in Christo" (*S. Jerome*).

The seed sown in the earth was Christ, as He Himself
says, "Except a corn of wheat fall into the earth and die, it
abideth alone ; but if it die it bringeth forth much fruit"
(John xii. 24).  Christ is the true Jezreel.  His Blood is the
Seed from which the Harvest of the Universal Church has
sprung up in the field of the whole world.

Great will be the day of Jezreel at the General Resurrection.  Christ's Death, Burial, and Resurrection are the seed-
plot of our Resurrection.  He is the First Fruits, we the Harvest (1 Cor. xv. 20—23).  Then all the glorified bodies of the
Saints will rise up like seed in an instantaneous harvest from
the furrows of the Grave in all parts of the earth ; then *great*
indeed will *be the day of Jezreel.*

Ch. II.  *Say ye—Ru-hamah*]  Ye Gentiles, who have become
the Israel of God in Christ, endeavour to win the Jews to God
by assuring them of God's favour.  Ye Gentile Christians, do
not despise the Jews, they are your *brethren and sisters ;* do
not irritate them by disdainful words, but provoke them to
godly jealousy (see Rom. x. 19 ; xi. 11) by accents of love, and
tell them, that though they are scattered abroad, yet God is
waiting to be gracious to them and to restore them to Him.
Cast aside the Hebrew negative prefix, *lo,* and in His Name call
them by titles of endearment, *Ammi* (*My People*) and *Ruhamah*
(*having obtained Mercy*).  Compare Rom. xi. 30, 31, where
St. Paul thus speaks to the Gentile Christians in regard to the
Jews : "As ye in times past have not believed in God, yet have
now *obtained mercy* through their unbelief, even so have these
also now not believed, that through your mercy they also *may
obtain mercy,*" where St. Paul refers to these words of Hosea.

2.  *Plead with your mother, plead*]  Thou, O Gentile Church
(says God here by the Prophet), remember that the Hebrew
Nation, though scattered and banished, is *thy mother ;* plead
with her and convert her to God.  Cp. Ezek. xx. 35, 36.

Hosea takes up here, as in other places (see on i. 2), the
language of the Song of Solomon, where the *Bride of Christ*
(i. e. the Gentile Church) desires to bring the Bridegroom to her
*mother's* house (i. e. to the house of the Hebrew Nation).  See
above, the notes on Canticles iii. 4, and especially the notes on
the eighth, the last chapter of that book, which forms an appropriate and harmonious prelude to this prophecy of Hosea.

As a proof of this harmony between Hosea and the Canticles, and as an evidence that the true interpretation of them both is
spiritual, it may be added that the Jewish Church is called both
a *mother* and a *sister* (see Cant. viii. 8) of the Gentile Church.
She is a *mother* in priority, and a *sister* in parity, of God's love.
Cp. Rom. ix. 7 ; xv. 5—9.

— *she is not my wife*]  The nation of Israel has divorced herself from me by her spiritual adultery.  As the *Targum* expresses
it, "The mother has played the harlot, the congregation has
gone a whoring after false prophets."

— *her breasts*]  Compare Ezek. xxiii. 3.

3 Lest <sup>c</sup>I strip her naked, and set her as in the day that she was <sup>d</sup>born,
And make her <sup>e</sup>as a wilderness, and set her like a dry land,
And slay her with <sup>f</sup>thirst,

4 And I will not have mercy upon her children;
For they *be* the <sup>g</sup>children of whoredoms.

5 <sup>h</sup>For their mother hath played the harlot:
She that conceived them hath done shamefully:
For she said, I will go after my lovers, <sup>i</sup>that give *me* my bread and my
water, my wool and my flax, mine oil and my † drink.

6 Therefore, behold, <sup>k</sup>I will hedge up thy way with thorns,
And † make a wall, that she shall not find her paths.

7 And she shall follow after her lovers, but she shall not overtake them;
And she shall seek them, but shall not find *them:*
Then shall she say, <sup>l</sup>I will go and return to my <sup>m</sup>first husband;
For then *was it* better with me than now.

8 For she did not <sup>n</sup>know that <sup>o</sup>I gave her corn, and † wine, and oil, and
multiplied her silver and gold, ‖ *which* they prepared for Baal.

9 Therefore will I return, and <sup>p</sup>take away my corn in the time thereof, and
my wine in the season thereof, and will ‖ recover my wool and my flax *given*
to cover her nakedness.

10 And now <sup>q</sup>will I discover her † lewdness in the sight of her lovers,
And none shall deliver her out of mine hand.

11 <sup>r</sup>I will also cause all her mirth to cease, her <sup>s</sup>feast-days, her new moons,
and her sabbaths, and all her solemn feasts.

12 And I will † destroy her vines and her fig trees, <sup>t</sup>whereof she hath said,
These *are* my rewards that my lovers have given me:
And <sup>u</sup>I will make them a forest, and the beasts of the field shall eat them.

13 And I will visit upon her the days of Baalim, wherein she burned incense
to them, and she <sup>x</sup>decked herself with her earrings and her jewels, and she
went after her lovers, and forgat me, saith the LORD.

14 Therefore, behold, I will allure her, and <sup>y</sup>bring her into the wilderness,
and speak ‖ † comfortably unto her.

---

**3.** *as in the day that she was born*] See Ezek. xvi. 16—
25, 39, which supplies the best exposition of this passage.
Ezekiel there describes the miserable state of the Israelitish
nation by nature, and displays God's love to her in the wilderness of Arabia (cp. Deut. xxxii. 10), and her unfaithfulness and
consequent punishment and misery.

**5.** *my lovers*] The false gods whom Israel worshipped instead
of the Lord, and to whom she ascribed the benefits received from
Him. Cp. r. 13, and Jer. ii. 25; xliv. 17, 18.

**6.** *I will hedge up thy way*] I will obstruct thy roving
vagrancy after thy idols; I will stop it up by afflictions and
banishment into a far-off land; and thus I will show thee the
vanity of thy idols, who cannot save thee in thy distress. As to
the metaphor here used, cp. Job xix. 8, and Lam. iii. 7, 9, "He
hath hedged me about—He hath enclosed my ways," which seems
to be grounded on this passage.

**7.** *Then shall she say, I will go and return*] The prophet
predicts the salutary effects of Israel's dispersion, which would
bring them to repentance and make them turn to God—like the
penitent prodigal in the Gospel (Luke xv. 18); and thus he
justifies God's severity as a discipline of love.

**8.** *she did not know*] Israel did not consider that I am the
Giver of all her blessings (Deut. vii. 13; xi. 14).

— *which they prepared for Baal*] Or, as some render it
(e.g. *Targum, Vulg., Syriac, Engl. Margin, Ewald*), *which
they made into idols*, whom they worshipped in the place of the God
Who gave them, and Who is their Maker and Judge. Cp. viii. 4,

" Of their silver and their gold have they made them idols, that
they may be cut off." The other interpretation, also, " which
they made for, or dedicated to Baal," has strong authority in
its favour. See *Hengst., Keil.*

**9.** *will I return*] They turned My gifts into idols, and therefore I will turn away Myself from them, and take away My
gifts.

**11.** *her feast days, her new moons, and her sabbaths*] Her
festal days, which she has appointed to be kept at Bethel, in
opposition to Mine at Jerusalem. See 1 Kings xii. 32.

This may be applied, also, to such festivals of the Levitical
Law as were still observed among the tribes of Israel, see
2 Kings iv. 23. Cp. Amos viii. 8, 10, and Tobit ii. 6, and the
lamentation of Jeremiah on their cessation (Lam. ii. 6), which
seems to refer to the words of Hosea.

**14.** *I will—bring her into the wilderness*] i.e. into far-off
lands in which they will be scattered. These various regions of
their future exile and dispersion are called by Ezekiel, " the
wilderness of Nations," and " the wilderness of the people."
See Ezek. xx. 35, 36, which are the best comments on this
passage.

God threatens here that He will bring Israel into the
wilderness of captivity and dispersion in Assyria, which was
designed to have the same merciful effect in chastening and
purifying the Ten Tribes, as the wilderness of Arabia after the
Exodus (cp. r. 15) was intended to produce on their forefathers
in their wanderings there. He brought them into that wilderness (as Moses says), that " He might humble them and prove

[15] And I will give her her vineyards from thence, and ' the valley of Achor for a door of hope : and she shall sing there, as in [a] the days of her youth, and [b] as in the day when she came up out of the land of Egypt.

[16] And it shall be at that day, saith the LORD, *that* thou shalt call me || Ishi ; and shalt call me no more || Baali. [17] For [c] I will take away the names of Baalim out of her mouth, and they shall no more be remembered by their name.

[18] And in that day will I make a [d] covenant for them with the beasts of the field, and with the fowls of heaven, and *with* the creeping things of the ground : and [e] I will break the bow and the sword and the battle out of the earth, and will make them to [f] lie down safely. [19] And I will betroth thee unto me for ever ; yea, I will betroth thee unto me in righteousness, and in judgment, and in lovingkindness, and in mercies.

[20] I will even betroth thee unto me in faithfulness : and [g] thou shalt know the LORD.

[21] And it shall come to pass in that day, [h] I will hear, saith the LORD, I will hear the heavens, and they shall hear the earth ; [22] And the earth shall hear

Before
CHRIST
About
763.

z Josh. 7. 26.
Isa. 65. 10.
• Jer. 2. 2.
Ezek. 16. 8, 22
60.
b Exod. 15. 1.
' That is, *My*
husband.
|| That is, *My*
lord.
c Exod. 23. 13.
Josh. 23. 7.
Ps. 16. 4.
Zech. 13. 2.
d Job 5. 23.
Isa. 11. 6—9.
Ezek. 34. 25.
e Ps. 46. 9.
Isa. 2. 4.
Zech. 9. 10.
Zech. 3. 10.
f Lev. 26. 5.
Jer. 23. 6.

g Jer. 31. 33, 34.
John 17. 3.

h Zech. 8. 12.

them, and to do them good at their latter end" (Deut. viii. 2—6) so as to qualify them for Canaan and for its heavenly antitype of everlasting rest.

— *speak comfortably unto her*] Literally, *to her heart*, in love. Cp. Gen. xxxiv. 3 ; 1. 21, and see Isa. xl. 1, 2, " Speak ye comfortably to Jerusalem," give to her a message of comfort from Christ, and from the Holy Ghost the Comforter.

Here the Prophet displays the love of God to His Ancient People in their dispersion and distress. They are represented as wanderers and outcasts, but it is that they may feel their misery, and yearn for the home of their reconciled Father in Christ. Cp. Deut. viii. 2—6.

15. *I will give her her vineyards from thence, and the valley of Achor for a door of hope*] Here is a reversal of the threat in vv. 9. 12. He continues the comparison of the foregoing verse :—As I prepared their forefathers by the probationary discipline of the Sinaitic Wilderness to enter Canaan, and to inherit its vineyards, so will I deal with their posterity the Ten Tribes. I will make their dispersion in Assyria to be a school for reception into a spiritual inheritance *from thence*, i. e. succeeding after it, and produced by it. I will bring them into the Vineyard of Christ's Church. Cp. on Isa. v. 1 ; lxi. 5. Ezek. xxviii. 26. Canticles i. 14 ; viii. 11.

And I will do more than this. As *the valley of Achor* (near Jericho, the first great city of Canaan which their fathers conquered) was, as its name indicates, a place of *trouble* (see on Josh. vii. 24. 26), but became *a door of hope* to them, on account even of the severe but salutary discipline there exercised, and thence they marched to victory "ibique aperta spes, ubi fuerat desperatio." *S. Jerome ;* so all the *Achors* of trouble, through which the Ten Tribes will pass, will be changed into *doors of hope* to them, by their penitential sorrow and God's gracious pardon and love. Hosea here chimes in with his contemporary, Isaiah, who says, " *The Valley of Achor* shall be a place for herds to lie down in" (Isa. lxv. 10). Even the destruction of Jerusalem and the Temple—the bitterest Achors of sorrow and humiliation to the Hebrew Nation—have become doors of hope to the true Israel of God, by weaning their affections from the material City and Temple, and by drawing them to the Spiritual Sion, the Church of Christ Universal (which has risen upon the ruins of the literal Jerusalem), and to the glories of the heavenly "Jerusalem, which is the mother of us all" (Gal. iv. 26).

This promise may be extended to all penitent believers. God gives to them in Christ such comforts as will be a foretaste of the sweet fruits of the heavenly Canaan of His eternal rest and bliss. The *Achor* of penitential sorrow becomes to them a *door of hope* to the heavenly kingdom of everlasting glory.

— *the days of her youth*] At the Exodus ; when Moses and Miriam sang their songs of joy (Exod. xv. 1. 20).

16. *Ishi*] My man, lit. *my man*. Cp. on Isa. liv. 5, " Thy *Maker* is thine husband."

— *Baali*] My baal, or lord. The word baal, whence *beulah*, *married*, in Isa. lxii. 4, though often used in a good sense (as Isa. liv. 5), yet shall be avoided by Israel, as being tainted with

idolatrous associations, "ne *rirum* nominans, idolum cogitet" (S. Jerome). Israel, once idolatrous, will so loathe idolatry, that even good and innocent words will be shunned by her, if they have been connected with idolatrous uses, and when there is any danger of a scandal arising from them.

Here is an important lesson for the Christian Church. Even innocent things, nay, even good things, if identified with idolatry, and scarcely separable from it, are to be avoided. See above, the notes on the case of Hezekiah and the brazen serpent, 2 Kings xviii. 4; Ps. xvi. 4; Zech. xiii. 2, "I will cut off the *names* of the idols out of the land, and they shall be no more remembered ;" words which are grounded on the divine precept, Exod. xxiii. 13, "Ye shall make *no mention* of the *names* of other gods, neither let it be heard out of thy mouth."

18. *will I make a covenant for them with the beasts of the field*] As Noah was at peace with the wild beasts in the Ark, and Daniel with the lions in the den, and our Lord with the wild beasts in the wilderness, so My people will walk unharmed amid dangers. Cp. Job v. 22, 23, and Isa. xi. 6, 7, describing, in poetical language, the happiness of the Christian Church. The union of all animals, savage as well as tame, in the sheet let down from heaven to St. Peter, symbolized the spiritual peace of the Gospel, and the union of nations formerly barbarous, in the Church of Christ. See on Acts x. 15 ; cp. on Mark xvi. 18.

— *I will break the bow*] Compare the description of Evangelical victory and peace in Isaiah, in Isa. ii. 4 ; xxxv. 9. Ezek. xxxiv. 25. Zech. ix. 10.

19. *I will betroth thee unto me for ever—in righteousness*] The Hebrew Nation, once betrothed to God at Mount Sinai, and loved by Him with the tenderest affection, and yet guilty of spiritual fornication and adultery, will be cleansed from its sins and washed pure by the blood of Christ, and be espoused to God as a chaste virgin (2 Cor. xi. 2), never to be divorced from Him. Her sins will not only be forgiven, but forgotten. Cp. John iii. 29. Eph. v. 25. Rev. xxi. 9. These blessed nuptials will be celebrated, on her repentance and conversion, through faith in Christ's righteousness, and in justification through Him alone, and in the free loving-kindness and mercy of God. Cp. Isa. lxii. 5 and *Theodoret* here. Here is a promise of perpetuity to the Church of God in Christ. Cp. Matt. xxi. 18.

" Ista meretrix " (says S. *Jerome*) "fornicata est, prophetis Sponsi sodalibus interfectis ; novissime autem venit Dei Filius Dominus Jesus, quo crucifixo et a mortuis resurgente desponsatur, nequaquam in legis justitia, sed in fide et gratia Evangelii."

This promise to Israel may be applied to every penitent soul which is espoused to Christ by repentance and faith.

THEY SHALL HEAR JEZREEL.

21, 22. *I will hear the heavens, and they shall hear the earth ; and the earth shall hear the corn, and the wine, and the oil ; and they shall hear Jezreel*] All Creation is here represented as hanging by a continuous chain of dependency on the Throne of God ; and when its due subordination is preserved, then a stream of prayer and intercession mounts upward from earth to heaven by that chain, and a stream of grace flows downward by it from

Before
CHRIST
about
787.

i ch. 1. 4.
j ver. 20.
Verily ver. 9.
1 ch. 1. 10.
2a ch. 1. 10.
Zech. 13. 9.
Rom. 9. 26.
1 Pet. 2. 10.
a ch. 1. 2.
b Jer. 3. 20.
† Heb. *of grapes.*

the corn, and the wine, and the oil; [i] and they shall hear Jezreel. [23] And [k] I will sow her unto me in the earth; [l] and I will have mercy upon her that had not obtained mercy; and I [m] will say to *them which were* not my people, Thou *art* my people; and they shall say, *Thou art* my God.

III. [1] Then said the LORD unto me, [a] Go yet, love a woman beloved of her [b] friend, yet an adulteress, according to the love of the LORD toward the children of Israel, who look to other gods, and love flagons † of wine.

[2] So I bought her to me for fifteen *pieces* of silver, and *for* an homer

† Heb. *lethech.*
c Deut. 21. 13.

of barley, and an † half homer of barley: [3] And I said unto her, Thou shalt [c] abide for me many days; thou shalt not play the harlot, and thou shalt not be for *another* man: so *will* I also *be* for thee.

d ch. 10. 3.

[4] For the children of Israel shall abide many days [d] without a king, and

---

heaven to earth; and thus all Creation, when harmonized by love and obedience to God, ministers to the comfort of man, who is *God's seed*, as well as to the glory of God.

All creatures are eager to serve man, when man serves God, and when he is a faithful *Jezreel*, or *seed of God*. The corn cries to the earth, the earth cries to the heaven, the heavens cry to God, that they may be enabled by Him to supply man's need, and minister to his comfort. Compare the true *seed of God*, owns its dependence on Him for all that it receives. The heavens pray to God, for they have no power of themselves to give rain (see on Jer. xiv. 22, and cp. Zech. x. 1, 2), in order that they may be empowered to hear the prayers of the Earth for rain; and God hears them, and allows them to pour forth genial showers upon the thirsty ground. The Earth hears the prayers of the corn and the wine and the oil for rain, and sends up their prayers heavenward; and they all listen to the prayers of *Jezreel*, and become its intercessors with God, Who hearkens to this chorus of prayer, and answers it in love.

How much more is this realized in the world of grace! There the Divine *Jezreel*, Who is Christ, and Who vouchsafed to become the *Seed* of the *Woman* (Gen. iii. 15), and to be the Seed of Abraham and David, and has thus joined God to Man in His own Person, and is our *Emmanuel* as well as our *Jezreel*, is ever praying for His People; and a shower of blessings descends from heaven to earth in answer to His prayers, and brings forth fruit an hundredfold. *Cp. S. Cyril* and *S. Jerome* here.

In this beautiful imagery we recognize a repeal of the divine threat, which was denounced on Israel for disobedience and represented heaven and earth as deaf to all human appeals; "Thy heaven that is over thy head shall be brass, and the earth that is under thee as iron" (Deut. xxviii. 23). The ears of the Element are unsealed by human obedience. If Man hearkens to God, all God's Creation will hearken to him.

23. *I will sow her unto me in the earth*] Not in her own land only, but every where. The seed of Abraham is sown in all lands where Christ is preached. The whole Earth, under the Gospel, has become a seed-plot for heaven, now that it has received seed from the Divine Sower, which is Christ, and has been sown by His Blood and by His Word, and is watered by the dews and rains of the Holy Ghost. Compare the prophetic imagery in Jeremiah xxxi. 27: "Behold the days come, saith the Lord, that I will sow the house of Israel and the house of Judah with the seed of men and with the seed of beasts;" and Isaiah lxi. 9—11. God is the Husbandman (John xv. 1), Jezreel is His husbandry (1 Cor. iii. 9); the field is the world (Matt. xiii. 24). The Apostles and their successors in all ages are the Sowers of the Seed; the Harvest is the End of the World (Matt. xiii. 39); the reapers are the Angels, and the Barn is Heaven. Cp. Rev. xiv. 15.

CH. III. 1. *Go yet, love a woman beloved of her friend, yet an adulteress*] Though Israel has been faithless to God, yet she is not utterly cast off; she is still beloved of her *friend* (cp. the use of the word *friend* in Cant. v. 16. Jer. iii. 1. 20), her companion, her lover, her husband, who is God (ii. 16). This is what is now represented by the Prophet, being commanded to take again to himself his wife Gomer (i. 3), notwithstanding her unfaithfulness to him.

— *and love flagons of wine*] Rather, *raisin-cakes*. See *Sept.*, *Vulg.*, *Syriac*, *Arabic*, and 2 Sam. vi. 19. Such cakes were offered to idols (Jer. vii. 18; xliv. 19). They who love such dainties are they who care not for the spiritual delights of

God's love, but only for that which gratifies their own sensual appetites. See above on *Diblaim*, i. 3.

2. *So I bought her to me for fifteen pieces of silver*] I did not espouse her to me for a wife, but I bought, or acquired (lit. by *digging*, cp. Deut. ii. 6. Job vi. 27; xlii. 11) her *for me* as a slave, at a mean price—fifteen shekels of silver (thirty shekels was the price of a slave—Exod. xxi. 32) and fifteen ephahs of *barley* (not wheat, cp. note on Rev. vi. 6), showing to how low a state of degradation and distress she was now reduced. This represents the condition of the Jewish People, no longer a loved or loving spouse, but in bondage (see Gal. iv. 25); and yet she is reserved for a happy time, when she will be delivered into the glorious liberty of the children of God (Rom. viii. 21).

3. *Thou shalt abide*] Lit. *thou shalt sit* (and so in v. 4) not as a harlot sitting by the way-side (Gen. xxxviii. 14), but waiting in patience till thy former Husband vouchsafes to take notice of thee, and restore thee to Himself. Cp. Deut. xxi. 13, which describes the preparatory discipline and purification of a captive woman before she is received into wedlock.

— *thou shalt not play the harlot*] Thou shalt not worship false gods: idolatry is spiritual fornication.

One of the happy consequences of the Jewish Captivity has been, that Israel has thus been weaned from idolatry. Cp. *Introd.* to Ezra, p. 299; and see v. 4 here.

THE DISPERSION OF ISRAEL, AND ITS FUTURE RESTORATION
IN CHRIST.

4. *without a king—teraphim*] Here is a remarkable prophecy, which has been literally fulfilled, as even the Jewish Rabbis confess. "These" (says Kimchi, ap. Pocock, 122) "are the days of the banishment in which we now are, wherein we have neither king nor prince of Israel, but are under the power of Gentile nations, and without a sacrifice: so are we at this time in this captivity, even all the children of Israel." "Who" (says S. Augustine, de Civ. Dei. vii. 28) "does not here recognize a prophetic representation of what the Jews are now? But let us hear what the prophet adds: 'Afterwards they shall return, and seek the Lord their God, and David their king.' Nothing can be more clear than this prophecy, inasmuch as Christ was made of David's seed (Rom. i. 3)."

Though God had promised to David perpetuity to his seed and throne, yet He here declares that Israel should remain many days without a king, and without a prince. Both prophecies have come true. David's monarchy ceased to be *visible* at the Captivity, and yet it is everlasting in CHRIST. See above, on Gen. xlix. 10, and on 2 Sam. vii.

Yet further. Although Israel has been many days without an *ephod* (Exod. xxviii. 4, 5. 1 Sam. xxii. 18; xxiii. 9), that is, without a visible *priesthood*, as the *Sept.* and *Arabic* rightly interpret it, yet it has never fallen into idolatry, as a nation, since the Babylonish Captivity. It has remained for more than 2000 years without an *image* (Exod. xxiii. 24; xxxiv. 13. Deut. vii. 5; xii. 3; xvi. 22. 2 Kings iii. 2; below, x. 1. Micah v. 13, where the same word is used as here), and without *teraphim*—i.e. without idols (as the Prophet says before in v. 3, they shall "not play the harlot"). See Gen. xxxi. 19. 1 Sam. xv. 23; xix. 13. 2 Kings xxiii. 24. Ezek. xxi. 21. Zech. x. 2.

And yet, though Israel has *not* been *guilty* of idolatry for 2000 years, it has been and is *punished* more severely than when it committed idolatry. What can be the cause of this? The reason is, because it is guilty of the sin of not believing in Christ.

without a prince, and without a sacrifice, and without † an image, and without an ᵉ ephod, and *without* ᶠ teraphim :

⁵ Afterward shall the children of Israel return, and ᵍ seek the LORD their God, and ʰ David their king; and shall fear the LORD and his goodness in the ⁱ latter days.

IV. ¹ Hear the word of the LORD, ye children of Israel : for the LORD hath a ᵃ controversy with the inhabitants of the land, because *there is* no truth, nor mercy, nor ᵇ knowledge of God in the land. ² By swearing, and lying, and killing, and stealing, and committing adultery, they break out, and † blood toucheth blood.

³ Therefore ᶜ shall the land mourn, and ᵈ every one that dwelleth therein shall languish, with the beasts of the field, and with the fowls of heaven ; yea, the fishes of the sea also shall be taken away.

⁴ Yet let no man strive, nor reprove another : for thy people *are* as they ᵉ that strive with the priest.

*Marginal references (right column):*
Before CHRIST about 785.
† Heb. *a standing, or, statue, or, pillar*, Isa. 19. 19.
e Exod. 28. 6.
f Judg. 17. 5.
g Jer. 50. 4, 5.
ch. 5. 6.
h Jer. 30. 9. Ezek. 34. 23, 24. & 37. 27, 24.
i Isa. 2. 2. Jer. 30. 24.
a Isa. 1. 18. & 3. 13, 14.
b Ezek. 38. 8, 16. Dan. 2. 28.
Micah 4. 1. about 780.
Jer. 25. 31.
ch. 12. 2.
Micah 6. 2.
b Jer. 4. 22. & 5. 4.
† Heb. *bloods*.
c Jer. 4. 28. & 12. 4.
Amos 5. 16. & 8. 8.
d Zeph. 1. 3.   e Deut. 17. 12.

---

In the captivity and dispersion of Israel, we recognize the hand of God's fatherly mercy and love. The destruction of the material fabric of the Temple, and of the Levitical Priesthood, prepared the Jews to look to Christ, the Eternal High Priest, and to the Spiritual Temple of His Universal Church ; the abandonment of their images and their teraphim—that is, of all idolatrous usages, has qualified them to be worshippers in that holy Temple. Alas ! that some Christian Churches should now be obstructing the approach of the Jews to Christ by acts of creature-worship—such as the adoration of saints and angels, and by setting up idols in the house of God ! It has been supposed, with good reason, that some severe judgments of God must overtake idolatrous Churches, before the Jews can be converted to Christianity.

5. *Afterward shall the children of Israel return, and seek the* LORD *their God, and David their king*] The Hebrew Nation, which said at the crucifixion of Christ, "We have no king but Cæsar" (John xix. 15),—thus rejecting her true King,—will remain many days without a visible Monarchy and Priesthood ; yet, in the latter days, they shall return and find *the* LORD *their God, and David their king* in CHRIST, Who is the Everlasting King and Priest (*S. Jerome*).

The Hebrew Rabbis themselves confess that this prophecy refers to the Messiah. See the *Chaldee* Paraphrase here and *R. Tanchum, Aben Ezra*, and *Kimchi*, in *Pocock*, 138, 139; and see above, note on *v.* 4. May God hasten the time !

It may be remarked here, in passing, that these words afford one refutation, among innumerable others, of the *literal* system of interpretation of Divine prophecy. *If* the promises of God to Jerusalem and Sion in Hebrew prophecy are to be localized, and to be limited to the literal City and Temple of the material Jerusalem (instead of being extended to the Spiritual Sion of Christ's Church Universal), then we ought, in reading the present prophecy, to say, that it predicts a personal resurrection of *David* the King, to sit on a throne in that earthly Jerusalem. But no; Jerusalem is Christ's Church; and David lives and reigns there for ever in CHRIST. See above, on Jer. xxx. 9. See xxxiv. 23, 24.

— *and shall fear the* LORD] Literally, *they shall go trembling to the Lord*. This must be the attitude and gesture of the Jews, if they are to be received again into the favour of God. See xi. 11, "They shall *tremble* as a bird out of Egypt, and as a dove out of the land of Assyria." Zech. xii. 10, and cp. Ps. ii. 11.

As was before observed, God's favoured people, the Jews (formerly addicted to idolatry, and therefore rejected by God), have now continued free from idolatry for many years (as the Prophet here foretells), and yet have remained outcasts from His favour ; and therefore it is certain that they must have been guilty, and still are guilty, of some more heinous sin than idolatry. What sin is that ? It is the rejection of God's own Son, crucified by them a short time before the destruction of Jerusalem and their own dispersion, which He Himself foretold would be the consequence of that act (Matt. xxiii. 38. *S. Chrysostom; S. Jerome*). Let the Jews only repent of that sin, and come trembling and mourning for it, and they will again be received with open arms by their heavenly Father. See below, on Zech. xii. 10—14; xiii. 1.

— *in the latter days*] It is a rule given by the Hebrew expositors, that, by the *latter days*, we are to understand the days

of the Messiah ; and we must conclude, that what is said to be done in the latter days, is to be fulfilled in the days of Christ— that is, in the times of the Gospel (*Pocock*, 143).

CH. IV.] Having anticipated the end in these introductory chapters, which are a PROLOGUE to the whole (see on i. 1), Hosea (as is usual with the goodly company of the Prophets) returns to his own age, and addresses his own people, "*Hear the word . . . ye children of Israel*." Observe, he takes up the words *children of Israel* from the foregoing chapter, and in a stirring apostrophe remonstrates with the people and their rulers, spiritual and temporal, for the sins which would be the cause of the misery which he has foretold, and thus he links on this portion of the prophecy to the preceding. See below, on v. 1, where another link of connexion, "*Hear ye*," is noticed.

2. *By swearing, and lying*] These are infinitive absolutes in the original. The preposition, *by*, should be omitted ; and thus there would be more vehemence in this prophetical outburst.

— *they break out*] Rather, *they break in*. The word describes violent aggression and irruption, like that of a house-breaker (*Gesen.* 691).

— *blood toucheth blood*] Literally, *bloods touch bloods*. The plural describes the frequency of the crime; waves of blood follow one another, like the billows of the sea in a ceaseless tide. . . . Alas ! that this description should be realized in some Christian countries in these latter days. What will the end be ?

It is not unworthy of consideration, that many Hebrew Expositors interpret these words *blood toucheth blood*, as applying to incestuous marriages, contracted within the forbidden limits of consanguinity. See the *Targum* here ; and *Pocock*, 149. If the words are received in that sense, here too is a warning to Christian nations.

3. *Therefore shall the land mourn—with the beasts of the field*] Cattle plagues are described by the Prophet here as punishments of the sins of men, who are sustained by the animal creation, and who suffer in its destruction by pestilence. See below, on Joel i. 18.

4. *let no man strive*] Impunity in sin is the greatest punishment. Cp. *v.* 17 ; and *Pocock*, 156.

— *thy people*] They are no longer God's people. Compare God's words to Moses after the idolatry at Horeb, "*Thy* people have corrupted themselves" (Exod. xxxii. 7. Deut. ix. 12).

— *as they that strive with the priest*] He repeats the word *strive*. Let no man strive by remonstrance with those who strive with God, by rebellion against His lawful representatives invested with His authority (Deut. xxxiii. 10. Mal. ii. 7). Their case is desperate ; they are given over to a reprobate mind. Cp. Deut. xvii. 8—13, where God says, that whoso wilfully and presumptuously rejected the lawful sentence of God, speaking by His priests, was to be put to death.

The Jews, to express great impiety, have a proverb which says, they are like those who "judge their judges" (*Pocock*, 158) ; and our Lord says of His Apostles, "He that despiseth you, despiseth Me" (Luke x. 16) ; and the Apostles specify this sin as an imitation of "the gainsaying of Korah," and as one of the characteristics of the latter days (2 Pet. ii. 10. Jude 8). The prevalence of this sin in our own age and country may

7

Before
CHRIST
about
780.

⁵ Therefore shalt thou fall ᶠ in the day, and the prophet also shall fall with thee in the night, and I will † destroy thy mother.

⁶ ᵍ My people are † destroyed for lack of knowledge: because thou hast rejected knowledge, I will also reject thee, that thou shalt be no priest to me: seeing thou hast forgotten the law of thy God, I will also forget thy children.

⁷ ʰ As they were increased, so they sinned against me: ⁱ *therefore* will I change their glory into shame.

⁸ They eat up the sin of my people,
And they † set their heart on their iniquity.

⁹ And there shall be, ᵏ like people, like priest:
And I will † punish them for their ways, and † reward them their doings.

¹⁰ For ˡ they shall eat and not have enough:
They shall commit whoredom, and shall not increase:
Because they have left off to take heed to the LORD.

¹¹ Whoredom and wine and new wine ᵐ take away the heart.

¹² My people ask counsel at their ⁿ stocks,
And their staff declareth unto them:
For ᵒ the spirit of whoredoms hath caused *them* to err,
And they have gone a whoring from under their God.

¹³ ᵖ They sacrifice upon the tops of the mountains,
And burn incense upon the hills,
Under oaks and poplars and elms, because the shadow thereof *is* good:
ᑫ Therefore your daughters shall commit whoredom,
And your spouses shall commit adultery.

¹⁴ ‖ I will not punish your daughters when they commit whoredom,
Nor your spouses when they commit adultery:
For themselves are separated with whores,

---

well suggest serious and sorrowful forebodings for what is coming.

5. *in the day—in the night*] Neither in day-time nor in night-time shalt thou be free from calamity.

— *thy mother*] The Hebrew Nation. Cp. ii. 2.

6. *of knowledge*] Literally, *of the* knowledge, the only true wisdom—the knowledge of God (Job xxviii. 12—20, Prov. i. 7).

— *no priest*] Thou, who wert a nation of priests (Exod. xix. 6), shalt be degraded from thy estate.

7. *As they were increased, so they sinned against me*] The more they prospered, the more they sinned against Me, the Author of their prosperity. Cp. Deut. xxxii. 15, "Jeshurun waxed fat, and kicked."

— *will I change their glory into shame*] Because they changed Me—their glory—for an idol, their shame (see ix. 10, and cp. Ps. cvi. 20), therefore will I change their glory into shame.

8. *my people*] They (the priests who ought to reprove sin) fatten themselves on the sins of the people. This was fulfilled specially in the fact that the priests encouraged the people to sin, in order that they themselves might feed upon the sacrifices which they commanded the people to bring in order to expiate their sins. See Lev. vi. 26; x. 17; and Pocock, 168.

— *they set their heart*] Or, *lifted up their soul* (literally, in the singular number, *every one lifted up his soul*) on the iniquity of the people; they encouraged them in it, in order that they might profit by it; like those in later days who connive at and abet sin, in order that they may enrich themselves with wealth gotten by absolution from it, and by commutation of penance.

The Prophet has been asserting the legitimate authority of the priesthood in the strongest terms ("thy people are as they that *strive with the priest*"); and therefore there is greater force in this censure and condemnation of the Priests who were treacherous to their solemn engagements.

9. *like people, like priest*] In sin and punishment. Cp. Isa. xxiv. 2.

Here is a warning to the Clergy. If the Priests of a

Church are untrue to their solemn vows and engagements, what will become of the people? How beautiful is the portrait of the "Good Parson," drawn by our great English poet of the fourteenth century, Geoffry Chaucer:—

"Wide was his parish, and houses far asunder,
But he ne left nought for no rain nor thunder,
In sickness and in mischief, to visit
The farthest in his parish touch and lite,
Upon his feet, and in his hand a staff;
This noble 'ensample to his sheep he yaf (gave),
That first he wrought, and afterward he taught;
Out of the Gospel he the wordes caught,
And this figure he added yet thereto,
That if gold ruste, what should iron do?
For if a priest be foul, on whom we trust,
No wonder is a lewèd man (lay man) to rust;
And shame it is, if that a priest take keep,
To see a foulèd shepherd, and clean sheep:
Well ought a priest ensample for to give
By his cleannesse, how his sheep should live."
( *Chaucer*, Prologue to "Canterbury Tales.")

12. *My people ask counsel at their stocks*] "Saying to a stock, Thou art my father" (Jer. ii. 27; x. 3). "Woe unto him that saith unto the wood, Awake" (Hab. ii. 19, and cp. Isa. xl. 20; xliv. 13—20).

— *their staff declareth unto them*] Their staff, or stick (see Ezek. xxi. 21), to which they resort (instead of to God and His Prophets, and Urim and Thummim), is *prophesying unto them.* They make the dumb wood their God. May not this also be applied to some in later days, who resort to forbidden arts for searching into futurity?

13. *They sacrifice upon the tops of the mountains*] Cp. Deut. xii. 2—5. 2 Kings xvii. 10, 11. Ezek. xx. 28.

— *elms*] Rather, the *terebinths.*

— *the shadow thereof is good*] Good for hiding their idolatrous and lustful purposes and practices.

14. *themselves*] The fathers and husbands *are separated,* or go aside, *with whores.*

And they sacrifice with harlots:

Therefore the people *that* ʳ doth not understand shall ‖ fall.

15 Though thou, Israel, play the harlot,

*Yet* let not Judah offend ;

ˢ And come not ye unto Gilgal,

Neither go ye up to ᵗ Beth-aven,

ᵘ Nor swear, The Lᴏʀᴅ liveth.

16 For Israel ˣ slideth back as a backsliding heifer :

Now the Lᴏʀᴅ will feed them as a lamb in a large place.

17 Ephraim *is* joined to idols :

ʸ Let him alone.

18 Their drink † is sour :

They have committed whoredom continually :

ᶻ Her † rulers *with* shame do love, Give ye.

19 ᵃ The wind hath bound her up in her wings,

And ᵇ they shall be ashamed because of their sacrifices.

V. ¹ Hear ye this, O priests ;

And hearken, ye house of Israel ;

— *harlots*] Consecrated as such to their false gods. See the note on Gen. xxxviii. 21, where the same word is used as here.

Gɪʟɢᴀʟ ᴀɴᴅ Bᴇᴛʜᴇʟ.

15. *Gilgal — Bethaven*] Gilgal and Bethel, two places once famous for God's mercies to their fathers ; the former celebrated in the history of Joshua, who initiated the people anew into covenant with God by circumcision there—whence it had its name *Gilgal*, or *rolling away* (Josh. v. 9) ; and it was "holy ground" (Josh. v. 15), and made glorious by his victories (see on Josh. iv. 19 ; ix. 6 ; x. 6) ; and famous also in the days of the Judges (ii. 1), and Samuel (1 Sam. vii. 16 ; x. 8 ; xi. 14 ; xv. 33).

The sin of Israel was aggravated by their desecration of such a place as Gilgal. Cp. below, ix. 15, 11. Amos iv. 4 ; v. 5. Cp. *A Lapide* here.

So *Bethel (house of God)* was once a holy place, but afterwards it was profaned. It was made famous in the history of Abraham and the other patriarchs by God's gracious revelation to them (Gen xii. 8 ; xxviii. 19 ; xxxi. 13 ; xxxv. 15), but was now perverted by idolatry into a *Beth-aven*, a *house of vanity* (1 Kings xii. 29, 32 ; xiii. 1. 2 Kings x. 29). Cp. v. 8 ; x. 5 ; and see below, on Amos v. 5.

There is no reason for supposing, with some modern Expositors, that the Prophets are speaking of *another* Gilgal than that which was near Jericho ; indeed, such a supposition much weakens the force of their remonstrances with Israel for desecrating, by their idolatry and other sins, such places as Bethel and Gilgal, which had been hallowed by the piety of their forefathers, and by God's gracious dispensations to them. Cp. on v. 1, and on vi. 9.

As Hosea himself says (ix. 15), " All their wickedness is in *Gilgal* "—even in Gilgal, where, when their fathers had been brought by Joshua out of the wilderness, they pitched their first camp in Canaan, and where they were consecrated to God by a second circumcision, even there they now set up their idols, and worship them instead of God (*S. Jerome*).

Observe here a specimen of that policy which has ever characterized the operations of the Evil One in the Church of God. He is ever attempting to pervert her holiest objects— her Bethels and her Gilgals—into scenes of idolatry, and to make them his own instruments for the destruction of souls. He is always endeavouring to change our Bethels into Beth-avens, Holy places, holy persons (even the Blessed Virgin herself), holy things (even the Word of God and Sacraments) are desecrated by him, and enlisted in his own service.

— *harlots, The Lᴏʀᴅ liveth*] Since ye worship *dead idols*, even at Gilgal and Bethel, instead of the *living* God, Who revealed Himself to your fathers in the wilderness, what monstrous inconsistency and absurdity is it for you to swear, "The Lord liveth :" you perjure yourselves by your acts.

16. *Israel slideth back as a backsliding heifer*] This image is suggested by the mention of Bethel. Israel worshipped a

calf there ; and by so doing became like "a calf that eateth hay," and like a refractory one, kicking against its owner.

— *a lamb in a large place.*] Observe the irony here. Israel kicks, like a restive and refractory heifer, against its Master's yoke, and desires freedom. Cp. Jer. v. 5. Israel shall have liberty—the liberty of wandering far and wide from its home in the wilderness of Assyria, to which it will be carried captive and be scattered there. The refractory heifer will become like a stray lamb, one not sheltered and fed in the fold, but feeble and exposed to wild beasts in the solitude of the desert. The service of God is the only perfect freedom. What the World calls liberty, is too often the slavery of Satan, hurrying the miserable soul from the city of God into a howling wilderness.

17. *Ephraim is joined to idols*] Idols will be the cause of misery to their votaries. The metaphor is kept up ; Ephraim has kicked against God's yoke, as a refractory heifer, and has joined or yoked itself to idols ; as it were, yoked itself to an idolatrous car ; and its punishment will be that God will let it alone (cp. Jer. vii. 16. Ezek. xx. 39), and leave it to itself to wander at large in a strange land.

18. *Their drink is sour*] Israel has degenerated, like milk turned sour, or like wine that has lost its flavour. Cp. Isa. i. 22, and our Lord's words, "if the salt has lost its savour" (Matt. v. 13).

— *rulers*] Literally, *shields*. Rulers, who ought to be "defenders of the faith" and protectors of the people, are called *shields* here, as in Ps. xlvii. 9.

— *Her rulers with shame do love, Give ye*] Rather, her rulers love, yea they love, shame (*Ewald, Pusey, Keil*) ; or it may mean, they love to say, Give ye shame, which offers the same sense. By serving idols they seek their own shame, and they woo their own woe.

19. *The wind—wings*] The wind has wrapped up Israel in its wings, in order to sweep it away captive into a distant land. Wind is personified as a winged creature, a powerful Bird of prey, which carries off its victims in its wings. Cp. the image in Zech. v. 1, 9, and Ps. xviii. 10 ; civ. 3. Isa. lvii. 13, and the representations of the Winds on "the Temple of the Winds" at Athens.

The metaphor is kept up. Ephraim has broken away from God's yoke, and bound itself to idols ; therefore, it will be tied up in the wings of a whirlwind, and swept away into the wilderness, as sand carried up and whirled about in the eddying vortex of a tornado in the desert.

— *ashamed*] Because they have *loved shame* (i. e. idols), they themselves will be reduced to shame. Cp. Isa. i. 29.

Cʜ. V. 1. *Hear ye this, O priests*] Observe the connexion ; he had said that if they turned to God, God would *hear* the voice of creation pleading for them (iv. 21, 22). But if not, he has a message of woe to Princes, Priests, and People. *Hear ye the word of the Lord*, iv. 1, and, *Hear ye this, O priests*. Cp. Joel i. 2. Amos iii. 1. 13 ; iv. 1 ; v. 1 ; vii. 16 ; viii. 1. Micah i. 2 ; iii. 1. 9 ; vi. 1. 2. 9.

And give ye ear, O house of the king;
For judgment *is* toward you,
Because <sup>a</sup> ye have been a snare on Mizpah,
And a net spread upon Tabor.

2 And the revolters are <sup>b</sup> profound to make slaughter,
  || Though I *have been* †a rebuker of them all.

3 <sup>c</sup> I know Ephraim, and Israel is not hid from me :
For now, O Ephraim, <sup>d</sup> thou committest whoredom, *and* Israel is defiled.

4 † || They will not frame their doings to turn unto their God :
For <sup>e</sup> the spirit of whoredoms *is* in the midst of them,
And they have not known the LORD.

5 And <sup>f</sup> the pride of Israel doth testify to his face :
Therefore shall Israel and Ephraim fall in their iniquity;
Judah also shall fall with them.

6 <sup>g</sup> They shall go with their flocks and with their herds to seek the LORD ;
But they shall not find *him ;* he hath withdrawn himself from them.

7 They have <sup>h</sup> dealt treacherously against the LORD :
For they have begotten strange children :
Now shall <sup>i</sup> a month devour them with their portions.

8   <sup>k</sup> Blow ye the cornet in Gibeah,
*And* the trumpet in Ramah :

Before
CHRIST
about
780.

a ch. 6. 9.

b Isa. 29 15.

* Or, *and, &c.*
† Heb. *a correction.*
c Amos 3. 2.

d Ezek. 23. 5, &c.
ch. 4. 17.
† Heb. *They will not give.*
‡ Or, *Their doings will not suffer them.*
e ch. 4. 12.

f ch. 7. 10.

g Prov. 1. 28.
Isa. 1. 15.
Jer. 11. 11.
Ezek. 8. 18.
Micah 3. 4.
John 7. 34.
h Isa. 48. 8.
Jer. 3. 20. & 5. 11.
i ch. 6. 7.
Mal. 2. 11.
i Zech. 11. 8.

k ch. 8. 1.
Joel 2. 1.

---

— *house of the king*] The royal family generally. He is not addressing the house of any one king of Israel specially (whether Jeroboam II., Zechariah, Shallum, Menahem, Pekahiah, or Pekah), but is speaking to them generally. The prophecies of Hosea are a summary of his exhortations and denunciations, uttered during his long ministry of more than sixty years.

— *on Mizpah*] Even Mizpah, the scene of God's revelations of favour to your great ancestor (Gen. xxxi. 49), and of other acts famous in your national history (Judges x. 17 ; xi. 11 ; xx. 1), and that other Mizpah, celebrated in the later days of Samuel (1 Sam. vii. 5, 6 ; x. 17), have been desecrated by you like Bethel and Gilgal (see iv. 15). Even there, on those high places, ye spread snares for souls, by waylaying them there in their journey to Jerusalem to worship in the place appointed by God (*Eben Ezra, Kimchi*), and by decoying them by the allurements of your idol worship,—as fowlers spread nets for birds on those mountains, and catch their prey there (S. *Jerome*).

Observe the paronomasia (or play upon the words) here. "Ye have been a snare on Mizpah (your strong watch-tower), therefore there is judgment—Heb. *Mishpat*—against you." If we pervert our *Bethels* into *Bethavens*, God will change our *Mizpats* into *Mishpats*.

— *Tabor*] Even there, where God showed His marvellous power, might, and mercy to Israel in the days of Deborah (Judg. iv. 6, 12).

2. *are profound to make slaughter*] Or rather, *made slaughter deep :* dug a deep pit and filled it with carnage—like the pit of *Mizpah* in the days of Jeremiah. See Jer. 7—9.

— *Though—all*] Or literally, "*but* I am *rebuke* (or *chastisement*) to them all" (cp. v. 9) for their sins." I, who am love, have become wrath to them. Cp. above, on P's. cix. 4. "I am prayer." Cp. Pocock, 218.

3. *Israel is defiled*] Has defiled itself.

4. *They will not frame their doings*] Or rather (see margin), their doings do not allow them to turn to God.

5. *the pride of Israel doth testify to his face*] The pride of Israel which witnesses against him. "As the rebel angels fell by pride (1 Tim. iii. 6), so did Ephraim. Ephraim, the descendant of Jacob, of the tribe of Joseph, and one of the most powerful and prosperous of the tribes, was impatient of the rule of Judah ; it envied Judah (Isa. xi. 13), and rebelled against the house of David in the days of Jeroboam (1 Kings xi. 26), and set up idols, in opposition to the Temple at Jerusalem. These were the fruits of its pride. These were the consequences of its haughtiness ; these its miserable results, in provoking God's wrath against Israel (till at length it was taken captive and

scattered), *testified* against Ephraim *to his face* openly, as Isaiah says (iii. 9). "The show of their countenance doth witness against them, they declare their sin as Sodom, they hide it not." This exposition seems preferable to the interpretation of some (e.g. Keil), that the "pride of Israel" (here and in vii. 10) is equivalent to "the glory of Israel" (in Amos viii. 7 ; cp. below, vii. 10), and is a title of Jehovah Himself.

— *Judah also shall fall with them*] Being tempted by Israel (as in the days of Athaliah, daughter of Ahab and Jezebel, and wife of Jehoram, the son of Jehoshaphat), to set up idols in Jerusalem (2 Kings viii. 18. 2 Chron. xxii. 2—4).

6. *They shall go with their flocks and with their herds to seek the LORD*] but though they drive all their flocks and herds to God's altar, and offer them there, they will not find Him, because they rebelled against Him. Cp. Isa. i. 11. Mic. vi. 6, 7, and below, vi. 6. All the holocausts and hecatombs in the world are profitless without obedience to God's Will and Word.

7. *Then have dealt treacherously*] They have acted perfidiously, like a faithless wife ; such is the meaning of the word used here (*bâgad*) and Jer. iii. 20. Mal. ii. 11. Hence we may explain what follows : "*they have begotten strange children*."

— *Now shall a month devour them with their portions*] Rather, "*Now shall the new moon devour them with their portions,* or inheritance. *The month, the new moon*—even their very feast-day—will be loathsome to God, and will be their day of doom (cp. Isa. i. 13, 14) ; it will devour them with their inheritance. See *Gesen.* 263, and Keil.

This prophecy was consummated in the crucifixion of Christ. The Paschal full moon brought hundreds of thousands of worshippers to Jerusalem, but it was the season in which the Jews killed Him who was the True Passover ; and that sin was the cause of their own destruction at the anniversary of the same Paschal Season, about forty years after, by the arms of Rome. See below, on Matt. xxiv. 1.

### THE FUTURE INVASION OF ISRAEL.

8. *Blow ye—the trumpet*] In order to summon the tribes of Israel together (cp. viii. 1. Jer. iv. 5 ; vi. 1. Joel ii. 1), to repel the invasion of their enemies the Assyrians. The Prophet foresees that invasion, and describes it. Compare the sublime

10

[l] Cry aloud *at* [m] Beth-aven,
[n] After thee, O Benjamin.
9 Ephraim shall be desolate in the day of rebuke:
Among the tribes of Israel have I made known that which shall surely be.
10 The princes of Judah were like them that [o] remove the bound:
*Therefore* I will pour out my wrath upon them like water.
11 Ephraim *is* [p] oppressed *and* broken in judgment,
Because he willingly walked after [q] the commandment.
12 Therefore *will* I *be* unto Ephraim as a moth,
And to the house of Judah [r] as ‖ rottenness.
13 When Ephraim saw his sickness,
And Judah *saw* his [s] wound,
Then went Ephraim [t] to the Assyrian, [u] and sent ‖ to king Jareb:
Yet could he not heal you, nor cure you of your wound.
14 For [x] I *will be* unto Ephraim as a lion,
And as a young lion to the house of Judah:
[y] I, *even* I, will tear and go away;
I will take away, and none shall rescue *him*.
15 I will go *and* return to my place,
† Till [z] they acknowledge their offence, and seek my face:
[a] In their affliction they will seek me early.
VI. 1 Come, and let us return unto the LORD:
For [a] he hath torn, and [b] he will heal us;
He hath smitten, and he will bind us up.
2 [c] After two days will he revive us:
In the third day he will raise us up,

Before CHRIST about 780.
l Isa. 10. 30.
m Josh. 7. 2. ch. 4. 15.
n Judg. 5. 14.
o Deut. 19. 14. & 27. 17.
p Deut. 28. 33.
q 1 Kings 12. 28. Micah 6. 16.
r Prov. 12. 4.
‖ Or, *a worm.*
s Jer. 30. 12.
t 2 Kings 15. 19. ch. 7. 11. & 12. 1.
u ch. 10. 6.
‖ Or, *to the king of Jareb*: or, *to the king* that *should plead.*
x Lam. 3. 10. ch. 13. 7, 8.
y Ps. 50. 22.
† Heb. *till they be guilty.*
z Lev. 26. 40, 41. Jer. 29. 12, 13. Ezek. 6. 9. & 20. 43. & 36. 31.
a Ps. 78. 34.
a Deut. 32. 39. 1 Sam. 2. 6. Job 5. 18. ch. 5. 14.
b Jer. 30. 17.
c 1 Cor. 15. 4.

---

prophetical picture in Isaiah (x. 28—31) pre-announcing the irruption of Sennacherib and his rapid march of destruction. We may also refer to the words of Ezekiel, declaring the duties of the watchman on beholding the approach of an enemy (Ezek. xxxiii. 2—6).

— *Gibeah—Ramah*] Two lofty eminences on the northern frontier of Benjamin. The mention of these places shows that in Hosea's prophetic eye the enemy was already in possession of the greatest part of northern and central Palestine.

— *Cry aloud*] *Sound an alarm*, as the word is rendered in Joel ii. 1.

— *Beth-aven*] Bethel. See iv. 15.

— *After thee, O Benjamin*] The enemy is already on thy rear.

**10.** *remove the bound*] Or landmark. Cp. Deut. xix. 14; xxvii. 17. Because they are guilty of this sin, I will remove them.

**11.** *in judgment*] Rather, *by the judgment*, of God.

— *the commandment*] Of Jeroboam. Israel obeyed, or *followed after, the commandment* (Hebr. *tsav*) of Jeroboam, ordering them to disobey God, and therefore God will break them by *judgment*. Compare Mic. vi. 16, "The *statutes of Omri* are kept—that I should make thee a *desolation*," and Matt. xv. 9. Mark vii. 7, "Teaching for doctrines the *commandments of men*."

**12.** *moth—rottenness*] Rather, *moth*, and *a worm*. That is, though Israel may seem to flourish (as it did in the days of Jeroboam II.), yet, because it is not sound at heart, God's anger is secretly corroding it, as a moth frets a beautiful garment, or as a canker preys on a fair shrub or flower; and, after much patient long-suffering, God's wrath will consume His people (*S. Jerome*). Cp. Isa. l. 9; li. 8. Ps. xxxix. 11. Job xiii. 28.

### KING JAREB.

**13.** *king Jareb*] Literally, *King adversary*. This title is given here to the king of Assyria, on whom Israel and Judah relied for help in trouble (2 Kings xvi. 8. 2 Chron. xxviii. 16—20), and to whom they resorted with gifts and fair speeches, as to a friend or lover, *oheb* (cp. ii. 5. 7. 10. 13); but who became a *yareb*, or *adversary* to them, and who *strove* and *fought* against them. Cp. x. 6. 2 Chron. xxviii. 16. 28; and see *Gesen*. 365. 368. 767; *Delitzsch* on Isa. xlix. 25.

For similar symbolical names (such as *Sheshach, Pekod, Merathaim*), formed by the Prophets to describe the characters of kings and cities with which Israel and Judah had to do, see the notes above, on Jer. xxv. 26.; li. 41. Ezek. xxiii. 23.

**14.** *I* will be] Do not suppose that Assyria will be strong against you by its own power. No; all its might is from God, Who uses it as His instrument. Cp. Isa. x. 5.

— *as a lion*] God, Who had been in His long-suffering like a moth (*v*. 12), and had seemed weak and powerless, will at length roar as a lion, and devour them suddenly.

**15.** *I will go* and *return to my place*] I will withdraw My presence from them, and will retire from their earthly Temple into My heavenly Sanctuary; and by making them feel their need of My help in their distress, I will bring them to repentance (*Targum*).

### PROPHECY OF THE REPENTANCE AND CONVERSION OF ISRAEL.

CH. VI. 1. *Come, and let us return*] God had just said that *He* would *return* to *His place*, and hide His Face from His People, and by the merciful discipline of affliction would bring them to repentance, and would draw them by affliction to seek Him (*v*. 15); and now the Prophet seems to behold the conversion of the Jews, and to hear their words of penitential prayer to God: "Come," they say, "*let us return* unto the Lord. He hath torn, and He will heal us; He hath smitten, and He will bind us up." Cp. 1 Kings viii. 46—51. Jer. xxix. 12—14; and note above, on Isa. lix. 7—10, and the language in Deut. xxxii. 39, which is adopted here.

**2.** *After two days will he revive us in the third day he will raise us up*] The fall of Babylon, and the consequent restoration of the Jews by Cyrus, came suddenly and unexpectedly. "Then were we like unto them that dream. Then said they among the heathen, the Lord hath done great things for them" (Ps. cxxvi. 1, 2).

After speaking of the marvellous deliverance of the Jews by Cyrus, the conqueror of Babylon, the Hebrew Prophets pass

Before
CHRIST
about
760
d Isa. 54. 17.
e 2 Sam. 23. 4.
1 Ps. 72. 6.
k mic. 5. 7.

h ch. 11. 8.

g Or, mercy, or,
kindness
i ch. 13. 3.

k Jer. 1. 10. &
5. 14.
l Jer. 27. 29.
Heb. 4. 12.
f Or, that thy
judgments might
be, &c.

m 1 Sam 15. 22.
Eccles. 5. 1.
Micah 6, 8.
Matt. 9, 13. &
12. 7.
n Ps. 50. 8. 9.
Prov. 21. 3.
Isa. 1. 11.
o Jer. 22. 18.
John 17. 3.
p Or, like Adam,
Job 31. 33.
p ch. 8. 1.
q ch. 5. 7.
r ch. 12. 11.
‖ Or, cunning for
blood,
s Jer. 11. 9.
Ezek. 22. 25.   ch. 5. 1, 2.    † Heb. with one shoulder, or, to Shechem.

And we shall live in his sight.

3 d Then shall we know, *if* we follow on to know the LORD :

His going forth is prepared e as the morning ;

And f he shall come unto us b as the rain,

As the latter *and* former rain unto the earth.

4 h O Ephraim, what shall I do unto thee ?

O Judah, what shall I do unto thee ?

For your ‖ goodness *is* i as a morning cloud,

And as the early dew it goeth away.

5 Therefore have I hewed *them* k by the prophets ;

I have slain them by l the words of my mouth :

‖ And thy judgments *are as* the light *that* goeth forth.

6 For I desired m mercy, and n not sacrifice ;

And the o knowledge of God more than burnt offerings.

7 But they ‖ like men p have transgressed the covenant :

There q have they dealt treacherously against me.

8 r Gilead *is* a city of them that work iniquity,

*And is* ‖ polluted with blood.

9 And as troops of robbers wait for a man,

*So* s the company of priests murder in the way † by consent :

on to speak of Christ, the divine Antitype of Cyrus (see above, on 2 Chron. xxxvi. 22), and of God's sudden liberation effected by Him. The fall of Babylon and the deliverance of the Jews were wonderful. Much more will be the destruction of the spiritual enemies of the Church. Her recovery from the bondage of sin, Satan, and death, and her hope of resurrection from the grave to life eternal, came suddenly and unexpectedly by the Death, Burial, and Resurrection of Christ. It came on *the third day.* As S. Jerome says, "God in Christ not only healed us when sick, but He raised us from death to life *after two days,* by Christ's Resurrection on *the third day* from the dead; and *we shall live* in *His sight*; we shall live for ever in the sight of Him Whose Resurrection from the dead is the pledge and earnest of our Resurrection (S. Jerome; see also Tertullian, c Marcion, iv. 43, adv. Jud. c. 13; Origen, Hom. 5 in Exod.; S. Cyprian, c. Judæos ii. 5 ; S. Cyril, Catech. 14 ; S. Aug. de Civ. Dei, xvii. 28; and so this passage of Hosea is interpreted by Mercer, Hammond, Pocock, Lyranus, Calvinus, A Lapide, M. Henry, and Pusey).

The Jewish Rabbis themselves allow that the Prophet is here speaking of the Messiah. See Pocock, 257 ; and cp. Job xix. 25—27. Isa. xxvi. 19—21. Ezek. xxxvii. 1—14.

Whether Hosea himself had a foresight of Christ's Resurrection on the third day, we cannot say ; but the Christian Church, looking at the event, has ever believed that the Holy Spirit, Who speaks by Hosea, here points to the Resurrection of Christ on the third day, as the source of all deliverance to the Israel of God. Cp. Pocock, 257, 258; and below, on xi. 1.

3. *Then shall we know, if we follow*] Rather, Then shall we know, and we shall *pursue*—like eager huntsman—after the knowledge of the Lord.

— *His going forth is prepared as the morning*] Many are the goings forth of Christ, and all were bright and glorious, like the Day-spring. Christ's going forth from the bosom of the Father in eternity ; His going forth by His Incarnation in time; His going forth as the Messiah to preach the Gospel after His Baptism; His going forth by His Resurrection from the grave—all these goings forth were *prepared* or decreed by God, like the orient beams of the *morning,* to give life and light to a world lying in darkness (Mal. iv. 2. Luke i. 68). The same word for *going forth* is used by Micah (v. 2). His great *going forth* will be on the dawn of the Day of Universal Resurrection and Judgment.

— *as the rain*] As the Psalmist says of Christ, "He shall come down as the rain on the mown grass" (Ps. lxxii. 6. Cp. 2 Sam. xxiii. 4).

5. *Therefore have I hewed them by the prophets*] I have hewed them by prophets, as blocks from the quarry of rough stone or marble are hewn, in order that they may be polished

12

and fitted to be lively stones (1 Pet. ii. 5) in the spiritual Temple of God's Church. As is sung by the Church in the Trochaic hymn, "In Dedicatione Ecclesiæ." See *Clictovei* Elucidationa, p. 41.

"Urbs beata Jerusalem
Dicta pacis visio,
Quæ construitur in cœlis
Vivis ex lapidibus.
* * * *
Tensionibus, pressuris,
Expoliti lapides
Suis coaptantur locis
Per manus artificis.
Dispununtur permansuri
Sacris ædificiis."

— *I have slain them by the words of my mouth*] Which are like the hammer that breaketh the rock in pieces (Jer. xxiii. 29). Cp. on Jer. i. 10.

MERCY, AND NOT SACRIFICE.

6. *For I desired mercy, and not sacrifice*] Although I require sacrifice, and have given minute and imperative directions for it in the Levitical Law, yet, *in comparison* with mercy, I do not desire it ; and I reject all sacrifices, however costly, unless they are offered in faith and love. See above, the note on Jer. vii. 22, which affords the best illustration of these words.

Observe the connexion with what has been said before: "They shall go with their flocks and with their herds to seek the Lord, but they shall not find Him " (v. 6). And why ? Because they did not practise mercy, which is the sacrifice of the heart that God requires, and without which all sacrifices are vain. Therefore all the sacrifices of all the flocks and herds on all their mountains and in all their pastures are of no avail. Cp. Ps. l. 8—13 ; li. 16, 17. Isa. i. 2—17. Mic. vi. 8. Matt. ix. 13 ; xii. 7; and Davison on Prophecy, 207.

7. *like men*] Or rather, like *Adam* ; so margin, and *Vulg.*

— *There have they dealt treacherously*] Even in the Holy Land, even in holy places—such as the Temple itself—have they transgressed, as Adam in Paradise. See what follows.

8. *Gilead is a city of them that work iniquity*—even] Even Gilead (an earthly Eden), where God showed His mercy to Jacob (Gen. xxxi. 21—25), and which God blessed with fertility and wealth—even that whole prosperous country or region (Num. xxxii. 1. Deut. iii. 12—15) has been desecrated by Israel, so as to become *a city of carnage.* It is *polluted,* or, rather, *tracked* or *trodden* with blood. Cp. above, on iv. 15.

9. *the company of priests murder in the way by consent*] Or,

For they commit ‖ lewdness.

¹⁰ I have seen ' an horrible thing in the house of Israel:
There *is* * the whoredom of Ephraim, Israel is defiled.

¹¹ Also, O Judah, * he hath set an harvest for thee,
² When I returned the captivity of my people.

VII. ¹ When I would have healed Israel,
Then the iniquity of Ephraim was discovered,
And the † wickedness of Samaria :
For * they commit falsehood, and the thief cometh in,
*And* the troop of robbers † spoileth without.

² And they † consider not in their hearts *that* I ᵇ remember all their wickedness:
Now ᶜ their own doings have beset them about ; they are ᵈ before my face.

³ They make the king glad with their wickedness,
And the princes * with their lies.

⁴ ' They *are* all adulterers,
As an oven heated by the baker, ‖ *who* ceaseth ‖ from raising after he hath
kneaded the dough, until it be leavened.

⁵ In the day of our king the princes have made *him* sick ‖ with bottles of wine ;
He stretched out his hand with scorners ;

⁶ For they have ‖ made ready their heart like an oven, whiles they lie in wait :
Their baker sleepeth all the night ;
In the morning it burneth as a flaming fire ;

⁷ They are all hot as an oven,
And have devoured their judges ;

Before
CHRIST
about
784.

Or, *enormity.*
† Jer 5. 30.
u ch.4. 12, 13, 17.
x Jer. 51. 33.
Joel 3. 13.
Rev. 14 15.
y Ps. 125, 1.

† Heb. *exits.*

a ch. 5. 1 & 6. 10.

† Heb. *strippeth.*

† Heb. *say not to.*
b Jer. 17. 1.
c Ps. 9, 16.
Prov. 5. 22.
d Ps. 10. 8.

e Rom 1. 32.

f Jer. 9, 2.

‖ Or, *the raiser will cease.*
‖ Or, *from waking.*

‖ Or, *with heat through wine.*

‖ Or, *applied.*

Fulfilled
about 771.

rather, *the company of priests murder in the way to Shechem*
(see margin), the sanctuary of God (*Shechem* means *shoulder*;
hence the confusion in the translation). Shechem, the scene of
God's mercies to the Patriarchs, is polluted by the sins of the
priests, who ought to teach the people to obey His law. On the
holiness of Sichem, or Shechem, as a national sanctuary, see
above on Gen. xii. 6; xxxiii. 18. Josh. xxiv. 1. Judges ix. 1.
1 Kings xii. 1. 25; and below, John iv. 5. Acts vii. 16; and
cp. note above on iv. 15. as to what is said on the desecration of
such sacred places as *Bethel* and *Gilgal*, and also of *Mizpeh*
and *Tabor.* See also the note on v. 1.

The consummation of these acts of wickedness of Israel,
polluting holy places with bloodshed, was seen in the Crucifixion of Christ Himself in the Holy City, and in the dreadful
carnage committed by the Jewish assassins in the Holy Place,
when God's House of Prayer became a "den of thieves." See
on Matt. xxiv. 15. All this bloodshed was visited upon them in
the slaughter of thousands of the Jews, and in the captivity of
many tens of thousands by the Roman armies, at the taking of
Jerusalem. See on Luke xxi. 25.

11 *he hath set an harvest for thee*] God hath appointed a
day of judgment—compared to a harvest—(Jer. li. 33. Joel iii.
13. Matt. xiii. 39. Rev. xiv. 15) for thee, Judah, as well as
for Israel. God first used the sword of Assyria against Israel,
and then used that of Babylon to execute this judgment on
Judah.

— *When I returned the captivity of my people*] Or, rather,
*in my turning of the captivity of my people.* Observe the words,
*My people*—that is, All My visitations upon the nation are
dispensed in love to the faithful remnant of My people. All
national afflictions are occasions and means of salutary discipline
and spiritual joy to them. All national *captivities* are *libera-
tions* to God's saints. The captivity of an Ezekiel and a Daniel
was a deliverance to them from the miserable thraldom and bondage of the sins which then enslaved Jerusalem; and it was a
season of deliverance to them from the trammels of earthly sorrow, and of admission to the glorious visions of heavenly joy.

The climax of this divine saying will be seen at the great
Harvest-Day of the World's Judgment. Then, when the harvest
is reaped, and the tares are cast into the fire, then will be the
time for the Saints of God to "look up, for their redemption"
(the *turning* of their *captivity* from the bondage of this world)
"draweth nigh" (Luke xxi. 28). And see Rom. viii. 21, and
8. Jerome here.

13

Ch. VII. 3. *They make the king glad*] The king and princes,
who, as God's vicegerents and ministers, ought to restrain and
punish national wickedness, connive at it; they even take
pleasure in it and encourage it. Cp. Rom. i. 32.

4. *heated by the baker*] Literally, *burning from the baker*, —
who has kindled it by fire from himself. So the sinner has an
oven which is kindled from the lusts in his own heart (Matt.
xv. 18).

— *raising*] Stirring the fire. The baker kindles the oven,
and when he knows that it is well heated, he ceases from
stirring it till the dough is leavened. Cp. r. 6; and see Rom.
i. 27, they burn in lust; and James iii. 6, where he calls the
tongue "a fire which setteth on fire the course of nature; and
it is set on fire of hell." Satan kindles for himself the fire of
literal and spiritual adultery in the heart of men, and leaves it
there to burn till the dough be leavened, and (so to speak) the
sin is made ready to be kneaded, and to be made into bread.

5. *In the day of our king*] The day of our *king* (not the
King of Judah, appointed by God, but the king whom we have
set up), the royal birthdays, the annual feast-days, instituted by
Jeroboam, instead of being days of spiritual joy and religious
praise and thankfulness to God, are perverted into days of
revelry and ribaldry.

— *have made him sick with bottles of wine*] Or, *are made
sick with heat of wine* (Gesen. 786). The king himself pro-
motes their debauchery, buffoonery, and scoffing against holy
things.

6. *whiles they lie in wait*] When they cease from actual sin, it
is not because they are desisting from sinful desires, but because
they are lying in ambush with deliberate purpose to commit it.

— *Their baker*] Satan, even of his prey, rests for a time from
his work, in order that he may return with greater force, and
make the embers of their passion to burst forth in a raging flame
of actual sin. Their lusts are like fire in an oven. But the
Day is coming, when that fire will kindle God's wrath, which
will burn *like an oven* to consume them (Ps. xxi. 9); "that Day
will burn as an oven." See Mal. iv. 1.

7. *They—have devoured their judges; all their kings are
fallen*] The heated oven of national sins, encouraged by kings
and princes, will consume those rulers who, instead of extin-
guishing it, have added fuel to it. This was fulfilled in the
political anarchy and confusion of the kingdom in the rapid
succession, and in the miserable end, of the kings of Israel after
Jeroboam the second, namely, Zachariah, Shallum, Menahem

Before
CHRIST
about
740.

g ch. 3, 4.
b 2 Kings 15. 10,
14, 25, 30.
i Ps. 14. 7.
k Ps. 106. 35.

l ch. 8. 7

† Heb. *sprinkled.*

m ch. 5. 5.

n Isa. 9. 13.

o ch. 11. 11

p See 2 Kings
15. 19, & 17. 4.
ch. 5. 13, & 9. 3.
& 12. 1.
q Ezek. 12. 13.

r Lev. 26. 14, &c.
Deut. 28. 15, &c.
2 Kings 17. 13, 18.

† Heb. *spoil.*

s Micah 6. 4.

t Job 35. 9, 10.
Ps. 78. 36.
Jer. 3. 10.
Zech. 7. 5.

‖ Or *chastised.*

u ch. 11. 7

⁸ All their kings ʰ are fallen :

ⁱ *There is* none among them that calleth unto me.

⁸ Ephraim, he ᵏ hath mixed himself among the people ;

Ephraim is a cake not turned

⁹ ˡ Strangers have devoured his strength, and he knoweth *it* not :

Yea, gray hairs are † here and there upon him, yet he knoweth not.

¹⁰ And the ᵐ pride of Israel testifieth to his face :

And ⁿ they do not return to the LORD their God, nor seek him for all this.

¹¹ ᵒ Ephraim also is like a silly dove without heart :

ᵖ They call to Egypt, they go to Assyria.

¹² When they shall go, ᑫ I will spread my net upon them ;

I will bring them down as the fowls of the heaven ;

I will chastise them, ʳ as their congregation hath heard.

¹³ Woe unto them ! for they have fled from me :

† Destruction unto them ! because they have transgressed against me :

Though ˢ I have redeemed them, yet they have spoken lies against me.

¹⁴ ᵗ And they have not cried unto me with their heart,

When they howled upon their beds :

They assemble themselves for corn and wine,

*And* they rebel against me.

¹⁵ Though I ‖ have bound *and* strengthened their arms,

Yet do they imagine mischief against me.

¹⁶ ᵘ They return, *but* not to the most High :

---

(see 2 Kings xv. 8—25), and finally in the captivity of the people and the ruin of the monarchy. Compare above, *Introd.* to Kings, p. ix, and Prov. xxviii. 2, "For the transgression of a land many are the princes thereof."

This prophetic denunciation may be addressed to all Rulers and States which seek to enrich themselves by national sins, instead of restraining them. In some cities, even in Rome itself, a large annual revenue is received from lotteries, and (not long since, if not still) from brothels. How much of the wealth of our Indian Government was received from the deadly trade in opium! How much of our own Excise Revenue arises from drunkenness, which is the root of most of the evil in our towns and villages, and which is encouraged by our multitude of haunts of intemperance! These are the fires which will burst forth upon those who kindle them, and will devour their kings and judges.

**8.** *Ephraim, he hath mixed himself among the people*] Literally, *among the peoples.* Israel, who was designed to be *separate* from the nations, and to be "a peculiar people" to God, has mingled "himself with the heathen, and has learned their works" (Ps. cvi. 35). Therefore he will be carried captive, and be scattered among the heathen in exile.

— *Ephraim is a cake not turned*] The metaphor of the oven in *vv.* 4—6 is kept up. Ephraim hath mixed himself with the heathen, but their mixing is of no profit ; he is like a thin round cake which is laid on the red-hot stones of the oven, and which, if not soon turned, is not fit to eat, but is scorched on one side with the fire, and burnt up, while the other side remains raw dough, and thus n[ei]ther side is palatable. See below, "the fire of enthusiastic zeal," &c.; comp. parts hereunto [illegible] of igniting ardour, circumduct[illegible].' S. *Jerome.*

Ephraim ought to be *turned* ; he ought to turn himself by repentance to God, &c., but, and then he would be preserved and be acceptable to God as an offering to Him.

**9.** *gray hairs are here and there upon him*] Literally, *hoariness of hair sprinkled itself upon him, and he knoweth it not*— "obrepit non intellecta senectus" [*Juvenal,* ix. 129). Israel has the seeds of decay and death in him, and he knows it not ; he imagines himself to be young, healthful, and prosperous, while he is approaching the verge of the grave. This was especially applicable to the times of Jeroboam II., when Israel wore the specious semblance of health and prosperity, but there was a deadly disease festering and rankling within.

**10.** *the pride of Israel*] Cp. v. 5.

**11.** *Ephraim also is like a silly dove*] Israel also is become

like a deluded dove without heart, i.e. without understanding, which does not perceive the net spread for it by the fowler : "She hastes to the snare, and knows not that it is for her life" (Prov. vii. 23). See above, on v. 1.

— *They call to Egypt, they go to Assyria*] Instead of fleeing for refuge to God, "like doves to their windows" (Isa. lx. 8), Ephraim, like a silly dove, flutters away for shelter to Egypt or Assyria, which are like "the snare of the fowler," and make it their pr[e]y. See on Isa. xxx. 3; xxxi. 1; xxxvi. 6. Jer. ii. 18, 36; and below, xii. 1; xiv. 3, "Asshur shall not save us."

**12.** *I will spread my net*] For this "silly dove." They who will not listen to God's invitations of mercy, must expect to feel His visitations of judgment.

— *I will bring them down*] However high they may soar, like a dove, into the air, God will bring them down into the net. He will use Egypt and Assyria as His nets to take them captive, for their sins against Him.

— *as their congregation hath heard*] In the solemn warnings of God's law, delivered to their forefathers at Mount Sinai, and on Mount Ebal. Lev. xxvi. 14. Deut. xxvii. 13—26; xxviii. 15—68. Josh. viii. 33. Cp. Jer. xvii. 5.

**13.** *Though I have redeemed them*] Literally, *And I have redeemed them;* and I would still redeem them, if they would hearken to Me. The imperfect has an optative sense (*Keil*).

**14.** *When they howled upon their beds*] Rather, *But they howled upon their beds.* They cried indeed, but their cry was not a devout ejaculation produced by faith, repentance, and love ; it was a howl of anguish, despite, and despair, like that of condemned spirits, who in [illegible] their tongues and gnash their teeth in terror and defiance. They did not call on God with a sincere heart, and therefore they were not heard. The cry of impenitent sinners in distress is not prayer, but howling ; it is like Cain's and Esau's bitter cry ; it comes not from sorrow for sin, but from pain for punishment. Compare notes above, on Job xxiv. 12, "Men groan from out of the city ;" and on Job xxxv. 9—12, which passage is the best comment on the present text.

— *they assemble themselves for corn and wine*] They clamour for temporal blessings, for corn and wine (as Esau did) ; they murmur if they are suffering from dearth or drought, and yet they rebel against God, in Whose hand the seasons are, and from Whom harvests come.

**15.** *I have bound—their arms*] I have instructed them, I have taught their fingers to fight (Ps. cxliv. 1). Cp. Ps. xviii. 34, "He teacheth my hands to war."

' They are like a deceitful bow:

Their princes shall fall by the sword for the *y* rage of their tongue:

This *shall be* their derision *z* in the land of Egypt.

VIII. ¹ *Set* *ᵃ* the trumpet to † thy mouth,

*He shall come* *ᵇ* as an eagle against the house of the LORD,

Because *ᶜ* they have transgressed my covenant,

And trespassed against my law.

² *ᵈ* Israel shall cry unto me, My God, *ᵉ* we know thee.

³ Israel hath cast off *the thing that is* good: the enemy shall pursue him.

⁴ *ᶠ* They have set up kings, but not by me:

They have made princes, and I knew *it* not:

*ᵍ* Of their silver and their gold have they made them idols,

That they may be cut off.

⁵ Thy calf, O Samaria, hath cast *thee* off;

Mine anger is kindled against them:

*ʰ* How long *will it be* ere they attain to innocency?

⁶ For from Israel *was* it also:

The workman made it; therefore it *is* not God:

But the calf of Samaria shall be broken in pieces.

⁷ For *ⁱ* they have sown the wind, and they shall reap the whirlwind:

It hath no ‖ stalk: the bud shall yield no meal:

If so be it yield, *ᵏ* the strangers shall swallow it up.

⁸ *ˡ* Israel is swallowed up:

Now shall they be among the Gentiles *ᵐ* as a vessel wherein *is* no pleasure.

⁹ For *ⁿ* they are gone up to Assyria, *ᵒ* a wild ass alone by himself:

Ephraim *ᵖ* hath hired † lovers.

¹⁰ Yea, though they have hired among the nations, now *ᑫ* will I gather them,

Before CHRIST about 760.
x Ps. 78. 57.
y Ps. 73. 9.
z ch. 9. 3, 6. about 760.
a ch. 5. 8.
† Heb. *the roof of thy mouth.*
b Deut. 28. 49
Jer. 4. 13.
Hab. 1. 8.
c ch. 6. 7.
d Ps. 78. 34.
ch. 5. 15.
e Tit. 1. 16.
f 2 Kings 15. 17, 17, 25. Shallum, Menahem, Pekahiah
g ch. 2. 8. & 13. 2.
h Jer. 13. 27.
i Prov. 22. 8. ch. 10. 12, 13.
‖ Or, *standing corn.*
k ch. 7. 9.
l 2 Kings 17. 6.
m Jer. 22. 28. & 43. 28.
n 2 Kings 15. 19.
o Jer. 2. 24.
about 721.
p Isa. 30. 6.
† Heb. *loves.*
q Ezek. 16. 37.
ch. 10. 10.

---

16. *a deceitful bow*] Ps. lxxviii. 57. Ephraim is a deceitful bow, when it relies on itself; but it will become a bow of power in the hand of Christ. See the noble contrast to this passage in Zech. ix. 13.

— *in the land of Egypt*] Egypt itself, the broken reed—on which they trust—will pierce their hands, and they shall be an object of scorn and derision to it. Cp. Isa. xxx. 3, 5.

CH. VIII. 1. *Set the trumpet to thy mouth—as an eagle*] Upon "the silly dove" (vii. 11), yea, rather even *upon the house of Jehovah*. The omission of the two verbs gives greater strength and suddenness to the exclamation, and shows the near approach of the danger. The foe is pouncing down as an eagle (cp. Ezek. xvii. 3, 7. Lam. iv. 19); therefore give immediate warning.

— *against the house of the* LORD] God's house would have been a defence to them if they had served Him faithfully there. But now God turns from them, and brings the eagle against His own people, which has become a feeble and timid dove (vii. 11).

This was fulfilled in the destruction of the Temple by the Babylonish Eagle, and afterward by the Roman Eagle. See our Lord's prophecy, Matt. xxiv. 1—26.

2. *Israel—thee*] Literally, and more emphatically, *To me will they cry, My God, we know thee—Israel*. Israel is reserved for the last place in the sentence, as the strongest plea for God's favour. Behold, O God, we turn to thee, we cry to thee, we know thee, we Israel, Thy people! The word *Israel* is re-echoed by the prophet in the next verse. If ye are Israel, God's people, why are ye casting off the good law and despising the grace which has been given you by the God of Israel.

4. *They have set up kings, but not by me*] First Saul (1 Sam. viii. 7), and then Jeroboam (1 Kings xi. 40; xii. 3), and many of his successors; who were not set up by God, or according to His law (Deut. xvii. 15).

5. *Thy calf, O Samaria, hath cast thee off*] It is not God that is the cause of thy rejection and captivity, but thou thyself, by the idol which thou hast set up instead of God. Thy calf hath cast thee off as a loathsome thing. God repeats here the

word (*zánach*) from the third verse. Thou hast *cast off* what is good, and hast chosen what is evil, and the object of thy choice has *cast thee off*. See *Gesen.* 219.

— *against them*] Observe, *them*. God turns His face from them, and speaks *of* them in the third person, and not *to* them, in the second person.

7. *It hath no stalk*] Lit. *stalk* (or grain growing on the stalk—*Gesen.* 734. Cp. Ex. xxii. 5) is *not to it*.

— *the bud shall yield no meal*] There is a play upon the words in the original, which have the form of a proverb. "*There is no stalk* (*kamah*) *to it*; the *tsemach* will yield no *kemach*, i. e. the *shoot* will yield no *fruit* (*Keil*).

9. *they are gone up to Assyria, a wild ass alone by himself*. *Ephraim* (that *hired lovers*) Israel is faithless to the Lord; and has gone to Assyria for help. Cp. v. 13; xiv. 3. Jer. ii. 18, 36. She has been faithless to her true Husband, and has hired lovers; such is her shamelessness; whereas lewd woman receive hire, she hath given hire to those with whom she plays the harlot in the spiritual fornication of Idolatry. The comparison of Israel to the *wild ass, alone by himself* (or rather, *alone for himself*, i.e. roving for his own pleasure, is best explained by Job xi. 12; xxiv. 5; and Jer. ii. 24; and the circumstance that here the reference is to a male wild ass, is explained by what has been said before, that Israel throws off all female modesty in her spiritual harlotry, and goes and seeks for paramours whom she hires. See what follows.

10. *though they have hired*] Though they have separated themselves from Me, and roved far and wide for the indulgence of their own lustful appetites in spiritual fornication (i. e. idolatry), yet I will bring them together into one herd—not, however, to their own land, but as captives to that very land (Assyria) to which they have looked for help, and for which they have forsaken Me.

The strong language which God uses in Hebrew prophecy, especially by Hosea, concerning idolatry, which he likens to adultery and harlotry, may well suggest a feeling of alarm and apprehension to Christian Churches in the present age. If they

15

Before
CHRIST
about
771.

And they shall ‖ sorrow ‖ a little for the burden of ' the king of princes.
11 Because Ephraim hath made ' many altars to sin, altars shall be unto him to sin.
12 I have written to him ' the great things of my law,
But they were counted as a strange thing.
13 ‖ They sacrifice flesh *for* the sacrifices of mine offerings, and eat *it ;*
* *But* the Lord accepteth them not ;
* Now will he remember their iniquity, and visit their sins :
' They shall return to Egypt.
14 * For Israel hath forgotten b his Maker, and c buildeth temples ;
And Judah hath multiplied fenced cities :
But d I will send a fire upon his cities,
And it shall devour the palaces thereof.

IX. 1 Rejoice not, O Israel, for joy, as *other* people :
For thou a hast gone a whoring from thy God,
Thou hast loved a b reward ‖ upon every cornfloor.
2 c The floor and the ‖ winepress shall not feed them,
And the new wine shall fail in her.
3 They shall not dwell in d the Lord's land ;
e But Ephraim shall return to Egypt,
And f they shall eat unclean *things* g in Assyria.
4 h They shall not offer wine *offerings* to the Lord,
' Neither shall they be pleasing unto him :
k Their sacrifices *shall be* unto them as the bread of mourners ;
All that eat thereof shall be polluted :
For their bread ' for their soul shall not come into the house of the Lord.
5 What will ye do in m the solemn day,
And in the day of the feast of the Lord ?

---

decline from the pure service of God to creature-worship, or to any thing that favours it, they must expect even a worse punishment than that which fell on Israel of old.

— *And they shall sorrow a little for the burden of the king of princes;* Or, literally, they shall *soon sorrow* (if the word in the original is from *chûl,* to *grieve*), or they shall *begin quickly* to suffer *from the burden of the king of the princes* (i. e. the Assyrian king—Isa. x. 8). Israel now goes after Assyria, and hires it to help her, but Assyria will punish and oppress her (cp. Isa. vii. 20, where Assyria is compared to a razor hired by God against His faithless people), and the hire which Israel paid to Assyria will be changed into a burden with which Assyria will oppress.

The word rendered *sorrow* is supposed by many to be the *hiphil* of *chalal,* which is used above fifty times, and always (except Num. xxx. 2. Ezek. xxxix. 7) in the sense of *begin* (cp. Pocock, 365), especially in the sense of a plague beginning to break out, as Num. xvi. 46; or, to *begin* to commit any sin (Gen. xi. 6. Num. xxv. 1); or to *punish* (2 Kings x. 32. 1 Sam. iii. 2. Ezek. ix. 6. Jer. xxv. 29). The sense of *begin*-*ning,* ought, it seems, to be recognized here; and the meaning is, they have begun to sin, and shortly they will begin to suffer.

11. *altars shall be unto him to sin.*] Israel has loved idols, therefore God will give them up to their sin, which will bring its proper punishment with it, and Israel will be carried away to a land of idols (cp. ix. 3) ; there shall eat unclean things in Assyria ; cp. Ezek. iv. 13, they shall eat defiled bread among the Gentiles.

12. *I have written—strange thing.*] I wrote to Israel the great and manifold things of My Law at Horeb : I wrote the Two Tables with My Own hand ; I wrote statutes and ordinances by the hand of My servant Moses. Thus Israel has been distinguished by Me, as a peculiar people, from all Nations (Deut. iv. 6) ; but Israel has counted them a *strange thing,* and has turned away from them to worship *strange gods.*

13. *They sacrifice flesh*] Their sacrifices are not sacrifices,

they are *mere flesh,* without any spiritual virtue. Cp. on Jer. vii. 21 ; xi. 15. I will not accept them ; because they have rejected Me.

— *They shall return to Egypt*] i. e. to captivity. Egypt is the synonym for " a land of bondage." Cp. ix. 3, 6 ; and note below, xi. 5. They shall be carried captive for their sins. Cp. Deut. xxviii. 68. Some suppose that this is to be understood literally, and that it was fulfilled after the destruction of Jerusalem by the Chaldeans. See Jer. xliv. 12. *A Lapide.* But that migration into Egypt was not effected by God, but was contrary to His express command. The former sense is preferable (cp. margin here and *Keil*), though, in a subordinate sense, the miseries endured by Jews in Egypt, after the fall of Jerusalem, may be within the scope of the prophecy. See on ii. 6.

14. *temples*] Especially for the golden calves at Bethel and Dan ; and for Baal.

Ch. IX. 1. *Thou hast loved a reward upon every cornfloor*] Thou hast prostituted thyself in the spiritual harlotry of idolatry upon every corn-floor, by praising thy false gods there for the fruits of the Earth, which are gifts of God. Cp. ii. 7, 8.

2. *The floor and the winepress shall not feed them*] Because they forget God, and worship and praise idols on their threshing-floors for His gifts ; therefore, the threshing-floor and wine-press (or, rather, the oil-press) shall bring no blessing to them. Observe the change of the pronoun from *them* to *them, her,* marking God's aversion from His people on account of their sins.

3. *Egypt*] See on viii. 13.

4. *Their sacrifices shall be unto them as the bread of mourn-ers*] That is, as unclean things, which have been polluted by contact with death. Cp. Num. xix. 14. Hag. ii. 13.

— *their bread for their soul*] Rather, *their bread is for their own soul*—i. e. for their own self-indulgence, not for God's glory ; therefore, *it shall not come into the house of the Lord.*

5. *What will ye do in the solemn day*] In your captivity, how will ye be able to celebrate the periodic festivals of the

16

⁶ For, lo, they are gone because of † destruction :
" Egypt shall gather them up, Memphis shall bury them :
‖ † The pleasant *places* for their silver, ° nettles shall possess them :
Thorns *shall be* in their tabernacles ;
⁷ The days of visitation are come, the days of recompence are come ;
Israel shall know *it :*
The prophet *is* a fool, ᵖ the † spiritual man *is* mad,
For the multitude of thine iniquity, and the great hatred ;
⁸ The �q watchman of Ephraim *was* with my God :
*But* the prophet *is* a snare of a fowler in all his ways,
*And* hatred ‖ in the house of his God.
⁹ ' They have deeply corrupted *themselves,* as in the days of ˢ Gibeah :
ᵗ *Therefore* he will remember their iniquity, he will visit their sins.
¹⁰ I found Israel like grapes in the wilderness ;
I saw your fathers as ᵘ the firstripe in the fig tree ˣ at her first time :
*But* they went to ʸ Baal-peor, and ᶻ separated themselves ᵃ unto *that* shame ;
ᵇ And *their* abominations were according as they loved.
¹¹ As for Ephraim, their glory shall fly away like a bird,
From the birth, and from the womb, and from the conception.
¹² ᶜ Though they bring up their children, yet ᵈ will I bereave them,
*That there* shall not *be* a man *left :*
Yea, ᵉ woe also to them when I ᶠ depart from them !
¹³ Ephraim, ᵍas I saw Tyrus, *is* planted in a pleasant place :
ʰ But Ephraim shall bring forth his children to the murderer.
¹⁴ Give them, O LORD : what wilt thou give ?
Give them ⁱ a † miscarrying womb and dry breasts.

VOL. VI. PART II.—17

---

Lord ? You will not be able to do this, because the Temple, at which the greatest of those festivals are to be celebrated, will be in ruins, and you yourselves far off from it in exile. See above, on ii. 11.

**6.** *Egypt shall gather them up*] They ought to have been gathered together as one man, to serve the Lord in His temple; but they have scattered themselves from Him to go after idols and serve them ; therefore, they shall indeed be gathered together, but it will be a forced and miserable gathering, viz. in a land of bondage and exile—another Egypt, in which they will be restrained as captives, separated from Canaan, and prevented from going up to Jerusalem to be gathered to the solemn festivals there.

— *Memphis*] The capital of Lower Egypt (Isa. xix. 13. Jer. ii. 16; xlvi. 1; xliv. 14. Ezek. xxx. 13. 16).

— *shall bury them*] This seems to be a prophecy of the events recorded in Jeremiah xliv. 11—27.

— *nettles*] Or, thistles (Gesen. 734). Cp. Isa. xxxiv. 13.

**7.** *the great hatred*] Against God and His laws, and His Prophets; as Ahab said of Micaiah, "I hate him" (1 Kings xxii. 8). Cp. Ps. l. 17.

**8.** *The watchman of Ephraim was with my God*] Or, rather, *Ephraim was a watchman with my God* (Sept., Vulg.). Israel was set by God to be a watchman *with God*, even by the side of Him, their King and Commander, in His Holy City. Cp. Jer. vi. 17. Ezek. iii. 17 ; xxxiii. 7. But they have fallen away and departed from God, and have become a snare of a fowler to catch birds.

There is a comparison between the watchman on his lofty tower (whence he looks forth in order to give notice of danger to his friends, and to defend the city), and the fowler who speculates from his position in order to catch birds. Cp. what is said of *Mizpah*, or watch-tower, above, v. 1.

They have also become *hatred* (cp. the use of the abstract in Ps. cxx. 7), even pure, intense enmity, instead of doing the work of God in love.

**9.** *as in the days of Gibeah*] When the men of Gibeah wrought that dreadful deed of cruel lewdness described in Judges xix., and the whole tribe of Benjamin abetted the crime, and was almost exterminated for its sin. This was an epitome of the history of Israel in crime and punishment. Israel's idola-

try is compared to the savage and lustful impurity of those men of Gibeah.

**10.** *I found Israel like grapes in the wilderness*] I loved Israel in the desert, as a thirsty traveller is delighted with the grapes which he finds in a barren wilderness ; or as one who is refreshed by the first ripe fruit on the fig-tree in its prime. Cp. above, i. 2, where God's espousal of Israel is described.

— *they went to Baal-peor,* even they, My own People; *and they consecrated themselves* (as Nazarites, or to Me their glory, but) *to shame.*

— *And their abominations*] Rather, *and they became abominations* (see above, v. 8, they became *hatred*) *according to their loves* (i. e. the objects of their love) they became cruel, brutish, and lustful, like the false gods which they worship. All idolaters become like the idols which they worship; as the Psalmist says, "They that make them are like unto them" (Ps. cxv. 8).

**11.** *From the birth—conception*] They will perish from every stage, even the earliest, of their being, so as to be utterly destroyed. This rendering (authorized by the ancient Versions; cp. v. 16) is preferable to that of some modern interpreters, "*no birth, no womb, no conception.*"

**13.** *Ephraim, as I saw Tyrus, is planted in a pleasant place*] Rather, *Ephraim, when I looked upon it (with favour), was like Tyre,* a noble and strong city, *planted in a fair place* (cp. Ezek. xxvii., xxviii.); but *I have departed* from Ephraim (see the foregoing verse), and they are wasted. Cp. Targum here. "Ephraim, ut vidi, Tyrus erat," is the rendering of the *Vulgate* here. Cp. S. Jerome.

**14.** *Give them a miscarrying womb and dry breasts*] The common consequences of barbarry. Here again the prophecies of Hosea are joined on to the Song of Solomon, and adopt its imagery and language; and they mutually illustrate one another. See Cant. viii. 8, where the Hebrew nation, in its state of rejection, is described by the true Bride, the Christian Church, as a "little sister, and she hath no breasts." See the note on that passage. On the other hand, the faithful Church of Christ is represented as a beloved wife and a fruitful mother of children. See Isa. xlix. 18—20; liv. 1—8; lxi. 10. Such will also the Hebrew Nation be, when it returns to God in Christ.

15 All their wickedness [k] *is* in Gilgal:
For there I hated them:
[l] For the wickedness of their doings I will drive them out of mine house,
I will love them no more:
[m] All their princes *are* revolters.
16 Ephraim is smitten, their root is dried up, they shall bear no fruit:
Yea, [n] though they bring forth,
Yet will I slay *even* † the beloved *fruit* of their womb.
17 My God will cast them away, because they did not hearken unto him:
And they shall be [o] wanderers among the nations.

X. 1 Israel *is* [a] ‖ an empty vine, he bringeth forth fruit unto himself:
According to the multitude of his fruit [b] he hath increased the altars;
According to the goodness of his land [c] they have made goodly † images.
2 ‖ Their heart is [d] divided; now shall they be found faulty:
He shall † break down their altars, he shall spoil their images.
3 [e] For now they shall say, We have no king, because we feared not the LORD;
What then should a king do to us?
4 They have spoken words, swearing falsely in making a covenant:
Thus judgment springeth up [f] as hemlock in the furrows of the field.
5 The inhabitants of Samaria shall fear because of [g] the calves of [h] Beth-aven:
For the people thereof shall mourn over it,
And ‖ the priests thereof *that* rejoiced on it, [i] for the glory thereof,
Because it is departed from it.
6 It shall be also carried unto Assyria *for* a present to [k] king Jareb:
Ephraim shall receive shame,
And Israel shall be ashamed [l] of his own counsel.
7 [m] *As for* Samaria, her king is cut off,
As the foam upon † the water.
8 [n] The high places also of Aven, [o] the sin of Israel, shall be destroyed:
[p] The thorn and the thistle shall come up on their altars;
[q] And they shall say to the mountains, Cover us;

Before CHRIST about 760.
k ch. 4. 15. & 12. 11.
l ch. 1. 6.
m Isa. 1. 23.
n ver. 13.
† Heb. *the desires.*
Ezek. 24. 21.
o Deut. 28. 64, 65.
about 740.
a Nahum 2. 2.
‖ Or, *a vine emptying the fruit which it giveth.*
b ch. 8. 11. & 12. 11.
c ch. 8. 4.
† Heb. *statues,* or, *standing images.*
‖ Or, *He hath divided their heart.*
d 1 Kings 18. 21. Matt. 6. 24.
† Heb. *behead.*
e ch. 3. 4. & 11. 5. Micah 4. 9. ver. 7.
f See Deut. 29. 18. Amos 5. 7. & 6. 12. Acts 8. 23. Heb. 12. 15.
g 1 Kings 12. 28, 29. ch. 8. 5, 6.
h ch. 4. 15.
‖ Or, *Chemarim,* 2 Kings 23. 5. Zeph. 1. 4.
i 1 Sam. 4. 21, 22. ch. 9. 11.
k ch. 5. 13.
l ch. 11. 6.
m ver. 3, 15.
† Heb. *the face of the water.*
n ch. 4. 15.
o Deut. 9. 21. 1 Kings 12. 30.
p ch. 9. 6.
q Isa. 2. 19. Luke 23. 30. Rev. 6. 16. & 9. 6.

15. *All their wickedness is in Gilgal: for there I hated them*] All their wickedness, their idolatry and licentiousness, is at *Gilgal*, even at the very place where, in the days of Joshua and their fathers, they worshipped Me, and where I was gracious unto them (see above, iv. 15; below, xii. 11); and at Gilgal, where *I once loved them*, and received them again into covenant with Myself, by the renewal of circumcision there, I now have cast them off *and hate them* for their sin. Cp. *S. Jerome* here. Gilgal was a type of Golgotha. See above on Joshua v. 9, p. 15.

17. *they shall be wanderers among the nations*] The Jews are a national Cain of nearly twenty centuries, for the murder of their Brother, the Good Shepherd, the Divine Abel. See above on Gen. iv. 11—15.

CH. X. 1. *Israel is an empty vine*] Rather, *Israel is a gadding vine*, stretching forth its branches far and wide (*Sept.*, *Vulg.*, *Arabic*; *Pocock*, 437; *Gesen.* 136), luxuriant, and pouring itself forth into foreign lands (Ps. lxxx. 9—12). There is a reference to Israel's tendencies to foreign alliances and idolatry (see vii. 11, and what follows); and though God gave her power to bring forth fruit, she *brought it forth unto herself*, for her own self-indulgence and not for Him. Cp. Deut. xxxii. 15. Prov. xiii. 7. Luke xii. 21. The more prosperity He gave her, the more unthankful and rebellious she was against Him. See iv. 7.

2. *Their heart is divided*] The literal meaning is, Ephraim *has divided their heart*, i.e. the whole Nation, by one simultaneous act of separation from God, has alienated the hearts of all her people from Him. The word rendered *divided*, is *chalak*, which, in *kal* (as here), has always a transitive sense; and so *Sept.* and *Arabic* here.

— *He shall break down*] God shall punish them with an outbreak of His fury, and will destroy their altars.

3. *they shall say, We have no king*] When scattered abroad and captive in Assyria and other lands, Israel will be forced to make this confession: "We have no king"—we, who have forsaken the Lord our King, and have set up kings for ourselves, have no king; and even if we had, what *should a king do to us?* Would he be able to help us in our present captivity and distress?

4. *words*] Words—mere words, and nothing else.

— *judgment springeth up as hemlock*] *Judgment*, which ought to be a good and salutary plant to human society, is perverted, and so becomes no better than a noxious weed which chokes the corn: and it *springs up* in pestiferous abundance every where, as hemlock (cp. Deut. xxix. 18, where the word (*rôsh*) is rendered *gall*, as usually in our Version; this is the only place where it is translated *hemlock*), which chokes the corn in the furrows of the field, and destroys the harvest. Cp. Amos v. 7, adopting Hosea's metaphor, they "turn judgment into wormwood," which explains this passage, and vi. 12, "ye have turned judgment into *gall* (*rôsh*).

5. *Beth-aven*] Bethel, *the house of God*, which has become Beth-aven, *the house of vanity* (iv. 15; v. 8).

— *the priests*] Heb. *Cemarim*. See 2 Kings xxiii. 5. Zeph. i. 4.

6. *to king Jareb*] The adversary king, the king of Assyria, to whom Israel looked for help, but who has become their enemy, and who fights against them. On the meaning of the word *Jareb*, see on v. 13.

7. *As the foam*] Or, as a splinter, or straw (*Gesen.* 738).

8. *they shall say to the mountains—and to the hills*] They

And to the hills, Fall on us.

9 ' O Israel, thou hast sinned from the days of Gibeah :
   There they stood :
* The battle in Gibeah against the children of iniquity did not overtake
   them.

10 ' *It is* in my desire that I should chastise them ;
And " the people shall be gathered against them,
|| When they shall bind themselves in their two furrows.

11 And Ephraim *is as* ˣ an heifer *that is* taught,
*And* loveth to tread out *the corn ;*
But I passed over upon † her fair neck :
I will make Ephraim to ride ;
Judah shall plow, *and* Jacob shall break his clods.

12 ʸ Sow to yourselves in righteousness, reap in mercy ;
ᶻ Break up your fallow ground : for *it is* time to seek the LORD,
Till he come and rain righteousness upon you.

13 ᵃ Ye have plowed wickedness, ye have reaped iniquity ;
Ye have eaten the fruit of lies :
Because thou didst trust in thy way,
In the multitude of thy mighty men,

14 ᵇ Therefore shall a tumult arise among thy people,
And all thy fortresses shall be spoiled,

Before CHRIST about 740. r ch. 9. 9.

s See Judg. 20.

t Deut. 28. 63.
u Jer. 16. 16. Ezek. 22. 40, 17.
ch. 8. 10.
§ Or, *when I shall bind them for their two transgressions, or, in their two habitations.*
x Jer. 50. 11. Micah 4. 13.
† Heb. *the beauty of her neck.*

y Prov. 11. 18.

z Jer. 4. 3.

A Job 4. 8. Prov. 22. 8. ch. 8. 7. Gal. 6. 7, 8.

b ch. 13. 16.

---

shall cry to those mountains and hills, where they once worshipped their false gods on their high places with fanatical cries of adoration (cp. 1 Kings xviii. 27), and shall say to them, "Cover us," "Fall on us." Cp. Isa. ii. 10.

Our Blessed Lord has generalized these words, and has applied them to the terrors of the Great Day, when men will cry out, and cry out in vain, to the mountains and hills of their own self-idolizing imaginations—such as worldly Policy, earthly Wealth and Power, and proud, unsanctified Philosophy—to hide them from the wrath of the Lamb. See Luke xxiii. 30. Rev. vi. 16.

Formerly Israel went up with festal joy to their high places to worship their idols there with music, dance, and jollity ; but the time will come, says the Prophet, when they will flee before the foe in panic and dismay, and wish themselves buried there beneath them, as in their graves. So it will be with the World at the Last Day, and with all its Gilgals and Bethels, which it has set up in opposition to God.

9. *from the days of Gibeah*] Thou hast continued those evil days of Gibeah, so that they form thy history. See above, on ix. 9.

— *There they stood : the battle in Gibeah against the children of iniquity did not overtake them*] They stood ; i. e. Israel continued obstinate in the sin of Gibeah. As the men of Gibeah, instead of punishing their own wicked citizens who violated the Levite's concubine, identified themselves with them ; and as the whole tribe of Benjamin made their cause their own, and pertinaciously stood and fought for it ; so do the ten tribes of Israel. Instead of punishing sin, they patronize it : Israel is one Gibeah. *The battle in Gibeah against* its cruel and lustful inhabitants shall not *overtake them ;* but a battle far worse—a battle (not of friends who are near, but) of heathen adversaries who will carry Israel away captive.

10. *the people*] Rather, *nations*—foreign, heathen nations, shall be gathered against them in battle.

— *When they shall bind themselves in their two furrows*] Or, in binding them in their two furrows (so Targum) ; and there seems to be some propriety in this old Jewish rendering, on account of the metaphor of the heifer, which follows. But the other ancient Versions render it, in *their two sins.* The difference of translation arises from the different pointing in the original (*Gesen.* 614. Cp. *Gesen.* 135 ; *Fuerst,* 1026). The sense is, " Heathen nations shall be gathered together against Israel, in binding them (or taking them prisoners and leading them away captive) in their two sins," i. e. in the two calves, at Dan and Bethel ; or in their twofold apostasy, from God, and

from the throne of David. The sins of Israel were the cause of their punishment : sin is the chain by which the sinner is led away captive.

11. *Ephraim is as an heifer that is taught*] Israel is like a heifer which *is taught ;* but all her learning consists in this, that she loves to tread out the corn because she can feed at pleasure, as the heifer was permitted to do when treading out the corn on the threshing-floor (Deut. xxv. 4). On this ironical use of the word "taught," compare 1 Tim. v. 13. " They *learn* to be idle, wandering about from house to house." All their learning consists in this. See the note there.

This describes the condition of Israel, serving God only for the sake of its own appetite ; *but I pass over her for neck, and make* the yoke to ride on Ephraim ; I will bring her into subjection to the enemy, and reduce Judah and Jacob to hard service for their sins.

EXHORTATION TO REPENTANCE, AND PROMISE OF GRACE.

12. *Sow to yourselves in righteousness*] Or rather, *for righteousness,* as your harvest. The agricultural metaphor is continued.

— *reap in mercy*] According to (God's) mercy ; that is, in gracious abundance from Him. They who sow the seed of good works, will receive a bountiful harvest from His love (2 Cor. ix. 6. Gal. vi. 7—9). Let us sow here in alms and prayers, that we may reap in blessing hereafter.

— *Break up your fallow ground*] Plough *for your own fresh soil.* Be not content with what ye have cultivated, but bring new ground into cultivation. Grow in grace ; forget what is behind ; reach forward to what is before ; add to your faith virtue, and every Christian grace ; and do you, who have been brought to God, bring others to Him.

On this text see *Bp. Bull's* Sermons, Sermon i.

— *rain righteousness*] Compare Psalm lxxii. 6. Isa. xlv. 8. The word rendered to *rain,* is translated by *teach,* in *Vulg.* and some other ancient Versions, and this is the usual sense of the *hiphil* of the verb *yarah,* used here ; and this is the only place where it is rendered *rain,* in our Version ; cp. vi. 3, where the *participle pad* is used. Especially compare below, the words of the next succeeding Prophet (Joel ii. 23). He will send you *a Teacher of righteousness.*" See the note there. These two passages of Hosea and Joel illustrate one another. Both of them speak of CHRIST, and touched the blessings of Justification and Sanctification which would be given by Him. See *Pocock,* pp. 484, 485.

As Shalman spoiled ᶜ Beth-arbel in the day of battle :
ᵈ The mother was dashed in pieces upon *her* children.
15 So shall Beth-el do unto you because of † your great wickedness ;
In a morning ᵉ shall the king of Israel utterly be cut off.
XI. ¹ When ᵃ Israel *was* a child, then I loved him,
And ᵇ called my ᶜ son out of Egypt.

---

14. *As Shalman spoiled Beth-arbel*] As Shalmaneser, king of Assyria (2 Kings xvii. 3), spoiled Beth-arbel ; probably the place called Arbela in 1 Macc. ix. 2, between Sepheris and Tiberias, and now perhaps called Irbid (Robinson).

15. *So shall Beth-el do unto you*] Your sin shall be the cause of your punishment. Your Bethel (or house of God) shall become your *Beth-arbel*, i.e. the house of the ambush of God, from which He will spring up to punish you. Such is the meaning of *Beth-arbel* (Hosea. 117 ; cp. *Pusey*, 70). All men's Bethels (houses of God), if they are made Bethavens (houses of vanity), become *Beth-arbels* (houses of ambush of God).

— *in a morning*] In the morning dawn ; quickly, before the dawn becomes day.

CH. XI. 1. *When Israel was a child, then I loved him*] At the Exodus. God loved Israel then, and in the wilderness ; but Israel has been faithless to God : and therefore is punished.

ISRAEL A TYPE OF CHRIST.

— *And called my son out of Egypt*] See Exod. iv. 22, 23. "Israel is My first-born ; let My son go, that he may serve Me." The Holy Spirit, speaking by St. Matthew (ii. 15), teaches us that when He Himself uttered these words by Hosea, His divine glance reached from the Exodus of Israel, God's son, to the Incarnation of Christ, and to His flight into Egypt, and to the return from it of the Son of God manifest in the flesh. And thus He has instructed us to see in Israel going forth as God's favoured child from Egypt—the land of the enemy of God—to Christ His truth throughout the Earth, a type of Christ, proceeding forth from the darkness of heathen Egypt, to evangelize and illuminate the World. The love of God to Israel was a fore-shadowing of God's love to Man in Christ, Who came of Israel, and Who has joined Man's nature to His own, and in His own person to God, and reconciles Man to God. Israel, God's beloved Son, was a prophecy of Christ, and Christ is the personal Antitype of a perfect Israel. See below, on Matt. ii. 15, and S. *Chrys.* and *Theophylact* on Matt. ii. 15, and *Theodoret* there, and S. *Jerome* here ; *Pocock*, 502—506; and *Matt. Henry* here ; and *Hengst.* on Micah, chap. v. ; and *Pfeiffer*, Dubia, p. 139; *Bp. Pearson*, On the Creed, Art. ii p. 89; *Fairbairn*, Typology, p. 146. Christ is the Antitype of Israel in God's love ; and is also the Antithesis of Israel in obedience to God.

S. Jerome tells us that the Emperor Julian, in the fourth century, made the following objections to St. Matthew (ii. 15) applying this prophecy to Christ. "The prophet Hosea is speaking of the Israelites, but Matthew the Evangelist has applied that prophecy to Christ, in order to deceive those simple people among the heathen who believe in Him." See S. *Jerome* here.

This objection of Julian the apostate has been repeated in later days by the author of the Scheme of Literal Prophecy ; Lond., 1727, p. 333, and by *Strauss*. It has been recently said by some among ourselves (Creed of Christendom, p. 104, Lond., 1851; *De Wette*, Erklärung des Evangeliums Matthäi, 3rd ed., Leipzig, 1845, p. 279, that the passage in question, which is in the eleventh chapter of Hosea, has "*not the slightest reference to Christ.*" And it has lately been affirmed by another in high place among us (Essays and Reviews, p. 418; see also Ibd., p. 400, that "the time will come, when educated men will be no more able to believe that the words, *Out of Egypt have I called my Son*, were intended by the Prophet (Hosea) to refer to the return of Joseph and Mary from Egypt, than they are now able to believe the Roman Catholic explanation of Gen. iii. 15, '*Ipsa conteret caput tuum,*' i.e. applying that prophecy to the Blessed Virgin Mary."

What shall we say here ?

*If* we imagined the Bible to be *not inspired*, we should be perplexed by these allegations. We should be embarrassed by them, *if* we supposed that the Prophets themselves were the original *Authors* of their own Prophecies. We should be staggered and confounded, if we supposed that the Prophets were like *sources* and *fountains*, *from* which the living water of divine prophecy *sprung*, and not rather like *channels*, *through* which it *flows* and is conveyed to us.

But we believe and profess in the Creed, that "the Holy Ghost spake by (through) the Prophets." We believe and profess

with St. Peter that the *Spirit of Christ* was in them (1 Pet. i 11), and prophesied by them, and that Prophecy *came not in old time by the will of men, but holy men of God spake, being moved (or borne along) by the Holy Ghost* (2 Pet. i. 21).

We readily allow, that *the Prophets* themselves, when they uttered their Prophecies, did *not fully understand* what was in the mind of the Holy Spirit Who spake by them. As *Bp. Sherlock* says (Discourse on Prophecy, ii., p. 21), "The Prophets did not clearly understand the things which they foretold, but employed themselves in searching the meaning of the prophetical testimonies of the Spirit which was in them" (1 Pet. i. 11). And *Bp. Marsh* (On the Interpretation of the Bible, Lecture x., p. 443) says ; "Most writers who treat of *secondary* senses (of Prophecies) contend that these *secondary* senses were unknown to the *Prophets themselves*; and that Divine Providence so ordered it, that the very persons who committed to writing the words which were dictated by the Holy Spirit, did not perceive *the whole extent of their meaning.*" The old Prophets did not clearly discern the extent and range of their own prophecies ; they did not fully understand their meaning. This the Prophet Daniel himself avows ; see Dan. viii. 26, 27 ; xii. 8. They were inspired to *prophesy*, but not to *interpret* their own Prophecies. Therefore the Apostle Peter says, that Prophecy was like *a light shining in a dark place, till the dayspring should dawn* in Christ, and dispel the darkness (2 Pet. i. 19). And he says, that the Prophets employed themselves in *inquiring diligently concerning the salvation* pre-announced in their own Prophecies; and in *searching what, or what manner of time*, the *Spirit of Christ, which was in them* did signify, *when it testified beforehand the sufferings of Christ and the glory that should follow* (1 Pet. i. 11).

Indeed, here is the proof of the divine origin of Prophecy. Almost every prophecy was "an enigma (as S. *Irenæus* says, iv. 26. 1; cp. *Archdeacon Lee* on Inspiration, pp. 198, 199) before its fulfilment ;" it was an enigma to the Prophets themselves. Time only could solve it. And wisely was this ordered ; because, otherwise, Divine Fore-knowledge might seem to control Human Will. But God's Fore-knowledge foresees every thing, and forces nothing. It does not touch Man's Free will. Whatever is foretold by God, will be done by Man ; but nothing will be done by Man, *because* it has been foretold by God. If the meaning of Ancient Prophecy had been clear before its fulfilment, it never could have had that probationary character, and have served those purposes of moral discipline, which God intended it should. God so ordered it, that it might be fulfilled by persons who were wholly unconscious that they were fulfilling it. And the fulfilment of Prophecies in a manner *unforeseen* by man, even by the Prophets themselves, is an evidence of their divine origin. The fulfilment of Prophecies by persons who were not aware that they were fulfilling them, as was the case with the Jews rejecting Christ, and so fulfilling the prophecies by condemning Him (Acts xiii. 27), and thus proving Him to be Christ while they rejected and condemned Him, and even *by* rejecting and condemning Him, is a proof that men were not *Authors* of the Prophecies—no, not the Prophets themselves—but that the true Author of Prophecy is GOD.

Let, therefore, the allegation just cited be true, that the Prophet Hosea did "*not intend* to refer to the return of Joseph and Mary," when he said *Out of Egypt have I called My Son.* But what is this to the purpose ? How is it relevant to the question at issue concerning the *Interpretation of Scripture?* If indeed it is alleged, that *because* the Prophet Hosea did not *intend* to refer to that Return, *therefore* that Return is not foretold by the *Prophecy*, then our answer is, that they who make such an allegation prove themselves thereby to be utterly incompetent to interpret Prophecy ; because they do not comprehend its nature—they do not understand *what* Prophecy is, nor *whence* Prophecy comes. They erroneously assume that Prophecy is a human thing proceeding from the mind of man, whereas Prophecy is a divine oracle issuing from the mouth of God.

The true question is, not what was *intended* by Hosea himself in what he uttered this prophecy, but what was intended by the Holy Ghost Who spake *by* Hosea. *That* is the question ; and a very important one it is.

<sup>2</sup> *As they called them, so they went from them :*
<sup>d</sup> *They sacrificed unto Baalim, and burned incense to graven images.*
<sup>3</sup> <sup>e</sup> *I taught Ephraim also to go, taking them by their arms ;*
*But they knew not that* ᶠ*I healed them.*
<sup>4</sup> *I drew them with cords of a man, with bands of love :*

Before
CHRIST
about
740
d 2 Kings 17 .. 
ch.2. 13. & 13.2
e Deut. 1 . 1, .
32. 10, 11, 12
Isa. 46, 3.
f Exod. 15 26.

And how is it to be decided?

Surely by the Holy Spirit Himself. For "*as man knoweth the things of God but the Spirit of God*" (1 Cor. ii. 11). And the Son of God has vouchsafed to decide that question. The Prophets of old were God's Messengers and Ambassadors, who brought sealed letters from Him ; and the Son of God has come from heaven, and has broken the seals of those letters, and has read them to us. The Holy Spirit has been pleased to inform us, by the Evangelist St. Matthew, what was in His own divine mind, when He spake, many hundred years before, by the Prophet Hosea. Hear His own words in the Gospel, "*Joseph arose and took the young child and his mother by night, and departed into Egypt, and was there until the death of Herod, that it might be fulfilled which was spoken by the Lord through the Prophet, Out of Egypt have I called my Son*" (Matt. ii. 15).

*S. Augustine* makes this excellent observation in his treatise De Doctrinâ Christianâ, iii.39 : "Whenever two or more senses are deducible from the same words of Holy Scripture, there is no harm in our not knowing *which* of those senses was *intended* by the *writer* himself ; provided it can be shown that those senses are authorized by *other* places of Holy Scripture. The writer himself may *not* have *intended* those senses, but we are sure that the *Holy Ghost*, Who used the agency of the writer, and worked *through* him, foresaw those senses and provided that those senses should be received by us. And herein we may admire the exuberant beauty of God towards us in Holy Scripture, in that the same words of Holy Scripture may have several meanings, which may be attested by His authority speaking to us in other places of Scripture."

And so *Bishop Butler*, Analogy, Part II., ch. vii. :—

"To say that the Scriptures and the things contained in them *can have no other or further meaning* than those persons thought or had, who first recited or wrote them, is evidently saying that those persons were the original, proper, and sole *Authors* of those books, i.e. that they *are not inspired*" (this is the saying of the writer in *Essays and Reviews* just quoted) ; "which is absurd, whilst the authority of these books is under examination, i.e. till you have determined that they are of no divine authority at all. Till this be determined, it must in all reason be supposed, not indeed that they have, for this is taking for granted that they are inspired, but that they *may have*, some further meaning than what the compilers saw or understood. And upon this supposition it is supposable also that this further meaning may be fulfilled.

"Now, events corresponding to prophecies, interpreted in a different meaning from that in which the prophets are supposed to have understood them ; this affords, in a manner, the same proof that this different sense *was* originally *intended*, as it would have afforded if the prophets had not understood their predictions in the sense it is supposed they did ; because there is no presumption *of their sense* of them being the whole sense of them. And it has been already shown, that the apparent completions of prophecy must be allowed to be explanatory of its meaning. So that the question is, whether a series of prophecy has been fulfilled in a natural or proper—i.e. in any real sense of the words of it. For such completion is equally a proof of *foresight* more than *human*, whether the prophets are, or are not, supposed to have understood it in a different sense. I say *supposed* ; for though *I think it clear, that the prophets did not understand the full meaning of their predictions*, it is another question how far they thought they did, and in what sense they understood them."

Here, therefore, a new light is shed by the Holy Spirit upon the prophecy of Hosea, and on the history of Israel in Egypt. We are taught that Israel was a type of Christ. The name *Israel*, a *Prince of God* (Gen. xxxii. 28), suggests this. In Israel, when a child, beloved of God, and called out of Egypt, we, who believe in St. Matthew's inspiration, have learnt to see a figure of Christ. The beloved Son of God, the Infant Jesus, was to be in Egypt till the Angel should bring Joseph word ; for Herod would seek the young child to destroy Him. He was there till the death of Herod. The death of the Persecutor was the signal for His deliverance and return. All this had been foreshewn by the literal Israel who had gone down from Canaan into Egypt. The Enemy of God worked by Pharaoh against Israel, as he did afterwards by Herod against Christ. God loved and protected

21

Israel in his childhood. In the infancy of the Nation, He shielded the young children from the rage of the King. He saved Israel *in* Egypt, and He saved Israel *from* Egypt ; and sent him forth to be a Witness and Preacher of His Truth to the World. All this was done for the sake of Christ, the Well-beloved Son of the Father, the Light of the World. God loved Christ in Israel, from whom Christ came according to the flesh. The first-born of Egypt were destroyed, and Pharaoh and his hosts were overthrown in the sea, and then Israel was delivered and went forth toward Canaan. So, the destruction of Christ's Enemies was the signal of *His* Exodus from Egypt, and of His return to Canaan. "When Herod was dead, behold, an Angel of the Lord appeared in a dream to Joseph in Egypt, saying Arise, take the young child and His mother, and go into the land of Israel, for they are dead which sought the Young Child's life. And he arose, and took the Young Child and His mother, and came into the Land of Israel."

Therefore, also, since the Enemies of the literal Israel are figures of the enemies of Christ, even of Death and the Grave, there is a peculiar propriety in the union of Hosea's prophecy concerning the exit of Israel out of Egypt, with another prophecy uttered by the same Prophet concerning the deliverance of the Spiritual Israel, the Israel of God, united in the whole mystical Body of Christ, and redeemed and ransomed by Him from their ghostly enemies, and concerning *their* glorious Exodus from the Egypt of Death, and the Grave, and their leading-forth from a land of bondage to the glorious inheritance of their heavenly Canaan in Christ. "*I will ransom them*" (says Christ Himself by Hosea) "*from the power of the Grave, I will redeem them from Death. O Death, I will be thy plagues. O Grave, I will be thy destruction*" (Hos. xiii. 14). And we may now take up the comment of the Holy Apostle St. Paul, "*O Death, where is thy sting? O Grave, where is thy victory? Thanks be to God Who giveth us the victory through our Lord Jesus Christ*" (1 Cor. xv. 55—57).

Shall we complain of these things? Shall we "*grieve the Holy Spirit*," Who spake by the Prophets? Shall we murmur at our Adorable Redeemer, because, in His tender love and mercy to us, He has given to us a clearer insight into a prophecy uttered by Hosea, than even Hosea himself had, when he uttered it? Shall we be impatient because Christ's gracious words are thus fulfilled in us : "*Blessed are your eyes, for they see, and your ears, for they hear : for verily I say unto you, that many prophets and righteous men have desired to see those things which ye see, and have not seen them, and to hear those things which ye hear, and have not heard them*"? (Matt. xiii. 16, 17. Luke x. 24. Heb. xi. 13.)

Shall we not rather be thankful to Him because He has revealed to us the meaning of Prophecies which we could never have explained for ourselves, and which therefore must ever have remained dark, without a revelation from Him? Shall we not rejoice in the light shed from Christ's glorious countenance, on the dark prophecies of the Old Testament? Shall we not exult in our Christian privileges, because He has opened our eyes, and has opened the Scriptures to us?

2. As *they called them*]  They (Moses and the Prophets) *called to them* (to Israel), but the more they called to Israel, the more rebellious Israel was ; *they sacrificed unto Baalim* (many forms of idolatry) instead of worshipping the one true God. Cp. Jer. ii. 23 : vii. 25 ; xxxv. 4. Zech. i. 4.

3. *I taught*]  I, even I, taught Ephraim to walk, as a Father teaches a child (Deut. i. 31).

— *taking them by their arms*]  Or, *He took them by His arms*. All the ancient versions render the *arms* here as referring to God. Cp. Pusey, Keil.

4. *I drew them with cords of a man*]  Not of a beast, a heifer (see x. 11), but of a rational and spiritual being. Compare Cant. i. 11, where the Bride says to the Bridegroom, "Draw me, and I will run after thee ;" and our Lord's words, "If I be lifted up, I will draw all men unto Me" (John xii. 32).

The *Vulgate* has here "*traham eos funiculis Adam*," and this prophecy was specially fulfilled in Christ : He took our Nature, and became the Second Adam, and draws us by the cords of His love in His Incarnation, which has made us to be one with Himself, and by which He espoused to Himself our Nature, sanctified to become His Bride in mystical wedlock, and joined the Church to Himself as His Eve.

Before
CHRIST
785.

g Lev. 2. 13.
4 Heb. 2. 14.
h Ps. 78. 17.
i Jer. 6. 6.
j See ch. 8. 13, 14.
2. 9.
k 2 Kings 17.
12, 11.
about
785.
They became
voluntary slaves to
Sennacherib.
l ch. 10. 6.
m Jer. 3. 6, &c.
8. 5, 5.
ch. 4. 16.
n. 5. 7, 12.
together
forsaken as 61.

o Jer. 9. 7.
ch. 6. 1
p Gen. 14, 8, &c.
19. 24, 25.
Deut. 29. 23.
Amos 4. 11.
q 1 Sa. el 23. 26.
Isa. 40. 13.
Jer. 31. 20.

r Num. 23. 19.
Isa. 55. 8, 9.
Mal. 3. 6.

s Joel 3. 16.
Joel 3. 16.
Amos 1. 2.
t Zech. 8. 7.

u Isa. 60. 8.
ch. 7. 11.

And **g** I was to them as they that † take off the yoke on their jaws,
And **h** I laid meat unto them.

5 **i** He shall not return into the land of Egypt,
But the Assyrian shall be his king,
**k** Because they refused to return.

6 And the sword shall abide on his cities,
And shall consume his branches, and devour *them*,
**l** Because of their own counsels.

7 And my people are bent to **m** backsliding from me :
**n** Though they called them to the most High,
† None at all would exalt *him*.

8 **o** How shall I give thee up, Ephraim ? *how* shall I deliver thee, Israel ?
How shall I make thee as **p** Admah ? *how* shall I set thee as Zeboim ?
**q** Mine heart is turned within me, my repentings are kindled together.

9 I will not execute the fierceness of mine anger,
I will not return to destroy Ephraim :
**r** For I *am* God, and not man ;
The Holy One in the midst of thee :
And I will not enter into the city.

10 They shall walk after the LORD :
**s** He shall roar like a lion :
When he shall roar, then the children shall tremble **t** from the west.

11 They shall tremble as a bird out of Egypt,
**u** And as a dove out of the land of Assyria :

---

— *I was that take off the yoke*] God, in His love to Israel, was as one who unyokes oxen and gives them fodder. In Christ, God takes off from our necks the yoke of sin, and the yoke of the Law, and puts His own easy yoke on us, and feeds us with the divine comfort of His holy Word and Sacraments.

5. *He shall not return into the land of Egypt, but the Assyrian shall be his king*] The Prophet had said before (vii. 13 ; ix. 3), that Israel would be carried back into Egypt, and he now explains the meaning of that phrase, viz. that *Egypt* is a typical name for a land of bondage, and *that* land will be Assyria. Or the sense may be, Israel will not look any more to Egypt for help against Assyria (8. *Jerome*).

6. *his branches*] Or, his *bars* and *bolts* (Heb. *baddim*). Cp. Exod. xxv. 13. Job xxvii. 16. viz. his strong men and fortresses, to which he looks for defence.

7. *are bent to backsliding*] Literally, are hung and fastened to apostasy from Me, instead of allegiance to Me.

This Section of Hosea, which is a prophetical commentary on the history of Jacob, from *v.* 7 to xii. 12, is the Haphtarah to Gen. xxviii. 10–xxxii. 3, which relates that history.

— *Though they called them*] Though God's prophets called Israel to Him, yet they were so obstinately riveted to apostasy, *together* though not—i.e. Israel as one man refused to exalt or extol God. On this use of the word rendered *to exalt* (the *pilel* of *ramah*), cp. Exod. xv. 2. Ps. xxx. 1 ; cxviii. 28 ; cxlv. 1. Isa. xxv. 1.

GOD'S LOVE TO ISRAEL ; THEIR CONVERSION.

8. *How shall I give thee up, Ephraim?*] We see here, as it were, an inward struggle between Justice and Mercy in the Divine Mind. Israel deserved utter rejection, but God, like a merciful Father, yet spares it ; He remembers His promises to Abraham, Isaac, and Jacob, and yearns over His undutiful son in tenderness and love.

— *Admah—Zeboim*] Cities destroyed with Sodom and Gomorrah. See Deut. xxix. 23, to which Hosea refers here. How can I bear to make thee like them ? No ; it must not be.

9. *The Holy One in the midst of thee*] Cp. Isa. xii. 6.

— *I will not enter into the city*] Rather, *I will not enter a city* ; I am in the midst of thee, and will not leave thee for an *other city* (Targum). God said (*v.* 5) that Israel would be carried captive from their own land to Assyria ; but He here says, I will not forsake thee, I will not exchange Zion (though

thou wilt be for a time an outcast and a wanderer in the wilderness of Assyria) for any noble fenced city, such as Nineveh and Babylon, of the heathen world.

The Hebrew word (*ir*) in the original is rightly rendered *city* here, as in several hundred other places. The sense of *rage* which is assigned to it here by some recent critics (and in Ps. lxxiii. 20 and Jer. xv. 8) is precarious and unsatisfactory.

Here is comfort to Israel in its present dispersion. The presence of the God of Israel is not, like that of the deities of the heathen, confined to one particular city ; it is not localized. No, "God is a Spirit," and the time is coming (as our Lord says) "when neither in this mountain, nor yet at Jerusalem, shall men worship the Father" (John iv. 21), "but in every place incense will be offered unto His Name and a pure offering" (Mal. i. 11). When the Jews receive the Gospel of Christ and turn to God, then, wherever they may be, throughout the whole world, they will find *the Holy One in the midst of them*, in the Universal Church of Christ. Zion will be every where.

10. *They shall walk after the LORD*] They will turn to Christ ; as has been already prophesied, "They shall abide many days without a king and without a sacrifice ; *afterward shall the Children of Israel return and seek the Lord their God, and David their king*." See also on iii. 4, 5.

— *He shall roar like a lion*] The Lord shall roar out of Zion (Joel iii. 16. Amos i. 2). Christ, the Lion of the Tribe of Judah (Rev. v. 5) shall roar with His voice (see on Rev. x. 3) in His Gospel, preached by Apostles sent forth from Zion, two of whom were called "sons of thunder" (Mark iii. 17). And by the terrors of His judgment—such as the destruction of Jerusalem—He will exhort them to repent and to flee from the wrath to come.

— *children shall tremble from the west*] Sons shall come trembling to God, not only from Egypt and Assyria (*v.* 11), but even from the isles of the sea (Isa. xi. 11). This was specially fulfilled in the conversion of vast multitudes by the preaching of St. Peter on the day of Pentecost to Jews "from every nation under heaven" (Acts ii. 5—11). Cp. Zech. viii. 7.

11. *as a dove*] As Isaiah says, speaking of nations flocking to the Church of Christ, "Who are these that fly as a cloud, and as the doves to their windows ?" See above, on Isa. lx. 8. Israel, without God, is described by the Prophet as a "silly dove without a heart" (vii. 11), and as falling into the snare of the fowler (ix. 8) ; but when the Holy Spirit came from heaven, then they

<sup>x</sup> And I will place them in their houses, saith the LORD.

<sup>12 y</sup> Ephraim compasseth me about with lies, and the house of Israel with deceit :

But Judah yet ruleth with God, and is faithful ‖ with the saints.

XII. <sup>1</sup> Ephraim <sup>a</sup> feedeth on wind, and followeth after the east wind :

He daily increaseth lies and desolation ;

<sup>b</sup> And they do make a covenant with the Assyrians,

And <sup>c</sup> oil is carried into Egypt.

<sup>2 d</sup> The LORD hath also a controversy with Judah,

And will † punish Jacob according to his ways ;

According to his doings will he recompense him.

<sup>3</sup>   He took his brother <sup>e</sup> by the heel in the womb,

And by his strength he † <sup>f</sup> had power with God :

<sup>4</sup> Yea, he had power over the angel, and prevailed :

He wept, and made supplication unto him :

He found him in <sup>g</sup> Beth-el, and there he spake with us :

<sup>5</sup> Even the LORD God of hosts ; the LORD is his <sup>h</sup> memorial.

<sup>6</sup>   <sup>i</sup> Therefore turn thou to thy God :

Keep mercy and judgment, and <sup>k</sup> wait on thy God continually.

<sup>7</sup>   He is ‖ a merchant, <sup>l</sup> the balances of deceit are in his hand :

He loveth to ‖ oppress.

<sup>8</sup> And Ephraim said, <sup>m</sup> Yet I am become rich, I have found me out substance :

‖ In all my labours they shall find none iniquity in me † that were sin.

Refer.
CHRIST
About
740
x Ezek. 28. 25,
26. & 37. 21, 25.
y ch. 12. 1.
‖ Or, with the
most holy.
about
725.
a ch. 8. 7.

b 2 Kings 17. 4.
ch. 5. 13. & 7. 11.
c Isa. 30. 6. & 57. 9.

d ch. 4. 1.
Micah 6. 2.

† Heb. visit upon.

e Gen. 25. 26.
† Heb. was a
prince, or,
behaved himself
princely.
f Gen. 32. 24, &c.

g Gen. 28. 12, 19.
& 35. 9, 10, 15.

h Exod. 3. 15.

i ch. 14. 1.
Micah 6. 8.

k Ps. 37. 7.

l. Or, Canaan:
See Ezek. 16. 3.
l Prov. 11. 1.
Amos 8. 5.

‖ Or, deceive.
m Zech. 11. 5.
Rev. 3. 17.
‖ Or, all my
labours suffice me
not: he shall
have punishment of iniquity in whom is sin.     † Heb. which.

partook of the glory and beauty of the Divine Dove, and were at peace in the Ark of the Church.

— *I will place them in their houses*] Wherever Christ is preached, there is His Church ; and there the true Israelites find their home in His Church. See above, on Ps. lxxxvii., and on Isa. ii. 1—4 ; lix. 20 ; lx.—lxii. ; lxv. 18 ; lxvi. 7—10. Jer.—xxxi. 5—12. Ezek. xx. 34—41 ; xxxiv. 13 ; xxxvi. 6—22 ; xxxvii. 16 - 19.

12. *But Judah yet ruleth with God*] Rather, *and even Judah is unruly toward God, and toward the Holy One, Who is faithful.* See above, on Jer. ii. 31, where the same word is used, and Gen. xxvii. 40, and Gesen. 759, and Keil here. Judah was not loyal to God, but was faithless as well as Israel, and therefore to be punished. See what follows immediately here concerning Judah's unfaithfulness (xii. 2). "The Lord hath a controversy with Judah, and will punish Jacob according to his ways ;" and cp. v. 5. 13, 14 ; vi. 4.

CH. XII. 1. *oil is carried into Egypt*] As a present ; to obtain its favour and help. Cp. above, v. 13. Isa. xxx. 2—7 ; and as to the history, see 2 Kings xvii. 4.

### JACOB'S EXAMPLE TO ISRAEL.

3, 4. *He took his brother by the heel—he wept, and made supplication unto him*] The Prophet, having mentioned Jacob in c. 2 as a name of the Israelitish nation, now proceeds to show how degenerate they are from their father Jacob, in faith and obedience ; and how deservedly, therefore, they are punished by God. Jacob, even in his mother's womb, strove for the birth-right (Gen. xxv. 22, 26) ; he coveted earnestly the best gifts (1 Cor. xii. 31). Jacob is represented as an example to the Israel of God, by that early act of bravery, and by that pious ambition for precedence, and by that eager zeal for the birth-right which Esau despised, and for despising which Esau is condemned as "a profane person" (Heb. xii. 16).

By his strength he had power with God, *for he wept and made supplication.* Prayers and tears were his weapons, and they must be the weapons also of penitent and returning Israel, if Israel is to prevail with God. They are the weapons of all true Israelites. Jacob prevailed, and became *Israel*, i. e. a *Prince of God*, when he wrestled with Him in faith and prayer for His blessing at Penuel. See above, the notes on Gen. xxxii. 24—32, where is a comment on this passage of Hosea, and

where it is shown that Jacob in his faith, his agony, his prayers and his tears, was a signal type of Christ, " Who, in the days of His flesh, offered up prayers and supplications with strong crying and tears unto Him that was able to save Him from death, and was heard in that He feared " (Heb. v. 7 ; and see S. Jerome here).

4. *He found him in Bethel*] Jacob was rewarded for his faith by *finding* God at Bethel, *the house of God*, so called because of God's appearing to him there twice (Gen. xxviii. 11 ; xxxv. 9) ; and there God confirmed to him the name of *Israel*, or *prince of God*. But ye Israelites, his descendants, have polluted *Bethel* by your idolatrous calf, and there you have forfeited God's favour and your own name. Jacob *found* God at Bethel by his faith, but ye have *lost* Him at Bethel—which you have made a Beth-aven (iv. 15).

— *there he spake with us*] God, in speaking to Jacob our father, spoke to us his children (cp. on Deut. i. 6 ; v. 3 ; below, Heb. vii. 9, 10) ; what God promised to Jacob, God said to *us*, i. e. to all Jacob's children by faith, to all true Israelites, even to the end of the world.

5. *Even the LORD God of hosts ; the LORD is his memorial*] Jehovah, the Lord God of the *hosts* of angels who appeared to Jacob at *Mahanaim* (the two camps or hosts) ; the Lord God of the starry hosts of heaven (whom ye worship as if they were God). See note on 1 Sam. i. 3. The Lord, Who revealed Himself by the Name JEHOVAH to Moses (Exod. iii. 13—15), the Everlasting, Self-existing One ; the One great Cause of all Causes, is *His Memorial* ; as He said to Moses (Exod. iii. 14), " I AM that I AM—the Lord God of your fathers, the God of Abraham, the God of Isaac, and the God of Jacob ;" this is My *Name* for ever, and this is My *Memorial* unto all generations.

7. *He is a merchant*] Rather, in Hosea's bold, abrupt style, *Canaan.* That is, Israel, is no longer worthy to be called *Israel*, the Son of Isaac, the Son of Abraham, but has become *Canaan* —the Son of Ham. Cp. Ezek. xvi. 3, " Thy father was an Amorite, and thy mother a Hittite." At the same time there is a reference to the mercantile character of Canaan, a name given to merchants generally (Job xli. 30). Isa. xxiii. 8. Prov. xxxi. 24. Gesen. 105) ; and therefore it is added, " the balances of deceit are in his hands." Cp. below, on Rev. vi. 5.

8. In *all my labours—sin*] *All my labours bring with them no iniquity that were sin* (*Vulg.*, *Keil*).

Before CHRIST about 725.

n ch. 13. 4.
o Lev. 23. 42, 43. Neh. 8. 17. [illegible]
p 2 Kings 17. 13.
† Heb. *by the hand.*
q ch. 5. 1. & 6. 8.
r ch. 4. 15. & 9. 15. Amos 4. 4. & 5. 5.
s ch. 8. 11. & 10. 1.
t Gen. 28. 5. Deut. 26. 5.
u Gen. 29. 20, 28.
x Exod. 12. 50, 51. & 13. 3. Ps. 77. 20. Isa. 63. 11. Micah 6. 4.
y 2 Kings 17. 11—18.
† Heb. *with bitternesses.*
† Heb. [illegible] see Ezek. 18. 13. & 24. 7, 8.
z Dan. 11. 18.
a Deut. 28. 37.
a 2 Kings 17. 16, 18. ch. 11. 2.
† Heb. *they add to sin.*
b ch. 2. 8. & 8. 4.
‖ Or, *the sacrificers of men.*
c 1 Kings 12. 28.

9 And [n] I *that am* the LORD thy God from the land of Egypt [o] will yet make
thee to dwell in tabernacles,
As in the days of the solemn feast.
10 [p] I have also spoken by the prophets, and I have multiplied visions,
And used similitudes, † by the ministry of the prophets.
11 [q] *Is there* iniquity *in* Gilead?
Surely they are vanity:
They sacrifice bullocks in [r] Gilgal;
Yea, [s] their altars *are* as heaps in the furrows of the fields.
12 And Jacob [t] fled into the country of Syria,
And Israel [u] served for a wife, and for a wife he kept *sheep*.
13 [x] And by a prophet the LORD brought Israel out of Egypt,
And by a prophet was he preserved.
14 [y] Ephraim provoked *him* to anger † most bitterly:
Therefore shall he leave his † blood upon him,
[z] And his [a] reproach shall his Lord return unto him.
XIII. 1 When Ephraim spake trembling, he exalted himself in Israel;
But [a] when he offended in Baal, he died.
2 And now † they sin more and more,
And [b] have made them molten images of their silver,
*And* idols according to their own understanding,
All of it the work of the craftsmen:
They say of them, Let ‖ the men that sacrifice [c] kiss the calves.

---

9. *And*] *But.* The conjunction here has an adversative sense. Although Ephraim says this, yet God will have pity on him.

— *will yet make thee to dwell in tabernacles*] I will restore thee to the condition in which thou wast in the wilderness, when thou wast My people. Thou shalt dwell in tabernacles, and shalt also celebrate the great and joyous Feast of Tabernacles—the crowning festival of the Hebrew year. The solemnity connected with the most glorious events of Hebrew history, and the typical foreshadowing of the Incarnation of the Son of God, *tabernacling* with men in their nature; and of their dwelling with Him, and of His dwelling with them for ever hereafter in heaven. See the notes on Lev. xxiii. 34. 42. Deut. xvi. 13. 16. 2 Chron. viii. 13. Ezra iii. 4; and below, Zech. xiv. 16—19; and on John i. 14; vii. 2. Rev. vii. 15; xxi. 3.

10. *I have also spoken by the prophets*] Or rather, *I have spoken upon the prophets;* I have come down upon them by My Spirit, and have spoken by their mouths. Cp. 2 Pet. i. 21.

— *visions*] Compare Num. xii. 6—8. Joel ii. 28.

— *similitudes*] Or parables, as when God compares Himself to a Husband (Isa. liv. 5) or to a Vinedresser (Isa. v. 1).

11. *Gilead*] Literally, *If Gilead* is *iniquity* (*Vulg., Arabic*). *If* even *Gilead* on the east of Jordan, as well as *Gilgal* on the west—the scenes of God's love to Israel—have become *iniquity* in the abstract (cp. on vi. 8), then Israel is come to nought.

Jacob prayed to God in Gilead, and was protected by Him. But in Gilead, ye who boast yourselves to be Jacob's posterity, rebel against God and worship idols; therefore ye shall perish, ye shall come to nought.

— *Gilgal*] Even in Gilgal, the scene of God's love to Israel. See above, on iv. 15; ix. 15.

— *their altars are as heaps*] *Their altars*, which are not God's altars, are no better than *heaps* of rude stones that are gathered together in the furrows of the field, and are to be carried away, because they mar the fertility of the soil.

12. *And Jacob*] Or, *yet Jacob*, your father, was an example of faith and obedience to God, Who mercifully preserved and blessed him in his exile and wanderings, as He blessed your fathers in the wilderness. Jacob served even Laban faithfully, for many years, when he was a wanderer in exile in Syria, a heathen and idolatrous land; and I greatly blessed him there, and brought him back from Padan Aram to Canaan.

But you, his posterity, who glory in his name, do not imitate Jacob; you will not serve God, even in the good land which He has given you; therefore, ye shall not enjoy Jacob's blessings, but be carried away captive from Canaan to a foreign and heathen country beyond Padan Aram.

Therefore, O Israel, do thou emulate thy father Jacob: weep and turn to God, wrestle with Him in prayer, and thou shalt prevail also, and recover thy name of *Israel* (*S. Jerome*).

13. *by a prophet*] By Moses, sent to your fathers to deliver them from Egypt, and to write the Law at Mount Sinai for them and for you. But ye have forgotten all these mercies.

— *was he preserved*] Literally, *was he kept.* Israel was *kept* (like a flock) by Moses, whom God appointed to be His shepherd. As the Psalmist says, "He led His people like sheep by the hand of Moses and Aaron" (Ps. lxxvii. 20). Hosea repeats the word from *v.* 12. Israel *kept* sheep for a wife; and Israel (his posterity) were *kept* like sheep by God. The *Vulgate* has, rightly, "*servavit*" in *v.* 12, and *servatus est* in *v.* 13.

14. *Therefore shall he leave his blood upon him*] God shall not wipe away Israel's blood-guiltiness from him, but leave it upon him. Cp. Josh. ii. 9. 2 Sam. i. 10.

How wonderfully has this been fulfilled in the execution of the imprecations which the Jews pronounced upon themselves when shedding the blood of Christ. "His blood be upon us and on our children!" (Matt. xxvii. 25).

CH. XIII. 1. *When Ephraim spake trembling—died*] Rather, *when Ephraim spake, there was trembling* (see *Targum* and *Aben Ezra, Kimchi*); that is, as long as Ephraim feared God, God made the nations to fear Ephraim (Deut. ii. 25; xi. 25, 1 Chron. xiv. 17. Cp. Esth. viii. 17; ix. 3. Job xxix. 21); *he exalted himself in Israel*, he became strong and prosperous, *but when he offended in Baal*, by idolatry and rebellion against God, then Ephraim, who was once so prosperous, perished. Cp. Amos ii. 2.

2. *They say of them, Let the men that sacrifice kiss the calves*] The grammatical rendering of this passage seems rather to be, *They say to them, Let sacrificers of men kiss calves.* And this is favoured by the greater number of ancient versions. See *Sept., Vulg., Syriac, Arabic;* and see the margin.

The sense is as follows:—The votaries of the golden calves at Bethel and Dan alleged that their form of religion was a reformation of heathen worship. Many of the Israelites (in the wilderness, and in the days of Solomon) had fallen away to the worship of Moloch, and had become *sacrificers of men* (1 Kings xi. 5. Amos v. 26. Cp. on Lev. xviii. 21. Deut. xviii. 10.

3 Therefore they shall be [d] as the morning cloud,
And as the early dew that passeth away,
[e] As the chaff *that* is driven with the whirlwind out of the floor,
And as the smoke out of the chimney.
4 Yet [f] I *am* the LORD thy God from the land of Egypt,
And thou shalt know no god but me:
For [g] *there is* no saviour beside me.
5 [h] I did know thee in the wilderness, [i] in the land of † great drought;
6 [k] According to their pasture, so were they filled;
They were filled, and their heart was exalted;
Therefore [l] have they forgotten me.
7 Therefore [m] I will be unto them as a lion:
As [n] a leopard by the way will I observe *them*:
8 I will meet them [o] as a bear *that is* bereaved *of her whelps*,
And will rend the caul of their heart,
And there will I devour them like a lion:
† The wild beast shall tear them.
9 O Israel, [p] thou hast destroyed thyself,
[q] But in me † *is* thine help.
10 ‖ I will be thy king: [r] where *is any other* that may save thee in all thy cities?
And thy judges of whom [s] thou saidst, Give me a king and princes?
11 [t] I gave thee a king in mine anger,
And took *him* away in my wrath.
12 [u] The iniquity of Ephraim *is* bound up; his sin *is* hid.
13 [x] The sorrows of a travailing woman shall come upon him:
He *is* [y] an unwise son;
For he should not [z] stay † long in *the place of* the breaking forth of children;

Before CHRIST about 725.
d ch. 6. 4.
e Dan. 2. 35.
f Isa. 43. 11. ch. 12. 9.
g Isa. 43. 11. & 45. 21.
h Deut. 2. 7. & 32. 10.
i Deut. 8. 15. & 32. 10.
† Heb. *droughts.*
k Deut. 8. 12, 14. & 32. 15.
l ch. 8. 14.
m Lam. 3. 10. ch. 5. 14.
n Jer. 5. 6.
o 2 Sam. 17. 8. Prov. 17. 12.
† Heb. *the beast of the field.*
p Prov. 6. 32. ch. 14. 1. Mal. 1. 9.
q ver. 4.
† Heb. *in thy help.*
‖ Rather, *Where is thy king?* King Hoshea being then in prison, 2 Kings 17. 4.
r Deut. 32. 38. ch. 10. 3. ver. 4.
s 1 Sam. 8. 5, 19.
t 1 Sam. 8. 7. & 10. 19. & 15. 22, 23. & 16. 1. ch. 10. 3.
u Deut. 32. 34. Job 14. 17.
x Isa. 13. 8. Jer. 30. 6.
y Prov. 22. 3.
z 2 Kings 19. 3.
† Heb. *a time.*

---

2 Kings xvi. 3; xvii. 17; xxi. 6; xxiii. 10. 2 Chron. xxviii. 3; xxxiii. 6. Ps. cvi. 36. Jer. vii. 31; xix. 5; xxxii. 35. Ezek. xvi. 21; xx. 26. 31. Amos v. 26. Jeroboam (it was pleaded by his adherents) wrought a change for the better among them. How could they scruple at, or be offended by, the milder worship of Jehovah under the form of calves set up by him? Let sacrificers of human victims turn away from their sanguinary orgies, and let them kiss the calves at Bethel and at Dan. On *kissing*, as an act of adoration, see on 1 Kings xix. 18. Job xxxi. 26, 27.

3. *smoke out of the chimney*] Or, out of the window—the lattice; the houses had no chimney.

5. *I did know thee*] I loved thee.

6. *According to their pasture*] The more abundantly I fed them, the more they kicked against Me. There is a reference here to Deut. viii. 11; xxxi. 20; xxxii. 15. The warnings which God gave them by Moses have been despised, and they have committed those very sins, against which the warnings were given.

7. *will I observe them*] I will lie in wait against them. Cp. Jer. v. 6.

9. *O Israel, thou hast destroyed thyself*] Rather, *O Israel, thy destruction* is from this, *that* thou art *against Me* who *am thy help*. Thou hast destroyed thyself by rebelling against thy Saviour. Here is a clear statement that men are authors of their own destruction, and not God, Who willeth that none should perish, but that all men should be saved: Jer. xxvii. 13. Ezek. xviii. 31, 32; xxxiii. 11. Cp. Isa. xlv. 22; and below, on 1 Tim. ii. 4. 2 Pet. iii. 9. *Bp. Sanderson*, iii. 150. *Bp. Andrewes*, v. 308.

10. *I will be thy king*] Rather, *Where is thy king, that he may help thee in all thy cities?* Cp. Deut. xxxii. 37—39. The word (*ehi*), rendered *where*, occurs also in *v.* 14. Cp. *Ewald*, § 104; *Gesen.* 16; and see the margin here.

11. *I gave thee a king in mine anger*] God, Who was the King of Israel, and Who was virtually rejected by them when they asked for an earthly king (1 Sam. viii. 7), gave to Israel, first Saul, and then to the Ten Tribes he gave Jeroboam, chosen by themselves; and He punished them by their own choice. So He had done to the men of Shechem who chose Abimelech. See Judges ix. 1—57. So God ever deals with those who sin against Him. He punishes them by means of their own sins. Cp. Isa. lxvi. 4. Jer. ii. 19.

12. *bound up*] As in a purse. See on Job xiv. 17. "My transgression is sealed up in a bag, and Thou sewest up mine iniquity." Cp. Deut. xxxii. 34, 35. "Is not this laid up in store with Me, and laid up among my treasures?" God notes men's sins, and keeps them in remembrance; and so men, by presuming on God's forbearance, and by obstinate continuance in sin, "treasure up for themselves wrath against the day of wrath" (Rom. ii. 5).

ISRAEL'S CONVERSION A SPIRITUAL CHILDBIRTH.

13. *The sorrows of a travailing woman*] Israel, enduring in exile the punishment of the sin which it has conceived, is compared to a woman suffering the pangs of parturition. But this chastisement of its banishment and captivity is a merciful one; it is designed to bring it to the blessedness of the new birth in Christ, and to a glorious resurrection from the womb of the grave, through Him Who is the first-born of every creature (Col. i. 15), the first-begotten of the dead (Col. i. 18. Rev. i. 5). We may compare the imagery in Micah iv. 10. Isa. xiii. 8; xxvi. 17; and especially our Blessed Lord's words, "A woman when she is in travail hath sorrow because her hour is come, but as soon as she is delivered of the child, she remembereth no more the anguish, for joy that a man is born into the world" (John xvi. 21). What a joyful day will that be, when (with reverence be it said) Christ shall have been conceived in the womb of the Jewish Nation (cp. St. Paul's words, Gal. iv. 19), and have been brought forth by its faith into the world!

— *He is an unwise son; for he should not stay long in the place of the breaking forth of children*] The metaphor derived from childbirth is continued. Israel is *an unwise child*; in that he lingers in the womb (in loco diruptionis vulvae; see 2 Kings xix. 3. Isa. xxxvii. 3), instead of being born into the light of day,

Before  
CHRIST  
about  
725.  
a Isa. 25. 8.  
Ezek. 37. 12.  
† Heb. *Or has*.  
b 1 Cor. 15. 54, 55.  

† or *luck*.  
Rom. 11. 29.  
d See Gen. 41. 52.  
& 48. 19.  
e Jer. 4. 11.  
Ezek. 17. 10. &  
19. 12.  
ch. 4. 19.  

† Heb. *vessels of desire*.  
Nahum 2. 9.  
‖ Fulfilled  
about 721.  
2 Kings 17. 6.  
1 2 Kings 18. 12.  
g 2 Kings 8. 12.  
a 15. 16.  
Isa. 13. 16.  
ch. 10. 14, 15.  
Amos 1. 13.  
Nahum 3. 10.  

a ch. 12. 6.  
Joel 2. 13.  

b ch. 13. 9.

14 "I will ransom them from † the power of the Grave ;  
I will redeem them from Death :  
b O Death, I will be thy plagues ;  
O Grave, I will be thy destruction :  
c Repentance shall be hid from mine eyes,  

15 Though d he be fruitful among *his* brethren.  
e An east wind shall come,  
The wind of the LORD shall come up from the wilderness,  
And his spring shall become dry, and his fountain shall be dried up :  
He shall spoil the treasure of all † pleasant vessels.  

16 ‖ Samaria shall become desolate ;  
f For she hath rebelled against her God :  
g They shall fall by the sword :  
Their infants shall be dashed in pieces,  
And their women with child shall be ripped up.  

XIV. 1 O Israel, a return unto the LORD thy God ;  
b For thou hast fallen by thine iniquity.

---

Israel is compared to a woman in childbirth, and to a babe to be born, because the characteristics of mother and infant are united in it. Israel, stubbornly lingering in the obstinacy and blindness of unbelief and impenitence, instead of hastening to be converted to the true faith, and to be spiritually born to light and life in Christ, is compared to a babe lingering in the darkness of the womb (on this use of the Hebrew verb *amid*, see 2 Sam. i. 10, 2 Kings iv. 6; xiii. 18), instead of hastening to be brought forth into the world.

Isaiah adopts the same metaphor: "Before she travailed she brought forth, before her pain came she was delivered of a man child. Who hath heard such things? Who hath seen such things? Shall the earth be made to bring forth in one day? or shall a nation be born at once? for as soon as Zion travailed she brought forth her children" (Isa. lxvi. 8).

There is a special propriety in the adoption of this figure here, in connexion with the Patriarch Jacob, whose example has just been propounded for the imitation of Israel, and who showed *his eager haste to be born* by laying hold of his brother's heel in the womb. See above, xii. 3. So ought Israel to feel a holy yearning, and to show an impatient alacrity, to be born into the pure and bright daylight of the Gospel of Christ. Observe, also, the beautiful connexion with what follows.

**THE BIRTH FROM THE GRAVE.**

14. *I will ransom them from the power* (or hand) *of the Grave*] Christ here speaks. He Who has given Himself a ransom for all (1 Tim. ii. 6), He Who has destroyed Death by dying on the cross (Heb. ii. 9, 14), He, the First-born of the Dead, delivers us by the glorious Childbirth of His Resurrection from the dark womb of Sin and the Grave, into the light and life of Immortality; see below, on John xvi. 21. Col. i. 18. Rev. i. 5; and the noble words of *St. Ignatius* at the prospect of *death*, as quoted below on Phil. i. 21. "My *birth* is now at hand; do not hinder me from being *born;* allow me to see the pure light; when I arrive there I shall be a man of God."

There is a happy harmony in the imagery here blended with what has gone before. Well may the Prophet now speak of the glory of the Resurrection, after speaking of Israel's conversion. For what will Israel's conversion be? It will be like the resurrection of the dead bones, in the valley of which Ezekiel speaks, and to which he compares it. See Ezek. xxxvii. "What," says the Apostle, "shall the receiving of them" (the Jews) "be, but *life from the dead?*" (Rom. xi. 15.)

The Christian Fathers apply these words to Christ (see *S. Jerome* here, and *S. Gregory*, Hom. xxii., in Evangelia; and *Eusebius,* Demonstr. Evang. iv. 12); and it is remarkable that the Hebrew Rabbis also understood these words as referring to the Messiah. See *A Lapide* here, who says, "The Hebrew Prophets are accustomed to subjoin joyful things to what is sorrowful, and to cheer the desponding nation by bright anticipations of the future; and to pass, by a rapid flight, from the miseries of their own times, to the gladsome days of Christ."

— *O Death, I will be thy plagues; O Grave, I will be thy*

*destruction*] So the passage is rendered by the *Vulgate,* and hence the Latin Fathers accept the sense as being, "O Mors, ero mors tua, ero morsus tuus, O Inferne" (*S. Jerome, S. Gregory, S. Aug.* See *A Lapide*); and this gives a very good sense. Cp. Heb. ii. 14.

But sound and sober criticism cannot assent to the assertion of the learned Roman Catholic expositor, *Cornelius A Lapide,* who does not hesitate to say, "Ex definitione Ecclesiæ (Romanæ) et Concilii Tridentini, sess. 4, sancientis Vulgatam Versionem esse genuinam Sanctam Scripturam, de fide certum est, hanc hujus loci esse sententiam, Ero mors tua, O Mors, ero morsus tuus, O Inferne, sic enim habet Vulgata Versio." Here is one proof, among many, of the fallibility of the Council of Trent, and of the Roman Church, and of the injury inflicted by them on Biblical Criticism. The right rendering of Hosea's words is, "O Death, where are thy plagues?" (see above, xiii. 10, and *Dr. Pusey* and *Kiel* here; and so they are translated by *Sept., Syriac, Arabic,* and by St. Paul (1 Cor. xv. 55), *O Grave, where is thy destruction?* (i.e. thy power to destroy.)

Christ here sounds the pæan of His victory over Death and the Grave, and enables and encourages every Christian believer to do the same. This chapter, therefore, and the following one, are fitly appointed by the Church to be read as proper Lessons on the Wednesday before the Festival of Christ's Resurrection (cp. *Bp.* Pearson, Art. xi., p. 387. *Bp.* Andrewes, ii. 256; iii. 229. *Derison* on Prophecy, Disc. vi. part ii., pp. 196, 197); and St. Paul's noble Sermon—the most glorious homily on the Resurrection that ever was preached—in which he adopts these words of Hosea, is fitly appointed to be read at the Burial of the Dead, for the purpose of ministering comfort to mourners, by the hope of Resurrection.

— *Repentance shall be hid from mine eyes*] Although thou hast been faithless to Me, I will never repent of My love to thee, and of My victory, by which thou art delivered. Compare the similar use of the word *repentance,* in Rom. xi. 29, "The gifts of God are without repentance;" He never revokes what He has once given to His Church. Cp. 1 Sam. xv. 29. Ps. lxxxix. 34. Ps. cx. 4.

15. *Though he be fruitful*] Rather, *Because* (so Sept., Vulg.) *he (Ephraim) will bear fruit* (as his name *Ephraim* signifies, see Gen. xli. 52) *among his brethren,* therefore the promise in the foregoing verse will stand firm. *Because* (or *when*) Ephraim is *fruitful among his brethren,* i.e. as soon as Israel begins to bring forth fruits of repentance and faith in Christ, then all these glorious promises will be fulfilled to him. A new paragraph begins with what follows; I have therefore altered the punctuation.

— *An east wind shall come*] God shall deprive Ephraim of his external prosperity, and prepare him for conversion by salutary discipline inflicted by the arms of Assyria, which will despoil Israel, and take Samaria, and carry the people captive. Cp. above, x. 14. 2 Kings xviii. 9—12. *But* this *chastisement* will eventually lead to the *conversion* of Israel. See what follows: "O Israel, return unto the Lord thy God" (xiv. 1).

2 Take with you words, and turn to the LORD:
Say unto him, Take away all iniquity, and ‖ receive *us* graciously:
So will we render the [c] calves of our lips.
3 [d] Asshur shall not save us; [e] we will not ride upon horses:
[f] Neither will we say any more to the work of our hands, *Ye are* our gods:
[g] For in thee the fatherless findeth mercy.
4 I will heal [h] their backsliding, I will love them [i] freely:
For mine anger is turned away from him;
5 I will be as [k] the dew unto Israel:
He shall ‖ grow as the lily,
And † cast forth his roots as Lebanon;
6 His branches † shall spread,
And [l] his beauty shall be as the olive tree,
And [m] his smell as Lebanon.
7 [n] They that dwell under his shadow shall return;
They shall revive *as* the corn, and ‖ grow as the vine:
The ‖ scent thereof *shall be* as the wine of Lebanon.
8 Ephraim *shall say,* [o] What have I to do any more with idols?
[p] I have heard *him,* and observed him:
I *am* like a green fir tree.
[q] From me is thy fruit found.
9 [r] Who *is* wise, and he shall understand these *things*?

Before CHRIST about 725.
‖ Or, *give good.*
c Heb. 13. 15.
d Jer. 31. 18, &c. ch. 5. 13. & 12. 1.
e Deut. 17. 16. Ps. 33. 17. Isa. 30. 2, 16. & 31. 1.
f ch. 2. 17. ver. 8.
g Ps. 10. 14. & 68. 5.
h Jer. 5. 6. & 14. 7. ch. 11. 7.
i Eph. 1. 6.
k Job 29. 19. Prov. 19. 12.
‖ Or, *blossom.*
† Heb. *strike.*
† Heb. *shall go.*
l Ps. 52. 8. & 128. 3.
m Gen. 27. 27. Cant. 4. 11.
n Ps. 91. 1.
‖ Or, *blossom.*
‖ Or, *memorial.*
o ver. 3.
p Jer. 31. 18.
q James 1. 17.
r Ps. 107. 43. Jer. 9. 12. Dan. 12. 10. John 8. 47. & 18. 37.

---

ISRAEL'S REPENTANCE; GOD'S GRACIOUS PROMISES TO THE JEWS ON THEIR CONVERSION.

CH. XIV. 2. *Take with you words*] God does not require costly sacrifices from the Jews; but He asks for heart-felt confession of sin and earnest prayer.

— *receive us graciously*] Literally, *receive good.* Israel, when it repents and believes in Christ, will no longer trust, as it has done, in its own merits; but will ascribe all to God's free grace, and say, Since Thou, O God, hast taken away our iniquity, receive as Thine own due whatever good is left in us. Receive Thy own gift, especially the merits of Christ imputed to us, Who is the perfect good, and the Giver of all good to men. "Whensoever," says *S. Augustine,* "we do any good, God works in us and by us; and whenever He rewards our acts, He crowns His own gifts."

Observe the affecting and pathetic dialogue which now follows between God and penitent and returning Israel. Their reconciliation to Christ, as here displayed by the Prophet, is like the embrace of Joseph and his brethren who had sold him, which was typical of that blessed event (see above, on Gen. xlv. 3—12); and like the scene in our Lord's Parable, where the father runs and falls on the returning prodigal's neck, and kisses him. See Luke xv. 20.

— *will we render the calves of our lips*] We will not any more worship the *calves* of *Bethel,* nor rely on the *calves* of burnt sacrifices; but we will offer the *calves of our lips* in confession of our sins to Thee, and in penitential prayer and joyful thanksgiving. As the Psalmist says (Ps. li. 15—19; lxix. 30, 31), "I will praise the name of God with a song, and will magnify Him with thanksgiving. This also shall please the Lord better than a bullock that hath horns and hoofs." Cp. Heb. xiii. 15, where the Apostle softens the metaphor into "the fruit of our lips:" the original would not have been so generally intelligible to his readers.

This Section, xiv. 2—10, with Joel ii. 15—27, is the Haphtarah, or Proper Prophetical Lesson, in some Synagogues, to Deut. xxxii. 1—52, the "Song of Moses," where he recounts God's mercies to Israel.

ISRAEL WILL BELIEVE AND REPENT, AND TRUST ONLY IN GOD.

3. *Asshur shall not save us*] Here follows Israel's confession to God: We will no longer look to Assyria for help (cp. v. 13; vii. 11; viii. 9), nor will we put our trust in horses from Egypt (Isa. xxxi. 1. Ps. xx. 7), but we will flee to Thee for succour, and rely on Thee, O God.

4. *I will heal*] God gives an immediate and gracious answer to the confession and prayer of Israel. Let the Hebrew Nation mark this and be encouraged by it.

GOD WILL HEAL ISRAEL IN CHRIST.

5. *He shall grow*] He shall blossom. Contrast this beautiful imagery of God's love and grace to Israel, with the description of Israel's desolation consequent on their sins (xiii. 15).

7. *They that dwell under his shadow shall return*] Rather, *They shall return; dwelling under his shadow they shall revive (as) corn, or, by corn* (*Sept., Vulg., Syriac, Arabic*). The *Targum* has the remarkable words, "*They shall dwell under the shadow of the Messiah.*" Christ shall give them corn—the bread of life, in Himself; and they *shall blossom as the Vine,* being engrafted as living branches in Him Who is the True Vine (John xv. 1—4).

8. *Ephraim* shall say, *What have I to do any more with idols?*] God's merciful dispensation in the captivity and dispersion of the Jews, may already be recognized in their abandonment of idolatry. Cp. above, *Introd.* to Ezra, p. 299. The rest will one day follow. May He hasten the time!

— *I have heard* him, *and observed him*] Israel, having forsaken idolatry, will have a vision of the True God. The veil will be taken from their eyes, and they will see Him in Christ (2 Cor. iii. 14—16).

—*fir tree*] Cypress.

— *From me is thy fruit found*] This is God's answer in Christ to Israel, when penitent and restored. A fir-tree, or cypress, is *unfruitful* in itself, but God enables it to bear fruit. Such is man: a dark, funereal, isolated, and barren Cypress by nature, but fruitful as a Vine, in luxuriant and joyful exuberance, by grace. As our Lord says (John xv. 4), "The branch cannot bear fruit of itself, except it abide in the Vine; no more can ye, except ye abide in Me."

This chapter is therefore appropriately appointed by the Church to be read, as on the Wednesday before Easter, when we thank God for the benefits derived from the Death, Burial, and Resurrection of Christ, Who, speaking of His future passion and of its fruitfulness, said, "Except a corn of wheat fall into the ground and die, it abideth alone, but if it die it bringeth forth much fruit" (John xii. 24). Ephraim (whose name signifies *fruitful*) derives its fruit from Christ. The conversion of the world—both of Jew and Gentile—is a Harvest which springs up in Christ, Who is the seed sown in the grave, and Who rose as the first-fruits from it (1 Cor. xv. 20).

GOD IS JUSTIFIED IN ALL HIS WAYS TO ISRAEL.

9. *Who is wise, and he shall understand these* things?] This

Before
CHRIST
about
725.
᷒ Prov. 10. 29.
Luke 2. 34.
1 Pet. 2. 8.

Prudent, and he shall know them?
For ᷒ the ways of the LORD *are* right,
And the just shall walk in them :
But the transgressors shall fall therein.

is the sum of the whole book. Hosea (whose name signifies *Saviour*) justifies God's ways to Israel, ever since His choice of Israel to be a favoured nation, even to the end of time.

To those who are *not wise*, but who cavil at God's doings and carp at His Word, the history of God's Ancient People, the Jews, is a hard problem, an unintelligible riddle, an insoluble enigma. They may even take occasion from it to charge God with weakness and caprice. But *he that is wise will understand these things*; he that is *prudent shall know them; for the ways of the Lord are right.* Hosea proves this. He shews that all the dispensations of God to Israel have ever been, and ever will be, dispensations of Love; and that in all of them *He is their Saviour* (Ps. cvi. 21. Isa. lxiii. 8), and that the Angel of His Presence is even now saving them if they will be saved, even in their affliction and by their chastisement; and that in His love and in His pity He redeems them (Isa. lxiii. 9). Even in their punishment there is mercy to Israel. Their captivity and dispersion, first by the arms of Assyria, and afterwards by those of Rome, were designed by God to wean them from their sins, and to bring them by faith and repentance to Himself. Already in great measure they have had that effect. The Jews have cast away their idols (*v.* 8). They no longer look to the Assyrian and Egypt, of this world for help. Many of them have been already brought to God in Christ. All the Apostles and Evangelists of Christ were Jews; Christ Himself was a Jew, and He said that "Salvation is of the Jews" (John iv. 22). The Gospel has gone forth from Sion; and the Christian Church, first planted at Jerusalem, and watered by the dews of the Holy Ghost descending there, as the dew fell at first on Gideon's fleece, is extending itself over the threshing-floor of the world; (see above, on Judges vi. 36 – 40). And in due time the dispersed

of Israel will believe in Christ, and will be united with their Gentile brethren in the Church, which is the true Zion, and is "the Jerusalem which is above, the mother of us all" (Gal. iv. 26), and will join with them in praising Him, and will acknowledge that "all the ways of the Lord are right; and the just shall walk in them."

This last verse, which is the Epiphonema of Hosea's prophecies, is an echo of that at the close of the 107th Psalm, which celebrates God's mercies vouchsafed to Israel, in redeeming them and gathering them from all countries of the world (Ps. cvii. 1—8), and to all mankind in His wonderful works of Creation and Redemption; and which ends with the words, "The righteous shall see it and rejoice, and all iniquity shall stop her mouth. Whoso is wise and will observe these things, even they *shall understand* the loving-kindness of the Lord" (Ps. cvii. 43).

The Prophet Jeremiah also, weeping over the ruin of Zion, declares that the judgment is just, and takes up Hosea's words and says, "*Who is the wise man, that may understand this,* and who is he to whom the mouth of the Lord hath spoken?" (see what follows there, Jer. ix. 12—16); and the Apostle St. Paul, in commenting on the history and prospects of Israel in his Epistle to the Romans (Rom. ix., x., xi.), where he grounds himself on the prophecies of Hosea (Rom. ix. 25, 26. Cp. Hos. ii. 23; i. 10), sums up his argument with an exclamation even of a more fervent character, "O the depth of the riches both of the wisdom and knowledge of God! How unsearchable are His judgments, and His ways past finding out. For of Him, and through Him, and to Him, are all things : to Whom be glory for ever. AMEN" (Rom. xi. 33. 36).

65

# JOEL.

I. ¹ THE word of the LORD that came to Joel the son of Pethuel.
² Hear this, ye old men,
And give ear, all ye inhabitants of the land.
³ Hath this been in your days,
Or even in the days of your fathers ?
³ ᵇ Tell ye your children of it,
And let your children tell their children,
And their children another generation.
⁴ ᶜ † That which the palmerworm hath left hath the locust eaten ;
And that which the locust hath left hath the cankerworm eaten ;
And that which the cankerworm hath left hath the caterpiller eaten.

Before CHRIST about 810.

a ch. 2, 2.

b Ps. 78. 4.

c Deut. 28, 38, 39, ch. 2. 25.
† Heb. 73 . . . . . . . . . . duced the palmer-worm.

CH. I.] The name JOEL signifies that JEHOVAH (the covenant God of Israel) is the GOD of all the world. *Joel*, in his name and in his prophecies, is, as we shall see, the precursor of *Ezekiel*.

The main design of his prophecy is, to show that Jehovah declares His judicial omnipotence in various ways, by which He punishes the ungodly, and maintains and vindicates His own glory and truth, and eventually rewards His own people. God does this by physical judgments, such as plagues of Locusts, Earthquakes, Pestilences, Famines, which are God's Prophets and Preachers to the World, and are like Heralds of Christ's Coming, and Apparitors of the great Assize. They call men to repentance, and prepare them for Resurrection, Judgment, and Eternity. Cp. Ezek. xiv. 21. Hos. ii. 11—13. Amos vii. 1—8. Nah. i. 6.

Joel also shows that God proclaims His judicial omnipotence by National Visitations—such as the invasion and captivity of Israel by the armies of Assyria, and such as the destruction of Jerusalem by the armies of Babylon and of Rome.

And lest it should be imagined that the God of Israel and Judah had been overcome by those heathen Nations who have been used by Him for the chastisement of the sins of His people, Joel reveals the future overthrow of *heathen* nations, and of all enemies of Christ and of His Church. He describes the grand consummation of the Last Day and Universal Judgment, when it will be proved by the supremacy of Christ, the King and Judge of all, that Jehovah, the Lord God of Israel, is indeed the God of the Universe, and the Saviour of His faithful people.

*Joel*, the Prophet of *Judgment*, follows *Hosea* (*Saviour*), the Prophet of *Salvation*. In this combination God's attributes of Mercy and Judgment are displayed. Thus Joel prepares the way for our Lord's prophecy on the Mount of Olives, when, looking down upon Jerusalem, He spoke of judgments in the natural world, "famines, pestilences, and earthquakes" (Matt. xxiv. 7), and of national judgments, especially the destruction of Jerusalem, as preparatory warnings of His own future Coming to judge the World (Matt. xxiv. 7—31; xxv. 31).

Indeed, by a sublime and magnificent process of prophetic *foreshortening*, Joel teaches us to see the majestic form of CHRIST standing in the background above all the Judgments, physical and political, from the Prophet's own age to the Day of Doom; and he enables us to descry the Great White Throne (Rev. xx. 11) towering in awful perspective above them all ; and he combines them all as hours in one grand diurnal generalization, which he calls "the Day of the Lord," which will have its Sunset in the Universal Doom of Quick and Dead.

Joel is quoted by Amos i. 2, who there takes up the warnings of Joel iii. 16, and who also closes his prophecy with gracious predictions similar to those of Joel (cp. Amos ix. 13. Joel iii. 18). Joel

is also cited by Isaiah (xiii. 6. See Joel i. 18). We may accept the opinion that he prophesied before Amos, i. e. before the twenty-seven years of the contemporaneous reigns of Uzziah and Jeroboam II., i. e. before B.C. 810 (*Ussher, Pusey, Keil*).

Joel is placed in the Hebrew Canon between Hosea and Amos, who, according to the inscriptions and contents of their prophecies, prophesied under Jeroboam II. and Uzziah ; his position in the Canon is tantamount to a testimony from the Hebrew Church, that he lived and prophesied at that time.

For further remarks on the prophecies of Joel, see the INTRODUCTION prefixed to this Volume.

1. *Joel*] i. e. *Jehovah* is *God*.

— *Pethuel*] i. e. *persuaded of God*.

4. *That which the palmerworm hath left hath the locust eaten*] Literally, *That which the gnawing* (locust) *hath left, the multiplying* (locust) *hath eaten*. These words (in Hebrew, *gázam, arbeh*) represent different kinds of locusts, distinguished by the characteristics which their names indicate (*Pocock, Pusey, Keil*).

Some interpreters have supposed them to mean the locust in its various phases of development ; but this opinion is not probable. The Prophet is describing successive swarms of locusts (see Lev. xi. 22), rapidly succeeding one another, and not gradual transformations of one genus of locusts after long intervals. The marvel (as S. Jerome observes) is, that they all come in one year.

— *that which the cankerworm hath left hath the caterpiller eaten*] Literally, *That which the licking* (locust) *hath left, the devouring* (locust) *hath eaten* (*Pocock* 215).

It has been supposed by some, that these locusts are symbolical of invading armies, and that these four different and successive swarms represent the four great nations hostile to God's people, viz. the Babylonians, Medo-Persians, Greeks, and Romans (*Ephraem Syrus, S. Cyril, S. Jerome, Haymo, Hugo, Lyranus, Hengstenberg, Hävernick*).

But though, doubtless, something more is meant by these locusts than what their name literally implies, and though it can hardly be doubted that the Prophet passes on from these physical locusts to hostile armies, especially from the North (ii. 20. Cp. on i. 9 and ii. 17, and *Pusey*, pp. 99—102), yet we must not discard the natural sense.

Indeed, the great lesson which the Prophet Joel teaches us is this, that God executes His judgments by His agents in the *natural* world, such as locusts, and thus displays His Justice and Omnipotence as the great Moral Governor of the Universe ; and speaks to men and nations by the voice of nature, and warns them by means of physical phenomena, which are instruments of His primitive retribution for sin, to prepare for a Judgment to come. The literal sense, with such a moral as this, has been

Before
CHRIST
about
810.
d Isa. 32. 10.
e So Prov. 30. 25,
26, 27;
ch. 2. 2, 11, 25.

f Rev. 9. 8.

g Isa. 5. 6.
† Heb. laid my
fig tree for a
barking.

h Isa. 22. 12.
i Prov. 2. 17.
Jer. 3. 4.
k ver. 13.
ch. 2. 14.

l Jer. 12. 11.
14. 2.

m Isa. 24. 7.
ver. 12.
|| Or, ashamed.
n Jer. 14. 3, 4.

o ver. 10.

p Isa. 24. 11.
Jer. 48. 33.
See Ps. 4. 7.
Isa. 9. 3.
q Jer. 4. 8.
ver. 6.

r ver. 9.

s 2 Chron. 20.
3, 4.
ch. 2. 15, 16.
t Lev. 23, 36.
|| Or, day of
restraint.
u 2 Chron. 20. 13.

x Jer. 30. 7.
y Isa. 13. 6, 9.
ch. 2. 1.

⁵ Awake, ye drunkards, and weep ;
And howl, all ye drinkers of wine,
Because of the new wine ; ᵈ for it is cut off from your mouth.
⁶ For ᵉ a nation is come up upon my land,
Strong, and without number,
ᶠ Whose teeth *are* the teeth of a lion,
And he hath the cheek teeth of a great lion.
⁷ He hath ᵍ laid my vine waste, and † barked my fig tree :
He hath made it clean bare, and cast *it* away ;
The branches thereof are made white.
⁸ ʰ Lament like a virgin girded with sackcloth for ⁱ the husband of her youth.
⁹ ᵏ The meat offering and the drink offering is cut off from the house of the
LORD ;
The priests, the LORD's ministers, mourn.
¹⁰ The field is wasted, ˡ the land mourneth ; for the corn is wasted :
ᵐ The new wine is || dried up, the oil languisheth.
¹¹ ⁿ Be ye ashamed, O ye husbandmen ;
Howl, O ye vinedressers,
For the wheat and for the barley ;
Because the harvest of the field is perished.
¹² ᵒ The vine is dried up, and the fig tree languisheth ;
The pomegranate tree, the palm tree also, and the apple tree,
*Even* all the trees of the field, are withered :
Because ᵖ joy is withered away from the sons of men.
¹³ ᑫ Gird yourselves, and lament, ye priests :
Howl, ye ministers of the altar :
Come, lie all night in sackcloth, ye ministers of my God :
For ʳ the meat offering and the drink offering is withholden from the house
of your God.
¹⁴ ˢ Sanctify ye a fast, call ᵗ a || solemn assembly,
Gather the elders *and* ᵘ all the inhabitants of the land *into* the house of the
LORD your God,
And cry unto the LORD,
¹⁵ ˣ Alas for the day ! for ʸ the day of the LORD *is* at hand,
And as a destruction from the Almighty shall it come.
¹⁶ Is not the meat cut off before our eyes,

---

maintained by *Theodoret* and many of the Rabbis, and by *Bochart, Pocock, Delitzsch, Pusey, Keil.*

We shall, however, see abundant reason for believing that the judgments of God, inflicted on His sinful people by means of locusts, real as they are, are symbolical of and introductory to, other judicial visitations, even to the Day of Doom. St. John, in the Apocalypse, adopts the imagery of Joel, and describes one of God's severest visitations under the figure of a swarm of locusts (see Rev. ix. 3), which the Prophet calls "God's great army" (ii. 25), spreading desolation every where.

6. *a nation is come* ] The devastations caused by the locusts, as described in these passages, are well illustrated from his own experience by Dr. *Thomson*, Land and Book, pp. 416—418, and by Dr. *Pusey*, pp. 985, 101, 103.

9. *The meat offering and the drink offering is cut off from the house of the Lord* ] Here is an intimation that the Prophet, when speaking of the plague of locusts, sees something beyond them, namely, a hostile army of invaders profaning the Temple of God ; and that his prophetic vision glances as it were with a lightning flash, to the times of the Chaldean Invasion, and to the cessation of the *daily sacrifice* in the time of Antiochus Epiphanes (cp. Dan. viii. 11, 12. 2 Macc. v. 15 ; vi. 1, 2—6 ; x.

1—5), and to a similar calamity in the Roman siege (*Josephus*, B. J., vi. 2. 1) ; and the destruction of Jerusalem by the Romans, and even to the Antichristian persecution of the Christian Church in the last days. Events which, in the course of history, follow one another in a long train at wide intervals, are here brought together into a single scene. This is a characteristic of Joel's style. He, the divinely-inspired Prophet of the Lord, speaks with the attributes of Him Who inspired him, and with Whom "a thousand years are as one day." See below, ii. 18—20. With marvellous celerity the prophet passes from his own age to the Day of Doom — "Alas for the day ! for the day of the Lord is at hand." Cp.

13. *Gird yourselves* ] With sackcloth. See Jer. iv. 8, who adopts the language of Joel.

15. *Alas for the day ! for the day of the Lord is at hand* ] Cp. Isa. xiii. 6, 9.

— *a destruction from the Almighty* ] Words adopted by Isaiah, xiii. 6. God is called Almighty (*Shaddai*) four times by the Prophets ; here, and in that passage of Isaiah, and twice in Ezekiel, i. 24 ; x. 5. Joel's special mission was to declare the Omnipotence of Jehovah the Lord God of Israel, the Judge of all the men and nations of the world.

Yea, ᶻjoy and gladness from the house of our God ?

¹⁷ The † seed is rotten under their clods,

The garners are laid desolate,

The barns are broken down ;

For the corn is withered.

¹⁸ How do ª the beasts groan ! the herds of cattle are perplexed,

Because they have no pasture ;

Yea, the flocks of sheep are made desolate.

¹⁹ O LORD, ᵇto thee will I cry :

For ᶜ the fire hath devoured the ‖ pastures of the wilderness,

And the flame hath burned all the trees of the field;

²⁰ The beasts of the field ᵈ cry also unto thee :

For ᵉ the rivers of waters are dried up,

And the fire hath devoured the pastures of the wilderness.

II. ¹ ª Blow ye the ‖ trumpet in Zion,

And ᵇ sound an alarm in my holy mountain :

Let all the inhabitants of the land tremble :

For ᶜ the day of the LORD cometh, for *it is* nigh at hand ;

² ᵈ A day of darkness and of gloominess,

A day of clouds and of thick darkness,

As the morning spread upon the mountains :

ᵉ A great people and a strong ;

ᶠ There hath not been ever the like,

Neither shall be any more after it, *even* to the years † of many generations.

³ ᵍ A fire devoureth before them ;

And behind them a flame burneth :

The land *is* as ʰ the garden of Eden before them,

**Margin references (right column):**

Before
CHRIST
about
810.

z See Deut. 12
6, 7, & 16. 11
14, 15.
† Heb. *grains.*

a Hos. 4. 3.

b Ps. 50. 15.

c Jer. 9. 10,
ch. 2. 3.
‖ Or, *habitations.*

d Job 38. 41.
Ps. 104. 21. &
145. 15.
e 1 Kings 17. 7.
& 18. 5.

a Jer. 4. 5.
ver. 15.
‖ Or, *cornet.*
b Num. 10. 5, 9.

c ch. 1. 15.
Obad. 15.
Zeph. 1. 14, 15.
d Amos 5. 18, 20.

e ch. 1. 6.
ver. 5, 11, 25.

f Exod. 10. 14.

† Heb. *of gene-*
*ration and gene-*
*ration.*
g ch. 1. 19, 20.

h Gen. 2. 8. &
13. 10.
Isa. 51. 3.

---

13. *How do the beasts groan!*] The sympathy of cattle with man in suffering, and even their punishment for his sin, as in the Flood, is a great mystery ; but the Hebrew Prophets, as Isa. xvi. 10; xxiv. 7. 11. Jer. xii. 4. Hos. iv. 3, and Joel here, the Prophet of Judgment, include the animal and the vegetable world in man's destiny, both for good and evil.

It is surely a solemn thought, that the sins of men and of nations are represented by Joel as adding to the groans of the brute creation, and as withering the fields, and blighting the shrubs and trees in the sylvan glades and noble forests of the natural world; and it is also a cheering thought, that he also displays man's repentance as having a beneficent and exhilarating effect on the herds and flocks of the pasture, and as imparting fruitfulness to the earth, and adding freshness to the landscape, and brighter colours to the flowers of the field. See below, ii. 21—24.

Why this is so, we do not yet know, but we shall know hereafter. That it is so, no devout reader of the prophetical Books of Holy Scripture can doubt.

We have also the comfort of believing, that though the Earth suffers now from man's sin, yet it will afterwards rejoice with our redeemed and glorified humanity, and be restored in new beauty, through the merits of Christ, and through the faith and obedience of His saints. See below, ii. 21, and Rom. viii. 22, 23.

19. *O LORD, to thee will I cry*] This is the only remedy in our distress, to cry unto Thee, O JEHOVAH, the Lord God of Israel. On the Name JEHOVAH, or JAHVE, see *Pocock* here, p. 252, and *Pusey*, on Hosea xii. 5, and above, on Exod. vi. 3.

CH. II. 1. *Blow ye the trumpet in Zion, and sound an alarm in my holy mountain*] Here is another proof that the Prophet passes, from God's judicial visitation inflicted by an army of locusts on His people for their sins, to another and severe divine Judgment, executed by a hostile force of terrible invaders, who are His instruments in the work of divine retribution. A trumpet is not blown, and an alarm is not sounded, to
31

muster the people to ward off a swarm of locusts ; but these warnings are uttered to gather together the people to repel the force of the invader. See Num. x. 9. Jer. iv. 5. Hos. v. 8; viii. 1; and Amos iii. 6, where the same language is used, and where the word rendered *cry aloud*, is the same as here translated *sound an alarm*. There is good reason, therefore, in S. Jerome's remark here, While we read of locusts, let us think of invading armies—" Dum locustas legimus, Babylonios cogitemus ;" and so S. Cyril and Theodoret.

— *the day of the* LORD *cometh*] The judicial visitation of this army of locusts reveals in the background other judgments of God on Jerusalem and on the world. The Prophet sees behind it the armies of Babylon and Rome, and the legions of Angels, with Christ coming at the Great Day to judge all Nations. The imagery of these several successive judgments, is blended together in a grand prophetic picture, as is done in our Lord's prophecy on the Mount of Olives, concerning His Coming to judge the world with legions of Angels (see below, on Matt. xxiv. 3, p. 85) : so that it is not easy to discern which phenomena in the prophetic scenery belong to the one event, and which appertain to the other.

— *nigh at hand*] The Day of the Lord is ever at hand ; it is present already in the eye of Him to Whom a thousand years are as one day ; it comes to every man virtually at his death, which cannot be far distant ; and it is foreshadowed in every physical and national visitation. See Phil. iv. 5. 1 Pet. iv. 7; and on 2 Pet. iii. 3—8.

2. *There hath not been ever the like*] Words repeated from the sacred history of Joshua commanding the sunlight to stand still—a prophetical figure of the act of the Divine Joshua at the Day of Doom. See above, the notes on Joshua x. 12—14.

3. *before them*] Rather, *before it*, before the Day. The Day of the Lord, by a magnificent abstraction, is revealed to the eye of the Prophet as a terrible Army. He sees it in the locusts ; he sees it in the invading forces of Babylon ; he sees it in the legions of Rome coming against Jerusalem—as in some sublime Alpine scenery, one ridge and range of mountains rises above

Before CHRIST about 800.

i And behind them a desolate wilderness;
Yea, and nothing shall escape them.
4 k The appearance of them *is* as the appearance of horses;
And as horsemen, so shall they run.
5 l Like the noise of chariots on the tops of mountains shall they leap,
Like the noise of a flame of fire that devoureth the stubble,
m As a strong people set in battle array.
6 Before their face the people shall be much pained:
n All faces shall gather † blackness.
7 They shall run like mighty men;
They shall climb the wall like men of war;
And they shall march every one on his ways,
And they shall not break their ranks:
8 Neither shall one thrust another;
They shall walk every one in his path:
And *when* they fall upon the ‖ sword, they shall not be wounded.
9 They shall run to and fro in the city;
They shall run upon the wall,
They shall climb up upon the houses;
They shall o enter in at the windows p like a thief.
10 q The earth shall quake before them;
The heavens shall tremble:
r The sun and the moon shall be dark,
And the stars shall withdraw their shining:
11 s And the LORD shall utter his voice before t his army:
For his camp *is* very great:
u For *he is* strong that executeth his word:
For the x day of the LORD *is* great and very terrible;
And y who can abide it?
12 Therefore also now, saith the LORD,

i Zech. 7. 14. k Rev. 9. 7. l Rev. 9. 9. m ver. 2. n Jer. 8. 21. Lam. 4. 8. Nahum 2. 10. † Heb. pot. ‖ Or, dart. o Jer. 9. 21. p John 10. 1. q Ps. 18. 7. r Isa. 13. 10. Ezek. 32. 7. ver. 31. ch. 3. 15. Matt. 24. 29. s Jer. 25. 30. ch. 3. 16. Amos 1. 2. t ver. 25. u Jer. 50. 34. Rev. 18. 8. x Jer. 30. 7. Amos 5. 18. Zeph. 1. 15. y Num. 24. 23. Mal. 3. 2.

---

another, and some grand gigantic peak towers above them all—so, the figure of Christ, the universal King, Conqueror, and Judge, and His judicial Throne, rise behind and above all these successive stages of judicial visitations.

— *escape them*] Escape it.

4. *The appearance of them*] *Its* appearance. It is to be regretted that our Translation has these words in the *plural* number: in the original they are in the *singular*, and refer to the Day of the Lord. The grandeur of the prophetic picture consists mainly in the concentration of various phenomena of Nature and History, past and future, into one great whole, "the Day of the Lord." Cp. *v.* 11.

— *of horses*] Locusts are often compared to horses by the Arabians (*Bochart*; *Pocock*, 261); and cp. Rev. ix. 7. "The shapes of the locusts were like unto horses prepared unto battle."

5. *Like the noise of chariots*] A prophetic image anticipated from the Assyrian invasion of Judah. See Isa. xxxvii. 24, "By the multitude of my chariots am I come up to the height of the mountains, to the sides of Lebanon."

6. *Before their face*] *Before its face*: the singular number. See on *v.* 4.

— *the people*] Rather, *peoples*, generally. All nations shall tremble at Christ's Coming to Judgment.

— *All faces shall gather blackness*] Some render it, *all faces shall withdraw their beauty* (*Gesen.*, *Keil*); but the verb *kabâts*, here used, occurs more than 120 times in the Bible, and by Joel himself three times besides in this passage, e.g. ii. 16; iii. 2. 11, and always in the sense of *to gather, to collect*. Cp. Lam. iv. 8. Nah. ii. 10.

— *blackness*] The ancient Versions connect the word here used (*pârur*) with *parur*, a pot, so called from a root signifying *to boil* (*Gesen.* 665, 689), and regard it as meaning "ollæ nigredinem," or "fuliginem." Modern Lexicographers render it *brightness* (*Gesen.* 665; *Fuerst*, iii. 2), and translate the phrase, *all faces draw in their brightness*, and become pale.

But, as was before observed, the sense of the word rendered *gather* (*kabâts*), is not to withdraw so that a thing may be absent, but to collect so that it may be present. Cp. *Pocock*, 261; *Pusey*, p. 117.

8. *fall upon the sword*] Here is another proof that the Prophet is not speaking merely of locusts. Men do not go forth against locusts with sword and spear, any more than they sound a trumpet to muster an army to repel them (*v.* 1). But this prophetic imagery declares that the executioners of God's judgments are irresistible.

9. *like a thief*] As our Lord Himself says, "Behold, I come as a thief" (Rev. iii. 3; xvi. 15); "The Day of the Lord so cometh as a thief in the night" (1 Thess. v. 2. 2 Pet. iii. 10). Cp. Matt. xxiv. 43. Luke xii. 39.

10. *before them*] Before it (in the singular number); i.e. the Day of the Lord.

11. *And the* LORD *shall utter his voice*] Rather, *And the* LORD *utters* (or, literally, *uttered*, in the perfect tense) *His voice*. The Prophet, in divine ecstasy, sees the judgment already present; he beholds the Day of the Lord; he hears the voice of the Archangel and the trump of God (1 Thess. iv. 16); the sun and the moon are dark, and the stars withdraw their shining. Compare our Lord's words concerning His Second Advent (Matt. xxiv. 29. Mark xiii. 24, 25).

— *his camp*] His *machaneh*, the word used by Jacob to describe the host of Angels at Mahanaim (Gen. xxxii. 2).

12. *Therefore also now*] Rather, *yet even now*: it is not yet too late, but it soon will be.

Before
CHRIST
about
800.
z Jer. 4. 1.
Hos. 12. 6. &
14. 1.
a Ps. 31. 18. &
51. 17.
b Gen. 37. 34.
2 Sam. 1. 11.
Jeb 1. 20.
c Exod. 34. 6.
Ps. 86. 5, 15.
Jonah 4. 2.
d Josh. 14. 12.
2 Sam. 12. 22.
2 Kings 19. 4.
Amos 5. 15.
Jonah 3. 9.
Zeph. 2. 3.
e Isa. 65. 8.
Hag. 2. 19.
f ch. 1. 9, 13.
g Num. 10. 3.
ver. 1.
h ch. 1. 14.
i Exod. 19. 10, 22.
k ch. 1. 14.
l 2 Chron. 20. 13.
m 1 Cor. 7. 5.
n Ezek. 8. 16.
Matt. 23. 35.
o Exod. 32. 11, 12.
Deut. 9. 26—29.
|| Or, *use a byword against them.*
p Ps. 42. 10. &
79. 10. & 115. 2.
Micah 7. 10.
q Zech. 1. 14. &
8. 2.
r Deut. 32. 36.
Isa. 60. 10.
s See ch. 1. 10.
Mal. 3. 10, 11, 12.
t See Exod. 10. 19.
u Jer. 1. 14.
x Ezek. 47. 18.
Zech. 14. 8.
y Deut. 11. 24.

<sup>z</sup> Turn ye *even* to me with all your heart,
And with fasting, and with weeping, and with mourning :
13 And <sup>a</sup> rend your heart, and not <sup>b</sup> your garments,
And turn unto the LORD your God :
For he *is* <sup>c</sup> gracious and merciful, slow to anger, and of great kindness,
And repenteth him of the evil.
14 <sup>d</sup> Who knoweth *if* he will return and repent,
And leave <sup>e</sup> a blessing behind him ;
*Even* <sup>f</sup> a meat offering and a drink offering unto the LORD your God ?
15 <sup>g</sup> Blow the trumpet in Zion,
<sup>h</sup> Sanctify a fast, call a solemn assembly :
16 Gather the people, <sup>i</sup> sanctify the congregation,
<sup>k</sup> Assemble the elders, <sup>l</sup> gather the children, and those that suck the breasts :
<sup>m</sup> Let the bridegroom go forth of his chamber,
And the bride out of her closet.
17 Let the priests, the ministers of the LORD, weep <sup>n</sup> between the porch and the altar,
And let them say, <sup>o</sup> Spare thy people, O LORD,
And give not thine heritage to reproach,
That the heathen should || rule over them :
<sup>p</sup> Wherefore should they say among the people, Where *is* their God ?
18 Then will the LORD <sup>q</sup> be jealous for his land, <sup>r</sup> and pity his people.
19 Yea, the LORD will answer and say unto his people,
Behold, I will send you <sup>s</sup> corn, and wine, and oil,
And ye shall be satisfied therewith :
And I will no more make you a reproach among the heathen :
20 But <sup>t</sup> I will remove far off from you <sup>u</sup> the northern *army*,
And will drive him into a land barren and desolate,
With his face <sup>x</sup> toward the east sea,
And his hinder part <sup>y</sup> toward the utmost sea,
And his stink shall come up, and his ill savour shall come up,

---

— *Turn ye even to me with all your heart*] This section, to v. 18, is appropriately appointed by the Church for the Epistle on the first of the Forty Days of Lent.

On this text see *Bp. Andrewes*, Sermons, i. 356.

**13.** *rend your heart*] Ps. li. 17. Ezek. xxxvi. 26, not only your garments. Cp. Hos. vi. 6.

**14.** *a meat offering*] Which had been taken away (i. 9, 13). Means of grace, the ministrations of the Word and Sacraments, are gifts of God, and proofs of His love, and will be vouchsafed in richer abundance as a reward to a penitent people.

**15.** *Blow the trumpet in Zion, sanctify a fast*] A remarkable expression. The true way of repelling our enemies, and averting the judgments which God sends by them, is by repentance. It is vain to blow the trumpet and sound an alarm to muster our armies (see *v.* 1), unless we obtain God's favour by repentance. The most effective trumpet is that which calls a Nation and a Church to wield its spiritual weapons of fasting and prayer in the Zion of the Church. The spiritual army of Christian congregations is the most powerful national defence.

**16.** *elders—children—bridegroom—bride*] Even they who were unfit to take part in a literal battle, or were exempt from going to war (Deut. xxiv. 5), must all form part of the spiritual army ; and a very important work they perform in it. Even the people of Nineveh recognized this truth. See Jonah iii. 5—10 ; cp. Judith iv. 9—13. The prayers of aged men and women, and of babes and sucklings, though disparaged by this world, are very powerful with God. As *Tertullian* says (Apol. 39), " Hæc vis Deo grata est." The Omnipotent allows Himself to be overcome by faith, and heaven itself is stormed by a siege of prayers.

**17.** *between the porch and the altar*] The brazen altar of
VOL. VI. PART II.—33

burnt-sacrifice. See above, 1 Kings vi. 3. 2 Chron. iii. 4 ; iv. 1 ; vii. 7 ; viii. 12.

— *That the heathen should rule over them*] Or, *scoff at them* (see margin), *saying* what follows. Here is another proof that the locusts mean a great deal more than a physical visitation. See the next verses.

**19.** *corn—wine—oil*] Here also Joel adopts the words of Hosea (ii. 22).

**20.** *I will remove far off from you the northern army*] The word "army" is not in the original, and would be better omitted. The promise is, " I will remove from you *the northern one*, or northman." Locusts did not come from the north to Palestine ; and this word is doubtless used to show that the judgment here described is not a mere physical plague. Cp. *Pusey*, 99. 123. The word *north* (*tsâphôn*) has an ominous sound. The north is, in Scripture, the quarter from which judicial visitations come (Jer. vi. 1 ; cp. above, on Jer. i. 11. Ps. xlviii. 2). This was realized to Israel and Judah in the invasions of Assyrians and Babylonians, and afterwards of the Romans, from the north. Cp. Isa. xiv. 31 ; xii. 25. Jer. i. 13—15 ; vi. 22 ; xv. 12 ; xxv. 9 ; r̄vi. 6. 10 ; l. 3. Ezek. xxvi. 7.

— *east sea*] The Dead Sea.

— *the utmost sea*] The hinder or western sea—the Mediterranean.

— *his stink shall come up*] The stench of the carcases of his army. This was signally verified in the destruction of the vast Assyrian army of Sennacherib before the walls of Jerusalem, in the Valley of Hinnom, or Tophet, the type of Hell, and in the deliverance of Jerusalem, in answer to the prayer of Hezekiah. See above, on Isa. xxx. 33 ; xxxiii. 11 ; xxxiv. 3 ; xxxvii. 36.

D

Before
CHRIST
about
>99.
† Heb. *he hath
magnified to do.*
a ch. 1. 18, 20.
a Zech. 8. 12.
See ch. 1. 19.

Because † he hath done great things.

²¹ Fear not, O land; be glad and rejoice :

For the LORD will do great things.

²² Be not afraid, ᵃ ye beasts of the field :

For ᵃ the pastures of the wilderness do spring,

For the tree beareth her fruit, the fig tree and the vine do yield their strength.

b Isa. 41. 16.
& 51. 10.
Hab. 3. 18.
Zech. 10. 7.
‖ Or, *a teacher of
righteousness.*
† Heb. *according
to righteousness.*
c Lev. 26. 4.
Deut. 11. 14. &
28. 12.
d James 5. 7.

²³ Be glad then, ye children of Zion, and ᵇ rejoice in the LORD your God : For he hath given you ‖ the former rain † moderately, and he ᶜ will cause to come down for you ᵈ the rain, the former rain, and the latter rain in the first *month.*

e ch. 1. 4.

f ver. 11.

²⁴ And the floors shall be full of wheat, And the fats shall overflow with wine and oil.

²⁵ And I will restore to you the years ᵉ that the locust hath eaten, the canker-worm, and the caterpiller, and the palmerworm, ᶠ my great army which I sent among you.

g Lev. 26. 5.
Ps. 22, 26.
See Lev. 26. 26.
Micah 6. 14.

²⁶ And ye shall ᵍ eat in plenty, and be satisfied, and praise the name of the LORD your God, that hath dealt wondrously with you : And my people shall never be ashamed.

h ch. 3. 17.
i Lev. 26. 11, 12.
Ezek. 37, 26,
27, 28.
k Isa. 45. 5, 21,
22.
Ezek. 39. 22, 28.
l Isa. 44. 3.
Ezek. 39, 29.
Acts 2. 17.
m Zech. 12. 10.
John 7. 39.
n Isa. 54. 13.   o Acts 21. 9.

²⁷ ʰ And ye shall know that I am ⁱ in the midst of Israel, And ᵏ that I am the LORD your God, and none else : And my people shall never be ashamed.

²⁸ ˡ And it shall come to pass afterward, *that* I ᵐ will pour out my spirit upon all flesh ; ⁿ and your sons and ᵒ your daughters shall prophesy, your

*That* destruction was a prophetic figure of the destruction of all the enemies of Christ and of His Church in the latter days. See above, on Isa. lxvi. 24.

— *Because he hath done great things*] Rather, as in the margin, *he hath magnified to do great things.* Such is the pride and presumption of the Sennacheribs of this world. They magnify themselves against God Himself. Cp. Jer. xlviii. 26. 42. Lam. i. 9. Dan. viii. 8—11. 25; xi. 36. Obad. 12. Zeph. ii. 8. 10, in all which passages the same word is used. But their haughtiness will be laid low; and the Lord will do great things and be magnified upon them.

21. *Fear not, O land*] Rather, *Fear not, O earth.* The Prophet had declared that the Earth and the animal and vegetable kingdoms are involved in suffering for man's sin; and he now reveals the joyful truth, that they will be renewed by God's mercy, on man's repentance and faith, which are made available by the Incarnation, Death, and Resurrection of Christ. Cp. Isa. lxv. 16, and the notes there. Amos ix. 13; and see the Apostolic development of this gracious assurance in Rom. viii. 19—22. 2 Pet. iii. 12, 13. Rev. xxi. 1.

THE TEACHER WHO WILL LEAD UNTO RIGHTEOUSNESS.

23. *he hath given you the former rain moderately*] Or rather, *he hath given you the Teacher for righteousness.* See margin and *Vulg.* and *Targum.* The word here rendered *former rain,* is, *moreh* (the *hiphil* participle of *yârâh,* to cast, to shoot, to lay foundations, to direct, to prescribe, whence *thôrah,* the *Law*); it is very rare in the sense of *early rain,* the word for which is *yôreh.* *Hengstenberg* denies that it is ever correctly rendered *rain.* See, however, the last clause of this verse. Ps. lxxxiv. 6, Isa. ix. 15; xxx. 10. Hab. ii. 18; and so *Pagnini, Munster, Castalio, Vatablus;* and so *Rabbi Japhet,* cited by *Aben Ezra,* and other Jewish Expositors; and *Abarbinel* says, "This is King Messias;" and so most Jewish Expositors (*Pocock,* 293). Joel seems to refer here to the words of Moses (Deut. xxxii. 2), "My *doctrine* shall drop as the *rain.*"

S. *Jerome* here says, "Vos quoque, quos justè post pœnitentiam voco filios Sion et Ecclesiæ, lætamini et gaudete, quia dedit vobis Deus Pater *Doctorem justitiæ,* et descendere facit pluvias temporaneas atque serotinas; juxta pluvia temporanea et serotina Vetus et Novum accipi Testamentum." Compare

*Hengstenberg* and *Keil,* who adopt the rendering, *Teacher;* and *Dr. Pusey* says, "It seems most probable that the Prophet prefixes to all the other promises that first, all-containing promise, of the Coming of Christ."

The promise is, that the Lord will send *the Teacher,* who will bring them *unto righteousness,* that is, not only guide them to it by His precepts and example, but make them partakers of righteousness, and give them justification by faith and mystical incorporation in Himself, Who is "the LORD our RIGHTEOUSNESS" (Jer. xxiii. 6). This has been declared by Hosea (x. 12), "Sow to yourselves in *righteousness,* reap in mercy, break up your fallow ground, for it is time to seek the Lord till He come and *rain righteousness* upon you." And thus the Hebrew Prophets prepare the way for the teaching of St. Paul (Rom. iii. 21—26), and this is confirmed by what follows, namely, by the promise of the sending of the Holy Ghost (v. 28). Justification by Christ must precede, in order that Sanctification by the Holy Spirit may follow. The sprinkling of Christ's Blood at the Passover must precede the sprinkling of the dews of the Spirit at Pentecost.

— *in the first month*] Or, *at the beginning;* or, *first of all.* See v. 23.

25. *cankerworm—caterpiller—palmerworm*] See i. 4.

27. *in the midst of Israel*] Though Israel is dispersed throughout the world, yet wherever they may be, the Lord will be "*in the midst*" of them, when they turn to Christ and become members of His Universal Church. They will find Zion there. Here, also, Joel adopts the words of his predecessor Hosea. See Hos. xi. 9.

28. *it shall come to pass afterward*] After the sending of the *Teacher of righteousness.* See v. 23.

THE PROMISE OF THE HOLY GHOST.

28—32. *I will pour out my spirit upon all flesh—shall call*] After the promise of the gift of the TEACHER Who will lead Israel unto *righteousness,* and Whose Coming will be to Israel an indwelling of the Lord JEHOVAH *in the midst* of them, the Prophet proceeds to speak of the Coming of the Holy Ghost, consequent on the Incarnation, Death, Resurrection, and Ascension of Christ. That this prophecy began to be fulfilled on the Day of Pentecost by the outpouring of the Holy Ghost at Jerusalem, we know from the Holy Spirit, speaking by St. Peter in Acts ii. 16—18, where the sacred writer adopts the words of the *Septuagint* here. The Spirit was poured upon *all flesh,* because "the Word was made flesh" (John i. 14), and of Him the old men shall dream dreams, your young men shall see visions : [29] And also upon [e] the servants and upon the handmaids in those days will I pour out my spirit. [30] And [q] I will shew wonders in the heavens and in the earth, blood, and fire, and pillars of smoke.

[31] [r] The sun shall be turned into darkness,
And the moon into blood,
[s] Before the great and the terrible day of the LORD come.

[32] And it shall come to pass, *that* [t] whosoever shall call on the name of the LORD shall be delivered :
For [u] in mount Zion and in Jerusalem shall be deliverance,
As the LORD hath said,
And in [x] the remnant whom the LORD shall call.

III. [1] For, behold, [a] in those days, and in that time, when I shall bring again the captivity of Judah and Jerusalem, [2] [b] I will also gather all nations, and will bring them down into [c] the valley of Jehoshaphat, and [d] will plead with

*Margin references (right):*
Before CHRIST about
[p] 1 Cor. 12. 13.
Gal. 3, 28.
[q] Col. 3, 11.
[q] Matt. 24, 29.
Mark 13, 24.
Luke 21, 11, 25.
[r] Isa. 13, 9, 10.
ch. 3, 1, 15.
ver. 10.
Matt. 24, 29.
Mark 13, 24.
Luke 21, 25.
Rev. 6, 12.
[s] Mal. 4, 5.
[t] Rom. 10, 13.

[u] Isa. 46, 13. & 59, 20.
Obad. 17.
Rom. 11, 26.
[x] Isa. 11, 11, 16.
Jer. 31, 7.
Micah 4, 7. &
Rom. 9, 27. &
11, 5, 7.
[a] Jer. 30, 3.
Ezek. 39, 11.
[b] Zech. 14, 2, 4.

[c] 2 Chron. 20, 26. ver. 12.  [d] Isa. 66, 16.  Ezek. 38, 22.

---

Baptist said, "He shall baptize you with the Holy Ghost, and with fire" (Matt. iii. 11). Cp. Acts i. 5.

The original, in *v.* 29, has, *upon the menservants* and *the maidservants.* This is paraphrased by the *Septuagint* into, *upon my manservants* and *upon maidservants*; and by St. Peter into, *on my servants* and *on my handmaidens,* implying that not only will the Spirit be poured out *upon all flesh* (i. e. Gentiles as well as Jews; see Isa. xi. 15. Acts ii. 39, "and all that are afar off;" cp. *Pocock,* 303), but that the humblest members of society, male and female slaves (cp. 1 Cor. vii. 21), will become God's servants in Christ by the unction of the Holy Ghost. St. Peter adds (Acts ii. 18), *and they shall prophesy,* which is not in the original—a cheering assurance, that even from the once-enslaved tribes of Africa, and from among the children of Ham, will be raised up Preachers of Christ.

The word *pillars* (like palm-trees, *Pocock,* 308) *of smoke*—probably referring to the pillar of cloud in the wilderness,—is paraphrased by the *Septuagint* and St. Peter into "*vapour of smoke;*" the allusion in the original (and in Cant. iii. 6, where see note) not being intelligible to non-Hebrew readers.

**31.** *The sun shall be turned into darkness*] In a certain sense, these prodigies were fulfilled in the Coming of Christ to punish Jerusalem, at the siege and capture of that city by the Romans. See *Joseph.* B. J. iv. 4. 5, and vi. 5. 3; and below, on Acts ii. 19. Cp. on Matt. xxiv. 6, 7. 29.

The Hebrew Rabbis suppose that these phenomena will be visible in the great battle of God's Church with the Powers of Gog and Magog (see *Pocock,* 310), that is, in the great conflict of the latter days. See above, on Ezek. xxxviii., xxxix.

But their full accomplishment is reserved for His Personal Advent at the Great Day. Cp. Matt. xxiv. 29. Luke xxi. 25. *Tertullian, Chrysostom, Theodoret.* Joel, as is usual with him, passes with a rapid flight from the one event to the other. There is a similar comprehensiveness in the Apocalypse (xiv. 14—20).

After the promise of Christ's Coming, and of the gift of the Holy Ghost, the Prophet proceeds to describe the awful phenomena of the Universal Judgment; for whoever despises the Gospel of Christ, and grieves the Holy Ghost, will feel the terrors of that dreadful Day (*A Lapide*).

— *terrible day*] The *Sept.,* and thence St. Peter (Acts ii. 20), call it "*notable day.*" It is probable that the *Sept.* substituted *nireah* (from *raah,* to see) for *norah* (from *yara,* to fear).

**32.** *whosoever shall call on the name of the LORD shall be delivered*] In the midst of this vision of Judgment there is Love. There is an universal Judgment to come; and there is an universal offer of Mercy to all who flee to Christ for Salvation; and this Salvation, which first began to be preached by the Apostles at Jerusalem, is freely offered to all in the spiritual Sion of His Church.

— *deliverance*] Rather, *a remnant delivered,* or *escaping* (Heb. *pelêytâh*). See *Sept.,* and cp. Isa. iv. 2; x. 20; xxxvii. 31, 32. Jer. l. 20. Ezek. xiv. 22; above, *v.* 3, and Obad. 14.

This word is exactly represented by the σωζόμενοι in the Acts of the Apostles. The words in Acts ii. 47, "those who should be saved," or, rather, "those who were escaping," refer to this passage of Joel.

— *as the* LORD *hath said*] Some suppose, said by Obadiah,

17. 21; but the opinion is more probable, that Joel here claims divine inspiration for himself, and characterizes his own words as words of God. Obadiah followed Joel. See on Obad. 10.

**RESTORATION IN CHRIST.**

**CH. III. 1.** *in those days—I shall bring again the captivity*] After the preaching of CHRIST, *the Teacher for righteousness* (ii. 23), and after the mission of the HOLY SPIRIT poured out upon all nations (ii. 28), I will *turn the captivity* (like a stream thrown back in its course; see Ps. cxxvi. 4; cp. Hos. vi. 11) of Judah and Jerusalem, and will bring them back to their home in Christ and His Church. Cp. above, on Ezek. xxxv.; note at the end of the chapter, pp. 238, 239.

Yet further, in a larger sense, *Judah* and *Jerusalem* comprehend and include Israel also. Those words not only denote that Nation according to the flesh, but include all the True Israel of God; all who are of the faith of Abraham, though not of his seed; all true believers, of what nation soever; all members of that heavenly new Jerusalem (Heb. xii. 22. Rev. iii. 12; xxi. 2), the Church of Christ, of which Judah and Jerusalem of old were an image and a type. Many of these may now be said to be strangers, pilgrims, and captives; but the promise is also to them. Cp. *Pocock,* 319.

**THE VALLEY OF JEHOSHAPHAT.**

**2.** *I will also gather all nations, and will bring them down into the valley of Jehoshaphat*] The restoration of Israel to God in Christ and His Church, will be followed by a judicial visitation of God on all hostile powers, and on all forms of Anti-christianism.

This is described here in prophetic language as the *bringing them down into the valley of Jehoshaphat.* They will be *brought down* from the lofty mountains of their arrogance, pride, and presumption, into a lowly valley, *the valley of Jehoshaphat,* which means, *judgment of the Lord.* Cp. *v.* 12, "Let the heathen come up" (or, let them rise up in insurrection against God, and come) "to the *valley of Jehoshaphat,* for there will I sit to *judge* the heathen round about."

It has been supposed by some (since the days of *Eusebius* and *Jerome*) that the Valley of Jehoshaphat had a local existence on the east side of Jerusalem, in the deep ravine more commonly called Kidron or Kedron, between the city and the Mount of Olives; and that name, since the fourth century of the Christian era, has been applied to that valley. *Mr. Grove* (Bib. Dict. i. 951) well observes, that "at what period the name was first applied to that spot is not known: there is no trace of it in the Bible or Josephus." And there is no reason to believe that the appellation *Valley of Jehoshaphat* was known to the ancient inhabitants of Jerusalem as a proper name, designating the Valley of Kedron, or any other in the neighbourhood of their city.

It is probable that the Valley of Kedron, as well as of Hinnom, was the scene of the great destruction of the immense Assyrian host of Sennacherib—a destruction which, as we have seen (on Isa. lxvi. 24. Jer. xxxi. 30; l. 21), was regarded by the Prophets as figurative of the future overthrow and extinction of God's enemies; and perhaps this circumstance

Before
CHRIST
about
860.

*e* Obad. 11.
Nahum 3. 10.

*f* Amos 1. 6, 9.
*g* Ezek. 25. 15,
16, 17.

† Heb. *desirable.*
Dan. 11. 38.
† Heb. *the sons
of the Grecians.*

*h* Isa. 43. 5, 6. &
45. 13.
Jer. 26. 8.

*i* Ezek. 23. 42.
*k* Jer 6. 20.
1 See Isa. 8. 9, 10.
Jer. 46. 3, 4.
Ezek. 38. 7.
† Heb. *Sanctify.*

*m* See Isa. 2. 4.
Micah 4. 3.

|| Or. *scythes.*

*n* Zech. 12. 8.

*o* ver. 2.

them there for my people and *for* my heritage Israel, whom they have scattered among the nations, and parted my land. ³ And they have ᵉ cast lots for my people; and have given a boy for an harlot, and sold a girl for wine, that they might drink.

⁴ Yea, and what have ye to do with me, ᶠO Tyre, and Zidon, and all the coasts of Palestine? ᵍ will ye render me a recompence? and if ye recompense me, swiftly *and* speedily will I return your recompence upon your own head;

⁵ Because ye have taken my silver and my gold, and have carried into your temples my goodly † pleasant things: ⁶ The children also of Judah and the children of Jerusalem have ye sold unto † the Grecians, that ye might remove them far from their border.

⁷ Behold, ʰ I will raise them out of the place whither ye have sold them, and will return your recompence upon your own head: ⁸ And I will sell your sons and your daughters into the hand of the children of Judah, and they shall sell them to the ⁱ Sabeans, to a people ᵏ far off: for the LORD hath spoken *it*.

⁹ ˡ Proclaim ye this among the Gentiles;

† Prepare war, wake up the mighty men,

Let all the men of war draw near; let them come up:

¹⁰ ᵐ Beat your plowshares into swords,

And your || pruninghooks into spears:

ⁿ Let the weak say, I *am* strong.

¹¹ ᵒ Assemble yourselves, and come, all ye heathen,

---

may have connected the name *Valley of Jehoshaphat* with them. There may have been this historical basis for the appellation. Joel may be foretelling here the destruction of Sennacherib's army, as a typical foreshadowing of the future overthrow of all the enemies of God and His spiritual Sion.

This name, *Valley of Jehoshaphat* (which does not occur any where else in the Holy Scriptures), seems to be formed by Joel, by a grand process of abstraction and generalization familiar to Hebrew poetry (like the name *Valley of decision*, or *of cutting to pieces*, in v. 14), as a symbolical representative of *Divine Judgment* wherever executed, and may be compared to the word *Armageddon* (i. e. *Mount of cutting to pieces*) in the Apocalypse. See below, on Rev. xvi. 13—16. We have seen many similar examples of this process, in the Song of Solomon, and in Jeremiah and Ezekiel. See above, *Introd.* to Canticles, p. 135; and on Jer. xxxi. 39; l. 21. Ezek. xviii. 23. This has been already observed by the Hebrew Rabbis, as *David Kimchi* here, "*Nominatur vallis Josaphat de nomine judicii Dei;*" and *S. Jerome*, "Omnis, qui judicatur propter peccata sua, in *valle positus est*, quae vocatur *Josaphat*, i. e. Dei judicium." *Munster* (on v. 19) says, "Joel here clearly shows that the *Valley of Jehoshaphat* is not limited to *any one place*; but wheresoever God executes judgment on the persecutors of His Church, there is a *Valley of Jehoshaphat*." Compare *Pocock*, 337.

In this view, this prophecy of Joel may be compared with the larger prophecy of Ezekiel, concerning the gathering together of infidel Powers in the latter days, against Christ and His Church, and their full and final discomfiture. See above, on Ezek. xxxviii, xxxix. "Nos" (says *S. Jerome*) "have juxta tropologiam eos qui contra Ecclesiam dimicant, et qui sub Anti-Christo adversus sanctos Domini pugnaturi sunt, accipere possumus; qui ideirco congregantur, ut pereant."

Joel's prophecies are like cartoons, which were afterwards enlarged and filled up in the grand pictures of Ezekiel. Cp. Ezek. xxxiv. to the end, with Joel. They close with the same cheering assurance of God's perpetual presence with His Church; and what has been said in the notes on those prophecies above, may serve as a commentary here.

— *they have scattered among the nations.* As the Assyrians did, and afterwards the Chaldeans and Romans. Joel foresees the dispersion of Israel and Judah.

3. *they have cast lots.*] As the Assyrians did (Nah. iii. 10). Cp. Obad. 11.

— *have given a boy for an harlot.*] They have sold a Hebrew boy to a harlot for her hire, and a Hebrew girl for a night's

revelry. This was done by Assyrians, Chaldees, and still more by the Romans. *Josephus* describes (B. J. vi. 2, 9) how Titus, the conqueror of Jerusalem, disposed of 97,000 Jewish captives. Some were executed; some sold as slaves; some reserved to fight in the arena with wild beasts; others to be led in the triumphal procession to the Capitol. In the times of the Jewish wars with Antiochus Epiphanes, a thousand slave-dealers followed the Syrian army, and carried chains with them for Jewish prisoners (1 Macc. iii. 41. 2 Macc. viii. 11. 25. *Joseph.* Ant. xii. 7. 3).

4. *what have ye to do with me*] How have I wronged you, O ye Philistines, Tyrians, Sidonians, that ye should inflict such injuries on My People? *Will ye render Me a recompence?* Have I done you any harm, that ye should seek to retaliate? Woe to you, if ye thus strive with Me. I have not injured you, but ye have spoiled Me.

The Philistines, Tyrians, and Sidonians are symbolical representatives of all those classes of persons who acrilegiously rob the Church of God, and who make merchandise of her people, for their own aggrandizement or gratification. See *A Lapide* here.

5. *ye have taken my silver and my gold*] In the time of Jehoram, son of Jehoshaphat, about B.C. 887. See 2 Chron. xxi. 16, 17.

6. *Grecians*] Heb. *Yevanim* (Gen. x. 2. 4. 1 Chron. i. 5. 7. Isa. lxvi. 19. Ezek. xxvii. 13. Dan. viii. 21; x. 20; xi. 2. Zech. ix. 13).

8. *I will sell your sons—into the hand of the children of Judah*] Probably on the defeat of the Philistines by Uzziah (2 Chron. xxvi. 6, 7), and by Hezekiah (2 Kings xviii. 8). See on Isa. xiv. 28, 29. 31. Perhaps there may be also a prophetic reference to the victories of the Maccabees.

This prophecy (says *S. Jerome*) is to be understood not only in a literal sense, but in a spiritual. The Prophet is foretelling the triumphs of the Israel of God—the Christian Church—which will overcome the heathen Nations, by the weapons of the Gospel, and will deliver them into the hands of the *children of Judah*, that is, of *true* believers, in order to be taught and guided by them in the faith of Christ. Compare note above, on Ps. cxliv. 7—9.

— *Sabeans*] See Job i. 15. Ezek. xxvii. 22.

9. *Prepare war*] Literally, *Sanctify a war*; by God's command, for the vindication of His glory. See above, on Jer. vi. 4.

10. *Beat your plowshares into swords*] The reverse of what is done in times of peace (Isa. ii. 4. Mic. iv. 3).

11. *Assemble yourselves*] Or, *Hasten* (Gesen. 616; Keil).

And gather yourselves together round about :

Thither ‖ cause ᵖ thy mighty ones to come down, O LORD.

¹² Let the heathen be wakened, ᵍ and come up to the valley of Jehoshaphat :

For there will I sit to ʳ judge ₐall the heathen round about.

¹³ ˢ Put ye in the sickle, for ᵗ the harvest is ripe :

Come, get you down ; for the ᵘ press is full, the fats overflow ;

For their wickedness *is* great ;

¹⁴ Multitudes, multitudes in ˣ the valley of ‖ decision :

For ʸ the day of the LORD *is* near in the valley of decision ;

¹⁵ The ᶻ sun and the moon shall be darkened,

And the stars shall withdraw their shining ;

¹⁶ The LORD also shall ᵃ roar out of Zion,

And utter his voice from Jerusalem ;

And ᵇ the heavens and the earth shall shake :

ᶜ But the LORD *will be* the † hope of his people,

And the strength of the children of Israel.

¹⁷ So ᵈ shall ye know that I *am* the LORD your God

Dwelling in Zion, ᵉ my holy mountain :

Then shall Jerusalem be † holy,

And there shall no ᶠ strangers pass through her any more.

¹⁸ And it shall come to pass in that day,

*That* the mountains shall ᵍ drop down new wine,

*(Marginal references, right column:)*

Before
CHRIST
about
80.

‖ Or, *the LORD*
*shall bring down,*
p Ps. 103. 20.
Isa. 13. 3.
q ver. 2.
r Ps. 96. 13. &
98. 9. & 110. 6.
Isa. 2. 4. & 3. 11.
Micah 4. 3.
s Matt. 12. 39.
Rev. 14. 15, 18.
t ver. 51, 23.
Hos. 6. 11.
u Isa. 63. 3.
Lam. 1. 15.
Rev. 14. 19, 20.
x ver. 2.
‖ Or, *concision,*
*or, threshing.*
y ch. 2. 1.
z ch. 2. 10. 31.
a Jer. 25. 30.
ch. 2. 11.
Amos 1. 2.

b Hag. 2. 6.

c Isa. 51. 5, 6.
† Heb. *place of*
*repair, or,*
*harbour.*

d ch. 2. 27.
e Dan. 11. 45.
Obad. 16.
Zech. 8. 3.
† Heb. *holiness.*

f Isa. 35. 8. &
52. 1.
Nahum 1. 15.
Zech. 14. 21.
Rev. 21. 27.

g Amos 9. 13.

---

### THE WORLD'S HARVEST AND VINTAGE.

**13.** *Put ye in the sickle—the press is full*] These are the words of Christ, the Lord and Judge of all, to "the reapers," "the Angels." See Matt. xiii. 30—39 (*S. Jerome*).

### THE FUTURE UNIVERSAL JUDGMENT.

Here are two metaphors, both of them symbolical of Judgment—the Harvest and the Wine-press. See below, on Rev. xiv. 14—20, where the same imagery is used. Christ is revealed as the principal Agent in these judicial visitations of the whole world. See Matt. xiii. 30. 39, and Rev. xix. 15, " He treadeth the wine-press of the fierceness and wrath of Almighty God."

In this prophetic description, God's judgments against the Nations, especially against the enemies of His People, which in the world's history may occupy a long period of time, are brought together and concentrated in one focus. They are comprehended in one great Harvest, and one great Vintage, the Harvest and Vintage of the GREAT DAY, to which they were preparatory, and of which they form a part, in the Eye of God, Who sees all things at one view, and in the eye of the Prophet, who is inspired by Him.

— *get you down*] Rather, *Tread ye*, trample under your feet, the ripe grapes of the nations in the wine-press of judgment.

**14.** *Multitudes, multitudes in the valley of decision*] Or, in *the valley of cutting to pieces,* like sheaves crushed on the threshing-floor by the sharp-toothed instrument which was formed with revolving cylinders, and by which they were threshed.

The *Valley of Jehoshaphat,* or Judgment of God (see v. 2), is the World's threshing-floor; and rebellious men and nations are compared to sheaves that have been reaped in the World's harvest, and are cast on the floor to be threshed. As *Mercer* well says, " *Vallis decisionis est ubicumque Dominus impios Ecclesiæ persecutores concidit.*" However numerous they may be in multitude, however furious the uproar they may make in their bold and blasphemous insurrection, raging against God (Ps. ii. 1, 2), yet He will gather them all together into the threshing-floor of His judgment, and cast them down prostrate there. Both ideas, namely of number and noise, are joined in the word *hamónim* used here, and rendered *multitudes.* See *Gesen.* 227. Cp. Judges iv. 7. 1 Sam. iv. 14; xiv. 19. Isa. xiii. 4; xvii. 12. Ezek. xxxi. 18; xxxix. 11. 15, " Gog and all his multitude," and the word *Hamon-Gog* used there, which connects that passage with the present, referring to the same great event. The vast aggregate of surging and tumultuous

multitudes will be mown down in the day of the World's harvest, and will be thrown into the Divine threshing-floor, with the same ease as that with which the reaper reaps a field, and flings the sheaves down on the floor (Mic. iv. 12) to be crushed by the sharp-toothed instrument (Hebr. *chárutz*). Cp. Isa. xxviii. 27; xli. 15, and below, on Amos i. 3 ; and note above, on Prov. xx. 26, " A wise king," especially *the* Wise King, Which is Christ the Judge of all, " scattereth the wicked, and bringeth the wheel over them," by which they are threshed. See also Isa. xxi. 10. Jer. li. 33. Mic. iv. 13, where the same metaphor is used ; and *Jahn,* Archæol. Bibl. § 64 ; and *Pocock,* 342, 343.

In the Apocalypse (as before observed) the word *Armageddon* (lit. *mountain of cutting* ; see below, on Rev. xvi. 16) expresses the same truth. That prophecy speaks of a time when the enemies of Christ and His Church will be gathered together in a great conflict ; the issue of which will be that they will be routed and cut to pieces.

**16.** *The LORD also shall roar out of Zion*] As a lion from his lair. Here, also, Joel again takes up the language of Hosea (Hos. v. 14). Cp. Amos iii. 4. Zion and Jerusalem here are not the city of the earthly Palestine, but the sanctified City of the Living God, which, taking its origin from Calvary, and from the place where the Holy Spirit came down at Pentecost, has become the Universal Church, and enfolds the World. See above, on Isa. ii. 2, 3, and on Ezek. xxxv ; the note at the end of the chapter.

Christ, the Lion of the Tribe of Judah, now roars from Zion. He preaches aloud with a voice of power in His Church ; and the Day is coming, when He will roar with a louder voice to destroy His enemies. He will deliver a fearful sentence of judgment, like the roaring of a lion, upon the ungodly, out of the Zion of the Church glorified " Depart from Me : ye cursed, into everlasting fire" (Matt. xxv. 41). *Bp. Hall, Pocock,* Diodati.

### THE GLORY OF THE CHURCH.

**17.** *Then shall Jerusalem be holy, and there shall no strangers pass through her any more*] Such will be the condition of the Church glorified and triumphant. She will then be the pure, holy Bride, arrayed in fair linen clean and white (Rev. xix. 8. 14 ; xxi. 2), and without spot, or wrinkle, or any such thing (Eph. v. 25—27). All things that offend will have been rooted out of her field (Matt. xiii. 41).

**18.** *the mountains shall drop down new wine*] Compare Amos ix. 13 ; Zech. xiv. 6 ; and especially Ezek. xlvii. 1—12, describing the happy condition of the Church of Christ, under the gracious

And the hills shall flow with milk,

ᵏ And all the rivers of Judah shall † flow with waters,

And ˡ a fountain shall come forth of the house of the LORD,

And shall water ᵘ the valley of Shittim.

19 ˡ Egypt shall be a desolation,

And ᵐ Edom shall be a desolate wilderness,

For the violence *against* the children of Judah,

Because they have shed innocent blood in their land.

20 But Judah shall ‖ dwell ⁿ for ever,

And Jerusalem from generation to generation ;

21 For I will º cleanse their blood *that* I have not cleansed :

ᵖ ‖ For the LORD dwelleth in Zion.

*Margin references (left column):*
Before CHRIST about 800
k Isa. 30. 25.
† Heb. go.
l Ps. 46. 4.
Ezek. 47. 1.
Zech. 14. 8.
Rev. 22. 1.
k Num. 25. 1.
m Jer. 49. 17.
Ezek. 25. 12, 13.
Amos 1. 11.
Obad. 10.
‖ Or, *abide.*
n Amos 9. 15.
o Isa. 4. 4.
p Ezek. 48. 35.
ver. 17.
Rev. 21. 3.
‖ Or, *even I the LORD that dwelleth in Zion.*

---

influence of the Holy Spirit, and of the Gospel of Christ, in similar imagery derived from the natural world.

THE FOUNTAIN FROM THE LORD'S HOUSE.

— *a fountain shall come forth of the house of the* LORD, *and shall water the valley of Shittim*] The fountain from the house of the Lord in Zion will flow down even to the land of Moab, and the barren valley of Shittim, far off from Jerusalem, once the scene of the sin of Israel's lust and idolatry (see Num. xxv.), but now to become the garden of the Lord. These words are not to be understood in a literal and carnal sense. No fountain ever did spring or could spring from the temple, such as to flow down into the plain of Moab (*A Lapide*). But the Prophet takes occasion from the existence of a real spring of water under the temple, to spiritualize that circumstance, and to apply it in a figurative sense.

This image is expanded by Zechariah (xiv. 8), and much more by Ezekiel, who describes the living waters of the Gospel, issuing forth from the Lord's house, and making beautiful trees to flourish on its bank, and flowing down even into the Dead Sea of human corruption, and cleansing and making it teem with life. See above, Ezek. xlvii. 1—12, and the RETROSPECT to it, pp. 286, 287, which may serve for a comment here.

In the words of S. Jerome, slightly modified and paraphrased, "a fountain will flow forth from the house of the Lord, which is the Church of Christ. It is described by Zechariah and Ezekiel at the close of their prophecies. Its beneficent purpose will be, to change our barren land of Shittim (or *acacias*), which yields only thorns and briars, into fallow land of the Lord; and to refresh our dry places with copious streams: so that, instead of brambles, we may yield flowers; and in order that in the same Moab, where Israel was guilty of harlotry, and was initiated into the foul orgies of Baalpeor, the lilies of chastity and roses of virgin modesty may flourish, and diffuse a sweet perfume."

Christ Himself, Who pours forth the living waters of the Spirit in His Word and Sacraments ministered in His Church, is ever irrigating the dry and barren wilderness of this world's wilderness, once defiled by Moabitish lusts and idolatries, and is changing them into a holy Eden, a spiritual Paradise.

19. *Egypt—and Edom*] Types of God's Enemies: Egypt, the foreign, open foe ; Edom, connected with Israel by origin, the

treacherous friend of the Church of God. See *Prelim. Note* to Isa. xiii., xxxiv., lxiii., and to Jer. xlvi. ; xlix. 7. Ezek. xxv. 14 ; xxix. 2.

20. *Judah shall dwell for ever*] From these words it is evident that the Prophet is *not* speaking of the *earthly* Jerusalem (as the Jews and Judaizers imagine), but of the Spiritual Zion, the Church of God, which will never be destroyed on earth (Matt. xvi. 18), and with which Christ will ever be present (Matt. xxviii. 20), and which will exist for ever in heaven (*A Lapide*). See also on v. 17.

21. *I will cleanse their blood that I have not cleansed*] I will wipe off the score of bloodguiltiness that I have not wiped off. In this world God seems for a time to leave sinners to themselves, and to let them escape with impunity. But the time is coming, when all unrepented sins of persons and nations, however they may seem to have escaped His notice, will be visited with full retribution. Cp. Ps. lviii. 10, 11, and Rev. vi. 10.

Or the sense may be (as S. Jerome suggests), In the Church of God I will cleanse the blood that I have not cleansed under the Levitical Law by the sacrifices offered in the Tabernacle and the Temple. Cp. Isa. iv. 4. "When the Lord shall have washed away the filth of the daughters of Zion, and have purged the blood of Jerusalem from the midst thereof by the Spirit of judgment, and by the Spirit of burning." By means of " *the fountain opened for sin and uncleanness in Zion,*" that is, by the Blood of Jesus Christ the Son of God, *which cleanseth from all sin* (1 John i. 7. Cp. Rev. i. 5; vii. 14). I will wash those clean who could not be washed by the ceremonial washings or blood-sheddings of the Levitical Law, or by any other means. This shall be done in the Church of God ; for *the Lord dwelleth in Zion.*

— *the* LORD *dwelleth in Zion*] The Prophet had promised that *Judah should dwell* (literally *sit, abide, or remain*) *for ever* (v. 20). That is, the elect of God shall dwell for ever in His holy habitation (*Bp. Hall*); and the reason is, because the Lord dwelleth, literally *tabernacleth, in Zion* (*Sept.*). Cp. Rev. xxi. 15 ; xxi. 3 where the same image is used.

The prophecies of Ezekiel are summed up in the same assurance (given in their final words, *Jehovah-shammah*) of the Lord's perpetual presence with His Church. "Lo! I am with you alway," says the Lord of all, "even unto the end of the world" (Matt. xxviii. 20).

# AMOS.

I. ¹ THE words of Amos, who was among the herdmen of ᵇ Tekoa, which he saw concerning Israel ᶜ in the days of Uzziah king of Judah, and in the days of ᵈ Jeroboam the son of Joash king of Israel, two years before the ᵉ earthquake.

² And he said, The LORD will ᶠ roar from Zion,
And utter his voice from Jerusalem;
And the habitations of the shepherds shall mourn,
And the top of ᵍ Carmel shall wither.

Before
CHRIST
787.
a ch. 7. 14.
b 2 Sam. 14. 2.
2 Chron. 20. 20.
c Hos. 1. 1.
d cb. 7. 10.
e Zech. 14. 5.
f Jer. 25. 30.
Joel 3. 16.

g 1 Sam. 25. 2.
Isa. 33. 9.

---

CH. I.] The prophecies of Amos are a sequel to those of Joel. Joel, whose name signifies "the Lord (Jehovah) is God," had displayed in one comprehensive view the judgments of God brought together and concentrated in a grand climax, "the Day of the Lord." He had foreshown the destruction of all the Lord's enemies; he had also displayed His Divine Supremacy, and His everlasting love for the spiritual Zion of His Church; He had closed his prophecies with an assurance of the Lord's perpetual abiding in her.

Amos, whose name signifies *bearer*, takes up the message and delivers it in several prophetic *burdens* of judgment (or *massas*; see on Isa. xxii., *Prelim. Note*) to the several Nations of the Earth.

He marks also his own connexion with Joel by adopting, at the beginning of his prophecy, the closing words of Joel, significant of God's judicial Majesty in His Church, "The Lord will roar out of Zion and utter His voice from Jerusalem" (i. 2). See Joel iii. 6. 16.

For further remarks on this subject, see above, the INTRODUCTION to the Minor Prophets generally.

1. *herdmen*] As he himself says (vii. 14), "I am no Prophet nor a Prophet's son, but a herdman and a gatherer of sycomore fruit."

Amos, the shepherd of Tekoa, in the wilderness of Judah, loves to introduce pastoral imagery in his prophecies. The lions roar (i. 2; iii. 4), the conflict of the shepherd with the lion (iii. 12), the kine of Bashan (iv. 3) driven through a gap in a hedge, the cart full of sheaves (ii. 13), the bird in the gin of the fowler (iii. 5), and other rural objects, were associated with his own life, and give a natural freshness to his writings.

— *Tekoa*] About six miles to the south of Bethlehem, according to S. *Jerome*, who says (on Jer. vi. 1) that he himself, residing at Bethlehem, had Tekoa daily before his eyes. In his preface to his Commentary on Amos, he repeats the same statement. "This Prophet" (he says) "was of the town of Tekoa," six miles south of the holy Bethlehem, which gave birth to the Saviour of the World. Beyond it is no village, nor even any cottages or huts; such is the desolation of that wilderness, which extends even to the Red Sea. But it affords a free range for shepherds, of whom was Amos the Prophet, "rude in speech, but not in knowledge" (2 Cor. xi. 6), for "One and the same Spirit spake by all the Prophets" (2 Pet. i. 21). Cp. *Hackett's* description in B. D. ii. 1146, and *Robinson*, i. 486, and *Dr. Thomson*, 606.

As to the position and history of Tekoa, see also above, on Josh. xv. 59. 2 Sam. xiv. 2; xxiii. 26. 1 Chron. ii. 24; iv. 5. 2 Chron. xi. 6; xx. 20. Neh. iii. 5. 27. Jer. vi. 1. It is now called *Tekua*.

It is observable that Amos, the shepherd of Tekoa, south of Bethlehem in Judah, directs his prophecies specially to the ten tribes of Israel. He thus presents an example of Divine kindness and tender sympathy for aliens and rebels; and in this respect is like the Good Shepherd, Who was born at Bethlehem, and laid down His life for His sheep when they had gone astray.

Amos tells us that he prophesied in the time during which Uzziah king of Judah and Jeroboam II. king of Israel were contemporary, viz. twenty-seven years, between B.C. 810 and B.C. 783. He, therefore, began his prophetic labours about the same time as Hosea (see Hosea i. 1), and he prophesied to Israel as Hosea did, and at Bethel, the seat of Israel's idolatry (vii. 10).

— *two years before the earthquake*] In the days of Uzziah (Zech. xiv. 5). *Josephus* (Ant. ix. 10. 4) connects this earthquake with the sin of Uzziah in invading the High Priest's office, and offering incense in the Temple. And this statement has been adopted by S. *Jerome*, S. *Cyril*, and most ancient interpreters, Christian and Hebrew. See *A Lapide* here.

It has been alleged that this is an error, because the earthquake took place, according to Amos, two years after he himself began to prophesy; and he prophesied while Jeroboam II. and Uzziah were contemporaries, that is, in some part of the twenty-seven years before Jeroboam's death; and Uzziah survived Jeroboam twenty-five years; therefore the earthquake must have been more than twenty-two years before Uzziah's death. But it is said that (as a consequence of his father's incapacity) Jotham his son was over the king's house judging the people of the land (2 Chron. xxvi. 21), and Jotham was only twenty-five years old at his father's death (2 Chron. xxvii. 1); and therefore it is alleged, that if the earthquake occurred when Uzziah was stricken with leprosy, it must have taken place *long after* Jeroboam's death, i.e. *long after* any of the time in which Uzziah and Jeroboam were contemporary, and much more than two years after the time in which Amos prophesied.

But this reasoning is grounded on the assumption, that Jotham *began* to be regent *immediately* after his father was stricken with leprosy, which is nowhere asserted in Scripture.

It is a noteworthy coincidence, that Isaiah's vision of the Seraphim in the Temple, and his message of mercy through Christ, is connected with the death of the leprous King Uzziah. See above, on Isa. vi. 1.

Amos mentions the *earthquake* as God's voice in nature (cp. Rev. vi. 12), echoing His voice in Prophecy; similarly Joel represents armies of locusts as harbingers of judgment.

2. *The LORD will roar from Zion, and utter his voice from Jerusalem*] Thus Amos joins on his own prophecy of judgment to that of Joel (iii. 16). God roared out of Zion by the voice of Joel, and of Amos himself, denouncing His judgments. And God roared by the voice of the Earthquake, confirming that denunciation by a solemn peal of subterranean thunder. The Earthquake was, as it were, an *Amen* to the prophecy.

— *the habitations of the shepherds shall mourn*] Amos, like Joel, notes the sympathy of the natural world with man in his punishment. See above, on Joel i. 18.

— *Carmel*] The fair and fruitful region, literally *garden* of God. See above, Cant. vii. 5. Isa. xxxiii. 9; xxxv. 2.

**3** Thus saith the LORD ;

For three transgressions of <sup></sup> Damascus, ‖ and for four, I will not ‖ turn away the punishment thereof ;

¹ Because they have threshed Gilead with threshing instruments of iron :

**4** ‖ But I will send a fire into the house of Hazael,
Which shall devour the palaces of Ben-hadad.

**5** I will break also the ¹ bar of Damascus,
And cut off the inhabitant from ‖ the plain of Aven,
And him that holdeth the sceptre from ‖ the house of Eden :
And <sup>m</sup> the people of Syria shall go into captivity <sup>n</sup> unto Kir, saith the LORD.

**6** Thus saith the LORD ; For three transgressions of <sup>o</sup> Gaza, and for four, I will not turn away *the punishment* thereof ;

Because they ‖ carried away captive the whole captivity,

---

### THE PROPHETIC BURDENS.

**3.** *For three transgressions of Damascus, and for four]* This is a prophetic formula which may be compared with the similar phrase in Proverbs xxx. 15, 18, 21, 29, where the numbers three and four are combined in a like manner. We may also compare the "torque quaterque beati" of *Virgil,* and the French use of *très,* in *très bon, très sage,* &c.

This prophetic formula is repeated eight times by Amos. It notes two things; first, God's long-suffering for a time, in order that men may repent and escape punishment; secondly, the certainty of that punishment.

It is remarkable that none of these *Burdens* of Amos are addressed to the greatest Powers of the heathen World, opposed to Israel and Judah—Assyria and Babylon. The Holy Spirit, Who spake by him, reserved the declaration of the destinies of these two great kingdoms for two other of the Twelve Minor Prophets. Assyria was reserved for Nahum; Babylon for Habakkuk. There seems, therefore, to have been Divine forethought in this omission. The desolation of Egypt (not mentioned by Amos), had been declared already by Joel iii. 19.

The Lord God of Israel, in delivering these *burdens* by Amos (the *bearer*), concerning the destiny of heathen lands, proved that He is not a local Deity (as the heathen thought their own gods to be), but is the Supreme Ruler of all Nations; and that their gods, who cannot help them, are mere vanities. By revealing also the judgments impending on His Own People Israel and Judah, He shows that these heathen nations which punished them for their idolatry (i. e. Assyria and Babylon), did not do it by their own power, but were executioners of His Divine Will, and were instruments in His hands for vindicating His own power, majesty, and truth.

Thus these prophecies of Amos are fraught with moral instruction not only to Israel and Judah (for if God punished the heathen who did not know Him, how much more would He chastise Israel and Judah for their sins), but also to the heathen world. Compare the notes above, on Isaiah's *burdens* (Isa. xiii. *Prelim. Note,* pp. 36—38), and the prophecies of Jeremiah and Ezekiel concerning the Heathen Nations of the World (Jer. xlvi.—li. Ezek. xxv.—xxxii.

On the spiritual interpretation of these prophecies, and their relation to the Christian Church, see above, on Isa. xiii. and the passages of Jeremiah (xlvi.) and Ezekiel (xxv.) just cited. Inasmuch as these prophecies of Amos are enlarged by the books of Isaiah, Jeremiah, and Ezekiel, it will not be necessary to repeat what has been already said concerning them in commenting on those books.

The prophecies of Amos are expanded by succeeding Prophets. Amos himself takes up the prophecy of Joel, whom he succeeds; Joel, by a magnificent generalization, had displayed all God's judgments in nature and history as concentrated in one Great *Day of the Lord.* Amos disintegrates this great whole, and particularizes those judgments. Joel declares that God will judge *all collectively.* Amos proclaims that He will judge each *singly.* And by saying that *for three transgressions and for four,* God will not reverse the judgment of each nation taken singly, he implies that each transgression is registered in God's book of reckoning.

— *Damascus]* The capital of Syria, which prospered under

Hazael, and invaded and subdued the eastern region of Israel (2 Kings x. 32, 33; xiii. 7; cp. 2 Kings viii. 12).

— *I will not turn away*] I will not reverse.

— *they have threshed Gilead with threshing instruments of iron*] Here again Amos adopts the imagery of Joel (see Joel iii. 14). The machine here mentioned is described by S. *Jerome* "as a kind of waggon which rolls on iron-toothed wheels, so that, the corn being shaken out of it, it may crush the straw on the threshing floor." The word here used (*chárúts*) is the same as that employed by Joel iii. 14, "Multitudes, multitudes, in the valley of decision" (*chárúts*). *Gesen.* 308.

Amos is referring here to the cruelties practised on Israel by *Hazael,* King of Syria, as foretold by Elisha:—"I know the evil thou wilt do to the children of Israel; their strongholds thou wilt set on fire, and their young men wilt thou slay with the sword, and wilt dash their children, and rip up their women with child" (2 Kings viii. 12). The Syrians cast the women of Israel like sheaves on the threshing-floor, and threshed them with sharp instruments of iron (*Theodoret*). Therefore God says, "I will send a fire on the house of *Hazael.*"

**4.** *Ben-hadad]* An official name of Syrian Kings, and signifying *Son of Hadad,* the sun-god worshipped by Syria (1 Kings xv. 18; xx. 2. 2 Kings vi. 24; xiii. 25).

These words, "*shall devour the palaces,*" are adopted by Jeremiah from Hosea viii. 14, and Amos here. See Jer. xvii. 17. The words "*shall devour the palaces*" (Hebr. *armenoth*) "*of Benhadad,*" are adopted from Amos by Jeremiah (xlix. 27).

The word *armon* (a palace) is a favourite one with Amos, who uses it four times in this chapter (rr. 4. 7. 10. 12. 14), and twice in the next chapter (vr. 2. 5), and in all these cases in connexion with the verb *deal,* to eat, to devour. It also occurs three times in the third chapter (rr. 9, 10, 11), and once in the sixth (r. 8), and only twice in any other of the Minor Prophets (Hos. viii. 14. Micah v. 5).

**5.** *plain of Aven]* Literally, *plain of vanity;* perhaps of Heliopolis, or Baalbek (*Ewald, Hitzig*). Its site has not been accurately defined; it seems to have been called *Aven* by the Prophet on account of the idolatry practised there. Cp. Hos. v. 8. It is contrasted with the *Eden* which follows. *Edens* become *Avens,* as *Bethels* become *Bethavens,* by idolatry.

— *Eden]* Literally, *pleasure;* one of the Paradises or Parks of the Syrian King. Its site is not known. Cp. B. D. i. 187.

— *Kir]* To the north of Armenia. This prophecy was fulfilled by Tiglath Pileser, king of Assyria, who carried the Syrians captive to Kir. See above, on 2 Kings xvi. 9.

**6—8.** *Gaza—Ashdod—Ashkelon—Ekron*] The great cities of Philistia (Josh. xv. 47. Judges i. 18; xiv. 19; xvi. 1. 1 Sam. v. 1. 6; vi. 17. Jer. xxv. 20. Zeph. ii. 4).

**6.** *they carried away—the whole captivity*] A captivity (of Israelites) in full number, so that none were spared (*S. Jerome*). This was done in the days of Jehoiachin (2 Chron. xxxvi. 10).

Here also Amos takes up Joel, who had threatened the Philistines with divine wrath for their cruelty in this capture and sale of Israelites (Joel iii. 6).

The judgments denounced in this chapter onwards to the end, and in the next chapter (ii. 1—3), were executed by Nebuchadnezzar and the Chaldeans. Cp. Jer. xlvii. 45. Ezek. xxv. 15.

Before
CHRIST
787.

ᵖ To deliver *them* up to Edom :

⁷ ᵠBut I will send a fire on the wall of Gaza,

Which shall devour the palaces thereof :

⁸ And I will cut off the inhabitant ʳ from Ashdod,

And him that holdeth the sceptre from Ashkelon,

And I will ˢ turn mine hand against Ekron :

And ᵗthe remnant of the Philistines shall perish, saith the Lord God.

⁹   Thus saith the Lord ; For three transgressions of ᵘTyrus, and for four,

I will not turn away *the punishment* thereof ;

ˣ Because they delivered up the whole captivity to Edom,

And remembered not † the brotherly covenant :

¹⁰ ʸ But I will send a fire on the wall of Tyrus,

Which shall devour the palaces thereof.

¹¹   Thus saith the Lord ; For three transgressions of ᶻEdom, and for four,

I will not turn away *the punishment* thereof ;

Because he did pursue ᵃhis brother ᵇwith the sword,

And † did cast off all pity,

ᶜ And his anger did tear perpetually, and he kept his wrath for ever :

¹² But ᵈI will send a fire upon Teman,

Which shall devour the palaces of Bozrah.

¹³   Thus saith the Lord ; For three transgressions of ᵉthe children of Ammon,

and for four, I will not turn away *the punishment* thereof ;

Because they have ‖ ᶠripped up the women with child of Gilead,

ᵍ That they might enlarge their border :

¹⁴ But I will kindle a fire in the wall of ʰRabbah,

And it shall devour the palaces thereof,

ⁱ With shouting in the day of battle,

With a tempest in the day of the whirlwind :

¹⁵ And ᵏtheir king shall go into captivity,

He and his princes together, saith the Lord.

II. ¹ Thus saith the Lord ; For three transgressions of ᵃMoab, and for four,

I will not turn away *the punishment* thereof ;

Because he ᵇburned the bones of the king of Edom into lime :

p ver. 9.
q Jer. 47. 1.

r Zeph. 2. 4.
Zech. 9. 5, 6.

s Ps. 81. 14.

t Jer. 47. 4.
Ezek. 25. 16.
u Isa. 23. 1.
Jer. 47. 4.
Ezek. 26. & 27,
& 28.
Joel 3. 4, 5.
x ver. 6.
† Heb. *the cove-*
*nant of brethren.*
2 Sam. 5. 11.
1 Kings 5. 1. &
9. 11—14.
y ver. 4, 7, &c.

z Isa. 21. 11. &
34. 5.
Jer. 49. 8, &c.
Ezek. 25 12, 13,
14. & 35. 2, &c.
Joel 3. 19.
Obad. 1, &c.
Mal. 1. 4
a Gen. 27. 41.
Deut. 23. 7.
Mal. 1. 2.
b 2 Chron. 28. 17
† Heb. *corrupted*
*his compassions.*
c Ezek. 55. 5
d Obad. 9, 10.
e Jer. 49. 1, 2.
Ezek. 25. 2.
Zeph. 2. 9.

‖ Or, *divided the*
*mountains.*
f Hos. 13. 16.
g Jer. 49. 1.

h Deut. 3. 11.
2 Sam. 12. 26.
Jer. 49. 2.
Ezek. 25. 5.

i ch. 2. 2.

k Jer. 49. 3.

a Isa 15, & 16
Jer. 48.
Ezek 25. 8.
Zeph. 2. 8.

b 2 Kings 3. 27.

---

*— to Edom*] The cruel and treacherous foe of their brethren of Israel. See on *v.* 11. Ps. cxxxvii. 7. Isa. xxxiv. 6; lxiii. 1. Jer. xxvii. 3. Ezek. xxv. 12; and Obadiah throughout.

9. *Tyrus*] See above, Isa. xxiii. 1—17. Jer. xxv. 22; xlvii. 4; and especially Ezek. xxvi., xxvii., xxviii., where this prophecy against Tyre is enlarged.

11. *Edom*] See on *v.* 6.

— *did cast off all pity*] Lit. *destroyed its own compassions* — as if pity were an evil thing, and to be extinguished.

12. *Teman*] The southern region of Edom (*S. Jerome*), the country of Eliphaz (Job ii. 11).

— *Bozrah*] The capital of Edom. See on Isa. xxxiv. 6; lxiii. 1.

14. *Rabbah*] The capital of Ammon. See above, 2 Sam. xii. 26, 27. 29. Jer. xlix. 2. Ezek. xxi. 20; xxv. 5, where this prophecy is enlarged.

Ch. II. 1. *Moab*] This prophecy of judgment is also enlarged in Isa. xv., xvi. ; and in Jer. xlviii. ; and in Ezek. xxv. 9.

— *he burned the bones of the king of Edom into lime*] This act of the king of Moab, burning the bones of the king of Edom into lime, was probably a sequel to what he is said to have done when harassed and distressed by the invasion of the three confederate kings of Judah, Israel, and Edom. He, the king of Moab, at that time in a fit of desperation, took his own eldest son (this is the true meaning of the passage; *cp. Josephus, Ant.* ix. 3. 2· and so *S. Jerome, Rufinus, Eusebius,* and most ancient

expositors) and offered him up as a burnt offering upon the wall. See on 2 Kings iii. 27.

Then the kings of Israel and Judah retired from Moab ; and then it was, as it seems probable, that the king and people of Moab, who before had attempted to attack Edom, but were prevented from executing their purpose by the two kings leagued with Edom, wreaked their vengeance on the king of Edom, being left isolated, and *burnt his bones into lime* as a holocaust to the spirit of the dead son of the king of Moab, whom, in a fit of desperate anguish, his father had offered as a burnt offering to win the favour of the cruel gods whom he worshipped.

This opinion is corroborated by the Hebrew tradition mentioned by *S. Jerome* here, "that the bones of the king of Edom, who had come up together with Joram king of Israel, and Jehoshaphat king of Judah, to attack Moab, were torn up from their grave by the Moabites, in a spirit of revenge, and were burnt."

Amos says, that the Moabites burnt the bones of the king of Edom *into lime* ; and the *Chaldee Targum,* and other expositors, explain this by saying, that in order to proclaim and perpetuate their act of vindictive cruelty, the Moabites daubed the walls of their houses with the lime made of the bones of the king.

This denunciation of the Prophet Amos against the king and people of Moab is designed to show that the Lord God of Israel is the God of the whole world, and takes judicial cognizance not only of things happening to Israel, but of the conduct of one heathen power, Moab, to another heathen power, Edom.

Before CHRIST 787.

c Jer. 48. 41.

d ch. 1. 14.

e Num. 24. 17. Jer. 48. 7.

2 But I will send a fire upon Moab,
And it shall devour the palaces of [c] Kirioth:
And Moab shall die with tumult,
[d] With shouting, *and* with the sound of the trumpet:
3 And I will cut off [e] the judge from the midst thereof,
And will slay all the princes thereof with him, saith the LORD.

f Lev. 26. 14, 15. Neh. 1. 7. Dan. 9. 11.

g Isa. 28. 15. Jer. 16. 19, 20. Rom. 1. 25.

h Ezek. 20. 13, 16, 18, 24, 30.

i Jer. 17. 27. Hos. 8. 14.

4 Thus saith the LORD; For three transgressions of Judah, and for four,
I will not turn away *the punishment* thereof;
[f] Because they have despised the law of the LORD,
And have not kept his commandments,
And [g] their lies caused them to err,
[h] After the which their fathers have walked:
5 [i] But I will send a fire upon Judah,
And it shall devour the palaces of Jerusalem.

k Isa. 29. 21. ch. 8. 6.

l Isa. 10. 2. ch. 5. 12.

m Ezek. 22. 11.

‖ Or, *young woman.*

n Lev. 20. 3. Ezek. 36. 20. Rom. 2. 24.

o Exod. 22. 26.

p Ezek. 23. 41. 1 Cor. 8. 10. & 10. 21.

‖ Or, *such as have fined, or, mulcted.*

q Num. 21. 24. Deut. 2. 31. Josh. 24. 8.

r Num. 13. 28, 32, 33.

s Isa. 5. 24. Mal. 4. 1.

t Exod. 12. 51. Micah 6. 4.

u Deut. 2. 7. & 8. 2.

6 Thus saith the LORD; For three transgressions of Israel, and for four,
I will not turn away *the punishment* thereof;
Because [k] they sold the righteous for silver,
And the poor for a pair of shoes;
7 That pant after the dust of the earth on the head of the poor,
And [l] turn aside the way of the meek:
[m] And a man and his father will go in unto the *same* ‖ maid,
[n] To profane my holy name:
8 And they lay *themselves* down upon clothes [o] laid to pledge [p] by every altar,
And they drink the wine of ‖ the condemned *in* the house of their god.
9 Yet destroyed I the [q] Amorite before them,
[r] Whose height *was* like the height of the cedars,
And he *was* strong as the oaks;
Yet I [s] destroyed his fruit from above, and his roots from beneath.
10 Also [t] I brought you up from the land of Egypt,
And [u] led you forty years through the wilderness,
To possess the land of the Amorite.
11 And I raised up of your sons for prophets,

---

2. *I will send a fire upon Moab*] For burning his own son with fire, and for burning the bones of the king of Edom.

— *Kirioth*] In Moab, now *Kereyat.* Cp. Jer. xlviii. 24. 41.

4. *Judah*] From judgments on heathen Nations he passes to Judah and Israel, the principal subject of his prophecies.

— *their lies*] Their idols.

5. *I will send a fire upon Judah—Jerusalem*] Observe, that though God by Amos denounces judgment both on Judah and Israel, yet it is only on Jerusalem that He threatens to send *fire* as the instrument of its destruction. Here is prophetic discrimination. And so it came to pass, Jerusalem was *burnt with fire* by the Chaldæans (2 Kings xxv. 9. 2 Chr. xxxvi. 19), and afterwards by the Romans. Samaria, the capital of Israel, was also taken, but it was not burnt with fire. There is a *speciality* (which proves their divine origin) in the prophecies concerning Jerusalem. Jerusalem was taken *seventeen* different times, but only *once* was it compassed by a trench cast around it by the invaders, viz. in the siege predicted by Christ (Luke xix. 43).

6. *they sold the righteous for silver*] They take bribes in judgment, and betray the innocent man, whom they ought to have defended from his enemy.

This portion, from ii. 6 to iii. 8, is the *Haphtarah* to Genesis xxxvii. 1 to xl. 23, which relates the history of the sale of Joseph, the type of Christ, for money, by his brethren, and the sin of Judah. "They sell *the righteous* for money," words certainly applicable in the deepest and fullest sense to the selling of *the* righteous One for thirty pieces of silver. It is one of the silent proofs of the inspiration of Hebrew Prophecy, that while it has literal subordinate fulfilments in historical acts of earlier days, it finds its full accomplishment in the person of CHRIST. "Christo hæc verba competunt, et ad Christum, quasi ad scopum et amorem suum, datâ vel levi occasione et similitudine, avolare solent Prophetæ" (*A Lapide*); a very true remark, which deserves the attention of the devout student of prophecy.

— *the poor for a pair of shoes*] They sell the precious souls of the poor for the meanest thing, with which they trample on the dust or in the mire (*S. Jerome*).

7. *And a man and his father*] This had been Reuben's sin (Gen. xxxv. 22), for which he lost his birthright (Gen. xlix. 3, 4). It was a sin to be punished by death (Lev. xviii. 7–15; xx. 11).

— *To profane my holy name*] So that it is blasphemed among the Gentiles (2 Pet. ii. 2), who abhor such a crime (1 Cor. v. 1, 2).

8. *they lay* themselves *down upon clothes laid to pledge*] This was another sin committed against another express law of God (Exod. xxii. 26. Deut. xxiv. 12, 13). Their consciences are so seared by sin, that they lay themselves down at ease to sleep on the garments of the poor debtor which he has pawned to them; and they do this *in the house of their god* by the side of *every altar* of their idol deities, and there they drink of the *wine* of the *condemned*—that is, wine bought by fines extorted from those whom they have amerced in judgment. Thus, with bold impiety, they sin against God and man at the same time.

9. *Yet destroyed I the Amorite before them*] This was Israel's ungrateful requital of all My mercies to them in destroying the Nations of Canaan for their idolatry and uncleanness; they were not thankful for My favour, nor did they profit by the warning, but they imitated the sins of the nations which I commanded them to exterminate for those sins.

— *Whose height was like the height of the cedars*] So that the spies quailed at the sight of them (Num. xiii. 28, 32, 33; xxi. 34).

And of your young men for ˣ Nazarites.

*Is it* not even thus, O ye children of Israel? saith the LORD.

<sup></sup>¹² But ye gave the Nazarites wine to drink;

And commanded the prophets, ʸ saying, Prophesy not.

¹³ ᶻ Behold, ‖ I am pressed under you, as a cart is pressed *that is* full of sheaves.

¹⁴ ᵃ Therefore the flight shall perish from the swift,

And the strong shall not strengthen his force,

  ᵇ Neither shall the mighty deliver † himself:

¹⁵ Neither shall he stand that handleth the bow;

And *he that is* swift of foot shall not deliver *himself:*

  ᶜ Neither shall he that rideth the horse deliver himself.

¹⁶ And *he that is* † courageous among the mighty shall flee away naked in that day, saith the LORD.

III. ¹ Hear this word that the LORD hath spoken against you, O children of Israel,

Against the whole family which I brought up from the land of Egypt, saying,

² ᵃ You only have I known of all the families of the earth:

  ᵇ Therefore I will † punish you for all your iniquities.

³ Can two walk together, except they be agreed?

⁴ Will a lion roar in the forest, when he hath no prey?

Will a young lion † cry out of his den, if he have taken nothing?

⁵ Can a bird fall in a snare upon the earth, where no gin *is* for him?

Shall *one* take up a snare from the earth, and have taken nothing at all?

*[Margin references:]*
Before CHRIST 787.
x Num. 6. 2. Judg. 13. 5.
y Isa. 30. 10. Jer. 11. 21. ch. 7. 12, 13. Micah 2. 6.
z Isa. 1. 14. ‖ Or, *I will press your place, as a cart full of sheaves presseth.*
a Jer. 9. 23. ch. 9. 1, &c.
b Ps. 33. 16. † Heb. *his soul,* or, *life.*
c Ps. 33. 17.
† Heb. *strong of his heart.*
a Deut. 7. 6. & 10. 15. Ps. 147. 19, 20.
b See Dan. 9. 12. Matt. 11. 22. Luke 12. 47. Rom. 2. 9. 1 Pet. 4. 17.
† Heb. *visit upon.*
† Heb. *give forth his voice.*

---

11. *Nazarites*] Separated and dedicated to God. See above, on Num. vi. 2—21. Judges xiii. 5. Lam. iv. 7.

12. *ye gave the Nazarites wine to drink*] Ye not only broke My law in your own persons, but ye tempted your children, who were dedicated to My service, to violate their vows to Me (Num. vi. 3).

This condemnation may be applied in Christian times to parents and others who deter children that have been baptized and confirmed (and are Christian Nazarites dedicated to God) from coming to the Holy Communion.

— *Prophesy not*] Because God's word was burdensome to them. Cp. vii. 10. Micah ii. 6; and above, Isa. xxx. 10. "Which say to the seers, See not," and Jer. xi. 21. The climax of Israel's sin is represented in our Lord's words: "O Jerusalem, Jerusalem, thou that killest the Prophets" (Matt. xxiii. 37). and in His own Crucifixion (Acts vii. 52).

13. *Behold, I am pressed under you*] Behold I, even I your God, *strain myself under you* and groan with the burden, being no longer able to bear your sins (as S. Jerome expounds it, and so Sept., Vulg., Arabic), *as a cart that is full of sheaves.* As God says by Isaiah, "Thou hast made Me to serve with thy sins, thou hast wearied Me with thine iniquities" (Isa. xliii. 24). Cp. Mal. ii. 17.

The propriety of the simile of the Cart, pressed down and groaning with its load of ripe sheaves, consists further in this, that the Cart bears them to the threshing-door and shoots them down there to be threshed. In like manner, Israel, wearying God with the weight of their sins, will be cast down by Him on the threshing-floor, to be crushed like sheaves by the sharp threshing instruments of divine judgment. "As a cart" (says S. Jerome), "loaded heavily with corn or hay, creaks and groans with the weight, so I, overburdened by your sins, utter my voice and say, 'The flight shall perish from the swift.'"

Amos here takes up the metaphor of the preceding Prophet, Joel (Joel iii. 14. See the note there).

Ch. III. 1. *Hear this word*] This address is repeated thrice (iii. 1; iv. 1; v. 1). See also vii. 16; viii. 4. It is like our Lord's emphatic saying, "He that hath ears to hear, let him hear," and the similar appeal seven times repeated in the Apocalypse. See Rev. ii. 7. It is taken up by Amos from his predecessors, Hosea v. 1, and Joel i. 2; and is continued by Micah i. 2; iii. 1. 9; vi. 1, 2. 9.

2. *You only have I known*] I have specially loved you. Cp. Hos. xiii. 5, and note below on Acts xv. 18, where it is said that

all God's works are *known*, i.e. loved by Him. Israel was loved by Him with a special love.

— *Therefore I will punish you*] Compare our Lord's words to Chorazin and Capernaum, and concerning those to whom His Apostles would preach (Matt. x. 15; xi. 21, 22. Mark vi. 11. Luke x. 13. Judgment begins with the house of God (Ezek. ix. 6. 1 Pet. iv. 17).

#### THE FIVE PARABLES.

In the following verses (vv. 3—6) are five Parables, all showing God's moral Government in the affairs of the World and of His Church; and that nothing in the history of either happens by chance, but is ordered by Him, using the natural Elements and the greatest Nations of the World as His instruments for the punishment of sins committed after deliberate warning, and for the manifestation of His Power and Glory.

3. *Can two walk together*] How can you expect God to walk with you and bless you, unless you conform to His will? Cp. "Agree with thine adversary quickly, whiles thou art in the way with him;" see Matt. v. 25, where "the adversary" is understood by many ancient expositors to mean, in a spiritual sense, the Word of God. Be of one mind with it, or be reconciled to it speedily, if you desire to be at peace.

4. *Will a lion roar*] Or, *Does a lion roar—and he has no prey?* The roar of a lion is a certain assurance that he has, or soon will have, the prey in his grasp. So the warning voice of the Lord by His Prophets (see i. 2) is a sure sign that He is coming to judge you.

5. *Can a bird fall in a snare—where no gin is for him?*] Or, as the Sept. paraphrases it, *Will a bird fall upon the earth without a fowler?*—literally, without a *springe.*

The fall of the bird is a sure sign of the fowler's presence. So, your punishment is not a mere matter of chance, but it is divinely designed. As our Lord says, "Not a sparrow falls to the ground without your Father" (Matt. x. 29). Much more, when Israel falls, let him recognize God's hand in his own fall, and repent of the sins which have caused it.

— *Shall one take up a snare*] Or, *shall the snare*, or trap, *rise up from the earth without having taken any thing.*

The springing up of the trap is a sign that it has caught something. It will not rise up without having done its work. So My instruments of judgment (such as the armies of Assyria and Babylon, whom I send against you, and set before you only as traps to take you) will not rise up and depart before they have executed upon you the judgment which I have set them to

<sup>6</sup> Shall a trumpet be blown in the city, and the people ‖ not be afraid?
<sup>c</sup> Shall there be evil in a city, ‖ and the LORD hath not done *it*?
<sup>7</sup> Surely the Lord GOD will do nothing, but <sup>d</sup> he revealeth his secret unto his
    servants the prophets.
<sup>8</sup> <sup>e</sup> The lion hath roared, who will not fear?
    The Lord GOD hath spoken, <sup>f</sup> who can but prophesy?
<sup>9</sup>   Publish in the palaces at Ashdod,
And in the palaces in the land of Egypt, and say,
Assemble yourselves upon the mountains of Samaria,
And behold the great tumults in the midst thereof,
And the ‖ oppressed in the midst thereof.
<sup>10</sup> For they <sup>g</sup> know not to do right, saith the LORD,
Who store up violence and ‖ robbery in their palaces.
<sup>11</sup> Therefore thus saith the Lord GOD;
    <sup>h</sup> An adversary *there shall be* even round about the land;
And he shall bring down thy strength from thee, and thy palaces shall be
    spoiled.
<sup>12</sup> Thus saith the LORD;
As the shepherd † taketh out of the mouth of the lion two legs, or a piece
of an ear; so shall the children of Israel be taken out that dwell in
Samaria in the corner of a bed, and ‖ in Damascus *in* a couch.
<sup>13</sup>   Hear ye, and testify in the house of Jacob, saith the Lord GOD, the God
of hosts, <sup>14</sup> that in the day that I shall ‖ visit the transgressions of Israel upon
him I will also visit the altars of Beth-el: and the horns of the altar shall be
cut off, and fall to the ground. <sup>15</sup> And I will smite <sup>i</sup> the winter house with
<sup>k</sup> the summer house; and <sup>l</sup> the houses of ivory shall perish, and the great
houses shall have an end, saith the LORD.

---

**perform.** Compare the metaphor in Ezekiel xii. 13, where God says, concerning Zedekiah king of Jerusalem, "My net also will I spread upon him, and he shall be taken in my snare"—i.e. by the Chaldaean army.

**6.** *Shall a trumpet be blown in the city*] Ye are alarmed at the sound of the trumpet announcing the approach of an earthly enemy (see on Hos. v. 8; viii. 1), and will you not much more fear when the prophetic trumpet of God's voice (Isa. lviii. 1, Ezek. xxxiii. 3, 5) is sounding an alarum in your ears and calling you to repentance (Joel ii. 1, 15), and preparing you for the sound of the trumpet of the Great Day, which will awaken you from your graves to Judgment?

— *Shall there be evil in a city*] Shall there be *physical* evil (not moral evil, though even this cannot exist without God's permission, and is overruled by Him to good), such as Plague, Pestilence, Famine, Earthquake, or War, and will ye attribute this to mere blind chance, and not to the deliberate will, sovereign power, and chastening hand of Him Who sends these things as His own sore judgments on guilty cities and nations (Ezek. xiv. 21), and who says to the World, "I form the light and create darkness, I make peace and create evil, I the Lord do all these things"? See on Isa. xlv. 7. *Bp.* Sanderson, iii. 77, 150; and *Pfeiffer*, p. 130.

**7.** *Surely the Lord GOD will do nothing—prophets*] Therefore ye ought to listen to the voice of the Prophets as the voice of God, declaring the secret counsel (Heb. *sôd*. See Job xv. 8; xxxiv. 4, where the same word is used) of His will, and fore-warning you of His dealings with you.

God has ever warned the World of coming judgments, in order that it may not incur them. As S. *Chrysostom* says, He has revealed to us hell, in order that we may escape hell. He warned Noah of the coming Deluge. He told Abraham and Lot of the future judgment on Sodom and the cities of the plain. He revealed to Joseph the seven years' famine, and to Moses, and to Pharaoh by Moses, the ten plagues; and to Moses, and Joshua, and the Prophets, all the chastisements of His People; and to

Jonah the destruction of Nineveh; and by Christ and His Apostles He foretold the fall of Jerusalem; and Christ has warned all of His own future Coming to judge the World. God does this in order that men may repent; and that, if they obstinately continue in sin, He may be justified in executing punishment upon them (*S.* Jerome; *Corn. a Lapide*).

**9.** *Publish in the palaces at Ashdod*] Even heathen nations are summoned to assent to the justice of God's judgment on His people. The Divine Judge appeals to them as His Jury, and asks for their verdict on Israel.

— *tumults*] Lawless anarchy, confusion, and violence.

**12.** *As the shepherd*] Only a small remnant of Israel will be saved from the general destruction. Only a pair of shin bones, or a lappet of an ear of the whole sheep, will be rescued from the mouth of the destroying lion of Assyria, "decem tribuum parvas reliquias de Assyriorum manibus narrat eruendas" (*S.* Jerome).

— *that dwell in Samaria in the corner of a bed, and in Damascus in a couch*] Only a small remnant shall be rescued of those voluptuous crowds of grandees who *dwell in Samaria*—i.e. (as he expresses it in vi. 1), who "trust in the mountain of Samaria"—relying on its earthly wealth and strength, and indulging in its comforts, like men who recline and loll at ease on couches themselves by pillows in the *corner of a bed* (i.e. in the corner of the divan—at the angle where two sides of the sofa meet—the most luxurious place), and *who recline on Damascus*, as *on a couch*—that is, who lean on Syria for help (as Pekah king of Israel did; Isa. vii. 2—8), instead of relying on God. "As a man who is weary" (says *S.* Jerome) "reposes on a couch, so Israel, when harassed by war, supported itself on Damascus." This seems to be the preferable interpretation of the passage, and is authorized by *Sept., Vulg., Syriac, Arabic, Targum*; and see *Pareq*, 154.

**15.** *the winter house with the summer house*] That is, both compartments of the palace. See on Jer. xxxvi. 22.

— *houses of ivory*] The palace which had rooms inlaid with ivory, like that of Ahab (1 Kings xxii. 39). Cp. Ps. xlv. 8.

IV. ¹ Hear this word, ye ªkine of Bashan, that are in the mountain of Samaria, which oppress the poor, which crush the needy, which say to their masters, Bring, and let us drink.

² ᵇ The Lord GOD hath sworn by his holiness, that, lo, the days shall come upon you, that he will take you away ᶜwith hooks, and your posterity with fishhooks. ³ And ᵈye shall go out at the breaches, every cow at that which is before her; and ‖ye shall cast them into the palace, saith the LORD.

⁴ ᵉ Come to Beth-el, and transgress; at ᶠGilgal multiply transgression; and ᵍbring your sacrifices every morning, ʰand your tithes after †three years: ⁵ ⁱand †offer a sacrifice of thanksgiving with leaven, and proclaim and publish ᵏthe free offerings: ˡfor †this liketh you, O ye children of Israel, saith the Lord GOD.

⁶ And I also have given you cleanness of teeth in all your cities, and want of bread in all your places: ᵐ Yet have ye not returned unto me, saith the LORD.

⁷ And also I have withholden the rain from you, when there were yet three months to the harvest: and I caused it to rain upon one city, and caused it

*[Marginal references:]*
Before CHRIST 787.
a Ps. 22. 12.
Ezek. 39. 18.
b Ps. 89. 35.
c Jer. 16. 16.
Hab. 1. 15.
d Ezek. 12. 5, 12.
‖ Or, ye shall cast away the things of the palace.
e Ezek. 20. 39.
f Hos. 4. 15. & ch. 5. 5.
g Num. 28. 3, 4.
h Deut. 14. 28.
† Heb. three years of days.
i Lev. 7. 13. & 23. 17.
† Heb. offer by burning.
k Lev. 22. 18, 21.
Deut. 12. 6.
l Ps. 81. 12.
† Heb. so ye love.
m Isa. 26. 11.
Jer. 3. 3.
ver. 8, 9.
Hag. 2. 17.

---

Ch. IV. 1. *ye kine of Bashan*] Ye voluptuous, effeminate rulers, who do not deserve to be called men, but animals; and not oxen, but cows (cp. Ps. xxii. 12. Ezek. xxxix. 18); or he may be speaking here of the haughty and luxurious women of Samaria.

— *their masters*] Their princes; or (if he is speaking of women) their husbands. Cp. Isa. iii. 16.

2. *he will take you away with hooks*] These words are adopted by Jeremiah : "Behold, I will send for many fishers, saith the Lord, and they shall fish them." Cp. Hab. i. 15. The execution of judgment will be personal and painful; not like the catching of fish in a net, so as they may be saved, but by a hook, which is followed by death.

3. *ye shall go out at the breaches*] Ye shall go through the breaches made in the walls of the captured city ; the prisoners will be so many that it would take too much time to drive them through the gates ; the ruin and captivity will be total.

— *every cow at that which is before her*] Every (woman, see v. 1) will be forced by the enemy to march straight onwards on the way which lies *before her*, without looking to the right or left (Josh. vi. 5. 20), like cows driven one after another through a gap in a hedge.

— *and ye shall cast* them *into the palace*] Rather, ye shall be cast towards the Harmon. The Hebrew letters are ha-harmôn-ah ; the final -ah signifies *motion to a place* like our final English *ward*, as heaven*ward* (see *Gesen.* Gram. § 90, p. 148) e.g. Babel-ah, to Babylon ; Assur-ah, to Assyria; ha-harrah, to the mountain ; midbarah-ah Dammesek, toward the wilderness of Damascus.

What the meaning is of the Hebrew word here used, *harmôn*, is disputable. One thing seems certain ; that it is designed to contrast with *armôn*, or *palace* (see above, on i. 4); and that it is used to announce that tney who rioted in their *armôn*, or palace (iii. 10), will be spoiled in their *armôn*, or palace (iii. 11), and that they will be flung out of their *armôn* to a *harmôn*.

The ancient renderings of *harmôn* are very various. Some think that the phrase, they will be cast out to *Armôn*, means that they will be driven as outcasts to *Armenia* (so *Symmachus*, *Targum*, *Syriac*, *Jerome*, *Bochart*); others, to *Mount Rimmon*, or *Reaman* (*Sept.*); others, to *Hermon*.

The sense is, ye will be hurled from a high estate to a low one ; ye, who were brought up in palaces, will hereafter "embrace dunghills" (Lam. iv. 5). And it is probable that the Prophet is here forming a word to mark the contrast between their present condition of pride and splendour, and their future state of abasement and shame. You, who now are revelling at ease in your *Armôn*, will be cast out to the *Ar*, or *hill*, of *Rimmon*, the god of Syria and Damascus (see 2 Kings v. 18), in whom ye trust (see iii. 12); and this is confirmed by what is said below (v. 27), "I will cause you to go into captivity beyond *Damascus*." This may have given rise to the rendering in the Septuagint here.

4. *Come to Beth-el and transgress—Gilgal*] Words uttered in a tone of bitter irony and indignation, as Ezekiel says (xx. 39), "Go ye, serve ye every one his idols ;" and our Lord to the Jews, "Fill ye up then the measure of your fathers" (Matt. xxiii. 32).

Amos, in thus speaking of Bethel and Gilgal, seats of Israelitish idolatry, is taking up the language of his predecessor Hosea. See Hos. iv. 15, "Come not ye unto Gilgal, neither go ye up to Beth-aven." Cp. ix. 15; xii. 11; and below, v. 5.

— *bring your sacrifices every morning, and your tithes after three years*] The strain of irony is continued. Go to, and imitate at Bethel the worship of the Temple; bring your sacrifices every morning, your *tithes after three years*, or, rather, after *every three days* (literally, after a *treble of days*); so *Sept.*, *Vulg.*, *Syriac*, *Arabic*, *Targum*, and so *Keil*. That is, Not only imitate, but go beyond, the requirements of the Levitical Law, which prescribed this payment after *three years* (Deut. xiv. 28 ; xxvi. 12).

This is a characteristic of idolatry and schism, to profess extraordinary zeal for God's worship, and go beyond the letter and spirit of His Law by arbitrary will-worship and self-idolizing fanaticism.

5. *offer a sacrifice of thanksgiving with leaven*] Contrary to the Levitical Law (Lev. ii. 11). You copy the Law in some things, and you innovate upon it in others, as seems best to your own private conceits. This was a characteristic of the worship set up by Jeroboam. See above, 1 Kings xii. 27—29. In some respects it was an imitation of the ceremonies of the Levitical Law, in others it was a deviation from it. Jeroboam chose what he liked, and left out what he liked. This is the essence of schism. It ends what pleases its fancy from God's Law and from the usages of God's Church. "This liketh you, O ye children of Israel, saith the Lord God."

— *proclaim and publish the free offerings*] Commit your sins of schism and idolatry with a bold face. Make no secret of them. Proclaim them by public announcements, so that all may know them. This is another characteristic of schism. It has no sense of shame in rending the seamless coat of Christ. It publishes itself to the world by demonstrations of disunion, and it even claims admiration for its zeal in breaking that Christian Unity for which Christ prayed (John xvii. 11, 21, 22).

6. *And I also have given you cleanness of teeth*] Your gifts to Me were such as I have described ; and what was My gift to you in return ? Ye defiled your teeth by feeding on idol-sacrifices, and I sent you *cleanness of teeth*, i.e. chastisement by Famine. But this was done in love. It was the only remedy left. God pleads with Israel in mercy while He announces this. He chastened them that they might return to Him (vv. 6, 9, 10, 11), and He says, "Seek ye Me, and ye shall live" (v. 4. 6).

— *Yet have ye not returned unto me*] God emphatically declares the loving design of His chastisement of Israel, by repeating this sorrowful ejaculation *four times* (vv. 6, 9, 10, 11).

7. *one city—one piece*] In order to call their attention to the fact that this visitation was not a thing of chance or necessity, but of design, God made it partial and extraordinary. For a like reason He made the light local in Goshen (Exod. x. 23), and afterwards at Beth-horon (see on Josh. x. 12); and sent a storm of thunder and rain in the time of wheat harvest, in the days of Samuel (1 Sam. xii. 17, 18).

45

Before
CHRIST
787.

n ver. 6, 10, 11.
f Hag. 2. 17.
¦ Or, the multi-
tude of your
gardens, &c. did
the palmer-
worm, &c.
p Joel i. 4. &
2. 25.
¦ Or, in the way.
q Exod. 9. 3, 6. &
12. 29.
Deut. 28. 27, 60.
Ps. 78. 50.
† Heb. with the
captivity of your
horses.
2 Kings 13. 7.
r ver. 6.
s Gen. 19. 24, 25.
Isa. 13. 19.
Jer. 49. 18.
t Zech. 3. 2.
Jude 23.
u ver. 6.

x See Ezek. 13. 5.
& 22. 30.
Luke 14. 31, 32.
¦ Or, spirit.
y Ps. 139. 2.
Dan 2. 28.
z ch. 5. 8. & 8. 9.
a Deut. 32. 13.
33. 29.
Micah 1. 3.
b Isa. 47. 4.
Jer. 10. 16.
ch. 5. 8. & 9. 6.
a Jer. 7. 29.
Ezek. 19. 1. &
27. 2.

b 2 Chron. 15. 2.
Jer. 29. 13.
ver. 6.
c Isa. 55. 3.
d ch. 4. 4.
e ch. 8. 14

not to rain upon another city: one piece was rained upon, and the piece whereupon it rained not withered. [8] So two or three cities wandered unto one city, to drink water; but they were not satisfied:

"Yet have ye not returned unto me, saith the LORD.

[9] "I have smitten you with blasting and mildew: ‖ when your gardens and your vineyards and your fig trees and your olive trees increased, [p] the palmer-worm devoured *them :*

Yet have ye not returned unto me, saith the LORD.

[10] I have sent among you the pestilence ‖ [q] after the manner of Egypt : your young men have I slain with the sword, † and have taken away your horses; and I have made the stink of your camps to come up unto your nostrils:

[r] Yet have ye not returned unto me, saith the LORD.

[11] I have overthrown *some* of you, as God overthrew [s] Sodom and Gomorrah, [t] and ye were as a firebrand plucked out of the burning:

[u] Yet have ye not returned unto me, saith the LORD.

[12] Therefore thus will I do unto thee, O Israel : *and* because I will do this unto thee, [x] prepare to meet thy God, O Israel.

[13] For, lo, he that formeth the mountains, and createth the ‖ wind, [y] and declareth unto man what *is* his thought, [z] that maketh the morning darkness, [a] and treadeth upon the high places of the earth, [b] The LORD, The God of hosts, *is* his name.

V. [1] Hear ye this word which I [a] take up against you, *Even* a lamentation, O house of Israel.

[2] The virgin of Israel is fallen ; she shall no more rise : She is forsaken upon her land; *there is* none to raise her up.

[3] For thus saith the Lord GOD ; The city that went out *by* a thousand shall leave an hundred, And that which went forth *by* an hundred shall leave ten, To the house of Israel.

[4] For thus saith the LORD unto the house of Israel, [b] Seek ye me, [c] and ye shall live :

[5] But seek not [d] Beth-el, nor enter into Gilgal, and pass not to [e] Beersheba :

9. *When your gardens—increased*] Or rather, a *multitude of your gardens* (see *Vulg., Targum, Syriac,* and the English margin) *the locust devoured.*

10. *taken away your horses*] By the sword of Hazael, king of Syria. Cp. 2 Kings viii. 12, with xiii. 3. 7.

13. *he—declareth unto man—his thought*] God knows what man thinks, and reveals man's thoughts to him (Ps. vii. 9; cxxxix. 2). The heart of man is deceitful (Jer. xvii. 9, 10), but God strips off the disguise and reveals man to himself. God did this by Nathan to David, by Elisha to Gehazi, by St. Peter to Ananias and Sapphira. How much more will He do it at the Great Day by Christ, Who "knows what is in man"? Therefore, O man, whoever thou art, "Prepare to meet thy God."

### PROPHECY OF JUDGMENT ON THE WICKED.

CH. V. 1. *Hear ye this—a lamentation*] The Prophet Amos now proceeds a step farther. He had warned Israel of coming judgment. He had declared the merciful calls they had received from God, in successive chastisements, exhorting them to repentance. He now sees judgment present, and describes it in a pathetic dirge over Israel.

*Hear this word,* this heavy *burden,* which, 1, Amos, the *bearer* (see above, on i. 1), *take up,* lift up, as a weight, to let it fall upon you from the hand of God. The consequence of this burden is, that the *Virgin of Israel* (cp. Isa. xlvii. 1) *is fallen;* she lies prostrate under it (*v.* 2).

2. *She is forsaken upon her land*] Rather, *she is cast down upon her soil* (*Vulg., Targum, Arabic*).

46

3. *shall leave*] Rather, *shall retain* as a remnant. He takes up the words of Deuteronomy (xxviii. 62), "Ye shall be left few in number, whereas ye were as the stars of heaven for multitude;" and he shows that God's blessings for obedience are turned into curses for disobedience. "One thousand shall flee at the rebuke of one; at the rebuke of five shall ye flee: till ye be left as a beacon upon the top of a mountain, and as an ensign on an hill" (Isa. xxx. 17); whereas, if they were obedient, "How should one of them chase a thousand?" (Deut. xxxii. 30. Josh. xxiii. 10). As the ancient Christian Poet says, "If the Lord is against us, our walls become cobwebs; but if the Lord is with us, even cobwebs become walls."

### PROMISE OF MERCY TO THE PENITENT.

4. *Seek ye me, and ye shall live*] Therefore this prophecy of judgment is designed to declare in mercy, that if Israel repents, the judgment will not be inflicted. He had before repeated four times His sorrowful complaint, "*Ye have not returned unto Me*" (iv. 6, 9, 10, 11); and now He repeats four times His gracious promise, *Seek ye Me, and ye shall live* (vv. 4, 6, 8, 14). Such was His long-suffering to Israel.

5. *pass not to Beersheba*] Bethel and Gilgal, on account of their ancient sacred reminiscences and associations, derived from patriarchal history, had been seized upon by Jeroboam (as Mahometans seize upon churches and change them into mosques), in order that he might destroy the connexion of Judah with them, and might avail himself of their sanctity as a lure for attracting votaries to his own form of religious worship. See on

For Gilgal shall surely go into captivity, and [f] Beth-el shall come to nought.
6 [g] Seek the LORD, and ye shall live;
Lest he break out like fire in the house of Joseph, and devour *it*,
And *there be* none to quench *it* in Beth-el.
7 Ye who [h] turn judgment to wormwood,
And leave off righteousness in the earth,
8 *Seek him* that maketh the [i] seven stars and Orion,
And turneth the shadow of death into the morning,
[k] And maketh the day dark with night:
That [l] calleth for the waters of the sea,
And poureth them out upon the face of the earth:
[m] The LORD *is* his name:
9 That strengtheneth the † spoiled against the strong,
So that the spoiled shall come against the fortress.
10 [n] They hate him that rebuketh in the gate,
And they [o] abhor him that speaketh uprightly.
11 Forasmuch therefore as your treading *is* upon the poor,
And ye take from him burdens of wheat:
[p] Ye have built houses of hewn stone, but ye shall not dwell in them;
Ye have planted † pleasant vineyards, but ye shall not drink wine of them.
12 For I know your manifold transgressions and your mighty sins:
[q] They afflict the just, they take ‖ a bribe,
And they [r] turn aside the poor in the gate *from their right*.
13 Therefore [s] the prudent shall keep silence in that time;
For it *is* an evil time.
14 Seek good, and not evil, that ye may live:
And so the LORD, the God of hosts, shall be with you, [t] as ye have spoken.
15 [u] Hate the evil, and love the good, and establish judgment in the gate:
[x] It may be that the LORD God of hosts will be gracious unto the remnant of Joseph.
16 Therefore the LORD, the God of hosts, the Lord, saith thus;

Before CHRIST 787.
f Hos. 4. 15. & 10. 8.
g ver. 4.
h ch. 6. 12.
i Job 9. 9. & 38. 31.
k Ps. 104. 20.
l Job 38. 34. ch. 9. 6.
m ch. 4. 13.
† Heb. *spoil*.
n Isa. 29. 21.
o 1 Kings 22. 8.
p Deut. 28. 30, 38, 39. Micah 6. 15. Zeph. 1. 13. Hag. 1. 6.
† Heb. *vineyards of desire*.
q ch. 2. 6.
‖ Or, *a ransom*.
r Isa. 29. 21. ch. 2. 7.
s ch. 6. 10.
t Micah 3. 11.
u Ps. 34. 14. & 97. 10. Rom. 12. 9.
x Exod. 32. 30. 2 Kings 19. 4. Joel 2. 14.

---

Hosea iv. 15. But Jeroboam was not content with appropriating Bethel and Gilgal in his own domain, for this purpose, but he also laid his hands on Beersheba (celebrated in the history of Abraham, and where God appeared to him (Gen. xxi. 33; xxvi. 33, 34), and to Isaac and Jacob (Gen. xxvi. 24; xlvi. 1, 2), and beyond the limits of Jeroboam's Kingdom of Israel, and even to the south of the kingdom of Judah, and he made it to be a place of religious pilgrimage for his people. That Beersheba was defiled with idolatry, is evident from 2 Kings xxiii. 8. Cp. below, viii. 14.

But all these arts of state-policy were of no avail, as the Prophet here declares. Bethel and Gilgal, notwithstanding their former sanctity, will be given up by God to destruction.

— *Gilgal shall surely go into captivity*] There is a paronomasia, or play upon words in the original, which renders it more expressive, "*Gilgal galoh yigleh*"—the place of *rolling away* (such was the origin of the name *Gilgal*, because there God *rolled away* the reproach of Egypt from Israel; see on Josh. v. 9) shall be clean *rolled away*. Cp. Isa. xxii. 18, "He will toss thee like a *ball* into a large country," as a "rota rotando rotabitur" (*A Lapide*).

This is the law of God's dealings with man; He "curses our blessings," if we do not use them aright (Mal. ii. 2). Christ, the Corner Stone, will break to pieces those who fall upon it; and it will grind to powder those on whom it falls (Matt. xxi. 44). Our holiest Gilgals—our Sacraments, our Scriptures, our Sermons, our Sundays—which were designed by God to roll away from us the reproach of Egypt, will be rolled away from us, if we do not use them aright; and will roll us downward into our destruction.

— *Beth-el shall come to nought*] Beth-el shall become *aven*, or vanity. See Hos. iv. 15, where it is called *Beth aven*, or house of *vanity*.

7. *Ye who turn judgment to wormwood*] A metaphor adopted from Hos. x. 4. See the note there, and cp. vi. 12.

— *And leave off righteousness in the earth*] Rather, *cast righteousness down to the ground*; as the Jews did when they killed "the Lord our righteousness" (Jer. xxiii. 6).

8. *that maketh the seven stars*] Ye who worship the stars are rebelling against Him Who made them. The *seven stars* (Heb. *cimah*, cluster or group) are the Pleiades. See above, on Job ix. 9; xxxviii. 31.

— *Orion*] Heb. *cesil*. See above, on Job ix. 9; xxxviii. 31. The "Seven Stars" and Orion are mentioned, as including the rest by a poetic *synecdoche*.

9. *That strengtheneth the spoiled*] Rather, *that maketh spoil* (see margin), or *desolation, to flash upon the strong*. Cp. *Sept.* and *Arabic*, and *Keil*.

— *So that the spoiled*] Or rather, *so that spoil*, or desolation, *cometh on the fortress* (*Sept.*, *Vulg.*, *Arabic*).

10. *They hate him that rebuketh in the gate*] In the place of public concourse, whether for deliberation or administration of justice. See on Job v. 4; xxxi. 21; and below, *v.* 15; and Isaiah's imitation of these words, they "lay a snare for him that reproveth in the gate." These words were fully accomplished in Christ (John vii. 7; viii. 45; xv. 25).

11. *ye take from him burdens of wheat*] Ye exact presents of wheat from the poor man, as bribes, for the administration of what you call justice.

On these verses see *Bp. Sanderson's* Sermons, ii. 353—356.

12. *They afflict—they turn*] Or rather, *afflicting, taking*. The words are participles.

13. *the prudent shall keep silence*] See above, on Prov. xxviii. 12. 28, "When the wicked rise, men hide themselves."

Before
CHRIST
787.

Wailing *shall be* in all streets ;
And they shall say in all the highways, Alas ! alas !
And they shall call the husbandman to mourning,

) Jer. 9. 17.

And such as are skilful of lamentation to wailing.
[17] And in all vineyards *shall be* wailing :

7 Exod. 12. 12.
Nahum 1. 12.
a Isa. 5. 19.
Jer. 47. 15.
Ezek. 12. 22, 27.
2 Pet. 3. 4.

For [z] I will pass through thee, saith the LORD.
[18] [a] Woe unto you that desire the day of the LORD !
To what end *is* it for you ?

b Jer. 20. 7.
Joel 2. 2.
Zeph. 1. 15.
c Jer. 48. 44.

[b] The day of the LORD *is* darkness, and not light.
[19] [c] As if a man did flee from a lion, and a bear met him ;
Or went into the house, and leaned his hand on the wall, and a serpent bit him.
[20] *Shall* not the day of the LORD *be* darkness, and not light ?
Even very dark, and no brightness in it ?

d Prov. 21. 27.
Isa. 1. 11—16.
Jer 6. 20.
Hos. 8. 13.
e Lev. 26. 31.
|| Or, smell your
holy days.
f Isa. 66. 3.
Micah 6 6, 7.
|| Or, thank
offerings.

[21] [d] I hate, I despise your feast days,
And [e] I will not || smell in your solemn assemblies.
[22] [f] Though ye offer me burnt offerings and your meat offerings, I will not
accept *them :*
Neither will I regard the || peace offerings of your fat beasts.
[23] Take thou away from me the noise of thy songs ;
For I will not hear the melody of thy viols.

g Hos. 6. 6.
Micah 6. 8.
† Heb. roll.

[24] [g] But let judgment † run down as waters,
And righteousness as a mighty stream.

h Deut. 32. 17.
Josh. 24. 14.
Ezek 20. 8, 16, 24.
Acts 7. 42, 43.
See Isa. 43. 23.
|| Or, Siccuth your
king.
i 1 Kings 11. 33.

[25] [h] Have ye offered unto me sacrifices and offerings in the wilderness forty
years, O house of Israel ?
[26] But ye have borne || the tabernacle [i] of your Moloch and Chiun your images,
the star of your god, which ye made to yourselves.

---

16. *such as are skilful of lamentation*] Professional mourners (2 Chron. xxxv. 25. Jer. ix. 17. Matt. ix. 23).

17. *I will pass through thee*] To destroy thee; as I passed through Egypt on that night when a great cry was made, " for there was not a house where there was not one dead " (Exod. xii. 12. 30);

18. *Woe unto you that desire the day of the* LORD!] This is to be explained from the foregoing prophecies of Joel. That Prophet had foretold the Coming of the *Day of the Lord*, when Jehovah, the God of Israel, would judge all the heathen, and deliver and exalt His people Israel and Judah. See Joel ii. 1, 2. 11. 31 ; iii. 2. 14. The words *day of the Lord* occur four times in the prophecies of Joel, but not in any earlier Prophet.

The Hebrew Nation had flattered itself that Joel's prophecy announced blessings to itself, because they were children of Abraham ; but Joel had warned them that only they who *call on the Name of the Lord*, i. e. who serve the Lord, and not any other god, would be saved (ii. 32), and that the Day of the Lord would be a terrible day to sinners.

A similar spirit manifested itself in those who said, in Jeremiah's day, " The Temple of the Lord, the Temple of the Lord, the Temple of the Lord are these " (Jer. vii. 4) ; and who prided themselves on their national religious privileges, but did not obey the Lord of the Temple, and were therefore condemned by the Prophet. A like temper was manifested after the Captivity. The Hebrew Nation was eager for the Messiah's Coming to the new-built temple ; but the Prophets reminded them that His Coming would be a day of fear and woe to the ungodly. See Mal. iii. 2.

19. *leaned his hand on the wall, and a serpent bit him*] Serpents often lurk concealed in the walls of Eastern houses (*Lane's Egyptians*, pp. 342, 343).

21. *I hate, I despise your feast days*] Language repeated by Isaiah (i. 11. 13, 14), and Jeremiah (vi. 20).

— *I will not smell*] Words derived from Leviticus xxvi. 31, " I will not smell the savour of your sweet odours." See the note there, and on Gen. viii. 21, " The Lord smelled a sweet savour," describing God's acceptance of Noah's sacrifice, typical of the one true and perfect Sacrifice well pleasing to God. See

Eph. v. 2, "Christ hath given Himself for us an offering and a sacrifice to God for a *sweet-smelling savour*."

23. *Take thou away from me the noise of thy songs ; for I will not hear the melody of thy viols*] *Or harps*. They thought to please God by vocal and instrumental music ; but it was an abomination to Him, because it came from hypocrites whose heart was far from Him. See below, on vi. 5. Compare the account given of the inventors of musical instruments in the history of the family of Cain (to be destroyed by the flood), Gen. iv. 21, and the note there ; and Job xxi. 12, 13 ; and Isa. v. 12, " The harp and the viol, the tabret and pipe, and wine, are in their feasts : but they regard not the work of the Lord, neither consider the operation of His hands." Here is a warning to all who think to please God by elaborate musical services in His house ; while they do not take heed to worship Him with their hearts, and to obey Him in their daily life.

24. *But let judgment run down as waters, and righteousness as a mighty stream*] The tide of music rolled down in a full stream of sound from many voices and harps, like the sound of many waters. Cp. Ezek. xliii. 2. Rev. i. 15 ; xiv. 2. But what did it profit when there was a drought of justice and righteousness ? Cp. Ecclus. xv. 9. Ps. i. 16.

25. *Have ye offered unto me*] Rather, *Did ye offer unto Me sacrifices in the wilderness, forty years, O ye house of Israel ?* No ; ye did not offer sacrifice to *Me*, but ye worshipped *idols*.

This is an important text, in answer to some recent allegations against the veracity of the Pentateuch (see note above, on Num. xv. 2), on the ground that the Israelites would not find a sufficient number of cattle in the wilderness for compliance with the sacrificial requirements of the Levitical Law. The fact is (as has been shown in that note), that the Levitical Law was given at Sinai under the supposition that Israel would obey God and would enter Canaan *within a few days after* the giving of the Law, and would observe it *there*. But it was not given with a view to their observance of it in the wilderness. And by their disobedience, they were excommunicated for thirty-eight years from God's favour, and condemned to wander in the wilderness, and were deprived of the privilege of observing it.

26. *But ye have borne*] Ye did not offer sacrifices to *Me*, ye

²⁷ Therefore will I cause you to go into captivity ᵏ beyond Damascus,
Saith the LORD, ¹ whose name *is* The God of hosts.

VI. ¹ Woe ᵃ to them *that* ‖ *are* at ease in Zion,
And trust in the mountain of Samaria,
*Which are* named ᵇ ‖ chief of the nations.
To whom the house of Israel came !

² ᶜ Pass ye unto ᵈ Calneh, and see ;
And from thence go ye to ᵉ Hamath the great :
Then go down to ᶠ Gath of the Philistines :
ᵍ *Be they* better than these kingdoms ?
Or their border greater than your border ?

³ Ye that ʰ put far away the ¹ evil day,
ᵏ And cause ¹ the ‖ seat of violence to come near ;

⁴ That lie upon beds of ivory, and ‖ stretch themselves upon their couches,
And eat the lambs out of the flock,
And the calves out of the midst of the stall ;

⁵ ᵐ That ‖ chant to the sound of the viol,
*And* invent to themselves instruments of musick, ⁿ like David ;

⁶ That drink ‖ wine in bowls,
And anoint themselves with the chief ointments :
ᵒ But they are not grieved for the † affliction of Joseph.

⁷ Therefore now shall they go captive with the first that go captive,

Before
CHRIST
787.
k 2 Kings 17.6.
Zech. 4. 14.
a Luke 6. 24
‖ Or, are secure.

b Ex. 19. 5.
‖ Or, first fruits.

c Jer. 2. 10.
d Isa. 10. 9.
Taken
about
781.
e 2 Kings 18. 4.
1 2 Chr. 26. 6.
g Nahum 3. 8.

h Ezek. 12. 27.
i ch. 5. 18. & 2. 16.
k ch. 5. 12.
ver. 12.
l Ps. 94. 20.
‖ Or, habitation
‖ Or, abound with
superfluities.

m Isa. 5. 12.
‖ Or, quaver.

n 1 Chr. 23. 5.

‖ Or, in bowls of
wine.

o Gen. 37. 25.
† Heb. breach.

did not adore *Me,* Whose glory dwelt in the moving tabernacle; *but ye took up,* and bore along with you, *the tabernacle of your king* (not the true King, Jehovah, the Lord of heaven and earth, and the Divine Protector of Israel, but *your* own chosen king, *Moloch*—which signifies *king*). Cp. 1 Kings xi. 7; and *Sept.* here; and the quotation by St. Stephen, Acts vii. 43, where the word *Moloch* is expressed.

— *and Chiun your images, the star of your god*] Rather, *and the stand* (pedestal, or basis; the word seems to be derived from the Hebrew *cûn,* to stand upright, *Gesen.* 386) *of your images* (so Ribera, Junius, Hengst., Keil, and, doubtingly, *Dr. Pusey*); others render it the *statue* of *your* images (so *Vulg., Gesen.* in Thes.). Others suppose that *Chiun* is the same as *Saturnus,* and as *Remphan* among the Egyptians, and that the *Sept.,* therefore, adopted the word *Remphan* for it. See *Fuerst,* 653; *Pfeiffer,* 439; *Surenhusius,* 415; and note below, on Acts vii. 43, and *Dr. Pusey,* 200; and *Gesen.* Lex. 395. Cp. *Turpie,* 181, who thinks that *Chiun* was a sun-god.

27. *Therefore will I cause you to go into captivity beyond Damascus*] Beyond the capital of Syria, in which you trust for help (see above, iii. 12), instead of relying on Me, the Lord God of Israel.

It was very appropriate, therefore, in Amos to use the word *Damascus* here; and it was no less proper for St. Stephen, in his speech at Jerusalem, to the Jewish Sanhedrin, where he refers to this prophecy, to use the word *Babylon,* " I will carry you away beyond Babylon," for such a carrying away had been foretold by Isaiah, and Jeremiah, xx. 4, 5. St. Stephen is quoting from "the Book of the Prophets," and nothing is more common among writers and speakers in the New Testament, than to combine into one several passages from various Prophetical Scriptures. See the note below, on Acts vii. p. 69, and the numerous instances of this practice collected in the excellent work of *Surenhusius* (Catallage, Amst. 1713), there cited.

Ch. VI. 1. *Woe to them that are at ease*] Cp. Isa. xxxii. 9.
— *named chief of the nations*] Rather, *the named* (i. e. the renowned princes; see Num. i. 16 ; xvi. 2) *among the chief of the nations,* i. e., Woe to the principal men of the princely nation of the Earth ! Woe to the princes of Israel, the first among the nations in God's favour (Exod. xix. 5).
— *To whom the house of Israel came*] To *which* (princes) the house of Israel resorts for help and guidance in affairs of state.

2. *Pass ye unto Calneh—Hamath—Gath*] Look to East, North, and West, and see whether any of the great kingdoms there *are* better (i. e. more favoured by God) than *these* kingdoms

VOL. VI. PART II.—49

of Israel. On Calneh in Babylonia, see Gen. x. 10. Isa. x. 10. Ezek. xxvii. 23. On Hamath in Syria, see Gen. x. 18. Num. xiii. 21 ; xxxiv. 8. Isa. x. 9. On Gath, see 1 Sam. v. 8.

These passages (vi. 1—6, and vii. 14, 15) are quoted by *S. Augustine* (de doct. Christ. iv. 16) as specimens of divine eloquence and inspiration in one who, like the prophet Amos, was "a herdman" (i. 1).

5. *That chant*] That *trill* (Heb. *pârat*), light ballads.
— *And invent to themselves instruments of music, like David*] Who flatter themselves that they will be blessed of God as David was, because they are *like* him in one particular—inventing musical instruments; but they invent them *to themselves,* not to God's glory—as David did.

On the flattering self-delusion of persons who imagine that, because they imitate good men in some particulars, they will therefore be favoured by God, see the excellent remarks of *Bp. Sanderson,* commenting on this text in his Lectures on Conscience (Lect. iii. § 13, vol. iv. p. 52).

6. *That drink wine in bowls*] Even in *sacrificial bowls* (Exod. xxxviii. 3. Num. iv. 14. 2 Chron. iv. 8); which they profane by sacrilegious revelry—as Belshazzar did at Babylon.
— *anoint themselves with the chief ointments*] Although in time of mourning all anointing was omitted (2 Sam. xiv. 2), yet they, in this crisis, when the divine wrath was about to break out upon the nation, and they ought to be sitting in sackcloth and ashes, are curious to procure the best ointment for their own use. Roman Patricians, in Cicero's days, cared only for their own fish-ponds, that their tables might be well supplied with mullets and other fish from them, when their country was in danger of being overwhelmed with a flood; they thought "only of the cock-boat of their own fortunes when the vessel of the State was being wrecked." The Emperor Nero was fiddling, when Rome was in flames. . . . . Here is another prophetic warning for our days of selfish luxury and lack of zeal for God.
— *are not grieved for the affliction of Joseph*] That is, (they grieve not themselves for the ruin (literally, breach) of their Church and country. Joseph, the ancestor of Ephraim, the head of the ten tribes, was afflicted by his own brethren, who saw the anguish of his soul, and were not moved by his tears (Gen. xlii. 21); and when they had sold him to the Ishmaelites, sat down, in heartless indifference, "to eat bread." See Gen. xxxvii. 25.

So their descendants, the Jews, feasted at the Passover after they had killed the true Joseph (John xviii. 28). How many dwelt in ceiled houses, and sing to the sound of the harp, and feast on the richest dainties, and care nothing for the sorrows of Christ and His Church ! nay, rather rejoice in them ! (Rev. xi. 10.)

E

Before
CHRIST
*v. 7.*
p Jer. 51.14.
Heb. c. 13, 17.
q Ps. 47. 4.
Heb. *hateth.*
Ps. 76.
r Heb. *the fulness
thereof.*

And the banquet of them that stretched themselves shall be removed.

⁸ ᵖThe Lord Goᴅ hath sworn by himself, saith the Loʀᴅ the God of hosts,

I abhor ᵠthe excellency of Jacob, and hate his palaces:

Therefore will I deliver up the city with all ʳthat is therein.

⁹ And it shall come to pass, if there remain ten men in one house, that they shall die.

¹⁰ And a man's uncle shall take him up, and he that burneth him, to bring out the bones out of the house, and shall say unto him that *is* by the sides of the house, *Is there* yet *any* with thee? and he shall say, No. Then shall he say,

r ch. 3. 13.
s ch. 8. 3.
t Or, *as we reckoned,
or, were wont.*
t Isa. 5. 30.
ch. 8. 6.
‖ Or, *droppings.*

ᵗHold thy tongue: ˢfor ‖ we may not make mention of the name of the Loʀᴅ.

¹¹ For, behold, ᵗthe Loʀᴅ commandeth,

And he will smite the great house with ‖ breaches,

And the little house with clefts.

¹² Shall horses run upon the rock?

Will *one* plow *there* with oxen?

x Hos. 10. 4.
ch. 5. 7.

For ˣye have turned judgment into gall,

And the fruit of righteousness into hemlock:

¹³ Ye which rejoice in a thing of nought,

Which say, Have we not taken to us horns by our own strength?

y Jer. 5. 15.

¹⁴ But, behold, ʸI will raise up against you a nation, O house of Israel, saith the Loʀᴅ the God of hosts;

z Num. 34. 8.
1 Kings 8. 65.
‖ Or, *valley.*

And they shall afflict you from the ᶻentering in of Hemath unto the ‖ river of the wilderness.

VII. ¹ Thus hath the Lord Goᴅ shewed unto me; and, behold, he formed

† Or, *green worms.*

‖ grasshoppers in the beginning of the shooting up of the latter growth; and,

---

**7.** *the banquet*] Rather, the cry of revelry (*Gesen.* 509).

**9.** *ten men*] A large number—they shall all die.

**10.** *a man's uncle*] Or, next of kin (*Gesen.* 191), whose duty it was to bury his deceased relative.

— *he that burneth him*] The Israelites did not burn corpses, but bury them; except in times of great mortality, which is implied here by this mention of *burning*.

— *by the sides of the house*] Or rather, at the back of the house, in its extreme corner.

— *No.*] They are all dead except one—myself.

— *Then shall he say*] Then shall the kinsman answer, *Hush! for there must be no mention of the name of the Lord.* This last man was expected by the kinsman to cry out in a piteous appeal for mercy to the Lord. But he, in an obstinate and godless fit of proud and sullen despair, checks and stifles the appeal, saying, "*Hush!*" Cp. viii. 3, where the same word is used.

— *for we may not make mention of the name of the Lord*] This represents the wretched, reprobate condition to which Israel would be reduced. As *S. Jerome* says, "Hoc commemorant ut ostendat, nec misericordiâ quidem posteâ et necessitate compulsos velle tenaci Dei conditori."

We see here a portraiture of the deathbed of the hardened infidel. He who has obstinately abused the intellectual powers given him by God, to cavil against God's truth, will be forsaken by Him at the last, and will not be able to utter His Name.

**11.** *with breaches—with clefts*] Or, *into breaches and shivers.*

**12.** *Shall horses run upon the rock?*] No; but *ye* do what is quite as preposterous. And, as horses tumble and wound themselves by running on sharp rocks; and as no harvest is to be expected from the ploughing of oxen there; so, in the self-chosen way of your own evil passions (which is preferred by you to the plain and even road of the law of God), you only lacerate yourselves, and reap no fruit from your labours.

— *ye have turned judgment into gall*] See v. 7.

**13.** *Have we not taken to us horns*] Horns are symbols of power (Deut. xxxiii. 17. 1 Kings xxii. 11). And these sinners ask, "Have we not acquired to ourselves help by our own might?" They speak like him who deified his own right hand and his own weapon, "Dextra mihi Deus, et telum, quod missile libro."

**14.** *a nation*] Assyria.

— *entering in of Hemath*] The northern boundary of Israel. See v. 12. Num. xxxiv. 8. 2 Kings xiv. 25, 28.

---

— *the river of the wilderness*] The southern boundary; the *Wady el Ahsy*, which separated Moab from Edom at the southern extremity of the Dead Sea (2 Kings iii. 25).

**Five Visions. Israel's Punishment and Restoration.**

Cʜ. VII. The last portion of the prophecies of Amos (ch. vii.–ix.) contains five Visions, which confirm what has been foretold in the foregoing portion.

Amos has five Parables (iii. 3–8) and five Visions.

The first four visions are distinguished from the fifth or last vision (ch. ix.) in this respect, that the first four begin with the same formula, "Thus hath the Lord God showed me;" the last begins with the words, "I saw the Lord."

They differ also in their contents. The first four symbolize the judgments which have already fallen in part on the Kingdom of Israel, and in part are still to fall; the last Vision, while it proclaims the overthrow of the ancient constitution of the Kingdom of Israel, reveals its *restoration* in a far more glorious and everlasting monarchy—that of Christ (ix. 11–15).

Of these four Visions the first two (vii. 1–6) contain a promise of divine *mercy* in reply to the Prophet's prayer; and thus they represent the memorable fact, that God was very patient with Israel, and that His judgments were not inflicted upon Israel at once, but after frequent admonitions and calls to repentance, and after many acts of divine love, sparing Israel when they deserved punishment. The second two Visions contain no assurance of mercy, because the divine long-suffering has been exhausted by Israel's sin, and is to be followed by *judgment*.

But Amos foretells, that eventually, in consequence of the infliction of salutary chastisement, Israel will be brought to repentance, and be reconciled to God in Christ, the beloved Son of God.

Thus we see that the Prophet Amos takes up and continues the strain of his predecessor Hosea, who has shown that all God's chastisements of Israel were due to Israel's sin, and were tempered with love, and will lead to the restoration of Israel to God in the Church of Christ. See Hosea xiii., xiv.

The Visions, like the Parables (iii. 3–8), begin with a prosaic *exordium*, which bursts forth into an impassioned, poetical, and antistrophical prophecy.

**1.** *he formed grasshoppers*] Rather, *he was forming locusts.* Cp. Nah. iii. 17, where the same word is used (*Gesen.* 161).

lo, *it was* the latter growth after the king's mowings.  ² And it came to pass, that when they had made an end of eating the grass of the land, then I said, O Lord GOD, forgive, I beseech thee : " || by whom shall Jacob arise ? for he *is* small.

³ ᵇ The LORD repented for this : It shall not be, saith the LORD.

⁴ Thus hath the Lord GOD shewed unto me : and, behold, the Lord GOD called to contend by fire, and it devoured the great deep, and did eat up a part.

⁵ Then said I, O Lord GOD, cease, I beseech thee : ᶜ by whom shall Jacob arise ? for he *is* small.

⁶ The LORD repented for this : This also shall not be, saith the Lord GOD.

⁷ Thus he shewed me : and, behold, the Lord stood upon a wall *made* by a plumbline, with a plumbline in his hand.  ⁸ And the LORD said unto me, Amos, what seest thou ? And I said, A plumbline. Then said the Lord, Behold, ᵈ I will set a plumbline in the midst of my people Israel :

ᵉ I will not again pass by them any more :

⁹ ᶠ And the high places of Isaac shall be desolate,

And the sanctuaries of Israel shall be laid waste ;

And ᵍ I will rise against the house of Jeroboam with the sword.

¹⁰ Then Amaziah ʰ the priest of Beth-el sent to ⁱ Jeroboam king of Israel, saying, Amos hath conspired against thee in the midst of the house of Israel : the land is not able to bear all his words.  ¹¹ For thus Amos saith, Jeroboam shall die by the sword, and Israel shall surely be led away captive out of their own land.

¹² Also Amaziah said unto Amos, O thou seer, go, flee thee away into the land of Judah, and there eat bread, and prophesy there : ¹³ but ᵏ prophesy not again any more at Beth-el : ˡ for it *is* the king's || chapel, and it *is* the † king's court.

*Margin notes:*
B-fore CHRIST 7.7.
a Isa. 51. 19. ver. 5.
2 Or, *who of for,*
3 Or, *Jacob shall stand?*
b Deut. 32, 36. ver. 6.
Jonah 3. 10. James 5. 16.
c ver. 2, 5.
d See 2 Kings 21. 13. Isa. 28. 17. & 34. 11.
Lam. 2. 8. e ch. 8. 2. Micah 7. 18. f Beer-sheba, Gen 26. 23. & g 1. ch 5. 5. & 5. 14. g Fulfilled, 2 Kings 15. 10. h 1 Kings 12. 32. i 2 Kings 14. 23.
k ch. 2. 12.
11 1 Kings 12. 32. & 13. 1.
2 Or, *sanctuary.*
† Heb. *house of the kingdom.*

---

Thus God shewed to Amos that the vast army of locusts described by Joel (i. 4) were creatures formed by Him to execute His purposes.

— *the latter growth*] The second crop; so that this would be consumed by the locusts.

— *after the king's mowings*] Therefore this first visitation was a merciful one. God might have formed the locusts so as to destroy the first crop; but He allowed the king to mow and to gather-in that. Thus He had dealt with Israel : He had given great successes to various Kings of Israel, especially to Jeroboam I. and to Jeroboam II. (see 2 Kings xiv. 27); but they were not drawn to God by these acts of kindness ; therefore, after these "King's mowings," He sends locusts to consume the *aftergrowth*. And even now He relents at the Prophet's penitential intercession (asking, *by whom shall Jacob arise?* or, *who is Jacob, that he should stand?* (*Gesen.* 469) and confessing his weakness, for *he is small*); and thus he shews that if Israel will repent, Israel will still be spared.

4. *by fire*] A severer judgment, sent because of Israel's impenitence under the former judgment. These successive judgments are like the successive plagues of Egypt, sent to bring Pharaoh to repentance.

— *it devoured the great deep*] The fire was devouring the ocean (cp. Gen. i. 2 ; vii. 11. Isa. li. 10), especially the Mediterranean sea, bordering Palestine. See the next note. The power of this fire shewed it to be a fire of God ; it was a precursor of the great conflagration which will consume the World —even the Sea itself—at the Great Day (2 Pet. iii. 10). Compare note on Jer. li. 32, where the fire of God, burning Babylon, is described as burning even in its lakes and moats.

— *did eat up a part*] Rather, *it devoured the portion* – God's favoured portion and inheritance, Israel. Deut. xxxii. 9, where the same word, *chélek*, is used. Cp. Micah ii. 4.

7. *with a plumbline*] The wall of Israel had been *built* by God with a plumb-line, and now it would be *destroyed* with a plumb-line (cp. 2 Kings xxi. 13. Isa. xxxv. 2. Lam. ii. 8); that is, there was, so to speak, an architectural design and plan in God's work of destroying Israel, no less than in His former favour to

Israel in building him up. God does every thing according to measure, number, and weight (Wisdom xi. 20). As one said of old, "The Deity is a perfect Geometrician." And the plumb-line of destruction was to be coextensive with the plumb-line of construction—it was to be total. This was fulfilled in the captivity and dispersion of Israel, which was so ordered as to be preparatory to the building up again and restoration of Israel, in Christ, and in His Universal Church, on the ruins of the literal Jerusalem. See below, ix. 11—15 ; and above, *Introd.* to Ezra, p. 299.

9. *the house of Jeroboam*] The *house* of Jeroboam II. (2 Kings xiv. 23—28). He does not say Jeroboam himself (as Amaziah, the priest of Bethel, falsely alleged, v. 11), who died in peace, but *the house* of Jeroboam, which came to a miserable end (2 Kings xv. 10).

10. *the priest of Beth-el*] The High Priest of the sanctuary of the golden calf there charges Amos, the Prophet of the Lord, with high treason against the King, and says that the land, i.e. the people, cannot *bear* his words ; that his prophecies are intolerable (cp. Wisdom ii. 12. 15) ; although the King's house, his dynasty, and his nation, would have been saved, if they had listened to his words ; they were eventually destroyed because they rejected his warnings.

12. *Judah*] Thy own country. See i. 1.

— *eat bread*] As if the design of Amos in prophesying was to gain a livelihood, like those false Prophets who prophesied, and those false priests who taught, for hire ! (Micah iii. 11.) Go thou to Judah, and *eat bread* there, and do not interfere with me, and let me *eat bread* in Bethel. Do thou live by thy trade there, and let me live by my trade here (S. *Jerome*).

13. *it is the king's chapel, and it is the king's court*] Bethel is the king's *sanctuary* and *house* of the *kingdom*—i. e. it is a chief shrine of the national worship. Observe, This priest of Bethel claims honour for it, not because it is the *Lord's* Sanctuary, but because it is the *King's* Sanctuary ; and not because it is the *house of God*, but the *house of Jeroboam*. All claims of reverence for a Church simply and merely as a *national establishment*, independently of Divine institution, are no better than these assertions of Amaziah. The first royal propounder of

Before
CHRIST
787.
m 1 Kings 20 35.
2 Kings 2, 5. 6.
4, 38, & 6. 1.
6, 14. 6. 1.
Zech. 13. 5.
* Or, *wild figs.*
† Heb. *gross*
*beast.*

o Ezek. 21. 2.
Micah 2. 6.
p See Jer. 28. 12.
& 29. 21, 25, 31, 32.
q Isa. 13. 16.
Lam. 5. 11.
Hos. 4. 13.
Zech. 14. 2.

a Ezek. 7. 2.

b ch. 7. 8.

c ch. 5. 23.
† Heb. *shall howl.*

d ch. 6. 9, 10.
† Heb. *be silent.*
e Ps. 14. 4.
Prov. 30. 14.

† Or, *month.*

f Neh. 13, 15, 16.
† Heb. *open.*

g Micah 6. 10, 11.

† Heb. *perverting
the balances of
deceit,* Hos. 12. 7.
h ch. 2. 6.

14 Then answered Amos, and said to Amaziah, I *was* no prophet, neither *was* I ᵐ a prophet's son; ⁿ but I *was* an herdman, and a gatherer of ‖ sycomore fruit : 15 and the LORD took me † as I followed the flock, and the LORD said unto me, Go, prophesy unto my people Israel.

16 Now therefore hear thou the word of the LORD :
Thou sayest, Prophesy not against Israel,
And ᵒ drop not *thy word* against the house of Isaac.

17 ᵖ Therefore thus saith the LORD ;
ᑫ Thy wife shall be an harlot in the city,
And thy sons and thy daughters shall fall by the sword,
And thy land shall be divided by line ;
And thou shalt die in a polluted land :
And Israel shall surely go into captivity forth of his land.

VIII. 1 Thus hath the Lord GOD shewed unto me : and behold a basket of summer fruit. 2 And he said, Amos, what seest thou ?
And I said, A basket of summer fruit.
Then said the LORD unto me, ᵃ The end is come upon my people of Israel ;
ᵇ I will not again pass by them any more.

3 And ᶜ the songs of the temple † shall be howlings in that day, saith the Lord GOD :
*There shall be* many dead bodies in every place ;
ᵈ They shall cast *them* forth † with silence.

4 Hear this, O ye that ᵉ swallow up the needy,
Even to make the poor of the land to fail, 5 saying,
When will the ‖ new moon be gone, that we may sell corn ?
And ᶠ the sabbath, that we may † set forth wheat,
5 Making the ephah small, and the shekel great,
And † falsifying the balances by deceit ?
6 That we may buy the poor for ʰ silver,
And the needy for a pair of shoes ;
*Yea,* and sell the refuse of the wheat ?

---

what is now called Erastianism, as far as we know, was Jeroboam I.; the first priestly advocate of it, as far as we know, was Amaziah. *S. Jerome*, in his note here, applies these words to the Arians, who appealed to Arian Emperors, supporting their dogmas and persecuting the orthodox teachers by the secular arm. When, in the fourth century, Catholic Bishops of Spain invoked the power of the Emperor Maximus, and would have put the Priscillianists to death, they were sternly rebuked and vigorously opposed by the saintly and apostolic Bishop, S. Martin of Tours (*Sulp. Sever.*, Hist. Eccl. ii. 50).

Observe, also, that it is often the lot of God's Prophets—indeed, it was the condition of Christ Himself (Luke xxiii. 2) and of His Apostles (Acts xvii. 7) to be taxed with disloyalty to the Crown, when they are discharging a duty of patriotism by upholding religious truth (which is the only safeguard of Thrones) in opposition to unbelief, heresy, schism, sacrilege, idolatry, and profaneness.

14. *I was no prophet, neither was I a prophet's son*] Literally, *"No prophet, I; no prophet's son* (or disciple, 1 Kings xx. 35. Matt. xii. 27), *I."* Thou chargest me with making myself a Prophet in order that I may *eat bread*, i.e. for the sake of a livelihood (see v. 12); but I have not sought that profession, I do not claim it. I am a mere herdman, and, so far from gratifying my appetite by prophesying, I am content with the simplest fare, the fruit of the mulberry-fig. See 1 Kings x. 27. Ps. lxxvii. 47. "In Palestine, at the present day, none but the very poor consent to be herdmen, and only such gather sycomore fruit or use it." (*Dr. Thomson*, the Land and the Book, 23).

16. *drop not thy word*] Cp. Deut. xxxii. 2. Ezek. xx. 16; xxi. 2. Micah ii. 6. 11. Probably Amaziah had used this word (*nataph*) in ridicule of the prophetic utterances of Amos.

17. *Thy wife shall be an harlot*] Thou teachest idolatry, which

is spiritual harlotry; and thou shalt be punished by harlotry in thy own house for thy sin.

— *thy land shall be divided by line*] According to my Vision (v. 7).

CH. VIII. 1. *a basket of summer fruit*] A basket of ripe fruit, signifying that Israel was ripe for judgment. Cp. Rev. xiv. 18. "Gather the clusters of the Earth, for her grapes are fully ripe."

2. *the end is come*] The *end*, Hebr. *kets*, with allusion to the Hebrew word *kaits*, summer fruit, used in the foregoing verse.

3. *the temple*] Or palace; the idol temple of Bethel.
— *they shall cast them forth with silence*] Literally, *"he* (i.e. every one) *casts them* (the corpses) *forth*, saying, *hush!"* See vi. 10, and Judges iii. 19. Neh. viii. 11. Zeph. i. 7. Zech. ii. 13.

4. *that swallow up the needy*] Rather, that pant after them to devour them, like a dog or wild beast panting and yelping after its prey. Cp. Job v. 5. Ps. lvi. 1, 2; lvii. 3; above, ii. 7. Eccles. i. 5, where the same word (*shaaph*) is used.

5. *the new moon*] The holy day when, according to the law, trade was suspended. Cp. Num. xxviii. 11.
— *the sabbath*] Cp. Neh. xiii. 15, 16.
— *set forth wheat*] Literally, open out wheat—i.e. throw open our granaries, closed on the holy day, and display the samples of our corn in our sacks, and sell their contents.
— *making the ephah small, and the shekel great*] Cheating by giving scant measure for the ephah by which ye sell (1½ of a bushel), and demanding greater weight than the right standard of the shekel, which ye charge as price for the goods sold.

6. *That we may buy the poor for silver*] To buy the poor by reducing him to the necessity of selling himself as a bondman (Lev. xxv. 39).
— *the needy for a pair of shoes*] Ch. ii. 6.

7 The LORD hath sworn by [i] the excellency of Jacob,
Surely [k] I will never forget any of their works.
8 [l] Shall not the land tremble for this,
And every one mourn that dwelleth therein?
And it shall rise up wholly as a flood;
And it shall be cast out and drowned, [m] as *by* the flood of Egypt.
9 And it shall come to pass in that day, saith the Lord GOD,
[n] That I will cause the sun to go down at noon,
And I will darken the earth in the clear day:
10 And I will turn your feasts into mourning,
And all your songs into lamentation;
[o] And I will bring up sackcloth upon all loins,
And baldness upon every head;
[p] And I will make it as the mourning of an only *son*,
And the end thereof as a bitter day.
11 Behold, the days come, saith the Lord GOD,
That I will send a famine in the land,
Not a famine of bread, nor a thirst for water,
But [q] of hearing the words of the LORD:
12 And they shall wander from sea to sea,
And from the north even to the east,
They shall run to and fro to seek the word of the LORD,
And shall not find *it*.
13 In that day shall the fair virgins and young men faint for thirst.
14 They that [r] swear by [s] the sin of Samaria,
And say, Thy god, O Dan, liveth;
And, The † manner [t] of Beer-sheba liveth;
Even they shall fall, and never rise up again.
IX. 1 I saw the Lord standing upon the altar: and he said,
Smite the ‖ lintel of the door, that the posts may shake:

Before CHRIST 787.
i ch. 6. 8.
k Hos. 8. 13. & 9. 9.
l Hos. 4. 3.
m ch. 9. 5.
791.
n Job 5. 14. Isa. 13. 10. & 59. 9, 10. Jer. 15. 9. Micah 3. 6.
o Isa. 15. 2, 3. Jer 48. 37. Ezek. 7. 18. & 27. 31.
p Jer. 6. 26. Zech. 12. 10.
q 1 Sam. 3. 1. Ps. 74. 9. Ezek. 7. 26.
r Hos. 4. 15.
s Deut. 9. 21.
† Heb. *way*: See Acts 9. 2. & 18. 25. & 19. 9, 23. & 24. 14.
t ch. 5. 5.
‖ Or, *chapiter*, or, *knop*.

---

**7.** *by the excellency of Jacob*] God Himself (1 Sam. xv. 29).

**8.** *it shall rise up wholly as a flood—drowned*] The whole land of Israel shall heave upward as a flood; it shall *rise up and then sink* downward, even as the *flood of Egypt*—the Nile. The land shall lose its stability, and become fluid, like the swollen flood of the river Nile in its inundations. Cp. below, ix. 5. Jer. xlvi. 7, 8. The word *by*, which is not in the original, would be better omitted.

**9.** *I will cause the sun to go down at noon*] This prophecy has been supposed by some (*Hitzig*) to have been fulfilled by an eclipse of the sun, B.C. 784, the year of the death of Jeroboam II. (but this is very questionable, see *Pusey*, 217); or by one of the eclipses in B.C. 791; or in B.C. 771; or in B.C. 770 (*Ussher*, Annales, A.M. 3213).

However this may be, the climax of the fulfilment was in the miraculous darkness at the Crucifixion of Christ; to which the words in the following verse may be applied (quoted as words of Amos in Tobit ii. 6). *I will turn your feasts into mourning.* Your great festival of the Passover (at which Christ was crucified) shall be turned into a day of lamentation (*S. Jerome* here, and *S. Irenæus*, iv. 66).

**10.** *the mourning of an only* son] Another reference to Christ. Cp. Zech. xii. 10.

**11.** *I will send a famine in the land*] *On the earth.* They in the land of Israel, who now despise God's Word, will, when dispersed, and wandering *from sea to sea*, and *from north to east* (v. 12), hunger after it. This will be one of the good effects of their banishment. They will be like the prodigal in the far-off land, feeding on husks, and yearning for the food once plentifully enjoyed and despised by him in his father's house.

Such is the present condition of the Jews. They roam in restless vagrancy about the world, and seek the word of God; but they find it not, because they have killed the Incarnate Word, revealed in the written word (*S. Jerome*). But they will feed upon the living bread of the written Word, when they are willing to see Christ there. See 2 Cor. iii. 14—16.

**14.** *the sin of Samaria*] The golden calf (iv. 4; v. 5) at Bethel.

— *The manner of Beer-sheba liveth*] Literally, *the way of Beersheba*—i. e. the religion there practised; so the word *way* is used in Acts ix. 2 (see the note there); or it may be, the way *to* Beersheba, the pilgrimage of unhappy votaries to the idolatrous shrine there. See above, v. 5.

CH. IX. 1. *I saw the* LORD] This is the fifth and last Vision. Before this Amos had seen the instruments employed by the Lord to execute His judgments (the locusts, the fire, the plumb-line, in the Lord's hands, and the basket of ripe fruit representing the ripeness of Israel for judgment), and to prepare the way for His Coming; but now the Lord Himself appears in all His Majesty.

— *standing upon the altar*] The altar which Jeroboam had set up at Bethel (*S. Cyril*, and so *Ruffinus, Clarius, A Castro, A Lapide, Ewald, Hitzig, Hoffmann, Pusey*), and against which the man of God from Judah prophesied, "O altar, altar, —behold this altar shall be rent" (1 Kings xiii. 1—3). Others (*S. Jerome, Theodoret, Hengst., Keil*) suppose the altar to be the brasen altar at Jerusalem.

— *Smite the lintel of the door*] Rather, *the knop*, or chapiter of the colonnade. Cp. the use of the same word (*captór*) in Exod. xxv. 31. 33; xxxvii. 17. In those two chapters of Exodus it occurs sixteen times, and is always rendered *knop*. See *margin* here, and in Zeph. ii. 14.

The command "Smite" is given by the Lord to the destroying Angel. Cp. Exod. xii. 12. 2 Sam. xxiv. 1. 15, 16. 2 Kings xix. 35; and Ezekiel's Vision (chap. ix. and x. 2. 7).

— *the posts*] Or *thresholds.* The idolatrous temple was to be shaken from top to bottom.

And ‖ ¹ cut them in the head, all of them ;

And I will slay the last of them with the sword :

¹ He that fleeth of them shall not flee away,

And he that escapeth of them shall not be delivered.

² ² Though they dig into hell, thence shall mine hand take them ;

⁶ Though they climb up to heaven, thence will I bring them down :

³ And though they hide themselves in the top of Carmel,

I will search and take them out thence ;

And though they be hid from my sight in the bottom of the sea,

Thence will I command the serpent, and he shall bite them :

⁴ And though they go into captivity before their enemies,

ᵉ Thence will I command the sword, and it shall slay them :

And ᶠ I will set mine eyes upon them for evil, and not for good.

⁵ And the Lord GOD of hosts *is* he that toucheth the land, and it shall ᵍ melt,

ʰ And all that dwell therein shall mourn :

And it shall rise up wholly like a flood ;

And shall be drowned, as *by* the flood of Egypt.

⁶ *It is* he that buildeth his ‖ ⁺ ʲ stories in the heaven,

And hath founded his ‖ troop in the earth ;

He that ᵏ calleth for the waters of the sea,

And poureth them out upon the face of the earth :

ᶠ The LORD *is* his name.

⁷ *Are* ye not as children of the Ethiopians unto me, O children of Israel ?
saith the LORD.

Have not I brought up Israel out of the land of Egypt ?

And the ᵐ Philistines from ⁿ Caphtor,

And the Syrians from ᵒ Kir ?

⁸ Behold, ᵖ the eyes of the Lord GOD *are* upon the sinful kingdom, and I

⁹ will destroy it from off the face of the earth ; saving that I will not utterly

destroy the house of Jacob, saith the LORD.

⁹ For, lo, I will command, and I will † sift the house of Israel among all

---

— *cut them in the head, all of them*] This is usually referred to the idolatrous fabric and its parts ; but it may be applied to the worshippers ; and this is confirmed by what follows ; and the sense then would be - cut them in the head, and I will slay the last, or remnant, of them with the sword : the worshippers from the head to the tail of them would be cut off, as well as the temple, from its summit to its threshold, be destroyed. See Isa. ix. 14, "The Lord will cut off from Israel *head and tail*."

2. *Though they dig into hell,* Cp. Ps. cxxxix. 8. Job xxvi. 6. Obad. 4. Jer. li. 53.

3. *top of Carmel*] Carmel, both from its height and numerous caverns (*Raumer, Richter, Schulz, Hengst., Pusey*), was used as a hiding-place ; as appears in the history of Elijah (1 Kings xviii. 19. 2 Kings ii. 25 ; iv. 25.

— *will I command the serpent,* God will command the venomous sea serpent to bite His enemies. The whale was commanded by God to swallow Jonah ; the fish to pay tribute for Christ ; the viper to spare St. Paul : all these were under Divine control. The "Old Serpent," Satan, is God's servant, and is used by Him to do His will in punishing the ungodly (Isa. xxvii. 33. Ps. vii. 130).

5. *shall be drowned,*] Shall sink, like the Nile (*Sept.*). See viii. 8.

6. *stories*] Or *steps*. Scripture speaks of the third heaven (2 Cor. xii. 2), the heaven of heavens (1 Kings viii. 27).

— *his troop*] Rather, his *vault* or *arch*. Literally, a *band* (Gesen. 10) ; the visible firmament (Gen. i. 7) which divides the water above the heavens from the water beneath the heavens. Cp. Gen. vii. 11.

7. *Are ye not as children of the Ethiopians* Ye people of Israel boast your close to be My special favourites, because I

chose your father Abraham, and brought him out of Mesopotamia into Canaan. And ye will be blessed by Me as My peculiar people, if ye walk in the steps of your father Abraham. But the fact of his call from Mesopotamia to Canaan was not, when considered irrespectively of the spiritual character of him who migrated at My call, any proof of My favour. I order and change the bounds of habitation of all nations. The Ethiopians are children of Ham, who came forth from the ark as well as Shem and Japhet ; and if ye do not obey Me, ye are no better than they are. I did bring you out of Egypt. Yes ; but I brought the Philistines also (whom ye despise as uncircumcised) out of Caphtor (probably Cappadocia—*Targum, Sept., Vulg.*: see Gen. x. 14) ; and I brought the Syrians from Kir (see i. 5). Ye cease to be Israelites ; ye become no better than Cushites, Philistines, and Syrians, if ye forsake Me ; indeed, ye become worse than them, in proportion as ye enjoy more spiritual light than they did. Compare St. Paul's statement, Rom. ii. 25—29 ; ix. 6, 7.

8. *the sinful kingdom*] Any and every kingdom that sins against Me. Cp. Isa. x. 6.

9. *I will sift the house of Israel* A beautiful image, representing clearly God's beneficent design in the captivity and dispersion of Israel. It seemed as if He, when He had given them into the hand of Assyria, had scattered them abroad and had utterly cast them to the winds. But no, they were safe in the divine sieve (cp. Jer. xv. 7 ; li. 1. Matt. iii. 12. Luke xxii. 31) ; and they were there for the purpose of being proved and tested. Those among them who were impenitent and godless, and did not profit by the chastisement, would be dispersed like chaff by the wind ; but the penitent and faithful would be preserved, and be made manifest by the sifting : they would be

nations, like as *corn* is sifted in a sieve, yet shall not the least † grain fall upon the earth. Before CHRIST 787. † Heb. *stone.*

10 All the sinners of my people shall die by the sword, [r] which say, The evil shall not overtake nor prevent us. r ch. 6. 3.

11 [s] In that day will I raise up the tabernacle of David that is fallen, s Acts 15. 16, 17.
And † close up the breaches thereof; † Heb. *hedge, or, wall.*
And I will raise up his ruins,
And I will build it as in the days of old:

12 [t] That they may possess the remnant of [u] Edom, t Obad. 19. u Num. 24. 18.
And of all the heathen, † which are called by my name, † Heb. *upon whom my name is called.*
Saith the LORD that doeth this.

13 Behold, [x] the days come, saith the LORD, that the plowman shall overtake the reaper, x Lev. 26. 5.
And the treader of grapes him that † soweth seed: † Heb. *draweth forth.*
[y] And the mountains shall drop ‖ sweet wine, y Joel 3. 18. ‖ Or, *new wine.*
And all the hills shall melt.

---

separated by that process from the chaff; and not a single grain (Hebr. *tserór;* literally, a thing bound together; any thing solid, as a pebble; a grain of corn, as opposed to the loose, dusty chaff; *Gesen.* 720)—would fall to the earth.

This image is adopted by the Evangelical Prophet Isaiah in that noble passage where Babylon is compared to a threshing-floor of God for the winnowing of Judah. See above, on Isa. xxi. 10, and compare xxviii. 23—29. Such is the whole World now. It is God's floor, in which Israel is being winnowed, in order that the remnant of good grain may be gathered into the garner of Christ's Church universal.

10. *prevent us*] Come before us, to meet us; confront us.

RESTORATION OF ISRAEL IN CHRIST; and CONVERSION of Israel's ENEMIES (symbolized by EDOM) and of the GENTILES.

11. *In that day*] The glorious day which is now revealed to the Prophet, the Day of Christ. Cp. *Bp. Chandler* on Prophecy, i. 139.

Having spoken of the Divine purpose in sifting Israel in its Captivity (*v.* 9), he now proceeds to speak of their Restoration to God in Christ, and in His Church. Amos foresees and foretells clearly that, before salvation comes to Israel, all that is dearest to Israel, all on which Israel dotes most fondly and relies most confidently, and of which they boast most proudly, will be destroyed, and Israel will be carried captive and dispersed; the House of David itself, to which God's promises of continuity were announced, will be in ruins. But the battle would be succeeded by peace. Calm would follow the storm. Building-up would grow out of destruction. Israel's Midnight would be changed by Christ into a glorious Noon.

— *will I raise up the tabernacle of David that is fallen*] Literally, the (pastoral) *hut* (or *booth*) *of David, the fallen* (hut) of the shepherd of Bethlehem; near which Amos himself kept cattle (i. 1).

He does not call it a royal palace, but a *hut* or *booth* (*succah*), and a *fallen* one, to show the low estate to which it would be reduced, and from which it would be raised in Christ; and thus he prepared the way for the prophecy of Micah concerning Bethlehem (see Micah v. 2), and for the prophecy of Isaiah concerning the rod springing forth from the roots of the hewn-down tree of Jesse. See on Isa. xi. 1; liii. 2. Ezek. xvii. 22—24.

The Hebrew Rabbis recognized in these words a prophecy concerning the Messiah (see the authorities in *Hengstenberg* here), and they call Him "the son of the fallen one," a title derived from this passage. See the Rabbinical Authorities in *Bp. Chandler* on Prophecy, i. 144.

Observe, the Prophet here tells the Ten Tribes of Israel that their own Restoration depends on the building-up of the house of *David*, from which they had severed themselves by the schism of Jeroboam (cp. Ezek. xxxvii. 15—25); and thus, while he cheers them with promises of recovery by Christ, the Seed of David, he does not suffer them to forget their own sin of schism and separation from David's House.

12. *That they may possess the remnant of Edom, and of all the heathen, which are called by my name, saith the* LORD *that doeth this*] These words, and those in the foregoing verse, are referred to by St. James, in the first Council of the Church, the Council of Jerusalem, when it was debated whether the Ceremonial Law of Moses was to be imposed as obligatory on the Gentile Converts, and whether they were to be admitted on any other terms, as of necessity, except faith in Christ, and by Baptism in His Name. See below, on Acts xv. 16, 17.

St. James, in dealing with this question, which concerned the Gentiles as well as the Jews, quoted the words of Amos here as they stand in the *Septuagint* Version, made by Jews at Alexandria, in the Greek language, the principal language of the Heathen World.

That Version was not designed to be a literal one, but a Paraphrase. Cp. below, on Micah v. 2. The Septuagint Version is a Hellenistic Targum. And when the Translators met with a passage, in the Original Hebrew, which, if literally rendered, would be unintelligible to Hellenistic ears, they did not hesitate to modify it, so as to preserve the spirit by deviating from the letter.

This they have done here. They did *not confound* the word *Edom* with *Adam* (man, or mankind) as some have imagined; but they deliberately substituted *Adam* for *Edom*, which contains the same consonants as *Adam*, mankind (with the exception of *vau*), and suggested *Adam* to them. And thus they gave, virtually, the true sense in a much clearer way to Greek readers than if they had preserved the *ipsissimam vocem*, *Edom.* To the *Hebrew* mind, Edom was a representative of the Nations of Mankind opposed to Israel; but this idea was *not* familiar to the *Greek* mind.

The substitution of *Adam* in the mind of the Translator, and its correlative Greek word, ἀνθρώπων, gave the true sense of Amos, for which he was cited by St. James, namely, that *all mankind* would be admitted into Covenant with God in Christ, Who is the Son of David, and Who builds up the tabernacle (or pastoral hut) of David, that had fallen down.

The same reason weighed with the Septuagint Translators for the modification of the other words of Amos, "that they may possess the *remnant.*" These words were intelligible enough to the Hebrew reader, who looked at *Edom* as symbolizing their enemies, and to whom it was promised that they themselves should possess Edom (see Num. xxiv. 18. Obad. 19)—a promise never accomplished literally by any of Zerubbabel's descendants, but fulfilled in Christ overthrowing the enemies of all true Israelites. See above, on Isa. lxiii. 1, "Who is this that cometh from *Edom?*" But these words, *They shall possess the remnant*, would be unintelligible to Greek ears; but *Edom* having suggested *Adam*, the word *yireshu* (*they shall possess*) suggested *yidreshu* (*they shall seek*), and thus the modification was completed, which imparted to Greek minds the true *sense* of the original by means of a *paraphrase* of the *words.* Cp. *Surenhusius*, pp. 430—434.

13. *the days come*] The days of the Messiah. See above, on Jer. ix. 25; xxiii. 5; xxx. 3.

— *the plowman shall overtake the reaper*] An image of evangelical joy and prosperity, derived from the Levitical Law.

— *the mountains shall drop sweet wine*] Words caught up from Joel iii. 18.

— *the hills shall melt*] Shall dissolve themselves into rivers of plenty and delight. There is a spiritual reference to the Mosaic

Before CHRIST 787.

z Jer. 30. 3.
a Isa. 61. 4. & 65. 21. Ezek. 36. 33-36.

14 z And I will bring again the captivity of my people of Israel,
And a they shall build the waste cities, and inhabit *them*;
And they shall plant vineyards, and drink the wine thereof;
They shall also make gardens, and eat the fruit of them.
15 And I will plant them upon their land,
And b they shall no more be pulled up out of their land which I have given them,
Saith the LORD thy God.

b Isa. 60. 21. Jer. 32. 41. Ezek. 34. 28. Joel 3. 20.

---

description of Canaan flowing with milk and honey (Exod. iii. 8, 17. Lev. xxvi. 5).

14. *I will bring again the captivity*] Rather, *I will turn the captivity.* The Captivity is regarded as a stream which is to be turned. Compare Ps. cxxvi. 4.

14, 15. *they shall build the waste cities—and they shall plant vineyards—and I will plant them upon their land, and they shall no more be pulled up out of their land which I have given them, saith the* LORD *thy God*] These prophecies received a subordinate and preparatory fulfilment when some of the Jews returned under Zerubbabel to Jerusalem; but this was only a foretaste of their full accomplishment in Christ. The opinion that they were fully accomplished in Zerubbabel, was broached by *Theodore of Mopsuestia*, but was condemned as heretical in the Second Council of Constantinople.

The Prophets speak of *conversion* to Christianity under the terms of *restoration*. Thus, a restoration is promised to *Moab* (Jer. xlviii. 47), to *Ammon* (Jer. xlix. 6), and even to *Sodom* and *her daughters*. Those prophecies *cannot be understood literally*, but they foretell the reception of heathen nations into the Church. See *A Lapide*, here. Similarly all these prophecies of Amos are fulfilled in all places wherever Israel is planted in the true spiritual Holy Land, the Church of Christ. Zion now enfolds the World, and will never be destroyed. Palestine extends to all places where Christ is preached and adored. The World has become a Holy Land in Him. See above, on Jer. xxx. 3; xxxi. 5; on Isa. lxv. 21, and chap. lxvi. 7—12. Ezek. xxxiv. 13; xxxvi. 33; xxxvii. 12; and on Joel iii. 20, 21.

An Ancient Father of the Church at the close of the Fourth Century, *S. Jerome*, who dwelt at Bethlehem in the immediate neighbourhood of Tekoa, the native place of Amos the Prophet, thus writes: "The Tabernacle of David had fallen down to those who said, 'Evil shall not overtake us' (*v.* 10), whom the Lord sifted and proved in His sieve, and whose threshing-floor He had purged by the fan of His Majesty, and the transgressors among whom He had slain by the sword.

"But now, according to the custom of Scripture, after a prophecy of chastisement, He adds promises of love and prosperity. He says, that He will *raise up* this *Tabernacle of David* that had *fallen down*, that He will build it all up again in the Resurrection of Christ the Son of David; so that what had fallen down in the Jewish Synagogue might rise up in the Christian Church; and that they who believe in Christ might *possess the remnant of Edom* and *of all the heathen*; so that whatever remains of the earthly and sanguinary kingdom of Edom, the enemy of Israel, might be changed into a kingdom of heaven; and that the heathen might be converted and return to the Lord; and so, when the fulness of the Gentiles had come in, all Israel should be saved (Rom. xi. 12).

"The prophecy of Amos which now succeeds, is understood by us who do not follow the letter that killeth (as some of the Jews now do), but the spirit that giveth life (2 Cor. iii. 6), to have been in part fulfilled, and to be in course of fulfilment, in the Christian Church. It is fulfilled in all who have fallen into ruin by sin, and who are built up by repentance. And when the Tabernacle of David, which had fallen down, is built up again in Christ, then, as the Prophet says, a time succeeds of universal abundance. They who before went forth weeping, bearing their good seed, now return again with joy, and bring their sheaves with them (Ps. cxxvi. 6). The ploughman overtakes the reaper, and the treader of grapes him that soweth seed. The vintage and seed-time will coincide. In that day the wine-press will be filled, the grapes will be trodden, and red wine will be poured forth from the blood of Christ and the Holy Martyrs, and this their blood will be the seed of the Church.

"*The mountains shall drop sweet wine, and the hills shall melt*, when every one, who ascends in a holy and virtuous life to the hills of spiritual contemplation, will taste the honey and the sweet wine which flow there; as the Psalmist says, 'Taste and see how gracious the Lord is.' 'Thy words are sweet to my mouth, sweeter than honey and the honeycomb' (Ps. xxxiv. 8; Ps. xix. 10; cxix. 103). And they who dwell beneath the mountains, on which the Bridegroom comes leaping in the Canticles (Song of Solomon ii. 8), will be planted like a Paradise of God; and all fruits of holy learning and knowledge will hang upon their boughs. Then he who once wandered in captivity, and did not then believe in the Name of the Lord, but is of the remnant of Israel, will *return to God and to his own land*, by faith in Christ, and he will recognize in the Gospels Him of Whom he once read in the Prophets; and after the Lord has thus turned back the Captivity of His people Israel, they will build up cities which before were desolate on lofty mountains, and dwell in them, according to our Lord's words, 'a city set upon a hill cannot be hid' (Matt. v. 14). They will also plant vineyards and drink wine of them, according to the invitation given by Christ in the Canticles (v. 1), 'Drink, yea drink abundantly, O beloved.' This is the grape of Sorec which we drink daily in the holy mysteries of the Lord's banquet. And they will plant gardens and water them, and no kinds of Christian graces and virtues will be lacking there; and they will eat the fruit of them. And thus the promise of Christ will be fulfilled, 'Blessed are the meek, for they shall inherit the earth' (Mat. v. 5). And the final promise of the prophecy here is, 'I will plant them upon their land, and they shall no more be pulled up out of their land which I have given them, saith the Lord of hosts;' whence we learn that, though the Church of God will be persecuted in the last days, it will never be destroyed; it will be assaulted, but it will never be conquered. And the reason of this is, because the Lord God Almighty, the Lord God of the Church, has promised this; and God's promise is Nature's law" (*S. Jerome*). Compare *S. Augustine*, De Civ. Dei, xviii. 28.

"We are *not* authorized to seek for a realization of this prophecy of Amos in the return of Israel from its Babylonish Captivity to Palestine, under Zerubbabel and Ezra; for this was no planting of Israel *to dwell for ever in the land*, nor was it a setting up of the fallen hut of David. *Nor* have we to transfer the fulfilment to the future, and think of a time when the Jews, who have been converted to their God and Saviour Jesus Christ, *will one day be led back to Palestine.* Canaan and Israel are types of the kingdom of God, and of the Lord's Church. Cp. Joel iii. 8. The raising up of the fallen hut of David began with the Coming of Christ, and the founding of the Christian Church; and the taking possession of Edom and all the other nations upon whom the Lord reveals His Name, took its rise in the reception of the Gentiles into the Kingdom of Heaven set up by Christ. The Land which will flow with streams of Divine blessing is not Palestine, but the domain of the Christian Church; it is the Earth, as far as it receives the benefits of Christianity. The people which cultivate this land are the members of the Christian Church, so far as it is grounded in living faith, and brings forth the fruits of the Holy Spirit" (*Keil*). See also *M. Henry* here, who says:—"This must certainly be understood of the abundance of spiritual blessings in heavenly things, which all those are and shall be blessed with, who are in sincerity added to Christ and His Church; they shall be abundantly replenished with the goodness of God's House, with the graces and comforts of His Spirit; they shall have bread—the bread of life—to *strengthen their hearts*, and the wine of divine consolations to *make them glad—meat, indeed*, and *drink, indeed*—all the benefit that comes to the souls of men from the Word and Spirit of God. In Gospel-times the mountains of the Gentile world shall be enriched with these privileges by the Gospel of Christ preached, and professed, and received in the power of it. When great multitudes were converted to the faith of Christ, and nations were born at once; when the preachers of the Gospel were *always caused to triumph in* the success of their preaching, then the *ploughman overtook the reaper*; and when the Gentile Churches were *enriched in all utterance, and in all knowledge*, and all manner of *spiritual gifts* (1 Cor. i. 5), then the *mountains dropped sweet wine*" (*M. Henry*).

# OBADIAH.

THE vision of Obadiah.
Thus saith the Lord God ² concerning Edom ;

Before
CHRIST
about
587.
a Isa. 21. 11. & 34. 5.    Ezek. 25. 12, 13, 14.    Joel 3. 19.    Mal. 1. 3.

## PRELIMINARY NOTE.

The prophecy of OBADIAH is linked on to the foregoing predictions of Amos by a particular word.

That word is EDOM.

In the last chapter of his prophecies, Amos had said that the Lord would "raise up the tabernacle of David that was fallen," and he had expressed its future glory and universal sovereignty under the sway of the Messiah, by saying that it would "possess the remnant of *Edom*" (ix. 11, 12).

The name *Edom*, as was there observed, represents not merely the literal Edomites, but all those persons and classes of society, which, being allied by nearness of birth or place to the Israel of God—that is, to the Christian Church (as Edom, or Esau, was to Jacob), have yet behaved to it in an unbrotherly, heartless, and treacherous manner.

That prophecy of Amos is now taken up and expanded by Obadiah, who follows next to Amos in the Hebrew Canon, and in the order of time.

That this is the proper place for Obadiah in the chronological sequence of the Prophets, and that he prophesied during, or soon after, the twenty-seven years in which Uzziah, King of Judah, and Jeroboam II., King of Israel, were contemporaries—i.e. between B.C. 810, and B.C. 783—was suggested 1400 years ago by *S. Jerome*, who says, "a great portion of Obadiah is contained in the Book of Jeremiah;" and this has been successfully proved, and is now generally admitted, by the best expositors, as Hengstenberg, *Pusey*, Keil; see also Kueper, Jeremias, p. 100; *Delitzsch* on Isaiah lxiii. 1—6; and the remarks of *Graf* (Der Prophet Jeremias, Leipz. 1863, pp. 559—570); and especially *Carl Paul Caspari* (Der Prophet Obadja, Leipz. 1842, pp. 6—42), who, however, thinks that Obadiah is speaking of the cruelty of Edom to Judah at the time of the Chaldean invasion. They have shown that Jeremiah in his prophecy concerning Edom (Jer. xlix. 7—22), has adopted the language of Obadiah.

The uncertainty of that modern Criticism which sets aside the authority of the Hebrew Canon, and has exhibited itself in the disquisitions on Obadiah of *Hitzig*, *Hofmann*, and others, is strikingly displayed in the fact that the former makes him to be the *latest* of the Prophets, and the other regards him as the *earliest*.

It is observed by *Caspari* (pp. 5—12), in examining the prophecies of Jeremiah concerning Edom, that we discover a great number of expressions which are peculiar to Jeremiah and often occur in his writings; but not a single one of these is found in Obadiah; which would be unaccountable, if Obadiah had followed and used the prophecies of Jeremiah, instead of *vice versâ*. On the other hand, nothing which Jeremiah has in common with Obadiah, in the prophecies concerning Edom, is found in any other part of Jeremiah. Obadiah's prophecies concerning Edom form one connected whole; Jeremiah intersperses his prophecy with phrases culled here and there from Obadiah.

From this demonstration we may derive the following inferences:—

1. It confirms our confidence in the arrangement of the Minor Prophets in the Hebrew Bible—an arrangement which, happily, has been adopted in our own Authorized English Version of the Old Testament.

2. The chronological position of Obadiah illustrates an important truth concerning God's dealings with mankind.

It may be laid down as a rule, that God never executes a judgment, or inflicts a punishment on a nation or an individual,

without having given some previous warnings, either special or general, as to the hateful character and dangerous consequences of the sins for which the judgments are inflicted. God warns men of hell, in order that they may escape hell, and attain heaven. He speaks of punishment, that He may not inflict it.

This was the law of His working with regard to even heathen nations. He did not denounce His judgments on Nineveh by Nahum before He had given a warning to Nineveh by Jonah; and He did not denounce His judgment on Edom by Jeremiah, before He had given warning of the approaching visitation by Obadiah.

3. It is to be regretted that in our English Version of Obadiah, the sin and punishment of Edom are represented as *already past*; whereas, the truth is, that they *are future*. Obadiah does not exult over Edom as *having been punished* for their sins against their brother Israel, by the Lord God of Israel, but he is sent by God, in His mercy, to *warn* Edom *against committing the sin*, in order that *they may escape the punishment*; see below, on v. 12.

4. The name *Obadiah* means *servant* of the *Lord* (Jehovah), the God of the Covenant of Israel. Obadiah performs his work as *servant* of *Jehovah*, by showing that the Lord God of Israel is Supreme Ruler of the Universe, and the destinies of all heathen Nations are in His hands; and that it is the duty and happiness of nations to acknowledge His supremacy; and that though heathen nations, like Edom, may for wise purposes be allowed to chastise Israel—the Church of God—yet, eventually, the Lord God of Israel (that is, of the true Church) will overrule all things to the good of His Church, which will endure for ever; and to the glory of the Great Name of the Lord God of Abraham, shedding blessings on all His faithful people of every nation, through the Seed of Abraham, in Whom "all families of the earth are to be blessed" —our Lord and Saviour JESUS CHRIST.

5. It may be observed, that, in order to bring out more clearly the supremacy of JEHOVAH, the Lord of Israel, Obadiah never uses the word ELOHIM.

6. In the series of *special* denunciations of warning against heathen nations, which form the *entire subject* of the writings of Three among the Minor Prophets, the denunciation of Obadiah against Edom holds the first place ;

It is followed by the special denunciations of Jonah and of Nahum against the great Assyrian capital, Nineveh.

These special denunciations by Obadiah against Edom, and by Jonah and Nahum against Nineveh, are again succeeded by Habakkuk's message of woe to Babylon. It has been shown above, concerning Edom, Nineveh, and Babylon, that each of them represents a particular type respectively of sin against God, and of enmity against His Church. See on Isa. xiii. *prelim. note.* Jer. xlix. 7; l. 1. 21. Ezek. xxv. p. 213 ; xxxi. p. 226.

Edom is the type of unfraternal and treacherous churchmanship.

Nineveh is the type of open blasphemy and infidelity.

Babylon is the type of proud and dominant Idolatry.

The priority of Obadiah to Jonah, Nahum, and Habakkuk may suggest the solemn truth, that Edonitish hatred against God's Church (that is, the malignant enmity of those who are connected with the spiritual Israel of God by ties of consanguinity or neighbourhood) calls for God's primitive retribution even before the sins of such distant foes as Nineveh and Babylon, who had not the same advantages as Edom enjoyed.

1. *Obadiah*] Servant of Jehovah. See the *Prelim. Note,* and *Caspari*, pp. 1, 2.

— *the Lord God*] Hebr. ADONAI JEHOVAH, declaring that

¹ We have heard a rumour from the LORD,
And an ambassador is sent among the heathen,
Arise ye, and let us rise up against her in battle.

² Behold, I have made thee small among the heathen:
Thou art greatly despised.

³ The pride of thine heart hath deceived thee,
Thou that dwellest in the clefts ᶜ of the rock, whose habitation *is* high;
ᵈ That saith in his heart, Who shall bring me down to the ground?

⁴ Though thou exalt *thyself* as the eagle,
And though thou ᶠ set thy nest among the stars,
Thence will I bring thee down, saith the LORD.

⁵ If ᵍ thieves came to thee, if robbers by night, (how art thou cut off!) would
they not have stolen till they had enough?
If the grapegatherers came to thee, ʰ would they not leave ‖ *some* grapes?

⁶ How are *the things* of Esau searched out!
*How* are his hidden things sought up!

⁷ All the men of thy confederacy have brought thee *even* to the border:
†ⁱ The men that were at peace with thee have deceived thee, *and* prevailed
against thee;

‡ *They that eat* thy bread have laid a wound under thee:
ᵏ *There* is none understanding ‖ in him.

⁸ ˡ Shall I not in that day, saith the LORD, even destroy the wise *men* out of
Edom,

---

JEHOVAH (the God of Israel) is the ADONAI, or Lord, the Creator, Ruler, and Judge of all Nations; as *S. Jerome* says here, "Visio Abdiae est servi Domini, quem mittit gentibus, Destructio Idumææ visio nationum est."

— *Thus saith the Lord God—We have heard a rumour* (or *report*) *from the Lord.* Some ancient writers regarded this passage as implying a *plurality* of Persons in the One Godhead. Compare on Gen. i. 26, "Let us make," and xix. 24, "The Lord rained fire from the Lord;" and see *S. Jerome* on Micah iv. and *Euseb.* Dem. Evang. v. 21; and this opinion is approved by some later Expositors (*Caccius, Calmet, Pfeiffer,* p. 442). It is certainly worthy of notice, that the Lord God (ADONAI JEHOVAH) is introduced as saying, *We* (which implies at least *two persons*) have heard a rumour from another Person, called the *Lord* (JEHOVAH). This coincides at least with the doctrine of Three Persons, each Divine, in the Unity of the Godhead.

— *Edom*. Connected with Israel by origin and neighbourhood, and therefore bound in duty to protect and help them; but perfidious and cruel in its conduct to Israel; and therefore a type of all who are allied to the Church of God, and that ought to defend her, but betray and persecute her. See above, on Isa. xxxiv. 1, and *Prelim. Note* on Isa. xiii. Cp. Jer. xlix. 7. Ezek. xxv. 12—14.

2. *Behold, I have made thee small*] Edom was great, but God will make it small. Cp. Jer. xlix. 15. The contrast to this is in the following prophecy of Micah concerning Bethlehem of Judah. Bethlehem was small, but God would make it great, by the birth of Christ there (Mic. v. 2, 3).

The fulfilment of this prophecy began to take place in the overthrow of the Edomites by Nebuchadnezzar; and was more completely executed under the Maccabees (*Josephus,* Ant. xii. 1s. 1; *Caspari,* 112—5).

3. *in the clefts of the rock*] In places of refuge in the rock (*Gesen.* 260). On the rocky fastnesses of Edom in Petra and other cities of its domain, see *Stanley,* Palest. pp. 87—89; *Burckhardt,* Syria, 421—427; *Robinson,* ii, 134—157; and *Keil* here, who says, "The Edomites inhabited the mountains of Seir, which are in the eastern side of the Ghor, or Arabah, stretching from the deep rocky valley of the river Aken, which extends northward, to the southern extremity of the Dead Sea, and stretches southward to the Elanitic gulf of the Red Sea. These mountains are formed of huge rocks of granite and porphyry, which terminate on the west in steep, walllike precipices of sandstone. Eastward they slope downward to the sandy desert of Arabia. They abound in clefts and caves, some

natural, some artificial. Hence its earliest inhabitants were called Horites, or dwellers in caves. The capital, Sela, or Petra, is proved to have been a place of great magnificence and strength by its numerous remains of temples, tombs, and other edifices. It was defended on the east and west by rocks like walls, which present an endless variety of bright colouring, from the deepest crimson, melting into the softest pale red, and sometimes shadowing off into orange and yellow. On the north and south it was guarded by mountains."

Jeremiah has adopted these words of Obadiah. See Jer. xlix. 16. Cp. Ps. lx. 9.

4. *Though thou exalt* thyself *as the eagle*] Cp. Job xxxix. 27—30, and Balaam's words concerning the Kenites (Num. xxiv. 21), "Strong is thy dwelling-place, and thou puttest thy nest in a rock. Nevertheless, the Kenite shall be wasted."

5. *If thieves came to thee*] The plundering of thieves would leave some remnant, and the gathering of grapes would leave some gleanings, "*but thou wilt be utterly spoiled and wasted.*"

6. *How are* the things *of Esau searched out!*] Literally, *How are Esau* out-searched; how are Esau rifled and ransacked. He uses the word *Esau* to remind Edom of its brotherly relation to Jacob or Israel. And so Jeremiah, in the parallel prophecy, says, "I have made *Esau* bare, I have uncovered his secret places" (Jer. xlix. 10).

— *hidden things*] Secret treasures.

7. *the men of thy confederacy*] Thine allies have spoiled thee, O Edom! Thou hast dealt treacherously with thy brother Israel, and thy confederates have dealt treacherously with thee; they *have sent thee to the border*; they have chased thee out of thy own land, as thou hast chased Israel.

— They that eat *thy bread have laid a wound under thee*] Literally, *thy bread have laid a snare* (see *Gesen.* 161) *under thee.* The abstract word *thy bread* represents the friends who lived upon the Edomites, and who had no other means of subsistence but from the nourishment which the Edomites gave them. Cp. Ps. xli. 9, "He who did *eat of my bread* hath lifted up his heel against me."

— *There is none understanding in him*] In Edom. They have lost all their wisdom, for which they were famous, and are infatuated and demented by sudden calamity. See what follows.

Edom is a type of worldly wisdom and secular policy, as well as of unbrotherly enmity to God's people. In both respects the punishment of Edom is a warning to all Machiavellian politicians in these latter days.

And understanding out of the mount of Esau?

9 And thy <sup>m</sup> mighty *men*, O <sup>n</sup> Teman, shall be dismayed,

To the end that every one of the mount of Esau may be cut off by slaughter.

10 For *thy* <sup>o</sup> violence against thy brother Jacob shame shall cover thee,

And <sup>p</sup> thou shalt be cut off for ever.

11 In the day that thou stoodest on the other side,

In the day that the strangers ‖ carried away captive his forces,

And foreigners entered into his gates, and <sup>q</sup> cast lots upon Jerusalem,

Even thou *wast* as one of them.

12 But ‖ thou shouldest not have ʳ looked on ˢ the day of thy brother in the day that he became a stranger ;

Neither shouldest thou have ᵗ rejoiced over the children of Judah in the day of their destruction ;

Neither shouldest thou have † spoken proudly in the day of distress ;

13 Thou shouldest not have entered into the gate of my people in the day of their calamity ;

Yea, thou shouldest not have looked on their affliction in the day of their calamity,

Nor have laid *hands* on their ‖ substance in the day of their calamity ;

14 Neither shouldest thou have stood in the crossway, to cut off those of his that did escape ;

---

9. *Teman.* See Amos i. 12. Jeremiah also adopts these thoughts and language in his prophecy concerning Edom (xlix.7).

10. *For thy violence against thy brother Jacob.* Words adopted from Joel iii. 19, and from Amos i. 11. Obadiah had used the word *Esau* in v. 6 ; he now uses the word *Jacob* in order to mark as strongly as possible the unbrotherly cruelty and treachery of the Edomites to their brethren.

11. *In the day that thou stoodest on the other side.* Rather, *in the day of thy standing against* (Israel) *in the day of strangers carrying away captive* his *strength.* Doubtless, Edom had been already guilty of many acts of wickedness to his brethren of Israel, ever since the days of their wandering in the wilderness (Num. xx. 14, 21, 22), and it persisted in this temper of hostility even to the time of the taking of Jerusalem by Nebuchadnezzar (Ps. cxxxvii. 7).

Obadiah *foresaw* the latter event (as has been rightly supposed by *Theodoret, Michaelis, Caspari, Hengstenberg, Pusey*) ; and he takes occasion from Edom's known disposition towards Israel, to warn Edom of the bitter consequences that *will* ensue to Edom itself, if it indulges in that virulent spirit of hatred and treachery to Israel at a crisis when the misfortunes of this brethren ought to excite its sympathy and to obtain its succour.

— *In the day*) Observe the pathetic repetition of these words, "*in the day,*" seven times, with every variety of sorrow to Israel, to be avenged *by the day of the* LORD (v. 15).

— *Even thou wast as one of them*] The word "*wast*" is not in the original, and ought to be expunged. The Prophet is *not* speaking of a *past* event, but of the *future*, and he is warning Edom against what he *will* be tempted to do, but *ought not* to do, and what the Prophet forbids him to do. This, therefore, is a proof of God's mercy to Edom. He endeavours to deter him from sin, so that he may not incur punishment. See above, *Prelim. Note.*

NOTE ON THE ENGLISH AUTHORIZED VERSION.

12. *But thou shouldest not have looked*] Rather, *And look thou not.* See the margin, Do not behold. It is a strong prohibition (so *Sept., Vulg., Syriac, Arabic, Junius, Tremellius, Piscator, Keil*, and cp. *Pusey*, p. 229).

This is important to observe. The translation given in the *text* of our AUTHORIZED VERSION is happily neutralized in the *margin* ; but it has tempted many readers to imagine that Obadiah is referring to a *past* event, especially to the unbrotherly conduct which was displayed by Edom towards Judah, when Jerusalem was taken by the Babylonian army under Nebuchadnezzar.

Thus many English readers have been led into an altogether inaccurate notion with regard to the prophetic character and

office of Obadiah, and also with regard to the time in which he lived ; and a prejudice has been raised against the Hebrew arrangement of the Books of the Minor Prophets.

These errors will be avoided by adopting the translation in the *margin* of our Authorized Version, instead of that in the *text*.

This may serve as an occasion for again expressing a desire, that the wish of our Translators, as uttered in their Preface to the Authorized Version (and why is that Preface so little known and so rarely printed with our Bibles ?) were complied with ; and that the renderings placed by them in the *margin*, should be consulted habitually by the reader of the Translation. Would it not be well that editions of our Authorized Translation were usually accompanied with the marginal renderings ? Indeed, it may be doubted whether any edition should be published without them. It may also be suggested for consideration, whether the ministers of the Church, who officiate publicly in reading the appointed Lessons of Holy Scripture, might not be at liberty to substitute, in such public reading, the rendering in the *margin*, in lieu of the rendering in the *text*. Such a substitution seems to be authorized by the *Keri* and *Chetib* of the Hebrew Synagogues ; and the advantage of it is obvious from such an example as that which is now before us in the Prophet Obadiah. If we are to have a new revision of our Authorized Version (which is a holy bond of union among all members and Churches of the Anglican Communion in all parts of the world, and also a sacred link of Christian connexion of our dissenting brethren with the whole Anglican Communion, and is of inestimable value in this respect), it deserves serious consideration whether this work of revision ought not, at least in the first instance, to be applied, not to the Text, but to the Margin. Considerable additions might be made to the Margin ; and if these additions, after careful examination and a sufficient time of probation, were generally approved, then (but not till then) they might be allowed to pass from the Margin into the Text. The remarks of *Dr. Pusey*, in his Introduction to the Minor Prophets, deserve the careful consideration of all who have a due regard for Church-Unity and Scriptural Truth.

— *Neither shouldest thou have rejoiced*—*neither shouldest thou have spoken*] Rather, *Rejoice thou not*—*speak thou not.* See the foregoing note. A similar correction is to be made in the two following verses, which are to be rendered, *Do not look*—*do not lay hands ; do not stand in the crossway. Do not deliver up the remnant.* The Prophet is here warning the Edomites against cruelty to their brethren of Judah in the day of the fall of Jerusalem, which he foresees.

This warning may be extended to all spiritual Edomites. Heretical and schismatical teachers, and treacherous friends, exult in the afflictions and distresses of God's Church. "Nos-

Before
CHRIST
about
787

Neither shouldest thou have ‖ delivered up those of his that did remain in the day of distress.

15 ⁱ For the day of the LORD *is* near upon all the heathen :
' As thou hast done, it shall be done unto thee :
Thy reward shall return upon thine own head.

16 ʸ For as ye have drunk upon my holy mountain,
So shall all the heathen drink continually,
Yea, they shall drink, and they shall ‖ swallow down,
And they shall be as though they had not been.

17 ᶻ But upon mount Zion ᵃ shall be ‖ deliverance,
And ‖ there shall be holiness ;
And the house of Jacob shall possess their possessions.

18 And the house of Jacob ᵇ shall be a fire,
And the house of Joseph a flame,
And the house of Esau for stubble,
And they shall kindle in them, and devour them ;
And there shall not be *any* remaining of the house of Esau ;
For the LORD hath spoken *it*.

19 And *they of* the south ᶜ shall possess the mount of Esau ;
ᵈ And *they of* the plain the Philistines :

---

*tram ruinam suam putant esse victoriam"* (*S. Jerome*). See on Rev. xi. 10.

But let them see their own punishment foretold here by Obadiah. All Edomites, who rejoice in the miseries of Sion, will bring worse woes on their own heads. The Day of the Lord is at hand ; *as thou hast done, it shall be done unto thee : thy reward shall return upon thine own head* (v. 15).

It is observable that this language is adopted in the Apocalypse, and is applied to the mystical Babylon—the Roman Church—as a judicial sentence upon her for her Edomitish hatred and persecution of her brethren in the Christian Sion, and for indulging a malignant pleasure in their sorrows. See Rev. xviii. 5, 6 ; and see above, on Jer. chap. li. 14, 24. 29. 49 ; and Baruch iv. 12.

JUDGMENT ON EDOM, AND ON ALL ENEMIES OF ZION.

15. *the day of the LORD is near*] A phrase adopted from Joel. See Joel ii. 1 ; iii. 14.

— *Thy reward*] Thy *recompense ;* compare Joel iii. 4. 7, where the same word (*gemul*) is used ; it is also adopted by Isa. lix. 18 ; lxvi. 6. Jer. li. 6. Lam. iii. 64, who (using the same word) calls God "the Lord God of *recompenses* (ii. 56).

16. *as ye have drunk upon my holy mountain*] As ye have profaned the Temple of God by your drunken revels and carousals.

— *So shall all the heathen drink*] Ye and all Zion's heathen enemies (of which Edom is a type) shall drink of the cup of God's wrath. See Lamentations iv. 21, "Rejoice and be glad, O daughter of Edom—the cup also shall pass through unto thee." Cp. Jer. xxv. 15, "Take the wine-cup of this fury at my hand, and cause all the nations to whom I send thee, to drink it." This, also, is applied in the Apocalypse to the mystical Babylon, the enemy of the Christian Sion, "In the cup which she hath filled, fill to her double" (Rev. xviii. 6). Cp. Rev. xiv. 10.

RESTORATION OF ZION IN CHRIST.

17. *But upon mount Zion shall be deliverance*] Words adopted from Joel ii. 32 ; iii. 17. As was observed in the former of these two passages, the word rendered *deliverance* (Heb. *peleytah*) would be better translated *as escaping,* i. e. the remnant who escape from God's wrath poured out upon the nations. This word is represented by the phrase οἱ σωζόμενοι in the Acts of the Apostles (Acts ii. 47 ; cp. Acts ii. 21. 40) ; and Joel and Obadiah are foretelling what the sacred historian of the Acts describes as fulfilled in Zion, the mother of Christendom, which stretches out her arms to enfold all who escape from God's wrath by repentance, and flee to her bosom with faith. Obadiah (says *S. Augustine*) is the briefest of all the Prophets ; but he, too, prophesies of Christ and of His conquests over the Gentiles, symbolized by Edom. He says that *in Sion will be salvation,* and that those who are saved, will "go forth from *mount Sion*" to

judge (*Augustine* has, "to defend ") the "mount of Esau," and the Kingdom will be the Lord's. This was fulfilled in part, when they who believed in Christ, especially the Apostles, went forth from mount Sion to save by their preaching those who were converted to Him, that they might be delivered from the power of darkness, and be translated to the Kingdom of God (*S. Augustine*, De Civ. Dei, xviii. 31).

— *there shall be holiness*] Or, a *sanctuary.* The Christian Zion is the *sanctuary,* not only of the Jews, but of all Nations. See Isa. ii. 2 ; lvi. 7. Joel iii. 17.

— *the house of Jacob shall possess their possessions*] Words taken up from Christ. Cp. on Num. xxiv. 18. God promised to Christ to give Him the heathen for an inheritance, and the utmost parts of the earth for a possession (Ps. ii. 8) ; and Christ, after His Resurrection, gave a commission to His Apostles to go into all the world and baptize all Nations, and to make them a possession for Himself (Matt. xxviii. 18, 19. Mark xvi. 15).

18. *the house of Jacob shall be a fire*] The living flame of God's Word, kindled by the fire that came down from heaven at Pentecost, when Christ baptized His disciples "with the Holy Ghost and with fire" (Luke iii. 16), will run with a holy conflagration of zeal and love, and consume all that is hostile to God, and will purify and refine the heart of the world. Cp. Isa. v. 24, and x. 17, "The light of Israel shall be for a fire, and His Holy One for a flame." And Jer. v. 14, "I will make my Words in thy mouth fire, and this people wood ;" and (xx. 9), "His Word was in mine heart, as a burning fire ;" and Mal. iii. 2, "He is like a refiner's fire ;" and ibid. iv. 1. "The day cometh that shall burn as an oven " to all who will not be purified by that refining fire of the loving discipline of the Gospel.

19. *they of the south shall possess the mount of Esau*] The Prophet refers to the territorial divisions of the literal Israel, and spiritualizes them. The *south* (Hebr. *négeb*) was the southern region of Judah. See Josh. x. 40 ; xv. 21 ; xviii. 5. Judges i. 9. The *plain* (Hebr. *shephêlah*), the lowland on the coast of the Mediterranean, west of Palestine. See Josh. x. 40 ; xv. 33.

The sense is, the Church of God will break forth in all directions from Zion, and subdue all the countries in its neighbourhood, till it has absorbed the World, and made it to become a Holy Land, a spiritual Jerusalem.

This prophecy began to be fulfilled when the Apostles and other disciples of Christ went forth from Zion to Idumea, and Philistia (Acts viii. 26 ; ix. 3. 32—43), and Samaria (viii. 1—7), and to the East of Jordan, and planted Christian Colonies there, according to our Lord's command, "Ye shall be witnesses unto Me both in *Jerusalem,* and in all *Judea,* and in *Samaria,* and unto the *uttermost parts of the earth* (Acts i. 8). "This prophecy" (says *S. Jerome*) "is daily being fulfilled in us, and has its accomplishment in the extension of the Church, which is the Kingdom of God."

And they shall possess the fields of Ephraim, and the fields of Samaria :
And Benjamin *shall possess* Gilead ;

<sup>20</sup> And the captivity of this host of the children of Israel *shall possess* that of the Canaanites, *even* <sup>e</sup> unto Zarephath ;

And the captivity of Jerusalem, ‖ which *is* in Sepharad, <sup>f</sup> shall possess the cities of the south.

<sup>21</sup> And <sup>g</sup> saviours shall come up on mount Zion to judge the mount of Esau ;
And the <sup>h</sup> kingdom shall be the Lord's.

Before
CHRIST
about
587.

e 1 Kings 17.9, 10

‖ Or, shall pos-
sess that which is
in Sepharad.
1 Jer. 32. 44.

g 1 Tim. 4. 16.
James 5. 20.

h Ps. 22. 28.
Dan. 2. 44, & 7.
14, 27. Zech. 14. 9. Luke 1. 33. Rev. 11. 15, & 19. 6.

**20.** *the captivity of this host—Zarephath*] Israel, once captive, shall take the World captive in the chains of the Gospel. Cp. above, the notes on Ps. cxlix. 8, 9.

Obadiah here enlarges on the prophecy of Joel. Joel had closed his prophecies with a promise that the Lord would bring again the captivity of His people Israel (Joel iii. 17); but Obadiah adds, that the *captivity* of Israel, i. e. they who once were carried captive to Assyria and Babylon, will *liberate* others and deliver them from the bondage of Sin and Satan, "into the glorious liberty of the children of God" (Rom. viii. 21).

This act of liberation, and this conquest of love, is described as being extended to *Zarephath*, the heathen city of Sidon, once the realm of Jezebel, who introduced the worship of Baal into Israel (see above, 1 Kings xvii. 9, 10, and below, Luke iv. 26); and thus the complete triumph of the Gospel going forth from Zion into heathen and idolatrous lands, is represented.

— *the captivity of Jerusalem, which is in Sepharad*] The sense is, The Jews of the Dispersion, both in the East and West, who were formerly carried away captive, but now Christianized, will extend themselves southward, and evangelize Egypt, Ethiopia, and the rest of Africa. *Sepharad* is a generic term, like *India*, applied both to East and West Indies, and represents Iberia in its twofold sense, viz. the Iberia on the Cimmerian Bosphorus in the East (*Vulg., S. Jerome*), and also the other or Western Iberia (colonized from the Eastern on the Cimmerian Bosphorus), and now called Spain (*Targum, Syriac, Arabic, Kimchi*, and other Hebrew expositors. *See Caspari*, 136; *Fuerst*, 994; and so *Lyranus, Vatablus, A Castro, A Lapide*, and others. It is not unworthy of remark, that the great Apostle of the Gentiles speaks of his own intention to go and evangelize Spain (Rom. xv. 24, 28). Obadiah (says *A Lapide*) is here speaking of Christ-

tian missions, of Apostles and apostolic men, many of whom were Jews, into the far West, and also to the East. Cp. *S. Augustine*, De Civ. Dei, xviii. 31.

**21.** *saviours*] Or *deliverers*. These were the Apostles and other preachers of the Gospel, who carried the glad tidings of salvation, which went forth originally from Zion, where Christ suffered, and where the Holy Ghost was given. See Isa. ii. 3. Christ is the Good Shepherd, and in like manner Jeremiah describes the Preachers of the Gospel as shepherds (Jer. xxiii. 4), "I will set up shepherds over them which shall feed them." Christ, Who is the light of the world (John viii. 12), and Who lighteth every one that cometh into the world (John i. 9), vouchsafed to say to His disciples, "Ye are the Light of the World" (Matt. v. 14). So the Saviour Himself enables His ministers to save others. "Sic Ipse Salvator Apostolos suos mundi voluit esse salvatores" (*S. Jerome*). Cp. 1 Tim. iv. 16, "Thou shalt both save thyself, and them that hear thee."

— *to judge the mount of Esau*] St. John, in the Apocalypse, beholds the saints of God standing on *Mount Sion* (Rev. xiv. 1); and here the Prophet says, that they who come up on *Mount Zion*—that is, in the Christian Church—will judge the *Mount of Esau*—that is, will overcome and condemn the Kingdoms of this World and the enemies of the Israel of God. So St. Paul says, that "the saints shall judge the world" (1 Cor. vi. 2). Cp. Matt. xix. 28).

— *the kingdom shall be the Lord's*] As the voices in heaven will proclaim, at the sounding of the last trump in the Apocalypse, "The Kingdoms of this World are become the Kingdom of the Lord and of His Christ" (Rev. xi. 15). Cp. Rev. xix. 6. 16.

# JONAH.

CHAPTER I.
B.C. ...
Matt. 12. 39.
Jonah
1 Kings 10. 11, 12.
ch. 3. 2, 3, 8.
4. 11.
c Gen. 18. 20, 21.  Ezra 9. 6.  James 5. 4.  Rev. 18. 5.

**I.** NOW the word of the LORD came unto a ‖ Jonah the son of Amittai, saying, ² Arise, go to Nineveh, that ᵇ great city, and cry against it; for ᶜ their wickedness is come up before me.

What is the design of the Book of JONAH?

In the previous prophetical books Almighty God had pronounced His judicial retribution on heathen Nations, whom He used, or would use, as His instruments to punish His people Israel and Judah for their sins. He had then revealed Himself as the Supreme Ruler and Moral Governor of the World. He had also declared His special love to Israel and Judah, and had foretold, that though they would be scattered for their sins, yet, on their repentance and faith, they would hereafter be restored in Christ.

Lest, however, it should be supposed that God's relation to the Heathen Nations was one only of power, terror, and judgment, and not also of love and mercy, He had announced by the prophet Amos that all Nations of the World would be brought into covenant with Him, on equal terms with the Jews, in Christ. See Amos ix. 11, 12, quoted by St. James at the Council of Jerusalem, Acts xv. 15—17, in proof of that statement.

He had also declared by the Prophet Obadiah, that He Himself, having used the Heathen Nations to punish and carry captive Israel and Judah for their sins against Him, would afterwards use Israel and Judah (who, after their captivity, and by their captivity, would be brought nearer to God in the Gospel) as His instruments for releasing the Heathen Nations from the bondage of Sin and Satan, and for bringing them back to Him in Christ. See Obad. 19—21.

He had also shown His kindness even to Edom itself, first by a salutary warning against the sin of malice and hatred toward Israel (Obad. 12—14), and next, He had cheered Edom with a promise of restoration, on condition of its faith and repentance, by means of Israel, converting it to Christ (Obad. 21).

Such Divine declarations as these must have seemed strange to some zealous Israelites. They would have been, in their days, what Saul of Tarsus afterwards was. They would have been fired with fervent enthusiasm for the Levitical Law, and for the privileges and prerogatives of Israel. They would almost have felt angry with God for such an extension of His favours to the Heathen. They would have thought that the gain of the Heathen was their own loss. And this narrow and exclusive spirit of Judaism towards the Heathen Nations of the world would be aggravated, exasperated, and intensified by the growing hostility, pride, and cruelty of Heathen Nations, especially of ASSYRIA, towards themselves, the favoured people of God.

But God would show the Jews that He had mercy for all. He would display this by His conduct to NINEVEH, the capital city of that very Assyrian Nation which was the most powerful and bitter enemy of Israel. He would thus teach Israel, that, if they were indeed His people, they must imitate His merciful spirit, and love their enemies, and embrace the Assyrians as brethren. We may compare the prophecy in Isa. xix. 24, "In that day shall Israel be the third with Egypt and with Assyria."

We have then a portraiture of the Jewish character (such as was afterwards displayed in the strongest colours in Saul of Tarsus) presented to us in the Prophet Jonah. He grudges God's mercy to the Heathen. He is angry with God's love to them. He shrinks from the commission of preaching repentance to Nineveh, the capital of Assyria. Perhaps he had heard that Assyria would be used by God to chastise Israel and carry it captive. He does not wish that Nineveh should repent. He is quite content, nay, he is almost eager, that it should perish. He sits down outside its walls, watching, to see them fall.

Almighty God graciously vouchsafed to correct this jealous temper. He would teach the Prophet Jonah to be merciful, like Himself; He would use him, although reluctant and shrinking back, in preaching repentance, and in delivering a message of pardon to Nineveh on its repentance; and in saving Nineveh from destruction.

Thus He anticipated the lesson inculcated in our Lord's parable, which exhibits the narrow-minded and sullen spirit of the Jew, in the elder brother murmuring at his father's love in receiving the penitent prodigal (Luke xv. 25—32). Thus He taught Jonah that while he was a Hebrew Prophet (i. 9), and therefore was justly full of love for the Hebrew Nation, and of zeal for the God of the Hebrews, he must also be like the God of the Hebrews—the God of Abraham, in whose Seed all the families of the Earth are blessed; and must feel sympathy for all Nations, even for Assyria, the greatest and most formidable foe of Israel; and must desire to promote the salvation of all, as children of one heavenly Father. He taught Jonah a lesson which was learnt in perfection by St. Paul, "the Hebrew of the Hebrews," the Apostle of the Gentiles, who would have sacrificed every thing for his brethren after the flesh, the Jews, and their salvation (Rom. ix. 1—5), and yet cheerfully incurred their wrath, and exposed himself to death at their hands (1 Thess. ii. 15, 16), Acts xiv. 5, 19), in order that he might preach among the Gentiles the unsearchable riches of Christ (Eph. iii. 8).

But Jonah (as we know from Christ Himself (Matt. xii. 39, 40; xvi. 4, Luke xi. 30) was also a type of a greater than St. Paul. Jonah, after his three days' burial and resurrection, preached Repentance to Nineveh, the great Heathen City. Christ, the Divine Antitype (in Whom we see in perfection the victors, opposite to all the failings of all His human types), went forth after His Resurrection and Ascension into Heaven, to preach by His Apostles; and He is ever going forth to preach by His Ministers, repentance and remission of sins to all Nations of the World.

The Book of Jonah is a prophecy of this great Missionary Work of Divine Mercy and Love, which has now been going on for 1800 years, and will go on to the Day of Doom.

Thus we see that, though the Book of Jonah may at first appear to be only a history, yet it is a prophecy. Jonah himself is not only a prophet, but is a prophecy as well. By his self-sacrifice for the sailors in the storm, he is a prophecy of the Propitiation and Atonement made by the Great Prophet, the Divine Jonah, Jesus Christ. The sudden cessation of the storm, the calm that followed Jonah's self-sacrifice, and the safe arrival at land of the weather-beaten ship of Joppa, are beautiful fore-shadowings of the World's Peace with God after the self-devotion on Calvary, and of its consequent safe anchorage in the haven of eternity.

Jonah was a prophet of Christ's Burial and of His Resurrection, and of the great Christian Doctrine of Universal Redemption by Him. He was a prophet of the gracious and blessed truth that God's mercy is over all His works. God desireth not the death of a sinner, and willeth not that any should perish, but that all (even the Ninevites) should be saved and come to the knowledge of His truth (1 Tim. ii. 4, 2 Pet. iii. 9); and that He offers salvation freely to all through Christ, Who "tasted death for every man," and gave Himself a ransom for all (Heb. ii. 9, 1 Tim. ii. 6).

[3] But Jonah [d] rose up to flee unto Tarshish from the presence of the LORD, [refs] and went down to [e] Joppa; and he found a ship going to Tarshish: so he paid [refs] the fare thereof, and went down into it, to go with them unto Tarshish [f] from [refs] the presence of the LORD.

[4] But [g] the LORD † sent out a great wind into the sea, and there was a [refs] mighty tempest in the sea, so that the ship was † like to be broken. [5] Then [refs] the mariners were afraid, and cried every man unto his god, and [h] cast forth [refs] the wares that *were* in the ship into the sea, to lighten *it* of them.

---

Such considerations as these, show that the Book of Jonah, though it may seem at first sight to be only a history, is rightly admitted among the Prophetical Books of the Old Testament. The history of Jonah is a prophecy. It prophesies of Christ—of His three days' Burial and Resurrection, and of the conversion of the Heathen and their reception into God's favour through faith in Christ. As is well said by *S. Augustine* (De Civ. Dei, xviii. 30), "Jonas non tam sermone quàm suâ quâdam passione prophetavit; profectò apertius quàm si Christi mortem et resurrectionem voce clamaret."

That the author of the Book of Jonah was Jonah himself, and that it was designed by him to be a representation of his own weaknesses and prejudices, and to be a penitential confession from his own lips; and to display God's love to the heathen, and to foreshadow their conversion, and thus to be a prophetical lesson to the world, will probably be evident to all who examine it with attention. See, for example, on i. 4, and his prayer in chapter ii.

CH. I. 1. *Now*] Or *And*. Thus this Book is linked on to the foregoing. See on Josh. i. 1. This copula shows that this Book is not an independent work, but belongs to the Hebrew Canon of Scripture.

— *the word of the* LORD *came*] There is a phrase used in the Old Testament not unfrequently, viz. "It was said unto" such and such a prophet "by the word of the Lord"(1 Sam. iii. 21; especially 1 Kings xiii. *passim*). The rendering should be "*in* the word of the Lord." This phrase seems to represent the "word of the Lord" as an atmosphere of kindling holy thought, a sphere of spiritual truth encompassing the Prophet, illuminating and moving his whole soul, and finally taking shape in language of exhortation, or prediction, or teaching, or resolve, as the case might be (*Canon Liddon*).

— *Jonah*] The name, like that of the other Prophets, is significant. Jonah means a *dove*, which, in Scripture, is said to *mourn* (Isa. xxxviii. 14; lix. 11). The name may serve to remind us of the mournful and plaintive spirit of the Prophet who bore it. In this book, Jonah relates that he had murmured against God's mercy to Nineveh; and that he had mourned for the seeming failure of his own prophecy (iv. 1, 2); and that he craved death; and that he mourned for the destruction of the gourd, and again wished to die (iv. 8). But, being brought to a better mind, he afterwards wrote this book, in which he mourns over his own backwardness and murmurings against God. He mourns for his own mourning, and utters a plaintive prophetic elegy for his own jealous and envious temper and sullen murmuring against God's love to the Gentiles; and thus he becomes at last like the dove who brought an olive branch of peace to Noah in the Ark, and a message of the ceasing of the Flood; he became even, like the Divine Dove, a figure of the love of the Holy Spirit Himself, coming down at Pentecost to enable the Apostles to preach the Gospel of Christ to the Nineveh of the Heathen World. As *S. Jerome* says (ad Paulinum), "Jonas, columba pulcherrima, naufragio suo" (quo pacem conciliat navigantibus, et fidem procellæ imponit) "passionem Domini præfigurans mundum ad pœnitentiam revocat, et sub nomine Nineve gentibus salutem nuntiat."

— *son of Amittai*] Of Gath-hepher, in the tribe of Zebulun, in the times of Jeroboam II. See 2 Kings xiv. 25.

2. *go to Nineveh*] God uses the Hebrew Prophet to convert the Heathen City. He is one of the numerous specimens of Israel's mission fulfilled in Christ to the World. "God always blessed those of the heathen who were brought into contact with His chosen people by a certain knowledge of Himself. The Egyptian kings and people learnt much of Him from Joseph in one generation, and from Moses in another. The Canaanites heard of Him from the Spies; the Philistines by the capture of the Sacred Ark; the Phœnicians on the Mediterranean coast through Hiram of Tyre; the Syrians of Damascus through captives like Naaman's Servant, and the Miracles of Elisha; the Babylonian and Persian kings through Daniel;

and the Persians, later, through Esther. The truth, which was already 'the glory of God's People Israel,' was, in a measure, 'a light to lighten the Gentiles'" (*Liddon*).

— *Nineveh, that great city*] See on Gen. x. 11. It formed a trapezium, or irregular parallelogram, the average length from west to east being about twenty miles, and the average breadth from north to south being about twelve miles, Nineveh proper (*Kouyunjik*) being at the north-west corner; another city (*Nimrûd*) being at the south-west corner; there was a third large city on the Tigris, about five miles north of *Nimrûd*; fourthly, the Citadel and Temple (now *Khorsabad*), near the north-east corner. See the Plan in *M. V. Niebuhr*, Geschichte Assurs, p. 284; and in *Dr. Pusey*, p. 254; *Rawlinson*, Anc. Mon. i. p. 316; *Dr. Smith*, Bib. Dict. ii. 550.

God, speaking to Jonah, says, "Their *wickedness is come up before Me*." God is brought before us in these words, as He sits above this waterflood of crime, as He remaineth in the moral world, a King for ever. He is the Great Judge, unseen by man, but witnessing all human acts, and words, and motives, seated even now upon His Throne of Judgment; and each crime of each member of that vast community mounts upwards, and is registered in His heavenly Court. The same phrase had already been used in the murder of Abel, and of the iniquity of Sodom and Gomorrah; it marks that special notice of sin which precedes judgment. God had waited long in His Patience and His Mercy, but the cup at length was full to overflowing (*Liddon*).

3. *Jonah rose up to flee unto Tarshish from the presence of the* LORD] Literally, *from the face of Jehovah*; that is, from doing this work, as a servant standing before his master and waiting for his orders, and as a prophet ministering before God (see *Pusey*, 247, 251); and from Palestine and the Temple at Jerusalem, where God specially vouchsafed His Presence visibly. See below, ii. 4. "I will look again toward thy holy temple."

— *Tarshish*] Tartessus, in Spain (1 Kings x. 22. Ps. lxxii. 10); the contrary direction to Nineveh.

— *Joppa*] On the Mediterranean, north-west of Jerusalem (2 Chron. ii. 16). He grieves at being chosen to go as a prophet to the Assyrians, the enemies of Israel, and to their capital city; and he fears lest, by the conversion of the Heathen, Israel should suffer loss. Therefore he becomes like Cain, and flees from the presence of the Lord (Gen. iv. 16. *S. Jerome*).

4. *the* LORD *sent out a great wind*] Literally, *the Lord cast forth*. The wind obeyed God, and preached a lesson to the Prophet, who was disobeying Him.

This is a penitential confession from Jonah's own lips. The whole history in this book is so composed as to exhibit God's power, and the obedience of His creatures to Him.

— *the ship was like to be broken*] The ship *thought* to be *broken*—to be wrecked. The living consciousness and apprehension of the ship, fearing to be wrecked in the tempestuous sea, is set in striking contrast to the lethargic stupor of the prophet, whose conscience was, as it were, entranced in a swoon; and though he was at that time guilty of the sin of disobedience against God, yet he thought nothing of his own danger of an eternal shipwreck, but lay fast asleep in the dark hold of the ship. Such is often the condition of the human soul. See on r. 5.

5. *the mariners—cried every man unto his god*] Jonah, the author of this book, makes his penitential reflections on his own history; he here contrasts the pious devotion of these heathens towards their false gods, with his own thankless and faithless resistance to his own God—the only true God.

— *cast forth the wares*] Cp. Acts xxvii. 18, 19, 38.

— *Jonah was gone down into the sides of the ship*] The lowest part of the ship "interiora navis" (*S. Jerome*). The word for *ship* (*sephînah*), from *saphan*, to board, or floor over) which occurs only here, is the usual word for *ship* in Arabic and Aramaic (*Gesen.*, 958).

Before
CHRIST
about
872.

But Jonah was gone down ¹ into the sides of the ship; and he lay, and was fast asleep.

⁶ So the shipmaster came to him, and said unto him, What meanest thou, O sleeper? arise, ¹ call upon thy God, ¹ if so be that God will think upon us, that we perish not.

⁷ And they said every one to his fellow, Come, and let us ᵐ cast lots, that we may know for whose cause this evil *is* upon us.

So they cast lots, and the lot fell upon Jonah.

⁸ Then said they unto him, ⁿ Tell us, we pray thee, for whose cause this evil *is* upon us; What *is* thine occupation? and whence comest thou? what *is* thy country? and of what people *art* thou?

⁹ And he said unto them, I *am* an Hebrew; and I fear ‖ the LORD, the God of heaven, ᵒ which hath made the sea and the dry *land*.

¹⁰ Then were the men † exceedingly afraid, and said unto him, Why hast thou done this? For the men knew that he fled from the presence of the LORD, because he had told them.

¹¹ Then said they unto him, What shall we do unto thee, that the sea † may be calm unto us? for the sea ‖ † wrought, and was tempestuous.

¹² And he said unto them, ᵖ Take me up, and cast me forth into the sea; so shall the sea be calm unto you: for I know that for my sake this great tempest *is* upon you.

¹³ Nevertheless the men † rowed hard to bring *it* to the land; ᵠ but they could not: for the sea wrought, and was tempestuous against them.

¹⁴ Wherefore they cried unto the LORD, and said, We beseech thee, O LORD,

l 1 Sam. 24. 5.

k 1. 5, 6.
l Joel 2. 14.

m Josh. 7. 14, 16.
1 Sam. 10. 20, 21.
& 14. 41, 42.
Prov. 16. 33.
Acts 1. 26.

n Josh. 7. 19.
1 Sam. 14. 43.

‖ Or, JE-
HOVAH.
o Ps. 146. 6.
Acts 17. 24.
† Heb. with great
fear.

† Heb. may be
silent from us.
‖ Or, grew more
and more tem-
pestuous.
† Heb. went.
p John 11. 50.

† Heb. digged.
q Prov. 21. 30.

*— was fast asleep.*] Literally, was cast into a deep sleep. The word here used (the niphal of *rādam*, to sleep heavily —Gesen. 758) is the same as that used to describe Sisera's deep sleep (Judg. iv. 21); and that of the Assyrians, in death (Ps. lxxvi. 6); and the trance of Daniel (viii. 18; x. 9).

Jonah, lying like one stupefied, in a heavy sleep, in the dark hold of the ship, ready to founder in the deep, is a type of the desperate sinner who has fled away from God, and is in peril of eternal perdition, and yet unconscious of his danger.

Jonah slept in the ship in the storm; Christ slept in the ship in the storm (Mark iv. 38). Jonah was flying from God; Christ was doing God's will. Jonah was awakened by the mariners; Christ by His disciples. Jonah is roused from his sleep, and the storm ceases; Christ, by His Divine Power, rebukes the storm, and there is a great calm.

6. *What meanest thou, O sleeper? arise, call upon thy God*] The prophet of God here relates that he himself was in such a state of physical and spiritual stupor, that he needed a powerful voice of alarm to awaken him; and that God mercifully rebuked him for his sin by sending a heathen shipmaster to be his prophet, and to awaken him from his slumber (*What meanest thou, O sleeper?*) and to excite him to watchfulness and prayer. The Apostle St. Paul speaks of this spiritual lethargy when he exclaims, "Awake, thou that sleepest, and arise from the dead" (the death of sin), "and Christ shall give thee light" (Eph. v. 14).

— *if so be that God will think upon us*] Rather, "if so be that *the* God" (Hebr. *ha Elohim*), the only true God, "will think upon us." Polytheism is put to flight by that inner sense of truth which often flashes on the mind in the hour of extreme danger, and gives vent to what *Tertullian* calls the "testimonium animæ naturaliter Christianæ."

7. *they cast lots, and the lot fell upon Jonah*] As the arrow, shot from the bow "drawn at a venture," but directed by God's hand, hit Ahab (though disguised) "between the joints of his harness" (1 Kings xxii. 34), so this lot fell on Jonah the Prophet, flying from the presence of the Lord; not "by any virtue in the lot itself, but by the Will of God, Who rules uncertain lots" even in the hands of heathens, when He thinks fit (*S. Jerome*. Cp. Josh. vii. 14, 18. 1 Sam. x. 20, 21; xiv. 41. Acts i. 26); as He sent the milch kine of the Philistines on the way to Bethshemesh, and thus declared His Will concerning the Ark, and proclaimed that their sufferings were

plagues inflicted upon them by Himself for their sin (1 Sam. vi. 1—12).

9. *I am an Hebrew; and I fear the LORD*] Jonah is brought by means of the storm, and by the appeal of the heathen mariners, and by the falling of the lot upon himself, to a sense of his sin, and now makes his confession of faith, and owns that he had fled from the presence of the Lord, and that the storm was on account of himself, and pronounces his own sentence, and therefore asks to be taken up and cast into the sea, in order that they may escape.

It cannot be doubted that the Prophet Jonah, in doing this, was under divine direction. "Against me the storm thunders; it is seeking me; it catches me; in order that you may live, the waves themselves command you to cast me into the sea" (*S. Jerome*).

Jonah was a type of Christ. None of the imperfections of the human types of Christ are ever seen in the Divine Antitype; but where the human types are blemished by sins, there the Divine Antitype shines by the opposite virtues. So it is here. Jonah had fled from the presence of God in faithless disobedience. Christ came forth from the bosom of the Father in filial love. Jonah, in a sense of personal sin, gave himself up to death, that the waves of God's wrath, raging against the mariners and the ship, might abate and the storm cease. Christ, the Holy One, without the least taint of sin, gave Himself up to die for the sins of the World—"the Just for the unjust" (1 Pet. iii. 18); and the waves of God's wrath, raging against the ship of the World, tossed by that furious tempest on account of the sins of the mariners who sailed in it, were lulled; and there is a great calm, and the ship will arrive safely at the harbour—the harbour of Eternal Life. Cp. *S. Jerome* and *A Lapide*, here.

11. *the sea wrought, and was tempestuous*] Literally, *the sea was going on and raging,* "ibat et intume sciebat" (*Vulg.*)

13. *the men rowed hard*] Literally, *they dug.*

14. *they cried unto the LORD*] The heathen mariners abandon their own gods, and cry to the LORD (JEHOVAH), the God of Israel, the only true God, Whom Jonah worshipped (v. 9), and Whom he had preached to them as the Creator, Lord of all. It is remarkable that the name JEHOVAH occurs three times in this verse. And in v. 16, it is added, that "they feared JEHOVAH exceedingly, and offered a sacrifice unto JEHOVAH, and made vows."

Here we see a prophetic glimpse of the conversion of the Heathen to the true faith, by means of Hebrew prophets and preachers.

we beseech thee, let us not perish for this man's life, and 'lay not upon us  <sup></sup> innocent blood : for thou, O Lord, 'hast done as it pleased thee.

<sup>r Deut. 21. 8.<br>s Ps. 115. 3.</sup>

<sup>15</sup> So they took up Jonah, and cast him forth into the sea : 'and the sea † ceased from her raging.

<sup>t Ps. 89. 9.<br>Luke 8. 24.<br>† Heb. *stood.*</sup>

<sup>16</sup> Then the men "feared the Lord exceedingly, and † offered a sacrifice unto the Lord, and made vows.

<sup>u Mark 4. 41.<br>Acts 5. 11.<br>† Heb. *sacrificed a sacrifice unto the Lord, and vowed vows.*</sup>

<sup>17</sup> Now the Lord had prepared a great fish to swallow up Jonah. And <sup>x</sup> Jonah was in the † belly of the fish three days and three nights.

<sup>x Matt. 12. 40. &<br>16. 4.<br>Luke 11. 30.<br>† Heb. *bowels.*</sup>

— *lay not upon us innocent blood*] What a striking contrast is presented by this prayer of these heathens to the imprecation of the Jews crucifying the Divine Jonah, " His blood be on us and on our children " ! (Matt. xxvii. 25.) The Jews rejected Christ ; but the Gentiles gladly received Him.

15. *the sea ceased from her raging*] When we consider the state of the world as it was before Christ's Passion, that it was like a Sea agitated by contrary winds and swelling waves of error and unbelief; and when we reflect how the vessel of Human Nature, sailing upon that boisterous sea, was in danger of being wrecked and of foundering in the deep, and how, after the Passion of Christ, there was a great calm of faith, peace, and safety, we shall recognize there a fulfilment of these prophetic words, *The sea ceased from her raging.*

17. *the Lord had prepared a great fish to swallow up Jonah*] *The Lord had prepared.* Literally, *The Lord numbered,* or *appointed.* The Hebrew verb *mânâh* (whence the Greek and Latin *mina*), to *divide,* to *number,* to *allot,* to *appoint,* is used four times in this book, in a remarkable manner. " The Lord *prepared* a great fish ;" " the Lord God *prepared* a gourd " (iv. 6) ; " God *prepared* a worm " (iv. 7) ; " God *prepared* a vehement east wind " (iv. 8)—showing that God is ever working in the government of the World—is alway *preparing* things for their appointed season and work,—and ordereth all things " by number, measure, and weight."

In the obedience of the fish whom God appointed to do His work, and who kept the Prophet in safe custody (as Daniel was kept in the lions' den, and as our Lord was safe "among the wild beasts" in the wilderness), and who, when "the Lord *spake* unto him, vomited out Jonah upon the *dry land*" (and *not* into the watery ocean), we see a contrast to Jonah himself, who had disobeyed God. The fish, like Balaam's ass, is a prophet to the Prophet himself, and teaches him obedience to God.

Let us hear in mind that Jonah himself (as is most probable) is the narrator of all this. This book was written by him ; and therefore we see here a frank confession of his own failings, and a proof of his own repentance.

" The great fish " (called *κῆτος* herein *Sept.* and in Matt. xii. 40) " was probably a large shark, or sea dog, 'canis carcharias,' which is common in the Mediterranean, and has so large a throat that it can swallow a man whole." See *Oken* and *Midler* (quoted by *Keil* here) who state that in the year 1758 a sailor fell overboard from a frigate in the Mediterranean, and was swallowed by a sea-dog ; and that the captain of the vessel ordered a cannon on the deck to be fired at the fish, and, that the fish, being struck by the ball, vomited up the sailor, who was taken up by a boat let down into the sea, and was received again alive and not much hurt. The fish, which was twenty feet long and nine feet broad, was harpooned ; it was drawn up on the frigate, and dried ; and was exhibited by the sailor in Erlangen, and at Nuremberg and other places.

*S. Augustine* mentions (Epist. 102), that in his time a fish was exhibited at Carthage which would have contained many men in its belly.

The fable of Arion and the Dolphin (*Herod.* i. 23) seems to have been derived from the history of Jonah.

The *reasons* for this miracle were many : (1) That the Ninevites, having heard of it from Jonah's own narration, and perhaps from some of the sailors who had cast him into the sea, might listen to his preaching, and repent. As Our Lord Himself said, " Jonah was a *sign* to the Ninevites," and they repented at his preaching (Matt. xii. 39 ; xvi. 4. Luke xi. 29—32. (2) That Jonah might be a type and prophecy of Christ's Death, Burial, and Resurrection. (3) That God's dealings with the Jewish Nation might be justified. The heathen city Nineveh repented in consequence of this miracle, and of Jonah's preaching, and was saved. Jerusalem did not repent after the greater miracle of Christ's Resurrection, and at the preaching of His Apostles, and was destroyed.

— *three days and three nights*] On the meaning of this Hebrew expression, see *S. Jerome* here, and the note below on Matt. xii. 40, where it is shown that it is equivalent to an assertion that Jonah rose from out of the whale's belly " on the *third day.*"

### JONAH IN THE WHALE'S BELLY THREE DAYS AND THREE NIGHTS.

Much has been written concerning this history. To the Christian reader it will be sufficient to remember, that its historical truth has been avouched and authenticated, and that its prophetical significance has been expounded, by Jesus Christ, Whom we can prove by incontrovertible arguments to be what He Himself affirmed—the Son of the Living God ; and therefore infinite in knowledge and truth. The proofs of this are given in the Editor's Four Lectures on the Inspiration of the Bible, Lecture ii, and need not be repeated here.

Well, therefore, might *S. Jerome* say, " *Hujus loci mysterium in Evangelio Dominus exponit* ; *et superfluum est, vel id ipsum, vel aliud dicere, quàm exposuit ipse Qui passus est.*"

The Christian reader will recollect that the Son of God has asserted the truth of this history, and has also applied it to Himself ; and has shown that there was an adequate reason for the miracle here wrought by God, inasmuch as it was a prophetical representation of the greatest events that have ever occurred in this world's history, namely, the Burial and Resurrection of Christ Himself. Jonah's grave in the belly of the fish for three days and three nights was a strange event, such as was never heard of before. But even in that respect he was a figure of Christ, Who was buried in a new tomb wherein no man before was laid (Luke xxiii. 53), and Who raised Himself from the dead, as He had declared that He would do - John ii. 19. Cp. Matt. xx. 19.

In Jonah's Burial and Resurrection, we may also see a foreshadowing of the great event still future, that concerns all mankind—namely, the Resurrection of all at the Great Day. Jonah's Resurrection was a type of Christ's Resurrection ; which is a pledge of our Resurrection. " As in Adam all die, even so in Christ shall all be made alive" (1 Cor. xv. 22).

The Burial of Jonah, unhurt in the whale's belly, affords to us a cheering illustration of what Jonah's predecessor, the prophet Hosea, said, as explained by the Apostle St. Paul—"O Death, where is thy sting ? O Grave, where is thy victory ?" (Hos. xiii. 14.) God can keep us *safe* in the jaws of the great Whale, and in the abysses of the great Deep ; namely, in the jaws of Death, and in the depths of the Grave. Cp. *S. Irenæus,* iii. 22 ; and v. 5 ; and *Tertullian,* De Resur. Carnis, c. 58.

Our Blessed Lord has distinctly affirmed that " Jonah *was* three days and three nights in the whale's belly ;" and He coupled that assertion as to the past, with a prophecy concerning the future – namely, " so *shall* the Son of Man be three days and three nights in the heart of the earth." *That* prophecy was fulfilled. Its fulfilment proved Christ's truth. It confirms our belief in His assertion, that the history of Jonah is true. All our difficulties with regard to this and other histories in the Old Testament are dissolved in the crucible of faith in Jesus Christ, the Son of God, Who received the Old Testament as true and divine, and commanded us to receive it as such. We accept the Written Word from the hands of the Incarnate Word. The Word of God is vouched to us as true, by the witness of the Son of God ; and we learn here to recognize a proof of the reality of our own future Resurrection, which Christ Himself has proclaimed to us as certain ; "The hour is coming, when all that are in the graves shall hear His Voice, and shall come forth ; they that have done good unto the resurrection of life, and they that have done evil unto the resurrection of damnation" (John v. 28, 29) ; and thus we too are stimulated to repent by the preaching of Jonah, and to rise from the death of sin now, that we may rise to glory hereafter.

F

II. [1] Then Jonah prayed unto the LORD his God out of the fish's belly,
[2] and said,

I cried || by reason of mine affliction unto the LORD, [b] and he heard me;

Out of the belly of || hell cried I, *and* thou heardest my voice.

[3] [c] For thou hadst cast me into the deep, in the † midst of the seas;

And the floods compassed me about:

[d] All thy billows and thy waves passed over me.

[4] [e] Then I said, I am cast out of thy sight;

Yet I will look again † toward thy holy temple.

[5] The [g] waters compassed me about, *even* to the soul:

The depth closed me round about, the weeds were wrapped about my head.

[6] I went down to the † bottoms of the mountains;

The earth with her bars *was* about me for ever:

Yet hast thou brought up my life [h] from || corruption, O LORD my God.

[7] When my soul fainted within me I remembered the LORD:

[i] And my prayer came in unto thee, into thine holy temple.

[8] They that observe [k] lying vanities forsake their own mercy.

[9] But I will [l] sacrifice unto thee with the voice of thanksgiving;

I will pay *that* that I have vowed.

[10] Salvation *is* of the LORD.

[10] And the LORD spake unto the fish, and it vomited out Jonah upon the dry *land.*

III. [1] And the word of the LORD came unto Jonah the second time, saying,

[2] Arise, go unto Nineveh, that great city, and preach unto it the preaching that I bid thee.

[3] So Jonah arose, and went unto Nineveh, according to the word of the LORD.

---

The remarks of S. *Augustine* on Jonah's history (Epist. 102, Sex Quæst. contra Paganos, vol. ii. p. 426; and De Symbolo ad Catechum., c. 6) are well worthy of attention. Their substance is as follows:—'The heathen (he says) scoff and sneer at the history of Jonah. How could he have been swallowed by a fish (they ask), and remain alive three days in its belly, and then be cast forth from it on dry land?' To which we reply, Either we must reject all miracles as incredible, or we must admit that there is no reason for not believing this miracle. If we are to abandon our faith because heathens and unbelievers scoff, we must cease to believe that Christ died, and was buried, and rose again the third day. We must cease to believe that Lazarus was brought forth out of his grave by Christ on the fourth day. We must cease to believe that those three men, who were cast into the fiery furnace at Babylon, walked in the fire, and came forth from it unhurt; and that the people of Israel—more than two millions in number—passed through the Red Sea, the waters of which stood as a wall on their right hand and on their left. Cp. S. *Irenæus*, v. 5, and S. *Jerome*, here. The history of Jonah is a type and prophecy of Christ. Christ Himself has assured us of this (Matt. xii. 39, 40). As Jonah went from the wood of the ship into the depth of the sea, so Christ went from the wood of the cross into the depth of the earth. As Jonah gave himself to death for those who were tossed by the storm in the Mediterranean Sea, so Christ Himself gave Himself to death for those who are tossed in the storm in the sea of this world. As Jonah rose from the whale's belly and from the depth of the sea, so Christ rose from the dead. As Jonah and his resurrection preached to the heathen of Nineveh, and they repented; so Christ after His resurrection preached by His Apostles to the Heathen World, and it repented at their preaching. The reality of the Antitype confirms the historical truth of the type. Jonah is prayed by Christ.

Ch. II. 1. *Then Jonah prayed unto the* LORD *his God*] Jonah prayed from the whale's belly in the depths of the sea;

and his prayer was heard. "Undique ad eelos tantundem est viæ." Heaven is equi-distant from all places of the earth. He prayed not only to Jehovah, but he prayed to Him as *his God.* Jonah, who probably wrote this book, thus declares his own repentance and conversion to God. He was sent to the Ninevites to call them to repentance, and to show that Jehovah his God was willing to be their God also.

The prayer here set down, which could be known to none but to God and Jonah, is a proof that we have here a communication from Jonah himself. As will be seen by reference to the margin, this prayer is derived mainly from the Psalms. Here also Jonah in his burial was a figure of Christ, Who, on the eve of His death (see Matt. xxvi. 39), and upon the cross, found utterance for His own feelings in the words of the Psalms (Matt. xxvii. 46).

Jonah, the type of Christ, was praying in his mystic grave of three days and three nights. This throws some light on the still more mysterious question concerning our Blessed Lord's employment in His Human Soul during the three days' Burial of His Human Body. See the note below, on 1 Pet. iii. 19—"He went, and preached to the spirits in prison."

3. *Thou hadst cast me*] Rather, *Thou didst cast me.*

3. *They that observe lying vanities*] Literally, *They that keep.* They who *keep* what is false, *lose* what is true. All who long a lie, lose God, Who is Truth and Love.

Ch. III. 3. *Jonah arose, and went unto Nineveh*] Observe the mysterious and inscrutable workings of God's Providence, by which His purposes are brought to pass. God had formerly sent Jonah to Nineveh. Jonah fled in the opposite direction, toward Tarshish. He fled the land and betook himself to the sea. God follows him, and raises a storm against the ship in which he is, and it is in danger of being wrecked. Jonah is cast into the sea, and is in peril of perishing. Jonah is swallowed by the whale, and is in danger of being destroyed. Jonah is cast forth out of the whale's belly—and into the sea, where the whale was, but on to the dry land. God did not bring him by a

Now Nineveh was an † exceeding great city of three days' journey.

⁴ And Jonah began to enter into the city a day's journey, and ᵃ he cried, and said, Yet forty days, and Nineveh shall be overthrown.

⁵ So the people of Nineveh ᵇ believed God, and proclaimed a fast, and put on sackcloth, from the greatest of them even to the least of them. ⁶ For word came unto the king of Nineveh, and he arose from his throne, and he laid his robe from him, and covered *him* with sackcloth, ᶜ and sat in ashes. ⁷ ᵈ And he caused *it* to be proclaimed and † published through Nineveh by the decree of the king and his † nobles, saying, Let neither man nor beast, herd nor flock, taste any thing: let them not feed, nor drink water: ⁸ but let man and beast be covered with sackcloth, and cry mightily unto God: yea, ᵉ let them turn every one from his evil way, and from ᶠ the violence that *is* in their

---

straight course to Nineveh. As S. *Chrysostom* says (Hom. 5, in Jonam). The sailors cast him into the sea, the sea gave him to the whale, the whale gave him to the land, the land gave him to God; and God gave him to the Ninevites; and God gave them pardon and peace. God's hand was in it all.

— *Nineveh was an exceeding great city*] Literally, *a great city to God*; that is, God regarded Nineveh, and God cared for it, though it was a heathen city, the enemy of Jerusalem; and therefore God sent Jonah to preach to it, and spared it on its repentance. Not only Jerusalem, but all cities of the World are cities *to God*. His eye is on them all.

Here is a tacit reproof from Jonah, reviewing his own history, and writing this book for the purpose of correcting the narrow spirit (by which he himself had once been influenced) which imagined that *no* city, except Jerusalem, was *a great city to God*.

Thus Jonah anticipates St. Stephen's speech to the Jewish Sanhedrim (see on Acts vii.), and St. Paul's language to the Jews, in his Epistle to the Romans (iii. 29), where he says, "Is He the God of the Jews only? is He not also of the Gentiles? Yes, of the Gentiles also."

— *three days' journey*] In circumference. *Diodorus Siculus* (ii. 3) says that the city was 150 stadia in length, and *Herodotus* (v. 53) reckons 150 stadia as a day's journey. Cp. *Pfeiffer*. p. 448. The city, or rather tetrapolis (for Nineveh consisted of four cities; see above on i. 2), was about ninety English miles in circumference. See *Marcus v. Niebuhr*, p. 277.

**4.** *Jonah began to enter into the city a day's journey*] He preached during one day in different parts of the city; beginning at the entrance into it from the west.

— *forty days*] This period of *forty days* (and also of *forty years*) often occurs in Holy Scripture as a time of probation. See S. *Jerome* here, and the note above, on Gen. vii. 4. Deut. ix. 9. 1 Kings xix. 8. and on Matt. iv. 2, and on Acts, p. 29.

This was the period of Nineveh's repentance, followed by escape from destruction; it was the period of the fast of Moses, followed by the reception of the Tables of the Law from the hand of God; it was the period of the pilgrimage of Elias, after which he had a vision of God in Horeb; it was the period of our Lord's fasting in the Wilderness, followed by Victory over Satan; it is therefore fitly appointed by the Church as the duration of the Lent fast, ending in the joy and victory of Easter.

Jonah, after his resurrection (from the whale's belly and the depth of the sea), preaching to Nineveh, was a type of Christ preaching after His Resurrection, by His Apostles, to Jerusalem.

Our Lord teaches us this; He says that Jonah was a *sign* to the Jews, and He adds that "the men of Nineveh will rise up in the Day of Judgment against that generation of Jews and condemn it; for they repented at the preaching of Jonah, and a greater than Jonah is here" (Matt. xii. 41).

Observe that other point of contrast. God gave Nineveh *forty days*, and they repented; He allowed Jerusalem *forty years* after Christ's resurrection, and they did *not* repeat, and perished.

— *be overthrown*] As Sodom and Gomorrah were. The same word is used here to describe the threatened *overthrow* as is applied to them. See above, note at Gen. xix. 25 on this word, which is of great importance for determining the manner in which the cities of the plain were destroyed.

**5.** *the people—proclaimed a fast*] Such was the readiness of

the people to listen to his preaching, that before the Prophet had begun his second day's work, the Ninevites believed, and *proclaimed a fast, and put on sackcloth, from the greatest of them even to the least of them.*

This alacrity of this great heathen city is mentioned to their honour by Christ Himself, and is contrasted with the obstinacy and unbelief of the Jews (Matt. xii. 41. Luke xi. 32).

— *the people—believed God*] Doubtless they had heard of Jonah's miraculous deliverance, and had been convinced thereby that he was a messenger sent from God. See above, on i. 16. *They believed God, and proclaimed a fast.* Here is a foreshadowing of the faith and repentance of the Heathen World after the Resurrection of Christ, and after the Preaching of the Gospel by the Apostles sent by Him to the Gentiles.

**6, 7.** *word came unto the king—and he caused it to be proclaimed*] Such was the effect produced by the preaching of Jonah; such was the alarm of the people; and such was their alacrity, that they would not defer their repentance till they could receive a command from the king; but, without waiting for a royal mandate, they proclaimed a fast. See c. 5. And such was the earnestness of the king, that when *word came*, or rather *the matter came*, to his ears, he was not offended by this act of his people, but he confirmed it by his own authority.

Nineveh was a vast city, and some time would therefore elapse before the king had tidings of what was done.

It is said by *Aristotle* (Polit. iii. 2), that such was the size of Babylon, and such were the intervals between its dwellings, that when the city had been taken by Cyrus, two days elapsed before tidings of its capture reached to the extremities of the city.

The name of the King of Nineveh at this time is uncertain. Some place him at as early a period as B.C. 860. *Rawlinson* supposes Jonah's preaching at Nineveh to have been at about B.C. 760 (*Rawlinson*, ii. 399—392). He seems to have resided in the royal palace at *Khorsabad*, in the north-east corner of the Tetrapolis of Nineveh.

The conquests of Shalmaneser II. had probably tended to increase the luxury and pride of Nineveh, which provoked God's anger against it.

**7, 8.** *Let neither man nor beast, herd nor flock, taste any thing—let man and beast be covered with sackcloth*] The King of Nineveh declared his consciousness of a great truth, that by the Providence of God the destinies of the animal creation, whether for joy or sorrow, whether for action or suffering, are linked in a mysterious chain of sympathy with those of man. See on Joel i. 18—20, and below iv. 11, where God declares His regard for *cattle*; and Ps. xxxvi. 7, "Thou, Lord, shalt save both man and beast."

We are informed by *Herodotus* (ix. 24), that when the Persian General Masistius was killed at Platæa, the whole Persian army, with Mardonius at their head, made a lamentation, shaving themselves and their horses, and the beasts of burden. Alexander the Great imitated this Persian custom in his mourning for Hephaestion (*Plutarch*, Alex. c. 72). The natural creation "was made subject to vanity" on account of man's sin at the Fall; and it yearns for deliverance, from the bondage of corruption, into a higher state of ease, joy, and felicity. See on Gen. iii. 17. Rom. viii. 19—23, 2 Pet. iii. 13.

**8.** *violence*] The besetting sin of the proud and warlike monarchy and nation of Assyria. Cp. Isa. xxxvii. 24—28, and the notes on 2 Kings xix. 37; xx. 12.

g 2 Sam. 12, 22.
Joel 2, 14.

h Jer. 18, 8.
Amos 7, 3, 6.

a ch. 1, 3.

b Ex. 34, 6.
Ps. 86, 5.
Joel 2, 13.
c 1 Kings 19, 4.

d ver. 8.

|| Or. Art thou
greatly angry?

|| Or. palmcrist.
† Heb. Kikajon.

† Heb. rejoiced
with great joy.

hands. ⁹ ᵉ Who can tell *if* God will turn and repent, and turn away from his fierce anger, that we perish not?

¹⁰ ʰ And God saw their works, that they turned from their evil way; and God repented of the evil, that he had said that he would do unto them; and he did *it* not.

IV. ¹ But it displeased Jonah exceedingly, and he was very angry. ² And he prayed unto the Lord, and said, I pray thee, O Lord, *was* not this my saying, when I was yet in my country? Therefore I ᵃ fled before unto Tarshish: for I knew that thou *art* a ᵇ gracious God, and merciful, slow to anger, and of great kindness, and repentest thee of the evil. ³ ᶜ Therefore now, O Lord, take, I beseech thee, my life from me; for ᵈ *it is* better for me to die than to live.

⁴ Then said the Lord, || Doest thou well to be angry?

⁵ So Jonah went out of the city, and sat on the east side of the city, and there made him a booth, and sat under it in the shadow, till he might see what would become of the city.

⁶ And the Lord God prepared a || † gourd, and made *it* to come up over Jonah, that it might be a shadow over his head, to deliver him from his grief. So Jonah † was exceeding glad of the gourd.

⁷ But God prepared a worm when the morning rose the next day, and it smote the gourd that it withered.

---

10. *God repented of the evil*] See Jer. xviii. 7, 8: "At what instant I shall speak concerning a nation and a kingdom, to pluck up, and to pull down, and to destroy it; if that nation, against whom I had pronounced, turn from their evil, I will repent of the evil that I thought to do unto them." God's unchangeable will to spare the penitent, is shown in changing His actions toward sinners on their repentance.

Ch. IV. 1. *it displeased Jonah*] Jonah was displeased for two reasons: (1) because his prophecy seemed to have failed of accomplishment, and he was liable to the charge of being called a false prophet (*Theodoret*). He preferred his own personal credit to the preservation of the city. (2) He was angry because God was merciful to the great heathen city, the enemy of God's people; and because Nineveh was spared. Cp. v. 11. How different is the conduct of the holy Angels, who rejoice when one sinner turns to God (Luke xv. 7). How different was the temper of the Lord of Angels, Who wept over Jerusalem because it would not repent (Luke xix. 41). But Jonah relates here his own infirmity; and doubtless he was inspired to record it as a sign that he repented of it, and to warn others against a similar sin.

2. *I know that thou art a gracious God*] Jonah, in an exclusive, jealous, envious, Jewish temper, murmurs at God's kindness to the heathen city; as the Elder Brother—the Jew—in the Parable, is angry, because his Father—Almighty God—was merciful to the returning and penitent prodigal, his younger brother—the Gentile—who had devoured his living with harlots (Luke xv. 28—31).

5. *Jonah went out of the city, and sat on the east side of the city*] He had come from the west, and had passed through it. The forty days had now expired.

— *a booth*] With interlaced twigs and leaves of trees. He would not enter into a house in Nineveh, for fear it might be overthrown, and fall on his own head; but he made a booth for himself outside the city wall.

— *till he might see what would become of the city*] Though the forty days had expired, yet he would not abandon all hope that the city might yet receive some punishment from God, in answer to his own remonstrance, and perhaps on account of a relapse of Nineveh into sin.

6. *The Lord God prepared*] Hebr. *Jehovah Elohim.* See Gen. ii. 4.

— *a gourd*] Hebr. *Kikaion*, the Palma Christi, or ricinus; the Coptic and Arabic *Kiki*; a tall biennial plant, cultivated in Eastern gardens; very rapid in growth; beautiful, succulent, and luxuriant, but a slight injury will cause it to fade and die (*Gesen.* 731; cp. *Rosenm.* here).

65

It grows to the size of a small fig-tree; its leaves are like those of a plane-tree, but larger, smoother, and darker. See *Pusey*, 259, 260.

S. Augustine, writing to S. Jerome (Epist. 71 and Epist. 82; cp. *S. Jerome* here), mentions that when this chapter was read according to S. Jerome's Latin translation, in a church in Africa, the congregation was much disturbed, because in that translation the word "hedera" had been substituted for the former Latin rendering, with which they were familiar, and which was derived from the Septuagint, "cucurbita;" and he takes occasion to offer some remarks concerning vernacular translations of Holy Scripture, which are well worthy of consideration at the present time.

7. *God prepared*] Hebr. *ha-Elohim; the God;* the only true God.

— *God prepared a worm—and it smote the gourd*] Which overshadowed Jonah's head.

Some of the Ancient Fathers (as *S. Jerome* and *S. Augustine*, Epist. 102) saw a typical representation in this incident also, as follows:—

Jonah was a figure of the Jews clinging to the ceremonial shadows of Judaism, and envying the Gentiles their privileges, and grieving at their repentance and at their reception into God's favour. When the doctrine of Repentance was preached by the Apostles, then the noonday Sun of the Gospel of Christ withered up the leaves of the Ceremonial Law, which was only a shadow of the Evangelical good things to come (Col. ii. 17. Heb. x. 1). Under its shadow many Jewish Jonahs sat at that time, placing themselves outside the Gentile World, and jealous of God's mercy to it, and even desirous to see its destruction. And those Jewish Jonahs were angry with God for withering the umbracular gourd of the Ceremonial Law, and were exasperated against the Apostles of Christ, especially against St. Paul (who himself had once been a Hebrew Jonah, rejoicing in that shadow), for accepting as a gracious dispensation of God's providence, the fact that the Jewish Gourd had faded beneath the rays of the Gospel of Christ, and that God had mercifully spared the Gentile Ninevehs, and had received them into covenant with Himself. They despised the Gospel as a worm; indeed, Christ Himself is called a Worm (Ps. xxii. 6), because He was rejected and trodden under foot as such by the Jews; and the Worm "smote the gourd that it withered."

As long as the Jews are like what Jonah was then—murmurers against God's dispensations—so long will they be like Jonah in Assyria, roaming there without a home, feeling the scorching heat of God's displeasure. But let them come to the Shadow of the Cross; let them sit down beneath the Tree of Life, whose leaves never wither, and which are "for the healing of

⁸ And it came to pass, when the sun did arise, that God prepared a ‖ vehe-   ‖ Or, silent.
ment east wind; and the sun beat upon the head of Jonah, that he fainted,
and wished in himself to die, and said, ᶜ *It is* better for me to die than to live.   c ver. 3.

⁹ And God said to Jonah, ‖ Doest thou well to be angry for the gourd ?   ‖ Or, Art thou
And he said, ‖ I do well to be angry, *even* unto death.   ‖ Or, I am greatly

¹⁰ Then said the LORD, Thou hast ‖ had pity on the gourd, for the which ‖ Or, spared.
thou hast not laboured, neither madest it grow; which † came up in a night, † Heb. was the
and perished in a night : ¹¹ and should not I spare Nineveh, ᶠ that great city, ᶠ ch. 1. 2. &c.
wherein are more than sixscore thousand persons ᵍ that cannot discern between ᵍ Deut. 1. 39.
their right hand and their left hand; and *also* much ʰ cattle ? ʰ Ps. 36. 6. &c.

---

the nations" (Rev. xxii. 2); then they will be refreshed with
health and joy, and will dwell in love and peace with their
Gentile brethren, under that hospitable shade in the Paradise of
God.

8. *God prepared*] Hebr. *Elohim*. These various titles of
God are designed to show that JEHOVAH, the Lord God of the
Hebrews, is also *Elohim*, the God of Creation and of Nature;
and that He is *the* God—that is, there is no other God besides
Him. And thus Jonah, while he encourages the heathen to look
to the Lord God of Israel as waiting to be gracious to them,
warns them against their own polytheism, which represents
various deities as exercising dominion in divers countries respectively, and as having several powers over the different
elements of the natural world.

— *a vehement*] Sultry and silent.

10. *the* LORD] JEHOVAH, the Lord God of Israel, sums up
the whole history, and teaches the lesson to be drawn from it.

— *which came up in a night*] Literally, *the son of a night.*

11. *sixscore thousand persons that cannot discern between
their right hand and their left*] These 120,000 were children ;
and therefore we may estimate the whole population of Nineveh
at about 650,000 souls (*M. v. Niebuhr*, p. 278).

Though Nineveh was a tetrapolis of about ninety miles in
circumference, we are not to be surprised that the population
was not greater than this; because, like Babylon and other
great Eastern Cities, it contained within its walls much pasture-
land and arable; as is implied by what follows, where it is
said that in it *was much cattle*. Cp. above, on iii. 6, 7.

— *and also much cattle*] This is a happy and appropriate
conclusion to the book. God cares even for *cattle*. How much
more, therefore, for *men*, for whose service cattle were created.
Therefore, let Jonah learn, and let him teach the world, that
God willeth all men to repent and to be saved, even the heathen
Ninevehs of this world, and to be united with the Jews in one
and the same faith, hope, and love, and in worshipping the same
Lord and Father of all, in the same Heavenly City, the Jerusalem that is above, which is the mother of us all (Gal. iv. 26).
This is the lesson which the Prophet Jonah learnt, and which
he is ever teaching in this Divine Book, read as divinely inspired
Scripture in the Church of every age ; and which has its
perfect fulfilment in CHRIST (the divine Jonah, i. 17), in Whom
there is neither Greek, nor Jew, barbarian, Scythian, bond nor
free, but He is all in all (Col. iii. 11. Gal. iii. 28) ; to Whom,
with the Father, and the Holy Ghost, be all honour and glory
now and for evermore. AMEN.

# MICAH.

Before
CHRIST
about
720.
a Jer. 26. 18.
b Amos 1. 1.

I. ¹ THE word of the LORD that came to ᵃMicah the Morasthite in the days of Jotham, Ahaz, *and* Hezekiah, kings of Judah, ᵇwhich he saw concerning Samaria and Jerusalem.

---

The name Micah signifies "Who is so *as JAH*, or JEHOVAH" (*Caspari*, after Micha, p. 11; cp. Exod. xv. 11; Deut. iii. 24; Ps. lxxxi. 8; below, vii. 18).

His prophecies are united to those of Jonah; and follow them in a logical sequence and harmonious order. As we have already seen, Jonah was not only a prophet, but a prophecy; a prophecy of Christ's Death, Burial, and Resurrection, and of the propitiation effected by His Sacrifice of Himself. His history foreshadowed the calm produced thereby in the Sea of this world, and it prefigured the preaching of Repentance after Christ's Resurrection to the Ninevites of Heathendom; and it exhibited God's desire that they should all be admitted into His Church, on their faith and repentance, upon equal terms with the Jews.

The Prophet Jonah, who had formerly been swayed by Hebrew prejudices, and had grudged the extension of God's mercy to the Heathen, especially to the Assyrians, the formidable foes of Israel and Judah, was brought by God to a better mind, and was chastened, and softened, and spiritualized by the holy discipline of Divine Love.

Jonah has written his own recantation in his prophetical book, and has preached to the world for 2500 years this holy lesson of universal charity, which he himself had been slow to learn; he has also delivered a gracious message of universal redemption by Christ, in that prophetic book, when expounded by the Light of the Gospel.

The Prophet Micah learnt this lesson, perhaps from Jonah's prophecy; and, so far from grudging the glad tidings of salvation to the Gentiles, he rejoices in the prospect of the reception of all Heathen Nations into the Church of God; spreading forth from Zion in the days of the Messiah, and enfolding them all in its arms. See iv. 1—5. He declares that the promised Shepherd, Who would be born at Bethlehem-Judah, the City of David, and "Whose goings forth are from everlasting," will "stand and feed in the strength of the Lord, and will be great *unto the ends of the earth*" (v. 4).

Thus, while Jonah declares the salvability of the Heathen, Micah proclaims the great truth afterwards expressed by Christ Himself in the words "salvation is of the Jews" (John iv. 22).

Zion is the mother of all Christendom. "It shall come to pass" (says the Prophet, rejoicing in the glorious vision of the Church Universal, elevated aloft so as to be visible to all Nations, and expanding itself with a living and growing power and energy, "that the mountain of the house of the Lord shall be established in the top of the mountains, and it shall be exalted above the hills; and people shall flow unto it. And many nations shall come, and say, Come, and let us go up to the mountain of the Lord, and to the house of the God of Jacob; and He will teach us of His ways, and we will walk in His paths. For the Law shall go forth of Zion, and the Word of God from Jerusalem" (Micah iv. 1, 2).

Micah thus reconciles the Jews to the admission of the Heathen within the pale of the Church of God. The Heathen are the spiritual offspring of Zion; and the Hebrew Mother is glorified in the multitude of her Gentile children.

Jonah had declared that God was willing and eager to be merciful even to Assyria and its great capital, Nineveh; and thus he comforted the Gentiles with a hope of being admitted into God's favour on a par with the Jews; and Micah, and Nahum after him, assure the Jews, that if the Ninevites of this world are obstinate in their hostility to God's Church, then the Messiah, the Son of David, will protect Israel and Judah (if they are faithful to God), and will deliver them from "the

Assyrian invader"—the proud and godless Sennacherib—and from all the enemies of the Church who are represented and typified by him. See below, v. 5, 6, 9.

Jonah declares the salvability of all Assyrian enemies of God's Church, if they repent; Micah proclaims the destruction of all Assyrian enemies of God's Church if they persist in their resistance and rebellion against Him.

The prophecies of Micah are divided into three parts, all beginning with *Hear ye*:—

> 1st. Chapters I., II.
> 2nd. Chapters III., IV., V.
> 3rd. Chapters VI., VII.

In the first part, the Prophet foretells the destruction of Samaria for its sins (i. 1—7), and the spoliation of Judah and the carrying away of its people (8—16); and grounds this threat on the iniquities of the Princes, Nobles, and false Prophets (ii. 1—11); and promises to Israel and Judah restoration on their repentance.

The second portion is a recapitulation of the former, with an enlargement containing a further declaration of their sins, in more minute and precise detail (iii.); and also a larger and fuller promise of recovery and restitution through the MESSIAH (whose birth-place he specifies, with a declaration of His Divine Nature and office), on their faith and repentance (iv. 1—7; v. 1—5), and a glorious display of His power and victories, and of the peace to be established by Him (v. 6—14).

The third portion declares God's gracious dispensation of love and mercy to Israel from the beginning; and Israel's ingratitude; and it contains a prophecy that Israel will hereafter be touched with remorse, consequent on their misery in their banishment and dispersion; and that they will confess their sins, and turn to God by repentance and faith; and that God will be gracious unto them, and deliver them from their enemies.

The prophecies of Micah may be regarded as standing in the same relation to those of Isaiah, as St. Mark's Gospel does to St. Matthew; or as the Epistle to the Galatians does to the Epistle to the Romans.

CH. 1. 1. *Micah the Morasthite*] From Moresheth Gath, in the lowland of Judah (see v. 14), south-west of Jerusalem, near Eleutheropolis (*S. Jerome*), which was about twenty miles south-west of Jerusalem, and eighteen miles west of Hebron. Cp. *Caspari*, 35.

— *in the days of Jotham, Ahaz, and Hezekiah*] After the death of *Uzziah*. Micah, therefore, was younger than Hosea, who prophesied under Uzziah (Hos. i. 1); and than Amos (Amos i. 1); and than Isaiah (see on Isa. i. 1; vi. 1); but, in other respects, the contemporary of that Prophet, who prophesied "in the days of Uzziah, Jotham, Ahaz, and Hezekiah, kings of Judah."

The salutary influence of Micah's prophetic warnings on the mind and conduct of the good King Hezekiah, is described in Jer. xxvi. 17—19.

On the genuineness and authenticity of this superscription, see *Caspari*, pp. 59—100, refuting the objections of *De Wette*, *Knobel*, *Maurer*, *Ewald*, *Meier*, and *Umbreit*.

We shall see that the invasion of Judah by the proud Assyrian conqueror Sennacherib, in the days of the good King Hezekiah, and the miraculous destruction of his army before the gates of Jerusalem, are treated by Micah in the same spirit as by Isaiah; that is, not only as instructive and cheering signs of God's protection to Hezekiah and Jerusalem, remaining firm in their allegiance to God, but as prophetic encouragements to

² † Hear, all ye people;
'Hearken, O earth, and † all that therein is:
And let the Lord God ᵈ be witness against you,
The Lord from ᵉ his holy temple.
³ For, behold, ᶠ the LORD cometh forth out of his ᵍ place,
And will come down, and tread upon the ʰ high places of the earth.
⁴ And ⁱ the mountains shall be molten under him,
And the valleys shall be cleft, as wax before the fire,
*And* as the waters *that are* poured down † a steep place.
⁵ For the transgression of Jacob *is* all this,
And for the sins of the house of Israel.
What *is* the transgression of Jacob? *is it* not Samaria?
And what *are* the high places of Judah? *are they* not Jerusalem?
⁶ Therefore I will make Samaria ᵏ as an heap of the field,
*And* as plantings of a vineyard:
And I will pour down the stones thereof into the valley,
And I will ˡ discover the foundations thereof.
⁷ And all the graven images thereof shall be beaten to pieces,
And all the ᵐ hires thereof shall be burned with the fire,
And all the idols thereof will I lay desolate:
For she gathered *it* of the hire of an harlot,
And they shall return to the hire of an harlot.
⁸ Therefore ⁿ I will wail and howl,
ᵒ I will go stripped and naked:
ᵖ I will make a wailing like the dragons,
And mourning as the † owls.

Before
CHRIST
...
f Heb. *H.....*
*people, ...*
*...m.*
c Deut. 31 1.
Isa. 1. 2.
† Heb. *in fulness
thereof.*
d Ps. 50 7.
Mal. 3. 5.
e Ps. 11. 4.
Jonah 2. 7.
Hab. 2. 20.
f Isa. 26. 21.
g Ps. 115. 3.
h Deut. 32. 13. &
33. 29.
Amos 4. 13.
i Judg. 5. 5.
Ps. 97. 5.
Isa. 34. 1, 2, 3.
Amos 9. 5.
Hab. 3. 6, 10.
† Heb. *a descent.*

k 2 Kings 19. 25.
ch. 3. 12.

l Ezek. 13. 14.

m Hos. 2. 5, 12.

n Isa. 21. 3. &
22. 4.
Jer. 4. 19.
o Isa. 20. 2, 3, 4.
p Job 30. 29.
Ps. 102. 6.
† Heb. *daughters
of the owl.*

---

the Church of God in every age, especially in the latter days. If she acts in the spirit of Hezekiah, all her Sennacheribs will be destroyed, and she will be delivered by God.

2. *Hear, all ye people*] Or, *Hear, nations all.* Micah takes up the appeal of his namesake *Micaiah*, speaking in the presence of Ahab and Jehoshaphat about 150 years before (1 Kings xxii. 28), *Hear, ye nations all.* The words are the same, and in the same order in both.

This appeal is not only to the people of Israel and Judah, but to *all nations.* See what follows—*Hearken, O Earth, and the fulness thereof* The God of Micah, the God of Israel and Judah, is the God of the Universe; all things are His creatures, and His witnesses. See Deut. xxxii. 1. Cp. Isa. i. 2, and Pocock here.

Micah follows Micaiah in rebuking the false prophets by which the king and people of Israel were seduced; and in reproving the rulers of Israel for their sins; and in showing to them the bitter fruits which those sins would produce.

He frequently adopts the imagery and language of Micaiah. Cp. the *lying spirit* (ii. 11) with the *lying spirit* in 1 Kings xxii. 22. 23; the *horn of iron* (iv. 13) with those in 1 Kings xxii. 11; the *smiting on the cheek* in v. 1 with 1 Kings xxii. 24.

Micah also often adopts the language of the Pentateuch. Here, in v. 2, Hearken, O Earth, he refers to Deut. xxxii. 1; and in v. 3 he refers to Deut. xxxii. 13; xxxiii. 29. In ii. 12; iv. 7, he refers to Exod. i. 7. 12; in vi. 4 he has his eye on Deut. v. 6; vi. 12; vii. 8; xiii. 5. See the important and interesting collection of passages in *Caspari*, pp. 420—427, in which it is shown that the prophecies of Micah are grounded on the Books of Moses, and supply a strong argument for their genuineness and inspiration. The same may be said of his testimony to the Book of Joshua and the Psalms and Proverbs (*ibid.* 427—432). In his turn Micah is referred to by Habakkuk, Zephaniah, Jeremiah, and Ezekiel, and by the Evangelists, *ibid.* 150—158.

3. *For, behold, the LORD cometh forth out of his place*] Words used also by Micah's contemporary, Isaiah (xxvi. 21).

4. *the mountains shall be molten*] As when the Lord came down in His glorious Majesty on Sinai (Judges v. 5. Psalm xcvii. 5).

5. *For the transgression of Jacob is all this*] All this is done to punish the falling away of Jacob; "judgment must begin at the house of God" (1 Pet. iv. 17).

— *high places of Judah—Jerusalem*] Even the Holy City and Temple are polluted by idolatry, and have become like the high places of heathen deities.

This was true specially in the days of King Ahaz, who made his children to pass through the fire to Molech, and made him altars in every corner of Jerusalem (2 Chron. xxviii. 3, 24, 25). Cp. xxxiii. 6; and 2 Kings xvi. 10—16. Ezekiel xvi. 31.

7. *the hires*] Gifts given to her for her spiritual harlotry; offerings for idolatrous worship. Micah here adopts the imagery and language of his predecessor Hosea (Hos. ii. 5, 8, 12; ix. 1).

— *they shall return to the hire of an harlot*] That is, her religious ornaments shall be carried away by her enemies and spoilers, to adorn the idolatrous temples of Assyria and other Heathen Nations. See the note on 2 Kings xvii. 5, where Sargon, King of Assyria, is cited as taking away 27,280 prisoners from Samaria. Doubtless he took away treasures also and religious vessels, and votive offerings to adorn the temples of Nineveh, his own harlot city (Nahum iii. 4—6). As Hosea prophesies, "It shall be also carried unto *Assyria*, for a present to *King Jareb*" (Hos. x. 6).

So Nebuchadnezzar took away the sacred vessels of the Temple at Jerusalem, to adorn the temple of his god at Babylon (Dan. i. 2; v. 1—4. Ezra i. 7).

The sense is, Because Samaria, the capital of Israel, fell away from her faithfulness to God, and lapsed into idolatry, which is spiritual harlotry—because she worshipped false gods, and attributed all her wealth and prosperity to them, instead of to the God of Israel—therefore her idolatrous images, and other precious ornaments, shall be carried away to other harlots—that is, to other idolatrous nations—viz. the Assyrians, who will give them as gifts to their false deities (*Targum*).

8. *dragons*] Jackals. See above, Job xxx. 29.

— *owls*] Ostriches. Literally, *daughters of the she-ostrich.* See on Job xxx. 29. Micah appears to be referring to that passage where Job describes himself "as a brother of dragons"

⁹ For † her wound *is* incurable ; for ʰ it is come unto Judah ;
He is come unto the gate of my people, *even* to Jerusalem.

¹⁰ ʲ Declare ye *it* not at Gath, weep ye not at all :
In the house of ‖ Aphrah ᵏ roll thyself in the dust.

¹¹ Pass ye away, ‖ thou † inhabitant of Saphir, having thy ˡ shame naked :
The inhabitant of ‖ Zaanan came not forth in the mourning of ‖ Beth-ezel ;
He shall receive of you his standing.

¹² For the inhabitant of Maroth ‖ waited carefully for good :
But ᵐ evil came down from the LORD unto the gate of Jerusalem.

¹³ O thou inhabitant of ⁿ Lachish, bind the chariot to the swift beast :
She *is* the beginning of the sin to the daughter of Zion :
For the transgressions of Israel were found in thee.

¹⁴ Therefore shalt thou ᵖ give presents ‖ to Moresheth-gath :
The houses of ‖ ᵠ Achzib *shall be* a lie to the kings of Israel.

¹⁵ Yet will I bring an heir unto thee, O inhabitant of ˢ Mareshah :
‖ He shall come unto ᵗ Adullam the glory of Israel.

¹⁶ Make thee ᶜ bald, and poll thee for thy ᵈ delicate children ;

b 2 Chr. 11. 7.
c Jut. i. 16.　Isa. 15. 2 & 22. 12.　Jer. 7. 29 & 16. 6, & 47. 5. & 48. 37.　d Lam. 4. 5.

Enlarge thy baldness as the eagle ;

For they are gone into captivity from thee.

II. ¹ Woe to them ª that devise iniquity, and ᵇ work evil upon their beds !

When the morning is light, they practise it,

Because ᶜ it is in the power of their hand ;

² And they covet ᵈ fields, and take *them* by violence ;

And houses, and take *them* away :

So they ‖ oppress a man and his house, even a man and his heritage.

³ Therefore thus saith the LORD ;

Behold, against ᵉ this family do I devise an evil,

From which ye shall not remove your necks ;

Neither shall ye go haughtily : ᶠ for this time *is* evil.

⁴ In that day shall *one* ᵍ take up a parable against you,

And ʰ lament † with a doleful lamentation,

*And* say, We be utterly spoiled :

ⁱ He hath changed the portion of my people :

How hath he removed *it* from me !

‖ Turning away he hath divided our fields.

⁵ Therefore thou shalt have none that shall ᵏ cast a cord by lot in the congregation of the LORD.

⁶ ‖ †¹ Prophesy ye not, *say they to them that* prophesy :

They shall not prophesy to them, *that* they shall not take shame.

⁷ O *thou that art* named the house of Jacob,

Is the spirit of the LORD ‖ straitened ?

*Are* these his doings ?

Do not my words do good to him that walketh † uprightly ?

⁸ Even † of late my people is risen up as an enemy :

Ye pull off the robe † with the garment from them that pass by securely as † men averse from war.

⁹ The ‖ women of my people have ye cast out from their pleasant houses ;

---

*Margin references (right column):*

*Before CHRIST about 750.*

ª Hos. 7. 1.
ᵇ Ps. 36. 4.

ᶜ Gen. 31. 29.

ᵈ Isa. 5. 8.

‖ Or, *defraud.*

ᵉ Jer. 8. 3.

ᶠ Amos 5. 13. Eph. 5. 16.

ᵍ Hab. 2. 6.

ʰ 2 Sam. 1. 17.
† Heb. *with a lamentation of lamentations.*

ⁱ Ch. 1. 15.

‖ Or, *instead of restoring.*

ᵏ Deut. 32. 8, 9.

*ˡ Or, Prophesy not as they prophesy.*
† Heb. *Drop, &c.* Ezek. 21. 2. Hos. 20. 10. Amos 2. 12. & 7. 16.
‖ Or, *restrained ?*

† Heb. *upright?*

† Heb. *yesterday.*

† Heb. *over against a garment.*

‖ Or, *wives.*

---

— *Enlarge thy baldness as the eagle*] Or rather, the vulture —vultur barbatus ; or perhaps, vultur percnopterus, which has the front part of the head bald (*Gesen.* 572 ; *Kamus* ; *Hassel-quist* ; *Keil*).

CH. II. 1. *Because it is in the power of their hand*] Rather, *because their hand is their God.* As Mezentius said,

"Dextra mihi Deus, et telum quod missile libro."
(*Virg.* Æn. x. 21.)

4. *lament with a doleful lamentation,* and *say*] Utter a lament (so *Gesen.* 536) ; but as the feminine form, *nihyah*, does not occur in this sense of *lamentation*, others suppose it to be *niphal* of *hayah*, to be, and to signify *actum est ! it is done ! it is all over !* (*Fuerst*, 910, and so *De Dieu*, *Ewald*, *Kleinert*, *Keil*; and the sense is, *they lament a lamentation.* "It is done," say they ; "we are utterly spoiled." There is a remarkable alliteration in the original, expressive of repeated lamentations (*nahah nehi, nihyah*).

— *Turning away he hath divided our fields*] Rather, *he hath divided our fields* (the fields of God's own people) *to one who turns away,* i. e. a *perverse* and *rebellious one*—to an infidel apostate—Assyria (*Kimchi*, *Pocock*, *Keil*). It is the same complaint as in Habakkuk, "the wicked (Chaldean) devoureth the man that is more righteous than he" (Hab. i. 13).

5. *thou shalt have none that shall cast a cord by lot*] Or, a *measure for a lot.* Thou, godless generation, shalt have none to partake in an inheritance. The reference is to the original assignment of the inheritances of the tribes in the Promised Land by lot under Joshua (Josh. xiv. 2).

6. *Prophesy ye not*] Literally, *drop not.* Micah adopts the word (*adtaph*, to *drop*, a word, a prophecy) used by Amos (vii. 16), and which is thence to be explained.

The false priests and prophets said to the true prophets, *Prophesy not* against Israel and her worship. See Amos ii. 12 ; vii. 13.

The sense is, *Prophesy ye not* (say the false prophets to Amos and to Micah, and to other true prophets), but they (the true prophets) shall *prophesy*; but *they shall not prophesy to these*; that is, they shall not be prophets to this godless people: it will not listen to their words, but will reject them, and will choose other prophets (viz. false prophets) for itself; *and it will not remove shame,* literally *shames* (plural); it will not put away its false gods, which are the cause of all its shame and misery. The word rendered *take* in our version is *násug*, which properly means to *remove*—to remove a landmark (Deut. xix. 14, Prov. xxii. 28. Hos. v. 10. Cp. *Gesen.* 552. Cp. below, vi. 14).

7. *Is the spirit of the LORD straitened ?*] Here is another reference to the words of Micaiah the true prophet in the time of Ahab, as contrasted with the false prophets of Israel ; and to the words of the false prophet saying to him. "Which way went the Spirit of the LORD from me to speak unto thee ?" (1 Kings xxii. 24.)

Do ye, O ye false prophets, imagine that ye can constrain the *Spirit of the Lord*, by forbidding His prophets to prophesy? *are these His doings ?* are your miseries caused by God ? are they not brought upon you by yourselves ? O Israel, *thou hast destroyed thyself* (Hos. xiii. 9). *Do not my words*—the words which I utter, as God's prophet—*do good*, and bring comfort to *him that walketh uprightly ?* e.g. to the good King Hezekiah, as contrasted with you, on whom I denounce judgment ?

8. *Even of late*] Even yesterday. Your wickedness is fresh, like a thing of yesterday. Cp. 2 Kings ix. 26, "Surely I have seen yesterday the blood of Naboth ;" and Ps. xc. 4, "A thousand years in Thy sight are but as yesterday."

From their children have ye taken away my glory for ever.

10   Arise ye, and depart ; for this *is* not *your* <sup>m</sup> rest :

Because it is <sup>n</sup> polluted, it shall destroy *you*, even with a sore destruction.

11   If a man ‖ <sup>o</sup> walking in the spirit and falsehood do lie, *saying*,

I will prophesy unto thee of wine and of strong drink ;

He shall even be the prophet of this people.

12   <sup>p</sup> I will surely assemble, O Jacob, all of thee ;

I will surely gather the remnant of Israel ;

I will put them together <sup>q</sup> as the sheep of Bozrah,

As the flock in the midst of their fold :

<sup>r</sup> They shall make great noise by reason of *the multitude of* men.

13   The breaker is come up before them :

They have broken up, and have passed through the gate,

And are gone out by it :

And <sup>s</sup> their king shall pass before them,

<sup>t</sup> And the LORD on the head of them.

---

Before CHRIST 710

m Deut. xii. 9.
n Lev. xviii. 25, 28

o Or, walking in the wind, and lie falsely.
o Ezek. xiii. 3.

p ch. iv. 6, 7.

q Jer. xxxi. 10.

r Ezek. xxxvi. 37.

s Hos. iii. 5.
t Isa. lii. 12.

9. *Have ye taken away my glory for ever*] Ye have robbed them for ever of the ornament which I gave them ; whereas the law prescribes, that thou shalt restore at night the garment thou hast taken in pledge from a poor debtor (Exod. xxii. 26). So *Keil*. But there seems to be something more in this prophetic declaration. Ye have not only despoiled the poor, but ye have robbed Me ; ye have divested Me, as far as ye are able, of My glory and excellency (Hebr. *hādār*, see Ps. viii. 5 ; xxix. 4. Isa. ii. 10, 19, 21 ; xxxv. 2, and usually applied to God).

He had said before (*v.* 6) that they would not *remove their own shame*, i.e. their own idols ; and now God says that they have *taken away His glory*.

10. *Arise ye, and depart*] A noble appeal to Israel and Judah ; representing to them that their future captivity will even be a blessing. *Arise ye, and depart*—quit your own home, for it is defiled by idolatry, which is the cause of your misery ; go ye into Assyria, depart ye to Babylon, there ye will be chastened for your sins, and purified by repentance.

11. *If a man walking in the spirit*] Rather, *walking in wind* as his element ; mere vanity. The sentence may be thus rendered, *If there be a man, walking in wind, forging lies and saying, I will prophesy unto thee of wine and strong drink*—*he shall be a prophet of this people*. Such an one, who is a prophet of this, is the only person fit to be their prophet, and the only one to whom they would listen. Cp. Ezek. xiii. 3, 4.

### PROMISE OF RESTORATION TO ISRAEL IN CHRIST.

12. *I will surely assemble, O Jacob, all of thee*] Observe the sudden transition from sorrow to joy. There is a similar change at the beginning of chapter iv.

The false prophets prophesied carnal delights, and deceived the people with lies. Micah, the true Prophet of the Lord, has nobler joys and purer pleasures to announce : " I foresee and foretell that thou, O Jacob, shalt be taken captive, and be scattered for thy sins ; but, I, saith the Lord, *will surely gather thee, I will gather together the remnant of Israel*," as Micah himself explains the words below (iv. 6), and as God says by Jeremiah (xxxi. 10), " He that *scattered* Israel will *gather him*, and keep him, as a shepherd doth his flock."

This prophecy is fulfilled in Christ, the Good Shepherd, who *gathers all* His sheep together into one fold. See *Pearson* here ; and cp. John x. 1—18 ; xvi. 28 ; and *Pusey*, p. 309.

The Prophet Micah, like Isaiah his contemporary, looks beyond the captivity of Israel by Assyria (i. 11, 16 ; ii. 4), which before befals, as Isaiah did ; and he looks also beyond the captivity of Judah at Babylon, which both these prophets pre-announced ; and he looks also beyond the liberation of Judah by the decree of Cyrus ; and his prophetic view extends to the time of that glorious spiritual restoration which is effected by Christ, of Whom Cyrus was a type. See above on Isa. xi. 1—12, which is the best comment on this prophecy.

— *the sheep of Bozrah*, in Edom ; famous for cattle (Isa. xxxiv. 6).

— *of a--*] He says *men*, in order that the comparison of Israel to a flock may be better understood.

74

### THE VICTORY OF CHRIST AND OF HIS PEOPLE, IN HIS TRIUMPHANT RESURRECTION FROM THE DEAD.

13. *The Breaker is come up before them*] A magnificent transition from Cyrus to Christ ; as in Isa. xl. 1—5. The Prophet sees the conqueror Cyrus breaking into Babylon, snatting asunder the bars which kept Israel captive as in a prison ; and how they went forth, after the issuing of his decree, in joy and triumph to their own land. And from this prophetical view of Cyrus and his victory, and its blessed consequences, he passes on, by a rapid prophetic flight, to speak of the Divine Cyrus, Jesus Christ, and of His triumph over Death and the Grave.

The *Breaker-up* is, by the confession of the Jews themselves, a title of the Messiah. See the Rabbinical authorities in *Bp. Pearson* on the Creed, Art. vi. p. 270, Note.

Christ has broken into the camp of our ghostly Enemy, and has spoiled the strong man, and has rescued us from his grasp, He has broken the gates of brass, and bars of iron in sunder (Ps. cvii. 16. Acts ii. 24), and has *gone forth* before us, as a triumphant king and captain at the head of a victorious army ; and He is no other than *the Lord Jehovah at our head* ; as the Lord went before His People, when He led them out of Egypt, at the Exodus (Exod. xiii. 21).

" There is no passing on nor going forth" (says *S. Jerome* here) "without Christ our King, Who is both King and Lord." "Christ" (says *Corn. a Lapide* here) "has delivered us from the bondage and prison-house of sin and Satan, and ye also will be able to break its bands, being strengthened by His grace, and ye will go forth with songs of joy to Zion—the Jerusalem above—which is free, and the mother of us all" (Gal. iv. 26). Christ, the Breaker, has gone up into heaven, and has sent His Spirit to lead all the faithful thither. All the saints of God, by virtue of the Death and Resurrection of this Divine Breaker, will burst through the prison-doors of the grave at the Day of Judgment, and be carried up, with Christ going before them, into His Heavenly Kingdom. He will pass on as a king at their head ; and the Lord God (for such He is) will lead them thither, that where He is they may be also.

For farther proofs and illustrations of this interpretation, see *Pfeiffer*, 451 ; *Hengstenberg*, and *Keil*. We may add the substance of the words of an English Expositor, who is often very happy in eliciting and in expressing the spiritual sense of Holy Scripture.—*Matthew Henry*:

" *Their breaker has come up before them* to break down all opposition, and to clear the road before them, and under His guidance they have *broken up* and have *passed through the gate*, and *have gone out by it*, having Omnipotence for their Vanguard. *Their King shall pass before* them, to lead them in the way—even *Jehovah* (He is their King), at the head of them, as He was at the head of the armies of Israel when they came out of Egypt, and followed the pillar of cloud and fire through the wilderness. Christ is the Church's King. He is Jehovah. He leads them ; passes before them ; brings them out of the land of their captivity (like Moses), and brings them (like Joshua) into the land of their rest. He is the *breaker*. He broke upon the powers of darkness, and broke through them, and rent the veil, and opened the Kingdom of Heaven to

III. [1] And I said, Hear, I pray you, O heads of Jacob,
    And ye princes of the house of Israel ;
    [a] *Is it* not for you to know judgment ?

[2] Who hate the good, and love the evil ;
    Who pluck off their skin from off them,
    And their flesh from off their bones ;

[3] Who also [b] eat the flesh of my people,
    And flay their skin from off them ;
    And they break their bones, and chop them in pieces,
    As for the pot, and [c] as flesh within the caldron.

[4] Then [d] shall they cry unto the LORD, but he will not hear them :
    He will even hide his face from them at that time,
    As they have behaved themselves ill in their doings.

[5] Thus saith the LORD [e] concerning the prophets that make my people err,
    That [f] bite with their teeth, and cry, Peace ;
    And [g] he that putteth not into their mouths,
    They even prepare war against him.

[6] [h] Therefore night *shall be* unto you, † that ye shall not have a vision ;
    And it shall be dark unto you, † that ye shall not divine ;
    [i] And the sun shall go down over the prophets,
    And the day shall be dark over them.

[7] Then shall the seers be ashamed, and the diviners confounded :
    Yea, they shall all cover their † lips ; [k] for *there is* no answer of God.

[8] But truly I am full of power by the spirit of the LORD,
    And of judgment, and of might,
    [l] To declare unto Jacob his transgression, and to Israel his sin.

[9] Hear this, I pray you, ye heads of the house of Jacob,
    And princes of the house of Israel,
    That abhor judgment, and pervert all equity.

[10] [m] They build up Zion with [n] † blood,
    And Jerusalem with iniquity.

[11] [o] The heads thereof judge for reward,
    And [p] the priests thereof teach for hire,
    And the prophets thereof divine for money :
    [q] Yet will they lean upon the LORD, † and say,
    *Is* not the LORD among us ? none evil can come upon us.

*Marginal references (right column):*

Before
CHRIST
710.

a Jer. 5, 4, 5.

b Ps. 14. 4.

c Ezek. 11. 3, 7.

d Ps. 18. 41.
Prov. 1. 28.
Isa. 1. 15.
Ezek. 8. 18.
Zech. 7. 13.

e Isa. 56. 10, 11.
Ezek. 13. 10. &
22. 25.
f ch. 2. 11.
Matt. 7. 15.
g Ezek. 13. 18, 19.

h Isa. 8, 20, 22
Ezek. 13, 23.
Zech. 13. 4.
† Heb. *from a vision.*
† Heb. *from divining.*
i Amos 8, 9.

† Heb. *upper lip.*
k Ps. 74. 9.
Amos 8. 11.

l Isa. 58. 1.

m Jer. 22. 13.
n Ezek. 22. 27.
Hab. 2. 12.
Zeph. 3. 3.
† Heb. *bloods.*
o Isa. 1. 23.
Ezek. 22. 12.
Hos. 4. 18. *
ch. 7. 3.
p Jer. 6. 13.

q Isa. 48. 2.
Jer. 7. 4.
Rom. 2. 17.
† Heb. *saying.*

---

all believers. *The breaker has gone before us* out of the grave, and has carried away its gates as Samson did Gaza's—bars and all—and by that break we go out and arise to glory.'

Ch. III. 1. *And I said, Hear, I pray you*] Here begins the second portion of Micah's prophecies. The following address to the Rulers of Israel and Judah is a recapitulation and enlargement of the former ; and as in that Address, so here also, denunciations of judgment are followed by promises of mercy in Christ. He contrasts evil shepherds with the Good Shepherd.

3. *Who also eat the flesh of my people*] Cp. Ps. xiv. 4, "They eat up My people as they eat bread ;" and Ezek. xxii. 27, "Her princes in the midst thereof are like wolves ravening the prey, to shed blood, and to destroy souls, to get dishonest gain. Cp. Ezek. xxxiv. 2—10.

5. *the prophets—that bite with their teeth, and cry, Peace*] The false prophets, as long as they receive any thing to put into their mouths, prophesy peace ; they prophesy for hire, and divine for money and for bread. See v. 11 ; and cp. above, on Amos vii. 12, where the idolatrous priest insinuates that the true Prophet Amos is like one of these false prophets, who, as

long as they are fed by their masters, are ready to promise peace to those who feed them ; like dogs, who fawn on those who give them meat ; and this is further explained by what follows : *he that putteth not into their mouths,* at him they snarl and growl, and *prepare war* (literally, *sanctify war* against him ; cp. on Joel iii. 9), as if the cause of their own appetite were the cause of heaven !

Such are false teachers in the Christian Church, who make a traffic of godliness (1 Tim. vi. 5), and corrupt the Word of God for their own benefit (see on 2 Cor. ii. 17), and whose "god is their belly" (Phil. iii. 19), and whose "gospel is their maw."

6. *the sun shall go down*] Words taken from Amos viii. 9.

7. *they shall all cover their lips*] As in mourning (Levit. xiii. 45), and in shame (Ezek. xxiv. 17). Those lips with which they spoke lies ; those mouths with which they devoured greedily what was given them, that they might prophesy (v. 5), shall be covered with sorrow and shame.

10. *They build up Zion with blood*] They build it up with blood as with cement. Cp. Jer. xxii. 13. Hab. ii. 12, "Woe to him that buildeth a town with blood."

Before
CHRIST
710.
r Jer. 26. 18.
ch. 1. 6.
s Ps. 79. 1.
t 1. 5. 5.
a Isa. 2. 2, &c.
Ezek. 17. 22, 23.

[12] Therefore shall Zion for your sake be ʳ plowed *as* a field,

ˢ And Jerusalem shall become heaps,

And ᵗ the mountain of the house as the high places of the forest.

IV. [1] But ᵃ in the last days it shall come to pass,

*That* the mountain of the house of the LORD shall be established in the top of the mountains,

And it shall be exalted above the hills;

And people shall flow unto it.

[2] And many nations shall come, and say,

Come, and let us go up to the mountain of the LORD,

And to the house of the God of Jacob;

And he will teach us of his ways,

And we will walk in his paths:

For the law shall go forth of Zion,

And the word of the LORD from Jerusalem.

[3] And he shall judge among many people,

And rebuke strong nations afar off;

---

**12.** *Therefore shall Zion for your sake be plowed as a field.*] This solemn warning of Micah was blessed by God with a salutary effect, and was remembered afterwards as having produced a reformation in Jerusalem, when, in the beginning of the reign of Jehoiakim (about B.C. 609), Jeremiah the Prophet was arrested by the priests and prophets of Jerusalem because he had stood forth in the Temple and had denounced, that woe would fall on Jerusalem for its sins unless it repented. But the princes (who were more just and temperate than the priests and prophets) interceded for him, and spake to all the assembly of the people—" *Micah the Morashtite*" (see above, i. 1) " prophesied in the days of Hezekiah, King of Judah" (Hezekiah's accession was about 120 years before that of Jehoiakim), "and spake to all the people of Judah saying, Thus saith the Lord of hosts, ' Zion *shall be plowed as a field*, and Jerusalem shall become heaps, and the mountain of the house' (the Temple) ' as the high places of a forest.' Did Hezekiah, King of Judah, put him at all to death? Did he not fear the Lord, and besought the Lord? and the Lord repented Him of the evil which He had pronounced against them."

Micah's prophecy produced a reformation in his own age; and it exercised a salutary influence a century afterwards, and induced the princes to protect Jeremiah, who was delivered out of the hands of his enemies (Jer. xxvi. 24), and continued to prophesy till after the fall of Jerusalem, which Micah and he himself had foretold.

Such is the energy of God's Word. It may seem to be dead for a time, like seed buried in the ground; but it springs up and brings forth fruit many years after it has been sown.

In a figurative sense, this prophecy of Micah extended even to the days of Christ. Then the heads of the house of Jacob and the princes of the house of Israel abhorred judgment, and perverted all equity. They condemned the Just One and built up Zion with blood, even with the Blood of Christ. Therefore Zion was ploughed as a field, and Jerusalem became heaps, and the mountain of the Lord's house—the Temple itself—became as the high places of the forest. Not one stone was left upon another by the Roman armies, but all was cast down, according to Christ's prophecy (Matt. xxiv. 2. Mark xiii. 2. Luke xix. 44; xxi. 6).

RESTORATION AND EXALTATION OF JERUSALEM IN CHRIST AND THE CHURCH.

CH. IV. **1.** *But in the last days*] Literally, *at the end of the days* of prophets; the *beginning* of the day of Christ.

— *it shall come to pass*] Here is a sudden transition from sorrow to joy, from humiliation to exaltation, like that in ii. 12. The transition in both cases is produced by the gleam which the Prophet catches of the glory of Christ. See v. 3.

He had described the abasement and desolation of the *mountain of the Lord's house* (iii. 12); he now foretells its exaltation in the Church of Christ (*Justin Martyr* c. Tryphon, § 109). Cp. above Isa. ii. 2, and *Pusey* here.

76

— *And people shall flow unto it.*] A marvellous prediction, which is fulfilled only in the world of grace. There rivers flow upward to hills, the powerful nations of the world flow to Zion which they had despised. The Church of Christ, which went forth from Jerusalem where Christ taught, worked miracles, and suffered, and rose from the dead; and to which He sent the Holy Ghost from Heaven, to enable His Apostles to go forth from Jerusalem to evangelize the World, was at first persecuted by the mighty Kingdoms of this world; but at length they were converted to Christianity, and bowed their necks meekly beneath the Cross. See above, on Isa. ii. 2, where the same prophecy is uttered, in order that in the mouth of two witnesses (Micah and Isaiah) this great truth might be established. Compare also the Vision of Ezekiel (xl.—xlviii.), describing the Catholic Church of Christ growing upward and stretching outward from Jerusalem to enfold all nations; which is the full expansion and development of the prophecy.

The *Law* of the New Dispensation, and the *Word of God*, which is the Gospel, are here represented as going forth from Zion, and from Jerusalem, the metropolis of the Old Dispensation, where the Temple stood, and sacrifices were offered, and to which, at stated periods, the Jews were obliged to go up to worship from all parts of the land.

The Gospel took its rise in Zion, in order to show that the Gospel was not set up in opposition to the Law, but grew out of the Law, and is the fulfilment of it.

In the Temple of Jerusalem Christ was presented, at Jerusalem He preached, worked miracles, died, and rose again; there the Spirit was poured out by Him when He had ascended into the Heavenly Jerusalem; there the Apostles were commissioned and enabled to begin to "preach repentance and remission of sins" to all Nations (Luke xxiv. 47); and thence they went forth with that gracious message into "Judæa, Samaria, and the uttermost parts of the earth" (Acts i. 8). The living waters of the Gospel, which has gushed forth from the well-spring in Zion, flow in ever-widening streams, to irrigate and fertilize the wilderness of heathenism, and to make it blossom as the rose. See *Bp. Pearson*, Art. ii. pp. 82, 89; and *M. Henry* here; and *Hengstenberg*.

It has been supposed by some (*Caspari*, 414; *Delitzsch* on Isaiah, ii. 2; *Hengstenberg*, and *Keil*) that Micah's prophecy was delivered *before* that of Isaiah; but see above, on Isa. i. 1, and vi. 1. However (as *Pocock* observes, p. 27), the matter is of little moment. The true Prophets were not like the false Prophets, who stole the word from others (Jer. xxiii. 30), but they were all full of power by the Spirit of the Lord (ch. 8. 2 Pet. i. 21); and what the Holy Spirit had spoken by the mouth of one Prophet, He often repeated by the mouth of another.

**3.** *He shall judge among many people*] Or *peoples*. Christ shall rule over all nations: " All kings shall bow down before Him, all nations shall do Him service" (Ps. ii. 8; lxxii. 8. 11; ex. 6); " At the Name of Jesus every knee shall bow" (Phil. ii. 10); " The Kingdoms of this World are become the Kingdoms of our Lord and of His Christ" (Rev. xi. 15).

And they shall beat their swords into <sup>b</sup> plowshares,

And their spears into ‖ pruninghooks :

Nation shall not lift up a sword against nation,

<sup>c</sup> Neither shall they learn war any more.

<sup>4</sup> <sup>d</sup> But they shall sit every man under his vine and under his fig tree ;

And none shall make *them* afraid :

For the mouth of the LORD of hosts hath spoken *it*.

<sup>5</sup> For <sup>e</sup> all people will walk every one in the name of his god,

And <sup>f</sup> we will walk in the name of the LORD our God for ever and ever.

<sup>6</sup>   In that day, saith the LORD, <sup>g</sup> will I assemble her that halteth,

<sup>h</sup> And I will gather her that is driven out,

And her that I have afflicted ;

<sup>7</sup> And I will make her that halted <sup>i</sup> a remnant,

And her that was cast far off a strong nation :

And the LORD <sup>k</sup> shall reign over them in mount Zion

From henceforth, even for ever.

<sup>8</sup> And thou, O tower of ‖ the flock,

The strong hold of the daughter of Zion,

Unto thee shall it come, even the first dominion ;

The kingdom shall come to the daughter of Jerusalem.

<sup>9</sup>   Now why dost thou cry out aloud ?

<sup>l</sup> *Is there* no king in thee ?

Is thy counseller perished ?

For <sup>m</sup> pangs have taken thee as a woman in travail.

<sup>10</sup> Be in pain, and labour to bring forth, O daughter of Zion,

Like a woman in travail :

For now shalt thou go forth out of the city,

**Margin references:**

Before CHRIST 710.
b Isa. 2. 4.
Joel 3. 10.
‖ Or, *scythes.*
c Ps. 72. 7.
d 1 Kings 4. 25.
Zech. 3. 10.
e Jer. 2. 11.
f Zech. 10. 12.
g Ezek. 34. 16.
Zeph. 3. 19.
h Ps. 147. 2.
Ezek. 34. 13, & 37. 21.
i ch. 2. 12. & 5. 3, 7, 8, & 7. 18.
k Isa. 9. 6, 7. & 24. 23.
Dan. 7. 14, 27.
Luke 1. 33.
Rev. 11. 15.
‖ Or, *Edar*;
Gen. 35. 21.
l Jer. 8. 19.
m Isa. 13. 8. & 21. 3.
Jer. 30. 6. & 50. 43.

---

— *they shall beat their swords into plowshares*] An image derived by inversion from Joel, speaking of times of war (Joel iii. 10).

This prophecy began to be fulfilled in the peaceful days of the first appearance of the Gospel. The World was in a quiet condition when Christ came to visit it. That universal peace was an earnest of the peace in earth and heaven which is the fruit of the Gospel of Christ (S. Cyril; Milton, Ode on the Nativity, stanzas 3, 4, 5).

4. *sit every man under his vine*] As in the days of Solomon, the peaceable—the type of Christ, the Son of David, the Builder of the true Temple, and the Prince of Peace (1 Kings iv. 25).

5. *For all people will walk*] All nations walk every one in the name of his god; i. e. though all nations should strengthen themselves in the name, and by the might, of their several gods, and combine against us, we will not fear, but will walk with our one true God, and shall prevail against them by His Name.

6. *In that day, saith the* LORD, *will I assemble*] Here is a promise of restoration similar to that in ii. 12.

— *her that halteth*] Cp. v. 7. I will make *her that halted* a remnant, and her that was cast off a strong nation; and Zeph. iii. 19, I will save *her that halteth.* She that *halteth* is the dispersed Israel, lame and worn out, like a flock by wandering, but gathered in Christ.

It is suggested that the history of Mephibosheth, the *halting* son of Jonathan, the son of Saul, is inserted in the Sacred History as being prophetic and typical of the Jewish Nation. See the note above, on 2 Sam. ix. 6.

Mephibosheth, who *halted*, was brought to David, and made to sit at his table (2 Sam. ix. 10). So the Mephibosheth of the Hebrew Nation, which now halteth, will be brought to sit at the table of the Divine Son of David, Jesus Christ.

7. *the* LORD *shall reign—in mount Zion—for ever*] These words are repeated from Joel iii. 20, 21. Obadiah 21.

Observe the contrast. On account of the rebellion of her people, Zion becomes a *ploughed field* (iii. 12), but through the obedience of Christ, the Lord will *reign in it for ever.* Cp. Ps. ii. 6, "Yet have I set my king upon my holy hill of Sion."

Isa. xxiv. 23, "The Lord of Hosts shall reign in Mount Zion." The Church of Christ is the Mount Sion which stands for ever. The Church is called *Mount Sion* by the Holy Spirit, Heb. xii. 22, "Ye are come unto *Mount Sion;*" and Rev. xiv. 1, " Lo, a Lamb stood on the *Mount Sion*, and with him an hundred forty and four thousand, having His Father's name written in their foreheads."

8. *And thou, O tower of the flock, the strong hold of the daughter of Zion, unto thee shall it (or he) come, even the first dominion*]. This is fulfilled in the Messiah (Targum). The strong hold or fortress of Zion, the royal palace and castle of David, the Shepherd and King (cp. Cant. iv. 4. 2 Sam. v. 9. 1 Kings ix. 15. 1 Chron. xii. 1. *Hengst., Keil*), shall become a sheepfold for the flock of Him Who is, like David, a King, a Conqueror, and a Shepherd. See below, v. 4, "He shall stand and feed in the strength of the Lord." Cp. vii. 14, "Feed thy people with thy rod, the flock of thine heritage."

To this pastoral fortress *the first dominion shall come;* all the primitive glory and majesty of the reign of Solomon and David shall come back to the Throne of David in Christ and His Church (Luke i. 32. Matt. xxi. 4, 5. John xii. 17).

Some of the Hebrew Rabbis supposed that this *tower of the flock* is the same as that *tower of the flock* which was near Bethlehem, and so *Pusey,* 327, and this deserves notice. See Gen. xxxv. 20. But the scenery of the prophetic description is at Jerusalem (see *Pocock,* 33; and *Keil* here; and so some Hebrew Rabbis; cp. *S. Jerome*, Tradit. Hebr. in Gen. xxxv.).

In a spiritual sense, this prophecy is accomplished in the true Zion, the Church of Christ. The Tower of the Flock (says *A Lapide*) is the Church of Christ, which had its origin in Jerusalem, and to which all nations are gathered, so as to make one flock and one Shepherd (John x. 16).

9. *Now why dost thou cry out aloud?*] He returns to the nearer vision of sorrow for the approaching misery of Zion. He sees the captivity of her kings (Jehoiachin and Zedekiah), and the confusion of her counsellors. She is represented as in anguish, like a woman in travail. See Hos. xiii. 13. Isa. xli. 14.

| | |
|---|---|
| Before CHRIST 710. | And thou shalt dwell in the field, |
| | And thou shalt go *even* to Babylon ; |
| | There shalt thou be delivered ; |
| | There the LORD shall redeem thee from the hand of thine enemies. |
| o Lam. 2. 16. | 11 °Now also many nations are gathered against thee, |
| | That say, Let her be defiled, |
| o Obad. 12. ch. 7. 10. | And let our eye °look upon Zion. |
| p Isa. 55. 8. Rom. 11. 33. | 12 But they know not ᵖthe thoughts of the LORD, |
| | Neither understand they his counsel : |
| q Isa. 21. 10. | For he shall gather them ᑫas the sheaves into the floor. |
| r Isa. 41. 15, 16. Jer. 51. 33. | 13 ʳArise and thresh, O daughter of Zion : |
| | For I will make thine horn iron, and I will make thy hoofs brass : |
| s Dan. 2. 44. | And thou shalt ˢbeat in pieces many people : |
| t Isa. 18. 7. & 23. 18. & 60. 6, 9. | ᵗAnd I will consecrate their gain unto the LORD, |
| u Zech. 4. 14. & 6. 5. | And their substance unto ᵘthe Lord of the whole earth. |
| | V. 1 Now gather thyself in troops, O daughter of troops : |
| | He hath laid siege against us : |
| x Lam. 3. 30. Matt. 5. 39. & 27. 30. | They shall ˣsmite the judge of Israel with a rod upon the cheek. |

**10.** *Thou shalt go even to Babylon*] As Isaiah also. Micah's contemporary, was enabled to foresee and foretell, in the days of Hezekiah, at a time when *Assyria* was the dominant power, and hostile to Judah, and *Babylon* was of little consideration. See above, the notes on Isa. xxxix. 3—8.

Here Micah also supplies a refutation of that modern sceptical Criticism, which ascribes the latter portion of Isaiah's prophecies to a later author than Isaiah, because they presuppose this captivity at Babylon. See above, on Isa. chap. xl. *Prelim. Note.*

— *There shalt thou be delivered; there the* LORD *shall redeem thee*] Micah also, as well as Isaiah, foretells the return of Judah from Babylon. Compare Isa. xl. 1—4; xliv. 26. Like Isaiah also, Micah was enabled by the Holy Spirit to look *far beyond* the captivity of Judah at Babylon, and beyond Judah's deliverance from it. He was empowered to see that glorious event, of which that deliverance was a type—namely, the deliverance of Judah and the World from the exile and bondage of sin and Satan by the mighty arm of Christ—the divine Cyrus. See above, ii. 12, 13; below, v. 3.

**11.** *let our eye look upon Zion*] Cp. Ps. liv. 7.

RESTORATION OF ISRAEL IN CHRIST.

**12, 13.** *he shall gather them as the sheaves into the floor. Arise and thresh, O daughter of Zion*] The Heathen Nations shall be like ripe sheaves cast together on the threshing-floor, to be trodden under the hoofs of some powerful horned oxen, drawing the threshing-machine over them, and trampling them under their feet (Deut. xxv. 4—horns are emblems of strength —Deut. xxxiii. 17. 1 Kings xxii. 11. Isa. xxi. 10; xli. 15. Amos vi. 13). See above, on Isa. xli. 15, 16, where similar imagery is used; and compare the note on Joel iii. 13, 14.

This prophecy received a primary and partial fulfilment in the victories of the Maccabees (1 Macc. v. 1, 2). But (as St. Jerome observes) its adequate accomplishment is in Christ. It is to be applied to the work of Apostles and Apostolic men, Missionaries of Christ, who are compared by St. Paul to oxen treading out the corn (1 Cor. ix. 9. 1 Tim. v. 18. Cp. Isa. xxxii. 20). Their work is indeed one of bringing the nations into subjection (2 Cor. ii. 11; also x. 5. Eph. vi. 12); but it is in subjection to the Law of Love, in order that the good grain, winnowed from the sheaves on the floor, may be gathered into the garner of heaven. Cp. note above, on Ps. cxlix. 8.

— *Thou shalt beat in pieces many people*] Rather, *thou wilt crush many nations* by threshing. Many Nations of the World will rise up against Christ and His Church, but He will enable her to overcome them all. This chaff and stubble will be burnt, but not a grain of good corn will be lost ; cp. Ezekiel's prophecy concerning the gathering together of the Antichristian Powers in the latter days, and their final overthrow. See above, on Ezekiel, chap. xxxviii. and xxxix. 9.

— *I will consecrate their gain unto the* LORD] Cp. Isa. xxiii. 18. Zech. xiv. 20.

**CH. V. 1.** *Now gather thyself in troops*] Rather, *Now shalt thou be cut in pieces, thou daughter of troops*; thou, O invading army (not Judah, as some expound the words), shalt in thy turn be *cut off*, or *spoiled*. Vata, *Targum*, R. *Tanchum, Rashchani, A Lap., Isa, Gesenius,* and *Pocock*. pp. 39—44.

The word here used is from *gâdad*, to *cut in pieces*; *Gen.* xlix. 19; *Theod.* 283; whence *Armageddon*, the *mount of cutting in pieces* (see on Rev. xvi. 16; and Joel iii. 14); and occurs in Deut. xiv. 1. 1 Kings xviii. 28. Cp. Jer. xvi. 6 ; xli. 5 ; xlvii. 5.

The sense is the same as in Isaiah (xxxiii. 1), " Woe to thee that spoilest—thou shalt be spoiled." This will be the fate of all the enemies of God and His Church. Cp. Rev. xiii. 10.

There is a play on the words between the verb here used and the noun *gâd*, a *troop*. Thou, who boastest of thy multitude *of troops*, wilt be assailed and conquered by an invader in thy turn, and be *cut in pieces*, for thy violence against us.

Observe also that this translation serves to show the connexion of what has gone before with what follows.

At the end of the last chapter, Zion, victorious over her enemies, is compared to one who threshes sheaves on a threshing-floor, with a sharp threshing instrument, and *cuts them in pieces* by it. And now it is said that the daughter of troops—that is, first, *Assyria*, the spoiler of Israel and the invader of Judah, and next, *Babylon*, the conqueror of Jerusalem, and the carrier-away of her people captive—will be *cut in pieces* by this threshing. Compare Joel's expression, " Multitudes, multitudes in the valley of *decision*," or of *cutting in pieces* (Joel iii. 14).

Next the Prophet Micah passes on to declare *Who* it is that gives to Zion this power and victory—namely, CHRIST.

— *he hath laid siege against us ; they shall smite,* The Chaldean has besieged us, and has smitten our King, Zedekiah (2 Kings xxv. 21. Lam. iv. 20); but will be smitten also.

Observe the noble contrast which now follows between the mighty Nineveh and Babylon of this world, and the lowly Bethlehem. That which is great in the world's sight, is small in God's eye ; and what is weak in man's sight, is strong by His power. The first shall be last, and the last first. All the proud Ninevehs and Babylons of this world will be put under the feet of Him Who came forth from obscure Bethlehem.

THE DELIVERANCE OF ZION BY CHRIST, BORN AT BETHLEHEM; THE RULER, THE SHEPHERD, THE EVERLASTING GOD.

The ensuing prophecy of Micah (v. 1—5), combined with what goes before and what follows, consummates the witness of the Old Testament concerning Christ, and is the groundwork of His History in the New. It completes the chain of predictions (as *Dr. Wsles* has observed) which appropriate the promised Seed of the Woman to the family of Shem, Abraham, Isaac, and Jacob, and to the Tribe of Judah, and to the Royal House of David at Bethlehem, where, as here foretold, He is to be

² But thou, ᵇ Beth-lehem Ephratah, *though* thou be little ᶜ among the ᵈ thousands of Judah,

*Yet* out of thee shall he come forth unto me *that is* to be ᵉ ruler in Israel ;

ᶠ Whose goings forth *have been* from of old, from † everlasting.

Prov. 8, 22, 23.   John i. 1.   † Heb. *the days of eternity.*

born. It carefully distinguishes that Human Nativity from His Divine Generation before the beginning of the World—even from Eternity. Thus it prepares the way for the Gospels of St. Matthew and St. Luke, which begin with a narrative of the wonderful events connected with His Birth at Bethlehem; and it is also like a prologue to the Gospel of the beloved Disciple St. John, declaring the mystery of His Godhead, and of His Eternal Generation from the Father. It foretells the dispersion and temporary rejection of the literal Israel, and the gathering in of the Gentiles into the Church by the instrumentality of the faithful remnant of Israel (the Apostles, and first preachers of the Gospel, who were Jews), and the final restoration of Israel to God in Christ and His Church. And thus it prepares the way for the preaching of St. Paul and the other Apostles in their Epistles; and it foretells and describes the full and final victory of Christ and His Church, over all the hostile powers of this world; and thus it anticipates the Apocalypse.

2. *But thou, Beth-lehem Ephratah*] Or, *And thou. On Beth-lehem Ephratah*, see Gen. xxxv. 19: xlviii. 7. Ruth iv. 11. *Bethlehem* signifies *house of bread*: *Ephratah* means *fruitful*. Both were appropriate names for the birthplace of Him Who is the *True*, the *Living*, *Bread* that came down from Heaven (John vi. 32—35); and Whose Birth, and Death, and Resurrection, are the germinant seed, and also the gracious nourishment, of all the spiritual *fruitfulness* of the Saints in this world, and of all their glory, beauty, and felicity in the world to come.

— *though thou be little among the thousands of Judah*] Or, too small to be reckoned among the thousands of Judah. See Keil and Pusey. The word *thousands* means *families* under a leader or head. See Exod. xviii. 21, 25. Num. i. 16; x. 36. Deut. i. 15. Judges vi. 15, where the word is rendered *family*.

In the Gospel of St. Matthew, when the wise men came to Jerusalem, saying, "Where is He that is born King of the Jews?" and when Herod asked the Chief Priests and Scribes where Christ should be born, we read that they answered that question by referring to this passage of the Prophet Micah, which is quoted in that Gospel in the following form :—"And thou, Bethlehem, in the land of *Judah*, art *not* the *least* among the *princes* of Judah."

From this quotation we may first gather the important inference, that the Jews in our Lord's age applied this prophecy of Micah to the Messiah; as the *Targum* here does. See also John vii. 42, where they say, "Hath not the Scripture said that Christ cometh out of the seed of *David*, and out of the town of *Bethlehem*, where David was?" And the Holy Spirit, recording the quotation thus interpreted, has set His Divine Seal upon that interpretation as true.

This leads us on to the conclusion, that, not only in this passage, but in many other prophecies, Micah is speaking of Christ. Cp. *Bp. Andrewes*' Sermon on this text, vol. i. 155.

It has been objected that the *form* of this quotation does not agree exactly with the original, nor with the Septuagint.

But, as was before observed with regard to the Septuagint (see on Amos ix. 12), it is rather to be regarded as a Paraphrase than a literal Version; and it imparts the sense and spirit more clearly to its Greek readers, because it is *not a literal version* of the Hebrew. So we may say here—the Council of Chief Priests and Scribes (if St. Matthew is giving their exact words), or St. Matthew himself, who was inspired by the Holy Spirit, is doing what the Septuagint had done, and what was familiar to all Hebrew expounders of Scripture; he is giving the *sense* of the Prophet Micah, and is giving it *more clearly* to his readers, even by *deviating* in some particulars from the *letter*, which would have been less intelligible to them. Thus, for example, he calls Bethlehem by the title of Bethlehem in *Judah*, and not *Ephratah*; and this for a good reason; because the name *Ephratah* was then obsolete. It was a fact that Bethlehem was in *Judah*, and the Evangelist thus reminds us of Jacob's prophecy that Shiloh should come from *Judah* (see on Gen. xlix. 10), and that the prophecy was now fulfilled in Jesus.

Next, he substitutes *princes* for *thousands*. This also was a reasonable and judicious paraphrase. He found the word *aláphim* (*thousands*) in the original of Micah. But this word,

however clear to the Hebrew mind, would not be so to those readers of the Gospel who were not familiar with Hebrew customs and history, and it suggested to the Evangelist the similar word *allaphim* (*leaders* or *rulers*), which would convey it to them; for the Hebrew *thousand* represented a certain organization, with a *leader* or *ruler* at its head. See the beginning of this note.

Further, whereas Micah says that *Bethlehem is little* to be among the thousands of Judah, St. Matthew says that *Bethlehem is not the least* among the princes of Judah. This also is a paraphrase, and it takes up the latter part of Micah's prophecy here, and makes it act upon the former. As much as to say, that since "out of thee shall He come forth unto Me, that is to be the ruler in Israel, Whose goings forth have been from of old, even from everlasting," therefore, though thou, O Bethlehem, art now fallen away from thy pristine grandeur and glory, which thou didst possess in the days of David, and thy very title, "City of David," has passed away from thee to Jerusalem, and thou hast dwindled down into a small and obscure village, and art therefore *little* (as Micah says) *to be reckoned among the thousands of Judah*; yet, by reason of what Micah also says concerning thee, thou (though thus fallen in the eyes of men, and in the esteem of the world) art *not little* in the eyes of God, Who will surely keep His promise to David, and Who loves to choose the weak and despised things of this world, to confound the mighty and the proud. No; thou art by *no means the least*; but, rather, thou art chief among the thousands and the rulers of the thousands of Judah; for out of thee shall come forth, *to Me* (says God) the Ruler of all Israel—Whose *goings forth*, or birth, are from thee, in time, but are from Me in Eternity. Cp. the note of *A Lapide* here, and *Pusey* on Daniel, p. 486; and for an excellent dissertation on this passage, in which its Christian character is triumphantly vindicated against the modern Jews and Unbelievers, see, especially, *Hengstenberg*, Christology, i. pp. 479—513, English Translation.

In thus dealing with the prophecy of Micah, the Evangelist acted in a manner familiar to Hebrew interpreters and expositors of Scripture, and consistently with the rules of sound reason, which does not scrutinize syllables, but endeavours to understand the sense, and to communicate the spirit, of God's Holy Word. On this subject see further below, the note on Matt. ii. 5, 6, and the excellent remarks of *Surenhusius*, Catallagé, pp. 170—188.

Lastly, observe how Micah agrees with his contemporary prophet Isaiah. Isaiah, speaking to the despairing King of Judah, Ahaz (when his throne and kingdom were menaced by the confederacy of Israel and Syria), guaranteed to him the stability of both (and the safety of all true believers in every age) by the promise of the birth of the Everlasting King Emmanuel, from the *Virgin* of the house of David. See on Isa. vii. 1—16. So Micah pledges God's word for the protection of Judah and Jerusalem, and of all faithful sons of *Zion*, from the Assyrian and Babylonian (and from all worldly enemies), by the promise of His Birth at *Bethlehem*. Isaiah's prophecy designates the *person* from whom He is to be born. Micah names the *place* of His Birth. Both declare His Manhood and Godhead.

— *shall he come forth unto Me*] God Himself speaks. The Father is declaring the Incarnation and Birth at Bethlehem, and also the Eternal Generation of the Son.

— *ruler*] Heb. *Moshel*. A word applied to Joseph as *Governor* over Egypt (Gen. xlv. 8, 26) ; to Solomon (1 Kings iv. 21); and to the *Ruler* (the Messiah) promised by God to David (2 Sam. xxiii. 3. 2 Chron. vii. 18). Compare Jer. xxx. 21, "Their Governor" (*Moshel*) "shall proceed out of them." Cp. Zech. x. 4.

— *from everlasting*] This is an illustrious testimony to the Divine Generation *before all time*, of Christ the Eternal Son of God, "God, of the substance of His Father, begotten before all worlds;" and also in *time* (according to what is said that He should come forth of Bethlehem), "made Man of the substance of His mother, and born in the world." Manifestly this prophecy belongs only to Him (*Pocock*, 44; and *Hengstenberg* here). Cp. note on Proverbs viii. 22, 23, where it is said, "I was set up *from everlasting*," the same word as here; and cp. John i. 1, 2; viii. 58.

79

Before
CHRIST
750.

³ Therefore will he give them up,
Until the time *that* ⁿ she which travaileth hath brought forth :
Then ᵒ the remnant of his brethren shall return unto the children of Israel ;
⁴ And he shall stand and ‖ ᵖ feed in the strength of the LORD,
In the majesty of the name of the LORD his God ;
And they shall abide :
For now ᵏ shall he be great unto the ends of the earth.
⁵ And this *man* ˡ shall be the peace,
When the Assyrian shall come into our land :
And when he shall tread in our palaces,
Then shall we raise against him seven shepherds,
And eight † principal men.

The Prophet Micah announces the Birth of the Messiah in human flesh, and His Coming forth from Eternity. This ought not to seem strange to us, when we remember that the Messiah is represented by Micah's contemporary prophet Isaiah, not only as a Child born to us, and as a Son given to us, but also as the Mighty God, the Everlasting Father, or, rather, the Father of *Eternity* ; i.e. the Father of the new, regenerate race of man— the Father of the new Creation ; of Whom Eternity is one essential attribute. See Isa. ix. 6.

3. *Therefore will he give them up, until the time that she which travaileth hath brought forth.* Because the Messiah will come forth from Bethlehem, the City of David, reduced to low estate, therefore it is appointed by Him Who is God as well as Man, that Israel and Judah should *be given up* to captivity and to humiliation, till the time of His Incarnation and Birth from His Mother at Bethlehem, in order that His Divine Power and Love may be shown by raising them from the depths of misery to a glorious elevation in Himself (*Cyril, Jerome, Pusey, Ewald, Hitzig, Keil*).

Here also Micah harmonizes with his brother prophet Isaiah, declaring the Godhead and Manhood of Christ ; and the one Prophet illustrates the other. "Behold, a Virgin" (or rather *the* Virgin ; the Virgin of the house of David ; the Virgin who is foreseen by the Divine Eye of the Holy Spirit, speaking by Isaiah's lips) "shall conceive, and bear a Son, and shall call His name Immanuel" (God with us) (Isa. vii. 14) ; and this was the proof to Ahaz, that though Judah would be brought low, it would never be destroyed. Cp. *Pusey*, p. 18.

—— *The remnant of his brethren shall return.* The remnant shall return, as the name *Shear-jashub* (Isaiah's son) declared (see Isa. vii. 3 ; x. 21), and they are called His *brethren* ; for since He is Man, and of the Seed of Abraham, He "is not ashamed to call them *brethren*." (Heb. ii. 11, 12) ; and they shall return unto Israel, because all will be united in that communion of love, and be the "Israel of God" (Gal. vi. 16).

4. *He shall stand and feed in the strength of the LORD.* He shall stand—that is remain—firm and immovable, in stately dignity, and royal and pastoral majesty ; and having a constant care for His people. He shall feed His flock like a Shepherd, in the strength of the Lord Jehovah ; for He is Son of God as well as Son of David, and is called *David* by the Prophets ; see in Ezek. xxxiv. 23, "I will set *one* Shepherd over them, even My Servant *David* ; He shall feed them, and He shall be their Shepherd."

So speaks Micah's contemporary, Isaiah : "Behold, the Lord God will come with strong hand, and His arm shall rule for Him. He shall *feed His flock like a shepherd* ; He shall gather the lambs with His arm, and carry them in His bosom, and shall gently lead those that are with young" (Isa. xl. 10, 11). Compare our Lord's words (John x. 1—12). His flock ranges over all lands, *even unto the ends of the earth.* Cp. Isa. lii. 10, Ps. ii. 8. All Men are His flock ; all the Earth is His fold. Cp. *Caspari* here, pp. 232—236.

5. *This man shall be the peace, when the Assyrian shall come into our land.* We have seen in the prophecies of Isaiah, that Sennacherib, the proud King of Assyria, blaspheming God, and invading Judah, and threatening Hezekiah and Jerusalem, in the days of Micah and Isaiah, was a type and figure of the godless Powers of this world raging against Christ and the spiritual Son of His Church ; and that the sudden destruction of the army of Sennacherib beneath the walls of Jerusalem, is a type and prophecy of the future discomfiture and overthrow of all the enemies of the Church of God. See

above, on Isa. lxvi. 24. This view is further displayed by Ezekiel in his prophetic description of the Anti-Christian conflict of the latter days. See above, on Ezek. xxxvii. 4. 17 ; xxxix. 2. 11. "*The Assyrian* is a type of Antichrist" (*Pusey*).

Christ is called *the Peace,* or *Our Peace.* The Hebrew word for *peace* means *safety* and all its attributes. Christ Himself explains it. "In Me ye shall have *peace* ; in the world ye shall have tribulation ; but be of good cheer, I have overcome the world" (John xvi. 33 ; xiv. 27). "He is our Peace," says St. Paul (Eph. ii. 14). Cp. Col. iii. 15.

"When the Assyrian shall come into our land." The words "*the Assyrian*" primarily represent Sennacherib coming against Judah ; and this prophecy of Micah suggests the conjecture that the "Angel of the Lord" (a title often given to Christ in the Old Testament ; see Gen. xvi. 7 ; xxii. 11. Exod. iii. 2. Judges vi. 12), who went out and smote the Assyrians at the walls of Jerusalem with that terrible stroke of destruction, in the days of Hezekiah, and brought *peace* to Jerusalem, was no other than He of Whom Micah is now speaking—namely, CHRIST.

In a second sense the name "*the Assyrian*" is a generic term for all the enemies of Christ and His Church. Cp. S. *Jerome* here, who applies this term to our ghostly enemy, the Evil One—the Adversary of Christ and of His People ; and so *Cora. a Lapide* and *Matthew Henry* here : "These words refer to the deliverance of Hezekiah and his kingdom from the power of Sennacherib in the type ; but under the shadow of that, it is a promise of safety to the Church from the designs and attempts of all the Powers of darkness" (cp. *Pusey* here).

—— *Then shall we raise against him seven shepherds, and eight principal men.* We will raise. Here, says S. Jerome, we may recognize a plurality of Persons in the Godhead. —We—the Father, Son, and Holy Ghost—will do this. Cp. Gen. i. 26.

In the numbers *seven* and *eight* used here, and applied to Christian Shepherds, who derive a royal power from Christ, there may perhaps be a reference to the *seven* and *eight* princes in Eastern Courts, "who saw the King's face" (see Esther i. 14, and Jer. xxxix. 3) ; and the contrast and antagonism of Christ and His Church to the secular Powers of the World, may perhaps be thus marked. But it must also be remembered that *seven* is the number of rest and completion, and *eight* is the number of resurrection, victory, and glory. See on Gen. ii. 2 ; xvii. 12, Exod. xii. 15 ; xxix. 30. 2 Chron. vii. 9, and the notes on Matt. v. 2 ; xxiii. 13 ; xxvii. 52. Luke xxiv. 1. Rev. i. 11 ; xi. 19, p. 229 ; xvii. 10, 11, and above, on Ezekiel, p. 280. Compare Eccles. xi. 2 : "Give a portion to *seven*, and also to *eight*," that is, give largely—let thy work of bounty be complete and overflow. And in Isaiah the *seven* women who take hold of the skirt of one Man who is a Jew (Isa. iv. 1), represent the sevenfold fulness of the Universal Church (symbolized by the seven golden Candlesticks in the Apocalypse, Rev. i. 12. 20) laying hold of the One Man, Christ Jesus, by the hand of Faith.

This prophecy of Micah, therefore, foretells the raising up of a complete and victorious army of Christ's faithful soldiers, the Apostles and their successors, the *principal men* in His Church, who will overcome the enemies of the Church by their holiness of living, their courage in preaching, and by their patience in suffering and dying.

Observe the word rendered *principal* men. It means *anointed*, and is so rendered by *Symmachus* and *Gesenius* (553). All the grace and power and royalty of Christians is from Christ, the Anointed One. "They have an unction from the Holy One" (1 John ii. 20). "Of His fulness have all we received, and grace for grace" (John i. 16).

[6] And they shall † waste the land of Assyria with the sword,

And the land of [m] Nimrod ‖ in the entrances thereof :

Thus shall he [n] deliver *us* from the Assyrian,

When he cometh into our land,

And when he treadeth within our borders.

[7] And [o] the remnant of Jacob shall be in the midst of many people

[p] As a dew from the LORD ;

As the showers upon the grass,

That tarrieth not for man,

Nor waiteth for the sons of men.

[8] And the remnant of Jacob shall be among the Gentiles in the midst of many people,

As a lion among the beasts of the forest,

As a young lion among the flocks of ‖ sheep :

Who, if he go through, both treadeth down, and teareth in pieces,

And none can deliver.

[9] Thine hand shall be lifted up upon thine adversaries,

And all thine enemies shall be cut off.

[10] [q] And it shall come to pass in that day, saith the LORD,

That I will cut off thy horses out of the midst of thee,

*Marginal notes (right):*

Before CHRIST 710.
† Heb. *ea'sp.*
m Gen. 10. 8, 10, 11.
‖ Or, *with her own naked swords.*
n Luke i. 71.

o ver. 3.
p Deut. 32. 2. Ps. 72. 6. & 110. 3.

‖ Or, *goats*

q Zech. 9. 10.

---

**6.** *they shall waste the land of Assyria*] Or it may mean, *they shall feed* (according as the word is derived from *rāāh*, to *feed*, or *rāu*, to break) *the land of Assyria with the sword.* Cp. Ps. ii. 9. Rev. ii. 7; and so *Sept.*, *Vulg.*, and *Keil.*

In the Church of God the work of pastoral teaching is always a work of warfare against error. In the escutcheon of the Church the sword is joined with the crook. Cp. above, on Psalm cxlix. 6—9.

The more widely the Gospel of Christ spreads itself among the nations of the world, the more bitter will be the spirit of Unbelief and Ungodliness (*Keil*). The conflict will wax hotter and hotter, till it is decided by the Coming of the Lord to Judgment. The more fierce the rage of Antichrist, the nearer will be the presence of Christ.

— *the land of Nimrod*] Babylon, the other great enemy of Judah. See Gen. x. 8—11.

— *in the entrances thereof*] Or, *gates.* The margin has *with her own naked swords.* The word in the original, *pethacheyah*, is from the same root (*pathach*, to open, to *unsheath*) with *pethichoth* (Ps. lv. 21), rendered *drawn swords*, and with *pethachim*, which signifies *entrances*; "and our Translators" (says *Pocock*) "being loth to determine, put one into the Text, and the other into the Margin. The Ancient Versions are in favour of the former; but many Hebrew Rabbis prefer the latter rendering;" and in that sense it may be said spiritually, with *Pocock*, 55, that "by the might and power of Christ, and of such as shall by Him be qualified and commissioned to spread and maintain His Truth, all that oppose it shall be beaten back with their own weapons"—as Goliath's head was cut off by David with Goliath's own drawn sword.

This sentence, *they shall waste the land of Assyria with the sword, and the land of Nimrod*, or Babylon, is the clue to the two next succeeding prophetical books—viz. of Nahum and Habbakuk, which foretell the overthrow respectively of the two great worldly powers hostile to God's ancient Church—viz. Assyria and Babylon; and under the type and figure of them, predict the destruction of the two forms of Antichristianism symbolized by them—viz. Infidelity and Idolatry. See above, on Isa. xiii., *Prelim. Note*, p. 38 ; xxi. 11.

— *Thus shall he deliver us*] Christ's ministers, his *principal men*, will fight valiantly; but the deliverance will be due to HIM.

**7.** *the remnant of Jacob shall be in the midst of many people* (or *nations*) *as a dew from the LORD—men*] The faithful *remnant of Israel* are the Apostles and all those among the Jews who believe in Christ, and preach Christ, God and Man, as revealed by the Prophet Micah, who loves to repeat this word *remnant* (ii. 12; iv. 7; v. 7, 8; vii. 18). Cp. Isa. i. 9. Rom. ix. 27; xi. 14.

This declaration is naturally subjoined to the prophecy that the God of Israel will raise up *seven shepherds* and *eight principal*

*men* (i. e. a victorious army of believers and preachers) against the enemy (v. 5).

The Apostolic Church of Christ, which derives its origin from Zion, is *in the midst of the Gentiles among many nations*, being diffused every where, and is like *a dew from the Lord upon the Nations*, and *like the shower upon the grass*, for the Church receives and diffuses the dews and showers of the Holy Spirit in the Word and Sacraments of Christ.

— *That tarrieth not for man, nor waiteth for the sons of men*] The Church is not like a cistern supplied with water pumped up by the force of some hydraulic mechanism of human device ; it is not like the irrigation of Egypt, "watered by the foot" (Deut. xi. 10) ; but it is moistened like Gideon's fleece— the type of the Church (see Judges vi. 39, 40) : it is saturated with silvery sparkling dew-drops, which distil graciously in abundance from heaven. Cp. above, the beautiful imagery in Ps. cx. 3. "Thou hast the dew of thy youth from the womb of the morning;" and in Ps. cxxxiii. 3, "Like as the dew of Hermon, that falls on the hill of Zion." In both those passages the congregations of Christian believers are compared to dew. See the notes above, on Ps. cx. 3, and on Ps. cxxxiii. 3, which illustrate this passage, and are illustrated by it.

**8.** *As a lion*] The Israel of God being strong in Christ, "the lion of the tribe of Judah" (Rev. v. 5), will be enabled to overcome its spiritual enemies. Cp. 1 Macc. iii. 4. It will be like Dew in gracious benediction, and like a Lion in invincible strength. See *S. Jerome* here ; and *Caspari*, 254.

**9.** *Thine hand shall be lifted up*] The following prophecy (9—14) is fulfilled by Christ, enabling all His faithful soldiers to do valiantly, to fight the good fight, and to overcome their enemies by His might. It reaches to the world's End (*Pusey*).

**10—14.** *I will cut off thy horses—cities*] These five verses may best be considered together. Israel had been accustomed to rely on Egypt and Assyria (see on Isa. xxxi. 1, 3 ; and Hos. xiv. 3); but the time will come, when the Church of God will not lean on an arm of flesh for support. The present prophecy declares that God will teach the Church in the latter days to rely solely on His Divine power and love, and not to look to the *horses* and *war-chariots* of secular allies (cp. Ps. xx. 7; and Isa. ii. 7; and Zech. ix. 10, "I will cut off the chariot from Ephraim, and the horse from Jerusalem "), and not to seek for refuge in the *strongholds* of temporal support; and will make her to "dwell safely without walls, and having neither bars nor gates" (Ezek. xxxviii. 11) ; and that He will root out of her that which caused her weakness and her misery; her witchcraft, sorcery, and idolatry ; and will pluck up her *groves*, or rather her idolatrous *wooden pillars, stems of trees* (Heb. *asherim*; see on Exod. xxxiv. 13. Deut. vii. 5. Judges iii. 7; vi. 25; 2 Kings xviii. 4; xxi. 3. 7, &c. Isa. xvii. 8; xxvii. 9. Jer. xvii. 2); and *will destroy her cities*—so most Ancient Versions. The

G

Before
CHRIST
710.

And I will destroy thy chariots :

[11] And I will cut off the cities of thy land,

And throw down all thy strong holds :

[12] And I will cut off witchcrafts out of thine hand ;

And thou shalt have no *more* ' soothsayers :

[13] ' Thy graven images also will I cut off,

And thy || standing images out of the midst of thee ;

And thou shalt ' no more worship the work of thine hands.

[14] And I will pluck up thy groves out of the midst of thee :

So will I destroy thy || cities.

[15] And I will ° execute vengeance in anger and fury upon the heathen,

Such as they have not heard.

VI. [1] Hear ye now what the LORD saith ;

Arise, contend thou || before the mountains,

And let the hills hear thy voice.

[2] ª Hear ye, O mountains, ᵇ the LORD's controversy,

And ye strong foundations of the earth :

For ᶜ the LORD hath a controversy with his people,

And he will plead with Israel.

[3] O my people, ᵈ what have I done unto thee ?

And wherein have I wearied thee ?

Testify against me.

[4] ᵉ For I brought thee up out of the land of Egypt,

And redeemed thee out of the house of servants ;

And I sent before thee Moses, Aaron, and Miriam.

[5] O my people, remember now what ᶠ Balak king of Moab consulted,

And what Balaam the son of Beor answered him ;

From ᵍ Shittim unto Gilgal ;

k Isa. 2. 6.

s Zech. 13. 2.

t Ot., diviners.

t Isa. 2. 8.

‡ Or, enemies.

u Ps. 149. 7.
ver. 8.
2 Thes. 1. 8.

a Deut. 32. 1.
Ps. 50. 1, 4.
Isa 1. 2.
b Hos. 12. 2.

c Isa. 1. 18. &
43. 4. & 43. 26.
Hos. 4. 1.

d Jer. 2. 5, 31.

e Exod. 12. 51. &
14. 30. & 20. 2.
Deut. 4. 20.
Amos 2. 10.

f Num. 22. 5. &
23. 7. & 24. 10, 11.
Deut. 23. 4, 5.
Josh. 24. 9, 10.
Rev. 2. 14.
g Num. 25. 1. &
33. 49.
Josh. 4. 19. & 5. 10.

*Targum* and our Margin has *thy enemies* (the word *areyca* may mean either ; *Pocock*, 60 ; *Gesen.* 659). The former rendering (*cities*—i. e. fenced cities) is confirmed by the context and r. 11, and S. Jerome here. It intimates that, when the Church has reached her consummation, she will have no need of fortifications ; God will be her defence. She will say, "We have a strong city ; salvation will God appoint for walls and bulwarks" (Isa. xxvi. 1). "The Lord is our King. He will save us" (Isa. xxxiii. 22). "He will be like a wall of fire round her." Cp. Zech. ii. 4. The extermination of idolatry by the good King Hezekiah, putting his faith and trust in God, and not in any arm of flesh, and his consequent deliverance from the invading army of Sennacherib, and the sudden destruction of that army by the Angel of the Lord—these things were figures and shadows of the last days of the Church. Cp. *Caspari*, 265. The Church is strong by holiness (cp. *Pusey*, 337).

CH. VI.] Here begins the third and last portion of Micah's prophecies. It is a hortatory application of what has gone before. God summons His people to hear His Voice, in the presence of all Creation, and He declares in the presence of that great public auditory, that all the miseries of the Hebrew Nation (and of Mankind) are due to their own sins ; and that He is ready to heal them. This passage (v. 6—vi. 8) is the *Haphtarah to Balaam's* history. Num. xxii. 2—xxv. 9.

1. *contend thou*] Stand thou, O Zion, plead with the mountains, which thou hast profaned with idols.

2. *Hear ye, O mountains*] For similar appeals to the Earth and Heaven, cp. Deut. xxxii. 1. Isa. i. 2. Jer. xxii. 29.

— *the* LORD *hath a controversy*] Jehovah condescends to become a litigant with His people ; and appeals to the Elements of the Universe, which had witnessed His dealings with them since the Exodus from Egypt, to decide the cause. Cp. Isa. i. 18, "Come, let us reason together ;" and Hos. iv. 1, "The Lord hath a controversy with the inhabitants of the land ;"

and Hos. xii. 2, "The Lord hath also a controversy with Judah."

3. *wherein have I wearied thee*] I have not wearied *thee*. No ; as He said by Isa. xliii. 23, "*I have not caused thee* to serve with an offering, nor wearied thee with incense." But, on the other hand, *thou hast wearied Me by* thy sins, as the same Prophet adds (xliii. 24). Cp. Amos ii. 13.

— *Moses, Aaron, Miriam*] The Lawgiver to command ; the Priest to atone ; the Prophetess to teach, and praise God.

5. *remember now what Balak king of Moab consulted*] Remember how Balak the King of Moab united with the elders of Midian in a desire and design to destroy thee (see the references in the Margin) ; and how he sent for Balaam, the Seer, from the East, and hired him to curse thee ; and how Balaam desired to curse thee ; but thy God turned that curse into a blessing (Deut. xxiii. 4, 5. Josh. xxiv. 10), and thus showed His love toward thee ; and how, even by the salutary discipline of love, chastising thee for harlotry and idolatry, unto which thou wast allured by Balaam's arts ; and also by the destruction of Balaam (Num. xxxi. 8), and by the punishment of the Midianites, He taught thee the wretched consequences of disobedience ; and how, by the example of zeal and courage in Phinehas, the son of Eleazar, and the benediction pronounced upon him, God showed thee the blessedness of obedience (Num. xxv).

— *From Shittim unto Gilgal*] That is, from the last station in the wanderings of Israel in the wilderness to the first station in Canaan, *Gilgal* (Num. xxii. 1 ; xxv. 1. Josh. iv. 19), where Israel's reproach was *rolled* away.

These words introduce a new consideration, and I have therefore inserted a stop after *him* ; the former sentences refer to mercies conferred under Moses, Aaron, and Miriam ; but the Prophet now appeals to the miracles of mercy vouchsafed by God to Israel under *Joshua*, in the passage over Jordan and in the overthrow of Jericho, and the new reception of Israel into covenant with God by circumcision at Gilgal.

That ye may know ᵇ the righteousness of the LORD.

6　Wherewith shall I come before the LORD,

*And* bow myself before the high God ?

Shall I come before him with burnt offerings

With calves † of a year old ?

7 ⁱ Will the LORD be pleased with thousands of rams,

*Or* with ten thousands of ᵏ rivers of oil ?

ˡ Shall I give my firstborn *for* my transgression,

The fruit of my † body *for* the sin of my soul ?

8　He hath ᵐ showed thee, O man, what *is* good ;

And what doth the LORD require of thee,

But ⁿ to do justly, and to love mercy, and to † walk humbly with thy God ?

9　The LORD's voice crieth unto the city,

And ‖ *the man* of wisdom shall see thy name :

Hear ye the rod, and who hath appointed it.

10　‖ Are there yet the treasures of wickedness in the house of the wicked,

And the † scant measure ᵒ *that is* abominable ?

11　‖ Shall I count *them* pure with ᵖ the wicked balances,

And with the bag of deceitful weights ?

12 For the rich men thereof are full of violence,

And the inhabitants thereof have spoken lies,

And ᑫ their tongue *is* deceitful in their mouth.

13 Therefore also will I ʳ make *thee* sick in smiting thee,

In making *thee* desolate because of thy sins.

14 ˢ Thou shalt eat, but not be satisfied ;

And thy casting down *shall be* in the midst of thee ;

Before
CHRIST
710.
h Judg. 5. 11.

† Heb. *sons of a year?*
i Ps. 50. 9, &c.
51. 16.
Isa. 1. 11.
k Job 29. 6.

† 2 Kings 16. 3, &c.
21. 6. & 23. 10.
Jer. 7. 31. & 19. 5.
Ezek. 23. 37.
† Heb. *belly.*
m Deut. 10. 12.
1 Sam. 15. 22.
Hos. 6. 6. & 12. 6.

n Gen. 18. 19.
Isa. 1. 17.
† Heb. *humble thyself to walk.*

‖ Or, *thy name shall see that which is.*

‖ Or, *Is there yet unto every man an house of the wicked, &c.*
† Heb. *measure of leanness.*
Amos 8. 5.
o Deut. 25.
14—16.
Prov. 11. 1. &
20. 10, 23.
‖ Or, *Shall I be pure with, &c.*
p Hos. 12. 7.
q Jer. 9. 3, 5, 6, 8.

r Lev. 26. 16.
Ps. 107. 17, 18.

s Lev. 26. 26.
Hos. 4. 10.

---

— *That ye may know the righteousness of the* LORD] All your history, from your deliverance out of Egypt under Moses, to your entrance into the Promised Land under Joshua, attests *the righteousnesses of the Lord*, His faithfulness to you, and His love of what is just and holy, and His hatred of sin.

6. *Wherewith shall I come before the* LORD] The Prophet takes up the word *the* LORD (JEHOVAH) from the foregoing clause, and supposes this question to be put by some persons who have heard of *the righteousness of the Lord* (the *righteous acts* of the Lord, in power, justice, and mercy. Cp. Judges v. 11. 1 Sam. xii. 7), and who profess, hypocritically, to be eager to offer any ritual sacrifices to Him.

On this passage, see *S. Augustine's* two Sermons, Serm. 48, 49.

It has been thought by some that Micah is supposing this question to be put by Balak when he consulted Balaam, and that the words in reply are what Balaam answered. So *Bp. Butler*, in his Sermon on the character of Balaam (Serm. vii. p. 104), who grounds some interesting and instructive inferences on that hypothesis; which is, however, questionable.

7. *rivers of oil*] Cp. Job xxix. 17. Oil formed a part of the daily *minchah*, or meat offering, and was added to burnt offerings (Num. xv. 1—16; xxxiii., xxix).

— *Shall I give my firstborn*] As a later King of Moab did (2 Kings iii. 27). Cp. Jer. vii. 31.

For a reply to *Tindal's* objection, that by this mention of human sacrifices together with legal rites, Micah appears to sanction them, see *Dr. Waterland,* Scripture Vindicated, p. 269.

8. *He hath showed thee—what is good*] As in Deut. x. 12. 1 Sam. xv. 22. Ps. l. 16, 17. Hos. vi. 6; and see Isa. i. 11; lxvi. 3. Jer. vi. 20; vii. 22. Amos v. 22—where God declares that He loathes all sacrifices where faith and obedience are not found in those who offer them.

It is observable that the inculcation of moral virtues by the prophets, as of superior and paramount importance, in comparison with ritual and ceremonial observances, though prescribed by the Levitical Law given by God Himself, is generally to be found, as here, in connexion with prophecies which predict the Fall of Jerusalem and the Temple, and the Captivity and dispersion of the Jews into foreign lands, where the observance of the ritual law would be impossible.

This was a merciful provision, in order that the Jews might not despond and despair because their City and Temple were in ruins, and they could not *come before the Lord with burnt offerings*, and *bow themselves before the High God* in His Temple. They could still hold spiritual communion with God; and He comforts them with the assurance that this spiritual communion would be exercised and its power intensified by the withdrawal and destruction of what was material and external; and that they would be able to serve and please God with what was good, and to render what the Lord required of them—namely, to *do justly* and *love mercy,* and *walk humbly with their God.* Cp. *Davison* on Prophecy (Disc. v. p. 208).

9. *The* LORD's *voice crieth unto the city*] The Lord's voice cries by His Prophets, and also by His penal visitations (such as plague, famine, and war—which are His "sore judgments"); *and Wisdom shall behold Thy Name;* Wisdom will recognize God's glorious attributes in all these manifestations, and will say, *Hear ye the Rod,* listen to God speaking by these visitations, and consider *Who hath appointed it.* Cp. Isa. xxvi. 11, "Lord, when Thy hand is lifted up, they will not see; but they shall see;" and Jer. ii. 31, "See ye the Word of the Lord." His voice cries in the ears of all (Prov. viii. 1—4), but only Wisdom sees His Name. The word here used for *Wisdom* literally means *what is* (see above on Job v. 12), i.e. is *real;* all mere worldly knowledge and policy is a vain phantom.

See the Sermon on this text, by *Dr. Pierce,* President of Magdalen College, before the King at Whitehall, A.D. 1665.

— *who hath appointed it*] Assyria was called "the rod of God's anger," and "His grounded staff" against Israel (Isa. x. 5; xxx. 32).

11. *Shall I count them pure with the wicked balances*] Rather, *Can I be pure with the wicked balance ?* That is, if I have it in my hand, can I be guiltless ?

14. *thy casting down*] "Thy destruction will be *in the midst of thee*" to stay thee, instead of thy God who was "in the midst of thee" to save thee (Isa. xii. 6. Hos. xii. 6).

Before
CHRIST
710.

And thou shalt take hold, but shalt not deliver;
And *that* which thou deliverest will I give up to the sword;

15 Thou shalt ᵗ sow, but thou shalt not reap;
Thou shalt tread the olives, but thou shalt not anoint thee with oil;
And sweet wine, but shalt not drink wine.

16 For ‖ the statutes of ᵘ Omri are ˣ kept,
And all the works of the house of ʸ Ahab,
And ye walk in their counsels;
That I should make thee ᶻ a ‖ desolation,
And the inhabitants thereof an hissing:
Therefore ye shall bear the ᵃ reproach of my people.

VII. 1 Woe is me! for I am as † when they have gathered the summer fruits,
As ᵃ the grapegleanings of the vintage:
*There is* no cluster to eat:
My soul desired the firstripe fruit.

2 The ᶜ ‖ good *man* is perished out of the earth:
And *there is* none upright among men:
They all lie in wait for blood;
ᵈ They hunt every man his brother with a net;

3 That they may do evil with both hands earnestly,
ᵉ The prince asketh, ᶠ and the judge *asketh* for a reward;
And the great *man*, he uttereth † his mischievous desire:
So they wrap it up.

4 The best of them ᵍ *is* a brier:
The most upright *is sharper* than a thorn hedge:
The day of thy watchmen *and* thy visitation cometh;
Now shall be their perplexity.

5 ʰ Trust ye not in a friend,
Put ye not confidence in a guide:
Keep the doors of thy mouth from her that lieth in thy bosom.

6 For ⁱ the son dishonoureth the father,
The daughter riseth up against her mother,
The daughter in law against her mother in law;
A man's enemies *are* the men of his own house.

---

† Deut. 28. 28,
30, 40.
Amos 5. 11.
Zeph. 1. 13.
Hag. 1. 6.

‖ Or, *he doth
much keep the, &c.*
u 1 Kings 16.
25, 26.
x Hos. 5. 11.
y 1 Kings 16.
30, &c. 21.
21, 25, 26.
2 Kings 21. 3.
z 1 Kings 9. 8.
Jer. 19. 8.
‖ Or, *astonish-
ment.*
a Isa. 25. 8.
Jer. 51. 51.
Lam 5. 1.
† Heb. *the
gatherings of
summer.*
a Isa. 17. 6. &
24. 13.
b Isa. 28. 4.
Hos. 9. 10.
c Ps. 12. 1. &
14. 1, 3.
Isa. 57. 1.
‖ Or, *godly, or,
merciful.*

d Hab. 1. 15.

e Hos. 4. 18.
f Isa. 1. 23.
ch. 3. 11.
† Heb. *the
mischief of his
soul.*

c 2 Sam. 23. 6, 7.
Ezek. 2. 6.
See Isa. 55. 13.

h Jer. 9. 4.

i Ezek. 22. 7.
Matt. 10. 21,
35, 36.
Luke 12. 53. &
21. 16.
2 Tim. 3. 2, 3.

— *thou shalt take hold*] Rather, *thou shalt remove, but not
save* (see *Gesen.* 552; and *Keil*); *thou shalt remove* thy goods
in thy flight from the enemy, but shalt not rescue them, or
save thyself by flight.

15. *Thou shalt sow, but thou shalt not reap*] From Levit.
xxvi. 25, 26. Deut. xxviii. 38, 40.

16. *the statutes of Omri are kept—works of the house of
Ahab*] Ye rebel against the Lord God, and break His Law, and
forget His mercies, to keep the statutes and follow the doings
of the worst kings of Israel (1 Kings xvi. 25, 31, 32. 2 Chron.
xxii. 2). Cp. Hos. v. 11. Ye "willingly walked after the commandment" of Jeroboam.

— *ye shall bear the reproach of my people*] Because ye
have oppressed My People, therefore ye, their rulers, shall bear
at the hands of the Heathen among whom you will be dispersed,
the reproach which they heap on My People. Cp. Ezek. xxxvi.
20.

This was fulfilled in King Zedekiah and his sons, and in
the princes and nobles of Jerusalem, upon whom the chief
weight of suffering and ignominy fell, in the Chaldæan invasion.

THE PROPHET FORETELLS THE PENITENTIAL PRAYER OF
THE JEWISH NATION, AND GOD'S PROMISES OF MERCY,
AND FAVOUR, AND GLORY TO HER IN CHRIST.

Ch. VII. 1. *Woe is me!*] The Prophet speaks in the name

of the ancient Church of Israel, and deplores her low estate
consequent on her sins.

1. *My soul desired the firstripe fruit*] I desired the early
fruit. I longed for the graces and virtues of primitive times,
but I did not find them. Cp. Hos. ix. 10, where Israel in its
youthful prime is compared to early fruit; but none is now
found in her.

God here speaks by the Prophet, and declares His dis-
appointment at the unfruitfulness of Israel. So Christ came
to the barren fig-tree,—the symbol of the Jewish Nation. He
hungered for fruit, but found nothing there but leaves. See
on Matt. xxi. 18, 19.

2, 3. *That they may do evil*] Rather, *For evil both hands* are
ready *to do it well* (i. e. as if evil were their good); but *to do good
the prince asketh* for a bribe.

— *a reward*] A bribe.

— *they wrap it up*] Or twist it together, to make it strong,
as a cart-rope (Isa. v. 18).

4. *The day of thy watchmen*] The day of visitation, foretold
by thy prophets, who warned thee, as thy watchmen (Ezek.
iii. 17: xxxiii. 7), of the coming doom.

5, 6. *Trust ye not in a friend*] Such is the wickedness of
the times, that the nearest friends and relatives cannot repose
any confidence in each other. Our Lord adopts these words in
His description of the latter days of the World (Matt. x. 21, 35,
36; xxiv. 12. Cp. Luke xii. 53; xxi. 16; and 2 Tim. iii. 2).

7 Therefore [k] I will look unto the LORD; k Isa. 8. 17.
I will wait for the God of my salvation:
My God will hear me.
8 [l] Rejoice not against me, O mine enemy: l Prov. 24. 17. Lam. 4. 21.
[m] When I fall, I shall arise; m Ps. 37. 24. Prov. 24. 16.
When I sit in darkness, [n] the LORD *shall be* a light unto me. n Ps. 27. 1.
9 [o] I will bear the indignation of the LORD, because I have sinned against him, o Lam. 3. 39.
Until he plead my cause, and execute judgment for me:
[p] He will bring me forth to the light, *and* I shall behold his righteousness. p Ps. 37. 6.
10 ‖ Then *she that is* mine enemy shall see *it*, ‖ Or, *And thou wilt see her that is mine enemy, and cover her with shame.*
And [q] shame shall cover her which said unto me, q Ps. 35. 26.
[r] Where is the LORD thy God? r Ps. 42. 3, 10. & 79. 10. & 115. 2. Joel 2. 17.
[s] Mine eyes shall behold her: s ch. 4. 11.
Now † shall she be trodden down [t] as the mire of the streets. † Heb. *she shall be for a treading down.* t 2 Sam. 22. 43. Zech. 10. 5.
11 *In* the day that thy [u] walls are to be built, u Amos 9. 11, &c.
*In* that day shall the decree be far removed;
12 *In* that day *also* [x] he shall come even to thee from Assyria, x Isa. 11. 16. & 19. 23, &c. & 27. 13. Hos. 11. 11.
‖ And *from* the fortified cities, ‖ Or, *even to.*
And from the fortress even to the river,
And from sea to sea,
And *from* mountain to mountain.
13 ‖ Notwithstanding the land shall be desolate because of them that dwell therein, ‖ Or, *After that it hath been.*
[y] For the fruit of their doings. y Jer. 21. 14. ch. 3. 12.
14 ‖ Feed thy people with thy rod, ‖ Or, *Rule*, Ps. 28. 9. ch. 5. 4.
The flock of thine heritage,
Which dwell solitarily *in* [z] the wood, in the midst of Carmel: z Isa. 37. 24.
Let them feed *in* Bashan and Gilead,

---

**8.** *Rejoice not against me, O mine enemy*] Zion warns Babylon not to exult over her; for Babylon will fall, and Zion will rise again (*S. Jerome, R. Solomon*). Cp. Jer. l. 11; and Isa. xlvii. 6.

The Church of Christ may apply these words to the mystical Babylon,—the corrupt and proud Church of Rome,—which exults in her distresses in these last times. The Jews themselves apply this text to Rome; and they say that some great blessing will be vouchsafed to Israel, when Rome is humbled and destroyed. See *Pocock*, 86. 88; and compare *Vitringa* on the Apocalypse, 792; *Mede's* Works, 902. And when we consider what hindrances the Roman Church places in the way of the conversion of the Jews to Christianity by her creature-worship and idolatry, and especially Mariolatry and adoration of the Roman Pontiff, to say nothing of her canonization of the Apocrypha, as if it were equal in authority and inspiration to the Hebrew Scriptures of Moses and the Prophets, we cannot doubt that the humiliation of the Roman Papacy is almost a necessary pre-requisite to the conversion of the Jews, and to their reception into the Christian Sion.

**11.** In *the day—built*] Or, *The day* (is coming) *for the building of Thy walls.* The day here spoken of cannot be the day in which the walls of the literal Jerusalem were rebuilt by Nehemiah, with a commission from Artaxerxes; for what follows was not fulfilled then. But this prophecy foretells the building up of Zion by the hand of Christ, Who came to Jerusalem, and laid the foundation of His Church there, and sent the Holy Spirit from heaven on the Day of Pentecost to the Apostles, the Master-builders under Him, to build up the walls of the spiritual city, so that it might enfold all Nations. See above, on iv. 1, 2.

— In *that day shall the decree be far removed*] Or rather, be extended and promulgated far and wide. God makes *the decree* (see Ps. ii. 7, 8, "I will declare the *decree*,"—where the same Hebrew word, *chŏk*, for *decree*, is used): "I have set My King upon My holy hill of Sion. I shall give thee the heathen for thine inheritance, and the uttermost parts of the earth for thy possession." Cp. Amos x. 11. Acts xv. 16; and *Pocock* here. Some suppose *the decree* to be the law of the enemy.

**12.** In *that day* also *he* (i. e. many persons) *shall come even to thee from Assyria, and* from *the fortified cities*] Or rather, *from the cities of Egypt* (Hebr. *Matsór*). See Isa. xix. 6; xxxvii. 25. *Gesen.* 501; and *Keil.* This began to be fulfilled on the Day of Pentecost, when multitudes from Assyria and Egypt were received by the Apostles into the Church of Christ. See Acts ii. 9, 10.

Here again Micah comes into contact with Isaiah, who, in foretelling the spread of the primitive Christian Church from Jerusalem by the ministry of the Apostles, who were Jews, says, "In that day shall *Israel* be the third with *Egypt* and with *Assyria.*" Cp. Isa. xix. 24; xxvii. 13.

Thus the Prophet Micah, although he has warned the Assyrians, and all other heathen Nations and worldly princes, that if they resist Christ, and persecute His Church, they will be broken in pieces, yet assures them (as God had done by Isaiah) that if they repent, and turn to Him, they will be graciously received by Him.

— *from the fortress*] Rather, *from Egypt* (Hebr. *Matsór*). See the foregoing note.

**13.** *Notwithstanding the land shall be desolate*] Rather, *And the earth* (as opposed to the kingdom of heaven, the Church of God) *shall be desolate, because of its inhabitants, for the fruit of their doings.* Cp. Rev. viii. 13; xii. 12, "Woe to the inhabiters of the earth," which may have been derived from this passage of Micah.

**14.** *Feed thy people*] Zion, that is, the Church, prays to Christ to feed His people in all regions of the spiritual Israel, represented by Carmel, the fruitful mountain-range on the western sea-coast (Isa. x. 18; xxxvii. 24), and by Bashan and Gilead, the rich pasture-land on the east of Jordan (Num. xxxii. 1. Deut. xxxii. 14). Cp. note on Jer. l. 19, "I will bring Israel again to his habitation, and he shall feed on Carmel and Bashan, and his soul shall on Mount Ephraim and Gilead." Micah resigns his pastoral office to "the Good Shepherd."

As in the days of old.

2 Ps. lxviii. 22, &
78. 12.

15 According to the days of thy coming out of the land of Egypt will I shew unto him marvellous *things.*

t. 1 a. 26. 11.

16 The nations <sup>g</sup> shall see and be confounded at all their might:

'They shall lay *their* hand upon *their* mouth,

Their ears shall be deaf.

a Ps. 72. 9.
Isa. 49. 23.
e Ps. 18. 45.
|| Or, *creeping
things.*
1 Jer. 33. 9.

17 They shall lick the <sup>d</sup> dust like a serpent,

'They shall move out of their holes like || worms of the earth:

'They shall be afraid of the LORD our God,

And shall fear because of thee.

g Exod. 15. 11.
h Exod. 34. 6, 7.
Jer. 50. 20.
i ch. 4. 7. &
5. 3, 7, 8.
k Ps. 103. 9.
Isa. 57. 16.
Jer. 3. 5.

18 <sup>g</sup> Who *is* a God like unto thee, that <sup>h</sup> pardoneth iniquity,

And passeth by the transgression of <sup>i</sup> the remnant of his heritage?

<sup>k</sup> He retaineth not his anger for ever,

Because he delighteth *in* mercy.

19 He will turn again, he will have compassion upon us;

He will subdue our iniquities;

And thou wilt cast all their sins into the depths of the sea.

l Luke 1. 72, 73.

20 <sup>l</sup> Thou wilt perform the truth to Jacob,

*And* the mercy to Abraham,

m Ps. 105. 9, 10.

<sup>m</sup> Which thou hast sworn unto our fathers from the days of old.

---

16. *They shall lay their hand upon their mouth*] In awe and dread. Cp. Job v. 16; xxi. 5; xl. 4.

— *Their ears shall be deaf* | With obstinate obduracy.

17. *They shall lick the dust*] Cp. the prophecy concerning Christ. "They that dwell in the wilderness shall bow before Him; His *enemies shall lick the dust*" (Ps. lxxii. 9), here extended to His Church. Cp. Isa. xlix. 23. It is grounded on God's malediction of the Old Serpent for tempting our first parents: "Upon thy belly shalt thou go, and dust shalt thou eat all the days of thy life" (Gen. iii. 14).

— *They shall move out of their holes like worms of the earth*] They who were once so proud, shall be like worms; and they who thought themselves impregnable, shall come trembling out of their strongholds. Cp. 2 Sam. xxii. 46.

18. *Who is a God like unto thee*] Micah, the Prophet, whose name signifies *Who is like unto Jehovah?* here alludes to his own name, as Isaiah alludes to his own name (see on Isa. viii. 1—4. 18) and Malachi to his own (iii. 1. *Caspari*, 26—28); and he asks, in the name of God's favoured nation, " *Who is a God like unto Thee?*" (Exod. xv. 11,) in that He has pardoned her iniquities, and has passed by the transgressions of the *remnant according to grace* (Rom. ix. 27; xi. 5), that is, of those among His ancient people Israel who have accepted His offers of salvation in Christ, and have become the preachers of His Gospel to the World.

19. *thou wilt cast all their sins into the depths of the sea*] He has washed away her sins by the blood of Christ, and will remember them no more (Ps. ciii. 12. Isa. xxxviii. 17. Jer. l. 20; xxxi. 34. 1 John i. 7. Rev. i. 5).

There is a special propriety in these words, " *Thou wilt cast all their sins into the depths of the sea*," because they are grounded on those words of Moses at the Exodus, and after the passage of the Red Sea (the mercies of which have just been commemorated by Micah, *v.* 15). In his song of victory, after that glorious deliverance, Moses said, " Pharaoh's chariots and his host *hath He cast into the sea.*" And Miriam said, "Sing ye to the Lord; for He hath triumphed gloriously: the horse and his rider hath He *thrown into the sea*" (Exod. xv. 4, 21).

The miraculous mercies of the Exodus, and of the deliverance of Israel by the blood of the Paschal Lamb, and by the way opened to them through the waves of the Red Sea, in which they themselves passed through a wall of waters on their right hand and on their left hand, from out of the land of bondage into the wilderness, on their way to Canaan, being baptized unto Moses in the cloud and in the sea (1 Cor. x. 2), were figurative of the far greater and more miraculous mercies which God bestows on all true Israelites in Christ, Who is the true Passover (1 Cor. v. 7. John xix. 36); and of their deliverance from the land of spiritual bondage, Sin, Satan, and Death, and of the overwhelming of their spiritual enemies in the Red Sea

of the Blood of Christ, through which they pass in their Baptism (as *Theodoret* here observes), out of the bondage of their ghostly Egypt, and enter on the way of salvation, which leads them on their earthly pilgrimage through the wilderness of this world to the heavenly Canaan of their everlasting rest. See the notes above, on Exod. xii. 7—15; and chap. xiv., *Prelim. Note*; and the words of the Church in her Baptismal Office (and how much is suggested by those few words!), "Almighty and everlasting God, Who of Thy great mercy didst save Noah and his family in the Ark from perishing by water, and also didst safely lead the children of Israel Thy people through the Red Sea, *figuring thereby Thy Holy Baptism.*"

Well, therefore, may Micah use these words, when he is foretelling the redemption of Israel by CHRIST, and the forgiveness of their sins, and the blessings received by them, and communicated to them by the Sacrament of Baptism, in which the Blood of Christ is applied to the washing away of sins, and to the purchase of His Universal Church (Acts xx. 28).

20. *Thou wilt perform the truth to Jacob, and the mercy to Abraham, which thou hast sworn unto our fathers from the days of old*] This is fulfilled in Christ, the Promised Seed of Abraham and Jacob, in Whom all Nations are blessed. And, therefore, we may sum up all, in the words of Zacharias the Priest of God, when, filled with the Holy Ghost, he prophesied, and said, "Blessed be the Lord God of Israel; for He hath visited and redeemed His people, and hath raised up an horn of salvation for us in the house of His servant David; as He spake by the mouth of His holy Prophets, which have been since the world began; that we should be saved from our enemies, and from the hand of all that hate us; to perform the mercy promised to our forefathers, and to remember His holy covenant; the oath which He sware to our father Abraham, that He would grant unto us, that we being delivered out of the hand of our enemies, might serve Him without fear, in holiness and righteousness before Him, all the days of our life" (Luke i. 68—75).

"There is no prophetic denunciation of judgment against Israel," says *Abarbinel*, "which is not concluded with promises of mercy." This he has shown from Hosea, Joel, Amos, Jeremiah; and Micah's last words declare how greatly God delights in mercy; because they not only give assurances of mercy to the literal Israel, on their repentance, but to all that shall in Christ, the Promised Seed, lay hold on His promise, made to Abraham, and in him to all the kindreds of the earth; so that the Gentiles, also, reading this prophecy, cannot but glorify God, and rejoice with His people, and sing unto Him that hymn which the Apostle puts into their mouth: "Praise the Lord, all ye Gentiles; and laud Him, all ye people" (Rom. xv. 11. *Dr. Pocock*).

# NAHUM.

I. [1] THE burden [a] of Nineveh. The book of the vision of Nahum the El- a Zeph. 2 13.
koshite.

[2] ‖ God is [b] jealous, and [c] the LORD revengeth;

‖ Or, The LORD
is a jealous God,
and revenger, &c.

b Exod. 20. 5 & 34. 14.  Deut. 4 24.  Josh, 24 19.    c Deut. 32. 35.  Ps. 94. 1.  Isa. 59. 18.

The connecting link between the prophecies of MICAH, which have preceded, and those of NAHUM and Habakkuk, which now follow, is to be found in Micah v. 6.

There that Prophet described the victory of Christ and His Church in these words:—"They shall waste the land of Assyria with the sword, and the land of Nimrod (or Babylon) in the entrance thereof. Then shall he deliver us from the Assyrian." See also Micah v. 5, "This man shall be the Peace when the Assyrian shall come into our land, and when he shall tread in our palaces; then shall we raise against him seven shepherds, and eight principal men."

These prophecies, as the context shows, and all the best Expositors agree, have not only a literal sense, which relates to the deliverance of Judah from Assyria in the days of Hezekiah, and also to the liberation of the People of God from Babylon by the arms of Cyrus; but they look far beyond those national mercies, and foreshadow the triumph of Christ and of His faithful people, and the overthrow of their enemies.

It is a legitimate inference from these prophecies, considered together with those of Isaiah, that the deliverance of the faithful Hezekiah and of the literal Jerusalem from the haughty and impious power of Sennacherib, the great Assyrian conqueror, and the destruction of his immense host before the walls of Jerusalem, by "the Angel of the Lord," was due to the might of Christ, Who is often called by that title in the Old Testament. See above, on Exod. iii. 2.  Judges xiii. 18.

Indeed, the words of Micah—which clearly point to Christ as the destroyer of the Assyrian invaders, whose conquests over Ethiopia and Egypt Micah himself saw, and whose overthrow he, as well as his contemporary prophet, Isaiah, foretold—being us irresistibly to this conclusion. Cp. above, on Micah v. 5.

They also lead us to regard the Assyrian King in his pride and blasphemy against the Lord, as a type of infidel and godless Powers which rise up against Christ, and which will be routed and crushed by Him in the last days.

This exposition, as we have seen, was accepted by ancient Interpreters, especially S. Jerome.

It prepares us for what follows.

There are three specific prophecies, which fill up the entire books of three of the Minor Prophets, and are directed against three different worldly powers, hostile to God and His people;

The first is that of OBADIAH, directed against EDOM— the faithless, treacherous, and cruel foe of Israel their brother. Edom is the type of powers which have some connexion with God's Church by neighbourhood or consanguinity, and who, in spite of this relationship, behave in a heartless manner to her in her distresses—as Edom did to Israel and Judah in the days of their calamity.

Edom is the type of faithless, insidious, and unbrotherly members of the Church.

The second prophecy is that of NAHUM, against NINEVEH, the capital of Assyria—the haughty and savage enemy of Judah.

NINEVEH is the type of the openly infidel and impious form of Antichristianism.

It is well said by a recent German Expositor, that the Prophet Nahum saw in Nineveh the representative of the Worldly Power opposed to God; and the destruction of Nineveh was a prophetic figure of the future overthrow of all such powers, even to the end of the world (Keil, p. 400).

The next is that of HABAKKUK, directed against BABYLON. Babylon is represented by the Prophets as professing herself very wise, and yet a votary of idols, a victim of gross and debasing superstition (Isa. xlvii. 10). Babylon is the figure of

the idolatrous form of Antichristianism, which makes presumptuous claims to superior intelligence and insight into the mysteries of the unseen world. Cp. what has been said on Isa. xiii., Prelim. Note.

We see these qualities brought to a climax in the Babylon of the Apocalypse, Papal Rome. The proofs of this identity are given by the Editor in another place, in his Notes on the Book of Revelation, and in a separate work, "On Union with Rome; or, Is the Church of Rome the Babylon of the Apocalypse?"

We have now arrived at the prophecy of Nahum. It has been said by some that there is no reference to Christ in this book. But the Holy Spirit, Who spake by the prophets (2 Pet. i. 20, 21), declares by the Apostles, that "to Him give all the Prophets witness" (Acts iii. 24; x. 43); and that the Spirit of Christ was in the Prophets, and that they inquired and searched diligently what that Spirit witnessed when it spake of His sufferings and of the glory that should follow (1 Pet. i. 10).

If we accept the interpretation now given, that the Assyrian was overthrown by Christ's power, and that the Assyrian is a type of godless Antichristian powers in these latter days, we shall see Christ in the prophecies of Nahum, as well as in all other; and we may adopt, with some modifications, the language of S. Jerome: "Micah is followed by Nahum, whose name signifies the Consoler. He consoles those of Israel who had been taken captive and dispersed by the Assyrian; he foretells the future downfall of Nineveh, the capital of Assyria; and, in a spiritual sense, he predicts the destruction of all godless Ninevehs in the latter days." And again (in his Epistle to Paulinus), S. Jerome says, "Nahum—the consoler of the world—rebukes the bloody city (iii. 1), and foretells its destruction, and after that event he exclaims, "Behold upon the mountains the feet of him that bringeth good things, that publisheth peace" (i. 15)—the Christian significance of which prophecy had already been declared by Isaiah (lii. 7.  Rom. x. 15).

The prophecy of Nahum (says S. Jerome in prolog.) is to be understood, not only historically, but figuratively; and in reading it we must rise from the level of the literal sense to the higher altitude of the moral and spiritual. The prophet speaks to us concerning the consummation of all things, and affords consolation to the faithful in the last days, in order that they may despise the pomp and power of this world as mere transitory phantoms and fleeting shadows, and may prepare themselves for the Day of Judgment, when the Lord will appear as the Avenger of His People against all Antichristian Assyrians.

So far, then, from its being true that Christ is not to be found in the prophecy of Nahum, rather we may say that He is the principal agent in it.

The date of Nahum's prophecy falls soon after those of Isaiah and Micah; namely, after the carrying away of the ten tribes of Israel by Assyria (B.C. 721), and after the destruction of the army of Sennacherib at the walls of Jerusalem (about B.C. 712—Vitringa, Keil), and before the fall of Nineveh, as to the date of which see on 2 Kings xxiii. 29.

CH. I. 1. The burden] Both the prophecies of Nahum and Habakkuk (which form a pair) are called burdens, or heavy messages from God, taken up by the two Prophets, and delivered to Nineveh and Babylon respectively. By this word (burden) these prophecies are connected with the similar predictions of Isaiah, which are also called burdens (Isa. xiii.).

— Elkoshite] A native of Elkosh in Galilee (S. Jerome).

* Heb. *hail hath*
*lords.*

d Exod. 34. 6, 7.
Neh. 9. 17.
Ps. 103. 8.
Jonah 4. 2.
e Job 9. 4
f Ps. 18. 7, &c. &
97. 2.
Hab. 3. 5, 11, 12

g Ps. 106. 9.
Isa. 50. 2.
Matt. 8. 26.

h Isa. 33. 9.

i Ps. 68. 8.
k Judg. 5. 5.
Ps. 97. 5.
Micah 1. 4.
l 2 Pet. 3. 10.

m Mal. 3. 2
† Heb. *stand up.*

n Rev. 16. 1.

o 1 Chr. 16. 34.
Ps. 100. 5.
Jer. 33. 11.
Lam. 3. 25.
|| Or, *strength.*
p Ps. 1. 6.
2 Tim. 2. 19.
q Dan. 9. 26. &
11. 10, 22, 40.

r Ps. 2. 1.

s 1 Sam. 3. 12.

t 2 Sam. 23. 6, 7.

u ch. 3. 11.

x Mal. 4. 1.

y 2 Kings 19.
23, 28.
* Heb. *a counseller of Belial.*

The LORD revengeth, and | *is* furious;
The LORD will take vengeance on his adversaries,
And he reserveth *wrath* for his enemies.

3 The LORD *is* d slow to anger, and e great in power,
And will not at all acquit *the wicked:*
f The LORD *hath* his way in the whirlwind and in the storm,
And the clouds *are* the dust of his feet;

4 g He rebuketh the sea, and maketh it dry,
And drieth up all the rivers:
h Bashan languisheth, and Carmel,
And the flower of Lebanon languisheth.

5 i The mountains quake at him, and k the hills melt,
And l the earth is burned at his presence,
Yea, the world, and all that dwell therein.

6 Who can stand before his indignation?
And m who can † abide in the fierceness of his anger?
n His fury is poured out like fire,
And the rocks are thrown down by him.

7 o The LORD *is* good, a || strong hold in the day of trouble;
And p he knoweth them that trust in him,

8 q But with an overrunning flood he will make an utter end of the place thereof,
And darkness shall pursue his enemies.

9 r What do ye imagine against the LORD?
s He will make an utter end:
Affliction shall not rise up the second time.

10 For while *they be* folden together t *as* thorns,
u And while they are drunken *as* drunkards,
x They shall be devoured as stubble fully dry.

11 There is *one* come out of thee, y that imagineth evil against the LORD,
† A wicked counseller.

---

3. *The LORD is slow to anger, and great in power*] God's mercy even toward Nineveh had been shown in the previous book of Jonah, who had even murmured at God's long-suffering. But Nineveh had now relapsed into sin; and therefore God, Who had shown His mercy by Jonah, declares His justice by Nahum.

Nahum, in the opening of his prophecy against Nineveh, manifestly refers to Jonah's appeal to God in regard to it (Jonah iv. 2).

It was for Nahum to exhibit the stricter side of God's dealings with that same city. God had shown by Jonah how He forgives on men's repentance. Nahum begins his book by declaring in the same form of words as that used by Jonah, that God is long-suffering, but will not spare the guilty. Cp. *Pusey* on Daniel, p. 509.

4. *Bashan—Carmel—Lebanon*] *Bashan* rich in pastures, *Carmel* in flowers, *Lebanon* in cedars, emblems of worldly wealth, glory, and power, languish and fade before God.

— *Bashan languisheth, and Carmel*] With these words, taken up from the last chapter of the foregoing Prophet, Micah (vii. 14), and from Isaiah (xxxiii. 9), Nahum links on his own prophecy to that of his predecessor. See also i. 3, compared with Micah vii. 18. And while the enemies of God and His People are described by Micah at the conclusion of his prophecy, as so humbled by Him, that they will *lick the dust* (vii. 17), Nahum declares, at the beginning of his prophecy, that such is God's Glory and Majesty, that the "*clouds are the dust of His feet*" (v. 3).

Nahum reminds his readers, in the beginning of his prophecy, that though the Assyrians were allowed to overcome the land of Israel, and to come up "to the sides of *Lebanon*, and into the forest of his *Carmel*" (Isa. xxxvii. 24), yet this was done by permission and commission of the God of Israel, to punish His People by "the Assyrian—the rod of His anger" (Isa. x. 5, 12), for their sins. God Himself said, "Hast thou not heard long ago how *I* have done it?" (Isa. xxxvii. 26.)

5. *the mountains quake*] Repeated from Amos ix. 13, *the earth is burned*, or heaved up by an earthquake.

6. *who can abide*] Or *rise up*. See *Margin.*

8. *the place thereof*] That is, of Nineveh; which occupies the whole scene in the Prophet's eye. See v. 1.

9. *Affliction shall not rise up the second time*] It will despatch Nineveh at one blow; it *had been* warned by Jonah.

10. *while they be folden together as thorns*] Or, *though they be twisted and matted together as thorns;* so as to appear impenetrable, and present to the enemy a front bristling with briars. Compare 2 Sam. xxiii. 6, 7. "The sons of Belial shall be all of them as thorns; the man that shall touch them must be fenced with iron;" and Isa. ix. 18. Micah vii. 4. "The best of them is as a briar, the most upright is sharper than a thorn hedge;" yet God will consume them.

— *while they are drunken*] The kings and nobles of Assyria, such as Sardanapalus (or Saracus) and his courtiers, were proverbial for their habits of intemperance and revelry. *Diodorus Siculus* (ii. 26) says that Nineveh was taken (under Sardanapalus) when the king and nobles were carousing in a drunken revel. The official name of *Rabshakeh*, the principal emissary of the King of Assyria, signifies *chief cup-bearer* (2 Kings xviii. 17).

11. *There is one come out of thee, that imagineth evil against the LORD*] Here is a reference to Sennacherib and his blasphemous message, delivered by Rabshakeh (2 Kings xviii. 22, 23. Isa. xxxvi. 14—20. *Theodoret*).

¹² Thus saith the LORD ;

‖ Though *they be* quiet, and likewise many,

Yet thus ² shall they be † cut down, when he shall ³ pass through.

Though I have afflicted thee, I will afflict thee no more.

¹³ For now will I ᵇ break his yoke from off thee,

And will burst thy bonds in sunder.

¹⁴ And the LORD hath given a commandment concerning thee,

*That* no more of thy name be sown :

Out of the house of thy gods will I cut off the graven image

And the molten image :

ᶜ I will make thy grave ; for thou art vile.

¹⁵ Behold ᵈ upon the mountains the feet of him that bringeth good tidings,

That publisheth peace !

O Judah, † keep thy solemn feasts, perform thy vows :

For † ᵉ the wicked shall no more pass through thee ;

ᶠ He is utterly cut off.

II. ¹ ‖ He ⁴ that dasheth in pieces is come up before thy face :

Before
CHRIST
about
715.

‡ Or. *If they
would have been
at peace, or,
should they have
been many, and
in should then
have been shorn,
and he should
have passed away,*
z 2 Kings 17.
35, 37.
† Heb. *ut ea.*
a Isa. 8. 8
Dan. 11. 10
b Jer. 2. 20 &
30. 8.

c 2 Kings 19. 37.

d Isa. 52. 7.
Rom. 10. 15.

† Heb. *feast.*
† Heb. *Belial.*
c ver. 11, 12.

f ver. 14.

‖ Or. *The
disperser, or,
hammer*
a Jer. 50. 23.

**12.** *Though they be quiet*] Though they be uninjured and unimpaired in strength, yet they shall be *cut down* when they *pass through* ; that is, when they imagine that they *will pass through* the land of Judah, in an easy march and resistless career of victory.

Such was the imagination of Sennacherib, marching in triumph from the conquest of Egypt and Ethiopia, and coming back from his southern campaign of victory to Jerusalem.

But his vast host was to be swept away there in a single night. See above, the notes on Isa. xx. 3 ; and xxxvii. 36 ; and compare the magnificent description of the sudden mowing down of Assyria's glory and power, in Isa. xvii. 12—14.

— *Though I have afflicted thee*] God afflicted Judah by the Assyrians—the rod of His anger—for their sins (Isa. x. 5—12), when Sennacherib took all their fenced cities and caused a terrible panic there. See Isa. x. 28—32, and the notes there ; and Isa. xxxvi. 1. Hezekiah's heart failed him, he cut off the gold from the Lord's house, as a bribe to the Assyrian ; and he said to him "That which thou puttest on me I will bear" (2 Kings xviii. 14). But this was of no avail. The threats of Sennacherib were repeated. God called Hezekiah to repentance by the Prophet Micah (Jer. xxvi. 18, 19), and then He encouraged him by Isaiah. Hezekiah sought the help of God by repentance and prayer, and he was saved, and his foes slain.

**14.** *thee*] O Assyrian : the gender is changed in the Hebrew.

— *I will make thy grave*] This was fulfilled in the murder of Sennacherib, in the house of Nisroch his god, by the hand of his own sons (2 Kings xix. 37). See also Isa. xxxvii. 38. The *Targum* and *Syriac* Version render this, *I will make there thy grave*, or, *I will make thy idol thy grave*; and so the Masoretic punctuation would lead us to understand the words. This interpretation has been accepted by *S. Jerome, Montanus, A Lapide, Junius, Tremellius, Drusius,* and others. "I will pollute thy idols by a dead body" (see 2 Kings xxiii. 20; cp. Ezek. vi. 5), "and *that* body will be thine own."

THE DELIVERANCE AND JOY OF JUDAH, FOR THE OVER-
THROW OF SENNACHERIB AND NINEVEH ; THE DELIVER-
ANCE AND JOY OF THE CHURCH FOR THE VICTORY OF
CHRIST.

**15.** *Behold upon the mountains the feet*] Like beacon-fires on the hills, telling glad tidings. These words, taken up from Isaiah proclaiming the Advent of Christ (Isa. lii. 7 ; cp. xl. 9 ; cp. St. Paul's exposition of them, Rom. x. 15) are used by Nahum in a double sense ; first, to describe the joy produced in Judah by the tidings of the destruction of Sennacherib, and afterwards of Nineveh, and Judah's consequent deliverance from its Assyrian enemies.

But beyond the horizon of this first sense, the Prophet sees into the far-off future, when he utters these words. The Holy Spirit, Who speaks in Nahum, and illumines his mind with divine light, reveals here the glad tidings which were brought to the Church of God by the news of Christ's Resurrection and

Victory over her ghostly enemies, Satan, Sin, and the Grave ; and foretells her future joy at her deliverance from the hostile Powers which will rise up against her in the latter days.

— *O Judah, keep thy solemn feasts*] Keep the feasts which were interrupted for three years by the occupation of Judah by the Assyrian invader, and by the alarm of his approach preventing the inhabitants from going up to Jerusalem. Keep them now that thine enemy is no more ; keep them with praise and thanksgiving to the Lord thy Redeemer.

Now that Christ has conquered our enemies, Satan, Sin, Death, and the Grave, the solemn feasts of Judah are kept under the Gospel, not in the shadow, but in the substance. We *keep the feast* of Passover at Easter. As the Apostle says, "*Christ our Passover is sacrificed* for us : therefore let us *keep the feast*" (1 Cor. v. 7).

We keep the *solemn feast* of Pentecost when we celebrate the Coming of the Holy Ghost at Whitsuntide. We keep the *solemn feast* of Tabernacles when we commemorate, in the season of Advent and at Christmas, the tabernacling of the Son of God in our flesh.

Well, therefore, might *S. Augustine* observe (De Civ. Dei, vii. 31), referring to this passage of Nahum, that "these words are said to the faithful of Judah, who belong to the New Testament, whose *solemn feasts* can never be superannuated and pass away, but are ever fresh as long as the world lasts."

In Holy Baptism we have a Spiritual Circumcision ; in the Holy Communion we feed on the true Paschal Lamb—"the Lamb of God which taketh away the sin of the World."

— *the wicked shall no more pass through thee*] The wicked (Hebr. *belial*) shall no more *pass through* thee. Nahum uses the word by which Isaiah describes the Assyrian army *passing through* Judah (Isa. viii. 8; xxviii. 15).

St. Paul adopts the word *Belial*, here used, and asks, "What concord has Christ with *Belial?*" (2 Cor. vi. 15) and leads us to recognize here a figure of Christ's enemies. "These words of rejoicing" (says *S. Jerome*) "may be addressed to the Church of Christ. Thine enemy is utterly cut off, Christ has come to thee. He Who formed thee from the dust, He Who, after His Resurrection, breathed into the face of His Apostles, and said to them, 'Receive ye the Holy Ghost' (John xx. 22), He it is, Who delivers thee from the enemy, who will no more pass through thee, Nineveh is destroyed. The World will pass away. Trouble and sorrow will pass away." These words may be applied also to every faithful soul which is delivered from the yoke of the Evil One. Cp. *v.* 13 ; and so *S. Cyril* and *Theodoret.*

CH. II. 1. *He that dasheth in pieces*] Rather, *the scatterer.* The prophet now turns to Nineveh, and announces her destruction. This was fulfilled by the combined forces of the Medes under Cyaxares, and of the Babylonians, probably under Nabopolassar, father of Nebuchadnezzar (*Herod.* i, 106). In the Book of Tobit (xiv. 15) that action is ascribed to Nabuchodonosor and Assuerus (Cyaxares). Cp. *Diod. Sic.* ii. 24—28,

Before
CHRIST
about
713.

b Jer. 51. 11, 12.
ch. 3. 14.
c Isa. 10. 12
Jer. 25, 29.
*f Or, the pride of
Jacob as the pride
of Israel*
d Ps. 80. 12.
Hos. 10. 1.

e Isa. 63. 2, 3.

*∥ Or, deep scarlet.*

*g Or, fiery torches.*

*† Heb. the shakes.*

*‡ Or, gallants.*

*† Heb. covering,
or, coverer.*

*∥ Or, molten.*

*¶ Or, that which
was established,
or, there was a
stand made:
‡ Or, discovered.
1 I. 35. 11 N
c² 11.*

²ᵇ Keep the munition, watch the way,
Make *thy* loins strong, fortify *thy* power mightily.

² ᶜ For the Lord hath turned away ∥ the excellency of Jacob,
As the excellency of Israel,
For ᵈ the emptiers have emptied them out,
And marred their vine branches.

³ The shield of his mighty men is made ᵉ red,
The valiant men *are* ∥ in scarlet :
The chariots *shall be* with ∥ flaming torches in the day of his preparation,
And the fir trees shall be terribly shaken.

⁴ The chariots shall rage in the streets,
They shall justle one against another in the broad ways :
† They shall seem like torches,
They shall run like the lightnings.

⁵ He shall recount his ∥ worthies :
They shall stumble in their walk ;
They shall make haste to the wall thereof,
And the † defence shall be prepared.

⁶ The gates of the rivers shall be opened,
And the palace shall be ∥ dissolved.

⁷ And ∥ Huzzab shall be ∥ led away captive,
She shall be brought up,
And her maids shall lead *her* as with the voice of ᶠ doves, tabering upon their
breasts.

---

whose narrative is derived from the Assyrian history of *Ctesias*, (see *Ctesiæ* Reliquiæ, pp. 426—440, ed. Bachr, Frankf. 1824) *Josephus*, Ant x. 22 ; and x. 5. 1. Cp. *Bp. Newton* on the Prophecies, Dissertation IX ; *Marcus v. Niebuhr*, pp. 39, 200, 466, who assigns the date B.C. 605 to that event, *Eb-Ers*, Handbuch, i. 206, places it in B.C. 610. See also *Duncker*, Geschichte, i. 316 ; *Keil* on the Lesser Prophets, pp. 390—500 ; and *Rawlinson*, Anc. Monarchies, ii. 520 ; iii. 188—195. The prophecy expands from Nineveh's fall to that of ANTICHRIST.

2 *For the Lord hath turned away the excellency of Jacob.* Rather, *the Lord restoreth the excellency of Jacob* (*Targum, Talg., Syriac, Kleinert*).

— *the emptiers*] *Spoilers* ; i.e. the Assyrians.

— *marred*] Destroyed.

— *their vine branches*] The branches of the Vineyard of the Lord. Cp. Isa. v. 1. Therefore the Lord interferes to restore them.

3. *The shield of his mighty men is made red.* The shield of the Lord's *mighty men* (those sent by Him against Nineveh, the Medes and Babylonians) is *made red* with vermilion, to inspire terrors (*Dewsius*).

— *scarlet*] The Oriental military cloak (*sagum*). The Prophet is describing the dress of the Median and Babylonian captains coming against Nineveh (*Grotius, Kleinert*).

— *flaming torches*] Or flashings, as of steel (*Fuerst*, 1141).

— *his preparation*] Or, *his equipment*, i.e. of the Lord's army.

— *fir trees. Cypresses* ; i.e. the spears, made of cypress wood, shall be brandished terribly by thy foes.

4. *They shall seem like torches*] The chariots of the Assyrians, as seen in the monuments of Nineveh, blaze with shining weapons, and the horses are caparisoned with red, and the poles are bright with metallic suns and moons ; the charioteers riding in them would also be bright in splendid armour, so that in their rapid motion they would have the appearance of flames and dashes of lightning (*Strauss, Kleinert, Layard*). See the engravings in *Rawlinson*, i. 294, 368, 429 ; ii. 2, 8, 11, 13, who observes (iii. 438) that the Babylonian chariots resembled the Assyrian. Cp. Hab. i. 7, 8. Jer. iv. 13.

5. *He shall recount his worthies : they shall stumble in their walk.*] The King of Assyria will muster his mighty men ; but they will be panic-stricken, and will totter and stumble

in their march, perhaps also reeling through intemperance. See on i. 10.

— *the defence shall be prepared*] The moveable tower, covered over for the protection of the soldiers working the catapult, for the projection of the missiles against the besieger. Cp. *Rawlinson*, ii. 78—83, where is a description of the covered towers, and battering-rams, and balistæ, used by the Assyrians in offensive warfare. Doubtless they had similar engines for defence.

6. *The gates of the rivers shall be opened*] The gates or sluices of the canals shall be opened by the enemy to let in a flood of water, in order to inundate the city (*Diod. Sic.* ii. 25—58; *Vatablus*. Cp. *Rawlinson*, iii. 191—193). On the fortifications of Nineveh, by means of its walls, and also by its water, canals, and moats, from the Khosru, which flows into the Tigris from the north-east, see *Layard*, Nineveh, p. 660; *Rawlinson*, i. 325 ; and the plan there, p. 316.

"There was an ancient prophecy," says *Diodorus* (ii. 26), "that Nineveh should never be taken till its river became an enemy to the city." It is a singular fact, that the rivers Tigris and Euphrates, which were the causes of the wealth and power of Nineveh and Babylon, and in which they trusted and exulted as their strength and glory, were turned into means for their destruction. So it will be with all worldly Ninevehs and Babylons, which rely on themselves, and resist God. The rivers of strength and wealth in which they trust, and of which they boast, will become the instruments of their destruction.

— *the palace shall be dissolved*] By the inundation. Compare *Diod. Sic.* ii. 27, who says that the city was overwhelmed by the bursting-in of the Tigris.

7. *Huzzab shall be led away captive*] Huzzab is a symbolical name for Nineveh, as *Sheshach, Pekod*, and *Merathaim* were for Babylon (see above, on Jer. xxv. 26; l. 21 ; li. 41. Ezek. xxiii. 23), and was formed or adopted by Nahum for the purpose of describing its character. *Huzzab* means *established, set firm* (Gen. xxviii. 12), and confident in its strength ; from *natsab, to set, to fix* (*Fuerst*, 915 ; *Gesen*, 560 ; *A Lapide* here). The sense is, that Nineveh, which seemed to be strongly rooted as a fortress on a rock, will be shaken, dismantled, and laid bare, and be stripped of its strength, and *be brought up*, or *be torn up*, and carried away captive.

— *her maids shall lead her*] Rather, *her maids shall be*

[8] But Nineveh *is* || of old like a pool of water :
   Yet they shall flee away,
   Stand, stand, *shall they cry* ; but none shall || look back.
[9] Take ye the spoil of silver, take the spoil of gold :
   || For *there is* none end of the store *and* glory out of all the † pleasant furniture.
[10] She is empty, and void, and waste :
   And the [g] heart melteth, and [h] the knees smite together,
   [i] And much pain *is* in all loins,
   And [k] the faces of them all gather blackness.
[11] Where *is* the dwelling of [l] the lions,
   And the feeding place of the young lions,
   Where the lion, *even* the old lion, walked,
   *And* the lion's whelp, and none made *them* afraid ?
[12] The lion did tear in pieces enough for his whelps,
   And strangled for his lionesses,
   And filled his holes with prey,
   And his dens with ravin.
[13] [m] Behold, I *am* against thee, saith the LORD of hosts,
   And I will burn her chariots in the smoke,
   And the sword shall devour thy young lions :
   And I will cut off thy prey from the earth,
   And the voice of [n] thy messengers shall no more be heard.
III. [1] Woe to the † [a] bloody city ! it *is* all full of lies *and* robbery ;
   The prey departeth not ;
[2] The noise of a whip, and [b] the noise of the rattling of the wheels,
   And of the pransing horses, and of the jumping chariots.
[3] The horseman lifteth up both † the bright sword and the glittering spear :

*Before* CHRIST *about* 713.
[ Or, *from the days that she hath been.*
[ Or, *cause them to turn.*
[ Or, *and their infinite store, &c*
† Heb. *vessels of desire.*

g Isa. 13. 7, 8.
h Dan. 5. 6.

i Jer. 30. 6.

k Joel 2. 6.

l Job 4. 10, 11.
Ezek. 19. 2—7.

m Ezek. 29. 3. & 38. 3. & 39. 1.
ch. 3. 5.

n 2 Kings 18. 17, 19. & 19. 9, 23.
† Heb. *city of bloods.*
a Ezek. 22. 2, 3. & 24. 6, 9.
Hab. 2. 12.
b Jer. 47. 3.

† Heb. *the flame of the sword, and the lightning of the spear.*

*sighing* or *sobbing* (*Gesen.* 536; *Fuerst*, 909), cooing sadly, like doves (cp. Isa. xxxviii. 14; lix. 11), *tabering*, i. e. smiting with their beaks on *their breasts* as upon timbrels (Ps. lxviii. 25), and thence producing a dirge-like sound. Cp. Luke xviii. 13 ; xxiii. 27, on the action of beating the breast in lamentation. Nineveh is compared to a Queen: her people and allies are like her handmaidens, who mourn with her and for her.

**8.** *But Nineveh is of old like a pool of water*] Rather, *And Nineveh has been like a pool* (Heb. *beréçah*, whence Spanish *Alberca*, through the Arabic) *or reservoir of water all her days.* The words *pool of water* are not here used in a bad sense, but in a good. The word *beréçah* is applied to the pool of Siloam, and of Gihon, and other royal pools at Jerusalem. See Neh. ii. 14 ; iii. 15. Eccl. ii. 6. Isa. vii. 3 ; xxii. 9, 11; xxxvi. 2, which, especially in hot and dry countries, were of great beauty and value.

The sense is, that Nineveh has been all her days a fair and richly-adorned reservoir, to which streams of many nations have flowed in commercial relations with her, and in tributary subjection to her (as *S. Jerome* well says : " Ninive tantos nutrierat populos, ut piscinarum aquis compararetur." Cp. *Rawlinson*, ii. 179—183, on the extensive commerce of Nineveh) ; but now they *shall flee* (like water flowing away), and shall not listen to her cry for succour, "Stand ye ;" and she shall be left like a dry and broken cistern.

In a somewhat similar manner the mystical Babylon is said in the Apocalypse to sit on *many waters,* which are *peoples, multitudes, and nations* (Rev. xvii. 1. 15) ; but they will all fail her in the hour of her distress (Rev. xviii. 10).

**9.** *Take ye the spoil*] This is said to the Babylonian invaders of Nineveh (*S. Jerome*).

**10.** *the faces of them all gather blackness*] Words adopted from Joel ii. 6. Cp. Jer. xxx. 6.

91

**12.** *The lion*] An Assyrian emblem of strength, and even of divinity, as seen in the Assyrian monuments. See *Rawlinson*, i. 173. The Man-Lion (there figured from *Layard*) was the emblem of Nergal, the Assyrian war-god.

The Lion was, in the language of prophecy, the fittest amongst animals to symbolize Assyria. The favourite national emblem—the Lion—was a true type of the people; blood and ravin are their characteristics in the mind of the Hebrew prophet (*Rawlinson*, i. 308).

*S. Jerome* interprets this in a figurative, as well as a literal sense, and says that " Leo Diabolus est " (1 Pet. v. 8), "et catulus Leonis, Antichristus."

**13.** *Behold, I am against thee*] Words repeated in iii. 5, and adopted by Ezekiel, and applied to Egypt (xxix. 3) and to Gog (xxxix. 1).

CH. III. **1.** *Woe to the bloody city*] Literally, *the city of bloods.* The savage temper, and sanguinary acts of Nineveh are recorded in her own history, written by herself, and still preserved in the cuneiform inscriptions recently discovered there. See some extracts from them above, in the notes on 2 Kings xvii. 4, 24; xix. 37, where Sargon, King of Assyria, father of Sennacherib, says, " I have ground to powder the nations, and have displayed the signs of my dominion to the four elements ;" and see, especially, the notes on 2 Chron. xxi. 1 ; and on Isa. x. 28—32; and xviii. 1.

**2.** *The noise of a whip*] The Prophet passes on to foretell the attack upon Nineveh by the confederate forces of the Medes and Babylonians ; he hears the cracking of the whips of their charioteers, and the rattling of the wheels) and the horses rushing to battle, and the chariots bounding over the plain ; and describes them with the vivid energy of poetic imagination.

**3.** *The horseman lifteth up both the bright sword*] The rider

And *there is* a multitude of slain, and a great number of carcases;
And *there is* none end of *their* corpses; they stumble upon their corpses:

<sup>4</sup> Because of the multitude of the whoredoms of the wellfavoured harlot,
     The mistress of witchcrafts,
That selleth nations through her whoredoms,
And families through her witchcrafts;

<sup>5</sup> "Behold, I *am* against thee, saith the Lord of hosts;
And <sup>e</sup> I will discover thy skirts upon thy face,
<sup>f</sup> And I will shew the nations thy nakedness,
And the kingdoms thy shame.

<sup>6</sup> And I will cast abominable filth upon thee,
And <sup>g</sup> make thee vile, and will set thee as <sup>h</sup> a gazingstock.

<sup>7</sup> And it shall come to pass, *that* all they that look upon thee <sup>i</sup> shall flee from
     thee, and say,
Nineveh is laid waste : <sup>k</sup> who will bemoan her ?
Whence shall I seek comforters for thee ?

<sup>8</sup>    <sup>l</sup> Art thou better than ‖ † populous <sup>m</sup> No,
That was situate among the rivers, *that had* the waters round about it,
Whose rampart *was* the sea, *and* her wall *was* from the sea ?

<sup>9</sup> Ethiopia and Egypt *were* her strength, and *it was* infinite ;
Put and Lubim were † thy helpers.

<sup>10</sup> Yet *was* she carried away, she went into captivity :

---

...king his horses *to mount upwards* (to the wall of the city), and the *flame of the sword and the flashing of the spear.*

4. *Because of the multitude of the whoredoms of the well-favoured harlot]* Nineveh professed love for other nations, and suggested to them that what she was doing was for their benefit, and was done in affection for them; and she allured and inveigled them by her crafty blandishments, as by magical arts, for her own benefit. Cp. Isa. xxiii. 17, where the same language is applied to the great commercial city, Tyre (*Abarbinel, Michaelis, M. Henry, Hengst., Keil*).

We have a specimen of this wily craftiness in Rabshakeh's speech to the Jews, in which he attempted to cajole and solace them from their allegiance to Hezekiah, by promises of temporal advantage to themselves (Isa. xxxvi. 16, 17).

The whoredoms of Nineveh (as Keil justly remark) are represented in this prophecy in that character, and not in the form of seduction to idolatrous worship; she is the emblem of godless, impious, and cruel worldly policy and power—in a word, of infidel Antichristianism. And in this respect she is distinguished from Babylon, the idolatrous form of seduction, and of rebellion against God. See Habak. ii. 18—20.

One of the worst features in the character of the Assyrians was their treachery. See v. 1; and Isa. xxxiii. 1. They were notorious as covenant-breakers (*Rawlinson*, i. 305).

— *selleth nations]* Enslaves them. It was the policy of Assyria, after the capture of cities, to sell their inhabitants into slavery. See the Assyrian inscriptions specified above, on v. 1. In one of these (quoted in the notes on 2 Chron. xxxii. 1), Sennacherib boasts that he carried away more than 200,000 captives, old and young, male and female, from cities of Judah in the days of Hezekiah.

Upon the Assyrian bas-reliefs still preserved, are long files of men bearing their booty out of the captured towns; and carts laden with spoil, succeeded by long trains of captives; their hands manacled before, or behind their backs, and letters attached to their feet, and even rings passed through their lips. And in this abject guise they are brought into the presence of the Assyrian King. On some he proudly places his feet; some he pardons; a few he orders for execution; many he sentences to be carried into slavery. See *Rawlinson*, ii. 86, 87. On the cruel modes of execution practised by the Assyrians, see *ibid.* pp. 87, 88.

7. *Whence shall I seek comforters for thee]* Nahum the Prophet, whose name signifies *consoler*, was raised up by God to comfort Israel and Judah with this prophecy concerning the overthrow of Nineveh, and the destruction of their Assyrian

enemy, and their own deliverance from him; but there was no comfort for Assyria herself.

In a spiritual sense this may be applied to the Church and the World. The Church has the divine promise of the perpetual presence of the *Comforter* (see John xiv. 16); but where will hereafter be any comfort to the worldly Ninevehs and their mighty men, who rebel against God and persecute His Church? They will cry, and cry in vain, to the hills to cover them.

8. *Art thou better than populous No?]* Rather, *Art thou better than No-Amon!* that is, than the Egyptian Thebes, the great city of Upper Egypt, which was called *No-Amon*—i. e. the *dwelling-place* or *portion* of the Egyptian god *Amon*; and called by the Egyptians *P-amun*, the *house* or *temple* of *Amun*, who was worshipped there (*Herod.*, i. 182; ii. 42. *Diod. Sic.*, i. 45). It is mentioned by Jeremiah xlvi. 25; and Ezek. xxx. 14—16. See the notes there.

— *situate among the rivers]* Thebes was built on both sides of the Nile (*Strabo*, xvii. p. 816; *Poole*, in Smith, B. D. ii. 576).

— *Whose rampart was the sea]* The Nile. See Isa. xviii. 2; xix. 5. The Nile is still called a *sea* (*bahr*) by the Arabs; and when it overflows it is very like a sea.

9. *Ethiopia and Egypt were her strength]* See above, on Isa. xviii.—xx. where these two countries are represented as combined against Assyria, and conquered by it.

— *Put]* In Northern Africa, stretching to Mauritania. See on Gen. x. 6; and Ezek. xxvii. 10.

— *Lubim]* Libyans. See on Gen. x. 13.

— *thy helpers]* He addresses No-Amon, or Thebes.

10. *Yet was she carried away]* Egypt and Ethiopia also were overrun by Assyria herself; and many of the inhabitants of their cities were carried captive by the Assyrian conqueror Sennacherib; and he returned in triumph from his victorious campaign in those countries, and expected to take Jerusalem as an easy prey; but his career was checked there, and his army was destroyed in one night by the Angel of the Lord.

These facts may be gathered from the eighteenth, twentieth, and twenty-seventh chapters of Isaiah, and from the Assyrian inscriptions recently discovered, and quoted in the notes on those chapters. Cp. *Rawlinson*, Anc. Mon., ii. 416; *Oppert*, Inscr. des Sargonides, p. 27.

Isaiah himself was commanded to symbolize prophetically in his own person this captivity of Egyptians and Ethiopians, whose King Tirhakah came forth to resist Sennacherib (Isa. xxxvii. 9). See Isa. xx. 3, "The Lord said, Like as my servant Isaiah hath walked naked and barefoot three years, for a sign

<sup>a</sup> Her young children also were dashed in pieces <sup>o</sup> at the top of all the streets:

And they <sup>p</sup> cast lots for her honourable men,

And all her great men were bound in chains.

<sup>11</sup> Thou also shalt be <sup>q</sup> drunken :

Thou shalt be hid,

Thou also shalt seek strength because of the enemy.

<sup>12</sup> All thy strong holds *shall be like* <sup>r</sup> fig trees with the firstripe figs :

If they be shaken, they shall even fall into the mouth of the eater.

<sup>13</sup> Behold, <sup>s</sup> thy people in the midst of thee *are* women :

The gates of thy land shall be set wide open unto thine enemies :

The fire shall devour thy <sup>t</sup> bars.

<sup>14</sup>    Draw thee waters for the siege,

<sup>u</sup> Fortify thy strong holds :

Go into clay, and tread the morter, make strong the brickkiln.

<sup>15</sup> There shall the fire devour thee ;

The sword shall cut thee off,

It shall eat thee up like <sup>x</sup> the cankerworm :

Make thyself many as the cankerworm,

Make thyself many as the locusts.

<sup>16</sup> Thou hast multiplied thy merchants above the stars of heaven :

The cankerworm ‖ spoileth, and fleeth away.

<sup>17</sup> <sup>y</sup> Thy crowned *are* as the locusts,

And thy captains as the great grasshoppers,

Which camp in the hedges in the cold day,

*But* when the sun ariseth they flee away,

And their place is not known where they *are*.

<sup>18</sup>    <sup>z</sup> Thy shepherds slumber, O <sup>a</sup> king of Assyria :

Thy ‖ nobles shall dwell *in the dust :*

---

and wonder upon Egypt and upon Ethiopia, so shall the king of Assyria lead away the Egyptians prisoners, and the Ethiopians captives, young and old, naked and barefoot, even with their buttocks uncovered, to the shame of Egypt" (Isa. xx. 3, 4).

Nahum here foretells the wonderful result, that the great Empire of Assyria, which a short time before the delivery of this prophecy had sent forth from Nineveh her mighty armies to overrun Egypt and conquer Thebes, will herself be spoiled by the invaders, and that Nineveh, her capital, be levelled with the dust. And so it came to pass.

**11.** *Thou also shalt be drunken*] From the cup of God's wrath (Jer. xxv. 17, 27. Obad. 16). As thou hast cruelly treated the Egyptians and Ethiopians, so wilt thou be treated by the Babylonians and Medes in return.

— *Thou shalt be hid*] Thou, who wast once so glorious, shalt be plunged in gloom. What a contrast between this description of Nineveh's fall and shame, and the vain-glorious boasting of Sennacherib, who marched forth from her gates to overrun Judah, Ethiopia, and Egypt, and conquered the two latter great nations, and then sent his messengers and his letters to vaunt his own invincibility and to blaspheme the living God! (Isa. xxxvi., xxxvii.)

So will it be hereafter with all Ninevehs—that is, with all the proud and infidel Powers of this World, which now glory in their might, and boast their own prowess, and vent words of defiance against the Most High, and oppress His Church.

**14.** *Draw thee waters for the siege*] O Nineveh, make preparations for filling thy cisterns, to provide thyself with water to drink during the siege: as Hezekiah did when thou didst besiege Jerusalem. Cp. on Isa. xxxvi. 2. 2 Chron. xxxii. 3, 4. 30. Ecclus. xlviii. 17.

— *Go into clay—brickkiln*] Make bricks for thy fortification.

**15.** *The fire*] Traces of fire may still be seen there (*Bonomi*).

**15.** *cankerworm*] Literally, the *licker*. Hebr. *yélék*. Translated *caterpillar* Ps. cv. 34; and Jer. li. 14, 27; and *cankerworm* in Joel i. 4; ii. 25; and here v. 16.

**17.** *Thy crowned*] *Thy princes*. So Kimchi, Gesenius, Kleinert, and others; but *Vulg.* has, *thy mixed troops*, and so *Arabic*; and this seems to be the true sense, *thy crowd of mercenaries* (*Fuerst*, 832; and *Keil*), who are compared to a swarm of locusts.

In a spiritual sense, this may be applied, with S. Jerome, to the strange, heterogeneous medley, the "mixtus populus" of forces (which Ezekiel has represented under the name of the *army of Gog*; see on Ezek. xxxvii., xxxix.), who are combined together under the banner of Antichristianism.

**18.** *Thy shepherds slumber*] (Hebr. *nâmu*) *have fallen asleep* in death. See on Isa. xxxvii. 36; and Ps. lxxvi. 1—12, where the same word (*nâmu*) occurs, v. 6. The destruction of the army of Sennacherib before Jerusalem, was like a prelude to the general destruction of the mighty men and of the countless hosts of Nineveh.

— *shall dwell*] Or, *are lying*. When all hope was lost, the King of Assyria, in a fit of desperation, committed suicide. Ctesias says (in *Diod. Sic.* ii. 25—28) that he burnt himself, with his concubines and eunuchs, and all his chief wealth, in his palace. Cp. *Rawlinson*, iii. 190—192.

Nahum's prophecy of the future destruction of Nineveh was fulfilled by the Medes and Babylonians (see above, on ii. 1); and, according to his prediction, the vast power of Nineveh completely vanished, and its glory was utterly eclipsed, so that in the year B.C. 401, Xenophon passed by the site without learning its name (*Xenophon*, Anab. iii. 4. 7). Four hundred years afterwards a small fortress was standing on the site, to guard the passage of the river Tigris (*Tacitus*, Ann. xii. 13), and opposite to it, on the west bank of the Tigris, has arisen

93

Ref. to
CHRIST
about
713.
b 1 Kings 22. 17.
† Heb. *wrinkling.*
c Micah 1. 9.
d Lam. 2. 15.
Zeph. 2. 15.
See Isa. 14. 8. &c.

Thy people is [b] scattered upon the mountains,
And no man gathereth *them*.
19 *There is* no † healing of thy bruise ; [c] thy wound is grievous :
[d] All that hear the bruit of thee shall clap the hands over thee :
For upon whom hath not thy wickedness passed continually ?

---

the city of Mosul. In the year 1776, Niebuhr visited the spot, and supposed that what were the heaps of ruins of Nineveh, were natural undulations in the soil (see the view in *Rawlinson*, i. 326). In more modern times it has been explored by Botta, the French Consul (in 1842), and more recently by Layard and others, who have brought to light those gigantic remains of palaces, statues, and other monuments which testify to the ancient grandeur of Nineveh, and those annalistic inscriptions which confirm the veracity of the prophecies of Nahum and of Isaiah, and of the historical narrative of Holy Scripture ; and bear witness to the divine foreknowledge of the HOLY GHOST, Who speaks in it ; to Whom with the FATHER and the SON, Three Persons and ONE GOD, be all honour and glory now and for evermore. AMEN.

# HABAKKUK.

I. [1] THE burden which Habakkuk the prophet did see.
[2] O Lord, how long shall I cry, [a] and thou wilt not hear?
Even cry out unto thee *of* violence, and thou wilt not save!
[3] Why dost thou shew me iniquity, and cause *me* to behold grievance?

---

The prophecy of HABAKKUK makes a pair with that of NAHUM. Both prophecies are called *burdens*; both are *visions* of the future. Nahum, the *comforter* (as his name signifies), consoles Israel, led captive by Assyria, with the assurance that the capital of that proud and cruel Empire would be overthrown by the Lord God of Israel, Whose universal sovereignty over the dynasties of this World, and Whose righteous attributes and tender regard for His exiled people, would then be declared; and that they would be delivered from the heavy yoke which pressed upon them.

Such is the literal sense of that prophecy; and in a spiritual sense it belongs to all time, especially to the last days of the World, and foretells that all haughty, infidel, and godless forms of Antichristianism will be eventually overthrown, and that the Church of God will be comforted by the Love of her Divine Lord and Saviour, to Whom all power in heaven and earth is given (Matt. xxviii. 18), and Who will make all His enemies His footstool (Ps. cx. 1. Matt. xxii. 44).

The Ten Tribes of Israel were carried captive by Assyria for their sins; but there was another proud and cruel Power, which was permitted, and indeed commissioned, by God, to chastise the other kingdom—that of Judah—which did not profit by the warnings of His wrath against idolatry, that had been displayed by the punishment of Israel, carried captive and dispersed by Assyria.

This was Babylon.

Babylon is displayed in Holy Scripture as the essence and type of all creature-worship, idolatry, and superstition, combined with a profession of much spiritual wisdom, and of a supernatural gift and ability to penetrate unseen mysteries, and to read the future; as evinced by its magical arts, its astrology, sorcery, and divination; and these characteristics were allied with vain-glorious vaunting of itself, its strong and magnificent city and vast extent of empire, consequent on the conquests of Assyria by Nabopolassar, and the successful campaigns of his son and successor, Nebuchadnezzar, in Asia and Palestine, where Jerusalem and Tyre had fallen before him; and in all the regions to the east and south-west of the Jordan, and in the land of the Pharaohs, who had been crushed by his victorious arms.

Habakkuk, the Levite (see iii. 19), who had ministered in the Temple of Jerusalem, was raised up by God to do the same work for Judah, with regard to Babylon, which Nahum the Elkoshite, of Galilee (Nah. i. 1), had done for Israel, with respect to the elder Empire of Asia—that of Assyria, which had fallen before the power of Babylon, and whose splendours had been eclipsed by its glory.

The name Habakkuk signifies a *loving embrace* (see Gesen. 258; Fuerst, 413, 414; Caspari on Micah, 31); and as *Nahum* was a *comforter* sent by God to console Israel, in captivity and affliction, so in *Habakkuk* (as *Luther* has suggested), we have a vision of God's *love, embracing* His people of Judah, whose captivity by the Chaldeans he foresees and foretells (i. 6). As *S. Jerome* says, "Prophetia" (Abacuc) "est contra Babylonem et regem Chaldæorum, ut quomodo prior Propheta Nahum, quem Abacuc sequitur, vaticinium habuit contra Nineven et Assyrios, qui vastaverunt decem tribus quæ vocabantur Israel, ita Abacuc prophetiam habet adversus Babylonem et Nabuchodonosor a quibus Juda et Jerusalem Templumque subversæ sunt."

"Both prophecies" (as *S. Jerome* also observes) "have a spiritual sense, and extend themselves to the last times." Both

are messages of consolation to the Church in her conflicts with Antichristianism, in two different aspects. Nahum comforts her with the assurance of the triumph of Christ over the Infidel form of Antichristianism. In Habakkuk God clasps His faithful people together to His own bosom, in a fatherly embrace of love, and assures them that the time is coming when they will have nothing to fear from the haughty pride, the vain-glorious boastings, the ambitious assumptions of universal Supremacy, and arrogant claims to Infallibility, and to divine knowledge in spiritual things; and that He will utterly destroy the fascinating superstitions and seductive Idolatries which are now the distinctive characteristics of the mystical Babylon, as displayed in the Apocalypse.

It may be observed that *Nahum* (the *comforter*) stands *seventh* in the order of the Minor Prophets; and *Habakkuk*, (the *embracer*) is *eighth*. *Seven* is the number of Rest after toil and distress. *Eight* is the number of Resurrection to *glory*. See above, on Ezek., p. 280. Nahum comforts us with a vision of rest; Habakkuk assures the faithful of a joyful embrace in the Kingdom of Glory, when their bodies will be raised and re-united to their souls, and they will embrace their friends and fellow-worshippers, and be embraced by God's love in Christ, in the Kingdom of Heaven. As *S. Jerome* says, we have "manifestissimam de Christo prophetiam in *octavo* Prophetâ, id est in *Resurrectionis dominicæ* numero" (*S. Jerome*, in cap. iii. prolog.).

Habakkuk prophesied in the reign of Josiah, probably near its close. He precedes Zephaniah, who foretold the fall of Nineveh (Zeph. ii. 13); for Zephaniah repeats thoughts and words of Habakkuk; see i. 7; cp. Hab. ii. 20), which took place a little before Josiah's death. See on 2 Kings xxiii. 29.

CH. I. 1. *burden*] See on Nahum i. 1.
— *did see*] So Nahum's prophecy is called a *vision*. As to the time of the vision, see ver. 5 and 6.

THE SINS OF JERUSALEM. ITS PUNISHMENT FORETOLD.

2. O LORD, *how long shall I cry*] Or, *how long have I cried, and thou heardest not!* O Lord God of Judah, how long have I cried to Thee concerning the wickedness of the people of Jerusalem, among whom I live? Dost Thou not observe these things? Wilt Thou not punish the proud and prosperous sinners, and deliver the righteous who are oppressed by them?

Yes (is the Lord's reply), I will bring the army of Babylon against the guilty princes of Jerusalem, and will punish them by the arms of the Chaldeans (*v.* 8).

Thus, at the beginning of his prophecy, Habakkuk protects the faithful people of Jerusalem against the notion that its future captivity would be due to the power of Babylon and her false gods; and teaches them to regard it as an act of God Himself, using the mighty empire of Babylon as His own vassal for doing His own work, in vindicating His own Majesty, and punishing offenders against His Law. Judgment must begin at the house of God; that is, at Jerusalem. But in order also to shew that the punishment of Jerusalem would not be inflicted by the power of Babylon independently of God, the Prophet further reveals that God's chastisements would extend to Babylon herself, because she would not take the warning which was given by the judgment executed by God on Jerusalem, for its idolatry and other sins, by her instrumentality.

3. *iniquity—grievance—strife and contention*] These are, as it were, personified by the Prophet, as they are by the Psalmist

For spoiling and violence *are* before me :
And there are *that* raise up strife and contention.

4 Therefore the law is slacked, and judgment doth never go forth :
For the " wicked doth compass about the righteous ;
Therefore ‖ wrong judgment proceedeth.

5 ' Behold ye among the heathen, and regard, and wonder marvellously :
For *I* will work a work in your days,
*Which* ye will not believe, though it be told *you.*

6 For, lo, " ‖ I raise up the Chaldeans, *that* bitter and hasty nation,
Which shall march through the † breadth of the land,
To possess the dwelling places *that are* not theirs.

7 They *are* terrible and dreadful :
‖ Their judgment and their dignity shall proceed of themselves ;

8 Their horses also are swifter than the leopards,
And are more † fierce than the " evening wolves :
And their horsemen shall spread themselves,
And their horsemen shall come from far ;
' They shall fly as the eagle *that* hasteth to eat.

9 They shall come all for violence :
‖ † Their faces shall sup up *as* the east wind,
And they shall gather the captivity as the sand.

10 And they shall scoff at the kings,
And the princes shall be a scorn unto them :
They shall deride every strong hold ;
For they shall heap dust, and take it.

---

(Ps. lv. 9, 10), "I have seen Violence and Strife in the city : Day and night they go about upon the walls thereof. Mischief also and Sorrow are in the midst of it. Deceit and Guile depart not out of her streets." The Prophet uses four words which the Psalmist had employed—*aven, amal, chamas, rib*—and in the same strain of complaint, for the sins of Jerusalem.

4. *the law is slacked*] Or benumbed, and paralyzed.

GOD ANSWERS THE PROPHET.

5. *Behold ye among the heathen, and regard*] Look forth, says Jehovah, *among the heathen;* for I will make use of a heathen nation (that of Babylon), the most powerful of all heathen nations) as My instrument for asserting My own righteous Majesty and vindicating My own holy Law and punishing the sins of My People, who defy the one and break the other.

These words are quoted by St. Paul, in his Sermon in the Jewish Synagogue, at Antioch in Pisidia ; "Behold, ye *despisers,* and wonder, and perish" (Acts xiii. 41). St. Paul's quotation is derived from the *Septuagint* (which is in harmony here with the *Syriac* and *Arabic*), and is, as has been before observed, a Paraphrase rather than a literal Version. See above, on Amos ix. 12. The Septuagint keeps the sense, but modifies the letter, of the Original. Instead of translating *bag-goyim* by, *among the Gentiles,* it adopts another rendering of it—O *despisers* (a rendering justified by the form of the word, as Dr. Pocock has shown, Not. Mis. in Port. Mos., Works, i. pp. 141—145); and instead of *be amazed,* the Septuagint has *vanish away* (or *perish*); that is, be stupefied by astonishment, and be confounded and faint away ; which is a justifiable rendering, and is authorized by Targum, Syriac, and Vulg. See Pocock, ibid., and Sacr. Arabes, Cavall. p. 427.

This passage of Habakkuk was very suitable to St. Paul's purpose. The Prophet is warning the Jews that they must expect a terrible retribution for faithlessness and disobedience to God. Precisely the same warning is addressed to them by the Apostle. The Prophet tells them that God would punish them with captivity and dispersion by the instrumentality of Heathen Babylon. Doubtless St. Paul, when he uttered those words, was looking forward to the similar punishments which

96

God would execute upon them by the hands of Rome (the Western Babylon), for like sins, and even more heinous, especially the sin of rejecting Christ and His Gospel.

6. *lo, I raise up the Chaldeans*] Behold, it is I, the God of Judah, Who do it. It is not done *by* the will and power of Babylon herself. Babylon is the servant of Jehovah. See Jer. xxv. 9, "I will send Nebuchadrezzar *My servant*;" and so in Jeremiah xxvii. 6 ; xliii. 10. God calls Nebuchadnezzar *My servant* for punishing Israel and Judah ; and He calls Cyrus *My shepherd,* for restoring them (Isa. xliv. 28). The punishment and the mercy both came from God.

— *Chaldeans*] A Semitic race, which dwelt from time immemorial in Babylonia, where they exercised the principal sway. (See Gen. xxii. 22. Isa. xxiii. 13 ; xliii. 14 ; xlvii. 1 ; xlviii. 14, 20. Jer. v. 15 ; xxi. 9 ; xxiv. 5 ; xxv. 12 ; xxxii. 4, 24. Ezek. xii. 13 ; xvi. 29 ; xxiii. 16, 23.)

7. *They are terrible and dreadful*] Rather, *terrible and dreadful is he.* The adjectives here, and pronoun, are in the singular number, and masculine gender. The nation is united and summed up in its Head.

— *Their judgment and their dignity shall proceed of themselves*] Or rather, *do proceed.* This verb, and the following verbs, would be better rendered in the *present* tense than in the future tense. The prophet says that the King of Babylon does not ascribe his power to God, as he ought to do, but arrogantly claims to be the source of his own pre-eminence.

This arrogance and vain-glorious impiety are exhibited in the speech of Nebuchadnezzar their King, for which he was smitten of God; "Is not this great Babylon, that I have built for the house of the Kingdom by the might of my power, and for the honour of my majesty ?" (Dan. iv. 30.)

8. *shall spread themselves*] Or rush forward.

9. *Their faces shall sup up as the east wind*] Or, more literally, the *gathering* of their faces is toward an east wind; i.e. for destruction (*Herald* ; cp. *Fuerst,* 760 ; cp. *Gesen.* 448).

— *the captivity a captivity* ; that is, hordes of captives.

10. *then shall heap dust, and take it*] Such is the case with which they storm and take a city. The raising an embankment against it is only like casting up a heap of dust, and the city falls before it.

Who enlargeth his desire ᵍ as hell,

And *is* as death, and cannot be satisfied,

But gathereth unto him all nations,

And heapeth unto him all people.

⁶ Shall not all these ʰ take up a parable against him,

And a taunting proverb against him, and say,

‖ Woe to him that increaseth *that which is* not his! how long?

And to him that ladeth himself with thick clay!

⁷ Shall they not rise up suddenly that shall bite thee,

And awake that shall vex thee,

And thou shalt be for booties unto them?

⁸ ⁱ Because thou hast spoiled many nations,

All the remnant of the people shall spoil thee;

ᵏ Because of men's † blood,

And *for* the violence of the land, of the city, and of all that dwell therein.

⁹ Woe to him that ˡ ‖ coveteth an evil covetousness to his house

That he may ᵐ set his nest on high,

That he may be delivered from the † power of evil!

¹⁰ Thou hast consulted shame to thy house by cutting off many people,

And hast sinned *against* thy soul.

¹¹ For the stone shall cry out of the wall,

And the ‖ beam out of the timber shall ‖ answer it.

¹² Woe to him that buildeth a town with ⁿ † blood,

And stablisheth a city by iniquity!

¹³ Behold, *is it* not of the LORD of hosts

ᵒ That the people shall labour in the very fire,

Before
CHRIST
about
626.

g Prov. 27. 20. &
30. 16.

h Micah 2. 1.

‖ Or, *Ho, he.*

i Isa. 33. 1.

k ver. 17.
† Heb. *bloods.*

l Jer. 22. 13.
‖ Or, *gaineth an
evil gain.*
m Jer. 49. 16.
Obad. 4.
† Heb. *palm of
the hand.*

‖ Or, *piece, or,
fastening.*
† Or, *witness
against it.*
n Jer. 22. 13.
Ezek. 24. 9.
Micah 3. 10.
Nahum 3. 1.
† Heb. *bloods.*
o Jer. 51. 58.

---

the former destroyed suddenly, the latter preserved to a good old age (Dan. i. 21; vi. 28).

— *enlargeth his desire*—*gathereth unto him all nations, and heapeth unto him all people*] Or, *peoples.* This was signally exemplified in the literal Babylon. See Dan. ii. 37, 38; iii. 4; iv. 1; Jer. xxvii. 7, 8; l. 23; li. 25.

May not this also be applied to the mystical Babylon, which sitteth as a Queen on many waters, "which are peoples and multitudes, and nations, and tongues," and requires that all should acknowledge her Supremacy? See below, on Rev. xvii. 1. 15. She too is intoxicated with pride, as was the literal Babylon. Her Sovereign King and Priest is now setting up a golden image (the idol of his own Supremacy and Infallibility) as Nebuchadnezzar did, who, like other Chaldean monarchs, united sacerdotal functions with royalty. She also has her Belshazzar's feast: her sins are like those of Babylon; and Babylon's doom will ere long be hers.

6. *Shall not all these take up a parable—a taunting proverb*] Habakkuk here adopts the words of Isaiah concerning Babylon (Isa. xiv. 4—" *Thou shalt take up this proverb against the King of Babylon, and say, How hath the oppressor ceased!*"), and connects his own prophecy of her fall with that of Isaiah.

— *ladeth himself with thick clay*] Or, *mass of dirt* (Hebr. *abtit*). So *Syriac* and *Vulg.*; but *Sept.* and *Arabic* render it *maketh his collar,* or yoke, to *press heavily.* The Hebrew word here used, *abtit,* occurs nowhere else, but seems to be connected with *abat,* to *knot together,* to *fasten;* and thence to lend, or borrow on a pledge (Deut. xv. 6. 8. *Fuerst,* 1006; *Gesen.*601.)

If we suppose the rendering in our Version to be correct, then the mention of *thick clay* (literally, *a cloud of clay*) derives additional interest from the fact that the city of Babylon was surrounded by enormous walls of clay ("coctilibus muris"). She deemed them to be impregnable (as Nebuchadnezzar boasts in his inscription still extant; cp. above, notes on Isa. xiii. 19; xiv. 21); yet they would be only like a grave for the burial of her glory.

On the whole, the rendering of *Sept.* and *Arabic* seems preferable. Babylon draws all nations to herself, and puts a

galling yoke and heavy burden on their necks. This is also true of the mystical Babylon. How different is her yoke and burden from the easy yoke and light burden of Christ! (Matt. xi. 29, 30.)

7. *Shall they not rise up suddenly that shall bite thee*] The Persian army, under Cyrus, *rose up suddenly* from the bed of the river of Babylon, the Euphrates, in which she gloried as the cause of her strength and wealth, and they rushed into the palace, and Babylon was taken in her hour of festal revelry, and Belshazzar was slain (*S. Jerome, Theophylact, Remigius*).

So will it be with the mystical Babylon, "In one hour shall her judgment come; in one hour shall her riches come to nought" (Rev. xviii. 10. 17). See above, the notes on Isa. xiii. 15—19; xiv. 1; xxi. 5. 8. 9. Jer. l. 1; and li. 30. 46, which may serve as a comment on this prophecy of Habakkuk concerning Babylon.

9. *That he may set his nest on high*] Cp. the language of Jeremiah, xlix. 16. Obad. 4; and the words of the King of Babylon himself, in Isaiah xiv. 14, where he says, "I will ascend above the heights of the clouds, I will be like the Most High;" and the words of the inscription written by Nebuchadnezzar himself, and quoted above on Isaiah xiv. 21, where he describes Babylon as impregnable; see also the note there on v. 14.

11. *the stone shall cry out of the wall*] This was literally fulfilled when the fingers of a man's hand came forth and wrote the doom of Babylon on the wall of the palace in which the kings of Babylon so much gloried (see the inscription referred to in the foregoing note), and in which one of them was feasting, on the anniversary of the festival of his god (Dan. v. 5—30).

12. *buildeth a town with blood*] Words adopted from Micah iii. 10.

13. *is it not of the* LORD—*the people shall labour in the very fire*] Rather, *Is it not the Lord's doing that the people*—i. e. nations like Babylon—*shall labour for the fire?*—i. e. to supply food for fire. Cp. Neh. ii. 13. Jer. li. 58, where the same words are applied to Babylon; see the note there.

This was literally fulfilled. The Babylonians baked bricks for immense walls which they thought would never be stormed,

| | |
|---|---|
| Before<br>CHRIST<br>about<br>626.<br>§ Or. in vain?<br>‖ Or. by knowing<br>the glory of the<br>LORD.<br>p Isa. 11. 9.<br>q Hos. 7. 5.<br>r Gen. 9. 22.<br>‖ Or. more with<br>shame than with<br>glory.<br>s Jer. 25. 26, 27.<br>& 51. 57.<br><br><br><br><br><br><br>t ver. 8.<br><br><br><br>u Isa. 44. 9, 10<br>& 46. 7.<br>x Jer. 10. 8, 14.<br>Zech. 10. 2.<br>† Heb. *the*<br>*fashioner of his*<br>*fashion.*<br>y Ps. 115. 5.<br>1 Cor. 12. 2.<br><br><br>z Ps. 135. 17.<br><br>a Ps. 11. 4.<br>† Heb. *be silent*<br>*all the earth*<br>*before him.*<br>b Zeph. 1. 7. Zech. 2. 13. | And the people shall weary themselves ‖ for very vanity?<br>14 For the earth shall be filled ‖ with the ᵖ knowledge of the glory of the LORD,<br>As the waters cover the sea.<br>15 Woe unto him that giveth his neighbour drink,<br>That puttest thy �q bottle to *him,* and makest *him* drunken also,<br>That thou mayest ʳ look on their nakedness!<br>16 Thou art filled ‖ with shame for glory:<br>ˢ Drink thou also, and let thy foreskin be uncovered:<br>The cup of the LORD's right hand shall be turned unto thee,<br>And shameful spewing *shall be* on thy glory.<br>17 For the violence of Lebanon shall cover thee,<br>And the spoil of beasts, *which* made them afraid,<br>ᵗ Because of men's blood, and for the violence of the land,<br>Of the city, and of all that dwell therein.<br>18 ᵘ What profiteth the graven image that the maker thereof hath graven it;<br>The molten image, and a ˣ teacher of lies,<br>That † the maker of his work trusteth therein, to make ʸ dumb idols?<br>19 Woe unto him that saith to the wood, Awake;<br>To the dumb stone, Arise,<br>It shall teach!<br>Behold, it *is* laid over with gold and silver,<br>ᶻ And *there is* no breath at all in the midst of it.<br>20 But ᵃ the LORD *is* in his holy temple:<br>†ᵇ Let all the earth keep silence before him. |

and for lofty palaces in which they hoped to reign gloriously; but all the labour of Babylon was only like fuel for the fire which was kindled by the Persian invaders and by which her glory was consumed. See the notes on Isa. xlvii. 14. Jer. li. 30, 32.

So it will also be with the mystical Babylon, the City and Church of Rome. See below, on Rev. xvii. 16; xviii. 18.

**14.** *the earth shall be filled—sea*] Words adopted from Isa. xi. 9. The Earth will not only be filled with *the glory of the* Lord (as it is in Isaiah), but with the *knowledge* of it. Men will *recognize* it. It will be filled with that knowledge, as the sea is covered with waters, which lie deep, spread far, and will never be dried up. Such is the knowledge of the glory of God in the face of Jesus Christ revealed in the Gospel (2 Cor. iv. 6). Such was the knowledge of His glory, manifested by the sudden destruction of Babylon, and the miraculous deliverance of His people (Ps. cxxxi. 1, 2). They who will not see God's glory in His mercy, will be compelled to own it in His judgments.

Habakkuk here describes the result of the overthrow of Babylon, and of all Powers that resemble it. Isaiah represents it as a consequence of the preaching of the Gospel of Christ. Destruction of error, and diffusion of the Truth—both are requisite for filling the Earth with the glory of the Lord.

Such will also be the result of the destruction of the mystical Babylon. It will give a great impulse to the spread of the Gospel.

**15, 16.** *Woe unto him that giveth his neighbour drink*] The Babylonians were notorious for their intemperance (*Curtius,* v. 1). Their religious festivals were celebrated with dissolute intemperance, even in the temples themselves (see *Rawlinson,* iii. pp. 464, 465); and, as a fit punishment for these sins, Babylon was taken at a religious festival and a time of revelry (Dan. v. 1. 30). Then God gave to her the cup of His wrath (*v.* 16). Cp. Jer. xxv. 27; and li. 57. Lam. iv. 21, concerning Babylon.

The mystical Babylon allures the nations, and intoxicates them with wine from the golden chalice of her false doctrines and alluring idolatries (Rev. xvii. 14); and she will be made to drink, in her turn, of the cup of the wrath of God (Rev. xvi. 19; xviii. 6).

**17.** *the violence of Lebanon shall cover thee*] The violence done by thee to Lebanon, the mountain of Israel, and the type of Israel's glory (see Jer. xxii. 6, 23. Isa. xxxv. 2), will be made to cover thee with shame. Isaiah says that at the fall of

Babylon the cypresses and cedars of *Lebanon* rejoiced. See Isa. xiv. 8, and the note there on *v.* 14, where it is shown from the King of Babylon's own words, that he made havock with the cedars and cypresses of *Lebanon,* to adorn the buildings of his own city. So the violence done by Rome to the true Church of Christ will recoil upon herself.

— *the spoil of beasts*] Hunted by thee. Cp. *Rawlinson,* iii. 438.

— *Because of men's blood, and for the violence*] On account of the blood shed by thee, and on account of the violence done by thee to land and city, and all that dwell therein.

**18.** *What profiteth the graven image—the molten image*] This is the climax of Babylon's sins—idolatry. Here also the prophet Habakkuk follows Isaiah, speaking of Babylon (xliv. 9, 10, 20), "Who hath formed a molten image that is *profitable for nothing—Is there not a lie in my right hand?*" Cp. xlvi. 1, 2, 6—8; and note there.

So the mystical Babylon will find in the day of her trial, that all her objects of will-worship will be of no avail to save her from the anger of a jealous God, Who will not give His honour to another; and Who said to the Evil One, the author of idolatry, "Get thee behind Me, Satan; for it is written, Thou shalt worship the Lord thy God, and Him only shalt thou serve" (Matt. iv. 10).

— *a teacher of lies*] The *teacher of lies* is here contrasted with the *Teacher of righteousness,* Joel ii. 23, which is Christ.

**19.** *Arise, it shall teach!*] Rather, Arise, Shall it teach? The antithesis is to be marked thus:—

> *Woe unto him that saith to the wood, Awake!*
> *To the dumb stone, Arise!*
> *Shall it teach?*

So *Vulg.* Cp. Isa. xliv. 9—20.

**20.** *the LORD is in his holy temple: let all the earth keep silence before him*] The Lord revealed Himself in His holy temple to Isaiah, who heard the Seraphim cry one to another, saying, "Holy, holy, holy, is the Lord of Hosts; the whole Earth is full of His glory" (Isa. vi. 3). Cp. Zeph. i. 7. "Hold thy peace at the presence of the Lord." Z ch. ii. 13, "Be silent, O all flesh, before the Lord. He is raised up out of His holy habitation."

In a spiritual sense, this is to be applied to the City and

III. ¹ A prayer of Habakkuk the prophet ª ‖ upon Shigionoth.

² O LORD, I have heard † thy speech, *and* was afraid :

O LORD, ‖ ᵇ revive thy work in the midst of the years,

In the midst of the years make known ;

In wrath remember mercy.

³ God came from ‖ Teman,

ᶜ And the Holy One from mount Paran.    Selah.

His glory covered the heavens,

And the earth was full of his praise.

⁴ And *his* brightness was as the light ;

He had ‖ horns *coming* out of his hand :

And there *was* the hiding of his power.

Before
CHRIST
about
626.
a Ps. 7, title.
‖ Or, according to
variable songs,
or, tunes,
called in Hebrew,
Shigionoth.
† Heb. thine report,
or, thy hearing.
‖ Or, preserve
alive.
b Ps. 85, 6.
‖ Or, the south
c Deut. 33. 2.
Judg. 5. 4.
Ps. 68. 7

‖ Or, bright beams
out of his side.

---

Temple of the Spiritual Zion, Christ's Holy Catholic Church, to which He has promised His presence, "even unto the end of the world" (Matt. xxviii. 20), and Who has this name, *Jehovah Shammah*—i.e. "The Lord is there." See Ezek. xlviii. 35.

CH. III. 1. *A prayer of Habakkuk the prophet upon Shigionoth.*] This is a *prayer* (Hebr. *tephillāh*), like Ps. xvii.; lxxxvi.; xc.; cii.; cxlii., which are the only places where this word (*tephillāh*) occurs in the titles of the Psalms.

It is a prayer, and it is also *upon Shigionoth*—that is, it is a prayer of an impassioned, literally, of an *erratic* strain; from *shagah*, to err; like the Psalm called *shiggaion* (Ps. vii.), characterized by vehement emotions and sudden transitions; as a magnificent lyrical ode, and a sublime and sacred dithyramb.

In this Prayer, which is also a Psalm, the Prophet reverts to the miraculous mercies of the Exodus, and of the wanderings in the wilderness, and of the triumphant march of Israel, under Joshua, into Canaan; and thence he derives a consolatory and cheering assurance, that, however God's people may for a time be tried by affliction, in the ruin of Jerusalem and the Temple, and in the captivity and exile at Babylon, and in the triumph of God's enemies over them; yet, if they turn to Him by repentance, wait patiently, and rely on Him with faith, the *vision will not fail*; but that God's love will manifest itself towards them, and His promises to Abraham will be fulfilled, and His might and majesty will be displayed in the overthrow of His enemies—especially such enemies as Babylon—and in the deliverance and restoration of His people from their captivity there; and much more in the deliverance of all true Israelites, by Christ, from the power of all their spiritual enemies, in the first coming of Christ in the flesh; and next, in the latter days; and, lastly, at His Coming in glory.

Therefore, whatever may happen, the Prophet declares his resolve thus—"I will rejoice in the Lord, I will joy in the God of my salvation" (v. 18).

Many ancient Expositors regarded the whole of this chapter as a triumphal Hymn, celebrating the victories of Christ. So *S. Augustine*, De Civ. Dei. xviii. 3, 4; *S. Jerome*, *Theodoret*, *Theophylact*, and others. There is a profound truth in that Exposition.

The Son of God was present with the people of God before His Incarnation, in the miracles of Egypt and of the Exodus, and in the mercies vouchsafed to Israel in the wilderness, as St. Paul has taught us (1 Cor. x. 4, 9. Heb. xi. 26). And this exposition opens to us a magnificent view of Christ, working in and for His Church in successive ages, even from the beginning to the end, when He will renew at once all the miracles of the Exodus and the deliverance from Babylon, and of the overthrow of the power of Egypt and Chaldea, and will sum up, as it were, all His might and majesty in that manifestation of His Presence and His Coming, when He will put all His enemies under His feet and receive His Church into glory.

2. *O* LORD, *revive thy work in the midst of the years*] So *Symmachus*, *Vulg.*, and *Theodotion*; *within the years*; literally, *in the inner years of years* (see il. 19, where the same word, *kěrěb*—derived from *kārab, to draw near*—is used), *within years*. So *Sept.*, and *Aquila*; "as years draw nigh."

As years pass on, do not delay, O Lord, to show Thy might and to revive Thy work of love and power, which Thou showedst to Thy People in the Exodus and in the wilderness. Do not defer it beyond *the appointed time*. See above, on ii. 3; *Lowth*, De Poes. Heb., p. 290.

There is a remarkable rendering here in the *Septuagint*,

*Syriac*, and *Arabic*: "*In the midst of the two animals thou wilt be known; when the years draw near thou wilt be recognized*.,

These words have been made the ground-work of the pictorial representations of the Infant Saviour in the stable at Bethlehem, lying between two animals, the Ox and the Ass. This translation, probably, arose from the interchange of *shenaim, two*, with *shānōth, years*; and of *chayyōth, animals*, with *chayyēhu, revive it*. This interpretation has been helped on by a mystical exposition of another prophetic passage (Isa. i. 3). "*The ox knoweth his owner, and the ass his master's crib*;" which have been applied in a figurative sense to Christ, the Lord of Creation, supposed to be recognized, even in His crib at Bethlehem, by irrational animals, while men slighted and despised Him; and this sense has been adopted in the Latin office for the Festivals of the Nativity and Circumcision, and is found as early as in writings of the fourth century; as in *S. Cyril Hierand.* Catechis. 12 ; *S. Jerome*, ad Eustoch., Epist. 27 ; and *S. Ambrose*, in Luc. ii. 7, from *Origen*, Hom. 13, in Luc.; and *S. Gregory of Nyssa*, and *S. Gregory Nazianzen*, Orat. in Nativit. See *Corn. a Lapide* here.

This interpretation, which has been so powerful in its influence on Christian Art, and so fruitful in its results, may be compared with that other interpretation in the *Vulgate*, of Exodus xxxiv. 29: "Moses ignorabat quod cornuta esset facies sua." See the note there.

— *remember mercy*] He does not say, Remember our merits; but, Remember thy own mercy (*M. Henry*).

3. *God (Eloah) came from Teman*] God came like a mighty warrior, in triumph and glory, from the land of Edom—the land of the enemies of Israel. Compare Obad. 9. Amos i. 12 ; and Deborah's Song, Judges v. 4, 5, "Lord, when Thou wentest out of Seir, when Thou marchedst out of the field of Edom ;" and the description of the Messiah coming from Edom, in Isa. lxiii. 1, "Who is this that cometh from Edom, with dyed garments from Bozrah ?" which displays Christ's victory over our spiritual enemies. (See the note).

In this splendid Epinicion, or song of victory, Habakkuk takes, as it were, the harp from the hand of Moses, who had sung a noble prelude to it in Deut. xxxiii.; and he also interweaves some notes from several of the historical Psalms, which describe God's victories in Egypt and in the Exodus, and in the passage through the Red Sea, and the crossing of the Jordan ; and such as Ps. xviii. and lxviii.; and also from the Book of Joshua, and the Song of Deborah (Josh. x. 12, 13. Judges v.: see the references in the Margin); and he makes them to culminate and burst forth at last in a grand Hallelujah to CHRIST.

— *from mount Paran*] At the north of Sinai. See Deut. xxxiii. 2. The glory of the Divine Presence coming to Sinai, filled the northern horizon from Edom to Paran. Num. x. 12.

— *Selah*] See on Ps. iii. 2.

— *his praise*] His brightness and glory.

4. *horns*] See the note on Exod. xxxiv. 29, 30, and Deut. xxxiii. 2, "From His right hand went a fiery *Law* for them ;" the Law of the Two Tables, perhaps resplendent with glory. Rays of glory beamed forth, like antlers of light, not only from His face, but His hands. His works are glorious, and shine in radiant emanations and brilliant coruscations of love to Israel. The *power* was *within*; it was dark with excess of light, and could not be seen and gazed upon by human eye (cp. Exod. xx. 21. 1 Kings viii. 12); but it gleamed forth in splendour on the world in the Incarnation of Christ. See John i. 18.

Before
CHRIST
about
626.

c Nahum i. 3.
d Or, *burning*
*coals*.
Vent. [?]. 14.
e Ps. 18. 8.
f Nahum i. 5.
g Gen. 49. 26.

i Or, *Ethiopia*.
‖ Or, *under*
*affliction*, or,
*vanity*.

h Deut. 33. 26, 27.
Ps. 68. 4. &
104. 3.
ver. 15.
‖ Or, *thy chariots*
*were salvation?*

[ Or, *Thou didst*
*cleave the rivers*
*of the earth.*
i Ps. 78. 15, 16.
& 105. 41.
k Exod. 19. 16,
18.
Judg. 5. 4, 5.
Ps. ch. 8. &
77. 18. & 114. 4.
l Exod. 14. 22.
Josh. 3. 16.
ra Josh. 10. 12, 13.

‖ Or, *thine*
*arrows walked in*
*the light, &c.*
n Josh. 10. 11.
Ps. 18. 14. &
77. 17, 18.

o Jer. 51. 55.
Amos 1. 5.
Micah 4. 13.

5 <sup>d</sup>Before him went the pestilence,

And ‖ <sup>e</sup>burning coals went forth at his feet.

6 <sup>f</sup>He stood, and measured the earth:

He beheld, and drove asunder the nations;

<sup>f</sup>And <sup>g</sup>the everlasting mountains were scattered,

The perpetual hills did bow:

His ways *are* everlasting.

7 I saw the tents of ‖ Cushan ‖ in affliction:

*And* the curtains of the land of Midian did tremble.

8 Was the LORD displeased against the rivers?

*Was* thine anger against the rivers?

*Was* thy wrath against the sea,

<sup>h</sup>That thou didst ride upon thine horses *and* ‖ thy chariots of salvation?

9 Thy bow was made quite naked,

*According* to the oaths of the tribes, *even thy* word.　　Selah.

‖ <sup>i</sup>Thou didst cleave the earth with rivers;

10 <sup>k</sup>The mountains saw thee, *and* they trembled:

The overflowing of the water passed by:

The deep uttered his voice,

*And* <sup>l</sup>lifted up his hands on high.

11 <sup>m</sup>The sun *and* moon stood still in their habitation:

‖ At the light of thine <sup>n</sup> arrows they went,

And at the shining of thy glittering spear.

12 Thou didst march through the land in indignation,

<sup>o</sup>Thou didst thresh the heathen in anger.

13 Thou wentest forth for the salvation of thy people,

---

5. *pestilence*] In Egypt; and on His own People, when disobedient (Num. xi. 33; xiv. 37; xvi. 16; xxxi. 16).

6. *He stood, and measured the earth*] Rather, He *stood, and shook the earth* (*Targum*, and so in substance, *Sept.* and *Arabic*, and *Gesenius, Delitz., Keil*). If the rendering *measured* is retained, then the reference is to the portioning out of Canaan by Joshua to the Tribes.

— *and drove asunder*] He agitated. He *made to tremble*. Cp. Nahum i. 5.

7. *Cushan—Midian*] Enemies of God and Israel. Ethiopians and Midianites, who trembled with fear when they heard of God's acts at the Exodus. Cp. Exod. xv. 14—16.

8. *Was the* LORD *displeased against the rivers?*] Was Thy wrath against the floods of the Red Sea and the Jordan, which Thou caudist to flee before Thee? See Ps. cxiv. 5, "What ailed thee, O thou Sea, that thou fleddest, and thou Jordan, that thou wast driven back?" No; Thy anger was not against the billows of the Red Sea and the waves of Jordan; but against the proud surges of haughty enemies, raging and foaming against Thee and against Thy People.

— *thine horses and thy chariots of salvation*] Opposed to the horses and chariots of destruction, of Pharaoh and of all Egyptian-like enemies of the Israel of God. Cp. v. 15.

9. *Thy bow was made quite naked*] Being drawn forth out of its cover, and revealed in all its terrible grandeur. Compare the description of Christ as a mighty Archer, in Ps. xlv. 5, and in the Apocalypse (vi. 2). The Prophet is referring to Deut. xxxii. 40—42.

— *According to the oaths of the tribes, even thy word.*] This, on the whole, appears to be the true sense of the passage. In a lyrical composition like this, we ought not to be surprised by conciseness and abruptness of style. It is thus paraphrased in the *Targum*, "Thou didst reveal Thyself in Thy Power on account of the Covenant which Thy Word made with the Tribes" (of Israel) "for many generations." Cp. *Vulg.* here. *The oaths of the tribes* are the oaths sworn by God to the Tribes, even from the time of Abraham (in whose loins they were, Heb. vii. 10), to the days of Jacob, and afterwards of David. Cp. Num. xxvi. 5; xxx. 1; xxxii. 28; xxxvi. 9. Josh. xix. 51.

Kings viii. 1. 2 Chron. v. 5, where the same word is used for *tribes*; and compare also the reference to the oath sworn by God to Israel, and fulfilled in Christ (Luke i. 73, and Acts ii. 30); and the mention of *the tribes* in the New Testament (Acts xxvi. 7. James i. 1).

— *Thou didst cleave the earth with rivers*] He is proceeding to recount God's miracles of mercy to His People at Rephidim. Cp. Ps. lxxiv. 15, "Thou didst cleave the fountain and the flood;" Ps. lxxviii. 15, 16, "He clave the rocks in the wilderness, and gave them drink as out of the great depths. He brought streams also out of the rock, and caused waters to run down like rivers;" Ps. cv. 41, "He opened the rock, and the waters gushed out. They ran in the dry places like a river."

10. *The overflowing of the water passed by*] This was true, when the Jordan, which then overflowed its banks, was parted asunder, and part of it passed on to the Dead Sea, and the other part of it flowed very far back, to Adam, near Zaretan. See the description (which has often been misunderstood) in Josh. iii. 15, 16, and the note there on that passage.

11. *The sun and moon stood still*] He refers to the staying of the sunlight at the prayer of Joshua (the type of Jesus), at Gibeon (*Targum*), in order that Israel might be enabled to rout their enemies. See the note above, at Joshua x. 12, 13, on the true character of that miracle, and its typical significance.

— *At the light of thine arrows they went*] Thy People went unhurt and marched safely to victory, while their enemies,— the armies of Canaan,—were overthrown and destroyed.

He refers to the terrible storm of hailstones by which the kings of Canaan were discomfited at Beth-horon (Josh. x. 11). The Israelites were not injured by it, but *went on* in their career amid the storm.

12. *Thou didst march through the land*] With Joshua and the victorious army of Israel. The defeat of the Canaanites, their extermination, and the planting of the Tribes of Israel in their land, were Thy doings, O Lord.

— *Thou didst thresh the heathen*] See Micah iv. 13.

13. *for the salvation of thy people, even for salvation*

102

*Even* for salvation with thine anointed;

ᵖ Thou woundedst the head out of the house of the wicked,

† By discovering the foundation unto the neck. Selah.

¹¹ Thou didst strike through with his staves the head of his villages:

They † came out as a whirlwind to scatter me:

Their rejoicing *was* as to devour the poor secretly.

¹⁵ ᵠ Thou didst walk through the sea with thine horses,

*Through* the ‖ heap of great waters.

¹⁶ When I heard, ʳ my belly trembled;

My lips quivered at the voice:

Rottenness entered into my bones, and I trembled in myself,

That I might rest in the day of trouble:

When he cometh up unto the people, he will ‖ invade them with his troops.

---

*with thine anointed*] Rather, even *for the salvation of thine anointed.* So Sept., Syriac, Arabic, Targum. Israel is called God's son, His firstborn (Exod. iv. 22), and so was a type of Christ, as the Holy Spirit declares, quoting Hosea xi. 1, "Out of Egypt have I called *My Son*;" and applying it to *Christ* (Matt. ii. 15). "And Israel was a holy nation, a nation of kings and priests" (Exod. xix. 6); and so a type of the MESSIAH in His Eternal Kingdom and Priesthood. Compare Ps. cv. 15, and 1 Chron. xvi. 19, "When ye were but few, even a few, and strangers in the land; and when they went from nation to nation, and from one kingdom to another people, He suffered no man to do them wrong, yea, He reproved kings for their sakes"—a saying which may be referred not only to the Patriarchs, but to the Nation of Israel, for whose sake God chastened Pharaoh (Exod. vii. 15—18), saying "Touch not Mine anointed."

This, therefore, is a declaration that Israel, the type of Christ, was protected by God's mighty arm from the days of the Patriarchs to the time of the Prophet, and its enemies overthrown. Much more will God exert His power for the exaltation of Christ, and the overthrow of His enemies in the latter days.

— *Thou woundedst the head—neck*] Thou smotest the head of the house of the wicked, so as to destroy it; and thou layedst bare the foundation of the house, even to the neck, in which its strength lay. The neck is the emblem of dignity and power (see Cant. iv. 4, "Thy neck is like the tower of David"), and sometimes of stubbornness and pride (Deut. xxxi. 27. Ps. lxxv. 5. Isa. xlviii. 4).

This was done, when God smote the firstborn of the enemies of His People in Egypt, from the firstborn of Pharaoh on the throne, to the firstborn of the maidservant behind the mill (Exod. xi. 5; xii. 12. 29; xiii. 15); and God's People was delivered, and went free from the land of bondage.

It was done afterwards at Babylon, when the city was taken and the royal family exterminated, and another dynasty planted in its place. As God said by Isaiah (xiv. 22), "I will cut off from Babylon the name and remnant, and son and nephew" (grandson). "saith the Lord."

So will it be in the latter days. The pride and power of the mystical Babylon will be overthrown, as a millstone plunged in the deep, and she will be destroyed (Rev. xviii. 21); and the Israel of God, the faithful people of Christ, will then be delivered from her yoke.

There is a remarkable sentence in the Targum (or Paraphrase) of *Jonathan*: "The kingdom of Babylon will not remain, nor exercise dominion over Israel, the *Romans* will be destroyed, and not take tribute from Jerusalem. And, therefore, on account of the marvellous deliverance which Thou wilt accomplish for Thine Anointed, and the remnant of Thy People, they will praise the Lord."

14. *Thou didst strike through with his staves the head of his villages*] Rather, *of his rulers* (Sept., Syriac, Arabic, Gesen., Fuerst, Kleinert*). The Prophet uses a rare verb (*smattch*) which has the threefold sense of *staff, sceptre,* and *tribe* (Gesen. 466: see Exod. iv. 4. Ps. cx. 2. Isa. ix. 4; ix. 5. 21), and which is rendered *tribe* in v. 9, where see the note. It was a fortunate circumstance that it had this threefold sense; for he is here describing the royal dignity and the victorious power of the tribes of Israel, who have a princely and judicial character (see v. 13), and were enabled by God to overcome the inhabitants of Canaan.

103

The Holy Spirit, Who is here delivering a prophecy which reaches to "the time of the end" (ii. 3). is foretelling the triumph which will be achieved by Christ, the King and Leader of all the tribes of the spiritual Israel (cp. Rev. vii. 4), who partake in His royalty, being made kings by Him; see Rev. i. 6; v. 10. The sense is, " *Thou* smotest *with* the sceptred and judicial *tribes* of Thine Anointed One *the heads of his rulers.* The word here used is from *páraz,* or *parats,* to divide, to judge, to rule (Gesen. 683; Fuerst, 1151). They professed to rule—literally, to decide, to divide; but they themselves will be divided and cut asunder. Cp. on Daniel v. 28, speaking (as Habakkuk here does) of Babylon, "Thy kingdom is *divided.*"

— *They came out—secretly*] That is, the rulers of Babylon (mentioned in the foregoing clause) *came out like a whirlwind* to scatter me (to divide me, and cut me asunder), who am Thy people; and *their rejoicing was as to devour the poor secretly.*

Such also is the character also of the mystical Babylon. It glories in the *Head of its rulers,*—the "Episcopus Episcoporum," the "Rex Regum et Pater Principum," as the Bishop of Rome is publicly addressed in his Coronation in St. Peter's Church. He comes forth like a whirlwind, to scatter all before him, and to devour the humble and meek; but his destiny is, to be smitten by Christ (2 Thess. ii. 2—4).

15. *Thou didst walk through the sea*] The Exodus is ever present to the Prophet's eye, as the type of all victories of the Israel of God, past, present, and future; and it will be consummated at the great and glorious day, when the victorious tribes of the spiritual Israel, the redeemed of God, who have stood firm against the mystical Babylon, and triumphed over the *θαπίαρ,* will stand on the margin of the calm crystal sea, with harps of God in their hands, and will sing the Song of Victory of Moses, and of the Lamb. See below, on Rev. xv. 2, 3.

16. *When I heard, my belly trembled—I trembled in myself*] God's voice sounded *in* the Prophet. See above, ii. 1. I will stand and watch to see what He will say *in me.*

See the use of *belly* in John vii. 38, where the carnal man is represented as changed and spiritualized; and in the Apocalypse, the voice, which God had been uttering within him, makes the animal man (Rev. x. 9. 11: cp. Ezek. iii. 3) to tremble; and the very lips, by which he had uttered God's voice from within him, quivered; his limbs tottered under him, and he fainted with awe. Compare Daniel's condition in his ecstasy (vii. 28; viii. 27; x. 8. 9. 15; xii. 8).

## THE PROPHET'S FAITH, HOPE, AND JOY IN THE PROSPECT OF FUTURE TRIALS, AND FINAL TRIUMPHS OF THE CHURCH.

— *That I might rest in the day of trouble—troops*] Literally, *I who shall rest.* I trembled with awe and alarm at the prospect before me. It was revealed to me that *he cometh* (that is, the Babylonian invader will come) against my own country, city, and people,—against Jerusalem, her king, and nation, and *will cut and break in upon them* (Gesen. 157. Gen. xlix. 19. Ps. xciv. 21). I trembled at the thought of this; even I, who was assured that *I shall find rest in that day of affliction.*

But the Prophet corrects himself; he recovers his confidence and courage, and at length bursts forth into that noble ejaculation of faith which follows. He utters a clear profession of unswerving and unwavering faith, even in times of darkest gloom and of agonizing distress. "Although *the fig-tree shall*

<sup>17</sup> Although the fig tree shall not blossom,
Neither *shall* fruit *be* in the vines;
The labour of the olive shall † fail,
And the fields shall yield no meat;
The flock shall be cut off from the fold,
And *there shall be* no herd in the stalls:

<sup>18</sup> Yet I will ‘ rejoice in the LORD,
I will joy in the God of my salvation.

<sup>19</sup> The LORD God *is* " my strength,
And he will make my feet like <sup>x</sup> hinds' *feet*,
And he will make me to <sup>y</sup> walk upon mine high places.
To the chief singer on my † stringed instruments.

---

*not blossom, and there be no fruit in the vines,* although *the labour spent in the olive fails, and the cornfield yield no fruit; although the flock is cut off from the fold, and no or be in the stall, yet I will rejoice in the Lord; I will joy in the God of my salvation.*

The last words of this sentence in the *Vulgate* Version here are remarkable, "Exultabo in *Deo Jesu* meo."

In a spiritual sense, this prophecy may be applied, with *S. Jerome*, to evil days in the Church, when the fig-tree of the Visible Church, which ought to be fruitful, seems to be stricken with barrenness, and to bear only leaves, as was the case with Jerusalem in the days when our Lord visited her (Matt. xxi. 19, 20), and although the Vine, planted by God's own hand, may be unfruitful, as it was then. Cp. Isa. v. 1—4, and the similar imagery in Prov. xxvii. 23—27, and the note there. Cp. the beautiful application by *S. Cyprian* (ad Demetrian. 20).

This is our comfort in these latter days.

Although the Visible Church of God may seem to be like that leafy fig-tree, barren and unfruitful; and though iniquity may abound, and charity wax cold (Matt. xxiv. 12), and though the Faith may be hard to find (Luke xviii. 8); and though the fields of Christ's husbandry may seem to yield little fruit; though the oxen of the Christian ministry (1 Cor. ix. 9, 1 Tim. v. 18) may flag in their work; and though the sheep of His pasture may be faint with hunger and thirst—in a word, however unpromising may be the condition and the prospects of the Visible Church on Earth, yet the true Prophet of God, the devout and faithful Habakkuk, clasps God's Word to his bosom in a loving embrace (see *Prelim. Note*), and he clasps it more firmly, the more fiercely the winds of the tempest of the dark night rages and howls about him. The true believer will never despair nor despond. His heart will never lose its confidence and courage; nay, rather, the worse the state of things in the Church and the World may be, and the more all earthly succours fail, the more firmly will he trust in the Lord, the more fervently will he rejoice in the God of his salvation. He will be like Habakkuk looking forward to the temporary triumph of Babylon, and even to the overthrow of Jerusalem, and to the captivity of her king and her people, and looking beyond it to the overthrow of Babylon, and to the restoration of Judah by Cyrus; and looking far beyond that typical overthrow, and that figurative deliverance, to the destruction of all Babylonish pride, all Babylonish presumption, all Babylonish usurpation, and all Babylonish idolatry by the divine power of CHRIST, and to the everlasting victory and glory of all faithful Israelites in the heavenly city, "the Jerusalem which is above, which is free, and which is the mother of us all" (Gal. iv. 26).

**19.** *The LORD God is my strength—places*] The Prophet

takes up again the language of the song of Moses (Deut. xxxii. 13; xxxiii. 29), and also of David, the true King of Israel, when persecuted by Saul (Ps. xviii. 33). So the Church in her persecution flies to Him Who is her Rock (Matt. xvi. 18), and finds refuge and strength in Christ.

— *To the chief singer on my stringed instruments*] That is, the Precentor, who is accompanied by the instrumental music of the harp. He adopts the title of Ps. iv. (see the note there),—a Psalm of trust and joy, written in a time of affliction.

He says, "*my* stringed instruments," whence it has been justly inferred that Habakkuk was one of the Levitical tribe, whose office it was to take part in the choral services of the Temple at Jerusalem.

In this respect Habakkuk, the Levite and Prophet, takes his place by the side of the priest and prophet Jeremiah, and the priest and prophet Ezekiel. They all once ministered in the Temple at Jerusalem (see above, on Jer. i. 1. Ezek. ii. 1; and *Introd.* to Ezek., pp. 152—156; they foresaw and foretold its destruction by Babylon; and they are ever ministering comfort to all faithful people of the true Sion, by assurances of God's presence and help in time of affliction, and by visions of her future glory. See on Ezek. xl.—xlviii., pp. 274—289.

Though the harps of Israel were for a time to be hung on the willows by the side of the waters of Babylon, and though the sacred courts of the Temple, in which Habakkuk had chanted the hymns and psalms of its daily service were ruined, and the desolate site itself would no longer resound with the songs of Sion (Ps. cxxxvii. 1), and perhaps the Prophet himself may have been among the captives who wept in that far-off land; yet the prophecy would cheer him and all faithful Israelites in their exile; and they would wait with patience and faith for its fulfilment. This prophecy was a *prayer* on *Shigionoth* (see *v.* 1), and also a *psalm of Neginoth*. Such are the songs which are ever in the mouth of God's Church, "in the house of her pilgrimage." They are prayers of faith and hope, and also hymns of praise. And the day may not be far distant when "the appointed time" will arrive (ii. 3), and God will revive His work—His work of the Exodus, and His work of the overthrow of Babylon, and the deliverance of His People, in the *midst of the years*; and the harps of all true Israelites will then be taken down from the willows, and the songs of the stringed instruments will be heard in the courts of the heavenly Sion, and they themselves will stand on the margin of a "sea of glass,"—a sea once of trouble and storm, but now crystallized into an everlasting heavenly calm; and "they will be there harping with their harps," and singing "the song of Moses, the servant of God, and the song of the Lamb" (Rev. xiv. 2; xv. 2, 3), to Whom, with the Father and the Holy Ghost, be all honour and glory now and for ever.

# ZEPHANIAH.

Before
CHRIST
about
630
† Heb. By taking
away I will
make an end.
† Heb. the face
of the land.

I. ¹ THE word of the LORD which came unto Zephaniah the son of Cushi, the son of Gedaliah, the son of Amariah, the son of Hizkiah, in the days of Josiah the son of Amon, king of Judah.

² † I will utterly consume all *things* from off † the land, saith the LORD.

---

ZEPHANIAH—whose name signifies, Whom *the Lord covers*, or shelters, in times of storm and distress (*Gesen.* 716)—holds a remarkable place in the Hebrew Canon. He is the last of the Minor Prophets before the Captivity: he follows Nahum and Habakkuk; and his prophecy is linked on to that of the latter. It opens with repeating Habakkuk's exhortation to the whole Earth to stand in silent reverential awe before Jehovah (see Zeph. i. 7: cp. Hab. ii. 20), and to the faithful *to wait in patience* till the prophecy is fulfilled. Cp. Zeph. iii. 8; and Hab. ii. 3.

The contents of his prophecy correspond to his position.

It has a retrospective, and also a prospective character.

The two preceding prophets, Nahum and Habakkuk, had foretold respectively the overthrow of the two great Powers of the ancient World, hostile to God and His People—Assyria and Babylon; and had cheered Israel and Judah with hopes of deliverance from them. And they minister consolation to the Church in every age, and animate all true Israelites with the spirit of patient trust in Christ, that God will protect the Christian Sion in all her dangers (whether from Infidelity or Superstition), and rescue her from all her enemies.

Zephaniah takes a more comprehensive view. He sums up and recapitulates the predictions of all preceding prophecy, and concentrates them in the bright focus of one great and concise prophetic denunciation against the World, whether outside the visible Church, or within it, as far as it is opposed to Jehovah, the Lord God of Israel, and is hostile to His faithful People.

Zephaniah prophesied when the tempest which was driven down from the northern regions of Chaldea, and which had been long hovering over Jerusalem, was about to burst with terrible fury upon the City, the Monarchy, the Priesthood, the Princes, and the People. He had a mission of mercy in that time of trouble. As his name suggests, he comforted the faithful of Jerusalem and of every age with the cheering assurance that *Jehovah* will *hide* and shelter them in all storms, political or ecclesiastical, however black and boisterous. "Though an host should encamp against me, my heart shall not fear; though war should rise up against me, in this will I be confident." "In the time of trouble He shall *hide* me in His pavilion; in the secret of His tabernacle shall He hide me" (Ps. xxvii. 3, 5). "Oh, how great is Thy goodness, which Thou hast laid up for them that fear Thee. Thou shalt *hide* them in the secret of Thy presence from the pride of man. Thou shalt *keep them secretly* in a pavilion from the strife of tongues" (Ps. xxxi. 19, 20). In both these passages the Psalmist uses the word *tsaphan* (to hide, to keep secretly), which is the root of the name *Zephaniah* (*Tsephan-yah*, whom *Jah*, or *Jehovah*, *hides*). The Prophet himself explains the sense of his name, when he says to the meek and righteous, "Ye shall be *hid* in the day of the Lord's anger" (ii. 3).

In another respect Zephaniah's prophecy corresponds to his position. He is the last of the Minor Prophets before the Captivity. And he takes up and renews the work of the first of that goodly fellowship—HOSEA.

Hosea had comforted Israel with the assurance that their own *captivity and dispersion* would be overruled by God to promote His glory and their own future happiness. He had consoled them by saying that they would be weaned by it from their besetting sin idolatry, and from dependence on heathen nations, such as Assyria, which caused their rejection. And he had cheered them with the reflection that God's truth would be communicated to the Heathen Nations of the World by their dispersion among them. He had foretold that the faithful remnant of Israel (the Apostles and first believers in Christ) would convert the Gentiles to Christianity; and that eventually the Gentiles, being received into Christ's Church would convert the rest of the Jews, and so "all Israel shall be saved" (Rom. xi. 26).

Hosea, the first of the Minor Prophets, was the Prophet of Israel; that is, of the Ten Tribes, who were to be carried captive and dispersed by Assyria.

Zephaniah, who was the descendant of King Hezekiah (i. 1), and who prophesied at Jerusalem in the reign of Josiah, was the Prophet to the two tribes, Judah and Benjamin; he does for them what Hosea had done for the ten. He predicts their *Captivity* and *dispersion*; but he foretells also that this also (as well as that of Israel) would be converted by God into a blessing to them and to the Heathen.

The great Heathen Nations of the World would all be humbled in their turn; the mighty powers of Ethiopia and Egypt would be subdued by Assyria; Assyria would be humbled by Babylon; Babylon would be used by God to overthrow Tyre and to overrun Moab, Edom, and Ammon, but would herself be captured by Persia and Media; Persia and Media would be subdued by Greece, and Greece by the arms of Rome. Thus the pride of all the Nations of the World would be broken, and they would lose their faith in the power of their own national deities, and would be prepared to receive Christianity, and would eventually become preachers of the Gospel; and having been themselves converted by Christian Jews, would at length convert the great body of the Jews, whom God would restore to Himself for ever in the true Zion,—the spiritual Jerusalem, the Church of Christ. See on iii. 8—20.

By foretelling these last conquests, the prophecies of Zephaniah are also joined on to those three prophecies which follow, namely, Haggai, Zechariah, and Malachi, the prophetical trio which stand nearest to the threshold of the Church. Zephaniah ends his prophecy with the cheering words, "I will make you a name and a praise among all people of the earth, when *I turn back your captivity* before your eyes, saith the Lord." He prepares the way for those three prophets, who prophesied when the Lord had *turned back the captivity* of Judah from Babylon, and who taught the Jews to see in it a foreshadowing of a far more glorious deliverance—the emancipation of all true Israelites from their own bondage and exile, under the powers of Sin, Satan, and the Grave, and their restoration to life, and hope of everlasting glory in the heavenly Jerusalem, by the might and love of CHRIST.

### THE COMING JUDGMENT.

CH. I. 1. *The word of the* LORD *which came unto Zephaniah —the son of Hizkiah, in the days of Josiah —king of Judah]* Zephaniah, the Prophet, was a descendant of the good King Hezekiah, and prophesied under another good king. Josiah; and he shows God's love to Judah in raising up for such good kings. He prophesies woe to Jerusalem, whose guilt was greater because she did not profit aright by the reformation attempted by them.

2. *the land*] Rather, *the earth*. He prophesies woe to the world, as far as it is opposed to God.

3 <sup>a</sup> I will consume man and beast; I will consume the fowls of the heaven, and the fishes of the sea, and <sup>b</sup> the ‖ stumblingblocks with the wicked; and I will cut off man from off the land, saith the LORD.

4 I will also stretch out mine hand upon Judah,

And upon all the inhabitants of Jerusalem;

And <sup>c</sup> I will cut off the remnant of Baal from this place,

*And* the name of <sup>d</sup> the Chemarims with the priests;

5 And them <sup>e</sup> that worship the host of heaven upon the housetops;

<sup>f</sup> And them that worship *and* <sup>g</sup> that swear ‖ by the LORD,

And that swear <sup>h</sup> by Malcham;

6 And <sup>i</sup> them that are turned back from the LORD;

And *those* that <sup>k</sup> have not sought the LORD, nor inquired for him.

7 <sup>l</sup> Hold thy peace at the presence of the Lord GOD:

<sup>m</sup> For the day of the LORD *is* at hand:

For <sup>n</sup> the LORD hath prepared a sacrifice,

He hath † bid his guests.

8 And it shall come to pass in the day of the LORD's sacrifice, that I will † punish <sup>o</sup> the princes, and the king's children, and all such as are clothed with strange apparel.

---

3. *fishes of the sea*] Words taken up from the foregoing Prophet, Habakkuk (i. 14).

4. *upon Judah*] He prophesies woes also to the visible Church, as far as it is apostate from God. It has been imagined by some, that the invasion of Judah and the woes of Jerusalem, here foretold by Zephaniah, were accomplished by an army of Scythians, mentioned by *Herodotus* (i. 15. 103—106; iv. 1). So *Ewald*, *Hitzig*, and *Bertheau*; and after them *Stanley*, Lectures, pp. 502, 503. But neither *Herodotus* nor the historical Books of the Old Testament mention any conquest of Jerusalem by the Scythians; and Jeremiah, who is very full and explicit in his details of Jewish history at this period, knows nothing of Scythians, but ascribes all God's judgments on Jerusalem at this time to Babylon. Cp. Keil, and *Kleinert*, p. 163.

— *the remnant of Baal*] The idolatry which still lurked in Judah, after Hezekiah's and Judah's reformation, and which thus aggravated the sin of those who still clave to it.

So the Reformation of the sixteenth century in Europe, when new light was shed upon the world by the diffusion of the Holy Scriptures, has greatly added to the guilt of those who still cling to the sins of idolatry and creature-worship, which are condemned in those Scriptures by God Himself, speaking not only by His Prophets in the Old Testament, but by Christ and His Apostles in the New.

The *remnant of Baal* is contrasted with the *remnant of the house of Judah*, or the residue of God's People, i.e. the believers in Christ. See ii. 7, 9; iii. 13. Zech. viii. 12; and note below, on ii. 7.

— *the name of the Chemarims*] Priests of the high places, who were put down by Josiah. See on 2 Kings xxiii. 5.

Even the *names* of such persons and things are hateful to God (see above, Exod. xxiii. 13; and Hos. ii. 17; and below, Zech. xiii. 2), and will be rooted out by Him. How much more the persons and things themselves!

— *with the priests*] Those who, being of the family of Aaron, and therefore Levitical Priests, have apostatized to idolatry (*Tarnovius, Grotius*).

*S. Jerome* applies this to Christian Bishops and Priests, "qui frustra sibi applaudunt in Episcopali nomine, et in Presbyterii dignitate, et non in opere."

5. *that worship the host of heaven upon the housetops*] Where they might better contemplate and adore the stars (*Theodoret*). See Deut. iv. 19. 2 Kings xxiii. 12. Jer. xix. 13; xxxii. 29.

— *that swear by the LORD, and that swear by Malcham*] Or, who swear *by their king* (i.e. Baal),—the king whom they have made for themselves—as well as by Jehovah.

The Prophet pronounces a severe censure against those who "halt between two opinions" (1 Kings xviii. 21), and endeavour, by ingenious shifts, to blend falsehood with truth; as is done by religious syncretism, which is one of the characteristics of these latter days. On the sin of religious compromise and indifference (what *Richard Hooker* calls "a mingle-

106

mangle of religion and superstition, light and darkness"), see the note above, at 2 Kings xvii. 29; and on the history of the judgment of Solomon (1 Kings iii. 22—25).

They that divide their affection and their adoration between God and idols, between the Creator and the creature, will, the Prophet warns us here, be punished in company with the worst idolaters. If Satan have half, he will have all. If God have only half, He will have none. "Ye cannot serve God and Mammon" (Matt. vi. 24). "What concord hath Christ with Belial?" (2 Cor. vi. 15).

6. *that have not sought the LORD*] It is a sin not to seek and diligently to inquire after Him. Diligent and persevering search after truth is necessary to salvation. The Evangelical merchantman *seeks* for goodly pearls (Matt. xiii. 45). The Bereans were more noble than they of Thessalonica, because they *searched* the Scriptures *daily*, whether those things were so (Acts xvii. 11). God is a rewarder of them that *diligently seek Him* (Heb. xi. 6).

7. *Hold thy peace at the presence of the Lord GOD*] Zephaniah takes up the words of the preceding prophet, Habakkuk, (ii. 20), and thus links on his prophecy to his predecessor's. "*The Lord is* in his holy temple; let the whole earth *keep silence before Him*," where the original words are the same as here.

— *the day of the LORD*] The Prophet here adopts the words of Joel i. 15; ii. 1, 11; iii. 14; and Amos v. 18. 20. Obad. 15. Isa. ii. 12; xiii. 6. See below, *vv.* 14, 15.

— *the LORD hath prepared a sacrifice*] Words repeated from Isa. xxxiv. 6. See the note there. Cp. Jer. xlvi. 10. Ezek. xxxix. 17. 19. These are the only passages in the prophetical books where the word *sacrifice* occurs in this sense.

The *sacrifice* which God hath prepared is the Jewish Nation; and He hath *bid His guests*, literally, He *hath sanctified His called ones to offer it.* Cp. Isa. xiii. 2. "I have commanded my *sanctified ones*." Jer. xxii. 7. "*Sanctify* destroyers;" and see Micah iii. 5. Joel iii. 9, where the words "*sanctify war*" occur. All men, either willingly or unwillingly, are *sacrifices* to God. They will be blessed for evermore, if they freely offer and present themselves, their souls and bodies, as living sacrifices to God, which is their reasonable service or worship (Rom. xii. 1). If not, they will be made to be sacrifices to His righteous indignation, against their own will. See above, on Isa. xxxiv. 6. Jer. xlvi. 10; and below, on Mark ix. 49, "Every sacrifice will be salted with salt." Cp. Rev. xiv. 7.

The contrast to this terrible picture is presented by the Prophet in the gracious revelation at the close of the prophecy, where God declares that the Gentiles, when converted to Christianity, will exercise a holy Priesthood, and will bring the Jewish Nation as an acceptable *offering* to Himself. See below, iii. 10.

8. *such as are clothed with strange apparel*] Such as mimic the manners of heathens, and adopt their costume. Cp. Lev. xix. 27, 28; xxi. 5. The Babylonian grandees wore splendid

[9] In the same day also will I punish all those that leap on the threshold, which fill their masters' houses with violence and deceit.

[10] And it shall come to pass in that day, saith the LORD, *that there shall be* the noise of a cry from *the fish gate, and an howling from the second, and a great crashing from the hills.

[11] *Howl, ye inhabitants of Maktesh,*

For all the merchant people are cut down ;

All they that bear silver are cut off.

[12] And it shall come to pass at that time, *that* I will search Jerusalem with candles, and punish the men that are † settled on their lees : that say in their heart, The LORD will not do good, neither will he do evil.

[13] Therefore their goods shall become a booty, and their houses a desolation :

They shall also build houses, but not inhabit *them ;*

And they shall plant vineyards, but not drink the wine thereof.

[14] The great day of the LORD *is* near, *it is* near, and hasteth greatly,

*Even* the voice of the day of the LORD :

The mighty man shall cry there bitterly.

[15] That day *is* a day of wrath, a day of trouble and distress, a day of wasteness and desolation, a day of darkness and gloominess, a day of clouds and thick darkness, [16] a day of the trumpet and alarm against the fenced cities, and against the high towers.

[17] And I will bring distress upon men, that they shall walk like blind men, because they have sinned against the LORD : and their blood shall be poured out as dust, and their flesh as the dung.

[18] Neither their silver nor their gold shall be able to deliver them in the day of the LORD's wrath ; but the whole land shall be devoured by the fire

---

scarlet and vermilion robes (Ezek. xxiii. 14. Dan. v. 7. 16, 29 : cp. Nahum ii. 3), and the Assyrians blue (Ezek. xxiii. 12) ; and the nobles of Jerusalem seem to have been dazzled with the splendour of their attire, and to have imitated it ; as the Macedonians, under Alexander the Great, adopted the gorgeous apparel of the Persian court of Darius.

**9.** *that leap on the threshold*] That leap over the threshold, violently rush into the houses of others to despoil them, and fill the houses of their masters with the rapine they have torn from them.

Many expositors explain this by what is recorded in 1 Sam. v. 4, 5, concerning the priests of Dagon, who would not tread on the threshold of his temple ; and so the *Targum* here. If this interpretation is correct, then the Prophet is to be understood as censuring the adoption of idolatrous practices from Philistia—practices which were the more blamable, because they were records of the humiliation of Dagon bowing down, and mutilated in his own temple before the Lord God of Israel (1 Sam. v. 3, 4)—as well as the *strange attire* of the Babylonians (*v.* 8).

**10.** *a cry from the fish gate*] A cry of distress, when, to punish the violence of those Jews who break into the houses of weaker citizens, the Chaldean invaders will come and rush into the fish-gate, on the north side of the lower city. Cp. 2 Chron. xxxiii. 14. Neh. iii. 3 ; xii. 39 ; and Jer. xxxii. 2.

— *the second*] Rather, the lower city (Acra), on the north of Zion. See above, on 2 Kings xxii. 14. Cp. Neh. xi. 9. Josephus, xv. 11. 5.

— *from the hills*] Of Jerusalem—Zion and Moriah. Cp. Isa. lxvi. 6 ; and *S. Jerome* here.

**11.** *Howl, ye inhabitants of Maktesh*] Literally, *of a mortar.* See *Gesen.* 421, 473. Prov. xxvii. 22. Judg. xv. 19, where the word denotes a hollow place in a rock.

The name *Maktesh,* or mortar, is here given to *Jerusalem,* because in her cruelty she pounded the poor and needy, as in a mortar ; and because she in her turn for her sins would be pounded, as in a mortar, by the Chaldaeans. Babylon itself is called a *hammer* by Jeremiah (l. 23). Similarly, Jerusalem is called a *pot,* or *cauldron,* by Jeremiah and Ezekiel. See on Jer. i. 13. Ezek. xi. 3 ; xxiv. 3. 6.

107

Such appellatives as these are frequent in the prophetical writings, and give much life and vigour to them. Jerusalem is called *Maktesh ;* so *Merathaim* and *Pekod* are names given to Babylon (Jer. l. 21. Ezek. xxiii. 23) ; *Gareb,* given to the King of Assyria (Jer. xxxi. 39) ; and *Buzzah,* given to Nineveh (Nahum ii. 7) ; and see the *Introd.* to the Song of Solomon, p. 125.

**12.** *I will search Jerusalem with candles*] I will search every corner and secret recess of the city, so that none may escape. (Cp. Prov. xx. 27. Luke xv. 8). This prophecy extends not only to the siege of Jerusalem by the Chaldeans, but also to her subsequent capture by the Romans, who searched all parts of Jerusalem, the drains, sewers, sepulchres, and caves, in order to drag forth to death those who lurked there (*Josephus,* B. J. vii. 17. 26 - 30).

So in the last day, the Judge will search every part of the Visible Church with candles. He searcheth every remote corner, and dark cranny, and chink of every heart. He will "bring forth to light the hidden things of darkness, and will make manifest the counsels of the hearts" (1 Cor. iv. 5). "Neither is there any creature that is not manifest in His sight ; but all things are naked and open to the eyes of Him with Whom we have to do" (Heb. iv. 13). Cp. *Bp. Sanderson,* ii. 327.

— *settled on their lees*] Men living in carnal security, and rooted in inveterate habits of sin and sensuality, are like wine that is not disturbed in order to be racked off ; and which, if it be bad wine, retains all its austere harshness and turbid thickness. See note above, on Jer. xlviii. 11 ; and Isa. xxv. 6.

True religion is diffusive. It is racked off, as it were, from the cask, and put into vessels for the refreshment of many. Selfishness is sin. It settles itself on the lees ; it stagnates and curdles, and thickens, till it becomes useless and noisome to the scent and to the taste.

— *The LORD will not do good*] This is the creed of the Deist and the Libertine. Cp. Ps. x. 11 ; xiv. 7. They deny God's providential government of the world. Things happen, they say, by chance or necessity. God will not reward piety and virtue, nor punish ungodliness and vice.

**17.** *their blood shall be poured out as dust*] Of as little value, and in as great quantity, as the dust in the streets of the city, or as in the sandy plain.

of his jealousy: for [c] he shall make even a speedy riddance of all them that dwell in the land.

II. [1] [a] Gather yourselves together, yea, gather together, O nation ‖ not desired;

[2] Before the decree bring forth, *before* the day pass [b] as the chaff, before [i] the fierce anger of the LORD come upon you, before the day of the LORD's anger come upon you.

[3] [d] Seek ye the LORD, [e] all ye meek of the earth, which have wrought his judgment; seek righteousness, seek meekness: [f] it may be ye shall be hid in the day of the LORD's anger.

[4] For [g] Gaza shall be forsaken, and Ashkelon a desolation: They shall drive out Ashdod [h] at the noon day, and Ekron shall be rooted up.

[5] Woe unto the inhabitants of [i] the sea coast, the nation of the Cherethites! the word of the LORD *is* against you;

O [k] Canaan, the land of the Philistines, I will even destroy thee, that there shall be no inhabitant.

[6] And the sea coast shall be dwellings *and* cottages for shepherds, [l] and folds for flocks.

[7] And the coast shall be for [m] the remnant of the house of Judah; they shall feed thereupon: in the houses of Ashkelon shall they lie down in the evening: ‖ for the LORD their God shall [n] visit them, and [o] turn away their captivity.

[8] [p] I have heard the reproach of Moab, and [q] the revilings of the children of Ammon, whereby they have reproached my people, and [r] magnified *themselves* against their border. [9] Therefore *as* I live, saith the LORD of hosts, the God of Israel, Surely [s] Moab shall be as Sodom, and [t] the children of Ammon as Gomorrah, [u] *even* the breeding of nettles, and saltpits, and a perpetual desolation: [x] the residue of my people shall spoil them, and the remnant of my people shall possess them.

---

JUDGMENTS ON THE NATIONS.—CALL TO REPENTANCE.

CH. II. 1. *O nation not desired*] Rather, O *nation not ashamed*; lost to all sense of shame, and therefore unwilling to receive correction, and incapable of amendment (*Sept.*, *Targum*, *Arabic*, *Syriac*). The radical idea of the word *câsaph*, here used (connected with *côseph, silver*), in the passive voice, is to become white, pale, or blank, as something which loses its colour and is eclipsed. Thence it is applied to a person who is put to confusion with shame. See *Gesen.* 409.

2. *before the day pass as the chaff*] Or, *day passes away like chaff*. The day of your life flies away like chaff. Cp. Isa. xxix. 5. "What is your life?" says St. James (iv. 14), "it is even a vapour, that appeareth for a little time, and then vanisheth away." Therefore repent, while ye have time. "Ccndum est ætate, cito pede præterit ætas." The day of man is contrasted with the Day of the Lord. The sentence is parenthetical; the word *before* (which is not in the original) ought to be omitted.

3. *ye shall be hid in the day of the LORD's anger*] Ye too shall be *Zephanizeh*. See above, *Prelim. Note* to chap. i. on the meaning of the Prophet's name.

4. *Gaza shall be forsaken*] The Prophet declares the judgments of the Lord God of Israel on the Nations of the Heathen World, and begins with that which is nearest to the judicial Throne of His Majesty at Jerusalem; namely, Philistia; thence he proceeds to Moab and Ammon; and so southward to Ethiopia.

These prophecies have not only a judicial and punitive significance, but also a merciful and gracious meaning. The *heathenism* of the Gentile World will be destroyed, and they will be converted to God in Christ. See vv. 7, 11; iii. 10.

*Gaza will be forsaken.* There is a play on the meaning of these words. Cp. above on Micah i. 10—14, "*Azzah*" (i.e. Gaza) "will be *azûbah*" (forsaken); "*Ekron* will be *tâîker*" (will be rooted out).

5. *Cherethites*] Perhaps a colony from Crete. See 1 Sam.

xxx. 14. 2 Sam. viii. 18. 1 Chron. xviii. 17. Ezek. xxv. 16. There is another play on the words here. The word *Cherethites* signifies *cutters off* (they were used as executioners in the royal army of Judah); and the sense is, I will *cut off* (from the verb *cârath*, to cut off, *Gesen.* 416) the *cutters off*.

6, 7. *the sea coast shall be dwellings—for shepherds, and folds for flocks—the coast shall be for the remnant of the house of Judah.* That is, the sea-coast shall become a sacred colony for those Jews who will believe in Christ and preach the Gospel. This is the true prophetic meaning of the words the *remnant of the house of Judah*. See r. 9, and Isa. x. 21; xi. 11; xxxvii. 32. Amos v. 15. Zech. viii. 11, and St. Paul's use of the word (Rom. ix. 27; xi. 5). This prophecy was fulfilled in the preaching of the Gospel in Philistia by St. Peter and by St. Philip, and by the erection of Christian Churches there. Cp. above on Ps. lxxvii. 4, and below, on Acts viii. 26, 40; ix. 32—35. These were "the dwellings and cottages for shepherds"—namely, Christian pastors—and "folds for flocks," Christ's sheep and lambs. Compare the similar imagery in the Evangelical prophecies of Isaiah (lxi. 5; lxv. 10), "Sharon shall be a fold of flocks;" Jer. xxxi. 5—14, and xxxiii. 12. Ezek. xxxvi. 38; and see S. *Jerome* and *A Lapide* here.

8. *I have heard the reproach of Moab*] Cp. Isa. xvi. 6. "We have heard of the pride of Moab." Cp. Jeremiah (xlviii. 29), and r. 10 here, "This shall they have for their pride." We, who have heard of its pride, will hear of its shame.

9. *the remnant of my people*] The faithful remnant. It is the same word as in v. 7. Here is a prophecy of the Christianization of those countries which were occupied by Moab. Cp. Jer. xlviii. 47, "I will bring again the captivity of Moab."

The prophecy declares that the heathenism of the nations here mentioned will be abolished, and that a faithful remnant of God's People will be gathered from them, by believing Jews—namely, by Apostles and primitive Disciples of the Christian Church, who went forth from Jerusalem—and will be incorporated in God's family in Christ.

[10] This shall they have ʸ for their pride,
Because they have reproached and magnified *themselves* against the people
of the LORD of hosts.

[11] The LORD *will be* terrible unto them :
For he will † famish all the gods of the earth ;
ᶻ And *men* shall worship him, every one from his place,
*Even* all ª the isles of the heathen.

[12] ᵇ Ye Ethiopians also, ye *shall be* slain by ᶜ my sword.

[13] And he will stretch out his hand against the north, and ᵈ destroy Assyria ;
And will make Nineveh a desolation, *and* dry like a wilderness.

[14] And ᵉ flocks shall lie down in the midst of her,
All ᶠ the beasts of the nations :
Both the ‖ ᵍ cormorant and the bittern shall lodge in the ‖ upper lintels of it ;
*Their* voice shall sing in the windows ;
Desolation *shall be* in the thresholds :
‖ For he shall uncover the ʰ cedar work.

[15] This *is* the rejoicing city ⁱ that dwelt carelessly,
ᵏ That said in her heart, I *am*, and *there is* none beside me :
How is she become a desolation, a place for beasts to lie down in !
Every one that passeth by her ˡ shall hiss, *and* ᵐ wag his hand.

III. [1] Woe to ‖ † her that is filthy and polluted, to the oppressing city !

[2] She ª obeyed not the voice ; she ᵇ received not ‖ correction ;
She trusted not in the LORD ; she drew not near to her God.

[3] ᶜ Her princes within her *are* roaring lions ; her judges *are* ᵈ evening wolves ;
They gnaw not the bones till the morrow.

[4] Her ᵉ prophets *are* light *and* treacherous persons :

*(marginal references)*
ᵇ Isa. 16. 6.
Jer. 48. 29.

† Heb. *make lean.*
ᶻ Mal. 1. 11.
John 4. 21.
ª Gen. 10. 5.

ᵇ Isa. 18. 1. &
20. 4.
Jer. 46. 6.
Ezek. 30. 9.
ᶜ Ps. 17. 13
ᵈ Isa. 10. 12.
Ezek. 31. 3.
Nahum 1. 1. &
2. 10. & 3. 15, 18.
ᵉ ver. 6.
ᶠ Isa. 13. 21, 22.
‖ *Or, pelican.*
ᵍ Isa. 34. 11, 14.
‖ *Or, knaps, or, chapiters.*

‡ *Or, when he hath uncovered.*
ʰ Jer. 22. 14.
ⁱ Isa. 47. 8.

ᵏ Rev. 18. 7.

ˡ Job 27. 23.
Lam. 2. 15.
ᵏ Ezek. 27. 36.
ᵐ Nahum 3. 19.
‖ *Or, gluttonous.*
† Heb. *crane*
ª Jer. 22. 21.
ᵇ Jer. 5. 3.
‡ *Or, instruction.*
ᶜ Ezek. 22. 27.
Micah 3. 9, 10, 11.
ᵈ Hab. 1. 8.

ᵉ Jer. 23. 11, 32.
Lam. 2. 14.
Hos. 9. 7.

---

*(footnote commentary, two columns)*

11. *he will famish all the gods of the earth*] By depriving them of their worshippers and sacrifices, and by converting the heathen nations to Himself.

This was the result of the chastisement of those nations by such conquerors as Sennacherib and Nebuchadnezzar, who were employed by the Lord God of Israel to punish them for their sins, and to break the neck of their pride, and to destroy their confidence in their own false national deities, which were not able to help them, and were carried away into captivity, never to be restored ; and thus to prepare them for the reception of a purer faith, and, eventually, for the incorporation of the neck and humble among them into the Church of Christ. See S. *Jerome* and *Theodoret* here. Cp. iii. 10. S. *Augustine* (De Civ. Dei, xviii. 33) applies these words to the conversion of the heathen to Christ ; and *Euseb.* also (Demonst. Evang. ii. 16) interprets this prophecy in that sense.

12. *Ye Ethiopians also, ye shall be slain by my sword*] Literally, "*Ye Ethiopians also*" (in the farthest south), "*shall be slain by my sword—even they.*" Ye shall be slain by *My* sword, wielded by the hand of the King of Babylon, Nebuchadnezzar, "*My Servant*" (Jer. xxv. 9 ; xxvii. 6 ; xliii. 10). Cp. Ezek. xxix. 19 ; xxx. 4, 9, 10. Jer. xlvi. 10.

13. *he will stretch out his hand against the north, and destroy Assyria*] Even Assyria, which carried away Israel captive, and had overrun Egypt and Ethiopia (Isa. xx.), shall be destroyed by the hand of the Babylonians. See above, on Nahum i. 1 ; ii. 1—7.

14. *cormorant and the bittern*] Or, *the pelican and the porcupine.* See on Isa. xxxiv. 11, whence the words are adopted here.

— *upper lintels*] Or knops of the pillars. See on Amos ix. 1.

— *Their voice shall sing*] There shall be *the voice of the songster in the windows;* birds shall perch and sing in the ruined windows of its palaces.

— *cedar work*] Cedars hewn in Lebanon, for Assyrian kings, for the construction of their palaces of Nineveh. See the note above, on Isa. xxxvii. 24.

15. *I am, and there is none beside me*] Such was the language of self-idolizing Nineveh, the type of the infidel and
impious powers of this World ; see above, Introd. to Nahum. In this respect, as in some others, that form of Antichristianism resembled the Babylonish or idolatrous form, to which these words are ascribed by Isa. xlvii. 8. Both these forms deify themselves, and defy God ; and both will be destroyed by Him, as He declares by His holy Prophets.

— *shall hiss, and wag his hand*] Cp. Jer. xix. 8. Micah vi. 16. The movement of the hand is an action of dismissal—"Away with thee ! begone out of my sight !"—and thus it intimates that the mighty Powers of this World, which once claimed homage from men bowing in silent awe before them, and kissing the hand in lowly adoration (1 Kings xix. 18), will be hissed and hooted off the stage of this world, and be motioned to be gone and to disappear, by those who once trembled in their presence.

The most terrible climax of this rejection and dismissal, will be in those awful words of the Judge of all at the Great Day, "Depart from Me, ye cursed, into everlasting fire."

WOE TO THE FAITHLESS AND UNRIGHTEOUS IN THE CHURCH OF GOD.

GOD'S TEMPORARY REJECTION OF THE JEWS, AND CHOICE OF THE GENTILES IN THEIR PLACE.

CH. III. 1. *Woe to her*] To Jerusalem.
— *that is filthy*] Rather, that is *obstinate* or *perverse* (Gesen. 505 ; Fuerst, 861 ; Kleinert, 177). See what follows. "she obeyed not the voice ; she received not correction."

3. *evening wolves*] Habak. i. 8.
— *They gnaw not the bones till the morrow*] Rather, *they lay not up the bones for the morrow.* They are wolves who prowl about in *the evening,* and are so ravenous when they seize their prey, that they leave not a single bone till morning-light. See Sept., Vulg., Syriac, Targum, and Gesen. 189 ; Fuerst, 300.

4. *Her prophets are light*] Rather, are boastful ; properly, *overflowing*—like a vessel which boils over—with profuse foam and scum of empty, vain-glorious, and wanton words. See Gen. xlix. 4. Judges ix. 4. Gesen. 672.

Her priests have polluted the sanctuary,

They have done ᶠ violence to the law.

⁵ ᵍ The just Lᴏʀᴅ ʰ *is* in the midst thereof;

He will not do iniquity:

ⁱ Every morning doth he bring his judgment to light, he faileth not;

But ʲ the unjust knoweth no shame.

⁶ I have cut off the nations:

Their ‖ towers are desolate;

I made their streets waste, that none passeth by:

Their cities are destroyed, so that there is no man,

That there is none inhabitant.

⁷ ᵏ I said, Surely thou wilt fear me,

Thou wilt receive instruction;

So their dwelling should not be cut off, howsoever I punished them:

But they rose early, *and* ˡ corrupted all their doings.

⁸ Therefore ᵐ wait ye upon me, saith the Lᴏʀᴅ,

Until the day that I rise up to the prey:

For my determination *is* to ⁿ gather the nations,

That I may assemble the kingdoms,

To pour upon them mine indignation, *even* all my fierce anger:

For all the earth ᵒ shall be devoured with the fire of my jealousy.

⁹ For then will I turn to the people ᵖ a pure †language,

That they may all call upon the name of the Lᴏʀᴅ,

To serve him with one †consent.

---

7. *I said, Surely thou wilt fear me*] I said to Judah, *Only fear thou me*. If thou wilt fulfil this one condition, then thou wilt be saved.

— *howsoever I punished them*] Or, in all my visitations of her.

— *they—corrupted all their doings*] The Jews rejected God's offers of mercy under the Old Dispensation and under the Gospel; therefore, as a Nation, they are cast off, and the Heathen are taken into His favour in their place. See what follows, and *S. Augustine*, De Civ. Dei, vii. 33, who cites these verses as a prophecy concerning the conversion of the Heathen to Christianity.

8. *Therefore*] Since salvation cannot come forth from the people, even of favoured Israel and Judah (for they have corrupted themselves and become abominable), wait ye for *Me*, says God, the only Saviour.

This is a prophecy of Christ, coming to visit and redeem His People (*S. Jerome*).

"Wait ye upon Me, saith the Lord." He repeats the exhortation of Habakkuk (ii. 3; the same word is used there), *to wait* in patience, and trust for the fulfilment of God's prophecies and promises; intimating that to many, in evil days of sore distress for the Church, the time will appear to be very long, and they will almost despair of the Lord's Coming to deliver them.

— *Until the day that I rise up*] The *Sept.* and *Vulgate* here has, "*In the day of My resurrection*," and ancient Christian Expositors have recognized here a prophecy of Christ's *rising up* (as He is described by Jacob, in Gen. xlix. 9) from the dead to divide the spoil. When He rose from the dead, He triumphed over Sin, Satan, and the Grave; and He gave a commission to His Apostles, to bring all Nations into subjection to the Gospel. See *Eusebius*, Dem. Evang. ii. 17, and *S. Jerome*, here; and *S. Augustine*, De Civ. Dei, xviii. 33.

— *For my determination is*] Rather, *it is my right judgment*; my judicial right and office (Hebr. *mishpat*; the word in v. 5, and Malachi iii. 5). I will come near to you *to judgment*.

God will inflict punishments on the Heathen Nations of the World, in order to bring them to Himself in Christ. God will judge the Nations; and in consequence of these judgments their conversion will take place. "O Lord, when Thy judgments are in the earth, the inhabitants of the world will learn *righteousness*" (Isa. xxvi. 9). See above, *Prelim. Note* to chap. i, and above, on ii. 11.

110

— *my determination (or judgment) is to gather the nations*] This is specially true of Christ, to Whom "the Father hath committed all *judgment*" (John v. 22), and Who, when He comes to judgment, will *gather before Him all nations* (Matt. xxv. 32).

Tʜᴇ Cᴏɴᴠᴇʀsɪᴏɴ ᴏꜰ ᴛʜᴇ Hᴇᴀᴛʜᴇɴ ʙʏ Iꜱʀᴀᴇʟ'ꜱ Fᴀɪᴛʜꜰᴜʟ Rᴇᴍɴᴀɴᴛ; ᴀɴᴅ ᴛʜᴇ ꜱᴜʙꜱᴇQᴜᴇɴᴛ Cᴏɴᴠᴇʀꜱɪᴏɴ ᴏꜰ ᴛʜᴇ Jᴇᴡꜱ ʙʏ Bᴇʟɪᴇᴠᴇʀꜱ ᴀɴᴅ Pʀᴇᴀᴄʜᴇʀꜱ ꜰʀᴏᴍ ᴛʜᴇ Hᴇᴀᴛʜᴇɴ.

9. *will I turn to the people a pure language*] Rather, *a clean lip* (the contrast to *unclean lips*; Isa. vi. 5). When I have chastened the Heathen, and weakened their faith in their own idols, I will *give back* to the Heathen Nations *a clean lip*; I will convert them to holiness. Their lips, which were created by Me, for My service and glory, have been polluted by worship of idols (Ps. xvi. 4); but I will cleanse and sanctify them by dedication to Myself; and they will render to Me the *calves of their lips*, as Hosea says xiv. 2.

Before the building of Babel, the *whole Earth was of one lip* (see on Gen. xi. 1); but pride, and defiance of God, produced confusion and a jargon of tongues. But when the Holy Ghost came down from Heaven, the Gospel sounded forth in the languages of all nations, and in the Christian Sion all nations meet together, in order that they may "with one mind and one mouth glorify God" (Rom. xv. 6).

This union, begun on earth, will be perfected in heaven. *There* will be one language; and that language will be Love.

— *with one consent*] Literally, and very forcibly, *with one shoulder*. Cp. Isa. xix. 23, 24, "Egypt will serve with Assyria, and Israel shall be a third with Egypt and Assyria, a blessing in the midst of the land."

What a noble picture is here! In ancient triumphal processions the victorious soldiers marched side by side, bearing the trophies of their conquest. Here all the great Nations of the World are personified, marching in order, side by side, and giving their shoulders and their necks, with one mind, to bear the one Gospel of Christ throughout the world, in a grand triumphal procession (cp. 2 Cor. ii. 14); and thus we see an anticipation of the glorious time when the voice will be heard in heaven, "The Kingdoms of this world are become the Kingdom of the Lord, and of His Christ" (Rev. xi. 15).

<sup>10</sup> ⁴From beyond the rivers of Ethiopia my suppliants,
'Even the daughter of my dispersed,
Shall bring mine offering.

<sup>11</sup>   In that day shalt thou not be ashamed for all thy doings,
Wherein thou hast transgressed against me :
For then I will take away out of the midst of thee them that ʳrejoice in thy
pride,
And thou shalt no more be haughty † because of my holy mountain.

<sup>12</sup> I will also leave in the midst of thee ˢ an afflicted and poor people,
And they shall trust in the name of the LORD.

<sup>13</sup> ᵗThe remnant of Israel ᵘshall not do iniquity, ˣnor speak lies ;
Neither shall a deceitful tongue be found in their mouth :
For ʸ they shall feed and lie down,
And none shall make *them* afraid.

<sup>14</sup>   ᶻ Sing, O daughter of Zion ; shout, O Israel ;
Be glad and rejoice with all the heart, O daughter of Jerusalem.

<sup>15</sup> The LORD hath taken away thy judgments, he hath cast out thine enemy :
ᵃ The king of Israel, *even* the LORD, ᵇ *is* in the midst of thee :

Before
CHRIST
about
630.
q Ps. 68. 31.
Isa. 18. 1, 7. &
60. 4, &c.
Mal. 1. 11.
Acts 8. 27.

r Jer. 7, 4.
Micah 3. 11.
Matt. 3. 9.

† Heb. *in my
holy.*
s Isa. 14. 32.
Zech. 11. 11.
Matt. 5. 3.
1 Cor. 1. 27, 28.
James 2. 5.
t Micah 4. 7.
ch. 2. 7.
u Isa. 60. 21.
x Isa. 63. 8.
Rev. 14. 5.
y Ezek. 34, 28.
Micah. 4. 4. &
7. 14.
z Isa. 12. 6. &
54. 1.
Zech. 2. 10. &
9. 9.

a John 1. 49.
b Ezek. 48. 35.
ver. 5, 17.
Rev. 7. 15. & 21. 3, 4.

**10.** *From beyond the rivers—mine offering*] Rather, *From beyond the rivers of Ethiopia they* (i.e. the Gentiles) *will bring my worshippers, the daughter of my dispersed ones* (i.e. the Jews scattered abroad), *as a meat offering to me.* Israel and Judah will be *dispersed* throughout the world for their sins, as God had foretold by Moses, "The Lord shall scatter" (or *disperse*) "you among the Nations" (Deut. iv. 27); and again "The Lord shall scatter" (or *disperse*) "thee among all people, from one end of the earth even unto the other" (Deut. xxviii. 64).

Already, in Zephaniah's time, this had been fulfilled with respect to the Ten Tribes captured and dispersed by Assyria. The dispersion of Judah also was near ; and, in course of time, the very name of the twelve tribes was "the *Diaspora*, or *Dispersion*." See below, John xi. 51, and on Acts iii. 2–6. James i. 1.

But Zephaniah has a message of comfort for them here. When Heathens have been converted to Christianity by the faithful remnant of Israel (i.e. by Apostles and other primitive Preachers of the Gospel, who went forth from Jerusalem), then they will convert the Jews of the different dispersions ; even in the far off region of Ethiopia, bordering on central Africa ; and they will present them as an offering (literally, a meat offering ; Hebr. *minchah*) to Me.

The best exposition of this passage will be found in the similar prophecies concerning the work of the Heathen in converting the Jews, in Isaiah lxi. 5, 6 ; lxv. 18–21 (where see the note) ; and in the Song of Solomon, iii. 4, and viii. 8, 9. St. Paul adopts this imagery (Rom. xv. 16), "That the *offering up* of the Gentiles might be acceptable, being sanctified by the Holy Ghost ;" and Phil. ii. 17, " I am *poured forth*" (my blood will be poured out as a drink offering) "upon the sacrifice and service of your faith."

On the *minchah*, the meat offering (an emblem of human labour mingled with divine grace) joined with the drink offering, and ever adjunct to the *whole burnt offering*, see on Levit. ii., *Prelim. Note*, and xxii. 13, which will explain the imagery here.

The Prophet had declared that the wicked would be a *sacrifice* to God's anger (Zeph. i. 7) ; He here declares that the Jewish Nation will be brought to Himself as an acceptable *sacrifice* by the Gentile Nations.

**11.** *In that day—mountain*] In that day, O Judah, when thou art converted to God, thou wilt no longer have cause to feel shame for thine iniquities ; for thou wilt repent and believe, and God will blot them out,—as Hosea says at the close of his prophecy (xiii. 12), "The iniquity of Ephraim is bound up, his sin is hid,"—and thou wilt no longer be proud of thy spiritual privileges, and feel a vain-glorious confidence in Jerusalem and its Temple (see on Jer. vii. 4) ; for the Gentiles will be admitted to equal privileges with thee ; and thou wilt embrace them as thy brethren in the spiritual Temple of Sion, the Universal Church of Christ.

**12.** *an afflicted and poor people*] A people bowed down and humbled with a penitential sorrow for sin ; such hath God chosen, says St. James, the first Bishop of Jerusalem (ii. 5). They will be left in thee ; they will be a precious remnant ; they will be comforted, and rest in peace and joy ; they will be fed by Me as a flock (Micah vii. 14) ; and none shall make them afraid (*v.* 13).

Perhaps there is something of a typical and prophetic significance in the words of the sacred historian and the Prophet (2 Kings xxv. 12. Jer. lii. 16), where they say that the Chaldeans, when they took Jerusalem, left "of the *poor* of *the land* to be *vinedressers and husbandmen,*" while the kings, princes, and nobles were taken prisoners. Certainly, in the first ages of the Gospel, and when Jerusalem was destroyed by Rome, God chose the poor, the meek, the humble and simple of this world ; not the mighty, and the noble, and the proud, to be *vinedressers* in His vineyard, and to be *husbandmen* in the field of His Church.

**13.** *The remnant of Israel*] The Israel of God, the children of faithful Abraham, the true believers in Christ. " This remnant " (says S. *Augustine,* De Civ. Dei, vii. 33) "are those of whom St. Paul " (quoting Isaiah x. 22) "speaks :—' Though the number of the Children of Israel be as the sand of the sea, a remnant (only) shall be saved' (Rom. ix. 27). This remnant are those of the Jewish Nation who believed in Christ." Cp. S. *Jerome* here.

#### SING, O DAUGHTER OF ZION.

Zephaniah closes his prophecy, as Hosea does, with a triumphant announcement of the restoration of God's ancient People to His favour in Christ. Hosea, the Prophet of the Ten Tribes, proclaims this blessed consummation to Israel ; Zephaniah, the Prophet of Jerusalem, completes the prophecy, and brings a joyful message of grace and glory both to Judah and Israel. He unites both together in one prophecy of God. " Sing, O daughter of Zion ; shout, O Israel ; be glad and rejoice with all thy heart, O daughter of Jerusalem." *Both the two sticks* are to be joined together in one stick, in the hand of Christ (see Ezek. xxxvii. 17) ; and the Gentiles are to be like almond blossoms on Aaron's rod, and to flourish upon it (Num. xvii. 8), in the hand of Christ, the Everlasting High Priest ; and to be laid up before God in the Holy of Holies of His Everlasting Temple, the heavenly Jerusalem. See the notes above on Ezek. xxxvii. 16—28, which afford the best exposition of this passage.

**15.** *The king of Israel, even the LORD, is in the midst of thee*] This joyful promise of God's presence and perpetual indwelling, is here repeated twice for greater assurance. See *v.* 17. It is taken up from Isaiah (see Isa. xii. 6, and the note on Isa. lxvi. 17, on the phrase "*in the midst*"), and from Hosea (xi. 9), who is the first of the Minor Prophets, and with whom Zephaniah, the last of the Minor Prophets before the Babylonish Captivity, loves to associate himself.

Before CHRIST about 630.
c Isa. 35. 3, 4.
d Heb. 12. 12.
‖ Or, *faint*
e ver. 15.
f Deut. 30. 9. Isa. 62. 5, & 63. 19. Jer. 32. 41.
† Heb. *he will be silent.*
g Lam. 2. 6.
† Heb. *the burden upon it was reproach.*
h Ezek. 34. 16. Micah 4. 6, 7.
† Heb. *I will set them for a praise.*
† Heb. *of their shame.*
i Isa. 11. 12. & 27. 12, & 56. 8. Ezek. 28. 25. & 34. 13. & 37. 21. Amos 9. 14.

Thou shalt not see evil any more.

16 In that day ᶜ it shall be said to Jerusalem, Fear thou not :
*And to* Zion, ᵈ Let not thine hands be ‖ slack.

17 The LORD thy God ᵉ in the midst of thee is mighty ;
He will save, ᶠ he will rejoice over thee with joy ;
† He will rest in his love, he will joy over thee with singing.

18 I will gather *them that* ᵍ *are* sorrowful for the solemn assembly,
*Who* are of thee, *to whom* † the reproach of it *was* a burden.

19 Behold, at that time I will undo all that afflict thee :
And I will save her that ʰ halteth,
And gather her that was driven out ;
And † I will get them praise and fame in every land †
Where they have been put to shame.

20 At that time ⁱ will I bring you *again,* even in the time that I gather you :
For I will make you a name and a praise among all people of the earth,
When I turn back your captivity before your eyes, saith the LORD.

---

This prophecy of the perpetual Divine Presence is fulfilled in God the Son, Emmanuel, "God with us" (Matt. i. 23); "God manifested in the flesh" (1 Tim. iii. 16), promising His perpetual presence to His Church (Matt. xxviii. 20); and in God the Holy Ghost, the Comforter, sent to abide with her for ever (John xiv. 16).

17. *he will rejoice over thee with joy*] As the Bridegroom with the Bride. The imagery is from Isa. lxii. 5, and cp. Jer. xxxii. 41.

— *He will rest in his love*] Literally, "*he will be silent in his love*" (*Vulg.*). He will acquiesce in thee, with full confidence in thy faithfulness and love. So the Psalmist compares himself to an infant, composed to sleep in tender trust and silent love on its mother's breast. He says that he lulled his soul to sleep (literally, *has made it silent*) like a weaned child, lying on the bosom of its mother; and he adds, "Let Israel trust in the Lord, from henceforth for evermore!" See the note on Ps. cxxxi. 2.

So the love of God reposes, as it were, in silent quietness and peace, on the devout soul of the believer, in full trust, that the soul, like a faithful spouse (cp. Isa. lxii. 5), will render love for love.

St. John, the beloved disciple, rested in silence on the bosom of Christ at the paschal supper; and when at death, after long tarrying (John xxi. 22), the Saviour came to him, St. John fell asleep in Christ.

18. *I will gather them that are sorrowful for the solemn assembly*] I will gather those who mourn for the cessation of the sacred feasts of Jerusalem (Lam. i. 7; ii. 6. Hos. ii. 11. Amos viii. 3), which were only shadows of the good things to come under the Gospel (Heb. xi. 1), and will comfort them by the restoration of those festivals in all their fulness, in the Sacraments of the Christian Church.

May we not apply these words to our own age and country? Many among us mourn and are sorrowful for churches closed during the week, from Sunday to Sunday; and for infrequent Communions; and for non-observance of the Fasts and Festivals of the Christian Church; and for the cold neglect of that spiritual edification which the Church provides in the Book of Common Prayer, in the examples of God's gracious working in holy men, Apostles, Evangelists, and Martyrs, whom He has

given to the Church; and for the loss of that Scriptural teaching provided by her in the Lessons, Epistles, and Gospels on these days. God sees the tears of the sorrowful; these things "are noted in His book" (Ps. lvi. 8). He will hereafter gather those who sorrow with this sorrow, and will make them rejoice for ever in an eternal festival in the Courts of His heavenly Sion.

— *Who are of thee*] They (that is, these faithful worshippers) *are of thee*; they proceed forth from thee, Zion was the Mother of Christendom. (See above, on Ezek. xxxv. 14, p. 239.)

— *to whom the reproach of it was a burden*] A burden to these holy mourners was the reproach which the Heathen uttered against Jerusalem, for her desolation and the cessation of her feasts (Lam. i. 7). They sympathized with her in her sorrows (cp. Ps. cxxxvii. 5); they were "grieved for the affliction of Joseph" (Amos vi. 6). The taunt of the Heathen against Zion wounded them to the quick.

Here is a promise of comfort to all who feel sadness of heart for the distresses and sufferings of the Church, which are inflicted upon her by the tyranny of evil men.

19. *I will save her that halteth, and gather her that was driven out*] A prophecy repeated from Isaiah (xxxiii. 23), "The lame take the prey;" and from Micah (iv. 7), where he is describing the blessed consequences of the birth of Christ, and the going forth of His Church from Jerusalem to enfold all Nations of the World. See Micah iv. 1—7, and v. 1—7, and the notes there.

20. *When I turn back your captivity before your eyes, saith the LORD*] Literally, *when I turn your captivities* (plural). Your various *captivities* (whether in Assyria, or Babylon, or Rome, or in other parts of the world) will all be turned back like a stream. As the Psalmist says, "Turn our captivity, O Lord, as the rivers of the south" (Ps. cxxvi. 5); they will all flow into the Church of Christ. See Isa. ii. 2, Micah iv. 1. "All nations shall flow into it."

The prophet here recapitulates the divine promises of restoration to the dispersed Israel and Judah (cp. Deut. xxx. 3, Ps. cxxvi. 4. Jer. xxiv. 11; xxxi. 23; xxxii. 44; xxxiii. 7, 11. Lam. ii. 14. Ezek. xxxix. 25. Hos. vi. 11. Joel iii. 1. Amos ix. 14), which are fulfilled in Christ; to Whom, with the Father and Holy Ghost, be all honour and glory now and for ever, AMEN.

---

At this point, in order of time, follow the prophecies of JEREMIAH, EZEKIEL, and DANIEL. Then succeed HAGGAI, ZECHARIAH, and MALACHI; the last of whom is called by the Jews, the "SEAL OF THE PROPHETS."

The reader is requested to refer here to the *Introductions* prefixed to the Prophets JEREMIAH and EZEKIEL; and also to the *Introductions* to the Books of EZRA and NEHEMIAH, as preparatory to what now follows in the prophetical writings.

# HAGGAI.

I. [1] IN [2] the second year of Darius the king, in the sixth month, in the first day of the month, came the word of the LORD † by Haggai the prophet unto

Before
CHRIST
about
520.

*a* Ezra 4. 24. & 5. 1.    Zech. 1. 1.    † Heb. *by the hand of Haggai.*

MORE than a hundred years elapsed between the prophecies of ZEPHANIAH and those of HAGGAI.

In that interval many predictions of foregoing prophets, namely, of Isaiah, Micah, Habakkuk, Zephaniah, Jeremiah, and Ezekiel, foretelling the capture and destruction of Jerusalem by the Babylonians, had been fulfilled.

In B.C. 605, the fourth year of Jehoiakim, Nebuchadnezzar took Jerusalem for the first time; but the city was still allowed to stand, and a time was granted to it for repentance. But it refused to listen to God's warnings of judgment from the prophets Jeremiah and Ezekiel; and it was again taken by Nebuchadnezzar, B.C. 597, and its king, Jehoiachin, was carried captive to Babylon. Still some further respite was granted it, but in vain. In the year B.C. 586, Jerusalem was taken; the Temple and the City were burnt with fire; its king, Zedekiah, and many of the princes, and nobles, and people were carried to Babylon; and the kingdom of Judah was destroyed.

Years passed on, and the time approached for the fulfilment of other prophecies—those which foretold the sudden capture of the great Chaldean City, Babylon, and the destruction of its dominion by Cyrus, "God's shepherd," and anointed one," leading the army of Medes and Persians to victory; and, as a result of that conquest, the restoration of the captives of Judah to their own land, and the decree for the rebuilding of the Temple of the Lord.

This fulfilment was in the year B.C. 536.

God had performed His work of wholesome discipline and loving chastisement to His People in their Captivity, by teaching them humility, and weaning them from idolatry, and healing the schism between Israel and Judah, and by sifting the faithful wheat from the careless and godless chaff, and had prepared the true Israelites, by the fulfilment of prophecies concerning themselves, for the reception of Christ, Who is the subject of all prophecy. See above, Introd. to Ezra, pp. 296—299.

The Temple began to be rebuilt in the year B.C. 535. But the work was thwarted by Samaritans (Ezra iv. 1—7. 23), and the builders themselves were disheartened, and began to doubt whether the time had arrived for the accomplishment of the prophecies which had foretold that the Temple would be restored, and whether the Temple which they were building, so inferior in grandeur to the Temple of Solomon, could be indeed the fabric of which such glorious things had been spoken by Isaiah, Jeremiah, and Ezekiel. "Many of the Priests and Levites, and chief of the fathers, who were ancient men that had seen the first house" (which had been destroyed fifty years before), "when the foundation of this house was laid before their eyes, wept with a loud voice" (Ezra iii. 12). "Who is left among you" (says Haggai, ii. 3) "that saw this house in her first glory? and how do ye see it now? Is it not in your eyes in comparison of it as nothing?"

In consequence of this opposition from without, and of this failure of faith and courage within, the work of building the Temple was intermitted for fifteen years, "unto the second year of Darius, King of Persia" (Ezra iv. 24). The foundations of the second Temple might have long continued to lie in this miserable condition; but God had ordered it otherwise. He would show that the work was not of man: "Not by might, nor by power, but by My Spirit, saith the Lord of hosts" (Zech. iv. 6). "Then the prophets, Haggai the prophet, and Zechariah, the son of Iddo, prophesied unto the Jews that were in Judah and Jerusalem, in the name of the God of Israel, even unto them. Then rose up Zerubbabel the son of Shealtiel, and Jeshua the son of Jozadak, and began to build the house of God which is at

Jerusalem; and with them were *the prophets of God helping them*" (Ezra v. 1, 2).

The first of these prophets was HAGGAI. His name signifies the *festal one* (S. Jerome here. Gesen. 260; Fuerst, 416; Hengst., Keil). One of the sources of the deepest sorrow to the mourners over Zion was this, that by reason of the destruction of her Temple, her solemn festivals could no longer be kept. "They wept, because the solemn feasts and sabbaths were forgotten" (Lam. ii. 6); and "all her mirth ceased, her feast days, her new moons, and her sabbaths, and all her solemn feasts" (Hos. ii. 11). But the promise of comfort to Zion was, that she should again "keep her solemn feasts" (Nahum i. 15); and the last Prophet before the Captivity, Zephaniah, in his final utterance before that event, had cheered the mourners with the assurance that God would gather those who were sorrowful for the cessation of the solemn assemblies (Zeph. iii. 18).

Very appropriate, therefore, is the name of the first Prophet after the Captivity, HAGGAI, properly *Chaggai*, from *Chag, a festival* (Gesen., Fuerst). He it was who was specially raised up by God to stimulate the flagging energies of the feeble company which had returned from Babylon to Jerusalem, and were dispirited and disheartened by opposition from without, and by lukewarmness and faithlessness from within, to resume the suspended work, and to complete the rebuilding of the Temple.

The significance of this name, Haggai, the festal one, will still further appear, if we remember that the Feast of Tabernacles was called specially by the Jews, *the chag*, or *feast*. See above, on Lev. xviii. 24. 1 Kings viii. 65. Ezra iii. 4; and below, ii. 2; and (as is shown in those notes) it was typical of the Incarnation of the Son of God, Who pitched His *tabernacle* in our flesh (John i. 14), and Who will *tabernacle* with His saints for ever. See Rev. vii. 15; xxi. 3.

The powerful motive, by which Haggai excited the Jews to prosecute and complete the work of building the Temple—which was begun at the Feast of Tabernacles (Ezra iii. 4)—was this, that, however insignificant this latter house might be in their eyes (from which tears flowed when they saw its foundation)—however in material respects, and in splendour of decoration, it was inferior to the former house, the Temple of Solomon—though no visible cloud of glory rested upon it (such as took possession of the Temple of Solomon at its dedication: see on 1 Kings viii. 10, 11)—though it had not the Ark of the Covenant, and the Two Tables of the Testimony in the Holy of Holies, nor the Urim and Thummim, nor the Fire from heaven on the Altar, nor the holy oil (cp. Bp. Pearson, Art. ii. p. 83)—yet, in fact, it would be far more glorious than Solomon's Temple. And why? Because the Lord God Himself, tabernacling in human flesh, would visibly appear there, and would "fill the house with the glory" of His presence, and "in that place would give peace, saith the Lord of hosts" (ii. 7—9).

When we consider that all the Hebrew festivals were fulfilled in Christ; that He is our Passover (1 Cor. v. 7); that by His Ascension, and sending of the Holy Ghost, all the shadowy glories of the Hebrew Pentecost are consummated (Acts ii. 1); that by His Incarnation we celebrate a perpetual Feast of Tabernacles in the spiritual Jerusalem of the Universal Church of Christ; and that all the Festivals of the Christian Church,—the weekly Festival of the Lord's Day, and the Sacrament of Regeneration, and the Festival of the Holy Eucharist, and all the Holy Days of the Christian Year,—derive all their virtue, beauty, and grace from the Incarnation, Death, Resur-

1

[1] Zerubbabel the son of Shealtiel, ‖ governor of Judah, and to [c] Joshua the son of [a] Josedech, the high priest, saying, [2] Thus speaketh the LORD of hosts, saying, This people say, The time is not come, the time that the LORD'S house should be built.

[3] Then came the word of the LORD [b] by Haggai the prophet, saying,

[4] [c] *Is it* time for you, O ye, to dwell in your cieled houses,
And this house *lie* waste?

[5] Now therefore thus saith the LORD of hosts; † [f] Consider your ways.

[6] Ye have [h] sown much, and bring in little;
Ye eat, but ye have not enough;
Ye drink, but ye are not filled with drink;
Ye clothe you, but there is none warm;
And [i] he that earneth wages earneth wages *to put it* into a bag † with holes.

[7] Thus saith the LORD of hosts; Consider your ways.

[8] Go up to the mountain, and bring wood, and build the house;
And I will take pleasure in it, and I will be glorified, saith the LORD.

[9] [k] Ye looked for much, and, lo, *it came* to little;
And when ye brought *it* home, [l] I did ‖ blow upon it.
Why? saith the LORD of hosts.
Because of mine house that *is* waste,
And ye run every man unto his own house.

[10] Therefore [m] the heaven over you is stayed from dew,
And the earth is stayed *from* her fruit.

[11] And I [n] called for a drought upon the land, and upon the mountains, and upon the corn, and upon the new wine, and upon the oil, and upon *that* which the ground bringeth forth, and upon men, and upon cattle, and [o] upon all the labour of the hands.

[12] [p] Then Zerubbabel the son of Shealtiel, and Joshua the son of Josedech, the high priest, with all the remnant of the people, obeyed the voice of the LORD their God, and the words of Haggai the prophet, as the LORD their God had sent him, and the people did fear before the LORD.

---

rection, and Ascension of "God manifest in the flesh," we may recognize here a witness in the name of the Prophet Haggai, whose mission it was to urge the Jews to rebuild the Temple, on the ground that the Lord Himself would glorify it with His Presence, and thus the "glory of the latter house would be greater than that of the former, saith the Lord of hosts." See the remarks above, on Ezra and Nehemiah, *Introd.*, pp. 296—299, which may afford some appropriate illustration here.

Ch. I. 1. *second year.*] See Ezra iv. 24.

— *Darius*] Hystaspes, who reigned from B.C. 521 to 486. On the meaning of the name, see above, at Ezra iv. 5.

— *first day of the month*] On the festival of the full moon. The prophecies of *Haggai* (the *festal*: see *Prelim. Note*) begin on the first festival of the sixth month.

— *Zerubbabel*] Of the royal seed sown at Babel, or Babylon. See 1 Chron. iii. 19; and Ezra i. 8—11; ii. 2; iii. 2; v. 14—16, as to the question how he is called *the son of Shealtiel* (asked of God), or Salathiel, as he is called also in Luke iii. 27.

— *Josedech*] That is *righteousness of Jehovah*. See Ezra ii. 2. 1 Chron. v. 11, as to the typical character of Zerubbabel, the representative of the royal seed of David; and of Joshua (*Saviour*), the son of Josedech (*righteousness of Jehovah*), the High Priest, both joined together in building the Temple, and thus together foreshadowing the work of Christ, Who was the True King of the seed of David, and is also our Great and Everlasting High Priest. "Historically" (*S. Jerome* says), "Zerubbabel, of the royal tribe, is one person, and Joshua, of the priestly dignity, is another person; but spiritually they are joined together in Him Who is our Lord and Saviour (Joshua), and our great High Priest, and also the King of all faithful Israelites." See above, *Introd.* to Ezra, p. 297. *S.*

114

*Jerome* says again here: "Hic Zorobabel de Tribu Juda, hoc est, de David stirpe descendens, typus est Salvatoris, qui verò destructum ædificavit Templum et reduxit populum de captivitate; et tam de veteris Templi lapidibus quàm de novis, qui priùs fuerant impoliti, ædificavit Ecclesiam, id est de reliquiis populi Judaici et de Gentium multitudine."

2. *The time is not come*] For the reason of this saying, see the *Prelim. Note.* The literal meaning is, [it is] *not time* [for us] *to come* [up to the site of the Temple]; [it is] *not time* for *building the house.*

4. *for you, O ye*] Rather, *for you yourselves.*

— *in your cieled houses*] In your houses *wainscoted* with cedar, and all costly woodwork (*Targum*). Cp. 1 Kings vii. 7. Jer. xxi; 14.

5. *Consider your ways*] Set your heart upon your ways,— an exhortation repeated v. 7; ii. 15. 18.

6. *Ye have sown much*] Cp. Deut. xxviii. 38. Hos. iv. 10. Mic. vi. 14. 15. God chastens you by dearth and drought, in order to make you consider your ways, and amend them, and to become fruitful in a spiritual harvest of good works.

8. *Go up to the mountain*] To the mountainous region; not to any particular mountain. See below, on Matt. v. 1.

9. *I did blow upon it*] And made it fly away, like chaff before the wind.

— *Because of mine house that is waste*] Observe the alliteration in the original: "Because my house *is chāreb*" (waste, or desolate),—the same word as is used by Nehemiah ii. 3, "the city of my father's sepulchres lieth *waste*;" and again ii. 17, "New Jerusalem lieth *waste*;" and Jer. xxviii. 10, 12,—"Therefore I have called upon you, *chóreb*, a *drought*" (v. 11).

<sup>13</sup> Then spake Haggai the LORD's messenger in the LORD's message unto the people, saying, <sup>q</sup> I *am* with you, saith the LORD. Before CHRIST about 520.<br>q Matt. 28, 44. Rom. 8, 31.

<sup>14</sup> And 'the LORD stirred up the spirit of Zerubbabel the son of Shealtiel, 'governor of Judah, and the spirit of Joshua the son of Josedech, the high priest, and the spirit of all the remnant of the people ; 'and they came and did work in the house of the LORD of hosts, their God, <sup>15</sup> in the four and twentieth day of the sixth month, in the second year of Darius the king. r 2 Chr. 36, 22.<br>Ezra 1. 1.<br>s ch. 2, 21.<br>t Ezra 5, 2, 8.

II. <sup>1</sup> In the seventh *month*, in the one and twentieth *day* of the month, came the word of the LORD † by the prophet Haggai, saying, <sup>2</sup> Speak now to Zerub-babel the son of Shealtiel, governor of Judah, and to Joshua the son of Josedech, the high priest, and to the residue of the people, saying, <sup>3</sup> <sup>a</sup> Who *is* left among you that saw this house in her first glory ? and how do ye see it now ? <sup>b</sup> *is it* not in your eyes in comparison of it as nothing ? † Heb. *by the hand of.*<br>a Ezra 3, 12.<br><br>b Zech. 4, 10.

<sup>4</sup> Yet now <sup>c</sup>be strong, O Zerubbabel, saith the LORD ; and be strong, O Joshua, son of Josedech, the high priest ; and be strong, all ye people of the land, saith the LORD, and work : for I *am* with you, saith the LORD of hosts : <sup>5</sup> <sup>d</sup> *According to* the word that I covenanted with you when ye came out of Egypt, so <sup>e</sup> my spirit remaineth among you : fear ye not. c Zech. 3, 2.<br><br>d Ex. 29, 45, 46.<br>e Neh. 9, 20.<br>Isa. 63, 11.

<sup>6</sup> For thus saith the LORD of hosts ; <sup>f</sup> Yet once, it *is* a little while, and <sup>g</sup> I will shake the heavens, and the earth, and the sea, and the dry *land ;* <sup>7</sup> and I will shake all nations, <sup>h</sup> and the desire of all nations shall come : and I will fill this f ver. 21.<br>Heb. 12, 26.<br>g Joel 3, 16.<br><br>h Gen. 49, 10.<br>Mal. 3, 1.

---

15. *In the four and twentieth day*] That is, the four-and-twentieth day of the month in which 'the Prophet had begun to exhort them, which he did on the first day of it (r. 1; and see ii. 18).

For the chronology of this period, see *Introd.* to Ezra, p. 295 ; and on Ezra v. 1; vi. 22.

THE GLORY OF THE SECOND TEMPLE.

Ch. II. 1. *In the seventh* month, *in the one and twentieth day of the month*] Of the second year of Darius ; twenty-four days after the foregoing appeal (in the former chapter), which had induced them to resume the work of rebuilding the Temple. It is observable that this prophecy was delivered on the *seventh day*, or the great day, of the great *Feast of Tabernacles* (see Lev. xxiii. 34), which was typical of the *Incarnation* of Christ, Who was presented in our flesh in this Temple, and filled this house with His glory. Cp. above, *Prelim. Note.*

The building was now prosecuted under great difficulties (Ezra v. 3—10) till it was finally completed and dedicated, in the sixth year of Darius—the twenty-first after the publication of the Edict of Cyrus, which, having been lost for a time, was providentially discovered at Ecbatana. See Ezra vi. 1. 15. 22. Ezra, the Priest and Scribe, did not come from Babylon to Jerusalem till fifty-three years afterwards, B.C. 458 (Ezra vii. 1). Nehemiah, the cup-bearer of Artaxerxes, the builder of the *Walls* of Jerusalem, came from Susa to Jerusalem fourteen years after Ezra's journey to Jerusalem. See *Introd.* to Ezra, p. 295.

Observe, therefore, how long the patience of God's people was tried. They only, who stood steadfast in patience, faith, and hope, were rewarded. Here is a lesson to our own age, when men's hearts fail, because they are sorely distressed by present trials, and do not firmly believe in the final triumph of Truth.

3. *Who is left among you that saw this house in her first glory ?*] See Ezra iii. 12, and above, *Prelim. Note.* It was now about sixty-six years since the destruction of the first Temple by the Chaldeans.

4. *be strong, O Zerubbabel*] Compare the words of Zechariah the Prophet (iv. 6—9) : "This is the word of the Lord unto Zerubbabel, saying, Not by might, nor by power, but by my Spirit, saith the Lord of hosts. Who art thou, O great mountain? before Zerubbabel thou shalt become a plain ; and he shall bring forth the head-stone thereof with shoutings, crying, Grace, grace unto it. The hands of Zerubbabel have laid the foundation of this house, his hands shall also finish it, and thou shalt know that the Lord of hosts hath sent me unto you." See also Zech. viii. 9. 13. "Let your hands be *strong.* . . . Fear not, let your *hands be strong.*"

115

5. *According to the word*] Rather, *the word.* The Word of God and the Spirit of God are with you. See the next note.

— so *My Spirit remaineth among you*] *Vulg., Syriac,* and see *Targum.* A remarkable expression, especially when explained by later events. Christ was in the ancient Church in the wilderness (see 1 Cor. x. 9. Heb. xi. 26) ; and now, when the Eternal *Word* became Incarnate, and when the *Holy Spirit* was sent to be *in the midst* of God's faithful people, then this prophecy was fulfilled.

6. *Yet once*] That is, *once more.* The first shaking was at Mount Sinai, to which the reference is in the foregoing verse. See Heb. xii. 26, and *S. Jerome* here.

6, 7. *I will shake the heavens, and the earth, and the sea, and the dry* land ; *and I will shake all nations*] The prophecy of shaking, as the Apostle to the Hebrews teaches us (Heb. xii. 26), was fulfilled in the Coming of Christ from heaven.

The shaking of all Nations took place *in a little while* after the Prophet's own days ; it was like the shock of an earthquake. It was felt in the breaking up of the Persian monarchy by Alexander the Great, and by the splitting up of his Empire, and by the crushing of the powers of the Nations of the World by Rome, which subjugated and humbled them, and destroyed their faith in their national deities, which were unable to save them, and thus prepared the way for the reception of a holier faith, that of the Gospel of Christ. See the excellent remarks of *Bp. Pearson* on this mission of the Roman Empire (in his 3rd Concio, Minor Works, ii. 35). Just before the Coming of Christ, "the Roman arms (says he) had broken the preconceived superstitions of the heathen concerning their false deities. Wherever Rome's victorious eagles flew, there the majesty of the ancient gods fell, and their authority was destroyed. As many conquests as Rome achieved over Nations, so many triumphs did she celebrate over their national deities. It was a very ancient notion, that the gods forsook the cities which were taken and occupied by enemies. Thus the armies of Rome had put to flight all the deities ; and the Romans had so learned to exult over the deities of other nations, that they scarcely worshipped their own, except with lukewarmness and indifference." Thus the Nations of the Earth were prepared for Christianity. Cp. *Hengstenberg* and *Keil* here.

THE DESIRE OF ALL NATIONS.

7. *the desire of all nations shall come*] So this passage was rendered by the ancient Jewish Expositors, as *R. Akiba* (Talm. Sanh. C. x. Sect. 30, *Maimon.* in Sanhed.; and this is acknowledged by *Jarchi*). And the Chaldee *Targum* here translates it thus, "The desire of all nations shall come;" and so the *Vulgate,* which understands it as applied to a Person, "Veniet desideratus

house with glory, saith the LORD of hosts.   [8] The silver *is* mine, and the gold *is* mine, saith the LORD of hosts.   [9] The glory of this latter house shall be

---

cunctis gentibus," i.e. "He who is desired by all Nations shall come." And so the Latin Fathers, as *S. Jerome* here, who (having mentioned the other interpretation of the *Sept.*, which will be noticed presently) says, "According to the Hebrew original, this signifies that He Who was desired by all Nations—the Lord and Saviour—will come; and then I will fill this house with greater glory than the former, saith the Lord of hosts. And because I know that nothing is so conducive to the edification of My glorious house as Peace, therefore, in this house I will give Peace—even the Peace that passeth all understanding. Therefore, O Zerubbabel, thou son of Josedech, and thou Joshua, the High Priest, be strong, take courage, and build this house."

The *Septuagint* (he observes) renders these words "the elect things, or choice things, of all Nations shall come." And, truly, to the Church of Christ have come the elect things of Corinth, Macedonia, and the elect of Babylon (1 Pet. v. 13), for the Apostles of Christ had a commission from Him to go and teach all Nations and bring them into the Church. So the *Septuagint.* "But" (adds *S. Jerome*) "it is better to understand it as it is in the Hebrew, which signifies that He Who was desired by all Nations would come to that Temple, and by His Coming to it would fill it with glory; so that its glory would be greater than that of the Temple of Solomon; inasmuch as the Lord of the Temple is greater than His servant who does His will." So S. Augustine, De Civ. Dei, xvii. 18, and *Remigius, Haymo, Hugo, Lyranus, Luther, A Lapide, Drusius, Grotius, Tirinus, Munster, Vatablus, Calovius, Glassius, Bp. Andrewes,* 240, Bp. *Pearson* on the Creed, Art. ii., Bp. *Chandler*, i. 77, *W. Lowth, Davison* on Prophecy, Disc. vi. p. 238. Hence *S. Bernard*,

> "Desidero Te millies,
> Mi JESU, quando venies?
> Me lætum quando facies,
> Dulcedo ineffabilis,
> Totus desiderabilis?"

and in the Hymn at the festival of the Ascension:

> "Jesu, nostra redemptio,
> Amor et desiderium,
> Tu esto nostrum gaudium.
> Et nostra in Te gloria
> Per cuncta semper sæcula."

These words of Haggai, applied to the Messiah, seem to be grounded on Jacob's prophecy, "The sceptre shall not depart from Judah, nor a lawgiver from between his feet, until *Shiloh come*; and to *Him shall the gathering of the people* (or peoples) *be.*" See on Gen. xlix. 10. And this interpretation, which applies Haggai's words to Christ, is confirmed by the language of his successor Malachi, who, speaking of the *latter house*, or second temple, says, "*The Lord*, whom ye seek, shall suddenly come to His temple, even the messenger of the covenant, whom ye delight in, behold He shall come, saith the Lord of hosts" (Mal. iii. 1). And the aged Simeon, when he took the Infant Jesus into his arms, at His presentation in that Temple, declared the fulfilment of the prophecy, when he said, "Lord, now lettest Thou Thy servant depart in peace: for mine eyes have seen Thy salvation, which Thou hast prepared *before the face of all people, a light to lighten the Gentiles, and the glory of Thy people Israel*" (Luke ii. 29).

Let us now consider the objections to this interpretation.

The Hebrew words here, *chamdath col-hag-gojim*, i.e. *et veniet* (plural) *desiderium* (singular) *omnium gentium.*

(1) First it is said that *chemdáh* cannot be applied to a person, and cannot signify an object of desire.

But this allegation does not seem of much force.

The substantive *chemdáh* is derived from the verb *chamad*, to desire, to long for, to delight in (*Gesenius*, 286; *Fuerst*, 456). As *Keil* says, "*chem-dah* signifies *desire* (2 Chron. xxi. 20); then, the *object* of desire," as costly things, valuables. We may compare "desiderium" in Latin; as *Cicero* addresses his wife, "Valete, desideria mea." Ep. xiv.

The cognate word *machmad* is often used in this sense of *object of desire*, as in 1 Kings xx. 6. Cant. v. 16. Lam. i. 10. Ezek. xxiv. 16, where Ezekiel's wife is called "the desire of his eyes." Cp. ibid. *vv.* 21, 25. Hos. ix. 16. Joel iii. 5.

Another objection is, that the singular noun *chemdáh* is joined to a plural verb, *bau*, and this is irreconcilable with the opinion that *chemdáh* represents a Person.

Doubtless, if the Person were any common Person, this objection would have much force.

But first let it be observed that in the original the verb
116

---

*precedes* the noun. It is *bau chemdah*, i.e. "There shall come" (plural) "the desire." The mind is kept for a time in suspense by *bau* (there shall come), and asks, *what* will come? The answer is *chemdáth col-hag-gojim* (the desire of all nations).

Now, let it be supposed, for argument's sake, that the version of the Targum and the Vulgate is correct, and that this is a prophecy of the Coming of the MESSIAH to the Temple, is it wonderful that the singular substantive here should be combined with a plural verb, when we consider that the Messiah contains in His own single Person the two distinct Natures of God and Man, and the three offices of Prophet, Priest, and King? Might He not be justly regarded as a collective Being? And collective nouns are often followed by a plural verb in Hebrew. See *Glass*, Philol. Sacr. Lib. iii., Tract iii., Canon 53; and *Gesen.* Gram. § 146; *Ewald*, Gram. § 307. 6. See Gen. xxxiii. 13; xli. 17. Num. x. 3. 1 Kings i. 10. 1 Chron. x. 6. Ezra x. 12. Ps. lxviii. 11.

The objection to our authorized translation (that in the original the verb is plural and the noun is singular), lies with still greater force against the other translation, which renders the noun as if it were plural, and explains it as "*desirable things*" so *Hengst., Keil*, and others. *Ewald* renders it "the *most longed-for of all nations.*" *Rückert* translates it "the *choicest nations*," and so *Hitzig.* They regard this as a prophecy of the offering of the treasures of the Gentiles to the Second Temple.

There is also another insuperable objection to the exposition which regards this prophecy as foretelling that the Gentiles would bring offerings to the Second Temple, and that therefore it would be more glorious than the Temple of Solomon. The fact is, the Gentiles brought offerings to Solomon's Temple. The Tyrians and Phœnicians hewed the cedars of Lebanon for it at its first erection; and in the days of Hezekiah many brought gifts unto the Lord to Jerusalem (2 Chron. xxxii. 23). But, on the other hand, the Heathen did *not bring* their desirable things to the *second* Temple. All the prophecies, such as those of Isaiah and others (Isa. lx. 5, 11. Micah iv. 13. Zech. xiv. 14), which are quoted in this sense, are distorted from their true meaning. They are all to be applied to the offerings which the Nations will bring of themselves and of their wealth to the spiritual Temple of Zion, the Christian Church (see below, on Rev. xxi. 24); and it is observable that some interpreters, who apply them here as predictive of oblations to the material Temple raised by Zerubbabel, have, in other places, rightly explained them, as pointing to contributions of the heathen, not to any material Temple at all, but to the Church of Christ. Nor, even if all the Nations of the Earth had united together in bringing their "desirable things" to the Second Temple—which they never did—could it ever be said, as a *consequence* of this, that God *filled this house with glory*; and in this house will I give peace (v. 9).

Observe that the *coming of what is desirable* to the Temple is put *first* by the Prophet, and then the *filling of the house with the glory* is represented as a result of the Coming; whereas the offerings of the Gentiles were consequent on the Coming of Christ. The filling the house with glory, with the *glory of the Lord of Hosts*, cannot be regarded as a *result* of the bringing of mere perishable gold and silver (which cannot be shown to have been brought at all) to the Temple of Zerubbabel; but can only be regarded as a consequence of the Divine Presence, seen in the Coming of Christ, the Lord God Himself, to the Temple.

Let any one examine the passages of Holy Scripture where this word glory (Hebr. *câbôd*) occurs, and where a place is said to be *filled with the glory of the Lord*, and he will be satisfied of this. See Exod. xl. 34, 35, concerning the *filling* of the Tabernacle *with the glory of the Lord*; and 1 Kings viii. 11. 2 Chron. v. 11; vii. 1, 2, 3, where the *glory of the Lord* is said to have *filled the Temple*; and compare the passages in Ezek. iii. 23; xliii. 4, 5; xliv. 4. This interpretation is further confirmed by the words of Haggai's brother-prophet, Malachi (iii. 1. 4), already quoted, "*The Lord*, whom ye seek, shall suddenly come to His *Temple*; behold, He shall come, saith the Lord of hosts; then shall the offering of Judah and Jerusalem be pleasant unto the Lord." The Coming of the Lord Himself to the latter house, and the benefits attendant on the Presence of Him "in Whom all the families of the Earth are blessed," filled the minds of both these Prophets with a vision of glory.

On the whole, we may adopt the words of Bp. *Pearson* (Art. ii. p. 88) on the text; and with them this note shall conclude.

"In the same manner the Prophet Malachi hath given an express signification of the Coming of the Messias while the greater than of the former, saith the LORD of hosts: and in this place will I give <sup>k</sup> peace, saith the LORD of hosts.

Before CHRIST about 520.
k Ps. 85. 8, 9.
Luke 2. 14.
Eph. 2. 14.

<sup>10</sup> In the four and twentieth *day* of the ninth *month*, in the second year of Darius, came the word of the LORD by Haggai the prophet, saying, <sup>11</sup> Thus saith the LORD of hosts;

l Lev. 10, 10, 11.
Deut. 33. 10.
Mal. 2. 7.

<sup>l</sup> Ask now the priests *concerning* the law, saying, <sup>12</sup> If one bear holy flesh in

Temple stood (Mal. iii. 1), ‘Behold, I will send My messenger, and he shall prepare the way before Me; and the Lord whom ye seek, shall suddenly come to His Temple, even the Messenger of the Covenant whom ye delight in.’ And Haggai yet more clearly (Hag. ii. 6, 7. 9), ‘Thus saith the Lord of hosts; Yet once, it is a little while, and I will shake the heavens, and the earth, and the sea, and the dry land, and I will shake all nations, and the desire of all nations shall come; and I will fill this house with glory, saith the Lord of hosts. The glory of this latter house shall be greater than the glory of the former, saith the Lord of hosts.’

“It is, then, most evident from these predictions, that the *Messias* was to come while the second Temple stood. It is as certain that the second Temple is not now standing. Therefore, except we contradict the veracity of God, it cannot be denied but the *Messias* is already come.

“Nothing can be objected to enervate this argument, but that these prophecies concern not the *Messias*; and yet the ancient Jews confessed they did; and that they do so cannot be denied.

“For, first, those titles, ‘*the Angel of the Covenant*,’ ‘*the Delight of the Israelites*,’ ‘*the Desire of all Nations*,’ are certain and known characters of the Christ to come.

“And, secondly, it cannot be conceived how the glory of the second Temple should be greater than the glory of the first, without the coming of the *Messias* to it. For the Jews themselves have observed that five signs of the divine glory were in the first Temple, which were wanting to the second—as the Urim and Thummim, by which the High-priest was miraculously instructed of the Will of God; the Ark of the Covenant, from whence God gave His answers by a clear and audible voice; the fire upon the altar, which came down from heaven, and immediately consumed the sacrifice; the divine Presence, or habitation with them, represented by a visible appearance, or given, as it were, to the King and High-priest, by anointing with the oil of unction; and, lastly, the spirit of prophecy, with which those especially who were called to the prophetical office were endued.

“And there was no comparison between the beauty and glory of the structure or building of it, as appeared by the tears dropped from those eyes which had beheld the former (Ezra iii. 12); for ‘many of the priests and Levites, and chief of the fathers, who were ancient men, that had seen the first house, when the foundation of this house was laid before their eyes, wept with a loud voice;’ and by those words which God commanded Haggai to speak to the people for the introducing of this prophecy (Hag. ii. 3):—‘Who is left among you that saw this house in her first glory? And how do ye see it now? Is it not in your eyes in comparison of it as nothing?’

“Being, then, the structure of the second Temple was so far inferior to the first, being all those signs of the divine glory were wanting in it with which the former was adorned; the glory of it can no other way be imagined greater, than by the coming of Him into it, in Whom all those signs of the divine glory were far more eminently contained; and this person alone is the *Messias*. For He was to be the glory of the people Israel, yea, even of the God of Israel; He, the Urim and Thummim, by whom the Will of God, as by a greater oracle, was revealed; He, the true Ark of the Covenant, the only propitiatory by His blood; He which was to baptize with the Holy Ghost and with fire—the true fire which came down from heaven; He which was to take up His habitation in our flesh, and to dwell among us that we might behold His glory; He who received the Spirit without measure, and from whose fulness we do all receive. In Him were all those signs of the Divine glory united, which were thus divided in the first Temple; in Him they were all more eminently contained than in those; therefore, His Coming to the second Temple was, as the sufficient, so the only means by which the glory of it could be greater than the glory of the first.

“If, then, the *Messias* was to come while the second Temple stood, as appeareth by God’s prediction and promise, if that Temple many ages hath ceased to be, there being not one stone left upon a stone; if it certainly were, before the destruction

117

of it, in greater glory than ever the former was; if no such glory could accrue unto it but by the Coming of the *Messias*, then is that *Messias* already come” (*Bp. Pearson*).

**8.** *The silver is mine, and the gold is mine, saith the* LORD *of hosts*] Therefore, do not be distressed because this latter house is not adorned with so much splendour of silver and gold as was the former house, the Temple of Solomon. All the Earth is My Temple. Every beast of the forest which is brought to Me for sacrifice is already Mine (Ps. l. 10). All the silver and gold in it are Mine by creation, and adorn that Universal Temple; as David, the father of Solomon, declared, when he offered to God what he had prepared for the Temple which was to be built by his son: “Thine, O Lord, is the greatness, and the power, and the glory, and the victory, and the majesty: for all that is in the heaven and in the earth is Thine. . . . Both riches and honour come of Thee; . . . and of Thine own have we given Thee” (1 Chron. xxix. 11—14).

These words may be rightly applied, with an ancient African Bishop, to stimulate the grace of Christian almsgiving: “When you hear the precepts of giving alms, take heed and remember that God is commanding thee to give, not of what belongs to thee, but of what belongs to Himself; lest when thou art bestowing thine alms on the poor, thou shouldest be puffed up with vain-glorious imaginations. ‘Mine is the silver, Mine is the gold’ (saith the Lord). It is not yours. O ye rich men of the earth, why therefore do ye hesitate to give of Mine to the poor? Or why are ye so proud when ye give it?” (*S. Augustine*, Serm. 50).

**9.** *The glory of this latter house shall be greater than of the former*] Because it will be filled with glory by the Coming to it of the *Lord of Glory*, as Christ is called, 1 Cor. ii. 8. Cp. James ii. 1. See above, on v. 7. In all other respects *this latter house* was as nothing in comparison with the former (v. 3). But having the *Lord of Glory* visibly presented in it, and teaching in it, it was filled with glory, and it had all the substance consummated in its splendour and majesty, of which all the ornaments, and all the sacrifices of the former house were only faint types and dim foreshadowings.

From this passage, and from that of Malachi (iii. 1), “The Lord shall suddenly come to His Temple,” we may conclude, against the Jews, that the Messiah is come, and that His coming is not future; for He was to come to His Temple, to that latter house, which was in course of being built when Haggai prophesied, to which Jesus of Nazareth did indeed come, and of which, as the same Jesus prophesied, not a single stone now remains upon another (Matt. xxiv. 2. Mark xiii. 2. Luke xix. 44), so that no Messiah can now come to it.

The registers of imperial Rome, the great heathen mistress of the world, by enrolling the names of Joseph, and Mary the mother of Jesus, in the census of Bethlehem, proved that He was born there; the armies of Rome, by destroying the Temple of Jerusalem, proved that the Messiah is come. And when the Roman Emperor Julian attempted to rebuild the Temple, in order to invalidate that argument, God intervened in a wonderful manner to frustrate the work (*Chrysost*, Orat. 3, in Judæos; *Ammian*. xxiii. 1; *Socrates*, iii. 17; *Theodoret*, iii. 15; *Sozomen*, v. 21; *Bp. Warburton’s* Julian; *Gibbon*, ch. xxii.; *De Broglie*, iv. 333). Thus Rome preaches Christ.

— *in this place will I give peace*] I will there give Him Who is the Prince of Peace (Isa. ix. 6), and through Whom we have peace with God; and Who has given us His peace (John xiv. 27; xvi. 33); and Who is Peace (Eph. ii. 14).

**10.** *In the four and twentieth day of the ninth* month, *in the second year of Darius*] A little more than two months after the delivery of the former prophecy (ii. 1). So soon was the prospect of things changed from sadness to joy, by the obedience of the people to the divine appeal, that now, near the end of the ninth month *Chisleu* (corresponding nearly to the latter part of our November and to the first part of December), when the sowing of the winter crops was finished, God gave them a respite from the drought, and a grateful supply of former rain, with a promise of an abundant harvest.

**11.** *Ask now the priests*] The Prophet of the Lord may

the skirt of his garment, and with his skirt do touch bread, or pottage, or wine, or oil, or any meat, shall it be holy?

And the priests answered and said, No.

m Num. 19. 11.

¹³ Then said Haggai, If *one that is* ᵐ unclean *by a dead body* touch any of these, shall it be unclean?

And the priests answered and said, It shall be unclean.

n Tit. 1. 15.

¹⁴ Then answered Haggai, and said, ⁿ So *is* this people, and so *is* this nation before me, saith the LORD: and so *is* every work of their hands; and that which they offer there *is* unclean.

o ch. 1. 5.

¹⁵ And now, I pray you, ᵒ consider from this day and upward, from before a stone was laid upon a stone in the temple of the LORD: ¹⁶ since those *days* were, ᵖ when *one* came to an heap of twenty *measures*, there were *but* ten: when *one* came to the pressfat for to draw out fifty *vessels* out of the press, there were *but* twenty. ¹⁷ ᑫ I smote you with blasting and with mildew and with hail ʳ in all the labours of your hands; ˢ yet ye *turned* not to me, saith the LORD.

p ch. 1. 6, 9.
Zech. 8. 10.

q Deut. 28. 22.
1 Kings 8. 37.
Amos 4. 9.
ch. 1. 9.
r ch. 1. 11.
s Jer. 5. 3.
Amos 4. 6, 8, 9,
10, 11.
t Zech. 8. 9.

¹⁸ Consider now from this day and upward, from the four and twentieth day of the ninth *month, even* from ᵗ the day that the foundation of the LORD's temple was laid, consider *it*.

u Zech. 8. 12.

¹⁹ ᵘ Is the seed yet in the barn? yea, as yet the vine, and the fig tree, and the pomegranate, and the olive tree, hath not brought forth: from this day will I bless *you*.

²⁰ And again the word of the LORD came unto Haggai in the four and twentieth *day* of the month, saying, ²¹ Speak to Zerubbabel, ˣ governor of

x ch. 1. 14.

---

not intrude into priestly functions, but must pay respect to the priesthood, as Christ did (Matt. viii. 4).

**12.** *If*] Literally, *Behold.*

— *holy flesh*] Sanctified and offered to the Lord in sacrifice.

— *pottage*] Literally, what is *boiled.*

— *No*] The offering is holy; but the thing touched by it does not become holy by the contact. The offering could not communicate holiness to what it touched. For the moral application of this, see what follows (*v.* 14).

**13.** *unclean by a dead body*] Literally, *unclean by a soul*—a phrase derived from the Levitical Law. See on Lev. xxii. 4. Cp. Num. v. 2; vi. 6; ix. 6, 10.

— *It shall be unclean*] For so it is declared in the Levitical Law (Lev. vi. 19. Num. xix. 11, 22).

**14.** *So is this people—and so is every work of their hands*] This people lives, it is true, in a holy Land, which is, as it were, an offering dedicated to the Lord; but the Land does not communicate any holiness to the People by any intrinsic virtue of its own, but it entails upon them all an obligation to personal holiness. They who live in the Holy Land, and draw near to the Presence of the Holy One in His holy house, ought themselves to be holy; just as they who feed on the holy flesh of the sacrifices are to be holy persons. See the note above, on Lev. vi. 18.

Yet further; if they themselves are morally dead in trespasses and sins, then the holiness of the Land will do them no good; nay, rather, since what is evil communicates its virulent poison by contact, they will pollute every thing that they touch with the foul taint of that moral and spiritual death.

We may here refer to the notes above (Lev. x. 6, 19), on the inner meaning of the Levitical Law concerning the contaminating influence of Death in the natural World, and on the blessed contrast produced in this respect by Christ's Incarnation, Death, Burial, and Resurrection, under the Gospel.

THE WINGS OR SKIRTS OF THE GARMENT.

In further illustration of those remarks, we may observe the words here used by the Prophet Haggai. He says that no *holy flesh* of a sacrifice carried in the *skirt* can *communicate* holiness.

The word used by him twice for *skirt* is *cânâph*, literally, *a wing.* Let us refer to his two brother prophets, Zechariah and Malachi. Zechariah predicts, that in the days of the Gospel, "Ten men shall take hold out of all languages, even shall take hold of the *skirt* (*cânâph*) of him that is a Jew, saying, We

118

will go with you; for we have heard that God is with you" (Zech. viii. 23). That is, all nations will take hold of the *skirt*, or hem, of the garment of Christ, Who is "the Word made *flesh.*" "God manifest in the *flesh*"—of Him Who is born King of the Jews. They will take hold of it by faith in His *Incarnation*, as the faithful woman laid hold of the hem of His garment; and virtue will go out from Him—from His holy flesh—to heal them, as it healed her. See Matt. ix. 20—23. Mark v. 30. Luke vi. 19.

Remark also, further, this contrast:—that whereas the flesh of a dead man, under the Levitical Law (as Haggai here reminds us), communicated defilement; and as Death under the Law was a source of pollution, now under the Gospel our only well-spring of Life and Purity is through the Death of Christ. It is from His *flesh*; it is from His blessed body, pierced for us, and hanging in death on the Cross, that the sanctifying, sacramental streams of blood and water flowed, which cleanse the heart of the believer. His Death is our Source of Life. By Death He overcame Death, and destroyed him who had the power of it (Heb. ii. 14), and has made us to be heirs of eternal life. But in order that this may be so, there must be faith on our part; there must be personal holiness in them that touch Him; and therefore Malachi, adopting the same word, *cânâph*, completes the statement of his brother prophets Haggai and Zechariah, by saying, "Unto you that *fear My Name*, the Sun of Righteousness" (Christ, "the Lord our Righteousness," as Jeremiah calls Him) "shall arise with *healing in His wings*," or *skirts* (*cenaphim*, Mal. iv. 2).

**15.** *before a stone was laid*] Literally, *from the not yet of laying stone to stone* (Keil, Fuerst, 526), or *before the beginning of laying* (Gesen. 325), when you were faithless and disobedient, then ye were chastened by God; but if ye return to Him, and build His house, He will hasten to be gracious to you.

The Prophet desires them first to look *backward* on their punishments for disobeying God, and then look *forwards* to their blessings for obeying Him.

**18, 19.** *Consider now from this day and upward*] Or, *from this day and forward*, or *onward*. Here is the contrast. It is still winter (see v. 10); the seed has only just been committed to the earth; it is not yet in the barn. There are no fresh leaves as yet on your fruit-trees—your vine, fig tree, pomegranate, and olive-tree—but ye have begun again to build the house of the Lord; and even from this day forward I will hasten to bless you.

**20.** *in the four and twentieth day of the month*] Even on the

Judah, saying, ʸ I will shake the heavens and the earth; ²² and ᶻ I will overthrow the throne of kingdoms, and I will destroy the strength of the kingdoms
of the heathen; and ᵃ I will overthrow the chariots, and those that ride in
them; and the horses and their riders shall come down, every one by the sword
of his brother.

²³ In that day, saith the LORD of hosts, will I take thee, O Zerubbabel, my
servant, the son of Shealtiel, saith the LORD, ᵇ and will make thee as a signet :
for ᶜ I have chosen thee, saith the LORD of hosts.

Before
CHRIST
about
520.

y ver. 6, 7.
Heb. 12. 26.
z Dan. 2. 44.
Matt. 24. 7.
a Micah 5. 10.
Zech. 4. 6. &
9. 10.

b Cant. 8. 6.
Jer. 22. 24.
c Isa. 42. 1. &
43. 10.

---

same day as the prophecy (c. 10). So eager was God to be
gracious to His penitent and obedient people.

### THE LORD'S SIGNET. CHRIST'S KINGDOM.

**21—23.** *I will shake the heavens and the earth—In that
day, saith the LORD of hosts, will I take thee, O Zerubbabel,
my servant, the son of Shealtiel, saith the LORD, and will
make thee as a signet : for I have chosen thee, saith the LORD
of hosts*] All other kingdoms shall be moved (see *v.* 7); but
the kingdom of the seed of David, which was represented by
Zerubbabel, the descendant of David, shall be destroyed. It
(see Matt. i. 12. Luke iii. 27. Cp. on 1 Chron. iii. 19. Ezra
ii. 2. Neh. vii. 7. Hag. i. 1), shall never be destroyed. It
will indeed be assailed; but it will break in pieces all kingdoms that resist it, and will scatter them like chaff of the
summer threshing-floor, but will never be removed (Dan. ii.
35. 44; vii. 14. 27. 1 Cor. xv. 24. Heb. xii. 28. Rev. xi. 15).

God promised by Jacob that the sceptre should never depart
from Judah. See the note on Gen. xlix. 10. God gave greater
clearness and force to that promise by assuring David, of the
tribe of Judah, that his Seed and Kingdom would continue
for ever (see the notes on 2 Sam. vii. pp. 85—87); and He
declared, by the Angel Gabriel, to the Blessed Virgin, that this
promise would be fulfilled in Jesus Christ. See Luke i. 31,
"Behold, thou shalt conceive in thy womb, and bring forth a
Son, and shalt call His Name JESUS. He shall be great, and
shall be called the Son of the Highest; and the Lord God
shall give unto Him the *throne of His father* David: and He
shall reign over the house of Jacob *for ever* and ever; *and of
His kingdom there shall be no end*."

This promise is here made to Zerubbabel, as the representative of the house of David, in a time of great humiliation
and distress. Just as it was with the Temple of Jerusalem, so
it was with her monarchy. The Temple seemed, in all external
respects, to be far inferior to the Temple of Solomon; but it
was to be made much more glorious than that Temple, by the
coming of the Lord of the Temple to it.

The family of David was now reduced to a low estate.
Zerubbabel, the representative of the house and monarchy of
David, was not called by the title of King; he appeared to
owe his position to the will of Persia, and to derive his dignity
from his office as Persian Governor (i. 1), or Sheshbazzar (Ezra
i. 11; ii. 2; v. 14. 16). But the promise was, that when they

seemed to be reduced to the lowest estate, then the seed and
kingdom of David would rise most gloriously. The diminution
of their earthly grandeur prepared the way for the increase of
their heavenly splendour. Isaiah had foretold this. He had
said that a rod should come forth out of the stem of Jesse,
and a branch should grow out of *his roots*—that is, when the
tree was hewn down to the very ground; and that the Messiah
should grow up as a tender plant, and as a root out of *a dry
ground*. See Isa. xi. 1; liii. 2.

From the time of the Captivity, the house of David never
recovered its royal title and insignia. But the monarchy was
safe in God's keeping. King Jeconiah, the faithless monarch
of Judah before the Captivity, was like a *signet plucked* from
God's right hand, and cast away (Jer. xxii. 24). But Zerubbabel,
the faithful governor, the leader of Judah from Babylonish
captivity to Jerusalem, the city of God, was made like a signet
on God's right hand. He was the builder of the Temple; and
by him God set a seal on His promises to Judah. He was
the descendant and representative of David, and the ancestor
and type of Christ. He was *a signet* (*chôthâm*) on God's hand
(cp. the use of the word *chôthâm*, repeated in Cant. viii. 6), and
this signet would ever remain on God's *right hand*. It would
be there for ever in CHRIST, the Divine Son of David, the true
King of Israel. By Him the royal charter of the Blessed
Gospel is sealed. He seals us as His own in Baptism, in Confirmation, in the Holy Eucharist. He has sealed us with His
own image and likeness, and has made us to become sons of God
(Rom. viii. 29). He gives us an earnest and pledge of immortal
glory to our souls and bodies, that, as we have borne the image
of the earthly, we shall also bear the image of the heavenly
(1 Cor. xv. 49); and that our vile bodies will be changed, so
as to be fashioned like unto His glorious body (Phil. iii. 21).
In Him all the promises of God are Yea and Amen. He, the
Everlasting Word, came down from heaven, and became the
Incarnate Word; and by the Witness which He gave to the
Old Testament, He set His Divine Seal on it; and by sealing
the Apostles and Evangelists with the seal of the Holy Spirit,
He avouched their writings to be divine. He has set His seal
on the whole Written Word, and has delivered the Holy Scrip-
tures to us as the lively oracles of God.

To HIM, therefore, with the FATHER and the HOLY GHOST,
be all honour and glory, in all the churches of the saints, now
and for ever. AMEN.

# ZECHARIAH.

Before
CHRIST
about
520.
a Ezra 4. 24.
Hag. 1. 1.
b Ezra 5. 1.
Matt. 23. 35.

I. ¹ IN the eighth month, ª in the second year of Darius, came the word of the LORD ᵇ unto Zechariah, the son of Berechiah, the son of Iddo the prophet, saying, ² The LORD hath been † sore displeased with your fathers.

† Heb. with displeasure.

---

### INTRODUCTORY NOTE.

The Book of ZECHARIAH is a sequel to that of Haggai; and it reveals the future from his own age even to the Second Coming of Christ. Zechariah was raised up by God, together with Haggai, to stimulate the flagging energies of the Jews who had returned from Babylon, and to excite them to resume the work of rebuilding the Temple, which had been suspended from the first year of Cyrus (B.C. 536) to the second year of Darius Hystaspes (B.C. 520), a period of about sixteen years. See Ezra iv. 24; v. 1; vi. 14; and *Introd.* to Ezra, p. 295.

Haggai had cheered the builders with the assurance, that however inferior the latter house would be to the former in material grandeur and external splendour, it would be made much more glorious than that by the Coming to it of Christ, Who would "fill it with the Glory of the Lord;" and He had encouraged them with the gracious promise, that in that house "He would give peace" (Hagg. ii. 6—9).

The Prophet Haggai had also declared, that all the nations of the world which resisted the power of God and oppressed His Church, would be placed beneath the feet of Christ,—the Divine Zerubbabel,—and that He would reign in everlasting glory at the right hand of God. See on Hagg. ii. 20—23.

Thus ended the prophecy of Haggai.

His prophecy is followed up and continued by Zechariah, and is carried on in a series of glorious visions to the Second Advent of Christ.

After a brief prologue (i. 1—6),—spoken in the interval between the penultimate and final prophecies of Haggai, and connecting Zechariah's predictions with them, and declaring that all God's promises of favour to His people depend for their fulfilment on their repentance and obedience to Him, and on their exercise of moral duties, and that if His people resist Him, they must look for chastisement at His hands, and that they will be cast off, as their fathers were,—the prophet proceeds to comfort them in the first vision, by saying that God is present with them in their low estate; and that though their enemies may seem to be enjoying prosperity, yet that their own present humiliation and the temporary exaltation of the heathen are not to be interpreted as signs of any indifference on God's part, or of any inability to protect them and to chastise His enemies; but that in His own good time, He will arise and punish the proud Powers of this world, and reward all His faithful servants who stand firm in the day of trial; and that the Lord is sore displeased with the heathen who afflict His people, and that He will yet comfort Zion, and will yet choose Jerusalem (i. 7—17).

The second Vision follows naturally after this gracious assurance. It reveals the four great Empires (designated as horns) which had oppressed God's people, and displays the four counteracting powers (called *carpenters*, or rather, *smiths*) employed by God to humble those Empires, and make them subservient to His own gracious purposes, for the advancement of His own glory, and for the trial and purification of His people, and for the building up of His Church. See i. 19—21.

An enlargement of this revelation succeeds. The next Vision displays the Coming of the Lord, and the redemption of His People by Christ (Who is the Divine Antitype of Cyrus the great conqueror of Babylon and the deliverer of God's people from its thraldom; see on 2 Chron. xxxvi. 22, and *Prelim. Note* to Isa. xl.); and reveals the building up of the Spiritual

Temple of His Church Universal, and the flowing in of the heathen to it (ii. 11).

These glorious evangelical events were foreshadowed by those things which Zechariah's countrymen had seen, namely, their own liberation by Cyrus, who had captured Babylon; and their restoration to their own country, the Holy Land, and the re-erection of the Temple by virtue of his royal decree. Therefore this Vision, which opens by taking up the words of the first Vision ("a line shall be stretched forth upon Jerusalem;" see i. 16, compared with ii. 1, 2) closes with a repetition of the promise there given, "The Lord shall inherit Judah his portion in the holy land, and shall choose Jerusalem again" (ii. 12). Cp. i. 17.

This has now been fulfilled in CHRIST.

The fourth Vision explains more fully the means by which this glorious restoration and exaltation of Israel into a Holy Nation and an Universal Church is to be achieved.

It is to be accomplished by Christ,—"the Angel of the Lord," Who is sent by Jehovah. It is done by Christ overcoming Satan, and delivering His people from Satan's grasp, and taking away the sins of the people, personified by Joshua their High Priest, and clothing them with the white robe of His own righteousness (see on iii. 1—5), and promising everlasting glory to His justified people, on condition of their obedience to His Will and Word.

The Angel of the Lord, Who is Christ, assures Joshua and the Priesthood of Israel, that they themselves are types of this blessed work of Justification. The Priesthood of Aaron was a thing "to be wondered at" (see iii. 8), that is, not to be looked at merely with the outward eye, but to be gazed at with the eye of faith, discerning, under the type of that Priesthood and of all its sacrifices, a marvellous prophetical adumbration of the Everlasting Priesthood of Christ—the Divine "Joshua the son of Josedech" (namely, Saviour, Son of Jehovah's righteousness; such is the meaning of those words)—and of His one Sacrifice, offered once for all, to take away the sins of the world.

Therefore, Christ is here introduced by Jehovah, saying, "Behold, I will bring forth My servant the BRANCH" (see on iii. 8); and He also is called the STONE, engraven with seven eyes (see iii. 9). And by Him the iniquity of the land is taken away, and peace and joy are given to all the Israel of God.

The enjoyment of all these blessings is represented as contingent on repentance, faith, and obedience; and therefore a solemn warning is here introduced against stubbornness and hardness of heart, and against hatred, malice, and uncharitableness; in order that the grace of God in Christ may not be received in vain.

This Vision of Christ justifying His People is followed by a Vision of His Church Universal. The Church is represented by a seven-branched lamp, and it is displayed to our eyes as illumined by the Holy Ghost the Sanctifier, filling it with the oil of His grace. Zerubbabel, the representative of the royal house of David, and the rebuilder of the Temple (as we have seen, on Hagg. ii. 20—23), is a typical personage, symbolizing the person and office of Christ, the True Seed of David, the Divine King of Judah, the Builder of the Spiritual Temple—the Universal Church,—from small beginnings, in troublous times. As Zerubbabel began and finished the building, so did Christ: He finished it by the gift of the Holy Ghost on the Day of Pentecost. "Not by might, nor by power, but by My Spirit, saith the Lord of Hosts" (iv. 5—10).

³ Therefore say thou unto them, Thus saith the Lord of hosts;
Turn ᶜ ye unto me, saith the Lord of hosts,

Before
CHRIST
about
520.
c Jer 25.5, 8.
3.13. Mich 7.19. Mal. 3.7. Luke 15, 20. Jam 4.8.

Hence we recognize the reason of the combination of the seven-branched Candlestick or Lamp-stand (the figure of the Church), and of the Olive-trees, with the plummet-line, and the foundation Stone. We have distinct figures of Christ's work as King, in the founding of the Church, and also in sending the Holy Ghost to finish the work, by His gracious agency, in sanctification and illumination. The Holy Ghost works upon the Church by the twofold office of Christ, namely, His Universal Monarchy and His Everlasting Priesthood. Christ's Kingly and Priestly offices are the two ever-verdant Olive-trees, through which the Oil of the Spirit is always flowing to fill the seven-branched Candlestick of the Universal Church with oil, and enabling it to diffuse the light of Divine Truth and heavenly grace throughout the world. See iv. 11—14.

But lest it should be imagined that the gracious work of Christ and the Holy Spirit in the Church can be effectual without the co-operation of the human Will, and lest these dispensations of God's love should be abused into occasions either of spiritual indolence, or of reckless licentiousness, a solemn warning is again interposed against the neglect of the moral virtues and practical duties of justice, mercy, and holiness, enjoined by the commandments of God. This is declared in the Vision of the Flying-Roll, proclaiming God's curses against all sin and unrighteousness; and in the sweeping-away of all wickedness (symbolized by the woman in the Ephah, pressed down by a weight of lead), from Sion the Church of God, the City of Truth and Peace, to the land of Shinar and Babylon, the land of confusion, and the city of exile and captivity. This judicial announcement is followed by a gracious declaration consequent on the former Visions of Christ and the Church. Observe the contrast which follows. Wickedness is to be carried to Babylon, the land of captivity; but Faith is to come from the land of captivity, and to do homage to Christ. (See v. 5—11).

This is symbolized in the seventh and last Vision. It reveals the Lord's universal sovereignty and His retributive justice exercised over all Nations of the earth (vi. 1—8). It pronounces the time when the Jews, who are now dispersed, will bring tribute to Christ and acknowledge Him, Who is the Branch from the root of David, to be the true Builder of the Spiritual Temple; and their offerings and their homage will be like silver and gold made into a royal crown formed of many diadems, and set upon the head of Him Who is the true High Priest, and therefore a recognition from them, that He is both King and Priest, and that He is the Messiah promised to their Fathers (vi. 9—15).

God's promises are again followed by warnings, lest any one should presume upon His love, and pervert His grace into an occasion for sin. He tells them that all religious observances, such as fasting and weeping and self-mortification, are of no avail without holiness (vii. 1—7). The enjoyment of all divine blessings is contingent on faith and obedience; and, therefore, another solemn warning is here introduced. The history of ancient Israel, chastened for its sin by God, in successive judicial visitations since the time of the Exodus even to the day of the captivity at Babylon, is propounded as a lesson to all their posterity, and to all future generations (vii. 8—14). If they listen to this warning, they will prosper; and the Church of God, going forth from Jerusalem to enfold the world, will be the source and well-spring of holy festivity and joy to all Nations of the world (viii. 1—23). This promise is followed by a prophecy foretelling the overthrow of all great worldly Powers opposed to the City of God; and the subjection of all Nations to Christ her King, and their incorporation in His Church (ix. 1—8).

The triumphal Entry of Christ into Jerusalem in lowliness and meekness is displayed as a prelude to that Victory; and the precious blood-shedding of Christ, which followed in a few days after that triumphal Entry, is revealed as the cause of the deliverance of His people from the prison-house of Sin and the Grave (ix. 9, 11).

The sending forth of the Apostles and first Missionaries, like arrows winged with feathers of the plumage of the Divine Dove, on the Day of Pentecost, discharged from the bow of the Divine Archer Jesus Christ, and shot forth from Jerusalem into all parts of the world, is represented as a consequence of Christ's Death, and Resurrection, and Ascension into Glory (ix. 13—17). Their warfare against His enemies will be a message of peace to His friends. "He shall speak peace unto the Heathen; His dominion shall be from sea to sea, and from the river to the ends of the earth." His Preachers shall be jewels in His Crown; and many shall rejoice in the beauty of Christ, preached by

them; and shall be strengthened and refreshed with spiritual food (ix. 13—17). Israel shall be gathered again (x. 8—12). This has been already fulfilled in part. All the Apostles were Jews. Many devout Jews from every country under heaven were united to Christ and His Church on the Day of Pentecost, and in the primitive ages of Christianity; and in His own due time God will restore the residue to Himself.

In the next prophecy, the destruction of Jerusalem by the armies of Rome is foretold (xi. 1, 2). The announcement of this sad catastrophe might well stagger and perplex the readers of this prophecy. Was it possible that the Hebrew people, who had been scattered by Assyria and Babylon, should derive so little benefit from those terrible calamities? Would they require another captivity? Yes, it would be so. And what would be the cause of this divine chastisement? Their own sin—even a sin far more heinous than any committed by their forefathers. This must have seemed almost incredible when Zechariah wrote his prophecies. But the words of the Holy Ghost speaking by him have been fulfilled. They were accomplished in the rejection of Christ, the Good Shepherd, valued at the miserable price of thirty pieces of silver (xi. 12). They were fulfilled in the Crucifixion of Him, Who is displayed by the prophet as no other than the Lord God (xi. 13). Therefore, the Hebrew nation would again be cast off; but still a remnant would be saved (xi. 11), and —oh! most merciful dispensation—in due time the heart of the Nation itself would be touched by the Spirit of God, and it would bleed with sorrow and remorse, and the Nation itself would turn with weeping eyes to Him Whom they had pierced, and would acknowledge Jesus Christ to be their Saviour, King, and God. A fountain would be opened to the house of David and to the inhabitants at Jerusalem—the fountain of His Blood —for sin and for uncleanness (xiii. 1). Israel would wash itself and be cleansed by the waters of that pool of Bethesda, would bathe in that Pool of Siloam, and be healed of its blindness (xiii. 1). The prophet foretells that Christ would be smitten (xiii. 7. Cp. Matt. xxvi. 31), and many would live by His death. The Kingdoms of the World will rise up in the last days against Him and against His Church, in a fierce Anti-Christian conflict, but they will all be scattered before Him. Then all Nations will be gathered before Him as their Judge. His Victory will be complete: "The Lord shall be King over all the earth: in that day shall there be One Lord, and His Name one" (xiv. 9). All the Israel of God, chastened by trial, and cleansed by those living waters which will flow forth from Jerusalem, shall be united for ever and ever in holy worship in the glorified Church of Christ (xiv. 8—21).

Zechariah is regarded by the Jewish Commentators as one of the most obscure of Hebrew Prophets. This is the opinion of *Abarbinel*, *Jarchi*, and other Hebrew Rabbis, concerning him. And no wonder, because they read his prophecies with a veil on their hearts (2 Cor. iii. 14). They cannot bring themselves to acknowledge that their own prophets have foretold that the Messiah would appear in a lowly guise and poor estate, and be rejected and put to death by His own People, as Zechariah foretells (ix. 9; xi. 12, 13; xiii. 13). But the veil is taken away in Christ. When they turn to the Lord, the veil will be taken away (2 Cor. iii. 14, 16); and this is what Zechariah himself predicts: "They will look on Him Whom they have pierced, and will mourn in bitterness for Him as one that mourneth for his firstborn" (xii. 9, 10). May God hasten the time!

On the erroneous theory of a *"double Zechariah,"* see below, *Preliminary Note* to chap. ix.

Ch. I. 1. *In the eighth month, in the second year of Darius*] About two months after Haggai's first prophecy (Hag. i. 1), and a few weeks after Haggai's second prophecy, foretelling the greater glory of the new Temple, by reason of the Coming of Christ to it (ii. 7—9).

— *Zechariah*] Namely, *whom the Lord remembers*; i. e. whom He cares for in times of trial. Compare the name of the Prophet *Zephaniah*, i. e. *whom the Lord hides* from a storm of trouble; and see the reference to the name of *Zechariah*, the father of the Baptist, in Luke i. 72.

— *Berechiah*] That is, *blessed of the Lord*. See below, on Matt. xxiii. 35.

— *the son of Iddo*] Cp. Ezra v. 1; vi. 14, where Zechariah himself is called "the son of Iddo," chief of one of the priestly families who returned from Babylon to Jerusalem with Joshua

And I will turn unto you, saith the Lord of hosts.

4 Be ye not as your fathers, 5 unto whom the former prophets have cried, saying, Thus saith the Lord of hosts; 6 Turn ye now from your evil ways, and *from* your evil doings: but they did not hear, nor hearken unto me, saith the Lord.

5 Your fathers, where *are* they? and the prophets, do they live for ever?

6 But 6 my words and my statutes, which I commanded my servants the prophets, did they not || take hold of your fathers? and they returned and said, 6 Like as the Lord of hosts thought to do unto us, according to our ways, and according to our doings, so hath he dealt with us.

7 Upon the four and twentieth day of the eleventh month, which *is* the month Sebat, in the second year of Darius, came the word of the Lord unto Zechariah, the son of Berechiah, the son of Iddo the prophet, saying, 8 I saw by night, and behold 9 a man riding upon a red horse, and he stood among the myrtle trees that *were* in the bottom; and behind him *were there* 9 red horses, || speckled, and white.

---

and Zerubbabel (Neh. xii. 4). Zechariah, like Jeremiah and Ezekiel, combined in his own person the offices of Priest and Prophet. Like them, he pre-announces Christ's everlasting Priesthood; like them, he displays Him as the great Prophet Who should come into the world; and also as the Universal King; and like them he proclaims His Divinity (xi. 13).

### CALL TO REPENTANCE.

3. *Turn ye unto me—and I will turn unto you.* Zechariah comes forth, like John the Baptist, and begins his preaching with a call to repentance, and warns the people, by the history of their fathers, that no spiritual privileges will profit them without holiness, but rather will aggravate their guilt, and increase their condemnation, if they disobey God. He declares to them that no outward profession of religion will avail; that all notions of self-righteousness are offensive to God; and that what He looks for is personal holiness, and a practical discharge of the duties of piety and mercy.

5, 6. *Your fathers, where are they?—dealt with us?* Your fathers have passed away. Yes; and you may reply that the Prophets have passed away likewise. True; but the Word of God, which was spoken by My servants the prophets, has not passed away. It took hold of your fathers; it was like an arrow, shot out of the divine bow, and it hit the mark; it has been fully accomplished in the punishment of your fathers for their sins. Therefore, do not imitate your fathers, who despised the warnings of former prophets, but listen to my prophecy.

### THE RIDER AMONG THE MYRTLES.—THE ANGEL OF THE LORD.

7. *Upon the four and twentieth day of the eleventh month.* Just five months after the resumption of the building of the Temple, in obedience to God's word by Haggai, which was followed by a promise of a blessing, even by a promise of Christ's coming to it (Hag. i. 12—15; ii. 7—9). The promise of a distant blessing had been followed, at an interval of exactly three months from the utterance of God's word by Haggai, exhorting the people to rebuild the house, by the assurance of an *immediate temporal* blessing, as a pledge and earnest of that *future spiritual* blessing (Hag. ii. 10, 18, 19); and now precisely two months afterwards Zechariah sees a series of Visions in a single night, which speak comfort to him, and through him to the people.

8—17. *I saw by night, and behold a man riding upon a red horse, and he stood among the myrtle trees that were in the bottom—the* Lord *shall yet comfort Zion, and shall yet choose Jerusalem*] These ten verses will best be considered consecutively in one note.

The Prophet sees a man, who appears to be also a divine personage, "the Angel of the Lord," the Son of God. See above, on Exod. iii. 2—8. Judg. xi. 22; xiii. 3—20; and see Ezek. i. 26; ix. 2; xl. 3. Dan. vii. 13; and so *Tarnovius* and other interpreters explain it here. He is revealed as a Rider. Such is Christ. See above, Ps. xlv. 1—3; and below, on

Rev. vi. 2; xix. 11—16. He is on a red horse,—the colour of blood. Some Expositors (as *A Lapide*) expound this as symbolizing His Incarnation. His human nature, by means of which He was enabled to die, and shed His blood, is, as it were, *that* on which He rides, as on a horse, to victory. Behind Him are other riders on horses, as in the Apocalypse (xix. 11—14). These, His followers and servants, are on horses of *red* (the colour of blood); *speckled*, grisly pale, or ghastly grey (see *Kliefoth*, 19; and compare the pale horse, in the Apocalypse, vi. 8); and *white*, the colour of victory (see on Rev. vi. 2), specially of Christ's victory.

This principal rider, followed by these three other riders, stood *amid the myrtles in the bottom*, "*in profundo*" (Vulg.), that is, in a low place, among lowly shrubs, myrtles, fragrant in smell, and beautiful in leaf. Esther was called *Hadassah*, or Myrtle, on account of her beauty. See Esther ii. 7. Cp. Isa. xli. 19; lv. 13, where the myrtle is mentioned among beautiful trees; and Neh. viii. 15, where it is specified with palms, olives, and pines, as furnishing branches for the joyful procession of the Feast of Tabernacles.

This Vision represents Christ's presence with Israel. Christ had been with them in the wilderness of Arabia (1 Cor. x. 4, 9. Cp. Heb. xi. 26); and He was with them in the days of Zechariah. Israel was no longer like a noble forest of stately cedars on a lofty Lebanon, but was like a lowly plantation of modest myrtles, in a lowly place, weak, surrounded by enemies. Such was the condition of the little band of exiles who had now returned to Jerusalem from Babylon.

But they had now been stirred by the Spirit of God; they were doing a work of holy faith and obedience in rebuilding the Temple. Therefore, though in a low place, they were like a beautiful, evergreen, fair-flowering, odoriferous grove of myrtles in God's sight; and the Angel of the Lord was among them.

The best commentary on the present vision of the Angel of the Lord among the myrtles in a low place, may be found in that other Vision of "the Angel of the Lord in the bush,"—the bush which was burning, but not consumed,—which Moses saw at Horeb, and which was also a type of God's people Israel, humble and afflicted in Egypt, but not destroyed, because God was with them. See the notes above, on Exod. iii. 2—4. "The Angel of the Lord," it is there said, was "in the midst of the bush;" and it is also said that "God spake to Moses out of the bush." The Angel was a divine Person, and He assured Israel by Moses of God's presence and protection.

So it is here.

Though Israel is like a myrtle-grove in a low place, yet God is in the midst of them. And the three riders on their red, speckled, and white horses, are perhaps symbolic of His Angel-ministers of War, Pestilence, and Victory, whom He sends forth to do His will in all parts of the world, and who return to Him and give to Him an account of their doings (*rv*. 10, 11); or, as some suppose (S. *Jerome, Kliefoth*), they represent the great worldly Powers,—Babylonian, Medo-Persian (a speckled or mixed power; cp. Dan. ii. 32; vii. 5; viii. 5), and Greek, symbolized as *white*, or blank, as not yet dominant. These (and all Earthly Dynasties) are God's servants, and do His will on the

122

9 Then said I, O my lord, what *are* these? Before CHRIST cir. 519.
And the angel that talked with me said unto me, I will shew thee what
these *be*.
10 And the man that stood among the myrtle trees answered and said, [k] These k Heb. 1. 14.
*are they* whom the LORD hath sent to walk to and fro through the earth.
11 [l] And they answered the angel of the LORD that stood among the myrtle l Ps. 103. 20, 21.
trees, and said, We have walked to and fro through the earth, and, behold, all
the earth sitteth still, and is at rest.
12 Then the angel of the LORD answered and said, [m] O LORD of hosts, how m Ps. 102. 13. Rev. 6. 10.
long wilt thou not have mercy on Jerusalem and on the cities of Judah, against
which thou hast had indignation [n] these threescore and ten years? n Jer. 25. 11, 12. Dan. 9. 2.
13 And the LORD answered the angel that talked with me *with* [o] good words ch. 7. 5. o Jer. 29. 10.
*and* comfortable words.
14 So the angel that communed with me said unto me, Cry thou, saying,
Thus saith the LORD of hosts; I am [p] jealous for Jerusalem and for Zion with a p Joel 2. 18. ch. 8. 2.
great jealousy. 15 And I am very sore displeased with the heathen *that are* at
ease: for [q] I was but a little displeased, and they helped forward the affliction. q Isa. 47. 6.
16 Therefore thus saith the LORD; [r] I am returned to Jerusalem with mercies: r Isa. 12. 1. & 54. 8.
my house shall be built in it, saith the LORD of hosts, and [s] a line shall be ch. 2. 10. & 8. 3.
stretched forth upon Jerusalem. s ch. 2. 1, 2.
17 Cry yet, saying, Thus saith the LORD of hosts; My cities through
† prosperity shall yet be spread abroad; [t] and the LORD shall yet comfort † Heb. good. t Isa. 51. 3.
Zion, and [u] shall yet choose Jerusalem. u Isa. 14. 1. ch. 2. 12. & 3. 2.

18 Then lifted I up mine eyes, and saw, and behold four horns. 19 And

---

earth. They report to Him that the heathen nations are at ease, i.e. secure, proud, and licentious, as if there were no God in heaven. See the use of the word *shaanān*, rendered *at ease*, in Isa. xxxii. 9. 11, "Tremble ye women that are at ease;" and Amos vi. 1, "Woe to them that are *at ease*," while His own people are in distress.

Such was the condition of the heathen in the second year of Darius Hystaspes. The contrast was great between their condition and that of God's chosen inheritance. The heathens were strong and joyous. Israel was weak and sorrowful. The walls of Jerusalem were as yet unbuilt, the city was still in a ruinous condition. The inhabitants were few. See Neh. i. 3, where he says, "The remnant in the province are in great affliction and reproach, the wall of Jerusalem is broken down, the gates are burned with fire;" and cp. Neh. ii. 3. 13—17, where the desolate condition of Jerusalem, as seen by him in his solitary ride by night round its ruined walls, is described. And see also Neh. xi. 2, with regard to the scantiness and weakness of its population at this time.

God's own favoured nation was indeed like a myrtle-grove in a low place. Therefore the Angel of the Lord, Whom we may reverently suppose to be the Son of God Himself, intercedes for Israel, and exclaims, "O Lord, how long wilt Thou not visit Thy people in mercy, with whom Thou hast been angry these seventy years?" (*v.* 12.)

The seventy years, here mentioned, date from the destruction of the Temple (B.C. 586). There are two periods of "*seventy years*" in the desolations of Jerusalem (Jer. xxv. 11, 12; xxix. 10. Dan. ix. 2; below, vii. 5), one period dating from the first Captivity in the fifth year of Jehoiakim, B.C. 605, and ending with the decree of Cyrus for the return of the Jews from Babylon, B.C. 535. See above, on 2 Chron. xxxvi. 22, 23. Ezra i. 1. The other period is that specified here.

This intercessory appeal calls forth a gracious reply from God (*vv.* 14—17): "I am jealous for Jerusalem and for Zion with a great jealousy. And I am very sore displeased with the heathen that are at ease: for I was but a little displeased" (with Israel), "and they helped forward the affliction. Therefore I am returned to Jerusalem with mercies: My house shall be built in it, saith the Lord of hosts: My cities through prosperity shall yet be spread abroad;" or rather, "they shall overflow with blessings" (*Sept.*, *Vulg.*, *Targum*). Cp. Prov. v. 16. And the Lord shall yet choose Jerusalem.

— *The angel that talked with me*] Lit. *in me.*

**18.** The reason why the Vision of the Four Horns is introduced with seeming abruptness, and is so slightly delineated, seems to be this, that the Prophet Zechariah presumes in his readers a familiar acquaintance with the prophecies of Daniel, where this imagery is displayed in greater fulness. Indeed, this prophetic rapidity and conciseness of Zechariah afford a strong argument for the genuineness of Daniel. Zechariah writes *from* Daniel, as being well known to himself and his readers. The Holy Spirit, Who had delivered prophecies by Daniel, *continues* those prophecies by Zechariah, and *completes* them in the Apocalypse by St. John.

The fulfilment of the foregoing promise is revealed in the next two Visions. They also are Visions of comfort.

First, the Prophet sees four *horns*, emblems of power (see Deut. xxxiii. 17. 2 Chron. xviii. 10. Ps. lxxv. 4, 5. 10; cxxxii. 17. Jer. xlviii. 25, and especially Dan. viii. 3. 9. 21), hostile to the people of God. See *vv.* 19. 21. These four horns are called "four kingdoms" in the *Targum* here, and the imagery is repeated from Daniel's Visions, and to be explained from them (cp. *Pusey* on Daniel, 357, 358), and doubtless they represent those worldly dynasties called horns of the Gentiles in *v.* 21, which afflicted and scattered God's people; especially the Assyrian and Babylonian, and afterwards the Persian and Roman Power (*S. Jerome*, *S. Cyril*, *Abarbinel*, *Hengst.*, *Kliefoth*, *Keil*).

But we must extend our view.

The horns, *four* in number (which in Holy Scripture is a symbol of universal space; see above, on Ezek. p. 276, and below, on Matt. xxviii. 19), may be regarded also in a wider sense, as representing, generally, all Earthly Powers which are hostile to the Church of God.

This explanation is suggested by the phrase "*the four winds*," in the next chapter, *v.* 6; and there is a promise here that these four horns will be broken,—as the Psalmist expresses it, "I said unto the fools, Deal not foolishly; and to the wicked, Lift not up the horn: Lift not up your horn on high, and speak not with a stiff neck. All the horns of the wicked also

Before
CHRIST
about
519
c Psa. l. 4, 7.
& 5, 5.

y Ps. 75, 4, 5.

a Ezek. 40, 3.

b Rev. 11, 1, &
21, 15, 16.

I said unto the angel that talked with me, What *be* these ? And he answered me, ˣ These *are* the horns which have scattered Judah, Israel, and Jerusalem.

²⁰ And the LORD shewed me four carpenters.

²¹ Then said I, What come these to do ?

And he spake, saying, These *are* the horns which have scattered Judah, so that no man did lift up his head : but these are come to fray them, to cast out the horns of the Gentiles, which ʸ lifted up *their* horn over the land of Judah to scatter it.

II. ¹ I lifted up mine eyes again, and looked, and behold ᵃ a man with a measuring line in his hand.

² Then said I, Whither goest thou ?

And he said unto me, ᵇ To measure Jerusalem, to see what *is* the breadth thereof, and what *is* the length thereof.

³ And, behold, the angel that talked with me went forth, and another angel went out to meet him, ⁴ and said unto him, Run, speak to this young man, saying,

---

will I cut off, but the horns of the righteous shall be exalted" (Ps. lxxv. 4, 5, 10).

Observe the phraseology in v. 19, "These are the horns which have scattered Judah, Israel, *and* Jerusalem;" where, in the original, the Hebrew note of the accusative (*eth*) is prefixed to Judah and also to Israel, but not to Jerusalem, which is put in apposition with them, combined by the copula *vau* with Israel, showing that all schism and separation between Judah and Jerusalem had now happily been healed by their dispersion, and that Judah and Israel are blended together in Jerusalem, as the common centre of all the people of God.

THE FOUR CARPENTERS, OR SMITHS.

The next Vision represents the *breaking* of these *horns*, and the full and final victory of God's people. The number *four* is a symbol of completeness, especially as to space. See ii. 6, and above, on Ezekiel, p. 276.

This Vision represents the agency by which this double work—first, of *destruction*, and, secondly, of *construction*—is to be accomplished.

The Prophet sees *four carpenters*, or smiths ; Hebr. *charáshim*, literally, *cutters, hewers, gravers,* and therefore, generally, *artificers* and *craftsmen* in wood, stone, or iron ; *carpenters, masons,* or *smiths,* or *engravers* ; and this word is rendered by all these seven words in our Authorized Version. See Exod. xxviii. 11. Deut. xxvii. 15. 1 Sam. xiii. 19. 2 Sam. v. 11. 2 Kings xxii. 6 ; xxiv. 14. 1 Chron. xiv. 1. 2 Chron. xxxiv. 11. Isa. xl. 19. Hos. viii. 6 ; xiii. 2 ; cp. *Gesenius,* 309.

These artificers *four* in number, signifying completeness in space (as was before observed), declare that *all* worldly powers which are hostile to God's Church in all the *four* corners of the earth, will be hewn in pieces, like stone, wood, or metal, by His Omnipresence, working by His artificers ; and that out of their materials, He will construct the Temple and City of Jerusalem.

We may compare God's words by Zechariah's contemporary Prophet Haggai, "I will overthrow the throne of kingdoms, and I will destroy the strength of the kingdoms of the heathen, and I will overthrow the chariots and those that ride in them, and the horses and their riders shall come down, every one by the sword of his brother" (Hagg. ii. 22). God uses one kingdom as His instrument against another, in order to prepare the way for His own kingdom, that will never be destroyed.

This prophecy of Zechariah was fulfilled in a subordinate sense by the building of the Temple and walls of Jerusalem by God's power, destroying Babylon as He had destroyed Assyria, and making the conqueror of Babylon, Cyrus, and his successors, Darius and Artaxerxes, and the materials supplied by them, to be like God's smiths and carpenters, building-up and adorning the literal Temple and City of Jerusalem.

But Zechariah's prophecies reach far beyond his own age. They stretch onward to Christ and His Church. Christ Himself is the great Artificer. Not without a mystery is He called " the Carpenter " (see Mark vi. 3), and He works by His

ministers. The fulfilment of this Vision is seen (as *S. Jerome* observes) in the work of the Preachers of the fourfold Gospel of Christ, spread forth to the four winds of heaven, and breaking the *horns* of all opposing powers. See the noble language of St. Paul, that great Christian conqueror and master-builder (1 Cor. iii. 10 ; 2 Cor. ii. 14 ; x. 5). "Thanks be to God, which always causeth us to triumph in Christ ; casting down imaginations, and every high thing that exalteth itself against the knowledge of God, according to the grace of God which is given unto me as a wise master-builder, I have laid the foundations—which is Jesus Christ."

May we not say that the greatest heathen Conquerors, such as Cyrus, Alexander the Great, and others, have been artificers in God's hands for the building-up of His Church ? The diffusion of the Greek Language by the conquests of the latter prepared the way for the spread of the Gospel of Christ, written in that universal language. The great military Roads made by Imperial Rome for her own legions marching to victory, became highways for the Prince of Peace. See below, *Introd.* to Acts of the Apostles, pp. 9, 10, and on Acts xxviii. 14, 15. So, in God's own due time, it will be seen that not only Christian Kings and Emperors—the Constantines, Justinians, Charlemagnes, and Alfreds, and others in later times, who, with pious purpose and intention, have advanced the Gospel, will be seen to have done service to it, and to have been instrumental in building the walls of Jerusalem ; but even the powers of those who have opposed it, will be overruled to the future glory of God and the edification of His Church,—" The kingdoms of this world will become the kingdom of our Lord and of His Christ " (Rev. xi. 15).

THE MAN WITH THE MEASURING-LINE.—VISION OF THE EXTENT AND GLORY OF THE SPIRITUAL JERUSALEM, OR UNIVERSAL CHURCH.

CH. II. 1, 2. *behold a man with a measuring line—To measure Jerusalem*] The promised work is here revealed as done. Jerusalem is seen as already rebuilt.

The work done by Nehemiah in building up the ruined walls in troublous times, and in spite of great opposition (see above, Neh. iii., iv., v., vi., xii.), was completed about seventy years after the delivery of this prophecy, and was doubtless stimulated by it.

This work was also figurative of another still greater and more durable one,—the building up of the spiritual Jerusalem by Christ Himself. See notes on Neh. xii. 27. 43. No one can read Zechariah's Vision, and compare it with the prophecies in Isa. xxxiii. 20—24 ; liv. 1—17 (as *S. Cyril* does), and the similar Vision of Ezekiel, which is the best illustration of it (see Ezek. xl. p. 252 ; and the notes at the end of Ezekiel, pp. 274—278), without recognizing that this vision reveals the erection and extension of the Universal Church of Christ. So *S. Jerome, S. Cyril, Theodoret, Haymo, Lyranus, Vatablus, A Lapide,* and others.

<sup>c</sup> Jerusalem shall be inhabited *as* towns without walls,
For the multitude of men and cattle therein :
<sup>5</sup> For I, saith the LORD, will be unto her <sup>d</sup> a wall of fire round about,
<sup>e</sup> And will be the glory in the midst of her.
<sup>6</sup> Ho, ho, *come forth*, and flee <sup>f</sup> from the land of the north, saith the LORD :
For I have <sup>g</sup> spread you abroad as the four winds of the heaven, saith the LORD.
<sup>7</sup> <sup>h</sup> Deliver thyself, O Zion,
That dwellest *with* the daughter of Babylon
<sup>8</sup> For thus saith the LORD of hosts ;
After the glory hath he sent me unto the nations which spoiled you :
For he that <sup>i</sup> toucheth you toucheth the apple of his eye.
<sup>9</sup> For, behold, I will <sup>k</sup> shake mine hand upon them,
And they shall be a spoil to their servants :
And <sup>l</sup> ye shall know that the LORD of hosts hath sent me.
<sup>10</sup> <sup>m</sup> Sing and rejoice, O daughter of Zion :
For, lo, I come, and I <sup>n</sup> will dwell in the midst of thee, saith the LORD.
<sup>11</sup> <sup>o</sup> And many nations shall be joined to the LORD <sup>p</sup> in that day,
And shall be <sup>q</sup> my people :
And I will dwell in the midst of thee,
And <sup>r</sup> thou shalt know that the LORD of hosts hath sent me unto thee.
<sup>12</sup> And the LORD shall <sup>s</sup> inherit Judah his portion in the holy land,
And <sup>t</sup> shall choose Jerusalem again.
<sup>13</sup> <sup>u</sup> Be silent, O all flesh, before the LORD :
For he is raised up <sup>x</sup> out of † his holy habitation.

III. <sup>1</sup> And he shewed me <sup>a</sup> Joshua the high priest standing before the angel

Before
CHRIST
547.
c Jer. 31. 27.
d Isa. 26. 1.
ch. 9. 8.
e Isa. 60. 19.
Rev. 21. 23.
f Isa. 48. 20. &
52. 11.
g Deut. 28. 64.
Ezek. 17. 21.

h Rev. 18. 4.

i Deut. 32. 10.
Ps. 17. 8.
2 Thess. 1. 6.
k Isa. 41. 1. &
19. 16.

l ch. 4. 9.
m Isa.12.6.&54.1.
Zeph. 3. 14.
n Lev. 26. 12.
Ezek. 37. 27.
ch. 8. 3.
John 1. 14.
2 Cor. 6. 16.
o Isa. 2. 2, 3. &
49. 22. & 60. 3, 4.&
ch. 8. 22, 23.
p ch. 3. 10.
q Ex. 12. 49.
r Ezek. 33. 33.
ver. 9.
s Deut. 32. 9.
t ch. 1. 17.
u Hab. 2. 20.
Zeph. 1. 7.
x Ps. 68. 5.
Isa. 57. 15.
† Heb. *the habitation of his holiness,*
Deut. 26. 15.
Isa. 63. 15.

a Hag. 1. 1.

---

**4.** *Jerusalem shall be inhabited as towns without walls*] Rather, *Jerusalem shall dwell as country villages*; namely, as unwalled towns in an open region (Esther ix. 19. Ezek. xxxviii. 11. *Gesen.* 689).

This imagery represents *extent* and *peace* ("apertis otia portis"). The prophecy was not accomplished in the literal Jerusalem, but is fulfilled in the spiritual Jerusalem, the City of Peace, the Universal Church of Christ, diffused throughout the world, and defended by the Divine protection as with a wall of fire (*v.* 5). See what follows here, and compare Ezekiel's sublime description of the spiritual Jerusalem as represented to him in a vision (Ezek. xl.—xlviii.).

**6.** *I have spread you abroad*] *I have scattered you* (Hebr. *perasti*) like the four winds, in storm and tempest. There is a reference to the preceding word, *perázoth*, *v.* 4. Ye have been spread abroad by dispersion (see Ezek. xvii. 21); but I will unite you again. This is fulfilled in the true Sion, the Christian Church, diffused throughout the world.

**7.** *Deliver thyself, O Zion*] In Zechariah's age, Zion had been in Babylon; part of it was still in Chaldæa; but let it flee thence, and it will be free, and become Zion indeed. Cp. Isa. xlviii. 2; iii. 11. Jer. li. 6, 7. 45.

In a spiritual sense this may be applied to those Christians who are captives in the mystical Babylon—the Church of Rome. See below, on Rev. xviii. 4, "Come out of her, my people." See also notes on Isa. xlviii. 20; lii. 11. Jer. li. 6, 7. 45.

**8.** *After the glory hath he sent me*] Jehovah sent the Angel of the Lord, Who is Christ; and He sent Him *after glory* in a double sense; i. e., from the glory which He had with the Father before the world was (John xvii. 5), and to promote His Father's glory by doing His will (John viii. 50).

— *toucheth the apple of his eye*] Compare Deut. xxxii. 10, "He kept him as the apple of His eye;" Ps. xvii. 8, "Keep me as the apple of an eye."

**8, 9.** *the nations which spoiled you—they shall be a spoil*] As the army of Sennacherib was. See Isa. xxxiii. 1. Christ, by the preaching of His Apostles, who were Jews, spoiled the nations which had spoiled Jerusalem. He brought them into the blessed captivity of His Gospel (*S. Augustine,* De Civ. Dei, viii. 30).

**9.** *I will shake mine hand upon them*] In anger, to terrify and to destroy. Cp. Isa. xix. 16. Or, as a General lifts up his hand or spear as a sign for attack (see Josh. viii. 18), and also as a signal that his foes will fall prostrate under it. Cp. Ps. cvi. 26, "He lifted up His hand against them, to overthrow them in the wilderness ;" and Isa. xlix. 22.

**10.** *I will dwell in the midst of thee*] Compare Isa. xii. 6; below, viii. 3. This is fulfilled in the Christian Sion, by the perpetual presence of Christ, and by the indwelling of the Holy Ghost.

**11.** *many nations shall be joined to the* LORD] In the Church of Christ. See Isa. ii. 2, 3; liv. 2, 3; lx. 3—5. 11. Micah iv. 2. The prophet declares that God will receive the Gentiles into covenant with Him on equal terms with the Jews, in Christ ; and that, through the preaching of the Gospel by the ministry of Jews, the Apostles and first teachers of Christianity, going forth from restored Jerusalem, He will establish an Œcumenical Sion. See *Kliefoth,* 34.

**12.** *the* LORD *shall inherit Judah—and shall choose Jerusalem*] God has now taken possession of Judah, and has chosen Jerusalem by setting up Christ as King in the spiritual Sion of the Church, the City of the Living God. See Ps. ii. 6; lxxxvii. 2, 5. Heb. xii. 22. Rev. xiv. 1. And *so S. Jerome* and *S. Cyril* here.

**13.** *Be silent, O all flesh, before the* LORD] Thus Zechariah's prophecy connects itself with that of Zephaniah (i. 7), "Hold thy peace at the presence of the Lord God ;" and of Habakkuk (ii. 20), "The Lord is in His holy temple, let all the earth keep silence before Him."

CH. III.] The following section (iii. 1—iv. 7) is the haphtarah to Numbers viii. 1—xii. 16, which describes the consecration of the Levites and their service, and other sacred ministrations of the Tabernacle.

JOSHUA THE HIGH PRIEST IS JUSTIFIED.

The following Vision continues what has gone before. It reveals the work of God in building up and cleansing His Church. Joshua, the High Priest, is the Representative of the

Before
CHRIST
B.C.
b Ps. 109.6.
Rev. 12. 10
c 2 Pet. 2. 11
a........
d Het. 6. ....
Ch. 7....
0.5. 4. 17.
Rom. 5. 2.
e Amos 4. 11.
Rom. 11. 5.
Jude 23.
1 Isa. 64. 6.
g 1 s. 61. 10.
Luke 15. 22.
Rev. 19. 8.
h Exod. 39. 6.
ch. 6. 11.

1 Lev. 8. 23.
1 Kings 2. 3.
Ezek. 44. 16.
* Or, ordinance.
k Deut. 17. 9.
Mal. 2. 7.
1 Pet. 5 while.
1 Ps. 4. 14 & 5. 2.

of the Lord, and [b]‖Satan standing at his right hand † to resist him.  [2]And the Lord said unto Satan, [c]The Lord rebuke thee, O Satan ; even the Lord that [d]hath chosen Jerusalem rebuke thee : *is not* this a brand plucked out of the fire?

[3]Now Joshua was clothed with [f]filthy garments, and stood before the angel.

[4]And he answered and spake unto those that stood before him, saying, Take away the filthy garments from him.  And unto him he said, Behold, I have caused thine iniquity to pass from thee, [g]and I will clothe thee with change of raiment.

[5]And I said, Let them set a fair [h]mitre upon his head.

So they set a fair mitre upon his head, and clothed him with garments.  And the angel of the Lord stood by.

[6]And the angel of the Lord protested unto Joshua, saying, [7]Thus saith the Lord of hosts ; if thou wilt walk in my ways, and if thou wilt [i]keep my ‖charge, then thou shalt also [k]judge my house, and shalt also keep my courts, and I will give thee † places to walk among these that [l]stand by.

---

Hebrew Nation in spiritual things.  Cp. Lev. iv. 3; xvi. 24. Heb. ix. 7.  The Hebrew nation, in God's sight, was as yet defiled by sin.  This is signified by Joshua's soiled attire.  But he is to be cleansed from his sin.  The Nation is to be justified; and how ?  There is one way, and one only.  And what is that ?  The Incarnation and Death of Christ.  All the blessings of justification and sanctification, and all the hopes of glory flow from His Incarnation, Death, Resurrection, and Ascension into Heaven; and from the indwelling of the Holy Spirit sent by Him (vv. 8—10).

We may cite here the words of an eminent Christian Father who lived in the second century.  Speaking to the Jews, he says, "In the prophecies of Zechariah ye may see, as in a figure, the mystery of Christ.  Joshua, the High Priest of the Hebrew People at Babylon, foreshadowed those things which were to be done by our Priest and God, Christ Jesus, the Son of the Father of the Universe.  In Him we are brands plucked from the fire.  He appears clothed with foul garments, because We bare our sins.  Satan stands at His right hand, because Satan desires to destroy us.  But He is stripped of these foul garments, and is attired with beautiful raiment, because in Him our sins are taken away and we are clothed in His righteousness" (S. Justin Martyr, Tryp. §§ 115—117).

**1.** *Satan—at his right hand*] Cp. Ps. cix. 6, "Set thou a wicked man over him, and let Satan stand at his right hand." Cp. Job xxx. 12.

In this Vision, Satan, the Adversary (cp. Job i. 6; ii. 1—6), "the accuser of our brethren" (Rev. xii. 10), who desires to have us as his own (Luke xxii. 31), is revealed as endeavouring to prevent and intercept the working of God's love to His people, by representing them as defiled by sin, and as utterly unworthy of His favour.  Satan stood at Joshua's right hand, and endeavoured to work his ruin.  So Satan stood at the right hand of our Joshua, on the pinnacle of the Temple at Jerusalem, and tempted Him to cast Himself down and fall (Matt. iv. 5, 6.  S. Jerome).  Satan stood at Christ's right hand when He was betrayed by Judas, into whom Satan entered (Luke xxii. 3) ; he tempted Him in His Agony, and in His Passion; and Satan is even still standing at Christ's right hand by his opposition to the preaching of the Gospel, and by sowing tares of heresy in His Church.

**2.** *The Lord rebuke thee*]  Compare Jude 9, "Michael the Archangel, when contending with the Devil, he disputed about the body of Moses, durst not bring against him a railing accusation, but said, *The Lord rebuke thee.*"  Here is a solemn warning against that sarcastic, bitter, and virulent spirit, which, in these last days, shews itself so often in speaking and writing against others, even against rulers temporal and spiritual.  The holy angels, even in contending against Satan, use mild words.  But these rash and reckless speakers and writers imitate Satan, who is called in Scripture Diabolus, or Calumniator, and Adversary, and "Accuser of the brethren" (Rev. xii. 10).  How can they hope to be with good Angels hereafter?  Must they not rather look to be with those wicked minds whom they imitate?

— *is not this a brand plucked out of the fire*]  Is not the Hebrew Nation (which (as S. Cyril observes, and as Hosea i.), is represented by Joshua, its High Priest, like a brand plucked out of the fire?  Compare Amos iv. 11.  Have I not shown my Love to them by their marvellous deliverance from Babylon?  Shall I now desert them?  No; they are indeed defiled by sin, but I

will cleanse them.  God bestows justification upon the High Priest, and in him upon the Nation at large, which is represented and personified by him.  Cp. Ps. cxxv. 7, 8.

**3.** *Joshua was clothed with filthy garments*]  He, the High Priest of the Hebrew Nation, was himself compassed with sin ; and he represented the People, who were defiled with iniquity.  Thus Joshua was also a type of Christ, Who, though Himself without sin, yet appeared in the likeness of sinful flesh (Rom. viii. 3), and was made sin for us (2 Cor. v. 21), and bare our sins in His own body on the tree (Isa. liii. 4, 11.  Heb. ix. 28.  1 Pet. ii. 24).  See S. Ambrose, in Ps. cxix.; S. Jerome here ; Eusebius, Dem. Evang. iv. 17 ; S. Gregory, Moral. xx. 18 ; A Lapide.

**4.** *Take away the filthy garments*]  Thus the acceptance of God's people, on their faith and repentance, is signified.

In a spiritual sense Joshua, the High Priest, is a type of Christ ; and being divested of his filthy garments and clothed with fair attire, he represents Christ, Who at His Passion was clothed with a scarlet robe in mockery, and was smitten and buffeted; and Who was put to death as a malefactor, and bare our iniquities ; but at His Resurrection and Ascension was clothed in heavenly glory, and had a royal crown of victory set upon His head; *Osiris*, in Lucam, Hom. 14, and *Eusebius*, Dem. Evang. iv. 17, whose words may deserve to be cited here: "This Joshua, the High Priest, appears to me to display a vivid image of our Saviour Jesus Christ.  He bears the same name, Jesus; and he led the people of Judah from the Captivity at Babylon; and our Jesus came and preached *deliverance to the captives* (Luke iv. 18).  Joshua brought the people to Jerusalem ; our Jesus carries us up even to the heavenly Sion.  Joshua is clothed in filthy garments; our Jesus condescended to wear our garb of slavery, and to bear our sins.  He it is, of whom the Baptist says, Behold the Lamb of God who bears and takes away the sins of the world.  Joshua is stripped of his filthy garments, and receives a fair robe and a goodly mitre.  So our Jesus, having died for us, and having conquered Death, is now attired in heavenly glory, and wears the brilliant mitre of an everlasting Priesthood at God's right hand."  Cp. *Tertullian* c. Jud. 14.

— *I have caused thine iniquity to pass from thee*]  God, Who is our merciful Father, offered to the Hebrew Nation the means of justification by faith in Christ.  He has taken away the filthy dress of our original guilt, and has clothed us with a white robe at our Baptism—the robe of Christ's righteousness ; for, as the Apostle says, "As many of you as have been baptized into Christ, have put on Christ" (Gal. iii. 27).  Therefore let us walk with Him in white (Rev. iii. 4 ; xvi. 15).  In the Parable of the Prodigal Son, God's mercy to him on his repentance is represented by the words, "Bring forth the best robe" (literally, *the first robe*, of original righteousness) "and put it on him" (Luke xv. 22).

**5.** *a fair mitre*]  Hebrew. *tsâniph*, the head-dress of priests and kings.  Cp. Job xxix. 14, Isa. lxii. 3, in which passages it is rendered *diadem*.  Joshua the High Priest is the representative of the Hebrew People, which was a kingdom of priests,—a royal priesthood (Exod. xix. 6), as all Christians are (1 Pet. ii. 5—9).  They, and we, were tainted with sin ; but there is pardon, grace, and glory for all true believers in Christ.  Christ is crowned with glory and honour.  We are crowned anew in Him ; let us hold fast what we have received, and let no man take our crown (Rev. iii. 11).  This is what is enforced in v. 7.

**7.** *I will give thee places to walk*]  The High Priest alone

<sup></sup> Hear now, O Joshua the high priest,

Thou, and thy fellows that sit before thee :

For they *are* " † men wondered at :

For, behold, I will bring forth " my servant the ° BRANCH.

<sup>9</sup> For behold the stone that I have laid before Joshua ;

<sup>p</sup> Upon one stone *shall be* ° seven eyes :

Behold, I will engrave the graving thereof, saith the LORD of hosts,

And <sup>r</sup> I will remove the iniquity of that land in one day.

<sup>10</sup> In that day, saith the LORD of hosts, shall ye call every man his neighbour

<sup>s</sup> under the vine and under the fig tree.

Micah 7. 19, 10. ch. 13. 1. ° ch.2. 11. † † Kings 4, 25. Isa. 36. 16. Micah 4. 1.

Before
CHRIST
519.

m Ps. 71. 7.
Isa. 8. 18. & 20. 3.
† Heb. *men of
wonder, or, men of
sign.*
Ezek. 12. 11. &
24. 24.
n Isa. 42. 1. & 49. 5.
& 52. 13. & 53. 11.
Luke 1. 32. 54.
o Isa. 4. 2. & 11. 1.
& 42. 1. & ver. 8.
ch. 6. 12. Luke 1. 78.
p Ps. 118. 22.
ch. 4. 10.
q ch. 4. 10.
Rev. 5. 6.
r Jer. 31. 34 & 50. 20.

could go, and only once a year, and that with blood, into the Holy of Holies, the figure of the true (Heb. ix. 24). But the vision declares that whole Nations, whom he represents, will have free access to God. The promise is, I will give thee a free approach to God in Christ, " through Whom we have access by One Spirit unto the Father" (Eph. ii. 18). Christ is the Way (John xiv. 6); and if we enter in and walk by Him, by the new and living Way, which He hath consecrated for us (Heb. x. 20), we shall come through the true Veil to the Holy of Holies, our heavenly home.

8. *Hear now, O Joshua the high priest—they are men to be wondered at*] Literally, *they are men of wonder,* that is, they are signs, mysterious portents, of something else; as Isaiah and his two sons were *signs* of Christ (Isa. viii. 18); and Ezekiel was a sign (Ezek. xii. 6). They are men who are to be gazed at with wonder, because they typify a great Mystery, which was no other than the Incarnation and everlasting Priesthood of Jesus the Son of God. Joshua the High Priest, and his associates with him, who constituted the Hebrew Hierarchy, and who were appointed to offer sacrifice, and to bless the people and to pray for them, were "typical men" (as *Bp. Chandler* renders it; and see *Eusebius,* Dem. Evang. iv. 17, and *S. Jerome, S. Cyril,* and *Hengst.* here): they prefigured the sacerdotal office of Christ. See *Introd.* to Leviticus, pp. ii–iv, and Lev. xvi., and Heb. ix. x. Even as early as in Ps. cx. Christ is represented as a Priest as well as a King; and in Isaiah (lii. 15) He sprinkles many nations, and presents an offering for sin, and bears the sins of the people (Isa. liii. 10—12). Observe, therefore, what follows,

MY SERVANT, THE BRANCH.

— *For, behold, I will bring forth my servant the BRANCH*] Here is the clue to the Vision. The cause of the justification of the Hebrew Priesthood, and of the Hebrew Nation represented by it, and of all the faithful Israel of God, the children of Abraham, in whose seed (which is Christ) all nations of the earth are blessed is this, that God brings forth *His Servant* (as the Messiah is named in Isa. xli. 1, 19; xlix. 6; lii. 13; liii. 11) the BRANCH (Heb. *Tsemach*), as the Messiah is called by Jeremiah xxiii. 5 ; xxxiii. 15, and below, "the Man whose Name is the BRANCH ;" for He sprouted forth from the root of the stem of Jesse and of David, when it was in a dry ground (Isa. xi. 1, 2 ; liii. 2). The Jewish Targum has here the remarkable words, " I bring forth My Servant the *Christ*."

THE STONE.

9. *For behold the stone—seven eyes ; behold, I will engrave the graving thereof*] The Messiah, Who has just been called the *Branch,* is now called the *Stone* (as He had been already named by Isaiah (xxviii. 16), and in Ps. cxviii. 22), lest any one should interpret this prophecy literally, and lest any one should imagine Him to be weak as a Branch. A Branch is *inoculated* with buds (called *eyes,* "Nec modus inserere atque *oculos* imponere simplex," *Virg.* Georg. ii. 73) ; and seven eyes are engraven on this Stone, which represents the Messiah. The Stone is not a dark, lifeless Stone, like other stones, but a *living, seeing* Stone. It has *seven eyes,* representing the sevenfold gifts of the Spirit with which, according to Isaiah (xi. 2), the Messiah is anointed, animated, strengthened, and enlightened (cp. *Kliefoth,* 49; or (as *S. Cyril* says), "Since the number *seven* denotes multitude and completeness, as in the phrase, "the barren hath borne *seven*" (1 Sam. ii. 5), the seven eyes denote the divine and ineffable nature of the Son, by which He beholds all things."

The ancient Expositors rightly affirm that Jesus Christ in His various attributes is typified by the High Priest, the Branch, and the Stone (*S. Jerome*). God declares that He lays, or rather, as the original signifies, that He *gives,* a stone

before Joshua : lit. *before his face,* to defend him, and in order that he may place it as the foundation and corner-stone of his building, which symbolized the Church, of which the corner-stone is Christ (Isa. xxviii. 16. Eph. ii. 20. 1 Pet. ii. 6).

This Stone is graven, like the precious stones in the breast-plate of the High Priest with the names of the Tribes upon them (Exod. xxviii. 21). Cp. below, 2 Tim. ii. 19. "The foundation stone (see the original) of God standeth sure, having this seal, " or gravure ; and Rev. xxi. 14, where the twelve foundation-stones (see again the original) of the heavenly city have twelve names graven upon them.

The gravure here is of *eyes,* emblems of light. Cp. Matt. vi. 22, and the wheel full of eyes in Ezekiel (i. 18), and the description of the Living Creatures full of eyes in the Apocalypse (Rev. iv. 1—6), and of the Lamb with seven eyes, which are the seven spirits of God sent forth into all the earth (Rev. v. 6), and below here (iv. 10), where these words are repeated.

These eyes are *seven,* signifying completeness (see below, on iv. 2, and above, on Ezekiel, p. 280), and representing the perfection of the spiritual illumination and perpetual watchfulness of Christ, the Messiah, anointed with the sevenfold gift (Isa. xi. 2) and unction of the Holy Ghost (Ps. lxxxii. 20. Acts iv. 27 ; x. 38. Heb. i. 9). God giveth not the Spirit by measure unto Him, but in infinite abundance (John iii. 31); and in Him all fulness of grace and light dwells (Col. i. 9; ii. 9) ; and from Him it flows as from a fountain, through all the spiritual life of the Church ; for of His fulness we all receive, and grace for grace (John i. 16).

This exposition is confirmed by ancient Interpreters, as *S. Jerome Remigius;* and *A Lapide* says, "Septem oculi sunt dona Spiritús Sancti, quæ plenissimé fuerunt in animâ Christi, quia hæc animam Ejus oculatam, illuminatam, et vigilantem fecerunt ;" and *S. Gregory,* Moral. xxix. 16, says, These seven eyes signify the spiritual plenitude of Christ, and that He has for ever the sevenfold gifts of the Spirit. One man has one gift, one another, which they *receive,* but Christ has always all spiritual gifts in Himself. In Him the spiritual Pleiad shines with eternal splendour.

— *of that land*] Rather, *of the earth,* the whole world, Christ is the Saviour of all.

— *in one day*] The day of Calvary ; the one day of Christ's Passion. See what follows, and below xiii. 1. " In *that day* there shall be a fountain opened for sin and for uncleanness."

Observe the poetical beauty and harmonious connexion of this prophetic vision. Christ is called the *servant* of God, the *Branch* ; this bespeaks His Condescension, His true Manhood ; from the root of David ; but He is also the *Stone,* the Corner-Stone, of the Church Universal ; and that Stone *is graven* with *seven eyes,* because He is filled with the Spirit, and by virtue of these attributes He became in *one Day,* the Day of His Death on the Cross, the True Sacrifice, atonement and propitiation for the sins of the whole world.

10. *In that day shall ye call every man his neighbour under the vine and under the fig tree*] In the day of Christ's Passion. All true Israelites were reconciled to God by the One Sacrifice offered once for all on Calvary by Him Who is our true and everlasting High Priest (Heb. vii. 27 ; ix. 12 ; x. 10), and thenceforth they enjoy peace through Him Who is our Peace (Eph. ii. 14), and they sit under their own vine and fig-tree, as in the days of Solomon. See 1 Kings iv. 25; and cp. on Micah iv. 4.

From speaking of the Passion of Christ, the Prophet next proceeds to speak of the CHURCH UNIVERSAL, purchased and cleansed by His most precious Blood, shed at Calvary. From the Bridegroom he passes to the Bride; and from the King to the Queen at His right hand (Ps. xlv. 9). As the Bride says to the Bridegroom in the Canticles, "Come, my beloved, let us

Before
CHRIST
547.
a ch. 2. 3.
b Dan. 8. 18.
c Exod. 25. 31.
Rev. 1. 12.
† Heb. *with her
bowl.*
d Exod. 25. 37.
Rev. 4. 5.
‖ Or, *seven several
pipes to the lamps,
&c.*
e ver. 11, 12.
Rev. 11. 4.

f Hos. 1. 7.
‖ Or, *army.*
g Jer. 51. 25.
Matt. 21, 21.
h Ps. 118. 22.

i Ezra 3. 11—13.

k Ezra 3. 10.
Hag. 2. 18.
m ch. 2. 9, 11. &
6. 15.
n Isa. 48. 16. ch.
2. 9.

IV. [1] And [a] the angel that talked with me came again, and waked me, [b] as a man that is *wakened out* of his sleep, [2] and said unto me, What seest thou? And I said, I have looked, and behold [c] *a* candlestick all *of* gold, † with a bowl upon the top of it, [d] and his seven lamps thereon, and ‖ seven pipes to the seven lamps, which *are* upon the top thereof: [3] [e] And two olive trees by it, one upon the right *side* of the bowl, and the other upon the left *side* thereof.

[4] So I answered and spake to the angel that talked with me, saying, What *are* these, my lord? [5] Then the angel that talked with me answered and said unto me, Knowest thou not what these be?

And I said, No, my lord.

[6] Then he answered and spake unto me, saying, This *is* the word of the LORD unto Zerubbabel, saying, [f] Not by ‖ might, nor by power, but by my spirit, saith the LORD of hosts. [7] [g] Who *art* thou, O great mountain? before Zerubbabel *thou shalt become* a plain: and he shall bring forth [h] the headstone *thereof* [i] *with* shoutings, *crying,* Grace, grace unto it.

[8] Moreover the word of the LORD came unto me, saying, [9] The hands of Zerubbabel [k] have laid the foundation of this house; his hands [l] shall also finish it; and [m] thou shalt know that the [n] LORD of hosts hath sent me unto you.

---

get up early to the vineyards, and see if the vine flourish" (Cant. vii. 12), so now that Christ is come, and the Gospel is preached everywhere, the vineyards of the Lord, which are Christ's Churches, flourish, and the fig-tree blossoms, and they bear fruit to the Lord. Cp. Isa. v. 1—7. Hab. iii. 17. *S. Cyril.*

CH. IV.] THE SEVEN BRANCHED GOLDEN CANDLESTICK, or rather, LAMPSTAND; the TWO OLIVE-TREES.

1. *wakened out of his sleep*] I had sunk down into sleep from exhaustion consequent on the wonderful and glorious revelations of the four preceding visions, and the angel waked me out of it. Compare Daniel's sleep after his vision, viii. 18; x. 8, 9; and St. Peter's sleep at the transfiguration (Luke ix. 32).

2. *a candlestick all of gold*] This imagery is derived from the Tabernacle and the Temple. Even to this day the seven-branched candlestick is seen in the sculptured bas-reliefs of the Arch of Titus at Rome, among the spoils of the Temple at Jerusalem, which were taken by him and carried in his triumphal procession along the Via Sacra to the Roman Capitol.

This Seven-branched Candlestick is a figure of the Universal Church of Christ. It is golden, as representing the preciousness, holiness, and glory of the Church. It is filled with oil, signifying the gift of the Holy Spirit flowing into it and through it; and it has seven branches, signifying its Universality, by which it diffuses the pure light of Divine Truth, derived from the oil of the Holy Spirit, throughout the world. See above, on Exod. xxv. 31—37; below, on Rev. i. 12, 13, 20, and on Rev. xi. 4, which is the best commentary on the present passage.

— *a bowl*] In the Candlestick of the Jewish Tabernacle and Temple there was no such bowl, because the lamps were trimmed and fed daily by the Priests (Exod. xxvii. 20, 21). But here the oil is supplied by God Himself through the Olive-trees, which represent the functions of Christ, Who is the great High Priest and King. The oil which flows in the candlestick of the Church is not from man, but from God. The light of the written Word is from Christ the Eternal Word (*S. Cyril*).

In this prophetic type and figure of the Church we see a warning against the error and sin of those who adulterate the divine oil with human admixtures, and "teach for doctrines the commandments of men" (Matt. xv. 9).

3. *two olive trees*] See below, on v. 11.

6. *by my spirit*] Not by human power, but by the might of the Holy Ghost, stirring up him and the people by the prophets was the Temple builded by Zerubbabel, the figure of Christ. See Ezra vi. 14. Hag. ii. 21, 23. The spiritual Temple of the Church of Christ was built by Him, sending the Holy Ghost on the Day of Pentecost to animate the builders, and to abide for ever with the Church (John xiv. 16).

It must be remembered in reading these prophecies, that, as David is the type of Christ, and not only so, but Christ Himself is also called *David* by the Prophets (see on Ezek. xxxiv.

163

23, 24; xxxvii. 24), so Zerubbabel (the seed of David, and leader of the people from captivity, and builder of the Temple) is not only a *type* of Christ, but Christ is *called* Zerubbabel. The author of Bresbith Rabba says, "The Messiah is called Zerubbabel and also David; because He was represented in both;" and so *Abarbinel.* Cp. *Bp. Chandler,* p. 266.

In the preceding verses, Joshua the High Priest is introduced in his priestly character, as the representative of the Nation in its consecration to God, and as a type of Christ, the Eternal Priest. So here Zerubbabel, the Civil Governor of the Hebrew Nation, and the seed of David, is also displayed in his princely functions as a representative of the Nation in its royal dignity, and as a figure of Christ, the Everlasting King. Hence we see the propriety of the transition to the imagery of the Candlestick, the symbol of the universal Church, set up by Christ, and filled by Him with the Oil of the Spirit, to enlighten the World.

THE MOUNTAIN SHALL BECOME A PLAIN.

7. *O great mountain*—thou shalt become *a plain*] The lofty mountains of worldly opposition were subdued into level plains by the Spirit of God, when Zerubbabel went forth from Babylon to build the Temple of the Lord. The great mountain of the worldly power of Babylon, which had carried Judah captive, was overthrown by Persia, and became a plain. The Jews, being freed by Cyrus, marched back to Jerusalem. The mountain of opposition from the Samaritans disappeared before their face. It became a plain. The Temple of God was built; Zerubbabel laid the foundation of it; and he finished it amid prayers and acclamations of the people, "*Grace, grace unto it!*"

Christ, Who was the Antitype of Zerubbabel, and the Giver of all grace (John i. 16, 17), came in person to that self-same Temple, and filled it with His glory (Hag. ii. 7). Therefore it may be truly said that this prophecy was accomplished by the Founder and Finisher of the Christian Church, Jesus Christ (*S. Cyril*). Mountains have become plains before Him; He has overcome Death by dying; He has conquered Sin and Satan by the Cross; He ascended in triumph into heaven, as in a chariot of victory, and was hailed by the acclamations of Angels, "Lift up your heads, O ye gates; and be ye lift up, ye everlasting doors; and the King of Glory shall come in" (Ps. xxiv. 7). And when He had ascended up on high and had led captivity captive, He gave gifts to men (Ephes. iv. 8). By the outpouring of His Spirit He made Jews to become Preachers of His Gospel; He changed St. Peter, who had thrice denied Him through fear, into a courageous Champion of the Faith. He changed the persecuting Pharisee Saul into the fervent Preacher St. Paul. He made the heathen nations to be builders of the Church. He has changed Temples and Basilicas into Churches. The Coliseum, where Christians were cast to the wild beasts and martyr'd, has been Christianized; the Cross stands there, and Christ has been preached there. He has made heathenism itself to become a spiritual Sion, on which the Church is built.

<sup>10</sup> For who hath despised the day of ° small things? ‖ for they shall rejoice, and shall see the ┼ plummet in the hand of Zerubbabel *with* those seven; ᵖ they are the eyes of the LORD, which run to and fro through the whole earth.

<sup>11</sup> Then answered I, and said unto him, What *are* these ᑫtwo olive trees upon the right *side* of the candlestick and upon the left *side* thereof?

<sup>12</sup> And I answered again, and said unto him, What *be these* two olive branches which ┼ through the two golden pipes ‖ empty ┼ the golden *oil* out of themselves?

<sup>13</sup> And he answered me and said, Knowest thou not what these *be*? And I said, No, my lord.

<sup>14</sup> Then said he, ʻThese *are* the two ┼ anointed ones,ʼ that stand by ʻthe Lord of the whole earth.

Before
CHRIST
515.
o Hag. 2. 7.
p Or, unto the
   seven eyes of the
   Lord it shall
   appear.
q Heb. stone
   of tin.
r 2 Chr. 16. 9.
s Rev. 15. 6.
   ch 3. 9.
t ...
   tit. betwixt the
   oil.
u Or, empty out
   of themselves oil
   into the gold.
t Heb. the gold.

Luke 1. 19.　1 See Josh. 3. 11. 13.　ch 6. 5.

10. *who hath despised the day of small things?*] Who, that desires to achieve great things, despises the day of small things? The work of building the "latter house" at Jerusalem was begun in days of weakness and amid tears, by a scanty band of labourers, and was encountered by much opposition; but finally was completed; and the house was dedicated with shouts of joy and singing, and was "filled with the glory of the Lord" by the Coming of Christ.

The Church of Christ was at first a little leaven, but it will leaven the world. It was a grain of mustard seed, but it will become a great tree, and all nations will sit beneath its shade.

Christ, the Stone cut out without hands, was despised at first, but He has become a Mountain and fills the Earth (Dan. ii. 35. 45), and will grind to powder all that resist Him (Matt. xxi. 44).

— *Zerubbabel with those seven; they are the eyes of the Lord*] Rather, a stop should be placed after the word *Zerubbabel*; the word *with*, which is not in the original, should be expunged. A new sentence begins after Zerubbabel. *Those seven, the eyes of the Lord are they, running over the whole world.* The "seven eyes" in the foundation-stone (see above, iii. 9) are "eyes of the Lord;" they are the fulness of spiritual illumination and perpetual vigilance in Christ, the True Foundation of the Church; and they run over the whole world in His fourfold Gospel preached to all Nations, even to all points of the four winds of heaven, by the Church Universal. He sees all; He is ever walking among the Churches, and watching them (see Rev. ii. 1); His eye is ever on them, and He illumines them.

The best illustration of the imagery in Zechariah is to be found in the Book of Revelation; indeed, the Apocalypse is the best commentary on Zechariah. There, as was before observed, the Lamb is displayed as having *seven eyes*, which are the seven spirits of God, sent forth into all the earth (Rev. v. 6). There the "four living creatures," representing the fourfold Gospel, are described as "*full of eyes*," full of the light of the Holy Spirit, radiating by them throughout the world. See on Rev. iv. 4—6, p. 182, and above on Ezek. i. 15—20.

11—14. *What are these two olive trees—What be these two olive branches* (lit. *ears*)—*These are the two anointed ones*] Literally, *they are the two sons of oil.*

It has been supposed that they represent the anointed Priesthood and Royalty; and that this was verified in a subordinate sense in the Hebrew nation, where the Monarchy and the Priesthood— both of which were consecrated with holy oil, the symbol of the outpouring of the Holy Spirit—were the appointed means and channels by which the favour and grace of God were conveyed and bestowed on the Hebrew People.

Some ancient and modern Expositors suppose the two olive trees to symbolize the two Churches, that is, the Hebrew and Gentile Church; and this interpretation derives confirmation from the fact that St. Paul describes the Jews and Gentiles as two olive trees (Rom. xi. 17. 24). But to this opinion it may reasonably be objected, first, that the Candlestick represents the Church; and next, that the Hebrew and Gentile Churches did not minister oil to the Candlestick, but were recipients of oil from Christ.

Rather, the two Olive Trees symbolize Christ's Priesthood and Monarchy. This is confirmed by what follows, ch. 13. By His Incarnation and Unction from the Holy Ghost, He has become the *Messiah*, the *Christ*, the *Anointed* One, the Everlasting King and Priest of the Universal Church. Olives produce oil; and oil supplies light to the Candlestick, and all the oil of the Holy Spirit flows, by the medium of His Messiahship in its twofold functions

of King and Priest, into the Candlestick of the Universal Church. We are Christians because we believe Jesus to be the Christ, and because we are incorporated in His Body. He which hath anointed us is God (2 Cor. i. 21). By faith in Him Who is anointed by God with the oil of gladness (Heb. i. 9), and by mystical union with Him, "we have *an unction from the Holy One*, and the anointing which we have received of Him abideth in us; and the same anointing" (being an anointing of illumination) "teacheth us all things, and is truth, and is no lie; and even as it hath taught us, we shall abide in Him" (1 John ii. 20. 27); and by virtue of His Incarnation, and Unction from the Holy Ghost, and of our mystical union with Him, He has "made us to be kings and priests to God" (Rev. i. 6; v. 10).

This Vision, interpreted in this sense, is fraught with doctrinal and practical instruction to all.

It teaches, that as all the light of the Moon is derived from God through the Son, so all the splendour and glory of the Church are received from the Father through Christ, "the Sun of Righteousness" (Mal. iv. 2). They flow from His Incarnation. He is the Eternal Son of God. "In Him dwelleth all the fulness of the Godhead bodily" (Col. ii. 9). And He is Very Man; and He communicates of that fulness to us all, whose nature He has taken (John i. 16). He has made us to be partakers of the Divine Nature (2 Pet. i. 4), by our mystical union with Himself, Very God and Very Man. And this communication of grace and glory is effectually accomplished by means of His twofold office of Priest and King. As our Priest, He has offered Himself for us, and has reconciled us to the Father; and the regenerating and refreshing, strengthening and sanctifying virtue of His Blood once shed, and of His Body once offered in the sacrifice of Calvary, is applied to each of us severally on the condition of our Faith and Obedience, in the Holy Sacraments of Baptism and the Lord's Supper.

By reason of His everlasting Royalty, the grace received by us through his Priesthood will be consummated in glory at that great Day when all earthly Powers will be put under His feet, and "the kingdoms of this world will become the kingdoms of the Lord, and of His Christ" (Rev. xi. 15), and He will "reign for ever and ever, KING of kings, and LORD of lords" (Rev. xvii. 14), and will say to all His faithful servants on His right hand, "Receive the kingdom prepared for you from the foundation of the world" (Matt. xxv. 34).

It is also a probable opinion, that the two Olive Trees symbolize the Old and New Testament; through which the Oil of the Holy Spirit is conveyed to the Candlestick of the Church which illuminates the world by the light thence received; and this interpretation is confirmed by the language of the Apocalypse, where are Two Olive Trees and Two Candlesticks, which are called God's Two Witnesses, and they are said to *stand before the Lord of all the earth*. See below on Rev. xi. 3, 4, pp. 216, 217.

On the whole, we may conclude that the two Olive Trees represent either the Incarnate Word or the Written Word.

12. *What be these two olive branches which through the two golden pipes empty the golden oil*] Literally, *empty the gold.* Observe, the Candlestick is golden, and the oil is called gold; it is like liquid gold. The Church must be pure and holy, and what she teaches and ministers to the People must be pure and holy also; not adulterated with the admixture of any novel doctrines, such as those which have been added by some to "the faith once for all delivered to the saints" (Jude 3), and imposed as necessary to salvation. "How is the gold become dim, and the fine gold changed!" (Lam. iv. 1.)

K

V. ¹ Then I turned, and lifted up mine eyes, and looked, and behold a flying
ᵃ roll.

² And he said unto me, What seest thou?

And I answered, I see a flying roll; the length thereof *is* twenty cubits, and
the breadth thereof ten cubits.

b Mal. 4. 6.

³ Then said he unto me, This *is* the ᵇ curse that goeth forth over the face of
‖ Or, *every one of
this people that
stealeth holdeth
himself guiltless,
as it doth.* the whole earth: for ‖ every one that stealeth shall be cut off *as* on this side
according to it; and every one that sweareth shall be cut off *as* on that side

c Lev. 19. 12.
ch. 8. 17.
Mal. 3. 5.
d See Lev. 14. 45. according to it. ⁴ I will bring it forth, saith the LORD of hosts, and it shall
enter into the house of the thief, and into the house of ᶜ him that sweareth
falsely by my name: and it shall remain in the midst of his house, and ᵈ shall
consume it with the timber thereof and the stones thereof.

⁵ Then the angel that talked with me went forth, and said unto me, Lift up
now thine eyes, and see what *is* this that goeth forth.

⁶ And I said, What *is* it?

And he said, This *is* an ephah that goeth forth.

He said moreover, This *is* their resemblance through all the earth.

‖ Or, *weighty
piece.* ⁷ And, behold, there was lifted up a ‖ talent of lead: and this *is* a woman that
sitteth in the midst of the ephah.

⁸ And he said, This *is* wickedness. And he cast it into the midst of the
ephah; and he cast the weight of lead upon the mouth thereof.

⁹ Then lifted I up mine eyes, and looked, and, behold, there came out two
women, and the wind *was* in their wings; for they had wings like the wings of
a stork: and they lifted up the ephah between the earth and the heaven.

¹⁰ Then said I to the angel that talked with me, Whither do these bear the
ephah?

e Jer. 29. 5, 28.
f Gen. 10. 10. ¹¹ And he said unto me, To ᵉ build it an house in ᶠ the land of Shinar: and it
shall be established, and set there upon her own base.

---

THE FLYING ROLL. THE WOMAN IN THE EPHAH.

CH. V.] This Vision follows as a natural sequel to the preceding one. The announcement of God's gracious favour to the
faithful in the former Vision is succeeded here by a solemn
warning to the ungodly.

The description of the faithful Church, the spiritual *Sion*,
in the foregoing chapter, is now followed by a representation of
its opposite, the faithless Church, whose place is a spiritual
*Babylon* (v. 11).

This Vision had in the first instance a message of warning
for the godless men at Jerusalem in Zechariah's own day, the
false swearers, extortioners, and adulterers, and others with
whom Nehemiah had to contend (cp. Mal. iii. 5); but it is
extended to the spiritual Jerusalem, the Church (S. *Cyril*).

2. *a flying roll* (or volume unrolled and spread out); *the
length thereof is twenty cubits, and the breadth thereof ten
cubits*] That is, its length was exactly equal to the dimensions
of the Holy Place of the Tabernacle; and to the Porch of the
Holy Place in Solomon's Temple, and of the House itself in
breadth, which was twenty cubits (see 1 Kings vi. 3), and it was
equal in its other dimensions, ten cubits, to the depth of the
Porch, so that if it had been laid down (as a carpet) in the
Porch, it would have covered the whole area.

This signifies that the warning here pronounced is universal
in its extent and application. None who enter the Porch of the
Visible Church may flatter themselves that they can escape
God's wrath and malediction, if they commit any of the sins
condemned by the comprehensive commination of this flying
Roll, which may be compared to a net, co-extensive with the
world, and drawn throughout the whole, from side to
side.

3. *that sweareth*] Namely, *falsely*. See v. 4.

6. *This is an ephah*] Literally, *the* ephah, the full measure of
iniquity (S. *Jerome*, *Theodoret*).

The Ephah was the measure by which corn was meted out
and dispensed. The Ephah or bushel is chosen here, because it

130

was the principal measure of capacity among the Hebrews: it
contained about eight gallons. See on Exod. xvi. 36.

What does it symbolize?

The members and ministers of God's Church ought to dispense
nourishment to others. They ought to measure out their gifts,
and to feed those around them with the wholesome food of divine
truth and holy example. If they do not do this, their privileges
will become the occasion and instrument of their punishment.
They will be like the woman (which represents *wickedness*) cast
into the ephah, and sealed up in it hermetically with lead, and
swept away by the winds of God's wrath, from the Sion of His
Church to the Babel of Confusion. Here is a warning to all
who adulterate God's truth, or refuse to impart it in purity and
simplicity.

9. *there came out two women, and the wind was in their
wings; for they had wings like the wings of a stork*] The Woman
in the Ephah is a corrupt Church; the other two women, who
carry her away, with wings like those of a stork, a bird proverbial for its filial love, and therefore called *chasîdah*, or *pious*
(see on Job xxxix. 13), perhaps represent faithful Churches; and
the meaning seems to be, that they will punish Error, because
they love the Truth. The stork is a migratory bird (Jer. viii. 7),
soaring aloft with sail-like, flapping wings, and frequents
ruinous and marshy places, like Babylon.

11. *To build it an house in the land of Shinar*] The place
where the tower of Babel, or Confusion, was built by rebels
against God (see on Gen. x. 10; xi. 9), and the scene also of
Israel's exile and punishment for sin (Isa. xi. 11. Dan. i. 2)
where Babylon was; the City of Confusion, opposed to Sion, the
City of Peace. See on Acts ii. 6.

The Prophet intimates to the Jews of his own age, that if
they sin against God by the sins here mentioned, their restoration to Jerusalem is frustrate and abortive; they are not, in
heart, in Sion the City of Peace, but in Babel the City of
Confusion; and though they may pride themselves in building a
city and temple at Jerusalem, yet their own proper place, where
their own house is built, is the land of Shinar.

Before CHRIST 519.

o Isa. 22. 24.

p Ps. 110. 4. Heb. 3. 1.

q Exod. 12. 14. Mark 14. 9.

And he [o] shall bear the glory,
And shall sit and rule upon his throne;
And [p] he shall be a priest upon his throne:
And the counsel of peace shall be between them both.
14 And the crowns shall be to Helem, and to Tobijah, and to Jedaiah, and to
Hen the son of Zephaniah, [q] for a memorial in the temple of the LORD.

---

*his throne: and the counsel of peace shall be between them both*] That is, the Priesthood and the Monarchy shall be united in a holy alliance, and shall produce eternal peace by their union in Him. This is fulfilled in Christ, and in Christ alone, "In unius gloriâ Domini Jesu utrumque consentit" (*S. Jerome*). This union had already been symbolized by the two Olive Trees in iv. 11–14.

It is an expansion of the divine words of Psalm cx., where Christ is revealed as a *King*, seated at God's right hand, till He makes his foes His footstool: and also, "as a Priest for ever."

The offering of silver and gold from *the people of the captivity*, and the formation of these precious metals so offered, into diadems for the crown of Joshua the High Priest, the leader of the captivity from Babylon, and the builder of the Temple with Zerubbabel, was typical of the homage to be paid to Christ by the Jewish dispersion and by all nations of the world who were once in the Babylonish bondage, and exile of Sin and Death, but have received liberty from Christ. *They that are far off* (it is added, v. 15) *shall come, and shall build in the Temple of the Lord*, namely, the Universal Church of Christ (*S. Cyril*), and do homage to Him. "All kings shall bow down before Him, all nations shall do Him service" (Ps. lxxii. 11). "The Kings of Tarshish and of the isles shall give presents, the Kings of Arabia and Saba shall bring gifts" (Ps. lxxii. 10). They shall cast their crowns down before Him. Therefore, the crowns or diadems here mentioned are described as *a memorial in the Temple of the Lord*, they were typical of what would take place hereafter, and they are inscribed with certan significant names, i. e. *Helem*, or *Chelem (strength)*; and *Tobijah (pleasing to the Lord)*; and *Jedaiah (whom the Lord knows)*; and *Chen (grace)*; *the son of Zephaniah (whom the Lord hides and protects)*. These names indicate the moral qualifications of those whose offerings will be accepted by Christ, "Per singulas virtutes nostras Dominus coronatur" (*S. Jerome*). Christ is crowned with gold and silver diadems of our faith and good works, and with the glory of our salvation (*S. Cyril*).

The following excellent remarks on these prophecies of Zechariah may here be submitted to the reader:—

"The first return of the Jewish people from Babylon was not to security and peace. Their establishment was opposed by the jealousy of the Samaritans, and the hatred of other surrounding enemies; the rebuilding of their Temple and their Walls was forcibly interrupted and delayed. The struggle affected their promised restoration as a Church and People; and the exercise of their religion was at stake in it.

"But Prophecy was instructed to supply the encouragement which the conflict of their misfortunes required. It did so by assurances of the repression of their enemies, and the complete re-establishment of their City, Temple, and public peace. 'Thus saith the Lord, I am returned to Jerusalem *with mercies; My house* shall be built in it, saith the Lord of Hosts, and a line shall be stretched forth upon *Jerusalem. My cities through prosperity shall yet be spread abroad*, and the Lord shall yet comfort Zion, and shall yet choose Jerusalem' (Zech. i. 16, 17). 'For thus saith the Lord of Hosts; *As I thought* to punish you, when your fathers provoked Me to wrath, saith the Lord of Hosts, and *I repented not; so again* have I thought *in these days to do well* unto Jerusalem and to the *house of Judah*: fear ye not' (viii. 14, 15).

"Such is the general scope of Haggai and Zechariah's predictions, as they relate to the affairs of the Jewish people.

"But these prophets introduce also the Gospel-subject; Zechariah especially, in mystic vision and by typical representation, which yet are sufficiently clear, as expressive of the kingdom of the *Christian Church*, and the concourse of Nations resorting to *that future Temple*. For here, in this æra, we have a *second* application of the same systematic form of prophecy which was employed in the establishment of the Temporal Kingdom. The nearer subject, in each instance, supplies the prophetic ground, and the prophetic images, for the future Christian subject.

"In the first instance, the Kingdom of Christ is delineated in connexion with, and by analogy to, the actual kingdom which was seen before men's eyes rising to view. In the second instance, His *personal Priesthood*, and His *Church*, are delineated in connexion with, and by an equal analogy to, the Priesthood and Temple of the Hebrew Church, at the time when the Priesthood was reinstated in its functions, and that Temple was rebuilt.

"As an example of this *symbolical* prediction, founded upon *the present scene* of things, consider the following oracle of Zechariah:—

"The prophet had been commanded to take *silver and gold*, and *make crowns*, and *set them*, or set one of them, upon *the head of Joshua*, the *son of Josedech*, the *high priest*, and then to deliver this prophecy: 'Thus speaketh the Lord of hosts, saying, *Behold the Man* whose name is the BRANCH and He shall grow up out of this place (or, there shall be a growth out of His place), and He shall build the Temple of the Lord: Even *He shall build the Temple of the Lord*, and *He* shall *bear the glory*, and *shall sit and rule upon His throne*, and the *counsel of peace* shall be between them both;' and 'the crown shall be for *a memorial* in the Temple of the Lord. And they that *are afar off* shall *come and build* in the *Temple* of the Lord, and ye shall know that the Lord of Hosts hath sent me unto you. And this shall come to pass if ye will diligently obey the voice of the Lord your God' (Zech. vi. 10–15).

"This oracle, I think, will justify and sustain the character I have assigned to it. Its mystic form, its sublime and emphatic spirit, its promise of glory, its union of the Priesthood and the Throne, its appointed memorial of the crown to be laid up in the Temple of the Lord, its assemblage of builders from afar, absolutely *refuse* to be confined to the *literal* idea of the *present* work of the Jewish restoration, in their national increase, their Priesthood, and their Temple. The whole principle of the prophecy meets us in the face, first in its ground of analogy, and next in its proper extent, an extent wherein it leaves the inferior subject, from which it springs, far behind.

"In truth, there is both reason and sublimity in Prophecy; and we shall scarcely understand it, unless we are prepared to follow it in both. Its sublimity is, that it often soars, as here, far above the scene from which it takes its rise. Its reason is, that it still hovers over the scene of things from which it rose. It takes the visible, or the temporal, subject as its point of departure (if I may borrow the phrase) for its enlarged revelation; and yet by that subject it governs its course.

"In this method of it, I believe that men of plain unsophisticated reason find it perfectly intelligible; and that it is only the false fastidiousness of an artificial learning which puts the scruple into our perceptions either of its consistency, or its sense. But when we consider that this structure of Prophecy founded on a proximate visible subject, had the advantage, both in the *aptitude* of the representation, and in *the immediate pledge* of the future truth; a sounder learning may dispose us to admit it, and that with confidence, whenever the prophetic text, or mystic vision, is impatient for the larger scope, and the conspicuous characters of the Symbol and the Fact concur in identifying the relation" (*Davison* on Prophecy, pp. 230–232).

Again, the same writer thus speaks:—

"The predictions joined with the building of Solomon's Temple are of a simpler kind; perhaps they relate purely and solely to the Temple itself. But the *second* Temple rises with a different structure of prophecy upon it. Haggai, Zechariah and Malachi have each delivered some symbolical prediction connected with it, or with its Priesthood and Worship.

"Why this difference in the two cases? I think the answer is clear; it is a difference obviously related to the nearer connexion which the *second Temple* has with the *Gospel*.

"When God gave them their First Temple it was doomed to fall, and rise again, *under* and *during* their first economy. The elder prophecy, therefore, was directed to the proper history of the First Temple.

"But when He gave them their Second Temple, Christianity was then nearer in view; through that second edifice lay the Gospel prospect. Its restoration, therefore, was marked by a kind of prophecy which had its vision towards the Gospel. And a great confirmation is derived to all this view of the structure of prophecy from the following fact, when it is deliberately weighed and examined. In the days of David and Solomon when the *temporal Kingdom* was set up, the *Christian Kingdom* was *copiously* and *eminently* foretold *at the same time*; but

<sup>15</sup> And 'they *that are* far off shall come
And build in the temple of the LORD,
And ' ye shall know that the LORD of hosts hath sent me unto you.
And *this* shall come to pass,
If ye will diligently obey the voice of the LORD your God.

VII. <sup>1</sup> And it came to pass in the fourth year of king Darius, *that* the word
of the LORD came unto Zechariah in the fourth *day* of the ninth month,
*even* in Chisleu; <sup>2</sup> when they had sent unto the house of God Sherezer and
Regemmelech, and their men, † to pray before the LORD, <sup>3</sup> *and* to <sup>a</sup> speak
unto the priests which *were* in the house of the LORD of hosts, and to the
prophets, saying, Should I weep in <sup>b</sup> the fifth month, separating myself, as I
have done these so many years?

<sup>4</sup> Then came the word of the LORD of hosts unto me, saying, <sup>5</sup> Speak unto
all the people of the land, and to the priests, saying, When ye <sup>c</sup> fasted and
mourned in the fifth <sup>d</sup> and seventh *month*, <sup>e</sup> even those seventy years, did ye at
all fast <sup>f</sup> unto me, *even* to me? <sup>6</sup> And when ye did eat, and when ye did drink,
did not ye eat *for yourselves*, and drink *for yourselves*? <sup>7</sup> ‖ *Should ye* not hear
the words which the LORD hath cried † by the former prophets, when Jerusalem
was inhabited and in prosperity, and the cities thereof round about her, when
*men* inhabited <sup>g</sup> the south and the plain?

<sup>8</sup> And the word of the LORD came unto Zechariah, saying, <sup>9</sup> Thus speaketh
the LORD of hosts, saying, <sup>h</sup> † Execute true judgment, and shew mercy and
compassions every man to his brother: <sup>10</sup> and <sup>i</sup> oppress not the widow, nor the

*Matt. 23. 23.*   † Heb. *Judge judgment of truth.*   ‡ Exod. 22. 21, 22. Deut. 24. 17. Isa. 1. 17. Jer. 5. 28.

cannot be said that *the Temple* set up in those same days had
an equal illustration of *Christian prophecy* cast upon it. The
*temporal kingdom*, which was then beginning its course, was
not to be restored, after it should once be taken away. But the
*Temple* was destined to fall, and be *restored*. Hence it should
appear that the *first* institution of the *kingdom*, and the *second*
building of the *Temple*, were equally the seasons wherein the
Christian prophecy, connected with each of those ordinances,
might be found with the most clear and significant adaptation.
And such is the actual case: such the date of the respective
predictions joined with and grounded upon the Jewish Kingdom
and Temple. Proceeding from these two *distant points* in the first
economy, Prophecy, in each, directs our view to that era which
unites together the Temple and the Kingdom, and completes the
divine promises and predictions, engrafted upon both, in the
Church and Kingdom of Christ" (*Davison on Prophecy*, p.237).

15. *they that are far off*] Distant nations, symbolized by these
missaries from Babylon, *shall come and build in the Temple of
the Lord*, the Church of Christ universal. See Isa. lx. 10.

— this *shall come to pass, if ye will diligently obey*] It shall
surely come to pass; but it shall be fulfilled only to those who
believe and obey the Gospel preached to them.

PROPHETIC REBUKES FOR SIN, ESPECIALLY HYPOCRISY.
THE MORAL VIRTUES ARE WHAT GOD REQUIRES. FASTING
IS PROFITLESS WITHOUT OBEDIENCE.

CH. VII.] Zechariah's seven typical and prophetical visions
are succeeded by practical instructions. All theological mysteries
are consummated in holiness and love.

1. *In the fourth year of king Darius—in Chisleu*] Two years
after the resumption of the building of the Temple, and two
years before it was finished. This prophecy is separated from
the foregoing by an interval of nearly two years.

The month Chisleu, the ninth month, coincided nearly with
our December. See above, on Ezra x. 9. Neh. i. 1.

2. *When they had sent unto the house of God*] Hebr. *Beth-el.*
There are four different renderings of this passage.
(1) They sent to Bethel.
(2) They sent to the house of God.
(3) Bethel (i.e. the inhabitants of it) sent.
(4) The House (or congregation of God) sent.

On the whole, the second interpretation, that in the text,
seems preferable. The sense is: " *They sent* " (literally, *one sent*)
" to the house of God," which was thus far advanced to completion. So *Vulg.*, R. *Salomon, Vatablus, Paynius, A Lapide.*

133

Compare Judges xx. 26, where there is the same difference of
rendering; and Judges xxi. 2.

3. *Should I weep in the fifth month, separating myself*]
From food and other enjoyments. Shall I continue to weep and
fast in the fifth month, on the tenth day, when the Temple was
destroyed by the Babylonians? See above, on Jer. lii. 12, 13.
Shall I do this now, when the Temple is rising from its ruins?

— *as I have done these so many years*] They did well to fast,
but not to boast of their fasting and self-mortification. Here
is a symptom of that Pharisaical reliance on outward works of
religion, which reached its height in our Lord's age (Matt. vi.
16, Luke xiii. 13) and became almost as detrimental to vital
religion as idolatry had been in the age before the Captivity.
The Jews suffered for each of these sins, in different times:
Idolatry was the cause of their captivity at Babylon, Pharisaism
led to their destruction by the arms of Rome. Surely it is a
miserable condition for a Church, when both these sins (idolatry
and Pharisaism) are combined in her. What then will the end
be?

5. *ye fasted—in the fifth and seventh month*] In the fifth
month for the destruction of Jerusalem, in the seventh month for
the murder of Gedaliah, the son of Ahikam, the Governor who was
set over the Jews by Nebuchadnezzar. See above, on Jer. xli. 1.

— *did ye—fast unto me*] No; ye fasted to yourselves.
Your fasting was not produced by a deep sense of shame and
remorse for sin, as hateful to Me and as the cause of your punishment from Me; it was not a fast of sorrow for My offended
Majesty, but for your own punishment. It was not a God-ward
sorrow, but a world-ward-sorrow (see on 2 Cor. vii. 10). And ye
fasted in order that ye might appear unto men to fast (Matt.
vi. 16), and in a vain-glorious self-conceit of your own righteousness. Cp. Amos v. 25. " Have ye offered unto Me sacrifices and
offerings in the wilderness forty years?" No, ye offered them not
to Me, but to the idols which ye made for yourselves to worship.

6. *And when ye did eat*] Ye did eat for yourselves, for your own
self-indulgence, not praising Me for your food, and not setting apart
thank-offerings from your abundance, to Me, and to the poor.

7. *the south*] Hebr. *negeb.* The region to the south of Judah
(Josh. xv. 21, 47).

— *the plain*] Hebr. *Shephelah.* The lowland, on the Mediterranean Sea (Josh. xv. 33).

9, 10. *Execute true judgment*] This is the fast which God
requires, and without which all fasting is useless, nay, is even an
hypocritical abomination in His sight. Fast from sin, and do
what is right in His eyes. Cp. Isa. lviii. 6, 7.

fatherless, the stranger, nor the poor; [k] and let none of you imagine evil against his brother in your heart.

[11] But they refused to hearken, and [†] pulled away the shoulder, and [†] stopped their ears, that they should not hear. [12] Yea, they made their hearts *as* an adamant stone, [b] lest they should hear the law, and the words which the LORD of hosts hath sent in his spirit † by the former prophets: [p] therefore came a great wrath from the LORD of hosts.

[13] Therefore it is come to pass, *that* as he cried, and they would not hear; so [q] they cried, and I would not hear, saith the LORD of hosts: [14] but [r] I scattered them with a whirlwind among all the nations [s] whom they knew not. Thus [t] the land was desolate after them, that no man passed through nor returned: for they laid [u] the † pleasant land desolate.

VIII. [1] Again the word of the LORD of hosts came *to me*, saying,

[2] Thus saith the LORD of hosts;
[a] I was jealous for Zion with great jealousy,
And I was jealous for her with great fury.

[3] Thus saith the LORD; [b] I am returned unto Zion,
And [c] will dwell in the midst of Jerusalem:
And Jerusalem [d] shall be called a city of truth;
And [e] the mountain of the LORD of hosts [f] the holy mountain.

[4] Thus saith the LORD of hosts; [g] There shall yet old men and old women dwell in the streets of Jerusalem, and every man with his staff in his hand † for very age. [5] And the streets of the city shall be full of boys and girls playing in the streets thereof.

[6] Thus saith the LORD of hosts; If it be ‖ marvellous in the eyes of the remnant of this people in these days, [h] should it also be marvellous in mine eyes? saith the LORD of hosts.

---

Here is a preparation for Our Lord's teaching in the Gospel; and for the woes pronounced by Him on that proud, self-righteous, pharisaical spirit, which brought down God's wrath upon Jerusalem. "Woe unto you, Scribes and Pharisees, hypocrites, for ye pay tithes of mint and anise and cummin, and have omitted the weightier matters of the law, judgment, mercy, and faith; these ought ye to have done, and not to leave the other undone" (Matt. xxiii. 23).

14. *they laid the pleasant land* (literally *the land of desire*) *desolate*] They themselves, the Jews, by their sins (rather than the Assyrians and Chaldeans by their arms), made their own land to be a wilderness. "O Israel, thou hast destroyed thyself" (Hos. xiii. 9).

THE BLESSINGS OF OBEDIENCE.

CH. VIII.] In the foregoing address the Prophet has declared the bitter consequences of disobedience to God's moral law: he now proclaims the blessings of obedience.

The rebuilding of the material Temple itself might prove a snare to them. They might be tempted to rely too much on the external forms of religion connected with that sacred fabric. He insists therefore on the need of personal holiness and of vital religion, and he promises to all true believers and faithful worshippers, those eternal blessings and heavenly glories which are bestowed by God on all devout worshippers in the spiritual Zion of the Church of Christ.

2. *I was jealous for Zion*] I glowed with love and zeal for Zion, whom I have espoused to Me, and with indignation against her enemies, who have treated her cruelly. He repeats the words from i. 14, "I am jealous for Jerusalem." Cp. Joel ii. 18, "The Lord will be jealous for His land, and pity His people."

3. *the mountain of the* LORD] The Church of God, "which shall be established in the top of the mountains, and exalted above the hills," in the Gospel Dispensation. See Isa. ii. 2. Micah iv. 1. Ezek. xl. 2.

This prophecy stretches onwards from the Prophet's age to the last days of the world. It received some faint gleams and dim glimpses of fulfilment in his own age, in the restoration of the Temple, and in the rebuilding of the Walls of Jerusalem;

but what was then effected fell very far short of the glorious revelations in this prophecy (see vv. 6—8. 20—23). It received a great accession towards its accomplishment after the Death, Resurrection, and Ascension of Christ, and in the Descent of the Holy Ghost on the Day of Pentecost, enabling the Apostles to go forth from Jerusalem and to preach the Gospel to all Nations, and to bring them into the spiritual Zion of Christ's Church, which will be extended to all the world, and be glorified for ever in heaven.

We assert (says an ancient Father) that these prophecies received a partial, preparatory and typical accomplishment under Zerubbabel and Nehemiah, when the people had returned from Babylon, and the Temple and City were rebuilt; but their complete fulfilment is in Christ, and in His Church, which is the true Jerusalem, to which all nations flow from the East and the West, to sit down in the kingdom of God (Matt. viii. 11). In *that* Jerusalem all the blessings that are promised here will be fully realized and enjoyed (*S. Jerome*).

4, 5. *old men—boys and girls playing*] This imagery, which represents a time when there is no alarm of war, or plague, or famine, but every thing is peaceful and joyous, describes, in a spiritual sense, the condition of the Church defended by Christ, and enriched with blessings by Him (*S. Jerome*).

4. *every man with his staff*] Men will live long, and will not die by any violent death, but of old age.

6. *If it be marvellous*] S. Jerome applies this prophecy to the times of the Church which succeeded the persecutions under the Roman Emperors, specially Diocletian, and says, "Who would have supposed that the same Imperial Power which destroyed our Churches and burnt our Bibles, should now rebuild the former at public expense, in splendour and magnificence of gold and various marbles, and restore the latter in golden, purple, and jewelled bindings (deauratos et purpuratos, et gemmarum varietate distinctos)?" But so it is. No doubt this was one of the marvels comprehended in the prophecy. But the greatest marvel of all is future. It will be in the deliverance of heathen nations from idolatry, and in the conversion of the Jews; and in the union of both in Christ. See what follows, and compare the Evangelical Prophecies of Isa. xi. 11, 12; xliii. 5, 6. Ezek. xxxvii. 21. Hosea ii. 19. Amos ix. 14. Mal. i. 11.

7 Thus saith the LORD of hosts; Behold, ¹I will save my people from the east country, and from ⁞ the west country; ²and I will bring them, and they shall dwell in the midst of Jerusalem: ᵇand they shall be my people, and I will be their God, ʲin truth and in righteousness.

9 Thus saith the LORD of hosts; ᵐLet your hands be strong, ye that hear in these days these words by the mouth of ⁿthe prophets, which were in °the day that the foundation of the house of the LORD of hosts was laid, that the temple might be built. 10 For before these days ‖ there was no ᵖhire for man, nor any hire for beast; ⁹neither was there any peace to him that went out or came in because of the affliction: for I set all men every one against his neighbour. 11 But now I will not be unto the residue of this people as in the former days, saith the LORD of hosts. 12 For the seed shall be ⁞ prosperous; the vine shall give her fruit, and ˢthe ground shall give her increase, and ᵗthe heavens shall give their dew; and I will cause the remnant of this people to possess all these things. 13 And it shall come to pass, that as ye were ᵘa curse among the heathen, O house of Judah, and house of Israel; so will I save you, and ˣye shall be a blessing: fear not, but ʸlet your hands be strong. 14 For thus saith the LORD of hosts; ᶻAs I thought to punish you, when your fathers provoked me to wrath, saith the LORD of hosts, ᵃ and I repented not: 15 so again have I thought in these days to do well unto Jerusalem and to the house of Judah: fear ye not.

16 These are the things that ye shall do; ᵇSpeak ye every man the truth to his neighbour; ⁺execute the judgment of truth and peace in your gates: 17 ᶜand let none of you imagine evil in your hearts against his neighbour; and ᵈlove no false oath: for all these are things that I hate, saith the LORD.

18 And the word of the LORD of hosts came unto me, saying, 19 Thus saith the LORD of hosts; ᵉThe fast of the fourth month, ᶠand the fast of the fifth, ᵍand the fast of the seventh, ʰand the fast of the tenth, shall be to the house of Judah ʲjoy and gladness, and cheerful ‖ feasts; ᵏtherefore love the truth and peace.

20 Thus saith the LORD of hosts; It shall yet come to pass, that there shall come people, and the inhabitants of many cities: 21 and the inhabitants of one city shall go to another, saying, ˡLet us go ‖ ⁞ speedily ⁺ to pray before the LORD, and to seek the LORD of hosts: I will go also. 22 Yea, ᵐmany people and strong nations shall come to seek the LORD of hosts in Jerusalem, and to pray before the LORD.

23 Thus saith the LORD of hosts; In those days it shall come to pass, that ten

Before
CHRIST
518.

n Isa. 3, 6, & 4. 1.

j 1 Cor. 14. 25.

about
517.

o Jer. 23. 33.

men shall [n]take hold out of all languages of the nations, even shall take hold of the skirt of him that is a Jew, saying, We will go with you : for we have heard [o]*that* God *is* with you.

IX [1]The [a]burden of the word of the LORD in the land of Hadrach,

---

from the type to the antitype (" Propheta avolat a typo ad antitypum ") from Jerusalem to the Church of Christ (*A Lapide*).

Some (as *S. Cyril*) interpret this as a prophecy of the time when many will join themselves to Christian believers, who are the genuine Jews and the true Israelites of God (Gal. vi. 15) ; as St. Paul says, " He is not a Jew, which is one outwardly ; neither is that circumcision, which is outward in the flesh : but he is a Jew, which is one inwardly ; and circumcision is that of the heart, in the spirit, and not in the letter " (Rom. ii. 28, 29. Phil. iii. 3) ; and the eagerness with which a large number of converts will flock from all parts to the Church of Christ, is represented by the statement that ten men out of all nations will take hold of the skirt of one believer in Christ, and say, " We will go with you." Cp. *Kliefoth*, 107.

But we must rise higher. This is a prophecy that all *Nations* will lay hold, by faith, on the hem of the garment of CHRIST, the Lord and Saviour of all (*S. Jerome*). Christ came of the Tribe of Judah, and was made "under the Law" (Gal. iv. 4). "Salvation is of the Jews" (John iv. 22). Ten is a number of completeness (*S. Cyril*). The words of the prophet may best be explained from the similar language of Isaiah, "In that day, *seven women shall take hold of one man* (Isa. iv. 1, where see the note). To take hold of the *skirt*, literally, *wing* (Hebr. *cánáph*) is an expression full of meaning, and runs through both Testaments, with special reference, of a typical and prophetical character, to Christ. To Him devout and faithful souls come, and lay hold of the hem of His garment, and virtue goes over from Him to heal them. See Matt. ix. 20 ; xiv. 36. Here is a beautiful picture of the act of faith, in all ages and countries, which lays hold of Christ in prayer, in Scriptures, and in Sacraments ; and receives spiritual comfort, pardon and grace, and life eternal from Him Who is the one Fountain and Well-spring of all our health and joy.

It is Christ, Who, by His Godhead joined indissolubly to the Manhood in His Person, protects the faithful soul which lays hold of the skirt, literally, the *wing*, of His garment : as Ruth the Moabitess, the future bride, the type of the Church coming from the Gentile world, was covered with the skirt of Boaz, the type of Christ. See above, on Ruth iii. 9. It is He Who, by His incarnation, cleanses all who lay hold of His skirt, or *wing*. See above, on Hag. ii. 12. It is Christ Who, by virtue of His perfect purity, arises as the *Sun of righteousness with healing in His wings* (Mal. iv. 2, where see the note).

In all these places the same word (*wing*) *cánáph* is used.

PRELIMINARY NOTE TO CHAPTERS IX.—XIV. OF ZECHARIAH.

There is a difference between the portion of this Book which has preceded, and that which follows.

In the former portion, a series of sublime visions has been presented to the view ; henceforward not a single vision occurs. In the former part, we have seen the ministry of angels ; no angel appears in this latter part.

It has been alleged by some, that this second portion of this Book was composed by a different person from the author of the former part ; and by a writer who lived at an earlier period.

This theory was propounded by the learned *Joseph Mede* (Epist. xxxi.), grounding an argument on the fact that a prophecy which is found in chapter xi. 12. is ascribed by St. Matthew (xxvii. 9) to Jeremiah. Mede was followed in this opinion by *Hammond, Kidder, Newcome* (see the note in his edition of the Minor Prophets, p. 303, ed. 1809), and others.

It is not to be forgotten, that though those critics assigned this second portion to an earlier writer than Zechariah, they all recognized its inspiration and canonicity. The arguments adduced by most of them were considered and refuted by *Blayney*, in his edition of Zechariah, Oxford, 1797. But since that time the genuineness of this latter portion has been impugned in Germany by *Bertholdt, De Wette*, and others, who ascribe it to the Zechariah mentioned in Isaiah viii. 2.

Other critics, as *Eichhorn, Corrodi, Paulus*, and *Gramberg*, have gone into the opposite extreme, and have assigned this second portion to a writer *later* than Zechariah, i. e. to a time posterior to the return from the Captivity.

These two opposite parties might well be left to answer one another ; and if the reader is desirous to see the evidence fairly and fully stated for the genuineness and integrity of Zechariah, 136

and to see an answer to the objections raised against it, he may consult the work of *Hengstenberg* on the subject (" Dissertations on the Genuineness of Daniel, and Integrity of Zechariah," Engl. Trans., Edin. 1848) ; *Hävernick*, Einleit. p. 408, and even *De Wette*, in the last edition of his Einleit. ; also the remarks of *Kliefoth*, 286, and of *Keil* (Introd. to Zechariah, p. 519, German edition).

In refutation of those theories it may be observed, that Zechariah lived at the time when the Canon of Holy Scripture was just on the point of completion by Ezra and others, and it is not at all probable, that his contemporaries, who collected the Canon, would make a large addition to his known writings, and call that addition by his name : the fact, that they, who lived in his age, called the whole Book by the name Zechariah, is a strong argument for its genuineness and integrity. To this consideration may be added, that, whereas in the writings of the more ancient prophets, as Isaiah and Micah, the spiritual deliverance to be wrought by the Messiah is connected with the temporal deliverance of Judah from Assyria and Babylon (because those nations were the enemies of Judah in those earlier days), this is not the case in Zechariah ; he grounds his prophecies of redemption by Christ on predictions of the deliverance of Israel and Judah, by the valour of the Maccabees, from the arms of Syria or of Greece. See ix. 13.

Every thing in the latter portion harmonizes with the former portion. The seven prophecies in the one grow out of the seven visions in the other ; and every thing in the latter, as well as in the former portion of this book of Zechariah, bespeaks an author who lived after the dissolution of the kingdom of the Ten Tribes of Israel, and also after the humiliation of the monarchy of Judah, and when the schism between Israel and Judah was healed, and all the Tribes looked to Jerusalem as their centre and their home ; and at a time also when the glories of Egypt, Assyria, and Babylon had waned and faded away ; and when the people of Judah had returned from captivity to Jerusalem, and were looking forward to the Advent of the Messiah, with no external obstacles and impediments between themselves and the kingdom of Christ, except those which were produced by those enemies whose rise and dominion were either contemporary with, or subsequent to, the days of Zechariah.

WOE TO ALL THE WORLDLY POWERS WHICH ARE OPPOSED
TO GOD.—THE LAND OF HADRACH.

CH. IX. 1. *The burden*] The prophetic message of woe. See above, on Isaiah xiii. 1. The burden signifies a denunciation of suffering, "verbum grave, et ponderis et laboris plenum " (*S. Jerome, Kliefoth*).

— *the land of Hadrach*] Hadrach is not a literal appellative of any specific region, as has been supposed by some (*Gesenius, Bleek, Maurer, Ebrard, Michaelis, Rosenmüller*, and others), but is a *symbolical* name (as *S. Jerome* has observed, and so *Hengst., Kliefoth*, and *Keil*) which designates the worldly Power at that time dominant, namely, Persia, which was then *powerful*, but was to be *weakened* by God using the arms of Greece, first at Marathon (B.C. 490), then at Salamis (B.C. 480), and at Plataea (B.C. 479), and Mycale (B.C. 478) ; and afterwards at Granicus (B.C. 334), at Issus (B.C. 333), and at Arbela (B.C. 331), in the conquests of Alexander the Great, who captured Persepolis and Ecbatana (B.C. 330), and finally died at Babylon (B.C. 323).

The Prophet had good reason to veil the hostile power of Persia under a symbolic name, as, in later days, St. Paul concealed the Roman Empire under the phrase, " He that now letteth." See below, on 2 Thess. ii. 7.

The word *Had-rach* is formed from two Hebrew words, viz. *had*, or *chad*, sharp, active, strong ; and *rach*, soft, weak. "*Ad-rach*" (says *S. Jerome*) "ex duobus integris nomen compositum ; AD, acutum, RACH, molle tenerumque significans." It designates the worldly Power once *strong*, but to be made *weak*. It may be compared to the Greek word *oxy-móron*.

This name, *Hadrach*, may also be compared with other *symbolical* names in the prophetical Books of the Old Testament, and applied by the Prophets to persons, nations, and cities, and expressive of their character or their destiny ; such as *Jareb*, a name for the king of Assyria (see on Hosea v. 13 ; x. 6) ; *Huzzab*, a name for Nineveh (see Nah. ii. 7) ; *Sheshach*, a name

And [Damascus] *shall be* the rest thereof :

When [the eyes of man, as of all the tribes of] Israel, *shall be* toward the Lord.

[2] And [Hamath also shall border thereby ;

[Tyrus, and [Zidon, though it be very [wise.

[3] And Tyrus did build herself a strong hold,

And [heaped up silver as the dust,

And fine gold as the mire of the streets.

[4] Behold, [the Lord will cast her out,

And he will smite [her power in the sea ;

And she shall be devoured with fire.

[5] [Ashkelon shall see *it*, and fear ;

Gaza also *shall see it*, and be very sorrowful,

And Ekron ; for her expectation shall be ashamed ;

And the king shall perish from Gaza,

---

for Babylon (see Jer. xxv. 26); *Pekod* and *Merathaim*, also names for Babylon (see Jer. l. 21. Ezek. xxiii. 23) ; *Dumah*, a name for Edom (Isa. xxi. 11) ; *Mokteeh*, a name for Jerusalem (see Zeph. i. 11). See also the notes above, on the words *Garêb* and *Goath* (Jer. xxxi. 39), and *Shoa* and *Koa* (Ezek. xxiii. 23), and the Valley of *Jehoshaphat* (Joel iii. 2), and *Azal* (below, xiv. 5), and the remarks above on symbolical names in the Song of Solomon ; see *Introd.* to Canticles, pp. 125, 126.

Hadrach is the designation of the Powers of this world generally (of which Persia was a specimen), strong for a while and proudly exulting in their strength, and opposing God, and persecuting His Church, and in His due time to be laid low and to be broken in pieces by Him. How many Hadrachs are now vaunting themselves as if they were all-powerful! how many are raging against Him, and how terrible will be their downfall!

*Damascus* *shall be* *the rest thereof*] The woe from God shall fall, and rest not only on Persia, but on Damascus, the capital of Syria. This was fulfilled primarily in the conquests of Alexander's general, Parmenio, in that country, B.C. 333. See *vv.* 2, 3.

For a learned commentary on the first eight verses of this chapter, see *Dean Jackson* on the Creed, book viii., chap. xvii., who shows that these prophecies were accomplished by Alexander the Great, and in the victories of the Maccabees in Philistia 1 Macc. x. 88; xi. 60, 61 ; xiii. 33—52). A recent writer thus comments on this passage :—

"In this chapter is a distinct prediction of the conflict of the Jews (i.e. under the Maccabees) with the Greeks, (i.e. Antiochus Epiphanes), and of their victories over them. And, where this war, there is a prophecy of a heavy calamity, which falls in succession upon Damascus, Hamath, Tyre, Zidon, and the maritime cities of Philistia, Ashkelon, Gaza, Ekron, abled ; in which calamity the temple of God was to be guarded, not by human power, but by His unseen Presence. *I will encamp about mine house, because of the army, because of him that passeth by, and because of him that returneth* (Zech. ix. ). And this, while God should *smite the power of Tyre in the a*. The selection of the places and of the whole line of country corresponds very exactly to the march of Alexander after the battle of Issus, when the capture of Damascus, which Darius had chosen as the strong depository of his wealth, of Persian women of rank, confidential officers and envoys (*Grote, Greece*, xii. 175), opened Cœle-Syria ; Zidon surrendered ; Tyre, specially marked at by Zechariah (ix. 3), was taken with great effort, after a seven months' siege (*Diod. Sic.* xvii. 40—45. *Arrian*, ii. 16—24. *Curt.* iv. 2) ; Gaza too resisted for five months, was taken, id, it is said, ploughed up (*Strabo*, xvi. 2—30) ; but Alexander passed by with his victorious army and returned, and Jerusalem remained uninjured. History gives no other explanation of Zechariah's prophecy than this conquest by Alexander: that conquest agrees minutely with the prophecy. No other event history does. But, apart from this, the victory of the Jews over the Greeks was, of all events of history, then the most improbable. There was not the most distant likelihood of collision between them ; they had no point of contact. The name of Greece was known to the Jews only as that of one of the many countries which traded with Tyre ; a distant nation, to whom Tyre and Zidon had, in their slave-trade, sold Jewish youths, *that they might remove them far from their border* ; but the guilt and the punishment belonged to Tyre and Zidon, not to them.

Joel had, for this sin, prophesied the punishment of Tyre (iii. 4—6), not of Greece. Eichhorn, whose form of unbelief exempted him from any necessity to explain prophecy of any other than its true object, avowed that this prophecy of Zechariah *did* relate to the march of Alexander and the victories of Jews over Greeks at the later critical period of their history. He said plainly, "The conquests of Alexander are described so clearly that they cannot be mistaken.' 'In what is said of Tyre, who can mistake Alexander's wonderful conquests?' 'All the chief places, which Alexander, after the battle of Issus, either took possession of or conquered, are named one by one, the land of Hadrach, Damascus and Hamath, Tyre and Zidon, Ashkelon, Gaza, Ekron and Ashdod.' Greece was, until Alexander, a colonizing, not a conquering nation; the Hebrews had no human knowledge of the site of Greece. There was not a little cloud, like a man's hand, when Zechariah thus absolutely foretold the conflict and its issue. Yet here we have a definite prophecy, given later than Daniel, fitting in with his temporal prophecy, expanding a part of it, reaching beyond the time of Antiochus, and fore-announcing the help of God in two definite ways of protection ; (1) *without war*, against the army of Alexander ; (2) *in* the war of the Maccabees ; and these, two of the most critical periods in their history, after the Captivity. Yet, being expansions of part of the prophecy of Daniel, the period to which they belong became clearer in the event by aid of the more comprehensive prophecies. They were two points in the larger prediction of the third empire" (*Dr. Pusey's* Lectures on Daniel, pp. 277—281).

In a spiritual sense, Damascus, the capital of Syria, is another form of worldly power opposed to God ; and so are the other heathen cities here mentioned. See above, on Isaiah xiii., *Prelim. Note*, and Jeremiah xlvi. 1.

— *When the eyes of man*—*toward the* Lord] Some render this, *for the Lord has an eye to man* (that is, to all mankind), *and to all the tribes of Israel* (Sept., Arab., Targum, Syriac) ; that is, Jehovah, the Lord God of Jerusalem, sees and cares for all Mankind, and especially the tribes of Israel ; and controls and disposes all the conquests of armies, and all the destinies of nations, to the advancement of His glory and to the spiritual welfare of His people.

Or the sense may be, *for the eyes of man and of all the tribes of Israel ought to look to the Lord* as their Saviour. Jehovah in Christ is the Redeemer of the World (*Kliefoth*).

2. *Hamath also shall border thereby*] Rather, *Hamath also which borders thereby*. Hamath, the great city of Syria, called "Hamath the great" (Amos vi. 2 ; see Numbers xiii. 21, 2 Kings xviii. 34. Ezek. xlvii. 16), shall suffer with Damascus.

— *Tyrus, and Zidon*] They also shall be humbled. This was fulfilled literally by the conquest of Alexander the Great, B.C. 332, after a seven months' siege. Tyre is a symbol of a particular form of earthly power, opposed to God. See above, on Ezek. xxvii., xxviii., and *Haggat*, here.

— *though it be very wise*] Rather, *because it is very wise* (*Sept.*). Because of its worldly wisdom, it shall be abased. Cp. Isa. xlvii. 10, "Thy wisdom and thy knowledge, it hath perverted thee.' Cp. *Kliefoth,* 117.

4. *The* Lord *will cast her out*] Alexander's victories are due to the Lord, Who beholds and controls all things. See *c.* 1.

5. *Ashkelon shall see it, and fear*] Ashkelon, and the other great cities of Philistia, shall see the fall of Tyre and shall fear for a like fate to themselves. Philistia is another form of hostility

Before CHRIST about 517.

And Ashkelon shall not be inhabited.

m Amos 1. 8.

6 And a bastard shall dwell [m] in Ashdod,
And I will cut off the pride of the Philistines.

† Heb. *bloods.*

7 And I will take away his † blood out of his mouth,
And his abominations from between his teeth:
But he that remaineth, even he, *shall be* for our God,
And he shall be as a governor in Judah,
And Ekron as a Jebusite.

n Ps. 34. 7. ch. 2. 5.

8 And [n] I will encamp about mine house because of the army,
Because of him that passeth by, and because of him that returneth:

o Isa. 60. 18. Ezek. 28. 24.

And [o] no oppressor shall pass through them any more:

p Exod. 3. 7.

For now [p] have I seen with mine eyes.

q Isa. 62. 11. ch. 2. 10. Matt. 21. 5. John 12. 15.

9 [q] Rejoice greatly, O daughter of Zion;
Shout, O daughter of Jerusalem:

r Jer. 23. 5. & 30. 9. Luke 19. 38. John 1. 49

Behold, [r] thy King cometh unto thee:

---

to God. Cp. Amos i. 6—8. Zeph. ii. 4, and Jer. xlvii., which is the groundwork of this prophecy.

6. *a bastard shall dwell in Ashdod*] A *bastard*, literally, one whose birth has some blemish in it. In Deut. xxiii. 2, the only other passage where it is found, it may mean a *stranger* (*Gesen.* 480). The sense is, Gaza will be humbled, and her citizens will be superseded and supplanted by a promiscuous immigration of a strange rabble of foreigners.

All these things (says *A Lapide*) have a mystical fulfilment in Christ and His Church. Christ and His Apostles have subdued the spiritual Philistines to the sway of the Gospel, and have made them to coalesce with the faithful Hebrew remnant in one People of God.

It has been supposed by some, that the words, *a bastard shall dwell*, point to a time when even they who were excommunicated by the Hebrew Law will be admitted, on their faith and repentance, to equal privileges with the Jews in the Church of Christ. See *Kliefoth*, 121.

This prophecy had a literal fulfilment in the victories of Alexander. In a spiritual sense it foretells the overthrow of worldly powers, which imitate Philistia in its sins, especially in its enmity to the Israel of God.

7. *I will take away his blood*] I will abolish the idolatrous sacrifices of the Philistines, who feasted on meats offered to their gods in their temples.

BENEFICIAL RESULTS OF ALEXANDER'S VICTORIES. CONVERSION OF THE GENTILES TO CHRIST.

— *he that remaineth—shall be for our God*] Rather, *and even he shall be left*, as a chosen and elect remnant *to our God, and shall be as a ruler in Judah*. That is, even from heathen nations men shall be saved, and be raised to a high place, as brethren, and as governors in the Church of Christ.

— *Ekron as a Jebusite*] The happy effect of this humiliation of the great worldly Powers of Persia, Syria, and Philistia was this, that they lost their confidence in their own false deities, and were prepared to receive a purer faith. The Prophet foretells this, and predicts also, that there will be a faithful remnant among those nations which will turn to the True God; and many among the heathens will become *governors* in Judah; many who were once Gentiles will become Preachers and Missionaries in Christ's Church. Even Ekron itself will become a *Jebusite*, a dweller in Jerusalem, the Church of God. Cp. *S. Cyril* here, and *Kliefoth*, 120.

What has already been observed with regard to the effects of the victories of Assyria, of Nebuchadnezzar, of Persia, and afterwards of Rome (see above, on Isa. xiv. 32; xvi. 1; xix. 23—25; xxiii. 18. Jer. xlviii. 6, 47; xlix. 39. Zeph. iii. 8—10) may also be applied to the conquests of Alexander the Great. They were all made ministerial to the conversion of the heathen from idolatry, and to their reception into the Church of God. See the *Introd.* to the Acts of the Apostles, pp. 7—14.

It would be well if History were written and read with an eye to this great truth, which is continually inculcated by the Holy Spirit in the writings of the Hebrew Prophets. We speak of the "connexion of sacred and profane history;" but *what* history can rightly be called *profane?* What history is there, rightly studied, which is not sacred? What history is there, in which we may not trace the footsteps of Christ? Alexander the Great was a fore-runner of Christ.

8. *I will encamp about mine house*] God here promises to encamp about the Church, says *S. Jerome*, who thus writes here, "These prophecies declare what God says to Christ by the Psalmist, 'Ask of Me, and I shall give Thee the heathen for Thine inheritance' (Ps. ii. 8); and again, 'The daughter of Tyre shall be there with a gift' (Ps. xlv. 12). This was typified by the faithful woman in the Gospel coming from Tyre and Sidon to Christ, and worshipping Him, and receiving a blessing from Him (Mark vii. 26). In the Acts of the Apostles St. Peter and St. Philip preach in Philistia, and there are Christian Churches there (Acts viii.; ix.; xxi. 3). Philistines will become Preachers of the Gospel, Ekron will become a Jebusite, that is, a citizen, of the spiritual Jerusalem, the Christian Church." See, therefore, what follows here. We have a vision of the triumphal entry of Christ, the mighty Conqueror—how different from Alexander the Great! and yet reaping the fruit of Alexander's victories, and making them ministerial to His own glory.

CHRIST'S TRIUMPHAL ENTRY INTO JERUSALEM.

9. *Rejoice greatly, O daughter of Zion*] The application of the foregoing prophecies, in a spiritual sense, to Christ and His Church, is corroborated by the fact that we have here a prophecy of Christ's triumphal entry into Jerusalem; we have an assurance to that effect from the Holy Spirit Himself in the Gospels (Matt. xxi. 5. John xii. 15).

Let us consider therefore the connexion of that triumphal entry with what the Prophet has been foretelling in the preceding part of this chapter.

Christ's victories are compared and contrasted with those of Alexander the Great. The conquests of Alexander were effected by fire and sword, and with the physical force of horses and chariots; and their effects were of short duration, except so far as they prepared the way for the Gospel. The victories of Christ are by peaceful and quiet agencies, and their results are universal and everlasting (cp. *Dean Jackson* on the Creed, book viii., chap. xvii., and chap. xviii., where is a commentary on this prophecy).

Observe how this is displayed by Zechariah.

Christ's riding on the young colt, the foal of an ass, in that triumphal procession into Jerusalem, was a figure of His peaceful victory over the heathen world,—typified by the foal of an ass, on which no man had ever ridden, and which was loosed by the Apostles, and brought to Him, and on which they laid their garments, and on which He rode to Jerusalem, the City and Church of God. This had been already foretold by the Patriarch Jacob, predicting the future victories of the Messiah, binding the foal (the figure of the Gentile Church) to the vine (the type of the Hebrew Church). Cp. here, Ps. lxxx. 8; Isa. v. 2; Jer. ii., 21; and see the notes above, on Gen. xlix. 10—12. The circumstances of the fulfilment of that prophecy, which is here repeated in greater fulness by Zechariah, are more specifically detailed in the notes below on the passages in the Gospel describing that fulfilment; to which the reader is requested to refer. See on Matt. xxi. 5—9; Mark xi. 2—10; John xii. 13—15, and *S. Cyril* here. Cp. *S. Justin Martyr*, contra Tryphon. § 53. It is remarkable that St. John's narrative of that triumphal

He *is* just, and ‖ having salvation ;
Lowly, and riding upon an ass,
And upon a colt the foal of an ass.
[10] And I ' will cut off the chariot from Ephraim,
And the horse from Jerusalem,
And the battle bow shall be cut off :
And he shall speak ' peace unto the heathen :
And his dominion *shall be* " from sea *even* to sea,
And from the river *even* to the ends of the earth.
[11] As for thee also, ‖ by the blood of thy covenant
I have sent forth thy ˣ prisoners out of the pit wherein *is* no water.
[12] Turn you to the strong hold, ʸ ye prisoners of hope :
Even to day do I declare *that* ᶻ I will render double unto the ;
[13] When I have bent Judah for me,

*Before*
CHRIST
*about*
517.

§ *Or, every kind of.*

t Hos. i. 7; & 7. 10.
Micah 5. 10.
Hag. 2. 22.

t Eph. 2. 14, 17.

u Ps. 72. 8.

§ *Or, whose covenant is by blood.*
Exod. 24. 8.
Heb. 10. 25.
x. 13. 20.
x Isa. 42. 7.
51. 14, & 61. 1.
y Isa. 40. 9.
z Isa. 61. 7.

Entry of Christ, riding into Jerusalem on the foal of an ass (the type of the Gentile world guided by Him into the Jerusalem of the Church), is immediately followed by the mention of an incident in the history : "Certain *Greeks* wished to see Jesus" (*c.* 20). The Entry itself was like a vision of the coming of the Greeks (i. e. of the Gentile world) to Jesus : these Greeks were its first fruits.

The foal on which Christ rode is followed by the mother ; both were brought to Jesus ; but Christ rode only on the colt. The Hebrew mother will follow the Gentile colt into the spiritual Sion of the Christian Church. Cp. Rom. xi. 25, 26, and *S. Cyril* here.

— *having salvation*] The Messiah, though lowly and now going to His Passion, is yet endued with help and power to save both Himself and the whole World from Death ; and to destroy all His enemies, and those of His People, by His Death.

— *riding upon an ass, and upon a colt*] Riding, not on a war-horse of victory (like the Bucephalus of Alexander the Great), but upon an ass, yea even (such is His humility) upon a young ass. See on Matt. xxi. 5 ; John xii. 13.

10. *I will cut off the chariot from Ephraim*] Although Christ is meek, and rides on the foal of an ass, in the days of His humiliation, into Jerusalem, yet He is a mighty King, and brings salvation with Him ; and *will cut off the chariot from Ephraim, and the horse from Jerusalem.* This prophecy declares that the Israel of God (His Church and People) shall dwell safely, and will not need earthly helps and supports (*S. Cyril*) ; and will no more trust in an arm of flesh, nor rely on chariots and horses, bows and spears, but on the power of Christ their Saviour ; as the Psalmist says, "I will not trust in my bow, it is not my sword that shall help me, but it is Thou that savest us from our enemies, and puttest them to confusion that hate us " (Ps. xliv. 7, 8). "Some put their trust in chariots, and some in horses, but we will remember the name of the Lord our God" (Ps. xx. 7). Cp. Hos. i. 7 ; ii. 18 ; Micah v. 9, 10, "I will cut off thy horses out of the midst of thee, and will destroy thy chariots."

— *he shall speak peace unto the heathen*] A clear prophecy concerning Christ, of whom the Apostle says, "He is our peace, Who hath made both to be one " (i. e. united the heathen and the Jews, "and hath broken down the middle wall of partition between us ; and came and preached peace to you which were afar off, and to them that were nigh " (Eph. ii. 14, 17).

— *his dominion shall be from sea even to sea, and from the river even to the ends of the earth*] The Prophet takes up the words of the Psalm, probably written by Solomon, the *peaceable* king—describing the work of his great Antitype, Christ, the Prince of Peace ; see above on Psalm lxxii. 1, 8.

11. *As for thee also, by the blood of thy covenant—no water*] Thou also, O daughter of Zion, for the sake, or by means, of the *blood* of thy covenant (that is, of the covenant made with thee), *I have delivered thy captives out of the pit wherein is no water.*

This is the true rendering of the passage, and not (*Vulg.* and *Sept.*) *thou hast delivered*, which is repugnant to the Hebrew original.

The Messiah here speaks to Sion, and declares the deliverance which He works for her by His own blood, shed on the Cross. God admitted the Israel of old into covenant with Him by blood at Sinai, when He delivered them from Egypt (see above, on Exod. xxiv. 5—8) ; and, as the Apostle teaches, this transitory covenant by blood, at the Exodus from a literal bondage, was a figure of the blood of Christ—the blood of the

Everlasting Covenant (Heb. xiii. 20), by which His People are delivered from the bondage of sin (Heb. x. 14—23).

By appointing this chapter to be read on *Easter Even*, the Church has happily led us to recognize the true meaning of these words ; namely, that Mankind was like Joseph in the pit where no water was (Gen. xxxvii. 24), and was like the prophet Jeremiah in the pit where was no water, but mire (see on Jer. xxxviii. 6) ; and that Christ, by His Death and Burial, descended into that pit (as He Himself says by the Psalmist in the Paschal Psalm, lxix. 2, "I sink in the deep mire where no ground is"), and raised Himself from it ; and by His Resurrection, He, Who is "the first-begotten of the dead," "the firstfruits of them that slept" (1 Cor. xv. 20), has raised us up also ; for "in Adam we all die," and sink into the pit, but "in Christ we all are made alive" (1 Cor. xv. 22), and rise up out of it ; and we, who once were *prisoners*, sullied in the mire of sin, being redeemed from our prison, and cleansed by the blood which He shed for us (1 Pet. i. 2, 19, 1 John i. 7), rise up to liberty, life, and glory through Him. "O Christe," exclaims *S. Jerome*, "in sanguine Passionis Tuæ eos qui in carcere vincti tenebantur inferni, in quo non est ulla misericordia, Tua clementia liberasti." See also *S. Cyril* here.

The Church of Rome has endeavoured to build on this text the dogma of Purgatory ; and has used it also as a groundwork for teaching that Christ after His Passion descended into what is called by her the "Limbus Patrum," and delivered some from it who were then confined there. See *Bellarmine*, vol. i. p. 175, De Animâ Christi, iv. 11.

But as to the action of Christ's human soul after His Death, see below on 1 Pet. iii. 19 ; and on Purgatory, see Luke xvi. 23 ; xxiii. 43, 1 Cor. iii. 14. What the Prophet is here announcing, is not the deliverance of a few persons at a particular time from the so-called "Limbus Patrum," nor the deliverance of some from an ideal Purgatory, but something far more blessed and glorious ; namely, the redemption of a lost world by the Blood of Christ. This is the sense which is clearly presented to us by the context, and this is the sense in which the prophecy was understood by the ancient Catholic Fathers, as *S. Cyril*, and *S. Jerome* already quoted, who says, "After the Lord arose from the dead, they who were held bound in the chains of Adam and of Death, arose with Him and appeared in the Holy City. And ye, who now lie bound in the deep pit, turn to Him, by Whose mercy ye are to be freed." And *S. Augustine* says, "The pit where is no water is the depth of human misery, where is the mire of sin." And *Theodoret* says, "When men were prisoners in this pit of sin and death, Christ the Lord loosed them, and brought them out of it, by His precious Blood, and led them forth into the path of life."

12. *Turn you to the strong hold, ye prisoners of hope*] Ye who once lay chained in a prison of despair, in a miry pit of sin and death, and were without hope (Eph. ii. 12), have now become prisoners of *hope* : ye have been begotten again to "a lively hope" (1 Pet. i. 3), "full of immortality," in Christ (Titus iii. 7), and have been brought forth from that dungeon of despair into a fortress of safety by Him. Cp. Isa. xlii. 7 ; xlix. 9 ; lxi. 1.

— *double*] Double measure of glory, instead of your former misery (Isa. lxi. 7).

CHRIST THE VICTORIOUS RIDER WITH BOW AND ARROWS.

13. *When I have bent Judah for me*] Literally, *For I have*

Before
CHRIST
about
517.

Filled the bow with Ephraim,

And raised up thy sons, O Zion, against thy sons, O Greece,

And made thee as the sword of a mighty man.

<sup></sup>14 And the LORD shall be seen over them,

a Ps. 18. 14.
& 77. 17.
& 144. 6.

And ª his arrow shall go forth as the lightning :

And the Lord GOD shall blow the trumpet,

b Isa. 21. 1.

And shall go ᵇ with whirlwinds of the south.

<sup></sup>15 The LORD of hosts shall defend them ;

‖ Or, subdue the
stones of the
sling.

And they shall devour, and ‖ subdue with sling stones ;

And they shall drink, *and* make a noise as through wine ;

‖ Or, shall fill both
the bowls, &c.
c Lev. 4. 18. 25.
Deut. 12. 27.

And they ‖ shall be filled like bowls,

*And* as ᶜ the corners of the altar.

---

*bent Judah for me as a bow, and have filled it with Ephraim* (as with arrows).

What is the connexion here ?

Christ has been represented by the Prophet as a King riding in triumph to Jerusalem (v. 9). That triumph was won by humility. His heavenly Glory was a fruit of His earthly Passion, to which He was going at that time.

After the vision of that triumphal Entry into Jerusalem, the Prophet proceeds to speak, in proper order, of Christ's Death, Burial, and Resurrection, and their blessed consequences to mankind.

He now reveals Him to us as no longer weak and lowly, but as a mighty Warrior, riding on a war-horse, with bow and quiver, to victory, and as the LORD and GOD.

He adopts the imagery of the Psalmist, addressing Messiah the King, " Gird Thee with Thy sword upon Thy thigh, O Thou most mighty : according to Thy worship and renown. Good luck have Thou with Thine honour : *Ride on*, because of the word of truth, of meekness, and righteousness ; and Thy right hand shall teach Thee terrible things. Thy *arrows* are very sharp, and the people shall be subdued unto Thee : even in the midst " (or, rather, *in the heart*) " of the King's enemies. Thy seat, O God, endureth for ever " (Ps. xlv. 4—7). Cp. note on Ps. cxxvii. 4.

Zechariah anticipates the words of St. John, revealing Christ's victories over all earthly powers, in the Apocalypse :—

" I saw, and behold a *white horse :* and He that sat on him had a *Bow*, and a crown was given unto Him : and He went forth *conquering* and to *conquer* " (Rev. vi. 2). And again, cp. Rev. xix. 11, " I saw heaven opened, and behold a *white horse :* and He that sat upon him was called Faithful and True, and in righteousness He doth judge and *make war*. His eyes were as a flame of fire, and on His head many crowns " (diadems on one crown); " and He was clothed with a vesture dipped in blood : and His Name is called the WORD of GOD ; and out of His mouth goeth a sharp sword, that with it He should smite the nations : and He shall rule them with a rod of iron : and He treadeth the winepress of the fierceness and wrath of Almighty God. And He hath on His vesture and on His thigh a Name written, KING of Kings, and LORD of Lords."

But what are Christ's Arrows ?

They are the *Apostles* (whose name means *sent forth*), whom, after He had risen from the dead and ascended into heaven (Ps. lxviii. 18; Eph. iv. 8 –11), He sent forth from His Bow, like Arrows winged with feathers from the plumage of the Holy Ghost—the Divine Dove Whose wings are silver wings and His feathers like gold (Ps. lxviii. 13). They are the Missionaries whom Christ is ever sending forth from the Bow of His Divine Commission, to subdue the world to Himself. These are His Arrows, His Quiver is full of them, and they will never fail of victory, " His sagittis totus orbis vulneratus et captus est," says *S. Jerome*. By these arrows all the world has been wounded, but these wounds (says *S. Cyril*) are not wounds unto death, but unto life; they are wounds of love, like those with which the Spouse in the Canticles is wounded by the Bridegroom (Cant. v. 8). For further illustrations of this exposition, see above on Psalm xlv. 5, cxxvii. 4, and below on Rev. vi. 1, 2.

The image is from Isaiah, where CHRIST Himself, who is *sent forth* from the Father, is compared to an *arrow* discharged from a Bow. " He hath made Me a polished shaft, in His quiver hath He hid Me " (Isa. xlix. 2). And, " As My Father hath sent Me " (says Christ to His Apostles), " so send I you " (John xx. 21). And S. Cyril here thus writes: " Zechariah here calls Israel *the Sons of Ephraim*, of whom were the Apostles, equipped with the

word of God, and made to be like a Bow and Arrows, which smote the nations with divine doctrines, and wounded them, not to death, but in love; as the Bride says in the Canticles that she is wounded with love (Cant. ii. 5). Cp. *A Lapide* here.

Judah and Ephraim are represented here as the Bow and Arrows of Christ, because the first Preachers of the Gospel were *Jews* and Israelites ; they were *sons of Zion* and children of Ephraim. And these apostolic sons of Ephraim are presented to us in noble contrast to those other *children of Ephraim*, of whom the Psalmist says that they, being *harnessed and carrying bows*, turned themselves back in the day of battle. These Evangelical sons of Ephraim are described as *mighty men* (see x. 7), and they never turn back from the enemy, but meet them boldly and put them to flight. And they are like Arrows discharged from Jerusalem against the *Sons of Greece*, or Javan (Dan. viii. 21), because they were sent forth from Zion against the Greek or Heathen World, to bring it into subjection to Christ.

— *And made thee as the sword of a mighty man*] Here is another reference to Isaiah. Christ Himself was like an arrow from the hand of God (Isa. xlix. 2), and Zechariah represents Christ's Apostles as arrows shot forth from Christ's bow. Of Christ it is said that God has made His mouth to be like a sharp sword (Isa. xlix. 2), and here Christ speaks of His Apostles as made to be " as the sword of a mighty man."

14. *The LORD shall be seen over them*] Christ is here called the LORD, and GOD ; and His majestic form is seen like that of a mighty Conqueror standing over the bow which he draws, and over the arrows which he places on the string in order to discharge them. A vivid illustration of this imagery may be seen in the engravings of Assyrian kings riding in their war-chariots, and drawing their bows, and discharging their arrows, from sculptures in Nineveh (in *Rawlinson*, Anc. Mon. ii. 8. 11. 13; cp. 32. 39). So the glorious form of Christ is ever visible to the eye of faith, standing over His ministers, whom He sends forth as arrows against His enemies, to subdue the world.

— *his arrow shall go forth as the lightning*] Such is the power and splendour of the preaching of the Gospel, flashing forth like lightning on the gloom of the world, and dazzling all eyes with its brightness.

Compare the act of Gideon and his men (figurative of the preaching of the Gospel), making the torches to flash forth from their pitchers, to dazzle and confound their enemies the Midianites. See above on Judges vii. 16—20. Two of the Apostles were called Boanerges, sons of Thunder (Mark iii. 17).

— *shall blow the trumpet*] Like the trumpets before which the walls of Jericho (the type of the city of this world, as opposed to Sion the city of God) fell down prostrate to the ground. See above, on Joshua, chapter vi., *Prelim. Note*.

— *with whirlwinds*] Like the mighty rushing wind, betokening the power of the Holy Spirit given to the Apostles on the Day of Pentecost (Acts ii. 1, 2).

15. *and subdue with sling stones*] So Sept., *Vulg.*, Arabic, *Targum*. Such as the Prophet here foretells was the power of the preachers of the Gospel, after the Resurrection and Ascension of Christ, and after the giving of the Holy Ghost by Him. The threatenings of Holy Scripture discharged by the preachers of the Gospel are like stones from a sling (*S. Jerome*).

— *they shall drink, and make a noise as through wine*] Being filled with the *new wine* of the Holy Spirit of God. See on Acts ii. 13; and cp. Cant. v. 1.

— *filled like bowls—corners of the altar*] Their power will be derived from the Blood of Christ. They will be filled with

[16] And the Lord their God shall save them in that day

As the flock of his people ·

For [d] *they shall be as* the stones of a crown,

[e] Lifted up as an ensign upon his land.

[17] For [f] how great *is* his goodness,

And how great *is* his beauty !

[g] Corn shall make the young men ‖ cheerful,

And new wine the maids.

X. [1] Ask ye [a] of the Lord [b] rain [c] in the time of the latter rain ;

*So* the Lord shall make ‖ bright clouds,

And give them showers of rain,

To every one grass in the field.

[2] For the [d] † idols have spoken vanity,

And the diviners have seen a lie, and have told false dreams;

They [e] comfort in vain :

Therefore they went their way as a flock,

They ‖ were troubled, [f] because *there was* no shepherd.

[3] Mine anger was kindled against the shepherds,

[g] And I † punished the goats :

For the Lord of hosts [h] hath visited his flock the house of Judah,

And [i] hath made them as his goodly horse in the battle.

[4] Out of him came forth [k] the corner,

Out of him [l] the nail,

Out of him the battle bow,

Before
CHRIST
about
517.

d Isa. 62, 3.
Mal. 3. 17.
c Isa. 11. 12.

f Ps. 31. 19.

g Joel 3, 18.
Amos 9. 14.
§ Or, *grow, ct. speak*

a Jer. 14. 22.
b Deut. 11. 14.
c Job 29, 23.
Joel 2, 23.
§ Or, *lightnings,*
Jer. 10. 13.

d Jer. 10. 8.
Hab. 2. 18.
† Heb. *teraphim,*
Judg. 17. 5.

e Job 13. 4.

§ Or, *answered that, se*
f Ezek. 34. 5.

g Ezek. 34. 17.
† Heb. *visited upon*
h Luke 1. 68.

i Cant. 1. 9.

k Num. 24. 17.
1 Sam. 14. 38.
Isa. 19. 13.
l Isa. 22. 23.

---

love of Him, and know nothing but Christ, and Him crucified (1 Cor. ii. 2). Thus they will be like sacrificial *bowls*, filled with the *blood* of a victim, and like *horns* of the altar, tinged with that blood.

16. *stones of a crown*] The faithful Preachers of the Gospel are jewels in the crown of Christ.

— *Lifted up as an ensign*] Their preaching will be clear and bold, like a standard lifted up on high. Cp. Ps. ix. 6. The banner of the Cross, unfurled in the eyes of the world, is leading them on to victory.

17. *how great is his goodness—beauty*] As the Psalmist says to Christ, "Thou art fairer than the children of men, full of grace are Thy lips, because God hath blessed Thee for ever" (Ps. xlv. 3). Cp. Song of Solomon ii. 3, 4; v. 10—16, and Isa. xxxiii. 17, "Thine eyes shall see the King in His beauty."

— *Corn—and new wine*] The spiritual blessings of the Gospel, especially in God's Holy Word and Sacraments, are the corn and new wine which strengthen and refresh chaste and holy souls, who are here compared to young men and maidens (*S. Cyril*). Cp. Joel ii. 19, and note on Jer. xxxi. 12.

RESTORATION OF ISRAEL IN CHRIST.

CH. X.) The Prophet, having foretold the victories of Christ over the *sons of Greece*, i. e., over the *heathen* Nations, by the Apostolic preaching of the Gospel, which is to go forth from Zion by the instrumentality of Jews, who are missiles discharged from the Bow of Christ, now proceeds to speak of the conversion of the Jews by means of the Gentiles; as the Apostle says, after the fulness of the Gentiles is come in, all Israel will be saved (Rom. xi. 25).

1. *Ask ye of the Lord*] Ask not of idols ; for none of the vanities of the Gentiles can cause rain (Jer. xiv. 22).

— *rain—latter rain*] Types of spiritual graces, shed in successive abundance on the field of Christ's Church in the Gospel. The former rain may represent the Old Dispensation, the latter the New.

2. *They were troubled*] Israel was troubled and perplexed, and scattered abroad among the Nations, because it forsook the Lord and worshipped idols. It was dispersed, and roamed in " the wilderness of the people " (see Ezek. xx. 25. Hosea ii. 14), like sheep without a shepherd.

3. *the shepherds*] The rulers of Israel, civil and ecclesiastical (Ezek. xxxiv. 2).

— *goats*] The chief and the evil among the people. See Jer. l. 8; h. 40. Ezek. xxxiv. 17.

— *the Lord of hosts hath visited his flock*] He has visited Israel with chastisement. He has scattered them in captivity and exile in Assyria and Babylonia; but it is with a loving design and merciful desire that they may be humbled and purified, and repent, and may turn to Him, and that He may gather them again. See Amos ix. 8, 9.

— *as his goodly horse in the battle*] Such will Israel be when they are converted to Christ. See the Bridegroom's words to the Bride, the Church : " I have compared thee, O my love, to a company of horses in Pharaoh's chariots " (Cant. i. 9). In the Apocalypse Christ is described as riding on the white horse, and His Saints follow Him on white horses (Rev. vi. 1, 2; xix. 14).

4. *Out of him came forth the corner*] Out of Judah came forth Christ the Lord, Who, as He Himself declares, is the Head Stone of the Corner (Matt. xxi. 42), and is called by the Apostles the Corner Stone, in Whom the two walls of the Gentile and Jewish People meet and are united, and on Which all the fabric of the Church rests (Eph. ii. 20, and so Isa. xxviii. 16, and 1 Pet. ii. 6).

This corner-stone is here described by Zechariah as from Judah ; and " it is evident," says the Apostle, " that our Lord sprang out of Judah " (Heb. vii. 14). The promise that Christ should come from Judah, was a pledge, that, however Judah might be chastened, it would never be destroyed, but would flourish anew in Him (see on Isa. vii. 14).

— *the nail*] The *peg* (Hebr. *yāthed*), by which a shepherd's tent was fastened to the ground. Christ is the Nail by which the pastoral Tent of the Church, in this world's wilderness, in its missionary-nomad life, is fixed ; and established in Him, is stands firm against all the winds and storms of Unbelief and Ungodliness. See on Matt. xvi. 18.

On this imagery of the *nail*, namely the wooden peg and pin, typical of Christ and His Cross, by which the Tent of the Universal Church is held fast, and immovable, see the notes above, on Judges iv. 21, 22, and on Isaiah xxii. 23, where the same word, *yāthed*, is used.

— *the battle bow*] See above, on ix. 13.

| | |
|---|---|
| Before CHRIST about 517. | Out of him every oppressor together. |
| | 5 And they shall be as mighty men, |
| m Ps. 18. 42. | Which ᵐ tread down *their enemies* in the mire of the streets in the battle : |
| | And they shall fight, because the LORD *is* with them, |
| † Or, *they shall make the riders on horses ashamed.* | And ‖ the riders on horses shall be confounded. |
| | 6 And I will strengthen the house of Judah, |
| | And I will save the house of Joseph, |
| n Jer. 3. 18. Ezek. 37. 21. | And ⁿ I will bring them again to place them ; |
| o Hos. 1. 7. | For I ᵒ have mercy upon them : |
| | And they shall be as though I had not cast them off : |
| p ch. 13. 9. | For I *am* the LORD their God, and ᵖ will hear them. |
| | 7 And *they of* Ephraim shall be like a mighty *man,* |
| q Ps. 104. 15. ch. 9. 15. | And their �q heart shall rejoice as through wine : |
| | Yea, their children shall see *it,* and be glad ; |
| | Their heart shall rejoice in the LORD. |
| r Isa. 5. 26. | 8 I will ʳ hiss for them, and gather them ; |
| | For I have redeemed them : |
| s Isa. 49. 19. Ezek. 36. 37. | ˢ And they shall increase as they have increased. |
| t Hos. 2. 23. | 9 And ᵗ I will sow them among the people : |
| u Deut. 30. 1. | And they shall ᵘ remember me in far countries ; |
| | And they shall live with their children, and turn again. |
| x Isa. 11. 11, 16. Hos. 11. 11. | 10 ˣ I will bring them again also out of the land of Egypt, |
| | And gather them out of Assyria ; |
| | And I will bring them into the land of Gilead and Lebanon ; |
| y Isa. 49. 20. | And ʸ *place* shall not be found for them. |
| z Isa. 11. 15, 16. | 11 ᶻ And he shall pass through the sea with affliction, |
| | And shall smite the waves in the sea, |
| | And all the deeps of the river shall dry up : |
| a Isa. 14. 25. | And ᵃ the pride of Assyria shall be brought down, |

— *every oppressor*] Every victorious ruler. Cp. Isa. iii. 12 ; lx. 17 ; and see above, on ix. 3, 4.

5. *they shall be as mighty* men] As the Apostle says, God always makes us to triumph in Christ (2 Cor. ii. 14).

6. *I will strengthen the house of Judah, and I will save the house of Joseph*] Joseph, the father of Ephraim, the chief of the Ten Tribes, will be united with Judah in Christ. He makes the *two sticks* of Ephraim and Judah to coalesce in one, so that there shall no longer be any rivalry between them, and they shall be gathered together in the spiritual Zion of His Church. See on Ezek. xxxvii. 19—22. Hosea i. 10, 11. They who were severed by Jeroboam's schism, will dwell together in Christ ; and there will be "One Flock and One Shepherd" (*S. Jerome*).

8. *I will hiss for them, and gather them*] As bees are gathered, by hissing or whistling, into a swarm and into a hive (Isa. v. 26 ; vii. 18, *Gesen.* 851). So easy will the conversion of the Jews be, by the power of God.

9. *I will sow them among the people*] The Jews, who are now scattered and bear no fruit, will be *sown* among all Nations as good seed in the field of the Church of Christ, which is diffused throughout the world (Matt. xiii. 28, 29) and will be gathered together in the great day of harvest into the garner of heaven. Cp. Jer. xxxi. 17. Hos. ii. 22, 23. They will be *Jezreel* indeed, i. e., the *seed of God*.

Zechariah takes up the imagery of Hosea, the first of the prophets, and repeats the gracious promises delivered by him. See above, on Hosea i. 10, 11. "Then shall the children of Judah and the children of Israel be gathered together, and appoint themselves one head" (Christ), "for they shall come up out of the land ; for great shall be the day of *Jezreel*."

10. *I will bring them again also out of—Egypt, and gather them out of Assyria*] Egypt, the house of bondage, and Assyria, the scene of Israel's captivity and dispersion, represent all lands where they are now scattered ; and the promise that God will

bring them thence is an assurance of their future liberation, and of their gathering together in Christ's Church. Compare *Kliefoth*, 145 ; above, Hos. xi. 11, "They shall tremble as a bird out of Egypt, and as a dove out of the land of Assyria ;" and above, on Isa. xi. 11, 16, and on xix. 23, 24, "There shall be a highway out of Egypt to Assyria. In that day shall Israel be the third with Egypt and with Assyria."

— *Gilead and Lebanon*] The rich pasture land on the east, and the great mountain range on the west of Palestine. There Christian Churches will arise.

These names are not to be confined to the literal signification, any more than Sion and Jerusalem are. They represent the rich spiritual pastures and lofty strongholds and mountains of religious contemplation, in the Holy Land of Christ's Universal Church, as is evident from a comparison of other prophetical passages of Scripture foretelling the conversion of the Jews. See *Kliefoth*, 145 ; and above, on Isa. lxv. 10, "Sharon shall be a fold of flocks." Jer. xxxi. 4—8. Ezck. xxxiv. 11 - 14, 23 - 31, with the *Retrospect* at the end of Ezekiel xxxv., which affords the best comment on this prophecy of Zechariah.

11. *he shall pass through the sea with affliction*] Or rather, "*the sea, the affliction,*" a phrase which shows that the Prophet is not speaking here of a *physical* sea, but the sea of troubles, like the Red Sea through which Israel passed from Egypt, the house of bondage, on their way to Canaan, the type of heaven.

— *And shall smite the waves in the sea*] As He smote the Red Sea for Israel to pass out of Egypt. This is equivalent to an assurance that all obstacles will be surmounted that now restrain the Jews in spiritual bondage, and that they will be delivered by a glorious Exodus from their present spiritual Egypt of darkness and thraldom into the glorious light and liberty of the Gospel in the Church of Christ. Cp. Isa. xi. 15, 16. See *S. Jerome* here, and *S. Cyril*, and *Keil*, who well says, "The principal fulfilment of this prophecy is of a spiritual kind, and was accom-

And ' the sceptre of Egypt shall depart away.

<sup>12</sup> And I will strengthen them in the LORD,

And ' they shall walk up and down in his name, saith the LORD.

XI. <sup>1</sup> Open <sup>a</sup> thy doors, O Lebanon, that the fire may devour thy cedars.

<sup>2</sup> Howl, fir tree ; for the cedar is fallen ; because the || mighty are spoiled :

Howl, O ye oaks of Bashan ; <sup>b</sup> for || the forest of the vintage is come down.

<sup>3</sup> *There is* a voice of the howling of the shepherds ; for their glory is spoiled :

A voice of the roaring of young lions ; for the pride of Jordan is spoiled.

<sup>4</sup> Thus saith the LORD my God ; <sup>c</sup> Feed the flock of the slaughter ;

<sup>5</sup> Whose possessors slay them, and <sup>d</sup> hold themselves not guilty :

And they that sell them <sup>e</sup> say, Blessed *be* the LORD ; for I am rich :

And their own shepherds pity them not.

<sup>6</sup> For I will no more pity the inhabitants of the land, saith the LORD :

But, lo, I will † deliver the men every one into his neighbour's hand,

And into the hand of his king :

And they shall smite the land, and out of their hand I will not deliver *them*.

<sup>7</sup> And I will <sup>f</sup> feed the flock of slaughter, || *even you*, <sup>g</sup> O poor of the flock.

---

lished in part through the gathering of the Jews into Christ's kingdom, which began in the days of the Apostles, and will continue on till the remnant of Israel is converted to Christ."

12. *they shall walk up and down in his name*] As Enoch walked with God, and pleased Him, and was translated (*S. Jerome*).

### THE DESTRUCTION OF JERUSALEM BY THE ROMANS, ITS PUNISHMENT FOR THE REJECTION OF CHRIST.

Ch. XI. 1, 2. *Open thy doors, O Lebanon*] Open thy gates to the enemy, that fire may devour thy cedars. These and the following words are prophetic of the devastation of the Holy Land by the Roman armies under Vespasian (A.D. 69 ; and the capture of Jerusalem by his son Titus (A.D. 70). See *S. Cyril* and *S. Jerome* here. The stately cedars of Lebanon, and the sturdy oaks of Bashan, are figurative symbols of the great men and glorious ornaments of the Holy Land. Cp. Isa. ii. 2, 13 ; x. 8, 19 ; xiv. 8. As is well said by these Christian expositors, the Prophet is here speaking of the Temple of Jerusalem, which was rebuilt by Zerubbabel, but afterwards destroyed by Titus. Lebanon opens its gates, that the armies of Rome may enter, and that the fire may devour the cedars, and that all the land may be laid waste and its rulers destroyed. It is said by *Josephus* (B. J. vii. 12), that seven years before the destruction of the Temple and the City, the great bronze eastern gate of the Temple, which required twenty men to shut flew open of its own accord in the sixth hour of the night, at a Passover ; and when a similar event happened, forty years before that destruction, some of the Hebrew doctors applied to it event the prophecy of Zechariah, "Open thy gates, O Lebanon" (*Galatinus, à Lapide*).

2. *the forest of the vintage*] Rather, "the *forest that is fenced* or *fortress*."

3. *the shepherds—young lions*] The shepherds are cruel as rulers, and the lions are symbols of such rulers as tyrannically oppress and devour the people. Cp. Jer. xxv. 34—36, ch. xix. 2, 3. Jer. iv. 10. These evil rulers roared like lions against Christ, even when hanging on the cross (*S. Cyril*).

4. *Thus saith the* LORD—*Feed the flock of the slaughter*] God had given a commission to the Priests and Rulers of Judea to feed His flock ; but they had made it a *flock of slaughtering*, as of food, but they slaughtered it, to fatten themselves ; therefore they themselves will be slain. See Ezek. xxxiv. 2, 3, "Woe to the shepherds of Israel that do feed themselves ! should not the shepherds feed the flocks ? Ye eat the fat, and ye clothe you with the wool, ye kill them that are fed : but ye feed not the flock." Therefore God revokes the commission and transfers it to the *Good Shepherd* (John x. 11), who is Christ (*S. Cyril, Theophlact*), and who, instead of slaying the flock, as the evil shepherds did, to feed themselves, gave His life for them, that they might live for ever, and is everything to them verily food (John x. 11 ; xxi. 16). Cp. Ezek. xxxiv. 23—31. Here is the same line of thought. The thirty-fourth chapter of Ezekiel is the best exposition of the present prophecy.

5. *they that sell them say, Blessed be the* LORD ; *for I am*

rich] Here is a prophecy concerning false teachers ; and it was fulfilled in our Lord's age. The language here described was that of the Pharisees, who corrupted the word of God (Matt. xv. 6) and sold the people, for gain to themselves (*M. Henry*). They were covetous and wealthy, and inferred, from their own worldly prosperity, that they were special favourites of Jehovah, and that all their doings were approved and blessed by Him. They insulted God by ascribing the gains of their own oppression and fraud to His favour. Compare Luke xvi. 14, and our Lord's teaching in that chapter, which is a protest against that Pharisaical notion.

6. *I will deliver—every one—into the hand of his king*] I will deliver the Jews into the hands of the Roman Power, of which they said, when they rejected and crucified their own true King, "We have no king but Cæsar" (John xix 15). Cp. *M. Henry* and *Hengstenberg* here.

### THE LORD JEHOVAH WILL FEED THE FLOCK. HIS LOVE FOR ISRAEL.

7. *I will feed the flock*] I (Jehovah says in Christ) will be the Shepherd of the flock, which is not fed, but slaughtered by its own shepherds (see v. 1) : I will feed even *you*, O poor of the *flock* (cp. v. 11) : I will not feed the wealthy and proud, but the poor and meek. "Blessed are the poor." He says ; and "Come unto Me, all ye that labour and are heavy laden, and I will give you rest. Learn of Me, for I am meek and lowly in heart ; and ye shall find rest unto your souls" (Matt. xi. 28, 29).

— *I took unto me two staves*] Two pastoral staves. Other shepherds have one pastoral crook ; Christ has two. Cp. Ps. xxiii. 4. Christ the Good Shepherd left His heavenly fold to seek the lost sheep (Luke xv. 4). He came to the lost sheep of the house of Israel (Matt. x. 6 ; xv. 24) : He gave all His pastoral care to them. He took into His hand two pastoral staves ; one of which He called "*Beauty*" or *favour* (Hebr. *nöam*, translated *beauty* in Psalm xxvii. 4 ; xc. 17—"*the beauty of the Lord*," and *pleasantness* in Proverbs iii. 17—"*ways of pleasantness*." Cp. xv. 26 ; xxi. 24, where the same idea is expressed ; and this is the most usual meaning of the adjective *nöam*).

The staff of *beauty, loveliness, favour, delight, pleasantness*, was indicative of God's love to Israel, of His delight in them, and of the pleasure He took in seeing their spiritual and temporal welfare and in promoting it. The Vineyard of the Lord of Hosts was the house of Israel, and the men of Judah His *pleasant plant*. What could have been done more to His vineyard, that He did not do in it ? See Isa. v. 1—7. Consequently the destruction of Jerusalem, which Zechariah here foretells, could not come from any design of God, but was caused by its own sins. Therefore our Lord wept over Jerusalem, and uttered those plaintive words in Matt. xxiii. 37 ; Luke xiii. 34.

The other Staff is called *Bands* ; for God's will was to join together Israel and Judah in one ; and to join them also to the Gentile world in Christ ; and to join them together in Christ to Himself. But they rejected God's counsel of love towards themselves. Cp. Luke vii. 30. They killed the Good Shepherd, and therefore God brake asunder those two staves. He

Before
CHRIST
about
547.
2 Or, *Binders*,
h Hos. 5. 7.
i Heb. *was
strait and for
them*.
i Jer. 15. 2. & 43.
11.
† Heb. *of his
fellow*, or,
*neighbour*.

[ Or, *the poor of
the flock, &c.,
certainly knew*.
k Zeph. 3, 12.
Ver. 7.
† Heb. *if it be
good in your
eyes*.
l Matt. 27. 15.
See Exod. 21, 32.
m Matt. 27.9, 10.

And I took unto me two staves; the one I called Beauty, and the other I called ‖ Bands : and I fed the flock.

[8] Three shepherds also I cut off [h] in one month ; and my soul † lothed them, and their soul also abhorred me.

[9] Then said I, I will not feed you : [i] that that dieth, let it die ; and that that is to be cut off, let it be cut off ; and let the rest eat every one the flesh † of another.

[10] And I took my staff, *even* Beauty, and cut it asunder, that I might break my covenant which I had made with all the people. [11] And it was broken in that day : and ‖ so [k] the poor of the flock that waited upon me knew that it *was* the word of the LORD.

[12] And I said unto them, † If ye think good, give *me* my price ; and if not, forbear. So they [l] weighed for my price thirty *pieces* of silver. [13] And the LORD said unto me, Cast it unto the [m] potter : a goodly price that I was prised at of them.

---

rejected His own people, and gave up their city to destruction, and received the Gentiles in their place.

— *Bands*] Or *binders*. The staff of God's covenant with the Jewish Nation ; that staff by which Israel and Judah were bound together in one. See c. 14. God joined all the tribes in one by a common worship, and especially by commanding them all to appear before Him at stated times in one place — Jerusalem.

— *I fed the flock*] Jehovah in Christ did the work of a Good Shepherd to the Jewish Nation during the whole of His earthly ministry. Cp. John x. 11. 14 ; xiv. 6. Heb. xiii. 20. 1 Pet. ii. 25 ; v. 4.

8. *Three shepherds also I cut off in one month*] The ancient Hebrew Nation was spiritually fed by Moses, Aaron, and Miriam. See Micah vi. 4," "I sent before thee Moses, Aaron, and Miriam," the representation of the Civil Government, the Priesthood, and the Prophecy. The Rulers, the Priests, and the Prophets were its three shepherds. And when the Jews rejected Christ, Who is the True King, Priest, and Prophet, then God cut off their *three shepherds*, took away from them their " place and nation" (John xi. 48), i.e. the *civil Power* and also the *Priesthood* and *Prophecy*. See *S. Cyril, S. Jerome*, and *Theodoret*. They have no longer any Ruler, no longer any Priest, no longer any Prophet or Preacher of Divine Truth. This was done *in one month*, even in *the first* month of the Hebrew year, " the beginning of *months*" (Exod. xii. 2), the month Nisan or Abib, the month of the Feast of the Passover, when they crucified their own *Prophet, Priest*, and *King*.

9. *that that dieth, let it die*] That which is spiritually dead, let it die and be buried. Cp. Matt. viii. 22. " The dry tree" of the Jewish Church and State was only fit for the fire. See Luke xxiii. 31.

— *let the rest eat—the flesh*] This was fulfilled in the terrible intestine feuds and civil bloodshed at Jerusalem, even in the Temple itself, when it was besieged by the Romans. See on Matt. xxiv. 15. And it was literally true, that some then ate the flesh of their neighbours ; even mothers ate the flesh of their children. See above, on Deut. xxviii. 54. 56, 57.

10. *that I might break my covenant which I had made with all the people*] Literally, *with all the peoples*. ' When the Most High divided ' to the Nations their inheritance, when He separated the Sons of Adam, He set the bounds of the people according to the number of the children of Israel, for the Lord's portion is His people, Jacob is the lot of His inheritance'' (Deut. xxxii. 8, 9). This was God's compact with all Nations, and with Israel. He assigned a special inheritance to Judah ; and no people could deprive them of it, as long as they were true to Him. But now that they have rejected Christ, He has broken that compact ; Jerusalem is trodden down by the Gentiles (Luke xxi. 24), and the Jews are wanderers and outcasts in all lands.

11. *the poor of the flock*— LORD] God rejected the wise and learned— the proud Priest and Pharisee ; but He accepted the lowly Galileans— the fishermen and publicans. The meek, humble, and docile disciples of Christ, who waited in patient trust on Him, Who is the Good Shepherd, recognized in His Crucifixion a proof of His Messiahship, because the Passion of Christ had been foretold by the Word of the Lord, namely here,

141

and by Isaiah (chap. liii.), and elsewhere. But the Cross of Christ was a stumbling-block to those who were proud and wise in their own conceits (Matt. xi. 25. Luke x. 21. 1 Cor. i. 23) ; and they fulfilled the words of the Prophets, as St. Paul declares, by condemning Him (Acts xiii. 27). The unbelief of the proud strengthens the faith of the lowly. That unbelief is foretold in Holy Scripture, and is therefore a proof of its truth.

12. *I said unto them*] Christ, the Shepherd of Israel, here speaks, and asks for His hire or the wages for His pastoral work.

## THE SHEPHERD'S PRICE.

— *So they weighed for my price thirty pieces of silver*] This miserable pittance, the price of a bondslave (see Exod. xxi. 32. Hos. iii. 2), is described here in bitter irony as the price of Him " that was valued, Whom they of the children of Israel did value " (Matt. xxvii. 9, 10). They weighed to Him thirty pieces of silver. Instead of wages, they offered to Him an insult. Thirty pieces of silver are so contemptible a sum, that the very offer of them from them, His own people, for such services as His, was more insulting than a positive refusal (*Hengst.*). This prophecy was fulfilled in the payment of this sum to Judas the Traitor, by the Chief Priests for the blood of Christ (Matt. xxvi. 14, 15 ; xxvii. 3—10).

## THE SHEPHERD IS JEHOVAH.

13. *And the LORD said unto me, Cast it unto the potter : a goodly price that I was prised at of them*] Jehovah speaks to Christ, the Good Shepherd, Who came from His Father to feed the flock ; and since He fed it in the Lord's Name, since the Father was in Him and He in the Father, and since He and the Father are One in substance, therefore His work was the work of Jehovah Himself. The rejection of Christ was the rejection of Jehovah. Christ is Jehovah. He is so called here by Zechariah, " The LORD said—a goodly price that I was prised at of them." The price at which Christ was estimated was the price at which Jehovah Himself was valued by His own people.

Christ, the Lord of all, says " Cast it to the Potter." What was done by Judas and the Jews in the betrayal of Christ, and in the purchase of the Potter's field with the price of His blood, was done with His permission.

No one could take away His life from Him. He laid it down of His own accord, and took it again (John x. 18). "Destroy this temple," He said, speaking of His own body, "and in three days I will raise it up" (John ii. 19). All this was done with the determinate counsel and foreknowledge of God, according to His inscrutable will (see on Acts ii. 23) ; and the proofs of His Messiahship were displayed by the fulfilment of such prophecies as these, even by those who rejected Him.

The similarity of language in which the Servant or Messenger of Jehovah is spoken of in both portions of Zechariah (see on chap. ix., *Prelim. Note*) is a strong argument for identity of authorship. The Messiah, the Servant of Jehovah, is distinguished from Jehovah, and yet is identified with Him as His equal in dignity and glory. See xii. 9, 10 : cp. xi. 13. In no prophetical book is the doctrine of the distinct Divine Personality, as well as the Humanity of the Messiah, more clearly and uniformly displayed than in this of Zechariah.

On the site of the Potter's field (probably the Valley of

And I took the thirty *pieces* of silver,

And cast them to the potter in the house of the LORD.

14 Then I cut asunder mine other staff, *even* ‖ Bands,

That I might break the brotherhood between Judah and Israel.

15 And the LORD said unto me,

" Take unto thee yet the instruments of a foolish shepherd.

16 For, lo, I will raise up a shepherd in the land, *which* shall not visit those that be ‖ cut off, neither shall seek the young one, nor heal that that is broken...

---

Hinnom) and on other incidents of a solemn and mysterious interest connected with that place, see above, on Jer. xviii. 2 ; xix. 2, and note after Jer. xix. 11, p. 44 ; and cp. Hengst. here.

From the words, " *Cast it to the Potter,*" it is probable that the potter may have been present in the Temple when the Chief Priests transferred the money (which Judas had cast into the Treasury) to the purchase of the field.

This prophecy, or rather a prophecy very like it, is ascribed to Jeremiah by St. Matthew (xxvii. 9).

When we bear in mind the fact that nothing is more usual in Hebrew Prophecy, than for the Holy Spirit to *repeat* by succeeding Prophets what He had said before by their predecessors; and that He does this in very many instances in Zechariah (who, as the Jews said, prophesied with the spirit of Jeremiah, *Sarenbusius*, 282), it cannot seem surprising that what is here said by *Zechariah* should have been said before with some slight additions by *Jeremiah* ; and that the Holy Spirit, speaking by St. Matthew, should have referred to that prophecy, which is no longer extant in his writings. The Holy Ghost, speaking by St. Jude, cites a prophecy from Enoch which is nowhere found in the Bible (Jude 14).

Further, it has been supposed (*Grotius, Hengstenberg, Eliefoth*) that the present prophecy of Zechariah is connected with, and grounded on, those events in Jeremiah concerning the Potter (xviii. 2; xix. 2), and that it is a renewal of those prophecies of Jeremiah which portend the destruction of Jerusalem, as a potter's vessel in the valley of Hinnom. If this is so, then St. Matthew, referring to the Prophets, specifies *Jeremiah* as the *elder*. It is usual for writers of the New Testament to *blend* several prophecies of the Old together, and to mention the name of one Prophet only. See below, on Matt. xxvii. 9, and *Sarenbusius*, p. 288. There is a remarkable instance of this in Mark i. 2, "As it is written in Esaias the Prophet" (such is the true reading), "Behold, I send my messenger before thy face, which shall prepare thy way before thee. The voice of one crying in the wilderness, Prepare ye the way of the Lord, make his paths straight ;" where St. Mark combines two prophecies, the first from Malachi iii. 1 ; and second from Isaiah xl. 3, and he mentions only the name of Isaiah as being the older prophet, although he places first the prophecy from Malachi.

There is a learned dissertation on this passage in *Dean Jackson's* work on the Creed, book VIII. ch. xxvii. and ch. xxviii.

14. *I cut asunder mine other staff—that I might break the brotherhood.*] The Twelve Tribes, which were joined together at Jerusalem in the solemn annual Festivals, have now been scattered abroad by God. This is a consequence of the destruction of Jerusalem ; the punishment inflicted upon them for the rejection of Christ (Matt. xxiii. 38, Luke xiii. 35).

#### THE FOOLISH, OR WICKED SHEPHERD.

15. *Take unto thee yet the instruments of a foolish shepherd*] This is said to the Prophet, who is commanded to personate the foolish or wicked shepherd (*folly*, in Scripture, is *impiety*, Ps. xiv. 1. Matt. v. 22 ; cp. note on Job ix. 9) by taking such accoutrements as he would appear in. The Jews, by their rejection of Christ, Who is the Light, have subjected themselves to the divine malediction. They rejected the True Shepherd, and they were given over into the hands of false and wicked shepherds. They were deceived by many false prophets and many false Christs (Matt. xxiv. 5); and they are under the dominion of false shepherds, who do not heal the sick and feeble, but commit ravages on the flock, by false doctrines, such as those which constitute the greater part of the later Rabbinical and Talmudical teaching. They have incurred the fearful retribution of judicial blindness and misery pronounced by the Messiah Himself, speaking prophetically by the Psalmist (see on Ps. lxix. 22—28, and St. Paul's explanation of those words in Rom. xi. 7—10) and by Christ, in His own Person, in those Eight Woes in Matt. xxiii. 13—39.

145

---

Good Shepherds (says *S. Cyril*) have a light pastoral staff, by which they guide the sheep; but the evil shepherd maltreats and belabours the sheep with rude handling. So, in spiritual things, the good Christian Pastor deals gently, tenderly, and lovingly with his flock ; but the bad Pastor is impatient, and rules them with roughness and violence; and does not bring back the sheep when astray, nor guard them against the wolf and the robber, nor heal those which are sick ; and does not feed them with the wholesome food of sound doctrine, but with poisonous heresies. See above, on Ezek. xxxiv. 2—4. 10. Such are the instruments of *an evil shepherd.*

#### THE IDOL SHEPHERD.

The Prophet, having spoken of foolish or godless shepherds in the Jewish Church and Nation, and having declared the miseries brought by them on that Church and Nation, and also on themselves, proceeds now to speak of pastoral folly or impiety in the Christian Church, and of its future destiny.

The characteristic feature of this form of folly and impiety is, that it claims *divine honour* for itself. The *Shepherd* makes himself to be an *idol*. The Prophet's words are, " Woe to the *idol* shepherd !" Literally, " Woe to the shepherd, *the idol*" (Hebr. *ha-elil*); the word is the same as in Leviticus xxvi. 1. " Ye shall make unto you no *idols*."

This is a mysterious prophecy, which reaches to the latter days. *S. Cyril* compares these words to those of St. Paul concerning "the Man of Sin," or "Lawless one," in 2 Thess. ii. 2—12; and *S. Jerome* says here, "O thou shepherd and *idol*!" This shepherd is so ungodly that he is not called a worshipper of idols, but is himself named an *idol*, inasmuch as he calls himself God, and desires to be *adored* by all men. This shepherd is described under another figure by Daniel the prophet (see on Dan. vii. 8. 11, 20, 21), and by St. Paul, writing to the Thessalonians, where he foretells the rise of a Power that would "sit in the temple of God" (or Christian Church), "and show itself as God." See the note below, on 2 Thess. ii. 3—12. *Theodoret* also applies this prophecy to the Antichristian Power that would arise in the Church of Christ in the latter days. And so *Remigius, Lyranus, Vatablus*, and others.

The question here offers itself for consideration—

Has any Person or Power, corresponding to this description, arisen in the Church of God ?

It cannot be denied that the Bishop of Rome claims to be a Shepherd, and even to be the Chief Shepherd of the Church of Christ ; he does not allow any Bishop or Priest to exercise any pastoral office in feeding the sheep and lambs of Christ, except by his own authority. All ordinations of Bishops, Priests, and Deacons are null and void (he says) without his sanction. And even a Bishop who is nominated to an Archbishopric, ceases for a time to be a Bishop, and (as may be seen in the Roman Pontifical p. 87, ed. Rom. 1818), he cannot exercise any episcopal function till he has received the pallium from the Roman Pontiff.

It would not be easy to point out any other Shepherd who makes himself to be an *idol*, except the Bishop of Rome. That the Bishop of Rome does make himself into an *idol*, is certain. The first act that he performs after his election to the papacy, is to go into the Church of St. Peter, and to take his *seat upon the High Altar there*; and while he is there sitting he claims and receives *adoration* from the Cardinals, who kiss his feet, which trample upon the Altar of God. He, as God, sitteth there in the Temple of God, showing himself as God. The present Pope, Pius IX., did this on Wednesday, June 17, 1846. This ceremony is called by Roman writers, "*Adoratio* Pontificis," " the *Adoration* of the Pope." The authorities for these assertions may be seen below, in the note on Revelation xiii. 14, pp. 233, 234. Among the medals struck in the Roman Mint, there is one which represents the Cardinals kneeling before the Pope whom they have elected, with this inscription, " Quem creant, *adorant,*" " Whom they create they *adore*" (Numismata Pontificum, p. 3, ed. Lutet., 1679); in

L

Before
CHRIST
about
517.

‖ Or, *bear.*
o Jer. 23. 1.
Ezek. 34. 2.
John 10. 12, 13.

broken, nor ‖ feed that that standeth still : but he shall eat the flesh of the fat, and tear their claws in pieces.

17 ° Woe to the idol shepherd that leaveth the flock !

The sword *shall be* upon his arm, and upon his right eye :

His arm shall be clean dried up,

And his right eye shall be utterly darkened.

XII. ¹ The burden of the word of the LORD for Israel, saith the LORD,

a Isa. 42. 5 & 44.
24. & 45. 12, 18.
& 48. 13.
b Num. 16. 22.
Eccles. 12. 7.
Isa. 57. 16.
Heb. 12. 9.
c Isa. 51. 17, 22, 23.
‖ Or, *slumber,* or, *poison.*

ª which stretcheth forth the heavens, and layeth the foundation of the earth, and ᵇ formeth the spirit of man within him. ² Behold, I will make Jerusalem ᶜ a cup of ‖ trembling unto all the people round about, ‖ when they shall be in the siege both against Judah *and* against Jerusalem.

3 ᵈ And in that day will I make Jerusalem ᵉ a burdensome stone for all

‖ Or, *and also against Judah shall he be which shall be in siege against Jerusalem.*   d. ver. 4, 6, 8, 9, 11. & ch. 13. 1. & 14. 4, 6, 8, 9, 12.   e Matt. 21. 44.

---

other words, "They worship *the idol* which they have made with their own hands."

One of the most eloquent French writers of the present day, himself a zealous Roman Catholic, Count Montalembert, in a letter written from his death-bed, dated Paris, Feb. 28, 1870, uttered an indignant protest against those votaries of the Papacy who, to quote his words, "trample under foot all our liberties and principles, in order to immolate justice and truth, reason and history, as a sacrifice to the *idol* which they have set up for themselves in the Vatican." The words of Count Montalembert are, "pour venir ensuite immoler la justice et la vérité, la raison et l'histoire, à l'*idole* qu'ils se sont érigée au Vatican." And he adds, "if this word *idol* seems too strong a one, let me refer you to the words used by Monseigneur Sibour, Archbishop of Paris, in writing to me, on Sept. 10, 1853. 'The new Ultramontane school is leading us to a double idolatry, idolatry of the temporal power of the Papacy, and idolatry of the spiritual. The Ultramontane Bishops have driven every thing to extremes, and have outraged all liberties both of the State and of the Church.'"

At the very time when the present note is passing through the press, the Roman Catholic Bishops, summoned by the Roman Pontiff to meet in Council at Rome, in St. Peter's Church, under his authority and influence, are debating whether they shall not ascribe to him an attribute of God,—Infallibility. If they promulgate this dogma, they will have supplied another argument to prove that the Bishop of Rome is the "*Idol Shepherd*" of Zechariah.

The doom of the "Idol Shepherd" is foretold in what follows :—

**17.** *that leaveth the flock*] Literally, *deserter of the flock.* Instead of defending the flock from grievous wolves who tear the flock, he exposes it to their attack. This is true of the "idol shepherd" described in the foregoing note. The Bishop of Rome does not feed the flock of Christ with the healthful food of the Holy Scriptures—he denies the use of God's Word to the People, and he exposes them to heretical teachers: he himself becomes a wolf and tears them.

— *The sword shall be upon his arm, and upon his right eye*] He claims to have the arm of Omnipotence for ruling the Universe,—the words addressed to every Pope, at his coronation by the person who crowns him, are, "Scias te esse Rectorem Orbis,"—and to have the eye of Omniscience for searching all mysteries of the faith. He has recently put forth a claim to this attribute by promulgating a new dogma (Dec. 8, 1854), which he enforces as an article of faith necessary to salvation, viz. that the Blessed Virgin Mary was exempt from original sin ; a dogma which exalts her to a participation in that original sinlessness which belongs only to Christ ; and by which therefore he endeavours to make the Blessed Virgin to be an instrument for outraging the honour of her Divine Son.

But the arm of the Idol Shepherd will be withered, and his eye be darkened. The sword of the Lord (says S. Jerome) will be upon his arm and upon his right eye; and all his might and boasting will be blighted, blasted, and dried up ; and the knowledge which he falsely arrogates to himself will be eclipsed in everlasting gloom. Cp. 2 Thess. ii. 8.

When will this be? Thou, O Lord, knowest.

THE PERSECUTIONS OF THE CHURCH OF GOD WILL RECOIL
UPON HER ENEMIES.
*Preliminary Note.*

**CH. XII.**] In these Prophecies which follow, to the end of

1 16

the Book, there is the same foreshortening as that which has already been observed in the Book of Joel.

It is the property of Omniscience to see all things at one glance ; and Divine Prophecy imitates this property by representing the future in one view.

In the following prophecies, the penitential act of contrite sinners, especially of Jews, looking at Him Whom they pierced (xii. 10), dates from the Day of Pentecost, and continues to the latter days, when it will be greatly intensified, and will produce blessed results, and is here concentrated into one focus.

The rising up of enemies of God against Christ's Church, which commenced at the same time, and has been continued in successive persecutions from Jews, Gentiles, and other unbelievers in every age, and which will reach its climax in the great Antichristian outbreak of the last times, and be confounded by the Coming of Christ to Judgment, is here summed up in one panoramic picture displayed at once to the eye.

**2.** *Behold, I will make Jerusalem a cup of trembling*] The cruelties which had been practised upon Jerusalem by Babylon had already, in Zechariah's age, brought God's wrath and indignation upon Babylon, which had afflicted her ; according to Isaiah's prophecy, "Behold, I have taken out of thine hand the cup of trembling" (the cup which causes reeling), "even the dregs of the cup of my fury, thou shalt no more drink it again. But I will put it into the hand of them that afflict thee," See on Isa. li. **17**—**23**.

Zechariah proceeds from that retributive act of God's justice, and enlarges it, and applies it to His dealings with the enemies of the *spiritual* Jerusalem, the universal Church of God, which is the subject of his prophecies in the latter part of the book. See xiv. 1, 2. And therefore he speaks here, not of one nation, such as the Chaldeans, or Romans, but of *all people* (or *peoples*) and *all nations* ; i.e., all those who rise up against God and persecute His Church. Thus Zechariah's prophecy here comes in contact with that of Ezekiel concerning the gathering together of Infidel Powers against Christianity in the latter days. See above, on Ezek. xxxviii., xxxix., and Joel iii. 1—16, which supply the best interpretations of this prophecy, revealing the confederacy of Worldly, Infidel, and Impious Powers against the Church of God in the latter days, and their future final doom and utter discomfiture.

It is impossible to apply these prophecies (as some have endeavoured to do) in all their breadth and fulness, to the *literal* Jerusalem. Doubtless they may have a partial reference to the days of the Maccabees and to Antiochus Epiphanes, the type of Antichrist. But no one who examines them carefully can say that they were exhausted by the events of that age. And therefore, with *S. Jerome, Theodoret,* and other ancient Expositors, and with *Ribera, Arias, Vatablus,* in more recent times, we must understand them as prophetic of the final triumph of Christ and the Christian Church.

The Christian Church from the commencement is the only legitimate continuation of "the Israel of God." The root is in Zion, but the branches over-shadow the earth. Cp. Rom. xi. 18. Eph. ii. 12. 19. Gal. vi. 16. See the note above, on Ezek. xxxv. 14, pp. 238, 239, which may serve to illustrate the present prophecies.

IN THAT DAY.

**3.** *in that day*] These words, *in that day,* occur sixteen times in this and the two following chapters (xii. 3, 4. 6. 8, 9. 11 ; xiii. 1. 2. 4 ; xiv. 4. 6. 8, 9. 13. 20, 21). It is not to be supposed that all the events here described are to occur *in one day,* or at one time. The words, *that day,* designate the Day present to people : all that burden themselves with it shall be cut in pieces, though all the people of the earth be gathered together against it.

⁴ In that day, saith the LORD, ⁴I will smite every horse with astonishment, and his rider with madness : and I will open mine eyes upon the house of Judah, and will smite every horse of the people with blindness.

⁵ And the governors of Judah shall say in their heart, ∥ The inhabitants of Jerusalem *shall be* my strength in the LORD of hosts their God.

⁶ In that day will I make the governors of Judah ᵉ like an hearth of fire among the wood, and like a torch of fire in a sheaf ; and they shall devour all the people round about, on the right hand and on the left : and Jerusalem shall be inhabited again in her own place, *even* in Jerusalem. ⁷ The LORD also shall save the tents of Judah first, that the glory of the house of David and the glory of the inhabitants of Jerusalem do not magnify *themselves* against Judah.

⁸ In that day shall the LORD defend the inhabitants of Jerusalem ; and ʰ he that is ∥†feeble among them at that day shall be as David ; and the house of David *shall be* as God, as the angel of the LORD before them.

⁹ And it shall come to pass in that day, *that* I will seek to ⁱ destroy all the nations that come against Jerusalem.

the Divine Eye of the Holy Ghost, Who inspired the Prophet, and to Whom "a thousand years are as one day" (2 Pet. iii. 8). He sees all things at one glance ; and to Him they are all concentrated in that day.

— *will I make Jerusalem a burdensome stone*] Literally, a *stone of burdening.* Jerusalem—the Holy City—was a burdensome stone to those who waged war against, and profaned the Temple of God ; such as Antiochus Epiphanes, Pompey, and Crassus, who came to a miserable end. See *A Lapide* here and Dean *Jackson* on the Creed, book I., chap. xix. It was not till Jerusalem had rejected and crucified the Lord of Glory that she ceased to be *a burdensome stone* to those who attacked her ; but when that sin was committed, then she was given up to destruction by the armies of Rome. Christ became a burdensome stone to her. As He Himself says, " Whosoever shall fall on this stone shall be broken : but on whomsoever it shall fall, it will grind him to powder " (Matt. xxi. 44). This stone will become a mountain, and break in pieces all powers that resist it, as Daniel foretells (Dan. ii. 44). And such is Christ's Church—a burdensome stone. Many have risen, and many more will rise up against it, but they will not prevail (Matt. xvi. 18) ; and if they resist it, and they dash themselves against it, they will be broken and crushed by it. See Ezek. xxxix. 1—28.

4. *I will smite every horse—of the people*] Rather, *if the peoples.* The Infidel and Worldly Powers which will rise up against the Church of Christ, are described as a mighty army of chariots and horses, rushing on to the charge ; but they are smitten and routed by God. Compare the words of the mighty Lost destroyed at Jerusalem and the representative of infidel powers assailing the Church. See above, on Isaiah lxvi. 24.

5. *the governors of Judah*] These are the holy Apostles, and all faithful rulers of Churches and Apostolic Pastors and teachers (S. Cyril).

— *my strength in the LORD of hosts*] In the last days *the governors of Judah*—that is, the rulers of Christ's Church—shall not trust in secular powers (which will be hostile to her) but in the *Lord of hosts* alone, and will say, " Some put their trust in chariots, and some in horses : but we will remember the Name of the Lord our God" (Ps. xx. 7). See on Micah v. 10, and above, ix. 10.

6. *will I make the governors of Judah like a hearth* (or a *pan*) *of fire among the wood*] The Apostles and Apostolic teachers of the Christian Church (on which the Holy Ghost descended in tongues of fire at Pentecost) will glow with flames of holy zeal and love, and consume every thing in a sacred conflagration (S. Cyril). Cp. Jer. v. 14.

— *they shall devour all the people*] Or all nations. No nations, however mighty, will be able to resist the power of Christ and His Church in the last days ; as it is said in the Apocalypse, "The kingdoms of this worldare become the kingdom of our Lord and of His *Christ*" (Rev. xi. 15). That Mountain (as described by Daniel) will fill all things, and destroy all that oppose it. God's Word will be like a fire, which will consume every thing as stubble that resists it.

147

— *Jerusalem shall be inhabited again in her own place*] Rather, literally, *Jerusalem shall dwell still under herself,* that is, the Church will not rely on earthly powers, which will be opposed to her, but she will dwell in continual stability, dependent upon herself (see the use of the word in vi. 12, *out of His place,* lit. *from under Himself*) and on her own spiritual strength, derived from her Divine Head, Christ.

7. *The LORD also shall save the tents of Judah first*] There shall be no local or personal supremacy in the Church of God. " The Church will recover her primitive glory " (S. *Jerome* says here), "and the *tents of Judah* will be saved ;" that is, there will be in the whole world Christian assemblies of faithful worshippers who belong to the "Jerusalem that is above, which is the mother of us all" (Gal. iv. 26). And the *house of David and the glory of the inhabitants of Jerusalem* will not magnify themselves, as if their power, honour, and victory were due to their own arm ; that is, "no rulers of the Church will imagine that any thing that they do is done by their own learning and wisdom, but will ascribe it to the help of the Lord." And none will domineer over the rest : according to the words of St. Peter, they will not be "lords over God's heritage," but will be ensamples to the flock" (1 Pet. v. 2, 3).

8. *In that day—he that is feeble among them—shall be as David ; and the house of David shall be as God*] This has been fulfilled in the Incarnation of Christ, Who is the True David. See above, on Ezekiel xxxiv. 23, 24, and xxxvii. 24, 25. " Of His fulness all we have received, and grace for grace" (John i. 16) ; and even the poorest and feeblest among us are made "kings and priests" to God (Rev. i. 6 ; v. 10 ; xx. 6, 1 Pet. ii. 59) by union with Him, the Everlasting King and Priest, and become "partakers of the Divine nature" (2 Pet. i. 4) by virtue of baptismal incorporation in Him, and spiritual indwelling in Him, Who is " Emmanuel, God with us" (Isa. vii. 14. Matt. i. 23), "God was manifest in the flesh" (1 Tim. iii. 16. John i. 14), especially by means of the Holy Communion received into the heart by faith.

By *Jerusalem* (says S. *Cyril*) the Prophet here, without doubt, means the Christian Church ; and he describes the strength, security, and quietness which she receives from Christ, the true David.

— *as the angel of the LORD*] The name of Christ. See above, on i. 11.

THE ENEMIES OF THE CHURCH WILL BE OVERTHROWN. CONVERSION TO CHRIST, ESPECIALLY OF THE JEWS.

9. *In that day—I will seek to destroy all the nations that come against Jerusalem*] This cannot be applied in all its fulness to the literal Jerusalem ; no such combination of *all nations* against Jerusalem ever has been formed.

This prophecy foretells a great insurrection and confederacy of Worldly Powers against the true Spiritual Jerusalem, the Church of Christ, and it predicts their destruction. The Lord will protect those who dwell in the Church " (says S. *Jerome*), "and will seek to destroy her enemies." See on xiv. 2, and the

Before
CHRIST
about
217.

k Jer. 31. 9, &
50. 4.
Ezek. 39. 29.
Joel 2. 28.
1 John 19. 24, 37.
Rev. 1. 7.
m Jer. 6. 26.
Amos 8. 10.
n Acts 2. 37.
o 2 Kings 23. 29.
2 Chron. 35. 24.
p Matt. 24. 30.
Rev. 1. 7.
† Heb. *families*,
*families*.
q 2 Sam. 3. 14.
Luke 3. 31.

[10] [k] And I will pour upon the house of David, and upon the inhabitants of Jerusalem, the spirit of grace and of supplications: and they shall [l] look upon me whom they have pierced, and they shall mourn for him, [m] as one mourneth for *his* only *son*, and shall be in bitterness for him, as one that is in bitterness for *his* firstborn.

[11] In that day shall there be a great [n] mourning in Jerusalem, [o] as the mourning of Hadadrimmon in the valley of Megiddon. [12] [p] And the land shall mourn, † every family apart; the family of the house of David apart, and their wives apart; the family of the house of [q] Nathan apart, and their wives apart; [13] the family of the house of Levi apart, and their wives apart;

---

prophecy in Ezekiel xxxviii., xxxix.; and in Revelation xvi. 16; xix. 11—21; and xx. 8, 9; and the notes there.

10. *I will pour upon the house of David, and upon the inhabitants of Jerusalem, the spirit of grace and of supplications*] The Prophet takes up the words of Joel (ii. 28), " *I will pour out my spirit* upon all flesh;" and Ezekiel xxxix. 29, " *I have poured out my spirit* upon the house of Israel." God will pour out His spirit of *grace*; and this grace from Him will excite in men a spirit of *supplication*.

This prophecy has been fulfilled in part, by the outpouring of the Holy Spirit on the Apostles, and on large multitudes of devout men from all countries, on the day of Pentecost; and upon Cornelius and his companions at Cæsarea, and on innumerable others after them; and will be completely accomplished in the Church of Christ. See what follows.

— *they shall look upon me whom they have pierced*] Observe that the Lord JEHOVAH here speaks, and says, "They shall look *upon Me*;" and we know from the Holy Spirit in the New Testament (John xix. 34. 37. Rev. i. 7) that these words are to be fulfilled in CHRIST. Therefore Christ is JEHOVAH. Compare *Bp. Pearson* on the Creed, Art. iv., p. 204, and *Dr. Waterland*, iii. p. 19; *Dr. Pusey* on Daniel, p. 486, who says here, "*I will pour out My Spirit.* To pour out the Spirit is plainly a Divine Act. When Zechariah prophesied, the Jews were familiar with that great prophecy of Joel in which God speaks, *I will pour out My Spirit* (Joel ii. 28). Here He foretells some outpouring, and that, as a fruit of it, they should gaze earnestly on *Himself*, Whom they had pierced."

These words of Zechariah predict the piercing of Christ; as the Holy Ghost Himself, speaking by the Evangelist St. John, has assured us (John xix. 33); and they foretell the turning of the eyes of the Jews to Him (*S. Cyril; Theodoret*); and, in a more general sense, they pre-announce the turning of the eyes of all penitent sinners—whether Jew or Gentile (see Rev. i. 7, where they are extended to " all kindreds of the earth ")—who have pierced Him with their sins, crucifying afresh the Son of God (Heb. vi. 6). They shall turn to the Cross of Christ with contrite hearts and weeping eyes, and shall look to Him with faith and repentance, and be saved from the ends of the earth (cp. Isa. xlv. 22), as the Israelites, when stung by the serpents, looked to the brasen serpent and were healed (John iii. 14). See an excellent sermon (a Good Friday sermon) in this general sense, by *Bp. Andrewes*, ii. 119—138.

This prophecy began to be verified on the Day of Pentecost, when many Jews at Jerusalem were "pricked in their heart" by St. Peter's sermon, and said. "What shall we do?" and were baptized (Acts ii. 37—41; cp. v. 14); and it will be fulfilled in a more signal manner (as *S. Augustine* observes in his De Civ. Dei, vii. 30) when the Jews come to Christ in the true Jerusalem of His Church, and weep for the sin they committed in rejecting Him. See on Isa. lxiv. 9—12. Jer. iii. 21; xxxi. 9; l. 4. Ezek. xxxix. 23—29.

On the rendering of the *Sept.* here, see *S. Jerome* and the note below, on John xix. 37. The framers of that Version, or rather Paraphrase, taking the word *dakaru* (they pierced) as figurative, and as equivalent to, " they pierced with pungent sarcasms of scorn," render it, "they *danced* against, or *insulted*;" being moved to this rendering by the similarity of the words (as written in Hebrew) *rakadu* (they danced) and *dakaru* (they pierced); on which principle of allusive analogy many of the renderings of the *Septuagint* may be accounted for. See above, on Amos ix. 11, 12.

The Jews themselves acknowledge these words to be spoken of the Messiah; but to escape the Christian inferences from this admission, they have invented the fiction of a double Messiah—a conquering and a suffering Messiah. See *Buxtorf*, Lexicon (in Armilius), and *Bp. Chandler*, p. 90.

— *they shall mourn for him*] Observe the change of persons here, "they shall look on *Me*," and " *they shall mourn for Him*."

Christ, being God, is one in substance with Jehovah, as He Himself says, " I and My Father are One " [substance] (John x. 30. Cp. John xvii. 21, 22.) But since He is Man as well as God, and distinct in Person from the Father, the Father speaks of Him in the third person.

— *as one mourneth for* his *only* son] *Only*, Hebr. *ydchid*, a word used with special typical reference to Christ, e.g., in the history of Isaac. See on Gen. xxii. 2. 12; and Judges xi. 34, with reference to Jephthah's daughter, whose history was a mysterious foreshadowing of Christ's sacrifice (see the note at the end of Judges xi. p. 129). Compare the use of this word in the great Paschal Psalm, xxii. 20, and xxxv. 17, which foretells the Crucifixion of Christ. Cp. Jer. vi. 26; Amos viii. 10.

11. *as the mourning of Hadadrimmon in the valley of Megiddon*] This prophecy implies the *Death* of the Messiah. It declares that the mourning of the Jews for Christ, and for their own sin in crucifying Him, will be like the bitter mourning for the death of Josiah the good King of Judah, who was slain at Megiddon (near to which, as *S. Jerome* says, was Hadadrimmon, now *Rammaneh*, or *Rummâne*); and for whom "all Judah and Jerusalem mourned, and Jeremiah lamented for him, and the singing women spake of him in their lamentations, for many generations " (2 Chron. xxxv. 23—25). Josiah was a signal type of Christ. See the notes above, on 2 Kings xxiii. 30, pp. 159, 160, which may serve for a comment here.

12. *every family apart*] Our mourning for Christ must be a personal mourning; a general one will not suffice; each one individually must have a separate consciousness of his own sin. See above, on Ezekiel, Introd., pp. 155, 156, and Ezek. xxiv. 23, " Ye shall pine away for your iniquities, and mourn one toward another."

12, 13. *the family of the house of David apart—of Nathan —of the house of Levi—of Shimei*] Four families are here mentioned—two of the royal line, under the names of David and Nathan (the son of David, from whom Zerubbabel descended, Luke iii. 27. 31) and two from the priestly line, Levi and Shimei. See Numbers iii. 17.18; where Shimei is mentioned as a son of Gershon and grandson of Levi. Cp. *Hengst.* and *Keil* here.

The prophet mentions one leading family (David) and one subordinate (Nathan) in the royal race; and one leading family (*Levi*), and one subordinate one (*Shimei*), in the priestly line (cp. *Dr. Mill* on the Genealogies, pp. 166—169).

This prophecy cannot be understood literally; first, because the genealogies of the families of David, Nathan, Levi, and Shimei are now lost; and next, because it cannot be imagined that other tribes than those of Judah and Levi will be excluded from this penitential confession and reconciliation. But these four names are representative names (as are the names of the tribes of Israel in the Apocalypse; see on Rev. vii. 4—8, p. 196). And these four names are used to intimate that *all* orders, high and low, of *both* classes, the civil and ecclesiastical, must confess their sins against Christ. The Rulers and Priests of Jerusalem joined together in rejecting and crucifying Him. They must both unite in mourning for Him. This prophecy, therefore, may be applied to describe the acts of penitence which are required of all orders of men, whether temporal or spiritual, for their manifold sins against Christ. It is only on this condition of repentance, and of conformity to the likeness of His death, by being crucified to the world, that they can obtain pardon of Him, and be saved. Every one must bear in his heart the marks—the stigmata—of the Lord Jesus (cp. Gal. vi. 17).

13. *their wives apart*] " Hoc significat, quòd tempore tribula-

he family ‖ of Shimei apart, and their wives apart; ¹⁴ all the families that remain, every family apart, and their wives apart.

XIII. ¹ In ᵃ that day there shall be ᵇ a fountain opened to the house of David and to the inhabitants of Jerusalem for sin and for † uncleanness.

² And it shall come to pass in that day, saith the LORD of hosts, *that* I will cut off the names of the idols out of the land, and they shall no more be remembered: and also I will cause ᵈ the prophets and the unclean spirit to pass out of the land. ³ And it shall come to pass, *that* when any shall yet prophesy, then his father and his mother that begat him shall say unto him, Thou shalt not live; for thou speakest lies in the name of the LORD: and his father and his mother that begat him ᵉ shall thrust him through when he prophesieth. ⁴ And it shall come to pass in that day, *that* ᶠ the prophets shall be ashamed every one of his vision, when he hath prophesied; neither shall they wear ᵍ † a rough garment † to deceive: ⁵ ʰ but he shall say, I *am* no prophet, I *am* an husbandman; for man taught me to keep cattle from my youth.

⁶ And *one* shall say unto him, What *are* these wounds in thine hands? Then he shall answer, *Those* with which I was wounded *in* the house of my friends.

---

*onis et luctús non debeamus servire conjugiis et operi nuptia-um. Unde et in Joel dicitur ad Judæos, Eræditatur sponsus 'cubículo suo et sponsa de thalamo suo"* (*S. Jerome,* Joel ii. 3). Cp. 1 Cor. vii. 5.

THE BLESSED CONSEQUENCES OF REPENTANCE AND OF TURNING TO CHRIST.

ABOLITION OF IDOLATRY AND HERESY.

CH. XIII. 1. *In that day there shall be a fountain opened*] The Prophet, having spoken of the piercing of Christ crucified, and of the looking of penitent souls to Him, Whom they have pierced with their sins, now speaks of the flowing forth of that blood from His side which cleanseth from all sin (1 John i. 7. Pet. i. 2. Rev. i. 5). The gushing forth of this stream, and its cleansing virtue, had been described in glowing imagery by Ezekiel (xlvii. 1—12) and by Joel (iii. 18). "Hic fons de domo i egrediens refertur ad 'Ecclesiam, et ad scientiam Scripturarum, et omnes renascamur in Christo, et in aqua baptismatis a which the cleansing virtue of Christ's blood is first applied to i nostra nobis peccata condonentur" (*S. Jerome*).

This fountain was opened at Calvary, and it flowed on the Day of Pentecost, and many were then cleansed by it (Acts iii. 19; v. 31), and it has ever been flowing to all the faithful, in the Word and Sacraments ministered in Christ's Church. In our pilgrimage through this world's wilderness to the Canaan of our heavenly rest, we drink of the smitten Rock—the spiritual Rock which followeth us, and that Rock is Christ, 1 Cor. x. 4, and John vii. 37, "If any man thirst, let him come unto Me, and drink." To those who dwelt in Jerusalem, a fountain was opened at Calvary; and the cleansing waters of that fountain are ever being applied to the soul in the holy Sacrament of Baptism (*S. Cyril*).

2. *I will cut off the names of the idols*] Not only all idolatrous worship will be abolished, but the very name of its objects will be cut off under the Gospel of Christ. See on Hos. ii. 16, 17. Here is a solemn warning to all who dally with idolatry in any shape.

— *the prophets and the unclean spirit*] The teaching of false doctrine is due to Satan himself, who is *the unclean spirit*, and is the author of what the Apostle calls "doctrines of devils" (1 Tim. iv. 1); and so St. John, Rev. xvi. 14.

3. *when any shall yet prophesy*] Having spoken of Satan, *the unclean spirit*, as the author of false doctrines, he now proceeds to speak of his emissaries, false teachers; they also shall be cut off (*S. Jerome*).

— *his father and his mother that begat him shall thrust him through*] Such will be their zeal for God, that they will execute on him the Law of Moses against teachers of false doctrines. See Deut. xiii. 6—9; xviii. 20. The *letter* of that law was abrogated under the Gospel. See below, on Luke ix. 55. Some Roman Catholic divines, indeed, as *A Lapide* here, make this text to be a divine command to kill heretics.

119

8. Martin of Tours was of a very different mind (see *Sulpicius Severus,* Hist. Eccl. ii. 50); and so *Tertullian,* ad Scap. 2., 'Religionis non est, religionem cogere;" and *Lactant.* Divin. Inst. v. 20, "Defendenda religio non est occidendo, sed moriendo; religio cogi non potest."

But this prophecy declares that no sound believer will give any quarter to heresy in his nearest and dearest relatives. It is the triumph of Christian faith and charity, to love the erring without loving their errors; and to hate their errors without hating the erring. Indeed, because the true Christian loves the erring, therefore he hates their error, and endeavours to deliver them from it, in order that they may be saved in the day of the Lord. Whereas the false teacher and treacherous brother abets the erring in their errors, and flatters heretics in their heresy.

4. *neither shall they wear a rough garment to deceive*] They shall not imitate Elias (2 Kings i. 8), or John the Baptist (Matt. iii. 4), or any other teacher, by their rough hairy garment and ascetic life; which some adopt in order to deceive others by specious semblances of sanctity. Cp. Micah iii. 5.

5. *But he shall say, I am no prophet—an husbandman*] He will no longer imitate the arrogance of false teachers, but will emulate the modesty of the true, like Amos (vii. 14).

6. *And one shall say unto him, What are these wounds in thine hands? Then he shall answer, Those with which I was wounded in the house of my friends*] To whom do these words refer?

Some reply—To the false prophet, wounded by his parents and friends for prophesying, whom he, being now penitent, calls his friends, because they punished him.

But this seems a doubtful interpretation. According to the Levitical Law, the false prophet was to be stoned (Deut. xiii. 10), not to be wounded in the hands.

Some think that by these wounds he means the gashes which he inflicted on himself in the worship of his false gods (1 Kings xviii. 28). But this notion seems still less tenable.

On the whole, it appears most reasonable to acquiesce in the opinion of those Interpreters (*Rupertus, Aquinas, Gelatinus, Ribera, Menochius, Tirinus, A Lapide, Bp. Chandler,* and others), who say that Zechariah, having spoken of the piercing of the Messiah (xii. 10), and of the fountain for uncleanness which gushed forth from His wounded side on the cross (xiii. 1), and of the blessed consequences of His passion to all penitents, here reverts to Him, and puts this question to Him, "*What are these wounds in Thine hands?*" The Holy Spirit had already revealed that the Messiah would be so wounded. "They pierced *my hands* and *my feet*," Messiah had said by the Psalmist (Ps. xxii. 16). And that these wounds would be received in the *house of His friends*, even among His own people the Jews, had been foretold by Isaiah (liii. 3—5).

This exposition is found even in so early a Christian writer as *S. Barnabas* (Epist. c. 6: see *Dressel's* note, p. 9); and it is

Before
CHRIST
about
517.

i Isa. 40. 11.
Ezek. 34. 23.
k John 10, 30.
& 14. 10, 11.
Phil. 2, 6.
l Matt. 26. 31.
Mark 14, 27.
m Matt. 18. 10,14.
Luke 12. 31.

n Rom. 11. 5.

o Isa. 48. 10.

p 1 Pet. 1. 6, 7.

q Ps. 50. 15.
& 91. 15.
ch. 10. 6.
r Ps. 144. 15.
Jer. 30. 22.
Ezek. 11. 20.
Hos. 2. 23.
ch. 8. 8.
s Isa. 13, 9.
Joel 2. 31.
Acts 2. 20.

b Joel 3. 2.

7 Awake, O sword, against [i] my shepherd,
And against the man [k] *that is* my fellow, saith the LORD of hosts:
[l] Smite the shepherd, and the sheep shall be scattered:
And I will turn mine hand upon [m] the little ones.

8 And it shall come to pass, *that* in all the land, saith the LORD,
Two parts therein shall be cut off *and* die;
[n] But the third shall be left therein.

9 And I will bring the third part [o] through the fire,
And will [p] refine them as silver is refined,
And will try them as gold is tried:
[q] They shall call on my name, and I will hear them:
[r] I will say, It *is* my people:
And they shall say, The LORD *is* my God.

XIV. 1 Behold, [s] the day of the LORD cometh,
And thy spoil shall be divided in the midst of thee.

2 For [b] I will gather all nations against Jerusalem to battle;

---

confirmed by what follows, "Smite the Shepherd, and the sheep shall be scattered," which refers to the Passion of Christ, as we know from Christ Himself. See Matt. xxvi. 31. Mark xiv. 27.

### THE PASSION OF CHRIST.

7. *Awake, O sword, against my shepherd*] Observe the connexion. In the foregoing verses, the earthly father and mother of the false prophet, or shepherd, are represented as smiting him and thrusting him through (v. 3). Here the Heavenly Father, Jehovah Himself, speaks concerning the true shepherd, "*Awake, O sword, against My Shepherd,*" the shepherd appointed by Me.

The salvation of the world by the sacrifice of Christ was by "the determinate counsel and foreknowledge of God," though that counsel was executed "by wicked hands." See on Acts ii. 23; and cp. note on 2 Sam. xxiv. 1, p. 131.

Christ Himself said to Pilate, "Thou couldest have no power at all against Me, except it were given thee *from above*," i.e. from heaven (John xix. 11).

— *Awake, O sword!*] This sword is that of which our Lord speaks to the Father in the Paschal Psalm, "Deliver my soul from the *sword*" (Hebr. *chereb*, the same word as here), "my darling from the power of the dog." And again in that other Paschal Psalm, "They persecute Him whom Thou hast smitten; and they talk to the grief of those whom Thou hast wounded," (Ps. lxix. 26). He, Who is the Good Shepherd, was smitten, as if He had been a false shepherd. That this prophecy points to Christ we know from His own words in Gethsemane, "All ye shall be offended because of Me this night; for it is written, I will smite the shepherd, and the sheep of the flock shall be scattered abroad" (Matt. xxvi. 31. Mark xiv. 27).

### THE GODHEAD OF CHRIST, THE TRUE SHEPHERD.

— *against the man* that is *my fellow*] Hebr. *âmîth*, a word only used in Leviticus, where it occurs eleven times, and is translated always (either in the text or margin) by *neighbour*, i.e. comrade and equal—one of the same nature and rank with another. See Lev. vi. 2; xviii. 20; xix. 11. 15. 17; xxiv. 19; xxv. 14, twice, 15. 17. This, then, is the sense in which the word is here used; and it is clear that the Shepherd, Who is here smitten, is equal to Jehovah, and a distinct Person from Him. Cp. *Hengst.* here, and *Keil*, and *Dr. Pusey* on Daniel, p. 488.

Christ Himself has assured us in the Gospel that Jehovah is here speaking of Him and of His Passion; and it is a wonderful mystery, that while Jehovah is thus foretelling the Death of Christ, to be slain by the hand of His own people, He proclaims Him to be not only a *Man* ("the *Man* that is My fellow"), but also declares Him of the same nature with Himself. The *Fellow* of Jehovah is no other than the equal of Jehovah. It is He Who said, "I and My Father are One" (John x. 30); "I am in the Father, and the Father in Me" (John xiv. 10).

He Who is smitten is Man, and so was able to die for us; He is also equal with Jehovah, and therefore is able to deliver us from death. He is the good Shepherd, Who gave Himself freely for us (John x. 11. 14—18), that we might live by His death.

— *Smite the shepherd, and the sheep shall be scattered*]
150

Words which were applied by Christ to Himself, as already noted (Matt. xxvi. 31. Mark xiv. 27).

— *I will turn mine hand upon the little ones*] Of whom the good Shepherd says, "Fear not, *little flock*" (Luke xii. 32; cp. Matt. xviii. 10—14). Immediately after our Lord had quoted these words of Zechariah, in the garden of Gethsemane, He added to the disciples who then forsook Him, "After I am risen, I will *go before you*" (He uses a pastoral word there; cp. John x. 4) "into Galilee."

That special fulfilment was like an earnest and pledge of the more general fulfilment still awaiting this prophecy; which is accomplished, whenever *the little ones,*—they who were once proud and great in their own conceit,—become meek and teachable, and go with faith and repentance to meet Christ. And it will be realized when the fulness of the Gentiles shall have come in, and the Jews turn to Christ with weeping eyes and contrite hearts, and look on Him Whom they have pierced (xii. 10).

8, 9. *Two parts therein shall be cut off—die; but the third shall be left therein. And I will bring the third part through the fire*] The division into three parts represents the time of trial for Jerusalem; and the falling away and reprobation of many, are represented by two-thirds, and the purifying and refining of a smaller number, are symbolized by one-third, in the salutary discipline of the fire of persecution. Cp. Rev. xix. 2; and see Ezek. v. 2. 12; Rev. viii. 7—12; ix. 15; xii. 4, where the *third* part represents what is smitten. With regard to the imagery of trial by fire, cp. Isa. xlviii. 10. Jer. ix. 16. Mal. iii. 3. 1 Pet. i. 7.

This purifying and refining work began immediately after the Crucifixion, in the last days of Jerusalem; and it will have its climax and consummation in the time immediately preceding Christ's Second Advent. The Prophet Daniel describes the purifying discipline of the persecutions in the latter days of the Church in xi. 35, "Some of them of understanding shall fall, to try them and to purge;" and Dan. xii. 10, "Many shall be purified, and made white, and tried."

### THE PERSECUTIONS OF THE LAST DAYS—THE FULL AND FINAL VICTORY AND GLORY OF CHRIST AND OF HIS CHURCH.

CH. XIV. 1. *thy spoil shall be divided in the midst of thee*] This prophecy was fulfilled, in a preparatory manner, when the Romans spoiled Jerusalem, under Titus; but it was not exhausted then, as is evident from v. 2. It will have its complete accomplishment in the last days, when the Church of God will be despoiled by her enemies.

2. *I will gather all nations against Jerusalem*] This was true, only in a very subordinate sense, when God brought the armies of Rome, under Titus, against the literal Jerusalem (cp. xii. 9); but it will be fulfilled by a general insurrection of Antichristianism against the spiritual Jerusalem, the Church of God, in the latter days. Compare Ezekiel's prophecy concerning that insurrection, xxxviii. 14—17, and the predictions in the Apocalypse, Rev. xvi. 12—14; xvii. 14; xx. 8. God is here said to gather the nations against Jerusalem, the Visible Church, as in Ezekiel xxxviii. 17, because what is done by them is done by

And the city shall be taken, and ' the houses rifled, and the women ravished ;
And half of the city shall go forth into captivity, and the residue of the
   people shall not be cut off from the city.
³ Then shall the LORD go forth, and fight against those nations,
   As when he fought in the day of battle.
⁴ And his feet shall stand in that day ᵈ upon the mount of Olives, which *is*
      before Jerusalem on the east,
And the mount of Olives shall cleave in the midst thereof toward the east
      and toward the west,
ᵉ *And there shall be* a very great valley ;
And half of the mountain shall remove toward the north, and half of it
      toward the south.
⁵ And ye shall flee *to* the valley of ‖ the mountains ;
   ‖ For the valley of the mountains shall reach unto Azal :

His permission (as in the campaigns of Nebuchadnezzar and the Romans against the literal Jerusalem), and for the trial and purification of His people, and for the punishment of their sins, and because the enemies of the Church will be gathered together in order to be destroyed by Him. Cp. on Joel iii. 2, " *I will gather* together all nations, and bring them down into the Valley of Jehoshaphat," (i.e. of *Judgment of the Lord*). " Assemble yourselves and come, all ye heathen, and gather together round about."

— *the residue of the people shall not be cut off.*] In the literal Jerusalem almost a total depopulation of Jerusalem was made by war, pestilence, famine, or captivity. "It is clear from this" (says *Keil*) "that the words do not refer to the destruction of Jerusalem by the Romans." The prophecy was not exhausted then, but it extends to the last days, and it is explained by Christ's promise of perpetual presence and protection to His Church, "On this Rock I will build My Church; and the gates of hell shall not prevail against it" (Matt. xvi. 18).

**3.** *Then shall the* LORD *go forth—as when he fought in the day of battle.*] In the day of slaughter. This is not applicable to the last days of the literal Jerusalem. The Lord *forsook* that guilty city which had rejected Christ, and gave it up to be trodden under foot by the Gentiles; but it will be fulfilled in the Christian Church, for which the Lord will fight in the great antichristian struggle, which even now seems near at hand; and He will destroy all her enemies. See the foregoing note, and on Ezekiel xxxviii. 18—23; xxxix. 1—8; and Rev. xix. 13—21, and xx. 8, 9, 10.

THE DAY OF DOOM.

**4.** *his feet shall stand in that day upon the mount of Olives.*] Christ ascended from the Mount of Olives in triumph to heaven, like a mighty conqueror and king, having overcome Satan, Death, and the Grave, and sat down in heavenly Glory, at the right hand of God ; and the angels announced His ascension in these words to the Apostles, who were standing on the Mount of Olives and were gazing up into heaven, " This same Jesus, Who is taken up from you into heaven, shall *so come in like manner as ye have seen Him go into heaven*" (Acts i. 10).

The Mount of Olives was the last spot on earth on which those Blessed Feet rested before His Ascension; and some have ventured to say that they left an impression there. See *A Lapide* here, and *Dean Jackson* on the Creed, book IX. chap. lxiii. Perhaps, when He comes in glory, it may please Him to stand there. Doubtless the *Mount of Olives* is mentioned here, and is referred to by Ezekiel (xi. 23, see the note there) with reference to His glorious Ascension from that place, and in order to connect His triumphant Ascension to Heaven with His future glorious Advent to judge the world. There was a subordinate and preparatory fulfilment of this prophecy when the literal Jerusalem was besieged and taken by the Roman armies. The judgment of God on Jerusalem is represented by Christ Himself (in Matt. xxiv.) as a type and rehearsal of the Universal Judgment of the world. See the notes below on that chapter. Christ delivered that prophecy on the Mount of Olives. He ascended from the Mount of Olives. The siege of Jerusalem began at the Mount of Olives. See below, on Matt. xxiv. 3. Christ's feet stood then, in a figure, on the Mount of Olives; for it was He Who led the armies of Rome; it was He Who sent Titus against

Jerusalem. The legions of Cæsar were armies of Christ, Who executed judgment by them on that guilty and rebellious city. Cp. *Dean Jackson*, vol. viii., p. 501.

— *a very great valley.*] This is the name given to the scene of the future Universal Judgment, which is called the *Valley of Jehoshaphat* (or of the *Judgment of Jehovah*) by Joel. See on Joel iii. 12—14.

There will be a great Earthquake (see Amos i. 1) which will shake all nations, and will raise the dead from their graves. All the pride, and pomp, and power of this World will then be depressed, as it were, into a lowly valley, and will be placed beneath the feet of Christ, the Almighty Judge (1 Cor. xv. 25).

**5.** *And ye shall flee to the valley of the mountains.*] Zechariah derives his prophetic scenery from the literal Jerusalem. As in the day of its destruction the true believers listened to Christ's warning, " Let them which be in Judea *flee to the mountains*" (see on Matt. xxiv. 16), and thus escaped the doom of the city; and as Lot of old fled from Sodom to the mountains, and found a refuge there (Gen. xix. 17. 30), so the true believers will take warning at the approach of the Great Day, and escape the wrath to come. Ye, who are my faithful people, *shall flee to the valley of the mountains*, or rather, *of My mountains*; ye shall flee from the great earthquake, and ye shall find shelter there : " When these things come to pass, lift up your heads, for your redemption draweth nigh " (Luke xxi. 28).

The wicked shall flee, and flee in vain, to *their mountains* in panic and alarm, and shall cry to the mountains, "Fall on us, and to the hills, Cover us, and hide us from the wrath of the Lamb" (Luke xxiii. 30. Rev. vi. 16). But ye shall look up to *My* hills from whence cometh your strength, and find safety there, as Lot fled from Sodom to the mountains, and was saved from the doom of the city.

He describes the Mount of Olives as cleaving asunder, so as to open a way for those who escape from the besieged city. The Mount of Olives would have hindered the flight of those who fled forth from Jerusalem; but by the earthquake a free passage is given to them, on account of their faith, according to our Lord's words, " If ye have faith as a grain of mustard seed, ye shall say unto this mountain, Remove hence to yonder place, and it shall remove" (Matt. xvii. 20).

— *unto Azal.*] *Azal* is a symbolical word, like many others in the prophetical writings (see above on *Hadrach*, ix. 1 ; cp. *Kliefoth* here, p. 265), signifying *nearness*, or *union*, from the Hebrew word *atsal*, to join together (*Gesen.* 71). Hence the *Vulgate* has "ad proximum."

The word *Azal* (says *S. Jerome*) signifies here *union*—the *union* of Jew and Gentile, the *union* of the Law and the Gospel —in one Church.

As Jeremiah describes the spiritual Jerusalem, i.e. the Christian Church, as extending to *Gareb* and *Goath* (two symbolical names), because the Church provides a spiritual remedy in Christ, for *sin* and death (see on Jer. xxxi. 39), so Zechariah describes the valley made by the *division* of the mountain of Christ's ascension, as extending to *Azal*, or *union*, because it *unites* all in Him.

In other words, the Valley of God's mountain, which is represented as near Jerusalem (the Mount of Olives), the site of Christ's Ascension, is here said to extend to *Azal*, that is to *union*, to enfold all the faithful, both Jews and Gentiles (who once were separated), in one Church; and this extension is to be

Yea, ye shall flee, like as ye fled from before the ᶠ earthquake in the days of Uzziah king of Judah :

ᵍ And the LORD my God shall come,
*And* ʰ all the saints with thee.

⁶ And it shall come to pass in that day,
‖ *That* the light shall not be † clear, *nor* † dark :
⁷ But ‖ it shall be ⁱ one day ᵏ which shall be known to the LORD,
Not day, nor night :
But it shall come to pass, *that* at ˡ evening time it shall be light.

⁸ And it shall be in that day, *that* living ᵐ waters shall go out from Jerusalem ;
Half of them toward the ‖ former sea,
And half of them toward the hinder sea :
In summer and in winter shall it be.

⁹ And the LORD shall be ⁿ king over all the earth :
In that day shall there be ᵒ one LORD, and his name one.

¹⁰ All the land shall be ‖ turned ᵖ as a plain from Geba to Rimmon south of Jerusalem :

---

both northward and southward, because all the faithful in both directions will be included in it. ᵉ *Duorum populorum* (olim separatorum sed) rursum in unâ fide *societas* inter duos montes placabili sede requiescet, quoniam et Vetus et Novum Testamentum sibi utrumque *jungetur*" (*S. Jerome*).

This union is a consequence of Christ's Ascension from the Mount of Olives. He sent the Holy Ghost from heaven, and enabled the Apostles to go forth from Jerusalem into all the world, to unite all nations in His Church, which holds both Testaments in her hands, and is the shelter appointed by God for all His people in all the world.

— *earthquake in the days of Uzziah*] See on Amos i. 1.

— *the LORD my God shall come*, and *all the saints with thee*] With Thee, O Christ, coming to judgment, the holy angels shall come also. *S. Cyril* here. Daniel vii. 13—27. Matt. xxv. 31. 1 Thess. iv. 16. 2 Thess. i. 7. Jude 14. He, to Whom all judgment is committed, is Christ (Gesen. v. 22) ; and He will come in the clouds with all His holy angels to judgment ; and it is expressly said here that the LORD God will come ; therefore Christ is Jehovah. Compare on xiii. 7.

6. *it shall come to pass in that day, that the light shall not be clear, nor dark*] Rather (according to the *Chetib*) *in that day there will not be light, the brightest things will be wrapped up* (that is, " the sun shall be darkened, and the moon shall not give her light, and the stars shall fall from heaven"—Matt. xxiv. 29. Mark xiii. 25. Cp. Joel ii. 31). The heavenly firmament, formerly expanded in its bright pages bespangled with constellations, will be wrapped together like a scroll, and be shrivelled up in the fire of the world's conflagration. Cp. Isaiah xxxiv. 4, " All the host of heaven shall be dissolved, and the heavens shall be rolled together as a scroll ;" and 2 Pet. iii. 7. 10, " The heavens and the earth are kept in store, reserved unto fire against the day of judgment and perdition of ungodly men. The day of the Lord will come as a thief in the night ; in the which the heavens shall pass away with a great noise, and the elements shall melt with fervent heat, the earth also and all the works that are therein shall be burned up." And compare Rev. vi. 12—17, describing the last day, "There was a great earthquake ; and the sun became black as sackcloth, and the moon became as blood ; and the stars of heaven fell unto the earth, even as a fig-tree casteth her untimely figs, when she is shaken of a mighty wind. And the heaven departed as a scroll when it is rolled together ; and every mountain and island were moved out of their places. And the kings of the earth, and the great men, and the rich men, . . . hid themselves in the dens and in the rocks of the mountains ; and said to the mountains and rocks, Fall on us, and hide us from the face of Him that sitteth on the throne, and from the wrath of the Lamb. For the great day of His wrath is come ; and who shall be able to stand ?"

The verb here used is *kâphâ*, which in *niphal* (as here) signifies, *to be drawn together*. See Gesen. 736 ; *Fuerst*, 1747 ; and so *Lud. de Dieu*, *Kliefoth*, *Hengst.*, *Hofmann*, *Kuehler*, and *Keil* here.

7. *it shall be one day—known to the LORD*] For, as our Lord

152

says, " Of that day knoweth no man—but My Father only" (Matt. xxiv. 36).

— *not day, nor night*] It will not be day, for the sun will be darkened ; nor will it be night, for moon and stars will disappear ; but there will be light from the countenance of Christ, and from the flaming stream of fire which will issue forth from the throne of the Judge, when He comes to judgment (Dan. vii. 9, 10. 2 Thess. i. 8).

### THE LIVING WATERS OF SALVATION.

8. *living waters shall go out from Jerusalem*] The Prophet, having described the terrors of the great Day, goes back to a higher point in the series of events, to justify God's judgments on the world, by declaring that in order to qualify and prepare men for that awful Assize, he will give them *living waters* of divine truth.

A remarkable instance of a similar process of *prophetic recapitulation* may be seen in the Apocalypse of St. John, who is continually reminding us of Zechariah. See the notes below, on Rev. xx. 1.

The Prophet takes advantage of the physical fact, that the literal Jerusalem was abundantly supplied with water, flowing in subterranean streams beneath the City and the Temple ; and the spiritual waters here described by Zechariah are represented as flowing forth from Jerusalem, where Christ suffered on the cross, and where the Holy Ghost was given to the Apostles, who went forth to preach the Gospel of salvation through the blood of Christ, to all nations, and to enfold the World in the spiritual Jerusalem of the Universal Church. See *S. Cyril, S. Jerome, Eusebius*, Dem. Evang. vi. 18, and *Theodoret* here.

These spiritual waters are described as going forth, half to the *former*, or eastern sea, i. e. the Dead Sea ; and half to the *hinder Sea*, i. e. the Mediterranean ; because the Gospel is diffused into all nations. And they are represented as flowing both in winter and summer (very different therefore from the literal brooks of Palestine), because the Gospel is not dried up in summer, and frozen in winter, but is perennial.

This imagery has been already displayed to us in the vision of Ezekiel, which exhibits these living waters as gushing from beneath the altar in the spiritual Temple, and flowing forth with salubrious streams to fertilize the world, and make it bring forth fruit, and to purify the Dead Sea of Human Corruption, and to make it teem with life. See above, on Ezek. xlvii. 1—12 ; and the *Retrospect* of Chapter xlvii., pp. 286, 287 ; and on Joel iii. 18, which may supply a comment on the present passage.

9. *one LORD, and his name one*] One Lord, One faith (Eph. iv. 5) ; and all will be baptized unto that One Name, the Name of the Ever-Blessed Trinity, according to Christ's command given to His Apostles, " Go and teach all nations, baptizing them *into* the Name of the Father, and of the Son, and of the Holy Ghost : and Lo ! I am with you alway (literally, *all days*, even unto the end of the world" (Matt. xxviii. 19, 20).

10. *All the land shall be turned as a plain from Geba*] Rather, all the land shall be changed (so as to become exalted)

And it shall be lifted up, and ‖ inhabited in her place,

From Benjamin's gate unto the place of the first gate, unto the corner gate,

ʼ And *from* the tower of Hananeel unto the king's winepresses.

11 And *men* shall dwell in it, and there shall be ʼ no more utter destruction ;

ʼ But Jerusalem ‖ shall be safely inhabited.

12 And this shall be the plague wherewith the LORD will smite all the people that have fought against Jerusalem ;

Their flesh shall consume away while they stand upon their feet,

And their eyes shall consume away in their holes,

And their tongue shall consume away in their mouth.

13 And it shall come to pass in that day, *that* ᵘ a great tumult from the LORD shall be among them ;

And they shall lay hold every one on the hand of his neighbour,

And ˣ his hand shall rise up against the hand of his neighbour.

14 And ‖ Judah also shall fight ‖ at Jerusalem ;

ʸ And the wealth of all the heathen round about shall be gathered together, gold, and silver, and apparel, in great abundance.

15 And ᶻ so shall be the plague of the horse, of the mule, of the camel, and of the ass, and of all the beasts that shall be in these tents, as this plague.

16 And it shall come to pass, *that* every one that is left of all the nations

---

*as the plain*, or high tableland, *from Geba*, about ten miles north of Jerusalem (Josh. xviii. 24) *to Rimmon*, on the *south of Jerusalem*, and on the borders of Edom, about fourteen miles north of Beersheba (Josh. xv. 32).

The meaning is, that all the land of Christ's Church will be elevated; according to the prophet's words, "It shall come to pass in the last days, that the mountain of the Lord's house" (the spiritual Temple), "shall be established on the top of the mountains" (Isa. ii. 2. Mic. iv. 1 ; and see above, on Ezek. xl. 1. p. 278, *Retrospect*). The Church of Christ is like a city set on a hill, which cannot be hid (Matt. v. 14).

Physically, the literal Jerusalem is lower than the hills that stand about it ; the prophecy of its elevation *above* the hills will be fulfilled in the glorification of Christ's Church, which will hereafter be exalted on earth *above* all worldly and temporal Powers, and will mount up in glory to heaven.

Zechariah does not foretell that the literal Jerusalem and Canaan will be glorified, but that the earth itself, the Universal Church, will be like a glorified Canaan, and a beatified Jerusalem (*Kliefoth*).

THE CITY SHALL BE SAFELY INHABITED.

— *it shall be lifted up, and inhabited in her place*] Literally, *be inhabited under herself*, by her own inherent spiritual strength.

The Church of Christ will no longer rely on secular powers, and be subject to them, which will call her and be arrayed against her ; but she will be lifted up and dwell securely in her own place, by virtue of Christ's presence and power always in her (Matt. xxviii. 20), and by reason of the indwelling of the Holy Ghost, given to her by Him to abide with her for ever (John xiv. 16).

On the use of the Hebrew word *tachath (under)* see above, vi. 12, where it is said of Christ, that "He shall grow up out of His place," literally, *from under Himself*.

The following prophecy of Zechariah is best explained by a comparison of it with that of Jeremiah, where he describes the building up of the Church of Christ, and the safety of its inhabitants in all parts of it, by imagery similar to the present, derived from the topography of the literal Jerusalem. See the notes above, on Jer. xxxi. 38, 39. pp. 77, 78.

Probably (as the ancient fathers suggest), the following names may have been chosen as symbolical, as is certainly the case in Jeremiah. See on Jer. xxxi. 38. *The corner gate* may be mentioned with reference to Christ, the *Corner Stone*; *Hananeel*, with reference to God's grace ; the *King's winepresses*, with allusion to the sufferings of Christ our King, Who in His passion was trodden like grapes in a winepress ; but Who rose and conquered by suffering, and Who will become like one who treadeth the *wine-press*, when He puts all His enemies under His feet. See on Isa. lxiii. 1—3.

153

— *From Benjamin's gate*] The gate on the north wall, toward Benjamin and Ephraim (2 Kings xiv. 13. Neh. viii. 16).

— *the first gate, unto the corner gate*] On the northwest. See on Jer. xxxi. 38, 39. The *first gate* may perhaps be the same as the *old gate* in Neh. iii. 6.

— *from the tower of Hananeel unto the king's winepresses*] Lit. from the northeast (Neh. iii. 1) to south (Neh. iii. 15); figuratively, from *God's grace* to Christ's act of *Judgment*. (See above.)

In order to mark the security of the universal Church, the gates on opposite sides of Jerusalem are specified. She is safe on all sides, even in the terrible day of doom.

11. *there shall be no more utter destruction*] literally, there shall be no more any accursed thing, and no loss of extermination, Hebr. *cherem*. See Josh. vi. 17, 18. where it signifies a *devoted* or *accursed* thing ; Mal. iv. 6. where it means a curse ; and compare Rev. xxii. 3. where it is said of the heavenly city, "there shall be no more curse."

The literal Jerusalem was devoted to destruction by a curse for its idolatry, and was destroyed by the Babylonians ; and it was again devoted to destruction for the rejection of Christ, and was destroyed by the Romans. But the Spiritual Jerusalem, the Church of Christ, will never be destroyed.

12. *the LORD will smite all the people that have fought against Jerusalem*] "Omnes persecutores, qui adflixerunt Ecclesiam Domini, tu Licentius de futuris cruciatibus, etiam in præsenti recompensæ passionem" says S. Jerome, who even plies this in the History of Valerian, Decius, Diocletian, Maximinianus, Maximinus, and Julian, and other persecutors of the Church.

13. *a great tumult (or confusion) from the LORD shall be among them*] The enemies of the Church, which have been confederate against her, and have raged against her with furious violence, will suddenly be checked in their mad career, and will be distracted and confounded, like the enemies of Jerusalem in Jehoshaphat's time (2 Chron. xx. 23).

14. *Judah also shall fight at Jerusalem*] All believers will be united in defending the Church of God.

— *the wealth of all the heathen—shall be gathered*] Compare Ezekiel xxxix. 10, describing the victory of the Church of God.

15. *so shall be the plague of the horse*] So complete will be the destruction of the enemy, that not merely they themselves, but all their instruments of warfare, here represented as horses, mules, and camels of a besieging army, will be consumed. Compare the similar description in Ezekiel xxxix. 4, 18, 20.

JOYFUL ANNOUNCEMENT OF THE CONVERSION OF THE HEATHEN. THE PURITY AND GLORY OF THE CHURCH.

16. *every one that is left of all the nations*—[*Hieronymus*] The manifestation of God's power and love in defending His

Before
CHRIST
about
517.

a Isa. 60. 6, 7, 9.
& ch. 23.
b Lev. 23. 34, 43.
Neh. 8. 14.
Hos. 12. 9.
John 7. 2.
c Isa. 60. 12.
† Heb. *upon whom there is not.*
d Deut. 11. 10.

‖ Or, *sin.*

‖ Or, *bridles.*
e Isa. 23. 18.

which came against Jerusalem shall even ᵃ go up from year to year to worship the King, the Lord of hosts, and to keep ᵇ the feast of tabernacles. ¹⁷ ᶜ And it shall be, *that* whoso will not come up of *all* the families of the earth unto Jerusalem to worship the King, the Lord of hosts, even upon them shall be no rain.

¹⁸ And if the family of Egypt go not up, and come not, † ᵈ *that have no rain;* there shall be the plague, wherewith the Lord will smite the heathen that come not up to keep the feast of tabernacles. ¹⁹ This shall be the ‖ punishment of Egypt, and the punishment of all nations that come not up to keep the feast of tabernacles.

²⁰ In that day shall there be upon the ‖ bells of the horses, ᵉ HOLINESS UNTO THE LORD ; and the pots in the Lord's house shall be like the bowls before the altar.

²¹ Yea, every pot in Jerusalem and in Judah shall be holiness unto the Lord of hosts :

And all they that sacrifice shall come and take of them, and seethe therein :

---

Church, and in defeating her enemies, shall have the blessed effect of turning many of the Heathen Nations (i.e. of unbelievers generally), to the true faith and worship of God.

The imagery is here also borrowed, as usual, from Hebrew customs, and from the literal Jerusalem. The conversion of the Nations to Christianity is described as a going up to Jerusalem to worship the *Lord at the Feast of Tabernacles*, because that Feast was the great and crowning festival of the Hebrew year, and was specially typical of Christ's Incarnation (by which He, Who is God from eternity, came down from heaven, and pitched His tent in our nature,—John i. 14,—and dwells for ever among us), and of all the blessed fruits of the Incarnation in time and eternity. Compare the notes above, on Isaiah lxvi. 23; Hos. xii. 9; and Lev. xxiii. 34. Deut. xvi. 13; xxxi. 10. 2 Chron. viii. 12, 13. Ezra iii. 4. John vii. 2.

**17.** *whoso will not come up of all the families of the earth unto Jerusalem to worship the King—even upon them shall be no rain]* No rain of God's grace will fall on those who despise the call to come to Christ and His Church. "There is none other Name under heaven, but that of Jesus, given unto men whereby we must be saved; neither is there salvation in any other" (Acts iv. 12); and "such as are being saved" are described in Holy Scripture as "added to the Church" (Acts ii. 47). The Church, says *S. Jerome* here, is the Jerusalem which is above, which is free, which is the mother of us all (Gal. iv. 26); and they who desire to partake of the grace and salvation provided by Christ, must "come to mount Zion, the city of the living God" (Heb. xii. 22). They must partake faithfully, joyfully, and reverently of the Word and Sacraments, and other means of grace which are ministered in His Church; and so the refreshing rain and dews of the Holy Spirit will fall upon them. But if they will not comply with these conditions, their souls will be parched and will wither away with spiritual drought.

**18.** *if the family of Egypt go not up]* Egypt is the representative of the enemies of the Israel of God (*S. Cyril*), and especially of such as rely on worldly wisdom and secular philosophy, science, and art, for which Egypt was famous. But she is not excluded from hope of salvation if she will turn to God and join the communion of His Church. But if God's adversaries will not repent, they cannot hope for His favour; they will have no rain of divine grace, but will be smitten with plagues, like those of Egypt. Egypt was not refreshed by rain from heaven, but was watered by artificial channels cut in the earth (Deut. xi. 10. *Plin, N. H.* v. 9). Such is the soul of man without divine grace; but the Egypts of this world will receive rain from God if they believe in Christ.

**19.** *This shall be the punishment]* Literally, *this will be the sin of Egypt* (Hebr. *chattath*), and so Sept., *Vulg.* God does not punish willingly. His enemies bring down His wrath upon themselves by their sins.

**20.** *In that day shall there be upon the bells of the horses, HOLINESS UNTO THE LORD]* Here is another proof, if proof were needed, that this prophecy does not concern the literal Jerusalem and the Hebrew Nation, otherwise than as united with the Church of Christ. For it was contrary to the Hebrew law to "multiply horses" (Deut. xvii. 16). But here

horses are mentioned as consecrated to God. The very words, Holiness to the Lord, which were engraven upon the golden plate of the mitre of the High Priest himself (Exod. xxviii. 36), are to be attached to the bells upon them.

The meaning is this – Horses are emblems of strength, war, and victory. See Ps. cxlvii. 10. Prov. xxi. 31. Jer. viii. 6. Hos. i. 7. Hab. iii. 15; above, x. 3. Rev. vi. 2; xix. 11–14, where Christ is described as a mighty Conqueror riding on the white horse, and followed by a train of riders on white horses. The consecration of horses (so that the housings, with which they are caparisoned, are to be like the mitre of the High Priest, inscribed with "Holiness unto the Lord") is an intimation that there will no longer be any need of horses for battle and destruction—"*men shall not learn war any more*" (Isa. ii. 4. Micah iv. 3), but that the instruments of War itself will be christianized, and that all power, and dignity, and victory, will be hallowed and dedicated to the honour and glory of God.

*— the pots in the Lord's house shall be like the bowls before the altar]* The meaning is, that there can be no future glory without holiness in this life. "Without holiness no man shall see the Lord" (Heb. xii. 14), "Blessed and holy is he that hath part in the first resurrection" (Rev. xx. 6).

This truth is expressed by means of imagery from the literal Temple at Jerusalem. In the Levitical Ritual, the pots in which the flesh of the sacrifices was boiled, were regarded as much less holy than the sacrificial bowls in which the blood "wherein is the life" was received, and out of which it was sprinkled or poured on the altar.

But in the Church, the spiritual Jerusalem, namely, the Church Universal when glorified, every vessel,—that is, every person, however humble in position he may be,—will be holy; and nothing that is unholy will find a place there, and therefore it follows, "*yea, every pot in Jerusalem and in Judah shall be holiness unto the Lord of Hosts.*" The words, "*every pot shall be holiness,*" may be illustrated by the word *vessel* in the New Testament: Acts ix. 15, "Go thy way, he is a chosen *vessel* unto me;" 1 Thess. iv. 4, "Let every one know how to possess his *vessel* in sanctification and honour;" 2 Tim. ii. 21, "If a man purge himself from these (sins), he shall be a *vessel* unto honour, sanctified and meet for the master's use." The "*earthen vessels*" (see 2 Cor. iv. 7) of the Church of God shall be glorified, and become like precious vessels of pure gold.

See here the blessings of repentance and of faith in Christ; thereby thy soul, which was once a vessel of shame, becomes a vessel of glory in the heavenly temple. As the ancient Hymn says—

> "Fit ex lebete phiala,
> In vas translata gloriæ
> Ex vase contumeliæ."

"Let all who are members of Christ's Church" (says *S. Jerome*) "consecrate all their strength and all their victories to Him. Let the bells of our horses be holy to the Lord. Let us endeavour to sanctify every thing, and dedicate it to Him. Let us hallow the vessels of Judaism, and convert them into vials of sweet odours before the altar of God."

And in that day there shall be no more the ᶠ Canaanite in ᵍ the house of the
Loʀᴅ of hosts.

ᶠ Isa. 35. 8.   Joel 3. 17.   Rev. 21. 27.   & 22. 15.      ᵍ Eph. 2. 19, 20, 21, 22.

**21.** *there shall be no more the Canaanite in the house of the* Loʀᴅ *of hosts*] The Church will then be purified, and all vestiges of idolatry and all sins of impurity by which the Canaanites were defiled will be rooted out (Gen. ix. 25. Lev. xviii. 28; xx. 23, Deut. vii. 2; ix. 4; xxix. 17). Cp. Isa. xxxv. 8; Obad. 17; Joel iii. 17; and Rev. xxi. 27, "There shall in no wise enter into the heavenly city any thing that defileth, neither whatsoever worketh abomination, or maketh a lie." Compare Rev. xxii. 15, and the last words of St. John's first Epistle, "Little children, keep yourselves from idols."

May the Loʀᴅ of Hosts grant (say The *elect* here) that no Canaanite may be seen among us, but that we may all live according to the laws of the Gospel of Christ, and may look for the blessed hope and glorious appearing of the great God and our Saviour Jesus Christ (Titus ii. 13.); to Whom, with the giving and praise in all the Churches of the Saints upon earth, and in the heavenly and eternal city of the Church glorified, the Jerusalem which is above, for ever and ever. Amen.

# MALACHI.

Before CHRIST about 400.

I. [1] THE burden of the word of the LORD to Israel † by Malachi.

[2] a I have loved you, saith the LORD.

† Heb. *by the hand of Malachi.*   a Deut. 7. 8. & 15. 1.

---

## PRELIMINARY NOTE.

The prophecies of MALACHI derive a special interest, not only from their contents, but from their position.

Malachi follows Zechariah; and he is called by the Hebrews "The Seal of the Prophets," as closing the prophetical Canon of the Ancient Dispensation. He completes the Old Testament, and prepares the way for the New. In this view his name *Malachi*, which means *Angel*, or MESSENGER, is very appropriate. He is the Angel of the Old Covenant, flying with joyful alacrity, to bring the glad tidings of the Gospel.

Malachi, in his immediate succession to Zechariah, discharges an office peculiar to himself. Zechariah is one of the most sublime and impassioned among "the goodly fellowship of the Prophets." It seems as if the Holy Spirit designed to teach the world by him, the last but one in the prophetic line, that if Prophecy was to become mute (as it became for an interval of about four centuries soon after Zechariah), its silence was not due to any failure or exhaustion of power in the Divine Author of Prophecy. No; the light of the sunset of Prophecy in Zechariah is as brilliant and glorious as its noonday splendours in Isaiah. The Visions of Zechariah, their rich colouring and varied imagery, their prophetic utterances reaching from his own age to the Day of Doom, display this truth. This has been shown already in the Introductory Note to Zechariah. Zechariah reveals to us the Birth of Christ, "the Man Whose Name is the Branch[1]" springing up from a lowly place; He sets Christ before us in a fair picture, riding in triumph "on the foal of an ass[2]" to Jerusalem; he also unfolds the scenes of Gethsemane and Calvary[3]; he declares to us His Royalty and His Priesthood, typified respectively by Zerubbabel and Jeshua the son of Josedech, the leaders of the returning exiles from Babylon to Jerusalem[4]; and he proclaims in clear tones His Godhead[5]; and finally, as with lightning's speed, he passes on to the future evangelization of the Heathen, the conversion of the Jews[6], and to the last struggle and overthrow of all Antichristian powers[7] and to the full and final victory of Christ, and the everlasting glory and felicity of His Church[7].

Let us now turn to Malachi.

What a striking contrast is here! All is quiet and sedate. We seem to have passed from the sight of some impetuous torrent, sweeping along in a violent stream, dashing over rugged rocks and hurling itself down in headlong cataracts, and carrying every thing with it in its foaming flood, to the contemplation of the clear mirror of a peaceful lake. The stream of Prophecy ceased to rush vehemently after Zechariah, and it tempers its vehemence "in the clear haven of a translucent pool" in Malachi; there it rested in peace for 400 years, till it flowed forth again in the Gospel.

Why was this?

The reason will be evident, if we examine the prophecies of Malachi.

They are all of an ethical character. They inculcate in clear, vigorous, stern, and severe language, made more expressive by sharp authoritative questionings, as if the Prophet were summoning the Nation in God's Name to a strict examination at His judicial bar[8], the great moral and religious duties of

piety to God, of justice and mercy to man, and of personal purity, holiness, temperance, and sobriety. They speak of, Christ's Coming. Like the Baptist, the Preacher of righteousness, the Prophet Malachi sees, even in Christ's First Coming to save, a vision of His future Advent to judge[9]. He calls back the minds of the people to a remembrance of the thunders and lightnings of Mount Sinai, and to the requirements of the Moral Law delivered by God to them by "Moses His servant[10];" and he concludes with carrying them onward to the terrors of the Great Day, and to the curse that will then be pronounced on all impenitent sinners. He speaks indeed of the rising of the "Sun of Righteousness with healing on his wings," but that genial and salutary Dayspring will beam only on those "who fear His Name[11]."

In the days of Malachi, the Temple of Jerusalem had been rebuilt; its ritual had been restored; a fragrant cloud of incense again arose in a silver steam from the golden altar before the veil in the Holy Place; sacrifices were offered again to God on the brazen altar before the porch of the Temple. The schism between the ten tribes of Israel and the two tribes of Judah and Benjamin had been healed in the Babylonish Captivity. The affections of all the tribes were now concentrated in Jerusalem. Idolatry had ceased. But in its place had arisen a cold, hard, rigid, self-complacent spirit of ceremonial formalism, which afterwards came to a head in the proud, vainglorious Pharisaism of our Lord's age. It had none of that penitential sorrow gushing forth from the contrite heart in a flood of tears, none of that living faith and ardent love showing itself in the daily self-devotion of a holy and religious life, which alone can make acts of worship to be pleasing and acceptable to God.

These considerations will explain the tone and tenour of Malachi's prophecies.

What are the practical inferences to be hence derived? What are the lessons to be deduced from the succession of the ethical teaching, commonitory precepts, and commonitory warnings of Malachi to the glowing imagery, and prophetic visions, and mysterious revelations of Zechariah? What are the lessons to be deduced from Malachi's position, not only as the last of the prophets, but also as the herald of the Gospel? They may be briefly stated as follows:—

The fruit of all spiritual teaching, even of the highest and transcendental kind, like the prophecies of Zechariah, is not in ecstatic emotions and enthusiastic raptures, but in the quiet discharge of moral duties; it is to be seen in holiness of life and in personal preparation for Death, Judgment, and Eternity. "Love is the fulfilling of the Law[12]." "On these two commandments" (love to God and our neighbour) "hang all the Law and the Prophets[13]." "He hath showed thee, O man, what is good; and now what doth the Lord thy God require of thee, but to do justly, and to love mercy, and walk humbly with thy God[14]?" "Prepare to meet thy God[15]."

Malachi is the Messenger of the Lord. He is like the Baptist, the great forerunner of Christ, Whose coming he announces, "Behold, I will send My Messenger, and he shall prepare the way before Me[16]." He is like the Baptist, a stern teacher of moral duties, and in boldly rebuking sin. The Temple had been rebuilt: sacrifices were again offered

---

[1] vi. 12.  [2] xiii. 7.
[3] xi. 1—10; iv. 6—11; vi. 10—15.
[4] xi. 13.  [5] xii. 10—11; xi. 7—16.
[6] xiv. 1—7.  [7] xiv. 8—21.
[8] See i. 1, 2. 6. 10; ii. 10. 14, 15. 17; iii. 7, 8.

[9] iii. 1—6.  [10] iv. 4.
[11] iv. 2.  [12] Rom. xiii. 10.
[13] Matt. xxii. 40.  [14] Micah vi. 8.
[15] Amos iv. 12.  [16] iii. 1.

Yet ye say, Wherein hast thou loved us ? *Was* not Esau Jacob's brother ?
saith the LORD : yet I loved Jacob, ³ and I hated Esau, and ᶜ laid his mountains and his heritage waste for the dragons of the wilderness.

⁴ Whereas Edom saith, We are impoverished, but we will return and build
the desolate places ; thus saith the LORD of hosts,

They shall build, but I will throw down ;

And they shall call them, The border of wickedness,

And, The people against whom the LORD hath indignation for ever.

⁵ And your eyes shall see, and ye shall say,

ᵈ The LORD will be magnified || † from the border of Israel.

⁶ A son ᵉ honoureth *his* father,

And a servant his master :

ᶠ If then I *be* a father, where *is* mine honour ?

And if I *be* a master, where *is* my fear ?

Saith the LORD of hosts unto you, O priests, that despise my name.

ᵍ And ye say, Wherein have we despised thy name ? ⁷ || Ye offer ʰ polluted

---

But in the priests and in the worshippers he saw a worldly,
formal, hypocritical spirit ; and he denounced it with intrepid
sternness and unflinching severity. "Ye offer polluted bread
upon Mine altar!." "And now, O ye priests, this commandment is for you—the priest's lips should keep knowledge—but
ye are departed out of the way². Ye have wearied the Lord
with your words³." And he threatens both people and priests
with God's judgments⁴ ; and, what is more, he foretells this
rejection for their sins, and the reception of the heathen in their
place⁵. The sight of the concourse of the worshippers in the
restored Temple at Jerusalem leads him to foretell the gathering
together of all Nations into the Church of Christ, Who would visit
that Temple, and Who would send forth the Priests of the Gospel
from Jerusalem to receive the whole world into His Church.
And the formality, and hypocrisy, and profaneness of the Jewish
Priests and People are contrasted with that holier faith and
service which God would accept from those who worship Him
in spirit and in truth in every nation in the world. "From the
rising of the sun even unto the going down of the same, My
name shall be great among the Gentiles ; and in every place
incense shall be offered unto Me, and a pure offering, for My
name shall be great among the heathen, saith the Lord of
hosts⁶."

The *reception* of the prophecy of Malachi into the Hebrew
Canon is a strong proof of its inspiration. It cannot be imagined
that the Hebrew Church and Nation would ever have consented
to receive a book containing such unpalatable announcements as
these—pronouncing such unmitigated censures on the Priesthood and People—predicting their future rejection, and foretelling the adoption by God of the heathen (whom they detested)
into His favour, in their own stead—unless they had been convinced, by incontestable proofs, that Malachi spoke by inspiration of God.

There are many valuable expository works on the prophecies of Malachi, such as the Commentary of *S. Jerome*, and
of *Dr. Pocock* in our own country ; and in our own age, of
*Hengstenberg* and *Keil*. But the best commentary is to be
found in the book of Malachi's contemporary, Nehemiah. The
reader is invited to refer to that book, with the *Introduction* to
it⁷, and notes upon it, in a former volume⁸. Compare especially
Malachi ii. 11—17 with Nehemiah xiii. 23—30, and Malachi
iii. 8—10 with Nehemiah xiii. 10—14.

CH. I. 1. *The burden*] Or prophetic message—usually of woe,
See on Nahum i. 1. Zech. ix. 1 ; xii 1. The present passage,
to ii. 7, is the *Haphtarah* to Gen. xxv. 19—xxviii. 9, the history
of Isaac, Jacob, and Esau. The reason of this juxtaposition is
obvious.

THE SINS OF THE JEWS.

2. *I have loved you, saith the* LORD. *Yet ye say, Wherein*

---

*hast thou loved us?*] These words must be explained (as
*S. Cyril* observes) by reference to the condition of the Jews at
this time. Malachi begins his prophecies with animadverting on
the ungrateful temper of the Hebrew Nation. They repined
and murmured against God. They were under heathen rule.
They were feeble and poor (Neh. ix. 36, 37). The former prophets
had foretold their return to Jerusalem and the rebuilding of the
Temple ; and these prophets had also preannounced the coming
of the Messiah. The Jews *had* returned ; the Temple *had been*
rebuilt ; but Messiah had not come. They were disappointed
and impatient, and murmured against God, and charged Him
with unfaithfulness, fickleness, and inconstancy. The prophet
replies to these allegations. He assures them of God's love ;
and teaches them that all their miseries were due to themselves.
Cp. Neh. ix. 31—33.

2, 3. *I loved Jacob, and I hated Esau*] See below, on
Rom. ix. 13. The doctrine there taught by St. Paul, which has
been much misrepresented and distorted by some Calvinistic
teachers, may be illustrated by the divine words here. The love
of God toward Jacob (as *S. Cyril* remarks) was not without
foresight of Jacob's faithfulness and piety as compared with Esau.
The hatred of God toward Esau, "a profane person who despised
his birthright" (Heb. xii. 16), was certainly no arbitrary or
capricious passion. And if we extend these words to the nation
which derived its descent from him—Edom, we find it represented in the historical and prophetical books as bringing
God's judgments on itself by its proud impiety, and by its
unmerciful and revengeful spirit towards Israel, its own flesh
and blood. See above, on Ps. cxxxvii. 7. Isaiah lxiii. 1.
Obadiah 8.

3. *dragons*] *Jackals*. Cp. Pocock here, p. 107.

4. *We are impoverished*] Rather, *we are broken in pieces*.
Observe Edom's pride and self-confidence. He says, We have
been broken in pieces, but we will mend ourselves. A vain
boast, for God had dashed them into fragments, and no man
could make them coalesce.

On the other hand, Judah, whom Edom has hated and
persecuted, has indeed been scattered by God ; but He will
gather them again. Observe the repetition of the word *border*
in the contrast between them. Edom is the *border (gebul)* of
wickedness ; but the Lord will show His power and love over
the *border (gebul)* of Israel (v. 5).

6. *If then I be a father, where is mine honour?*] This is
God's question to Israel, His "firstborn" (Exod. iv. 22). Israel
has received special favour from God's fatherly love. Observe
the characteristics of the Lord's words to Israel by Malachi.
They are distinguished by a series of *interrogations* (see *Proëm,
Note*). The nation is arraigned at God's judgment-seat, and
God puts questions to it, as He did to Adam. We have here a
rehearsal of the questionings of the great day of reckoning, to
which Malachi appeals (iv. 1—6).

7. *polluted bread, Bread* (Hebr. *lehem*) is the Levitical word
for sacrificial offerings. See Lev. iii. 11, 16 ; xxi. 6, 8, 17,
21, 22. Pocock, iii. Hence the term *lehem* here for *altar* ;
polluted *bread* is equivalent to what is described as "blind,
lame, and sick," in v. 8.

¹ i. 7.  ² ii. 1—8.  ³ ii. 17.
³ iii. 18 ; iv. 1.  ⁴ i. 11.  ⁵ i. 11.
⁷ pp. 295—300.  ⁸ Vol. iii. pp. 325—357.
157

Before CHRIST about 397.

i Ezek. 41. 22. ver. 12.
k Lev. 22. 22. Deut. 15. 21. ver. 14.
† Heb. *to sacrifice.*
l Job 42. 8.
† Heb. *the face of God.*
m Hos. 13. 9.
† Heb. *from your hand.*
n 1 Cor. 9. 13.
o Isa. 1. 11. Jer. 6. 20. Amos 5. 21.
p Ps. 113. 3. Isa. 59. 19.
q Isa. 60. 3, 5.
r John 4. 21, 23. 1 Tim. 2. 8.
s Rev. 8. 3.
t Isa. 66. 19, 20.

bread upon mine altar; and ye say, Wherein have we polluted thee? In that
ye say, [i] The table of the LORD *is* contemptible.
8 And [k] if ye offer the blind † for sacrifice, *is it* not evil? and if ye offer the lame and sick, *is it* not evil? offer it now unto thy governor; will he be pleased with thee, or [l] accept thy person? saith the LORD of hosts.
9 And now, I pray you, beseech † God that he will be gracious unto us: [m] this hath been † by your means: will he regard your persons? saith the LORD of hosts.
10 Who *is there* even among you that would shut the doors *for nought?* [n] neither do ye kindle *fire* on mine altar for nought. I have no pleasure in you, saith the LORD of hosts, [o] neither will I accept an offering at your hand.
11 For [p] from the rising of the sun even unto the going down of the same my name *shall be* great [q] among the Gentiles; [r] and in every place [s] incense *shall be* offered unto my name, and a pure offering: [t] for my name *shall be* great among the heathen, saith the LORD of hosts.

---

**8.** *offer it now unto thy governor*] Thy *governor* (Hebr. *pechâh*), the ruler set over thee by the Persian king. Such were those who are called "*governors* beyond the river" in Nehemiah ii. 7, such was Nehemiah himself, who was appointed to that office by Artaxerxes (Neh. v. 14), and who says of himself, "I did not eat nor required I the *bread* of the *governor*" (Neh. v. 14—18). Cp. xii. 26. Such had been Zerubbabel before him (Hagg. i. 1. 14; ii. 2. 21).

The sense is, Ye treat your God in a worse manner than the deputy of a heathen power. Ye put polluted *bread* on His *table*; ye would not dare to present such *bread* at your *governor's table*, Hebr. *shulchan*, a word also used by Nehemiah, the governor, to describe the abundant supply of food prepared for his own *table* (Neh. v. 17. 18). What a contrast between that provision and the miserable supply (the lame, the blind, the sick) for the Lord's table, as here described by the prophet!

**9.** *this hath been by your means*] Such sins have ye committed; will God then accept you? No; not except ye repent. It is useless for you to pray and offer sacrifice, except ye amend your own practice.

**10.** *Who* is there *even among you*—nought] The sense is rather as follows: *Who* is there among you, or, *Oh! that there were even some among you, who would* not open My sanctuary to such profane intruders, but *would close the doors* (of My house, the Temple at Jerusalem) against such worshippers and such sacrifices as these! *and would not kindle the fire* on Mine altar to no *purpose!* "Away with your vain oblations! What purpose is the multitude of your sacrifices to Me!" Would that some one would drive them from My house! Cp. Isa. i. 11. Jer. vi. 20. Amos v. 21.

The interrogative *Who would*, often expresses a wish, and is equivalent to *Oh that!* See 2 Sam. xv. 4. Ps. iv. 6. Jer. ix. 12. Hagg. ii. 3. Cp. *Theodoret, Vatablus, A Lapide, Pocock*, 113, and *Keil* here.

THE RECEPTION OF THE GENTILES.

**11.** *For from the rising of the sun—Gentiles*] Ye will be cast off from My presence for your sins. Yes; and ye think that God cannot exist without the Temple and without your worship; and that, if I cast you off, I shall be left without votaries. No; this will not be so, for I have resolved to receive the Heathen in your place. Compare Isa. lxiv. 10—12; lxv. 1—9, where the Lord meets the allegations of the Jews by a similar reply.

Here is an anticipation of our Lord's declaration to the Jews, "The kingdom of God shall be *taken from you, and given to a nation* bringing forth the fruits thereof" (Matt. xxi. 43).

All earthly calamities are represented by the prophets as preparing the way for the preaching of the Gospel throughout the world. Cp. Habakkuk ii. 13, 14.

— *in every place*] Not only in the Temple at Jerusalem, but every where; as our Lord declared to the Samaritan woman (John iv. 21—23), and St. Paul (1 Tim. ii. 8).

Here was a bold leap into futurity. And here is a striking proof of Malachi's inspiration. God had declared in the Levitical Law that sacrifices were to be offered only in *one place*, and not "*in every place*" (Deut. xii. 13). The Hebrew Nation was jealous of any extension of God's favour to the Heathen (see this feeling exemplified above in the Prophet Jonah); but Malachi has overcome this prejudice (cp. Micah iv. 1), and even revokes the Divine command to offer sacrifice in one place. Who could do this but God Himself?

— *incense* shall be *offered unto my name, and a pure offering*] This passage is grounded on Leviticus ii. 1, where the *offering* (*minchah*, the word used here) is combined with incense: "When any will offer a *meat offering* (*minchah*) unto the Lord, his offering shall be of fine flour, and he shall pour oil upon it, and put *frankincense* thereon." The *minchah*, being made of flour (produced by a concurrence of human labour and divine goodness) and being joined with *oil* and *frankincense*, the one (oil) the symbol of the unction of the Holy Spirit, the other (frankincense) the emblem of prayer (Rev. v. 8; viii. 3—11; and see *Irenæus*, iv. 33, referring to this passage of Malachi) represents two things:—

(1) In relation to Christ, the *minchah* symbolizes His offering of Himself, the heavenly corn of wheat (see John xii. 24) given by God's goodness and bruised by suffering and obedience, the act of His own will and work; and sanctified by the unction of the Holy Ghost, and consummated in His mediatorial office in the heavenly Temple by the incense of prayer offered by Him as our Great High Priest in the golden censer of His merits.

(2) In respect to man, the *minchah*, with its accompaniments of oil and incense, represents God's goodness working with our will, sanctified by the Holy Ghost, and offering up prayer and thanksgiving, going up to God, as it were, in a fragrant silver cloud of incense from the altar of our hearts.

The prophecy of Malachi, therefore, foretells that Christ's sacrificial offering and mediatorial office would be universal and everlasting, as *S. Augustine* says (De Civ. Dei, xviii. 37), "We see this sacrifice offered by the Priesthood of Christ after the order of Melchizedek in all the world; but the Jewish sacrifices have ceased, as the Prophet here predicts; and that men in all places would respond to it by a correlative offering of themselves." The ancient Christian Fathers have applied this prophecy to the Holy Eucharist, and have regarded it as a prediction that this commemorative sacrifice, representing the Sacrifice once offered at Calvary, and pleading its efficacy and applying it to the faithful receiver, and being sanctified by the invocation and illapse of the Holy Spirit, and by the prayers of the faithful, would be offered in all the world. See *S. Justin Martyr*, C. Tryphon. §41, where he says that this is a "figure of the bread and the cup of the Eucharist;" and *S. Irenæus* (iv. 32, Grabe) says that Christ taught us "the new oblation of the New Testament, which (oblation) the Church, having received it from the Apostles, offers up in all the world to God, Who gives to us nourishment; and presents to Him the first fruits of His own gifts, according to the words of Malachi" (i. 10, 11). In the words of *Joseph Mede* (Works, 355), "This place of Scripture was once, in the eldest and purest times, a text of eminent note, and familiarly known to every Christian, being alleged by their Pastors and Teachers as an express and undoubted prophecy of the Christian Sacrifice, or solemn worship of the Eucharist, taught by our Blessed Saviour unto His

<sup></sup>¹² But ye have profaned it, in that ye say, " The table of the LORD *is* polluted; and the fruit thereof, *even* his meat, is contemptible. ¹³ Ye said also, Behold, what a weariness *is it!* and ye have snuffed at it, saith the LORD of hosts; and ye brought *that which was* torn, and the lame, and the sick; thus ye brought an offering: should I accept this of your hand? saith the LORD.

---

Disciples, to be observed of all that should believe on His Name. It is quoted in this sense by Fathers of the second and third centuries, and is inserted in this sense in ancient Liturgies, as in that of S. Mark.

*Tertullian* (C. Jude x. c. 5; C. Marcion, iii. 22, iv. 1) generalizes the words into a prophecy of spiritual offerings of prayer, and praise, and thanksgiving; and so *Cyprian*, *Euseb.* (Dem. Evangelic. i. 6) applies them to the pure offering of prayer and good works to God; and S. *Cyril* says here, "God thus declares that the sweet perfume of spiritual incense will be offered to Him every where in reverence and holiness, namely, the oblation of faith, hope, and charity, and good works."

The sacrifice is called *pure* by the Prophet, as being offered by a pure conscience (*Iren.* iv. 34, *Tertullian*, C. Scap. c. 2), or else in respect to Christ, Who offered the only pure sacrifice, contrasted with the sacrifices of the Jews. Compare *Mede*, pp. 358, 359, in his essay on this text, where he shews in what sense the Eucharist is called a sacrifice (a commemorative one) by the Ancient Fathers, pp. 360–379; and see *Waterland* on the Service of the Eucharist considered in a Sacrificial View, vol. vii. pp. 341–591, or chap. xii. of his Review on the Doctrine of the Eucharist.

### THE CHRISTIAN SACRIFICE.

As a very imposing superstructure has been built on this text by the Divines of the Roman Church, both in doctrine and practice, with regard to the sacrificial character of the Holy Eucharist (see *A Lapide* here), it may not be amiss to dwell a little longer on this subject.

Undoubtedly the Fathers, especially S. *Chrysostom* and S. *Augustine*, and others in the fourth and fifth centuries, speak of the Eucharist as a *Sacrifice*.

But what is their definition of the word Sacrifice? " A true Sacrifice," says S. *Augustine* (De. Civ. Dei. x. 6), " is every act which is performed in order that we may cleave unto God in holy communion; such act being referred to Him as our Sovereign Good, by which alone we can enjoy true felicity."

Undoubtedly also they say that " Christ is daily offered in the Sacrifice of the altar."

But the sense in which they use these words is explained by other expressions in their writings. Thus S. *Chrysostom* says, in expounding our Lord's words, "Do this in remembrance of Me," in his commentary on Hebrews x. 9, " We do not offer another Sacrifice, as the High Priest did formerly, but always the same;" and then, explaining himself, he adds, "or rather we make a *commemoration* of a Sacrifice" (ἀλλὰ θὲ ἀνάμνησιν ἐργαζόμεθα θυσίας).

And S. *Augustine* (C. Faust. xx. c. 18) thus speaks: " Christians, in the holy oblation and participation of the body and blood of Christ, celebrate a *memory* of the same Sacrifice that *has been accomplished.* ' *Percepti ejusdem Sacrificii memoriam celebrant.* '" And again he says (Epist. ad Bonifac. xxiii. p. 267, ed. Benod.), " Was not Christ offered once in Himself? And yet He is offered in the Sacrament at Easter and every day; nor does any one say what is false when he affirms Him to be offered. For if Sacraments had not a *resemblance* to the things of which they are Sacraments, they would not be Sacraments at all. But from this *resemblance* they derive the names of the things themselves" (which they represent).

Let not the words of the Fathers be cited partially, but as a whole. When this is done, it will be granted by candid reasoners that those expressions in which the Fathers speak of the Eucharist as a Sacrifice are to be qualified by those *other* phrases in which they speak of it as a memory or similitude of a Sacrifice; and *not vice versâ.* A writer, especially when speaking rhetorically, may call a picture by the name of the person or thing of which it is a picture; but the living person or thing would never be *called* a picture of itself. The statue of Homer may be called Homer; a view of Athens may be called Athens; but Homer could never be called a statue of Homer, nor Athens be called a view of itself. A map of Greece may be called Greece, but Greece could never be called a map of Greece. The Fathers, believing the Eucharist to be, by Christ's appointment, a perpetual representation and memory of the Sacrifice of the Cross, which is ever represented by our Great High Priest to His Father in Heaven, and to be

159

the means by which the virtue of that Sacrifice is communicated to us, and we are united to Christ and receive His body and blood in our hearts by faith, might well speak of the Eucharist as a Sacrifice; but if the y had thought the Eucharist to be no other than the very Sacrifice of the Cross itself contained or renewed, they never could have called it, as they do, a *memory or resemblance of a Sacrifice that is past.*

Hence *Bishop Andrewes* (Ad Card. Bellarmin. Apolog. Responsio, p. 184) thus writes, " Credunt nostri homines instituram a Domino Eucharistiam in Sui Commemorationem, etiam Sacrificii Sui, vel si ita loqui libeat, in *Sacrificium commemorativum.* . . . *Memoriam* ibi fieri Sacrificii damus non inviti, sacrificari ipsi Christum denuo factum nonquam damus." And in his sermon on Acts ii. 42, vol. v., p. 66 : " The Church of Rome many times celebrate th this mystery without any breaking (of bread) at all. Whereas it is of the nature of an Eucharist or peace-offering which was never offered but it was eaten, that there might be a *representation* of the *memory of that Sacrifice,* and together an application to each person by partaking of it."

Similarly *Archbishop Laud* (Conference with Fisher, ed. Oxon. 1839, p. 256) : " And since here is mention happened of Sacrifice, my third instance shall be in the sacrifice which is offered up to God in that great and high mystery of our redemption by the death of Christ. For as Christ offered up Himself once for all, a full and all-sufficient sacrifice for the sins of the whole world, so did He institute and command a memory of this sacrifice in a sacrament, even till His coming again. For at and in the Eucharist we offer up to God three sacrifices: one by the priest only; that is, the commemorative sacrifice of Christ's death, represented in bread broken and wine poured out; another by the priest and people jointly, and that is the sacrifice of praise and thanksgiving for all the benefits and graces we receive by the precious death of Christ; the third by every particular man for himself only; and that is the sacrifice of every man's body and soul, to serve Him in both all the rest of his life, for this blessing thus bestowed on him. Now thus far these dissenting Churches agree, that in the Eucharist there is a sacrifice of duty, and a sacrifice of praise, and a sacrifice of commemoration of Christ. Therefore, according to the former rule (and here in truth too), it is safest for a man to believe the commemorative, the praising, and the performing sacrifice; and to offer them duly to God, and leave the Church of Rome in this particular to her superstitions—that I may say no more."

And in like manner *Bishop Bull* (Works, vol. ii. p. 256, ed. Oxon. 1827) : " The first article (of the Roman Creed) I shall take notice of is this; 'I profess, that in the Mass is offered to God a true, proper, and propitiatory sacrifice for the living and the dead; and that in the most holy sacrifice of the Eucharist there is truly, and really, substantially the body and blood, together with the soul and divinity of our Lord Jesus Christ; and that there is wrought a conversion of the whole substance of the bread into the body, and of the whole substance of the wine into the blood, which conversion the Catholic Church calls transubstantiation.' Where this proposition ( that in the Mass there is offered to God a true, proper, and propitiatory sacrifice for the living and the dead,) having that other of the 'substantial presence of the body and blood of Christ in the Eucharist' immediately annexed to it, the meaning of it must necessarily be this, that in the Eucharist the very body and blood of Christ are again offered up to God as a propitiatory sacrifice for the sins of men. Which is an impious proposition, derogatory to the One full satisfaction of Christ made by His death on the cross, and contrary to express Scripture, Heb. vii. 27; and ix. 12, 25, 26, 28; and x. 12, 14. It is true the Eucharist is frequently called by the ancient Fathers προσφορά, θυσία, an oblation, a sacrifice. But it is to be remembered that they say also it is *θυσία λογικὴ καὶ ἀναίμακτος, a reasonable sacrifice, a sacrifice without blood;* which how can it be said to be, if therein the very blood of Christ were offered up to God?

" They hold the Eucharist to be a commemorative sacrifice, and so do we. This is the constant language of the ancient Liturgies, 'We offer by way of commemoration,' according to our Saviour's words when He ordained this holy rite, *Do this in*

Before
CHRIST
about
397.
y ver. 8.
‖ Or, *in whose flock is.*
z Ps. 47. 2.
1 Tim. 6. 15.

14 But cursed *be* ‖ the deceiver, ‖ which hath in his flock a male, and voweth, and sacrificeth unto the Lord a corrupt thing : for ²I *am* a great King, saith the LORD of hosts, and my name *is* dreadful among the heathen.

II. ¹ And now, O ye priests, this commandment *is* for you.

*commemoration of Me.* In the Eucharist, then, Christ is offered, not hypostatically, as the Trent Fathers have determined (for so He was but once offered), but commemoratively only : and this commemoration is made to God the Father, and is not a bare remembering, or putting ourselves in mind of Him. For every sacrifice is directed to God, and the oblation therein made, whatsoever it be, hath Him for its object, and not man. In the holy Eucharist, therefore, we set before God the bread and wine, as 'figures or images of the precious blood of Christ shed for us, and of His precious body' (they are the very words of the Clementine Liturgy), and plead to God the merit of His Son's sacrifice once offered on the cross for us sinners, and in this Sacrament represented, beseeching Him for the sake thereof to bestow His heavenly blessings on us.

"To conclude this matter : the ancients held the oblation of the Eucharist to be answerable in some respects to the legal sacrifices; that is, they believed that our Blessed Saviour ordained the Sacrament of the Eucharist as a rite of prayer and praise to God, instead of the manifold and bloody sacrifices of the Law. That the legal sacrifices were rites to invocate God by, is evident from many texts in Scripture. See especially 1 Sam. vii. 9, and xiii. 12. Ezra vi. 10. Prov. xv. 8. And that they were also rites for praising and blessing God for His mercies, appears from 2 Chron. xxix. 27. Instead therefore of slaying of beasts, and burning of incense, whereby they praised God, and called upon His Name under the Old Testament, the Fathers, I say, believed our Saviour appointed this Sacrament of bread and wine, as a rite whereby to give thanks and make supplication to His Father in His name. This you may see fully cleared and proved by the learned Mr. Mede, in his Treatise, *The Christian Sacrifice.* The Eucharistical Sacrifice, thus explained, is indeed λογικὴ θυσία, *a reasonable sacrifice,* widely different from that monstrous sacrifice of the Mass taught in the Church of Rome."

And so *Robert Nelson* (Life of Bishop Bull; Works, Life, p. 414, ed. Oxon. 1827) : "This learned divine" (Bishop Bull) "had in his answer to the Bishop of Meaux's inquiries, asserted the doctrine of the *Eucharistical Sacrifice;* that it was an oblation of bread and wine, instituted by Jesus Christ, to represent and commemorate His sacrifice upon the cross; and that its being representative and commemorative no more hindered it from being a proper sacrifice, than the typical and figurative sacrifices of the old law hindered them from being proper sacrifices; for as to be a type doth not destroy the nature and notion of a legal sacrifice, so to be representative and commemorative doth not destroy the nature of an evangelical sacrifice. He thought this doctrine plain from Scripture, and from the unanimous and universal tradition of the primitive Church; nay, that it was not only her language, but her avowed and general practice, to offer up the bread and wine to God the Father in the Eucharist, as an oblation appointed by our Saviour Christ, to commemorate the oblation of Himself upon the cross, and as representative of that full, perfect, and sufficient sacrifice for the sins of the whole world.

"Now in his sermon concerning *the antiquity and usefulness, &c., of common prayers* (Sermon xiii.), he observeth the wonderful consent of all the Christian Churches in the world, however distant from each other, in the prayer of oblation in the Christian Sacrifice of the holy Eucharist. He assureth us, all the ancient Liturgies agree in this form of prayer, almost in the same words, but fully and exactly in the same sense, order, and method. 'Which,' saith he, 'whoever attentively considereth, must be convinced, that this order of prayer was delivered to the several Churches in the very first plantation and settlement of them. Nay, it is observable, that this form of prayer is still retained in the very *Canon of the Mass* at this day used in the Church of Rome, though the form doth manifestly contradict and overthrow some of the principal articles of their new faith. For from this very form, still extant in their Canon, a man may effectually refute these two main doctrines of their Church, that of *Purgatory,* and that of *Transubstantiation.*' [All they who have departed this life in the faith and fear of God are there said to *sleep in peace,* and the Eucharistic bread after consecration is called *bread.*] The antiquity of this prayer shews that the doctrine of the oblation was a part of the faith once delivered to the Saints. Now, as this notion of the Eucharist

is founded upon Scripture, and runneth through all the great writers of the first three ages; as it is highly honourable to God, and no less comfortable to all devout Christians; so it hath this advantage, that it secureth us a bulwark against those innovations of the Church of Rome which relate to this primitive doctrine. The popish sacrifice of the Mass supposeth the oblation of the same body of our Lord and Saviour Jesus Christ which suffered upon the cross, and consequently, that it propitiateth by its own virtue and merit; whereas according to the primitive doctrine, though the Eucharist be a proper sacrifice, yet it is only representative and commemorative of that sacrifice upon the cross; and it renders God Almighty propitious to us, only as it represents and communicateth the benefits of the great sacrifice; and consequently, as long as it is believed to be but representative, it is impossible it should be the thing itself."

It has been supposed by some that this passage authorizes and prescribes the use of *incense* in the Christian Church; but this seems to be a strained interpretation. If the word *incense* is to be taken literally, so ought the word *minchah,* or offering, in the same sentence, to be taken literally; in other words, if we are obliged to burn incense in our churches, we ought also to offer *fine flour;* but, as has been already observed, the Ancient Fathers understood *incense* to be here a symbol of *prayer,* and so the word is interpreted in the Apocalypse, viii. 4.

Terms relating to Hebrew sacrifices are often used in a *spiritual* sense (says *Hengst.*) on account of the spiritual meaning of the sacrifices of the Old Testament. Compare Ps. l. 23; li. 19. Hos. xiv. 2; and especially Isaiah lxvi. 20, where the presentation of a spiritual *minchah* or meat offering by the heathen is foretold, as in the present passage. In the New Testament the spiritual use of such terms may be seen in Rom. xii. 1. Heb. xiii. 15. 1 Pet. ii. 5.

Observe, lastly, there was something very appropriate in this prophecy concerning the acceptance of the spiritual worship of the Gentiles. At this time the High Priest had surrendered, for profane use by a heathen Ammonite, Tobiah, the very Chamber of the Temple at Jerusalem where the incense and meat-offering were kept. See above, on Nehemiah xiii. 9; "I commanded, and they cleansed the chambers : and thither brought I again the *meat-offering* (*minchah*) and the *frankincense.*"

— *my name* shall *be great among the heathen*] Ye despise *My Name* (v. 6), but it will be magnified by all Nations. Cp. Isaiah ii. 2; lvi. 7 : "Them will I bring to My holy mountain, and make them joyful in My house of prayer: their burnt offerings and their sacrifices shall be accepted upon Mine altar; for Mine house shall be called an house of prayer for all people" (or nations). Cp. Mark xi. 17.

In Malachi's age the Jews longed to see God's judicial chastisement of the heathen, who oppressed them, as they did in our Lord's time; but God tells them plainly, that they themselves will be ejected for their hypocrisy and self-righteousness, and that the Heathen will be accepted in their place.

There is a learned essay on this text by *Joseph Mede* (On the Christian Sacrifice, Works, p. 355).

13. *ye have snuffed at it*] To blow it away, as a thing contemptible and offensive (*Gesen.* 556).

— *torn*] Stolen. Ye would not give of your own; but rob others, in order to sacrifice the fruit of your rapine to God, by way of propitiation for your crime.

— *lame, and the sick*] Strictly forbidden by the Levitical Law (Lev. xxii. 19—24).

14. *a male*] Which the Law required in certain cases, especially at the passover (Exod. xii. 5), and in some other sacrifices (Lev. i. 3—10; iv. 23; xxii. 19—23).

— *a corrupt thing*] Rather, a thing *blemished.* Cp. note below, on the sacrificial office of our Blessed Lord as our Great High Priest and Judge, minutely scrutinizing all the sacrifices offered to God; Heb. iv. 13 : "All things are naked and opened" (literally, anatomized even to the back bone), by the searching examination "of Him with Whom we have to do," i. e. to Whom we have to render our account at the Great Day.

### WARNING TO THE PRIESTS.

CH. II. 1. *And now, O ye Priests*] He proceeds to announce the punishment due for their sin just specified.

160

| | | Before CHRIST about 397 |
|---|---|---|

²ᵃ If ye will not hear, and if ye will not lay *it* to heart,
　To give glory unto my name, saith the LORD of hosts,
　I will even send a curse upon you,
　And I will curse your blessings :
　Yea, I have cursed them already, because ye do not lay *it* to heart.

³ Behold, I will ‖ corrupt your seed,
　And † spread dung upon your faces,
　*Even* the dung of your solemn feasts ;
　And ‖ *one* shall ᵇ take you away with it.

⁴ And ye shall know that I have sent this commandment unto you,
　That my covenant might be with Levi, saith the LORD of hosts.

⁵ ᶜ My covenant was with him of life and peace :
　And I gave them to him ᵈ *for* the fear wherewith he feared me,
　And was afraid before my name.

⁶ ᵉ The law of truth was in his mouth,
　And iniquity was not found in his lips :
　He walked with me in peace and equity,
　And did ᶠ turn many away from iniquity.

⁷ ᵍ For the priest's lips should keep knowledge,
　And they should seek the law at his mouth :

---

**2.** *I will curse your blessings*] Even the blessings received by you from Me shall be turned into a curse. So in Ps. lxix. 22, the Messiah, speaking by David, foretells the doom of the Jews for rejecting Him; "Let their table be made a snare before them, and that which should have been for their welfare, let it become a trap."

On the other hand, God says to them, "If ye will repent, I will pour out upon you a *blessing*." See below, iii. 10. Cp. Ezek. xxiv. 26. Joel ii. 14.

The very blessings which men receive become a bane to them unless they use them aright. Scriptures, Sacraments, Sermons, Sundays, all have a double edge ; if used well, they lead men to heaven ; but if despised or misused, they aggravate men's sin, and increase their condemnation. See below, on Luke ii. 34, 2 Cor. ii. 15, 16, and on Rev. v. 5.

**3.** *Behold, I will corrupt your seed*] Literally, *I will rebuke or reprove your seed.* The word rendered *corrupt (ghar)* means twelve times, and the cognate substantive fourteen times; and they are always translated by *rebuke* or *reprove*, except here.

The meaning may be illustrated by the use of the word, "He *rebuked* the Red Sea, and it dried up" (Ps. cvi. 9). Cp. Nahum i. 4. Isa. l. 2. As at God's *rebuke* the Sea itself was dried up, so your seed will be withered. Cp. *Gesen.* 177. Drought and dearth are significant symbols of God's wrath and f man's misery. Cp. Joel i. 17. "The seed is rotten under the clods;" and Hagg. i. 11. "I called for a drought upon the corn and upon the oil, and upon that which the ground bringeth orth ;" and Hagg. ii. 17; and Jer. xiv. 3.

The Levites had neglected the service of the Temple, and ad betaken themselves to farming ; therefore this threat was ery appropriate. See above, on Nehemiah xiii. 10. Here is a arning to ecclesiastical persons who follow secular pursuits, to ie neglect of their spiritual duties.

— *spread dung upon your faces—(the dung of your solemn feasts*] According to the requirements of the Levitical Law, the ung (Hebr. *peresh*, excrements, &c.) of the victims offered in acrifices was to be carried away by the Priests out of the abernacle to an unclean place outside the camp, and burned here (Exod. xxix. 14. Lev. iv. 12 ; viii. 17 ; xvi. 27. Num. ix. 5).

But, in order to show the condition of contempt and momiuy to which the Priests degraded themselves, by despising od's commands, and by not offering such sacrifices, and in such manner, as He required of them, He says, that the dung of their sacrifices, which, on account of its uncleanness, ought be burnt, would be spread by God upon their faces, which howed no sense of shame for their sin. A solemn lesson to bristian Priests who do not discharge aright their holy duties.

— *and one shall take you away with it*] That is, ye will be

swept away, together with the dung spread on your faces; as God says of Jeroboam, "I will take away the remnant of the house of Jeroboam, as a man taketh away dung, till it be all gone" (1 Kings xiv. 10; and cp. *Pocock*, 121).

**4.** *That my covenant might be with Levi*] Rather, *that this may be my covenant with Levi;* that is, that this judicial sentence, pronounced upon you for your sins, may take the place of "My covenant of peace." I gave to Levi (that is, to you, the priestly tribe) a pledge of favour; but ye have forfeited it (see v. 8), and it is now therefore turned into a threat of reprobation for your sins. This is now "My covenant with Levi." No longer a covenant of peace, but of woe.

**5.** *My covenant was with him of life and peace*] Such was originally My covenant with the Levitical Priesthood, a covenant of life and peace; but ye have made it, by your sins, to become a covenant of death and destruction. The continuance of God's covenant with us depends on their faith and obedience. As long as the Levitical Priesthood feared Him, and as long as the law of truth was in their mouths, and as long as—in duty bound (for "the Priest's lips should keep knowledge")—they turned many to righteousness, so long it went well with them; but now all this had been rescinded and annulled by their iniquities.

**7.** *the priest's lips should keep knowledge, and they should seek the law at his mouth*] A memorable statement. The offering of sacrifice was indeed an essential part of the priestly office ; but Malachi declares that all sacerdotal sacrifices are of no avail without religious knowledge, sound learning, and wholesome teaching. The first duty of the Levitical Priests —and how much more of the Christian!—was to *keep*, or *preserve, knowledge;* the knowledge of God, as revealed in His Holy Word; and so to discharge their sacred office, that, according to the Word of God (Deut. xvii. 9—11; xxiv. 8; xxxiii. 10. Lev. x. 11), the people should resort to them for instruction in holy things, and not resort in vain; and unless this was done by them, all their offerings and sacrifices were nugatory, and God would "spread dung on their faces" (v. 3) in token of His displeasure.

Here is a solemn warning to the Christian Clergy. If such was the duty of the Levitical Priesthood, and such the penalty for not performing it aright, how much more imperative is the obligation of the Christian Priest to "keep knowledge," and to instruct the people in sound doctrine ; or, as St. Paul expresses it, "to give attendance to reading, to exhortation, to doctrine, to meditate on these things, and give himself wholly to them" (1 Tim. iv. 13, 15) ; "to speak the things which become sound doctrine" (Titus ii. 1) ; "to hold fast the faithful word, so that he may be able by sound doctrine to convince the gainsayers" (Titus i. 9). And how much soever will be his punish-

Before CHRIST about 397.

h Gal. 4. 14.
i 1 Sam. 2. 17. Jer. 18. 15.
‖ Or, *fall in the law.*
k Neh. 13. 29.
l 1 Sam. 2. 30.
‖ Or, *lifted up the face against.*
† Heb. *accepted faces.*
m 1 Cor. 8. 6. Eph. 4. 6.
n Job 31. 15.
‖ Or, *ought to love.*
o Ezra 9. 1. & 10. 2. Neh. 13. 23.
‖ Or, *him that waketh and him that answereth.*
p Neh. 13. 28, 29.
q Prov. 5. 18.
r Prov. 2. 17.

[h] For he *is* the messenger of the LORD of hosts.
8 But ye are departed out of the way;
Ye [i] have caused many to ‖ stumble at the law;
[k] Ye have corrupted the covenant of Levi, saith the LORD of hosts.
9 Therefore [l] have I also made you contemptible and base before all the people,
According as ye have not kept my ways, but ‖ † have been partial in the law.
10 [m] Have we not all one father?
[n] Hath not one God created us?
Why do we deal treacherously every man against his brother,
By profaning the covenant of our fathers?
11 Judah hath dealt treacherously,
And an abomination is committed in Israel and in Jerusalem;
For Judah hath profaned the holiness of the LORD which he ‖ loved,
[o] And hath married the daughter of a strange god.
12 The LORD will cut off the man that doeth this,
‖ The master and the scholar,
Out of the tabernacles of Jacob,
[p] And him that offereth an offering unto the LORD of hosts.

13 And this have ye done again,
Covering the altar of the LORD with tears, with weeping, and with crying out,
Insomuch that he regardeth not the offering any more,
Or receiveth *it* with good will at your hand.
14 Yet ye say, Wherefore? Because the LORD hath been witness between
thee and [q] the wife of thy youth, against whom thou hast dealt treacherously:
[r] yet *is* she thy companion, and the wife of thy covenant.

---

ment, if he fails to discharge it! Compare Titus i. 7—9. 2 Tim. ii. 2. It is to be feared that this warning is greatly needed in the present day. The Clergy of the Eastern Church, especially in Asia and Greece, have been degraded to a low condition with regard to religious and secular knowledge. Celebrated Roman Catholic writers deplore the ignorance of a great part of their Clergy, consisting of mere illiterate Mass-Priests (see *Rosmini*, Cinque Piaghe, pp. 20—45, and *Dr. Döllinger*, "The Church and the Churches," p. 401). In Protestant Germany the Theological Chairs of the Universities are filled by laymen, who are not united by any common profession of the Christian Faith; and have no pastoral experience in the care of souls, and have none of that wisdom which is found at the side of sick-beds, and death-beds, and in church-yards at the grave; and have no mission from Christ, and no unction from the Holy Ghost; and many among them treat the Holy Scriptures as if they were a mere common book. The science of Divinity has been divorced from the Christian Priesthood; scarcely any great theological works in Germany have been produced in recent times by clergymen. Hence the theological teaching of the Schools has contracted a dry, hard, unspiritual and unpractical character; and the result has been disastrous to Christianity, to Literature, and to Society.

The importance of these considerations to the Church of England, and to English Universities, and the great issues which depend on the observance of Malachi's declaration, "the Priest's lips should keep knowledge, and they should seek the law at his mouth," may, it is hoped, serve as an apology for these observations in this place.

— *he is the messenger of the* LORD *of hosts*] The Priest is the *messenger* (Hebr. *maleac*), the *Angel* of God. Such he is by his office, and such he ought to be in his practice; the herald of God's Word to men. Cp. Hag. i. 13. Malachi refers to his own name. Compare a similar reference in Micah vii. 18; below, iii. 1.

**9.** *have been partial*] Have had respect to persons, which St. Paul forbids; see 1 Tim. v. 21, "Doing nothing by partiality;" and St. James, ii. 1—4.

STRANGE MARRIAGES.

The connecting link between what has gone before, concerning the sins of the priests, and what follows, is supplied by the book of Nehemiah (xiii. 28), whence it appears that Eliashib the High Priest himself countenanced a strange marriage in his own family. Nehemiah's words are, "One of the sons of Joiada, the son of Eliashib the High Priest, was son-in-law to *Sanballat* the *Horonite*; therefore I chased him from me. Remember them, O my God, because they have defiled the Priesthood, and the *covenant* of the priesthood, and of the *Levites*." Nehemiah uses the same words as Malachi (*v.* 8), "Ye have corrupted the *covenant* of *Levi*." See above, on Neh. xiii. 29. Cp. Ezra ix. 1, 2, where the Priests and Levites are mentioned as guilty of this sin.

Thus the historical book of Nehemiah explains and illustrates the prophecies of Malachi. Cp. below, iii. 8.

**10.** *Have we not all one father?*] The Lord God of Israel.

— *Why do we deal treacherously—by profaning the covenant of our fathers?*] Why do we deal treacherously with our brethren, by marrying a heathen wife and putting away a Hebrew wife, and thereby profane the covenant which God made with our fathers as a holy nation and peculiar people? (Exod. xix. 6; xxiv. 8. Deut. xiv. 2).

**12.** *The* LORD *will cut off the man that doeth this, the master and the scholar*] Literally, the *watcher and the answerer*. Probably a metaphor derived from the practice of the Levites keeping watch and ward in the Temple; one of whom, who watched in turn, was to call out, and the others to answer when challenged by him. Cp. Ps. cxxxiv. 1. *Lightfoot*, Temple Service, chap. vii. sect. 1. *Gesenius*, 615. Hence its use here, where the Prophet is addressing the Priests and Levites. This phrase was employed as a proverbial expression, to signify what Isaiah has expressed more in detail (xxiv. 2), "As with the people, so with the priest; as with the buyer, so with the seller," &c.

— *him that offereth an offering*] Any Priest or Levite of this class; and any one who offers a sacrifice for others.

DIVORCE CONDEMNED.

**13.** *And this have ye done again, covering the altar of the* LORD *with tears*] The tears of your wives, whom ye have put away, and who mourn and supplicate to the Lord of Hosts for comfort and protection against their own husbands (*S. Jerome*).

[15] And ᵉ did not he make one ? Yet had he the ‖ residue of the spirit. And wherefore one ? That he might ʄ ᵗ a godly seed. Therefore take heed to your spirit, and let none deal ‖ treacherously against the wife of his youth.

[16] For ᵃ the LORD, the God of Israel, saith ‖ that he hateth ‖ putting away : for *one* covereth violence with his garment, saith the LORD of hosts : therefore take heed to your spirit, that ye deal not treacherously.

[17] ˣ Ye have wearied the LORD with your words. Yet ye say, Wherein have we wearied *him ?* When ye say, Every one that doeth evil *is* good in the sight of the LORD, and he delighteth in them ; or, Where *is* the God of judgment ?

III. [1] Behold, ᵃ I will send my messenger,
And he shall ᵇ prepare the way before me :
And the Lord, whom ye seek, shall suddenly come to his temple,
ᶜ Even the messenger of the covenant, whom ye delight in :
Behold, ᵈ he shall come, saith the LORD of hosts.
[2] But who may abide ᵉ the day of his coming ?
And ᶠ who shall stand when he appeareth ?
For ᵍ he *is* like a refiner's fire.

before
CHRIST
412.

a Matt. 19. 4, 5.
1 Or, excellent.
4 Heb. a residue.

b Gen. 2. 7.
1 Or, seeth.
1 Cor. 7. 11.
1 Or, wilfully party.
a Deut. 24. 1.
Matt. 5. 32.
19. 3, 9.
1 Or, if he hate
her, put her away.
Matt. 1. put
away.
x Isa. 43. 24.
Amos 2. 13.
ch. 2. 14, 15.
a Matt. 11. 10.
Mark 1. 2.
Luke 1. 76.
& 7. 27.
1 Isa. 40. 3.

c Isa. 63. 9.

d Hag. 2. 7.

e ch. 4. 1.

f Rev. 6. 17.

g See Isa. 4. 4.
Matt. 3. 10, 11, 12.

---

**15.** *And did not he make one ?—godly seed.*] Rather, "*And no one did it*" (i.e. divorced his wife), "*and a remnant of the spirit was in him*" (R. Tanchum, Keil). That is, no one who has the least remnant of that Spirit which God breathed into man, from whom He formed woman, will put away his wife, as ye do, on frivolous pretences, or in order to contract a marriage with some fairer or wealthier heathen woman. Or the sense may be, interrogatively, *And did not one* (viz. Abraham) *do it* (i.e. put away his wife, Agar), *and yet he had a remnant of the Spirit* ?

— *And wherefore one ?*] The Hebrew has the definitive article here—"*the one.*" Some (R. Kimchi, Calvin, Drusius, Keil) suppose that by "*the one*" the prophet means Abraham ; and the sense then is as follows :—*And* (ye may therefore ask by way of objection) *why did the one* (that is, Abraham, the one father of all the family of Israel—the Hebrew has the definitive article here—*the one*) *do it ?* Why did he put away Hagar ? The answer is, He was justified in doing so, because God commanded him to "cast away the bondwoman and her son," and *because he sought a godly seed*—literally, a seed of God—the seed promised to him in Isaac, the son of Sarah (Gen. xxi. 12).

— *take heed to your spirit.*] Which ye have from God, for no one retains even the least portion of that Spirit who puts away his wife. See the foregoing note.

**16.** *one covereth violence with his garment.*] So Pagnin, R. Tanchum, Junius, Tremellius, Piscator. The literal sense is, One covereth violence under his garment, so as to wrap his garment over it. The phrase seems to be from the Hebrew custom of espousals. The bridegroom cast the skirt of his garment over her whom he betrothed to himself, and covered her with his garment, as is seen in the history of Boaz and Ruth. See Ruth iii. 9, where Ruth says, "I am Ruth thine handmaid ; spread, therefore, thy skirt over thine handmaid, for thou art a near kinsman." (Cp. the note there, Ezek. xvi. 8.)

Ye, who put away your wives, reverse this order ; ye cast your skirt over iniquity, and betroth violence to yourselves for a bride ; ye espouse to yourselves rapine and covetousness. This figure was more appropriate, because money and other possessions were often carried in the fold or lap of the garment.

### THE DAY OF THE LORD.

**17.** *Ye have wearied the LORD.*] This verse belongs to what follows ; and it is to be regretted that the chapter ends with it. God answers the murmurs of the godless sceptics by an announcement of judgment to come. Cp. 2 Pet. iii. 4–10.

### JOHN THE BAPTIST.

**Ch. III. 1.** *Behold, I will send my messenger.*] Declared to be John the Baptist in Matt. xi. 10 ; Mark i. 2 ; Luke vii. 27. In the words of the Evangelist (John i. 6), "There was a man *sent from God* whose name was John," there may be a reference to this prophecy, "Behold, I *send* My Messenger." The Church declares her judgment in this matter by appointing this chapter to be read on the Festival of St. John the Baptist.

Observe how, throughout his prophecy, *Malachi* (the

messenger), the last of the goodly company of Hebrew Prophets, prepares the way for Christ. Hebrew Prophecy in Malachi resigns its charge to the personal forerunner and immediate messenger of Christ, and expires with the Gospel on its lips. See S. *Cyril* here ; and cp. *Davison*, 253.

— *he shall prepare the way before me.*] Words adopted from Isaiah xl. 3, speaking of John the Baptist.

— *the Lord.*] Malachi gives to Christ the Name (the *Lord*) which belongs to God only (*Pusey* on Daniel, 380).

— *shall suddenly come to his temple.*] Since the Temple is said to be the Temple of Him Whose coming is prepared by the Messenger, therefore He Who cometh is God.

Since, also, the Temple has now been destroyed to which the Messiah was to come (see above, on Haggai ii. 7–9 ; *Pocock* here, 150 ; and *Bp. Chandler* on the Prophecies, p. 84), therefore the Messiah is now come. His Coming is past, not future, as the Jews imagine. Jesus of Nazareth was presented in the Temple forty days after His birth. He came suddenly to His Temple, when few (only an aged man and woman) knew of His Coming. See Luke ii. 21–38.

The Church has therefore appointed this passage (vv. 1–8) to be read as the Epistle on the Festival of our Lord's Presentation in the Temple.

— *whom ye seek—whom ye delight in.*] Ye are impatient and disappointed because the promised Messiah is not come (see above, *Prelim. Note*) ; ye earnestly seek Him ; *ye delight in* Him ; ye eagerly desire Him. But are ye prepared for His Coming ? Will ye receive Him gladly when He comes ? Are not your actions such as He, Who is the Holy One, must condemn and punish when He comes ? The answer to this question is found in St. John's Gospel (i. 11), "He came into His own, and His own received Him not."

On this text see *Dr. Mill's* Lent Sermons, p. 193.

**2.** *who may abide the day of his coming ?*] Malachi, like John the Baptist, sees the future Judge in the present Saviour. The White Throne and the opened Books are in the background of the Baptism at Jordan. "His fan is in His hand" (said the Baptist, who proclaimed Him as the Bridegroom and also as the Lamb of God), "and He shall throughly purge His floor" (the world), "and shall gather the wheat into His garner, and burn up the chaff with unquenchable fire" (Matt. iii. 12).

Our Lord Himself said, that He had come into the world for judgment (John ix. 39) ; and "This is the condemnation, that Light is come into the world, and men loved darkness rather than light, because their deeds were evil" (John iii. 19) ; and "The Prince of this World is judged" (John xvi. 11).

The Word of God is ever revealing what men's tempers and moral dispositions are ; and thus a judicial process is for ever going on. The Day of the Lord *began*, in a certain sense, with our Lord's first appearance upon earth ; and it will have its climax and consummation in His Second Advent.

Therefore S. *Augustine* (De Civ. 18c, xviii. 35) says of this prophecy of Malachi, "Primum et secundum Christi denuntiat Adventum."

— *refiner's fire.*] Jer. vi. 29. Zech. xiii. 9.

Before
CHRIST
about
397.
h Isa. 1. 25.
Zech. 13. 9.

And like fullers' soap :

3 And ʰ he shall sit *as* a refiner and purifier of silver :

And he shall purify the sons of Levi,

And purge them as gold and silver,

i 1 Pet. 2. 5.

That they may ⁱ offer unto the LORD an offering in righteousness.

k ch. 1. 11.

4 Then ᵏ shall the offering of Judah and Jerusalem be pleasant unto the LORD,

‖ Or, *ancient*.

As in the days of old, and as in ‖ former years.

5 And I will come near to you to judgment ;

And I will be a swift witness against the sorcerers, and against the adulterers,

Zech. 5. 4.
James 5. 4, 12.
‖ Or, *defraud*.

ˡ and against false swearers, and against those that ‖ oppress the hireling in *his*

wages, the widow, and the fatherless, and that turn aside the stranger *from his*

*right,* and fear not me, saith the LORD of hosts.

m Num. 23. 19.
Rom. 11. 29.
James 1. 17.
n Lam. 3. 22.

6 For I *am* the LORD, ᵐ I change not ;

ⁿ Therefore ye sons of Jacob are not consumed.

o Acts 7. 51.

7 Even from the days of ᵒ your fathers ye are gone away from mine ordinances,

and have not kept *them.*

p Zech. 1. 3.

ᵖ Return unto me, and I will return unto you, saith the LORD of hosts.

q ch. 1. 6.

ᵍ But ye said, Wherein shall we return ?

8 Will a man rob God ? Yet ye have robbed me.

But ye say, Wherein have we robbed thee ?

r Neh. 13. 10, 12.

ʳ In tithes and offerings.

9 Ye *are* cursed with a curse : for ye have robbed me,

*Even* this whole nation.

s Prov. 3. 9, 10.
t 1 Chron. 26. 20.
2 Chron. 31. 11.
Neh. 10. 38, & 13.
12.

10 ˢ Bring ye all the tithes into ᵗ the storehouse,

That there may be meat in mine house,

And prove me now herewith, saith the LORD of hosts,

u Gen. 7. 11.
2 Kings 7. 2.
† Heb. *empty out.*
x 2 Chron. 31. 10.

If I will not open you the ᵘ windows of heaven,

And †ˣ pour you out a blessing, that *there shall* not *be room* enough *to*

*receive it.*

y Amos 4. 9.

11 And I will rebuke ʸ the devourer for your sakes,

---

— *fullers' soap*] Lye, or alkali. Jer. ii. 22.

3. *he shall sit*] He shall come and *sit as* a Judge. He shall *sit* down on His judgment-seat, to execute justice. Christ is ever judging the World, and will continue doing so till He has finished it at the Great Day.

— *he shall purify the sons of Levi*] This prophecy began to be fulfilled when Christ purged the Temple at Jerusalem (Matt. xxi. 12. John ii. 13—25).

This purifying process is ever going on in the Church, by the moral probation of its ministers. Her Priests and Levites are purified by the Messiah; He applies to them the smelting process of severe trial for the faith; such as the Levite of Cyprus had to endure (Acts iv. 36); and such as those of the Priests had to endure who were obedient to the Faith; and such as all Christian Priests must expect to endure, if they are true to their profession as guardians and champions of the Faith.

4. *Then shall the offering of Judah—be pleasant—as in former years*] Literally, *the minchah (or meat-offering) shall be pleasant.* He uses the same words as in i. 11, "a *pure offering.*" The essence of all sacrifice is the same in every age. No sacrifice is pleasing to God, if not accompanied with the sacrifice of the heart and will, and of all the faculties, intellectual, spiritual, and bodily, of the offerer; and no sacrifice is pleasing to God, except by virtue of its reference to the One Sacrifice of the dearly-beloved Son in Whom He is well pleased (Matt. iii. 17. 1 Pet. ii. 5).

The Prophet foretells that the offerings made by faithful Christian Priests and Christian Levites (see on Isa. lxvi. 21) in the Spiritual Sion, the Church of Christ, will be acceptable to God, like the sacrifices offered by Abel, Noah, Abraham, and Aaron. Cp. Zech. xiv. 16—21, and above, i. 11.

This great predictive revelation of the Gospel, is at once a

prophecy and a moral parable. It puts to shame the corrupt Priesthood of the days of Malachi, by exhibiting in reverse the holiness and spirituality of the New Covenant and its purified ministers. See *Davison* on Prophecy, p. 252.

5. *sorcerers*] Cp. Acts viii. 9; xiii. 6.

— *adulterers*] John viii. 9.

— *false swearers*] Cp. on Matt. v. 33—35. James v. 12.

— *oppress the hireling*] James v. 4.

6. *Therefore ye—are not consumed*] Ye shall be purified by the fire of trial, but not consumed. Cp. Amos ix. 9.

8. *In tithes and offerings*] Literally, *in the tithe and the heave-offering.* Another passage illustrated by Malachi's contemporary, Nehemiah. See above, Neh. xiii. 10—12, and the notes there. On the various kinds of *tithes* among the Hebrews, see notes on Lev. xxvii., Num. xxviii. 21. On the heave-offering, see Exod. xxix. 27.

9. *Ye are cursed with a curse*] Compare Nehemiah xiii. 25. Perhaps Malachi is referring to the solemn act described by Nehemiah. See the note there, and below, iv. 6.

10. *Bring ye all the tithes into the storehouse*] Here again Nehemiah illustrates Malachi. He says, " *All Judah brought a tithe into the treasuries.*" See on Neh. xiii. 12, where the word for *treasury* is the same as that for *storehouse* here. Probably the stirring words of Malachi produced the act which is recorded by Nehemiah. The coincidences between Malachi and Nehemiah are full of interest and importance.

— *that there shall not be room enough*] Rather, *till there be not enough,* i.e. *no more supply*; till all My abundance is exhausted. And since this can never be, therefore it means, "*for ever*" (*Kimchi; Gesen.* 195). I will give you all that I have, Who have infinity at My command.

11. *the devourer*] The locust. Cp. Joel i. 4.

And he shall not { destroy the fruits of your ground ;

Neither shall your vine cast her fruit before the time in the field, saith the
LORD of hosts.

¹² And all nations shall call you blessed :

For ye shall be ᵏ a delightsome land, saith the LORD of hosts.

¹³ ˡ Your words have been stout against me, saith the LORD.

Yet ye say, What have we spoken *so much* against thee ?

¹⁴ ᵐ Ye have said, It *is* vain to serve God :

And what profit *is it* that we have kept { his ordinance,

And that we have walked { mournfully before the LORD of hosts ?

¹⁵ And now ⁿ we call the proud happy ;

Yea, they that work wickedness { are set up ;

Yea, *they that* ᵒ tempt God are even delivered.

¹⁶ Then they ᵖ that feared the LORD ᵠ spake often one to another : and the
LORD hearkened, and heard *it*, and ʳ a book of remembrance was written before
him for them that feared the LORD, and that thought upon his name. ¹⁷ And
ˢ they shall be mine, saith the LORD of hosts, in that day when I make up my
{ ᵗ jewels ; and ᵘ I will spare them, as a man spareth his own son that serveth
him.

¹⁸ ᵛ Then shall ye return, and discern between the righteous and the wicked,

Between him that serveth God and him that serveth him not.

IV. ¹ For, behold, ᵃ the day cometh, that shall burn as an oven ;

And all ᵇ the proud, yea, and all that do wickedly, shall be ᶜ stubble :

And the day that cometh shall burn them up, saith the LORD of hosts,

That it shall ᵈ leave them neither root nor branch.

² But unto you that ᵉ fear my name shall the ᶠ Sun of righteousness arise

---

**14.** *Ye have said, It is vain to serve God.* This sceptical and murmuring spirit had been rebuked by Zephaniah (i. 12).

— *we have kept his ordinance.* Literally, that *we keep his keeping, or observe his observance.* It seems here specially to refer to the ceremonial ordinances prescribed by the Levitical Law. Cp. Num. iii. 6—8. Ezek. xliv. 8.

— *walked mournfully.* Literally, *walked in black,* squalid, and sordid—in sackcloth, and with ashes on the head (Ps. xxxv. 13, 14; xxxviii. 6).

**15.** *And now we call the proud happy.* We call. The Prophet condescends to identify himself with those whom he reproves. " *We* call the proud happy; yea, *we* say" (he is adopting the words of the murmurers), "they that work wickedness are set up." Therefore it is vain to serve God. But he suddenly quits the seat of the scorners. He retires aside from the crowd, who proudly rely on their own popular verdicts, vaunting their own intelligence, and setting at nought the decrees of God; and, standing aloof from them, he joins the smaller company of the faithful few who wait and fear the Lord, and think upon His Name, and look up to heaven, and with the eye of faith behold the Almighty Judge holding a book of remembrance in His hand, and noting down the acts, speeches, and thoughts of the dwellers upon earth; and he listens, with the ear of faith, to the promises of God, assuring His righteous servants of a future eternal reward.

**17.** *they shall be mine—jewels.* Rather, *they shall be to Me for a peculiar treasure,* Hebr. *segullâh,* the word used in Exod. xix. 5, whence it is derived here : " Ye shall be to Me a peculiar treasure;" and in Deut. vii. 6; xiv. 2; xxvi. 18. Ps. cxxxv. 4. *On that day which I am making* (Sept., R. Tanchum, Vatablus, Hengst., Keil, that is, in the last Day, the Day of the Lord, the Day which the Lord is always *making,* when He calls men by death to Himself; and for which He is preparing in all His visitations on Men and Nations.

In God's divine eyesight that Day of Doom is now present; and, by a grand process of foreshortening, the holy Prophets, especially Joel, represent all God's judgments in the world as hours (if we may so speak) marked on the dial plate, and struck by the alarum, of that Great Day. Men vainly imagine that

165

they can determine questions of morals and religion—that they can set aside the Bible, or recast the Creed of the Church, according to what they call "the needs of the age." They would even be making the Day of Judgment, if they could, to be an Assize Day of their own judicial supremacy; but *that* Day is the Day which God knows, and which God *makes*—and He only.

**Ch. IV. 1.** *the day cometh, that shall burn as an oven* (or furnace); *and all the proud—shall be stubble.* The Baptist (to whom Malachi has referred) adopts this imagery (Matt. iii. 1) when he sees Christ coming to his baptism, and foresees His coming to Judgment. "He will burn up the chaff with unquenchable fire" (Matt. iii. 12).

— *the proud.* The proud, whom "ye call happy" (see iii. 15), and who think themselves to be happy. He uses the same word here as there.

— *leave them neither root nor branch.* Another phrase adopted by the Baptist, speaking of Christ's Coming. "Behold now the axe is laid to the root of the trees. Every tree that bringeth not forth good fruit is hewn down, and cast into the fire" (Matt. iii. 10. Luke iii. 9).

Our Lord says, "The Law and the Prophets (i. e. the Old Testament) were until John" (Luke xvi. 16). Malachi twice foretells the coming of the Baptist as the forerunner of Christ (iii. 1; iv. 5); and it is interesting to observe how the Baptist, at the beginning of the Gospel, takes up and repeats the language of Malachi, the last of the Prophets.

St. John the Baptist, standing at the threshold of the New Testament, echoes the voice of Malachi, standing at the exit of the Old; and he reaches forth his hand, and takes from the hand of Malachi the torch of divinely-revealed truth, which had been delivered down in an unbroken series through successive generations of inspired men for a thousand years, from the hand of Moses.

**2.** *But unto you that fear my name shall the Sun of righteousness arise with healing in her wings.* Observe the word *wings.* The Hebrew word for *wing* (*cânâph*) signifies the *skirt* or *hem* of a garment. The skirt of a garment was

Before
CHRIST
about
397.
*c* 2 Sam. 22. 43.
Micah 7. 10.
Zech. 10. 5.

*h* Exod. 20. 3, &c.

*i* Deut. 4. 10.

*k* Ps. 147. 19.

*l* Matt. 11. 14.
& 17. 11.
Mark 9. 11. Luke 1. 17.

With healing in his wings;
And ye shall go forth, and grow up as calves of the stall.
3 *c* And ye shall tread down the wicked;
For they shall be ashes under the soles of your feet
In the day that I shall do *this*, saith the LORD of hosts.

4 Remember ye the *h* law of Moses my servant,
Which I commanded unto him *i* in Horeb for all Israel,
*With* *k* the statutes and judgments.

5 Behold, I will send you *l* Elijah the Prophet

---

cast by a Bridegroom over a Bride in espousals (see on Ruth iii. 9); and persons laid hold on the skirt of a garment in order to receive the guidance and protection of those who wore it. See above, Zech. viii. 23, "Ten men shall take hold of the *skirt* of him that is a Jew;" and compare Isa. iv. 1, "In that day" (the day of the Messiah) " seven women" (representing the Universal Church) " shall lay hold of one man" (Christ).

Malachi, foretelling Christ's Advent, takes up this imagery, and in a glorious picture describes Him as the *Sun of Righteousness.* Compare Ps. xix. 5, where is a reference to Christ as the Sun, and as a Bridegroom, and Jer. xxiii. 6, "The LORD our RIGHTEOUSNESS." This "Day-Spring from on High" (Luke i. 78) is invested in glorious apparel, clothed with light as with a garment (Ps. civ. 2); and from the wings—the very hem and skirt of His raiment—healing is shed upon *all who fear His Name.*

How signally was this exemplified when the faithful woman came trembling, and knelt behind Christ, and took hold of the hem of His garment; and immediately virtue went forth from Him, to heal her in body and soul (Matt. ix. 20—22. Mark v. 30). What a beaming forth of healing light was there from the solar orb of His Righteousness, what a flood of luminous glory streamed forth from Him, when they might only touch His Name "besought Him that they might only touch the hem of His garment, and as many as touched it were made perfectly whole" i. e. whole, not only in body, but in soul (Matt. xiv. 36); or, as St. Luke expresses it, "virtue went out of Him, and healed them all" (Luke vi. 19).

The Baptist saluted Christ as the Bridegroom, and the Church as His Bride (John iii. 29). Christ, the Divine Bridegroom, the Sun of Righteousness, casts the skirt of His pure spotless robe over His Spouse, as Boaz did over Ruth (see on Ruth iii. 19). He, dying on the cross, cleansed her with His own blood (Eph. v. 25, 26. Acts xx. 28. Rev. i. 5. 2 Cor. xi. 2; and hath clothed her with His own righteousness; and therefore she is represented in the Apocalypse as the " woman *clothed with the Sun* " (Rev. xii. 1). The Church is clothed with Christ. And every baptized person has put on Christ (Gal. iii. 27), the new man (Rom. xiii. 14. Eph. iv. 24. Col. iii. 10), and wears Christ, and *walks in white* (Rev. iii. 4). All *who fear His Name,* and come to Him with humility, and take hold of the skirts of His clothing, in His holy Word and blessed Sacraments, with the hand of faith—to them virtue goes forth from Him, and they are healed; to them " the Sun of Righteousness arises," in genial radiance illumining the dark places of their souls, "with healing on His wings."

— *ye shall go forth, and grow up as calves of the stall*] Rather, *ye will go forth and leap, skip,* or *vault* (Sept., Vulg.), *like calves* well-fed *in the stall*; which exult with joy when let loose out of their stalls to go forth to pasture.

Such is the joy of the Saints of God even now, being delivered by Christ from the bands of sin and Satan, and exulting with spiritual joy in their Evangelical liberty, purchased for them by the death and resurrection of Christ (S. Cyril); and such and much more will be their joy hereafter. At the sound of His Divine Voice, they will spring forth from their graves, and renew their strength, and mount up with wings like eagles (Isa. xl. 31), and be caught up in the clouds to meet the Lord in the air, and so be ever with the Lord (1 Thess. iv. 17).

3. *ye shall tread down the wicked*] The metaphor is kept up. As oxen tread the sheaves under foot on the threshing-floor at the harvest; so, at the Great Day which is the world's harvest, shall the Saints (who are now trodden under foot by the proud oppressor) trample on all ungodliness. See Rom. xvi. 20. This metaphor is taken up from Micah iv. 12; vii. 10. Isa. xli. 15, 16. Cp. Joel iii. 14. Zech. x. 5.

REMEMBER THE LAW OF MOSES.

4. *Remember ye the law of Moses my servant*] Malachi, who

is called by the Hebrews "The Seal of the Prophets," concludes the Old Testament with a solemn admonition to the Hebrew Nation and to all ages, that they should remember what is contained in the earliest portions of that Book—the Pentateuch.

The Holy Spirit, speaking by Malachi, here sets His divine seal on the Pentateuch, as it was received by the Jews in his days. And the Old Testament in our days is precisely the same as it was in the days of Malachi.

Whosoever, therefore, despises or disparages the Pentateuch, is chargeable with sin against the Holy Ghost, Who commands us here to remember, that is, to revere and observe it.

It is remarkable, that at the conclusion of the Gospel (John xx. 31; xxi. 24, 25), and at the end of St. Paul's Epistles (2 Tim. iii. 15—17, the last Epistle written by St. Paul), and at the close of St. Peter's Epistles (2 Pet iii. 15, 16), and in the last words of the Revelation of St. John (xxii. 18, 19), we have similar retrospective references to the *preceding* portions of Holy Scripture. The Holy Spirit has taken care, in all His farewell utterances, to inculcate on our minds the paramount importance of the careful study of God's written Word, and of devout veneration for it. Malachi, the last of the prophets, preaches of Christ, and exhorts us to remember Moses. He thus teaches us that the Gospel is no new thing, but was foreshadowed in the Law, and dates from the earliest times. The fulness of the Law and the Prophets is Christ.

ELIJAH THE PROPHET.

5. *Behold, I will send you Elijah the prophet*] Our Lord expressly tells us that " *Elias* is come already, and they knew him not;" and the Evangelist adds, " then the disciples understood that He spake to them of *John the Baptist* " (Matt. xvii. 9—13. Mark ix. 11—13). Cp. Matt. xi. 13. Cp. *Pocock,* 148—192.

The Jews, interpreting these words of Malachi literally, suppose that Elijah, who is still alive, will appear in person before the Second Advent of the Messiah, and "restore the tribes of Jacob." (Ecclus. xlviii. 10); and many ancient Christian Expositors, as *Justin Martyr, Hippolytus, Origen, S. Cyril, Gregory Nyssen, S. Chrysostom, Tertullian, S. Hilary, S. Ambrose, S. Jerome, S. Augustine, S. Gregory,* using the *Septuagint* Version, which has here " Elijah the *Tishbite* " (and so *Arabic*), imagined that Elijah will come in person before the Second Advent of Christ. See the authorities quoted below, in the note on Matt. xvii. 10, and on Rev. xi. 3, 4; the passages cited in *Suicer,* Thes. v. Elias; and in the Catéchisme de Montpellier, i. 375, and by *Heugst.* here, Christol. iv. 219—224, English translation.

In the face of such strong catholic evidence in favour of a belief in a personal coming of Elias before the Second Advent of Christ, it would seem to be presumptuous to deny the possibility, or even the probability, of such an event. But the words of the Prophet Malachi, especially as interpreted by the Gospel, do not seem to require, perhaps not to admit, such a belief; and the opinion of these early Greek Fathers may, perhaps, be ascribed to the fact that they used the Septuagint Version, rather than the Hebrew Original; and perhaps the Latin derived their opinion from them. The *Vulgate* has " Eliam *prophetam,*" and so the Syriac—not " *Thesbiten;*" but the early Latin Version has " *Thesbiten.*"

As Christ Himself is called *David* by the Prophets, because He is the true King and Shepherd of Israel, and because all the promises which were made to David are fulfilled in Him Who is David's Seed (see on Jer. xxx. 9. Ezek. xxxiv. 23; xxxvii. 24. Hosea iii. 5), so John the Baptist is called *Elias,* who was the representative of the Prophets, just as Moses is the representative of the Law; and therefore Moses and Elias were illumined in Christ's glory at the Transfiguration (Matt. xvii. 3. Mark ix. 4. Luke ix. 30). "Dominus atque Salvator trans-

" Before the coming of the great and dreadful day of the LORD :
6 And he shall turn the heart of the fathers to the children,
And the heart of the children to their fathers.
Lest I come and smite the earth with a curse.

*ignatus in monte loquentes secum habebat Moysen et Eliam in candidis vestibus, qui et dicebant ei quae passurus erat in Jerusalem : Lex enim et omnis prophetarum chorus Christi redent passionem" (S. Jerome).*

All the Law and the Prophets testified of Christ, and are lighted up by Him, Who is the Sun of Righteousness, and by His Gospel. John the Baptist was not only the antitype of Elias in his dress, his office, his character, and his courageous acts, especially in his reproving kings (see on Matt. iii. 4; xiv. 2; Mark ix. 12, 13), but he also consummated the prophetical work of which Elias was the exponent and representative. " The Law and the Prophets prophesied until John, since that time the kingdom of God is preached, and every man presseth into " (Matt. xi. 12. Luke. xvi. 16).

The Church declares her judgment on this matter by appointing this chapter, as well as the third, to be read on the stival of St. John the Baptist.

— *Before the coming of the great and dreadful day of the* LORD | Words adopted from Joel ii. 31. See the note there.

*6. he shall turn the heart of the fathers to the children* the angel Gabriel, when he appeared to Zacharias, the father of John the Baptist, quoted these words and applied them to the Baptist, whose birth he foretold. " He shall go before Him in the spirit and power of Elias, *to turn the hearts of the fathers to the children,* and the disobedient to the wisdom of the just " Luke i. 17 ; whence we may observe that the angels themselves read the Scriptures. Cp. Eph. iii. 10. 1 Pet. i. 12.

The sense is, He shall unite the fathers, who are our fathers, to us Christians, who are their children (S. Jerome, Theodoret, and S. Chrysostom, in Matt. xvii.).

This blessed work will be done by him who preaches the kingdom of heaven ; many will come from the East and the West, and sit down with Abraham, Isaac, and Jacob in the kingdom of God (Matt. viii. 11. Luke xiii. 28). This is fulfilled even now in the Church ; for we are children of Abraham by faith in Christ, Who is Abraham's Seed (Gal. iii. 7—9).

St. John the Baptist also adopted these words of Malachi when he said, " God is able of these stones to raise up *children* unto *Abraham*" (Matt. iii. 19) ; the Father of the faithful, Abraham is our father, and we are his children, and his heart turned to our heart, and our hearts are turned to his heart, by faith in Christ.

Yet further, it is not to be denied or forgotten, that according to the Christian Fathers who supposed that Elias will appear again in person before the Second Advent of Christ (see above vv. 5, 6), one of the principal purposes assigned for that appearance is, that he may convert the Jews to Christianity. So Theodoret here, and S. Chrysostom and Theophyl. in Matt. xii. ; S. Gregory, Hom. 12 in Ezechiel.

It may suffice to quote the words of S. Augustine in this case. In his book De Civ. Dei, xx. 29, he thus writes, " It is a very prevalent opinion in the discourses and hearts of the faithful, that by the instrumentality of Elias, the great and wonderful prophet, expounding to them the true meaning of the Law of Moses, in the latter days before the final Judgment, the Jews will be brought to believe in the true Christ. With good reason the appearance of Elias is hoped for, before the Advent of our Saviour and Judge ; because with good reason he is believed to be still alive, inasmuch as he was carried up from this world in a chariot of fire. When, therefore, Elias comes, he will expound the Law spiritually, which the Jews now understand carnally, and will turn the hearts of the fathers to the children, that is, the Jews, who are the children, will understand the Law in the same sense as their fathers the Prophets understood it."

— *lest I come and smite the earth with a curse*] Rather, *with the ban* (Hebr. *cherem*) of extermination. The word here used (*cherem*) has a double sense, like *sacer* or *devotus* in Latin, dedicated for a blessing, or doomed to a curse. It is not the same as that used in iii. 9, but as that rendered *utter destruction* in 1 Kings xx. 42, and in Zech. xiv. 11, " There shall be no more *utter destruction,* but Jerusalem shall be safely inhabited."

The sense is that the *earth* is opposed to the *kingdom of heaven* will be the another Canaan—under a curse—as the seven nations of Canaan were, unless it listens to the preaching of the Gospel of Christ, Whose herald the Baptist was.

This was fulfilled in the utter destruction of Jerusalem—which was symbolized by the act of Christ, visiting the barren leafy fig-tree with a curse, which withered it (Mark xi. 21), and in the ban of extermination executed on Judæa for the rejection of Christ at His first coming. Jerusalem and Judah became as Canaan for their sin against God.

But this prophecy extends also to the time of Christ's Second Coming.

Malachi ends his prophecy as his predecessor Zechariah had done, " The Lord will *smite with a plague* all the people that have fought against Jerusalem," that is, who war against Christ and His Church (Zech. xiv. 12) ; " and there shall be no more the Canaanite in the house of the Lord of Hosts" (Zech. xiv. 21). Whoever is a Canaanite in heart, will become like Canaan in fate (Lev. xxvi. 14. Deut. xii. 29 ; and xxiii. 3. If we do not offer ourselves as a holy *cherem* (Lev. xxvii. 28), by self-dedication to God, we shall be doomed *as a cherem* for extermination by Him. Cp. on Mark ix. 29. If we do not devote ourselves a willing *àvábnµa* to God, we shall be an unwilling *àváðnµa.*

This concluding sentence of Malachi—this final utterance of the Holy Spirit—is a solemn warning to these latter days.

Some of the Jews wished to shift this verse from its proper place, in order that the Old Testament might have a joyful termination. The *Septuagint* ends with the fourth verse of this chapter ; and the fifth and sixth are made to precede it. The Masorites prescribed that in the synagogue the *penultimate* verse should be read again at the *end* of Isaiah, Lamentations, and Ecclesiastes, in order to escape the dirge-like tones of the *last* verses of those books. The same was to be done here, at the end of what the Jews call " the Twelve," i.e. Minor Prophets, in order that the Old Testament might not conclude with words of terrible denunciation. Cp. Prock, 201.

But the Holy Spirit knows what is best for us. He warns us of future punishment, in order that we may escape it, and that we may inherit everlasting glory. " Knowing the terror of the Lord," He would " persuade men" (2 Cor. v. 11). And the character of these latter days, when the Evil One is endeavouring to lure men into his own grasp, and to make them his victims for ever, by dissolving God's attributes into one universal fulness of undiscriminating love ; and by endeavouring to persuade them that His Justice and Holiness are mere ideal theories and visionary phantoms, and that there is no Judgment to come, and that the terrors of Hell are but a dream—in defiance of the clear words of Him Who is the Truth (see on Mark ix. 44—48. Matt. xxv. 46. Cp. on Isa. lxvi. 24)—shows that there is divine foresight in this warning by Malachi. Let it not be forgotten, that the Apostle of love, St. John, ends his Epistle with a warning against idolatry, and that at the close of the Apocalypse there is a solemn declaration against all who tamper with any words of that book, which speaks in the clearest tones concerning Judgment, Heaven, Hell, and Eternity (Rev. xx. 11—15 ; xxi. 27 ; xxii. 18, 19). May we have grace so to profit by this solemn warning, that we may escape the malediction of those on the left hand at the Great Day, and inherit the blessing which will be pronounced to them on the right hand, by the Almighty and Everlasting Judge!

NOW UNTO THE KING ETERNAL, IMMORTAL, INVISIBLE, THE ONLY WISE GOD, BE HONOUR AND GLORY FOR EVER AND EVER. AMEN (1 Tim. i. 17).

# PUBLICATIONS BY CHR. WORDSWORTH, D.D., BISHOP OF LINCOLN.

The HOLY BIBLE; with Notes, Introductions, and Indexes. Particulars may be seen in the Advertisement prefixed to this Volume.

On the INSPIRATION of the BIBLE. *Eighth Edition.* 1s.

On the INTERPRETATION of the BIBLE. 3s. 6d.

The HOLY YEAR; or, Original Hymns, for Sundays, Holy Days, and Daily Use. *Fifth Edition, large type, price* 1s.; *smaller type* 6d. With Texts, edited by W. H. Monk. 4s. 6d.

THEOPHILUS ANGLICANUS; or, Manual of Instruction on the CHURCH UNIVERSAL, and on the ANGLICAN CHURCH. *Cheaper Edition.* 2s. 6d.

ELEMENTS of INSTRUCTION on the CHURCH; an Abridgment of the above. 6d.

The HISTORY of the CHURCH of IRELAND. (1869.) 6s.

MANUAL of CONFIRMATION. *Fourth Edition.* 9d.

SCRIPTURAL OBLIGATION of the LORD'S DAY. 6d.

On UNION with ROME; or, Is the CHURCH of ROME the BABYLON of the APOCALYPSE? An Essay. *Seventh Edition*; with a Postscript on passing Events, considered with reference to the Apocalypse. 1s.

S. HIPPOLYTUS, and the CHURCH of ROME in the beginning of the Third Century, from the newly-discovered "Philosophumena." 8s. 6d.

LETTERS to M. GONDON, on the DESTRUCTIVE Character of the CHURCH of ROME in Religion and Polity. *Third Edition.* 7s. 6d.

A SEQUEL to the ABOVE. *Second Edition.* 6s. 6d.

THEOCRITUS, Codicum MSS. ope recensitus et emendatus, cum Indicibus locupletissimis. 10s. 6d.

CORRESPONDENCE of RICHARD BENTLEY, D.D. 2 vols. 2l. 2s.

MEMOIRS of WILLIAM WORDSWORTH. 2 vols. 30s.

GREECE, Historical, Pictorial, and Descriptive. *Fifth Edition.* 1l. 8s.

ATHENS and ATTICA; Journal of a Residence there. *Third Edition.* Crown 8vo. 8s. 6d.

INEDITED ANCIENT WRITINGS, or GRAFFITI, from the walls of POMPEII. 2s. 6d.

A DIARY in FRANCE; concerning Education and the Church. *Second Edition.* 5s. 6d.

NOTES at PARIS. A Sequel to the above. 4s.

TOUR in ITALY; with reference to the Prospects of Religion there. *Second Edition.* 2 vols. 15s.

The LAW of the CHURCH on RITUAL: a Letter to the Archbishop of Canterbury. 1868. 1s.

On the VATICAN COUNCIL at ROME of 1869. 1s.

RESPONSIO ANGLICANA LITTERIS APOSTOLICIS REDDITA PII PAPÆ IX. 1s.

"An ANGLICAN ANSWER," &c.; being an ENGLISH TRANSLATION of the above. 2d.

A PRIMARY CHARGE to the Diocese of Lincoln. 1870. 2s.; *Smaller Edition,* 6d.

On DIOCESAN SYNODS and DIOCESAN CONFERENCES, their distinctive Character and Uses; an Address at the Diocesan Synod at Lincoln, 1871, with the Form and Order of its Proceedings. 1s.

On COLLEGE STATUTES, COLLEGE FELLOWSHIPS, AND COLLEGE LEGISLATION. 1s.

The MACCABEES and the CHURCH; or, The History of the Maccabees, a Warning to Ourselves. Two Sermons preached before the University of Cambridge, 1871. 2s. 6d.

SPEECH at the COLOGNE CONGRESS, &c., 1873.

TWELVE ADDRESSES on CHURCH MATTERS (e. g. Fasting Communion, Eastward Celebration, Confession, Non-Communicating Attendance, &c.). 3s. 6d.

On CONFESSION and ABSOLUTION. *Second Edition.* 3d.

PASTORAL to the WESLEYANS. *Tenth Edition.* 3d.

On the SALE of CHURCH PATRONAGE and SIMONY. *Second Edition.* 3d.

On TEMPERANCE SOCIETIES. *Third Edition.* 1d.

On CREMATION. *Second Edition,* 1874. 6d.

On PERVERSIONS to ROME, 1874. 3d.

On the REVISION of the NEW LECTIONARY, 1874. 1s.

RESULTS of a DIOCESAN ENQUIRY on RITUAL, with Proposals for Peace. *Second Edition.* 1d. 1875.

RIVINGTONS, 3, WATERLOO PLACE, LONDON; AND AT OXFORD AND CAMBRIDGE.

[OVER.

Milton Keynes UK
Ingram Content Group UK Ltd.
UKHW011221280324
440101UK00005B/506